Governance and Auditing

Critical Governance in the New Global Economy

Series Editors: Kevin Keasey
Leeds Permanent Building Society Professor of Financial Services and Director of the International Institute of Banking and Financial Services, Leeds University Business School, UK
Steve Thompson
Professor of Strategic Management, Nottingham University Business School, UK
Mike Wright
Professor of Financial Studies and Director of the Centre for Management Buy-out Research, Nottingham University Business School, UK

Wherever possible, the articles in these volumes have been reproduced as originally published using facsimile reproduction, inclusive of footnotes and pagination to facilitate ease of reference.

For a list of all Edward Elgar published titles visit our site on the World Wide Web at
www.e-elgar.com

Governance and Auditing

Edited by

Peter Moizer

Professor of Accounting
Leeds University Business School, UK

CORPORATE GOVERNANCE IN THE NEW GLOBAL ECONOMY

An Elgar Reference Collection
Cheltenham, UK • Northampton, MA, USA

Published by
Edward Elgar Publishing Limited
Glensanda House
Montpellier Parade
Cheltenham
Glos GL50 1UA
UK

Edward Elgar Publishing, Inc.
136 West Street
Suite 202
Northampton
Massachusetts 01060
USA

A catalogue record for this book is available from the British Library.

ISBN   1 84376 830 5

Printed and bound in Great Britain by MPG Books Ltd, Bodmin, Cornwall

Contents

Acknowledgements

The editor and publishers wish to thank the authors and the following publishers who have kindly given permission for the use of copyright material.

American Accounting Association for articles: Chee W. Chow (1982), 'The Demand for External Auditing: Size, Debt and Ownership Influences', *Accounting Review*, **LVII** (2), April, 272–91; Zoe-Vonna Palmrose (1988), 'An Analysis of Auditor Litigation and Audit Service Quality', *Accounting Review*, **LXIII** (1), January, 55–73; Jere R. Francis and Earl R. Wilson (1988), 'Auditor Changes: A Joint Test of Theories Relating to Agency Costs and Auditor Differentiation', *Accounting Review*, **LXIII** (4), October, 663–82; Zoe-Vonna Palmrose (1989), 'The Relation of Audit Contract Type to Audit Fees and Hours', *Accounting Review*, **LXIV** (3), July, 488–99; Randolph P. Beatty (1989), 'Auditor Reputation and the Pricing of Initial Public Offerings', *Accounting Review*, **LXIV** (4), October, 693–709; Joseph V. Carcello, Roger H. Hermanson and Neal T. McGrath (1992), 'Audit Quality Attributes: The Perceptions of Audit Partners, Preparers, and Financial Statement Users', *Auditing: A Journal of Practice and Theory*, **11** (1), Spring, 1–15; April Klein (2002), 'Economic Determinants of Audit Committee Independence', *Accounting Review*, **77** (2), April, 435–52; Joseph V. Carcello and Terry L. Neal (2003), 'Audit Committee Characteristics and Auditor Dismissals Following "New" Going-Concern Reports', *Accounting Review*, **78** (1), January, 95–117.

Blackwell Publishing Ltd for articles: Terrence B. O'Keefe, Dan A. Simunic and Michael T. Stein (1994), 'The Production of Audit Services: Evidence from a Major Public Accounting Firm', *Journal of Accounting Research*, **32** (2), Autumn, 241–61; Clive S. Lennox (1999), 'Audit Quality and Auditor Size: An Evaluation of Reputation and Deep Pockets Hypotheses', *Journal of Business Finance and Accounting*, **26** (7/8), September/October, 779–805; William L. Felix, Jr., Audrey A. Gramling and Mario J. Maletta (2001), 'The Contribution of Internal Audit as a Determinant of External Audit Fees and Factors Influencing This Contribution', *Journal of Accounting Research*, **39** (3), December, 513–34.

Elsevier for articles: Linda Elizabeth DeAngelo (1981), 'Auditor Independence, "Low Balling", and Disclosure Regulation', *Journal of Accounting and Economics*, **3** (2), 113–27; Linda Elizabeth DeAngelo (1981), 'Auditor Size and Audit Quality', *Journal of Accounting and Economics*, **3** (3), 183–99; Michael E. Bradbury (1990), 'The Incentives for Voluntary Audit Committee Formation', *Journal of Accounting and Public Policy*, **9** (1), Spring, 19–36; W. Bruce Johnson and Thomas Lys (1990), 'The Market for Audit Services: Evidence from Voluntary Audit or Changes', *Journal of Accounting and Economics*, **12** (1–3), 281–308; Christopher Humphrey, Peter Moizer and Stuart Turley (1992), 'The Audit Expectations Gap – Plus ca Change, Plus c'est la Meme Chose?', *Critical Perspectives on Accounting*, **3** (2), June, 137–61; Brian T. Pentland (1993), 'Getting Comfortable with the Numbers: Auditing and the

Micro-Production of Macro-Order', *Accounting, Organizations and Society*, **18** (7/8), October/November, 605–20; Don Anderson, Jere R. Francis and Donald J. Stokes (1993), 'Auditing, Directorships and the Demand for Monitoring', *Journal of Accounting and Public Policy*, **12** (4), Winter, 353–75; Krishnagopal Menon and Joanne Deahl Williams (1994), 'The Use of Audit Committees for Monitoring', *Journal of Accounting and Public Policy*, **13** (2), Summer, 121–39; Allen T. Craswell, Jere R. Francis and Stephen L. Taylor (1995), 'Auditor Brand Name Reputations and Industry Specializations', *Journal of Accounting and Economics*, **20**, 297–322; Michael Power (1996), 'Making Things Auditable', *Accounting, Organizations and Society*, **21** (2/3), 289–315; Larry Rittenberg and Mark A. Covaleski (2001), 'Internalization Versus Externalization of the Internal Audit Function: An Examination of Professional and Organizational Imperatives', *Accounting, Organizations and Society*, **26** (7/8), 617–41.

David Flint for his own article: (1971), 'The Role of the Auditor in Modern Society: An Exploratory Essay', *Accounting and Business Research*, **1** (4), Autumn, 287–93.

Journal of Managerial Issues, Pittsburgh State University for article: Lawrence P. Kalbers and Timothy J. Fogarty (1998), 'Organizational and Economic Explanations of Audit Committee Oversight', *Journal of Managerial Issues*, **X** (2), Summer, 129–50.

James C. Lampe and Steve G. Sutton for their own article: (1994), 'Evaluating the Work of Internal Audit: A Comparison of Standards and Empirical Evidence', *Accounting and Business Research*, **24** (96), July, 335–48.

Every effort has been made to trace all the copyright holders but if any have been inadvertently overlooked the publishers will be pleased to make the necessary arrangement at the first opportunity.

In addition the publishers wish to thank the Library of the University of Warwick and the Library of Indiana University at Bloomington, USA for their assistance in obtaining these articles.

Introduction

Peter Moizer

---

1. Introduction

This edited volume collects together some of the important research papers relating to the role that auditing plays in the governance of corporations. The principal function of auditing is to give assurance that the financial statements prepared by the directors of a company can be relied upon to provide reasonable guidance as to what has happened to that company in the past. Stakeholders can then assess whether the results achieved by the directors are satisfactory. Hence, audited financial statements are a key information resource for stakeholders wishing to know what has happened to a company. However, users of audited financial statements face a problem in that they have no clear guidance on the extent of the reliance they can place on the work of the auditor. Most audit reports are identical, merely indicating that the auditors are satisfied that the information provided in the financial statements fairly represents what has happened. However, users of financial statements are also aware that auditors are in effect appointed and remunerated by the directors of the company on whom they are reporting. Auditors compound this effect by speaking of the directors of the company as their 'client' even though they are in theory 'agents' of the shareholders. Indeed, the letter setting out the terms of the audit engagement is a private one between the auditors and the directors of the company. Hence, for all but the most credulous stakeholder, there is a problem of trust, which is summed up in the famous quotation from the satires of Juvenal, '*Quis custodiet ipsos custodes*?' (who will guard the guards themselves?).

The structure of this introductory chapter is as follows. In the next section, the role played by auditors is sketched out in relation to the three actors in the process: managers, owners and auditors. What constitutes the audit activity is briefly described in Section 3, which discusses the choices that auditors have to make and what influences those choices. The important question of what is meant by the quality of an audit is discussed in Section 4 as well as how users assess audit quality. The readings themselves are grouped into four areas to provide a focus for their consideration. The next four sections discuss each of these groups of articles: the role of auditing in the governance process (Section 5), audit quality and auditor reputation (Section 6), governance and the audit committee (Section 7) and the relationship between internal and external auditors (Section 8). Section 9 contains a brief summary of the conclusions that can be drawn from this survey of the literature.

2. Role of Auditors

To understand the role played by auditors, it is helpful to consider first a simplified description of the auditing process as consisting of three individuals (the owner, the manager and the auditor). The need for the audit activity arises if the owner does not have complete confidence that the manager is acting so as to maximize the interests of the owner, however defined. If the owner had such complete confidence, then there would be no need for the owner either to spend any of his or her time auditing the work of the manager or to employ someone else to do it. Two aspects of this lack of confidence can be identified: *technical competence* and *integrity*. The technical competence aspect involves not only the technical ability of the manager to do the job, but also the extent to which the manager understands the objectives of the owner, since a technically competent manager might perform some activity well, but it might be the wrong activity in the eyes of the owner.

The aspect of integrity relates to the need of the owner to trust that the manager is performing in the owner's interest rather than in the manager's own self-interest. The two principal ways in which the manager can 'cheat' his or her owner are in the amount of effort the manager expends on the owner's behalf and in the personal consumption of the owner's assets. The activity of auditing can help improve the owner's confidence in two ways. Firstly, the visible nature of the process should act as an incentive to the manager to improve his or her performance. The results of motivational studies show that performance improves when individuals know their performance is being monitored. Secondly, the auditor is providing confirmation that the report given by the manager is a faithful representation of the events occurring during the period. The owner can, therefore, attach more credence to the account.

The above analysis of the need to audit the work of the manager can also be applied to the need to audit the work of the auditor, and so on *ad infinitum*. The owner might have doubts about the technical competence of the auditor in the same way that he or she has doubts about the technical competence of the manager. The owner might also have doubts about the integrity of the auditor, since the auditor is no less likely to follow his or her own self-interest at the expense of the owner than is the manager. Managers and auditors are both human beings and the owner has no reason to assume that the motivations of managers differ from those of auditors. It is interesting to note that in a game-theoretic analysis of the above situation (Antle, 1982), in which the auditor and the manager have the same motivational drives (maximizing their own economic self-interest), the auditor and the manager tend to act together to the detriment of the owner.

Extending the analysis to the modern corporation, the three individuals become three groups. The owner becomes those individuals who control the company's shares, who for the most part are doing so as agents themselves, their clients being pension fund members, insurance policy holders, investment trust shareholders and mutual fund holders. The manager is a board of directors or a chief executive or a combination of the two, depending on the extent to which the chief executive wields absolute power. The individual auditor becomes a partner in a firm of registered auditors and the partnership name will appear on the auditor's report.

The main role of the modern company auditor is to express an opinion on whether a company's financial statements present a true and fair view of the financial position and operations of the company. The audited financial statements are, therefore, the result of a joint process using inputs supplied by both client company management and the auditor. Management produces draft financial statements and the auditor gathers evidence which either substantiates or contradicts the information contained in them. The nature, timing and extent of audit procedures will vary depending on the philosophy of the audit firm and the type of client involved.

The service the auditor provides is the independent verification of the credibility of the information contained in a company's financial statements. Hence, the value of the auditor's service can be measured by the increased confidence felt by readers when using audited accounts as opposed to unaudited ones (Wallace, 1980). An audit improves the quality of the information presented in the financial statements by reducing two possible distortions: noise and bias (Ng, 1978). The term *noise* refers to the unintentional errors that occur in the financial reporting process. The auditor can reduce noise in two ways: by discovering errors during the normal routine of audit testing and by increasing the standard of care adopted by employees who are conscious that their work will be subject to independent scrutiny. The second distortion, termed *bias*, refers to the creation of intentional errors by management, intent on window dressing their own performance. Bias can be introduced either by creating deliberate mistakes (such as valuing an obsolete inventory product as if it were part of the current range) or by the choice of accounting methods which do not accord with generally accepted accounting principles (e.g. defining the date on which a sale took place to be the date on which the sales order was received rather than the date on which the order was despatched to the customer). By reducing noise and bias, the auditor is helping to reduce the uncertainty faced by users when interpreting accounting information.

3. Choices Faced by Auditors

In the simple case, it could be possible for the auditor to check all the transactions of the manager and to check the existence and state of all the assets of the owner. However, the modern corporation is so large that it is impossible to check all the transactions. Hence, the auditor will have to examine only a small sample and verify only a small proportion of the assets and liabilities, and revenues and expenses. The auditor has, therefore, to choose the amount of audit work he or she considers necessary. This choice is not a simple one and involves trading off the benefits and costs of undertaking audit work. Broadly speaking, the more audit work the auditors undertake, the greater will be their confidence that the financial statements are not misstated in a significant way. However, more audit work means more time and hence more cost. Occasionally more audit work means more audit fee income, because the client has been persuaded to pay a higher fee as a result of the need to perform the extra audit work, but this is unusual and it is more likely that the audit fee income is relatively fixed. Hence, the auditor has to decide how much audit work to undertake on the grounds of increased confidence and extra cost alone.

Having chosen the extent of the audit work to be performed and having performed the audit tests and reviews, the auditor may have to make a second choice, depending on whether the audit procedures reveal that the financial statements are misstated in some material way. If the financial statements are materially misstated, then the auditor has to decide what to do about it. There are essentially two options. First, the auditor can decide to do nothing, in which case the status quo is maintained. The auditor has, however, the longer-term risk that the misstatement will eventually become public knowledge (e.g. as a result of a take-over by another company) with the attendant costs (e.g. legal claims for damages, higher insurance premiums, loss of fee income as a result of the adverse publicity, loss of personal prestige and loss of self-esteem). Alternatively, the auditor can ask management to change the financial statements to correct the misstatement. This act alters the status quo and could alter some of the various courses of action that the readers of the financial statements might take. As a consequence, the management of the company could react favourably or unfavourably, depending on how it felt that users of the financial statements would react. Accordingly, the auditor might receive praise or blame for bringing the misstatement to the attention of management. To a large extent the attitude of the company management will depend on the nature of the misstatement. If the misstatement was caused by a genuine error, then the auditor is likely to receive praise for discovering it, unless the effect of the alteration is to make management's performance look significantly less favourable. However, if the misstatement was caused by some deliberate act on the part of company management, then the auditor would not expect a favourable reaction to his or her request to make good the misstatement. If company management refuses to change the financial statements, then the auditor has to decide whether or not to reveal the misstatement in the auditor's report. Such a course of action is bound to incur the displeasure of management and lead to an impairment in the relationship between the auditor and company management. The effects of this are that it will be more likely another firm of auditors will be appointed and hence the audit fees and any other associated revenues from this particular client will disappear.

4. Audit Quality

The value of the auditor's report ultimately depends on the quality of the work performed. The classic definition of audit quality has been provided by DeAngelo (1981, p. 186): 'The quality of audit services is defined to be the market-assessed joint probability that a given auditor will both (a) discover a breach in the client's accounting system, and (b) report the breach.' The value of this definition is that it stresses the twin aspects that are required of a quality audit: technical competence and independence. By *technical competence* is meant the auditor has sufficient technical expertise to know what evidence needs to be collected and the skill to interpret it correctly, so that all the significant errors and omissions present in a set of financial statements can be identified. An *independent* auditor will ensure that either all significant errors and omissions are corrected or that they are fully disclosed in the auditor's report. In reality, the concepts of expertise and independence are interrelated. An auditor who is not independent may choose to act in such a way that errors or omissions are not discovered; that is to say, to behave in a technically incompetent fashion. An illustrious example of the practice was given in 1801 at the Battle of Copenhagen, when Nelson put his telescope to his blind eye to avoid seeing the signal commanding him to withdraw his ships from battle. Auditors can choose to act in a similar fashion by studiously avoiding those areas where errors or omissions might be found. Since the audit tests have failed to produce any embarrassing revelations, the auditor can produce an unqualified opinion without apparently compromising his or her integrity.

The practical difficulty with DeAngelo's market definition is that it is not clear how the market can make its joint probabilistic assessment of technical expertise and independence. To assess audit quality, consumers will have to judge not only the technical competence of the audit work done but also the independence of the auditor. To assess the technical competence of an audit requires access to the audit working papers and involves the reviewer assessing how well the work done compares with established professional standards. One example occurs when the auditors of a holding company (primary auditors) evaluate the quality of the work of another firm of auditors auditing a subsidiary company (secondary auditors). In this case, quality is judged by assessing the extent and appropriateness of the audit work conducted by the secondary auditors, using the primary auditors' own 'feel' for what audit work should have been carried out. Assessing independence is more difficult, since ultimately independence is an attitude of mind and depends on the ethical and moral beliefs of the individual audit partner. However, it is possible to catalogue those visible aspects of the auditor–client management relationship which might deter the auditor from disclosing a breach by management; for example, the length of time the auditor partner has been involved with the company; the percentage of the total fees of the firm accounted for by this one audit; any family relationships between the auditor and client management, and so on.

Apart from the formidable problems of acquiring the information necessary to make a judgement on the quality of a particular audit, there is also a more fundamental problem which relates to the nature of the auditing activity. Unlike a manufacturing process, an audit is not a well-defined activity. The audit procedures followed will be the result of a series of planning decisions made in response to client-specific factors, such as the strength of the internal control system, the number of independent sub-units, the types of business activities undertaken by the client, and so on. The auditor will have to decide which areas to investigate and in how much depth. He or she will need to decide which tests are appropriate, how they are to be conducted and which criteria should be used to evaluate their results. The scope of the audit work has to be sufficient to allow the auditor to be reasonably satisfied that the financial statements are fairly presented in accordance with generally accepted accounting principles. However, the determination of how much audit work is appropriate is very subjective and the phrase 'professional judgement' is usually invoked to explain how this decision is made, for example:

> By far the most important consideration to the auditor in determining how much auditing depth is enough is deciding what constitutes reasonable satisfaction. To some this may seem a non-answer – too subjective, too circular to be useful. Like beauty, reasonable satisfaction lies in the eye of the beholder. But after all, this is the real world. A professional is identified by the exercise of informed, independent judgement. Were there a check-list or formula to tell us how far to go or when we have a basis for reasonable satisfaction, we would cease to be members of a profession. (Hall, 1978, p. 134)

As the above quotation implies, auditors have only a very approximate feel for the extent of the audit work necessary to provide a specific level of audit quality. It is very difficult to determine the probability that audited financial statements might contain a material error, even with a complete knowledge of what audit work has been done. The relationship between input (audit work) and output (audit confidence) is not sufficiently well understood to allow output audit quality to be readily linked to input quality.

As far as readers of audited financial statements are concerned, the only time they become aware of audit quality is when subsequent events show that the financial statements passed by the auditors were not in fact fairly presented. With the benefit of hindsight, it is usually fairly easy to argue that an auditor either failed to find or failed to report a breach by management because a poor quality audit had been conducted. Such a judgement is not necessarily fair, since audit opinions are always probabilistic statements. Indeed, the DeAngelo definition is couched in probabilistic terms. As the auditor cannot check all the transactions of a company, it is inevitable that there must be some probability that a significant error or omission has gone undetected. The decision an auditor must make is to select the level of audit quality he or she is aiming to achieve. Whatever level is selected, the auditor must expect that in the long run undetected errors will come to light in roughly the same proportion as the probability of non-detection. This is the essence of the audit risk assumed by auditors when they confirm that a set of financial statements show a true and fair view.

The main check on the quality of audit work occurs whenever audit failure is suspected and a case pursued for damages in a court of law. Such cases represent the acid test for auditors, since their work is set against the expectations of the court as to what is an appropriate standard of auditing. It is reasonable to suppose that auditing firms which appear regularly in court will gain a reputation for sub-standard audit work. Wilson and Grimlund (1990) found that audit firms involved in disciplinary actions by the Securities and Exchange Commission tended to lose market share relative to their competitors. They also had more difficulty in retaining clients than other public accounting firms. The difficulty faced by users (and researchers) in Europe is that few cases reach the courts and so there is little public information available. There are a number of reasons for this depending on the country concerned. In the UK, for example, there are two main reasons: one relates to the difficulty of pursuing an effective action for negligence against auditors following the 1990 Caparo decision and the second relates to the penchant of the insurance companies to settle cases out of court. However, despite the lack of many examples, it has to be assumed that there exists a level of minimum audit quality which is set by courts of law, albeit heavily influenced by statements of standard practice issued by the auditing profession.

Having provided a brief introduction to the process of auditing and how the quality of an audit might be judged, we can now turn to the selected articles and what they tell us about auditing and its relationship to governance.

5.   Readings Relating to the Role of Auditing in the Governance Process

The earliest article is by Flint (1971) and this sets out the role auditing has from the perspective of the accountability a corporation has to its stakeholders. Flint's basic position is that in a democratic society, power is not absolute and those who exercise it should be accountable for their actions. Flint sees the audit function as critical to ensuring accountability in the broadest and deepest sense. Chow (1982) uses an agency theory framework to analyse firms' incentives to hire external auditors. He argues that the major reason for firms to hire external auditors is to help to control the conflict of interests among firm managers, shareholders and bondholders. Furthermore, regardless of who nominally takes the decision to employ external auditors, this choice is guided by the expected effects of external auditing on the resource activities of the various parties. The probability that a firm will voluntarily hire external auditing increases with leverage, size and the number of accounting-based debt covenants. Anderson et al. (1993) extend the agency theory approach by viewing external auditing together with a larger set of monitoring mechanisms that can be used for corporate governance to include both internal auditing and directorships. They develop the argument that the comparative advantage of each type of monitoring in particular production-investment environments means that the substitutions among monitoring mechanisms are imperfect and that the mechanisms complement each other in the determination of the efficient mix of monitoring from these three sources. In stark contrast, both Pentland (1993) and Power (1996) take a view of the auditing process that emphasizes the social and contextual aspects of the work. Pentland sees auditing as a form of ritual purification in which the production of order within the audit process is the product of both tacit and formal knowledge which are combined to create 'comfort'. To reach a conclusion, in the face of an essentially unknowable situation, auditors must rely on the emotional resources generated by the audit ritual: 'gut feel'. Pentland sees that for society at large, the sanctity of the audit ritual is largely taken for granted, presupposed as a shared cultural resource. Power argues that auditing actively constructs the legitimacy of its own knowledge base and seeks to create the environments in which this knowledge base will be successful. Thus in this analysis, quality control procedures function less to make quality observable and more to construct and define quality itself. For Power, making things auditable is a constant and precarious project of a system of knowledge that must reproduce itself and sustain its institutional role from a diverse assemblage of routines, practices and economic constraints.

Finally in this section, the article by Humphrey et al. (1992) sets out to demonstrate that ever since modern corporate auditing started in the late 1800s, there has been a gap between what consumers of the audit service think they are receiving and what auditors think they are providing. Such an 'expectations gap' becomes visible when there has been some failure of corporate governance, usually as a result of fraud. In such circumstances, the first question is inevitably 'where were the auditors?'. The paper shows that this gap has been a regular concern for auditors and regulators, but that it never appears to be bridged and concludes it is unlikely that it ever will be. Auditors will see the existence of fraud at a client as a failure of the corporate governance process, while outsiders will see auditors as the primary control within the corporate governance process.

6. Readings Relating to Audit Quality and Auditor Reputation

A crucial element in the value of the audit in the governance process is the view of users of the quality of the audit work performed. DeAngelo's two 1981 articles have become seminal in providing a model for considering the quality of an audit. As noted earlier, the essence of her model is that audit quality depends on both the auditor's technical competence and independence. In her first paper, DeAngelo concentrated on independence, arguing that an auditor must have some incentive to tell the truth when the news is bad from the perspective of company management. Her main contention is that incumbent auditors possess cost advantages over competitors in future audits of a given client. These advantages occur because of the significant start-up costs in audit technology and transactions costs of switching auditors. When incumbent auditors possess these advantages, they can raise future audit fees above the avoidable costs of producing audits; that is to say, incumbent auditors earn client-specific quasi-rents. The expectation of receiving quasi-rents has two effects. Firstly, the optimal level of auditor independence is less than perfect independence, and secondly competition for these property rights to incumbency forces auditors to 'low ball' in the initial period (set an audit fee below cost). Hence in her model, low balling becomes a natural competitive response and does not reflect a lessening of audit quality, although it should be borne in mind that the analysis keeps technical quality and hence the costs of the audit as a constant, independent of audit fees charged. DeAngelo's second paper shows that when existing auditors earn quasi-rents, audit quality is not independent of firm size. These quasi-rents, when subject to loss from discovery of a lower-than-promised audit quality, serve as collateral against such opportunistic behaviour. The implication is that the larger the auditor as measured by the number of current clients and the smaller the client as a fraction of the auditor's total quasi-rents, the less incentive the auditor has to behave opportunistically and the higher the perceived quality of the audit. This result led to hundreds of later academic papers using a dichotomous variable for the Big Eight/ Six on the assumption that the large international accounting firms produce an audit of superior quality. One good example of the genre is Beatty (1989), which looks at the relationship between the reputation of the auditor of an initial public offering (IPO) and the initial return earned by an investor. He shows that US companies that hire more reputable audit firms exhibit lower initial returns than clients which choose to hire an audit firm with less reputational capital at stake. This means that the price paid by investors is higher for IPOs involving a large audit firm. Beatty's results suggest that the traditional Big Eight/non-Big Eight classification may measure audit firm reputation with error, particularly for the smaller Big Eight and larger non-Big Eight firms. Crasswell et al. (1995) also consider whether there is some reputational premium to industry specialization by an audit firm. They looked at Australian audit fees and found that, on average, industry specialist Big Eight auditors earned a 34 per cent premium over non-specialist Big Eight auditors. The Big Eight brand name premium over non-Big Eight auditors averaged around 30 per cent. These results support the argument that industry expertise is a dimension of the demand for higher quality Big Eight auditors and a basis for within-Big Eight product differentiation.

Palmrose (1988) and Lennox (1999) used litigation against auditors as an inverse measure of audit quality. Following DeAngelo and the professional literature, Palmrose (1988) defines audit quality as the probability that financial statements contain no material omissions or misstatements. Higher levels of assurance correspond to higher quality services. An important implication of this definition is that audit failures (financial statements with material omissions or misstatements) become less likely with higher quality services. Audit failure as defined is assumed to result in litigation because clients or users suffer losses as a consequence of materially false or misleading audited financial information. This suggests that users can view auditors with relatively low litigation activity as higher quality suppliers. Palmrose considered 472 US litigation cases for the period 1960–85. The results indicate that non-Big Eight firms as a group had higher litigation occurrence rates than the Big Eight, which Palmrose interpreted as being consistent with research showing the Big Eight to be quality-differentiated auditors. As well as the reputation hypothesis used by Palmrose, Lennox (1999) also considers the 'deep pockets hypothesis' as an explanation for litigation activity. The essence of the deep pockets hypothesis is that auditors with more wealth at risk should have more incentive to issue accurate reports, because larger auditors have deeper pockets and, therefore, have more to lose. Lennox looked at all UK publicly quoted companies in the period 1987–94. His sample, therefore, represents a later period than that in Palmrose as well as a different legal environment. Lennox's analysis uses not only cases where writs were issued against audit firms, but also news items in which the work of auditors received criticism. Both measures of litigation and criticism showed a strong relationship between auditor size and litigation activity, indicating that large auditors were more prone to litigation despite their supposed superior accuracy. He could not find any evidence that criticized auditors suffered any client losses or lower audit fees compared with similar uncriticized auditors. Lennox interprets this result as indicating that reputation effects do not seem to have an influence on the consumers of the audit service. In his view, it is the threat of litigation rather than the loss of client-specific rents that drives the superior accuracy of large auditors. The most likely explanation for the differences between Lennox and Palmrose is that the legal environment changed in the mid-1980s in both the US and the UK, when it became much more common for aggrieved users of audited financial statements to sue the auditors. In addition, the Big Eight/Six had become relatively much larger than the remaining medium sized audit firms and so the forces underpinning the deep pockets hypothesis would have become much stronger.

Another area of study which can give an insight into quality perceptions of the work of auditors is when there is a change of auditor. Francis and Wilson (1988) looked at 676 US auditor changes that took place in the period 1978–85. The essence of their approach is that given a change in auditor has occurred, is the choice of the new auditor associated with a change in agency costs? Audit firm quality was defined in two ways: as a categorical variable, Big Eight or not, and as a continuous size variable based on total client sales audited by the audit firm. The results provided support for the proposition that there is an association between agency cost proxies and the choice of brand name Big Eight audit firm, but there was no consistent association using the continuous size proxy for audit quality. After controlling for client size and growth, the individual agency cost proxies that were at least weakly significant were: the presence of accounting-based incentive bonus plans, diffusion of ownership, leverage and the new issue of securities following the auditor change. However, the overall explanatory power of the models is low, indicating that other factors are also influential. Johnson and Lys (1990) continue the analysis looking at 490 companies that replaced their auditor in the period 1973–82, a similar period to that used by Francis and Wilson. They argue that voluntary client–auditor realignment can generally be explained as an efficient response to competition among audit firms. They argue that audit firms specialize by adopting distinctive production technologies which reduce the costs of supplying audit services to particular market segments. Clients wish to purchase audit services from the least cost supplier and so change auditor when the incumbent can no longer provide the level and type of services required at the lowest cost. As the production functions of audit firms are not observable, Johnson and Lys used relative audit firm size as a proxy for cost structure variations (relative size being measured in terms of the total sales of clients of an audit firm). They also looked at the effects of auditor switches on share price returns. They found a general absence of systematic abnormal returns over the three days centred on the announcement of an auditor switch.

As well as focusing on the output side of the audit process, some studies have looked at the audit production process. Two examples are included: Palmrose (1989) and O'Keefe et al. (1994). Palmrose obtained data on audit fees and the total number of hours spent on audit engagements in the 1980–81 time period. Her primary aim was to see whether the type of audit contract (fixed fee or cost reimbursement) affected audit fees and audit hours. She noted that fixed-fee contracts tended to be used more in the early years of an audit engagement. While *ceteris paribus* fixed-fee contracts appeared to result in lower audit fees, there was no significant effect on audit hours, suggesting that the greater incentives for efficiencies under fixed-fee contracts did not result in a reduction in audit hours. There is one particularly interesting finding which is buried in footnote 8 on page 496 (p. 300 of this volume). This notes that the variable relating to the number of years that the auditor had been retained was not significant in the audit fee regression, but that it was negatively significant in the audit hour regression. This suggests that auditors did less work as they became more and more familiar with the client, but this did not result in lower audit fees. This is consistent with DeAngelo's arguments of pricing advantages to incumbency; an audit firm's profit margins improve over time. O'Keefe et al. extended the work of Palmrose by obtaining disaggregated labour hour information by rank (partner, manager, senior and staff). The major drawback of the O'Keefe et al. study is that their data relate to only one Big Eight firm for 249 of its audits performed in 1989, and hence this limits the generalizability of their results. They found that the cross-sectional variation in the quantity of labour inputs could largely be explained by the same client size, complexity and risk measures found to be important in previous research on audit fees. However, the client size and risk measures were also associated with significant changes in the mix of labour inputs, which were not used in fixed proportions. Certain risk measures had a statistically significant effect only on some classes of labour. They found no evidence of auditor learning over time for any class of labour.

The final paper in this section is Carcello et al. (1992), which looks at audit quality from the perceptions of 245 Big Six audit partners, 264 Fortune 1000 controllers (preparers) and 120 financial statement users (fund managers and bankers). The factors that were viewed as being most important to audit quality were: (i) audit team and firm experience with the client, (ii) industry expertise, (iii) CPA firm responsiveness to client needs, and (iv) CPA firm compliance with general audit standards. However, among the three groups there were significant differences in the importance assigned to each factor.

7. Readings Related to Governance and the Audit Committee

The establishment of audit committees in the US was recommended by the Securities and Exchange Commission as early as 1940, but it is only within the last 30 years that the role of audit committees in the corporate governance process has increased dramatically. Hence most of the important studies of the workings of audit committees tend to be recent. Both Bradbury (1990) and Menon and Williams (1994) use an agency theory approach to explain the voluntary formation of audit committees. Essentially, this model predicts that audit committees will be voluntarily employed in situations of high agency costs to enhance the quality of the information flows between principal and agent. Bradbury's sample consisted of 135 companies listed on the New Zealand stock exchange and he examined their 1981 financial statements. The most obvious result from Bradbury's study is that in a voluntary environment very few companies form audit committees. He found no significant relationship between voluntary audit committee formation and auditor incentive variables or to agency cost variables arising from the separation of ownership and control. However, a relationship was found between voluntary audit committee formation and directors' incentives. Both the number of directors on the board and intercorporate ownership were found to be the more important determinants of voluntary audit committee formation. Menon and Williams constructed a randomly selected US sample of 200 over-the-counter (OTC) firms for which data on audit committees existed. The period chosen was 1986–87, when OTC firms were not required to form audit committees. Forty-four firms out of the sample of 200 firms did not maintain an audit committee. However, while the majority of firms had an audit committee, many of these firms did not rely on them. Fifty-seven audit committees did not meet at all or met only once during the year studied and nineteen were staffed by insiders. The multivariate analysis showed that audit committee formation was related to the type of auditor employed by the firm and the proportion of outsiders on the board of directors. However, auditor type was not associated with measures of reliance on audit committees, suggesting that the big accounting firms might have encouraged the formation of an audit committee but went no further in persuading boards to rely on them. There was a size effect, with larger companies having more active audit committees than smaller ones. The empirical analysis provided little support for the agency theory variables, management stock ownership and leverage.

Following on from the work of Bradbury, Menon and Williams and others, Kalbers and Fogarty (1998) use institutional theory to discuss the inability of agency theory to explain the voluntary formation of audit committees. Institutional theory offers a sociological approach that questions the sufficiency of technical rationality for understanding corporate governance. Hence, as a result of the importance of creating ceremonial structures for the benefit of constituencies, control structures may not exist primarily to accomplish control objectives. The theory suggests that outcomes, such as effectiveness, are more attributable to an internal 'core' logic not derivable from external structures. This core escapes the attention of external parties and is therefore unconstrained by their influence. As well as testing the traditional agency theory variables, Kalbers and Fogarty introduce two derived from institutional theory. The first is that the level of agency costs is not directly related to audit committee effectiveness and the second that publicly available measures of audit committee attributes are not directly associated with audit committee effectiveness. The sample consisted of data from 79 companies and from 164 individuals who responded to a questionnaire survey instrument. The effectiveness data were taken from the questionnaire results. The findings of the study support the conclusion that audit committee effectiveness emanates from sources close to the actual functioning of the committee. The formal empowerment of the audit committee appears to be designed for the consumption of external parties with some interests in the adherence to adequate forms of corporate control. Kalbers and Fogarty conclude that the true relevance of corporate structures that establish and maintain audit committees is the linkages they forge with the power exerted by the individuals that serve monitoring functions within organizations. A key sentence in their conclusions is that 'In sum, corporate governance cannot be left to rational economic incentives' (p. 396 of this volume).

As demands for improving corporate governance increase, the audit committee has become a favoured regulatory solution. Accordingly, researchers have started to look at how audit committees operate. Klein (2002) looks at the independence of audit committees, using the percentage of outsiders on the audit committee as a measure of its independence. She makes the assumption that audit committee members who are independent of management are better monitors of the firm's financial reporting process. This better monitoring should produce more transparent financial statements containing more unbiased financial accounting numbers. Her sample consisted of the non-financial companies listed on the Standard & Poor 500 Index in the US as of 31 March 1992 and 1993, producing a sample of 803 firm-years representing just over 400 companies. During that time, exchange rules allowed more flexibility with respect to audit committee independence and many firms opted for audit committees with less than 100 per cent outside directors. Klein found that audit committee independence increased with board size and the percentage of outsiders on the board, consistent with the hypothesis that audit committee independence depends on the supply of available outside directors on the board. In contrast, audit committee independence decreased with the firm's growth opportunities and when the firm reported net losses in each of the two preceding years. This result supports the hypothesis that audit committee independence is related to management's and shareholders' demand for scrutiny of the firm's financial accounting process, the argument being that the financial statements become less value relevant when a firm makes losses. Klein also allows an alternative explanation which is that the negative association between losses and audit committee independence arises because such firms have greater difficulty attracting outside directors to serve on their audit committees as a result of fears over additional personal liability concerns.

One key role of the audit committee is to defend external auditors from pressure from management to modify their opinion using the threat of dismissal if the auditors do not accede to management's wishes. Carcello and Neal (2003) examine the extreme case of what happens when auditors are faced with the decision of whether or not to issue a going-concern qualification in their audit report. This represents an extreme form of qualification because the auditor is raising doubts about the future existence of the company. Carcello and Neal wanted to test the impact of audit committees and so they created two sets of matched pairs of companies that had audit committees. To create the first match pair, they identified a sample of 62 non-financial companies that had received a new going-concern qualification and had subsequently dismissed their audit firm. These were then matched with 62 companies that had also received a going-concern qualification but which had not dismissed their audit firm. A further sample was also created of 125 companies that had received a clean audit opinion but which had dismissed their auditors in the following year. This sample was then matched with 125 companies that had received a clean audit opinion but which did not change their audit firm. One of their key explanatory variables was the percentage of audit committee members who were classed as 'affiliated' directors. These were directors who had or had had some link with the company as a result of employment, trading, professional or personal relationships. Carcello and Neal's results suggest that an audit committee that is more independent (that is to say, has a lower than average percentage of affiliated directors on the audit committee), with members who sit on more boards (governance expertise) and who own less company stock, is more effective in protecting the auditor from dismissal following the issuance of a going-concern report. These results appear to be caused by the contentious nature of the issuance of a going-concern report, as there was no equivalent relationship for companies dismissing their auditor after having received a clean audit opinion. These results provide an explanation for the results of an earlier paper (Carcello and Neale, 2000), which showed that audit firms were less likely to issue going-concern reports to financially distressed clients whose audit committees lacked independence.

8.   Readings on the Relationship between Internal and External Auditors

The relationship between internal and external auditors is an important one from the perspective of corporate governance. Both groups can help reduce the business risk of a company and also ensure that its financial statements fairly reflect the underlying economic reality. Unfortunately, internal audit is something of a Cinderella subject, both for practising auditors and researchers.

As a result, there have been few academic studies and only three have been selected for inclusion in this volume. The lack of research is disappointing, because since the early 1990s there has been somewhat of a revolution in internal audit, with it becoming much more focused on risk evaluation and less on its traditional role of compliance testing. This focus of internal audit has mirrored the change in external audit, which itself has become more focused on risk assessment and less concerned with compliance and substantive testing to judge the truth and fairness of a set of financial statements.

One of the key elements bringing about this change in the focus of internal audit has been the development of control self-assessment (CSA), and interested readers are referred to the book of readings edited by Keith Wade and Andy Wynne (1999). CSA promises to liberate internal auditors from being a profession dominated by low-value-added compliance testing and reporting into one in which internal auditors are routinely using and adapting sophisticated conceptual control models to assess, design and report on the status of control and risk in their organizations. Internal auditors are thus enabled to undertake root cause analysis and powerful profiling of behavioural forces at work in organizations. CSA is in essence a bottom-up approach to risk management. Its key objectives are to identify and measure organizational risks and then to improve related controls and organizational processes to help improve the organization's performance. CSA provides a means to achieve these objectives by having a formal procedure for extracting knowledge from both senior management and the persons who work within a process for their assessment of the risks and controls in their particular process.

The first article is by Lampe and Sutton (1994), who look at the specific guidance issued by UK, US and Canadian professional bodies to external auditors when using the work of internal auditors. Professional auditing standards recognize that internal auditors may contribute to the financial statement audit by either working as assistants under the direct supervision of the external auditors or independently performing relevant work throughout the audit year on which the external auditors can rely. The article describes the traditional roles of the internal audit department and the use made of its work by external auditors. The article primarily focuses on the UK Auditing Practices Board's Exposure Draft SAS 500, *Considering the Work of Internal Auditors*. It then describes a two-phase research study of the key elements used by internal auditors when evaluating the quality of internal audit work. These results are then compared with the SAS 500 and it is found that there is much in common, but that there are differences, which the paper documents.

The second article by Felix et al. (2001) looks at the contribution of internal audit as a determinant of external audit fees. Felix et al. had a unique data set comprising publicly available archival data and matched survey responses from internal and external auditors affiliated with 70 non-financial services Fortune 1000 firms. They found that the extent to which internal audit contributes to the financial statement audit is a significant determinant of external audit fees: the greater the contribution, the smaller external audit fees. While this result is not surprising, Felix et al. also show that the contribution made by internal audit is influenced by internal audit quality as assessed by the external auditors. They found that as inherent risk increased, there was a diminution in the effect of the assessment of the external auditors of whether the internal audit department had time available to assist in the performance of the financial statement audit. However, as inherent risk increased, there was a greater influence of the co-ordination variable, which related to the degree of integration judged by external auditors to exist in their relationship with the internal auditors.

One of the logical extensions of the results of Felix et al. is that there may be synergies to be had were external auditors to undertake the internal audit work as well, hence eliminating any co-ordination problems. Additionally, as indicated at the beginning of this section, the working practices of internal audit are changing and becoming more like those of the external audit, being focused on business risk assessment. Hence, given these two forces, it is perhaps not surprising that there has been a recent trend for external auditors to seek to gain internal audit work. Rittenberg and Covaleski (2001) looked at this clash between the public accounting profession and the internal auditing profession over the provision of internal audit services. They used two literature perspectives: (i) the sociology of the professions and (ii) outsourcing. Their article is interesting because it tries to analyse what it is that constitutes external auditing and internal auditing. At one level, the difference relates to the possession of a body of abstract knowledge on which each of the two professions bases its claims for the exclusive right to control specific work activities. The Big Five audit firms' jurisdictional claim was judged to fit both theories as the Big Five highlighted their attributes of being global knowledge professionals having unparalled access to public information. For its part, the internal audit profession claimed unique local knowledge and command of private information.

9. Conclusions

The selected articles should provide a good indication of the academic research in relation to auditing and governance. Much work has been done and there is now a body of knowledge of how auditing can contribute to the process by which outside stakeholders monitor the activities of corporate management. The problematic element in the relationship between auditors and stakeholders is the fact that it is corporate management who effectively control who are a company's auditors and how much they should be paid. Auditing standards exist and set out what auditors should do in particular circumstances and so offer some protection against the temptation to cut corners and hence make the audit more profitable. However, the main worries of users of audited financial statements concern auditor independence and the temptation for auditors to do, not what they know they should, but what is likely to be acceptable to management. The problem for external stakeholders is that the work of the auditors is not observable and so they must use indirect indicators of quality. The one that seems to have the most significant effect is whether the audit firm belongs to the top tier of international accounting firms, which was once the Big Eight, then the Big Six, more recently Five and now Four. There is a deep irony in the fact that while this classification appears empirically to be significant in many areas, it was a Big Five firm, Andersen, that imploded so spectacularly following the collapse of Enron. With this exception, the Big firms have weathered many scandals without any noticeable effect on their perceived competence and independence. However, as Humphrey et al. have observed (Chapter 6), the gap between the level of assurance expected by stakeholders of auditors and what level of assurance auditors themselves expect to provide is one that is unlikely ever to go away: *plus ça change, plus c'est la meme chose* (no superficial or apparent change alters the essential nature).

However, regulators do worry about the auditor expectation gap and in particular about auditor independence, and one of their favoured solutions is a strong audit committee. Research in this area is still in its infancy, but it is clear that the quality of audit committee members will have to come under similar scrutiny to that which they are supposed to subject external auditors. The blurring of the roles of internal and external auditor is also a recent phenomenon that awaits more academic research as its effects are not yet clear. The main conclusion, therefore, is that there is still much research work that needs to be done on the relationship between auditing and governance.

Additional References

Antle, R. (1982), 'The Auditor as an Economic Agent', *Journal of Accounting Research*, Autumn, 503–27.

Carcello, J.V. and T.L. Neal (2000), 'Audit Committee Composition and Auditor Reporting', *Accounting Review*, **75**, 453–67.

DeAngelo, L.E. (1981), 'Auditor Size and Audit Quality', *Journal of Accounting and Economics*, December, 183–99.

Hall, W.R. (1978), 'How Much Auditing is Enough? Critique – An Auditor's Viewpoint', *Proceedings of the Arthur Young Professors' Roundtable Conference*, pp. 133–41.

Ng, D.S. (1978), 'Supply and Demand for Auditing Services and the Nature of Regulations in Auditing', *Proceedings of the Arthur Young Professors' Roundtable Conference*, pp. 99–124.

Wade, K. and A. Wynne (1999), *Control Self Assessment*, Chichester: John Wiley and Sons.

Wallace, W. (1980), *The Economic Role of the Audit in Free and Regulated Markets*, Touche Ross Foundation.

Wilson, T.E. and R.A. Grimlund (1990), 'An Examination of the Importance of an Auditor's Reputation', *Auditing: A Journal of Practice and Theory*, **9**, Spring, 43–59.

Part I
Role of Auditing in the Governance Process

The Role of the Auditor in Modern Society: An Exploratory Essay

David Flint

It is now 75 years since the memorable and much quoted remark of Lord Justice Lopes in the Kingston Cotton Mill[1] case: 'An auditor is not bound to be a detective . . . he is a watchdog, but not a bloodhound.' Whatever may have been the case in 1896 the inherent philosophy of such an approach is entirely irrelevant to the needs of today. It is passive and protective with some hint of reserved power to be brought into play if sufficiently provoked. What is needed in auditing is something dynamic, a critical, penetrating, enquiring attitude of mind, and a deep conviction of a vital social purpose. In some respects this last aspect is the most important. The practice of auditing cannot evolve satisfactorily in a changing world if it is not conceived and exercised in the context of a social philosophy of audit and accountability.

There is an urgent need for clearer understanding of what that social philosophy is because at the present time the audit function is under challenge. Auditors for what they conceive to be their duty and for how they discharge that duty are under even greater public challenge. This is a matter which is serious and fundamental. The public are right to question and to challenge. Matters of public interest are at issue. It fails to measure up to the problem, or to appreciate the nature of the challenge, for auditors to retreat behind the defence that the public really do not understand what auditors do or for what they take responsibility; or for auditors to deplore the ignorance and intolerance of the public in the context of the growing volume and size of claims for damages and the prospect of criminal prosecution for negligence.

There may indeed be a need for better communication, better understanding, better public relations and some institutional action should be taken to deal with this. However, the really critical social issue is what should be the concern of the modern audit. What is the role of the auditor in modern society? Is

the present responsibility – however onerous – the right one in the context of the society of the 1970s and prospectively of the last quarter of the twentieth century? There is no evidence that this issue is the subject of serious consideration and research.

It is true that audit practice has changed and is changing; new methods and techniques are being developed and used; auditing standards have been raised. Yet, how can it be determined if they are adequate until it is certain that the objective they are designed to achieve is right. Against what criteria can the adequacy of practice be judged in the absence of a basic philosophy. The theoretical basis of the audit function has received little attention in the past and yet it is an evolving function reacting to social change and need. The doubt and uncertainty of the public about the audit function and suspicion as to its inadequacy in terms of satisfying a social need is almost mirrored by the lack of comprehension by auditors of the wider relevance of what they do and of the underlying nature of the public disquiet. This is not intended to criticise the integrity and competence of professional auditors. Far from it. Without doubt, the immediate and explicit objects of any audit are well understood and it is not the purpose of this paper to elaborate on them. However, these objectives must not be seen as an end in themselves but as a means only of fulfilling the audit function in the particular social institution and it is to this that the auditor should address his attention.

The terms of reference of any audit can only imperfectly convey the principle of the audit and it is this which should determine practice. The Companies Acts, the Nationalised Industries Acts, the Savings Banks Acts, the Building Societies Acts, the Friendly Societies Acts, etc. do not set out why there has to be an audit; they specify very little about what is required in the audit. There is a widespread acceptance that audit has some well understood meaning and significance. Yet, professional literature does not

---

[1] In re Kingston Cotton Mill Co Ltd (1896), 2 Ch. 279.

attempt to explain the social function and the conceptual principles of audit. For example, explanations from the statements of the professional bodies read –

'The term "audit" as used throughout this study refers to an auditor's examination – performed without restriction by management as to scope – of the basic, general purpose financial statements of business conducted in corporate form.'

'The principal function of the auditor is to express a professional opinion on the financial statements of his client.' (*Accountants International Study Group*)[2]

'The purpose of the work of the auditors is to enable them to express an opinion as to whether the accounts presented to the members show a true and fair view.' (*Institute of Chartered Accountants in England and Wales*)[3]

'The objective of the ordinary examination of financial statements by the independent auditor is the expression of an opinion on the fairness with which they present financial position and results of operations.' (*American Institute of Certified Public Accountants*)[4]

and, from a selection of the leading texts –

'The object of a modern audit . . . has as its ultimate aim the verification of the financial position disclosed by the balance sheet and the profit and loss account of the undertaking.'[5]

'The object of an audit is to ensure that the accounts on which the auditor is reporting show a true and fair view and are not misleading.'[6]

'An audit is an examination of accounting records undertaken with a view to establishing whether they correctly and completely reflect the transactions to which they purport to relate.'[7]

This representative selection is clear on the immediate objectives but goes no further and does not help in an enquiry as to the underlying purpose of these objectives. These objectives must be set in some wider social context and it is this which must be sought.

'Without audit, no accountability; without accountability, no control; and if there is no control, where is the seat of power' states Professor W. J. M. Mackenzie[8] and this looks more like a pointer to the social

framework of the audit function.

Accountability

Admittedly the comment is made in relation to government but it is equally apposite in other social institutions, in business, finance, social and other services. The powers of directors, managers, administrators, governors – whatever may be the name of those entrusted with decision making authority in these diverse institutions – is not absolute. The power is granted and is exercised at the behest of some other group which society has placed in this superior position, generally with the force and sanction of law. Directors, managers and administrators have this duty of accountability, a duty to demonstrate the quality of their performance within the constraints of the limited responsibility which has been entrusted to them. It is in this context that society has conceived the audit function whereby the performance of, and the account of their performance, submitted by the directors, managers, etc. may be subject to some scrutiny on behalf of those to whom the directors, managers, etc. are accountable. The starting point therefore is to establish what degree of accountability is required. For this purpose it is not too important to establish where the law stands – or is thought to stand – at the moment. The position is taken that the law is the creature of society and may be enacted to give sanction to what society has determined to be desirable or to what has on some criteria been determined by legislators to be desirable, in the best interests of society. The issue under examination is the role of the auditor in modern society as it is emerging and evolving to meet the social needs of society. Nor is it relevant to this study to consider whether the role as so conceived could be filled by those who are educated and trained by reference to present professional requirements. Education and training have to be developed to meet the need – as has been done in the past and is being done, for example, in relation to computers.

Although society has increasingly concerned itself with, for example, conditions of work and employment, with qualities and standards and with amenity and public interest, has legislated in these areas, and has made institutions accountable for their actions it is only in relation to financial affairs that the concept of accountability subject to audit has developed – and an analysis of the character of this accountability shows that it is not a fixed but an evolving concept. At an early stage, at the time of the growth of corporations with limited liability from the middle of the nineteenth century, particularly with the increasing incidence of separation of management and capital, the primary need was seen to be honesty and regu-

[2] Accountants International Study Group *The Independent Auditor's Reporting Standards in Three Nations*, para 7.

[3] The Institute of Chartered Accountants in England and Wales, *General Principles of Auditing*, p. 6.

[4] American Institute of Certified Public Accountants, *Auditing Standards and Procedures*, p. 9.

[5] *Practical Auditing*, Spicer and Pegler, 15th Edition, 1969, p. 2.

[6] *Manual of Auditing*, VRV Cooper, 2nd Edition, 1969, p. 1.

[7] *Auditing*, L. R. Dicksee, 18th Edition, 1969, p. 1.

[8] *The Accountability and Audit of Governments*, E. L. Normanton, Foreword, p. vii.

larity in financial affairs. Indicative of the general nature of accountability in business carried on by limited companies was the nature of periodic account required – a balance sheet only – and the standard or quality of reporting required – 'a true and correct view'. It was not until 1929 that a profit and loss account was required – the details of it were not specified and it was not required to be embraced in the audit report. Not until 1948, was there specified in some detail the information required to be presented in the balance sheet and the profit and loss account and at the same time the standard or quality of reporting required was revised to 'a true and fair view'.

These dates and others which can be quoted over 100 years when different matters of accounting were specified in statute are merely milestones recognising what was an evolutionary change in society's concept of accountability in limited companies. The earlier requirement for honesty and regularity, demonstrated by a balance sheet giving a true and correct view, was not too concerned with profit measurement provided the profit was not over-stated to the possible prejudice of creditors' interests and provided it was not misappropriated to the prejudice of shareholders. However, progressive social change over a century has resulted in considerable change. The increased size and complexity of business units, the development of a class of professional managers with little or no stake in the capital, greater sophistication in the techniques and practices of management, much more informed scrutiny and review of business performance and accounts have been the principal factors contributing to the development of a wider and more demanding interpretation of what management were accounting for. The influence of economists and others in the direction of affairs, accompanied by an understanding of the economic significance for society of the policies and decisions of major national and international business groupings has resulted in much greater interest in the efficient utilisation of resources and accordingly in the quality of managerial performance. Over the period profit came to be recognised as a yardstick with which to measure management performance. Parallel with this development, as a consequence of the increasing complexity of business operations and of the industrial process it became recognised that even in the limited context of honesty and regularity, as a quality of the balance sheet, 'correct' was too absolute for a view which was substantially dependent on the opinion and judgement of management in relation to material items. However, when 'fair' was introduced as the requisite standard in 1948 honesty and regularity were still the keystones of management accountability, and it was

in this context that their performance and their report were to be judged.

Introduction of the concept of 'fairness' in financial reporting prompts some speculation on the influence of social values on the quality of financial accountability and reporting. It is part of the thesis of this paper that the quality of accountability expected in business is a reflection of the ethics and standards of society and is the product of the attitudes of society to the responsibilities in respect of the exercise of which the accountability is due. Society's views of what should be expected of directors and managers will fashion the accountability and changes in social thinking will, accordingly, result in changed expectations. There is no doubt that changes in social, economic and political thought over a century and a half have changed the quality of accountability expected of directors and managers. The change is very much greater than is implied in even the fairly extensive changes in specification in the statute, and in the movement from 'correct' to 'fair'. The real essence of the change has not been effected by statute at all. The important change has been the evolution from a standard of honesty and regularity to one of efficient utilisation of resources. While this change has taken place in the quality or character of accountability the criteria of the test of the report of accountability have remained the same – truth and fairness in presentation – i.e. the matters of which the truth and fairness is in issue have changed.

From a test of what was true and correct in relation to honest intromission, the character of the report revealing the quality of the accountability in business has developed, through what was a true and fair view of the resources in respect of which honest intromission was required, to what is a true and fair view of what is required to be presented to investing shareholders to meet information needs – not only in relation to honesty and regularity of management, but in relation also to efficiency of management in the allocation, utilisation and control of resources, as a basis of decision, not so much on directors' appointments and dividend distribution, although these still apply, but as a basis of decision on investment.

The implications of this for the auditor are clear. The function in its basic concept is unchanged but the demands of the function have changed immensely and the social significance of the function has changed from being one of mainly private concern to being one of considerable public concern. Since the auditor is the expert scrutineer with the responsibility of ensuring that the quality of management accountability is maintained and demonstrated he must understand and keep abreast of the evolutionary changes in the quality of accountability that is required.

The fact that the audit function does change and adapt to the views of society can be verified from the professional texts. In 1896 detection of errors seems to have been the primary objective.

'An Audit, to be effectual, that is, to enable the auditor to certify as to the accuracy of the accounts presented, may for practical purposes be divided into three parts, namely, to guard against,

1. Errors of omission;
2. Errors of commission; and
3. Errors of principle.'[9]

However, by 1919, the detection of fraud ranks more significantly.

'The object of an audit may be said to be threefold
1. The detection of fraud.
2. The detection of technical errors.
3. The detection of errors of principle.

On account of its intrinsic importance the detection of fraud is clearly entitled to be considered an "object" in itself, although it will be obvious that it can only be concealed by the commission of a technical error, or of an error of principle. It will be appropriate therefore to combine the search after fraud with search for technical and fundamental errors; but it can never be too strongly insisted that the auditor may find fraud concealed under any item that he is called upon to verify. His research for fraud should therefore be unwearying and constant.'[10]

and by 1969 both fraud and error have been relegated to subordinate importance.

'The main object of an audit is to give a report on the view presented by the accounts and statement prepared by the client (and his staff), in accordance with the terms of the auditor's appointment. Although of great importance, detection of fraud and error must be regarded as incidental to this main object.'[11]

This current view was confirmed by James C. Stewart writing in 1956

'I take the main objective of an audit to be to enable the auditor to express an opinion for the guidance and protection of proprietors; the detection and prevention of fraud or error may be incidental results of the audit but are not, in my opinion, objectives in themselves.'[12]

and by John A. Stewart in 1958

'The prevention and detection of error and fraud

---

is not regarded as a primary purpose of the audit.'[13]

Fraud and errors

Reassuring as this view may be to the auditor there are good grounds for asking if society so readily accepts it or if in the event of having to decide the issue the courts might see it quite so clearly. Admittedly it is a question of emphasis and relative importance.

This emphasises the importance of developing a concept of what it is that the ethics and standards and social philosophy of society shape as the kind of accountability which is expected, and, through audit, exacted of directors and managers and others.

Within the context of the accountability so conceived society is entitled to expect to be advised, as a result of audit, if in any respect performance has fallen short.

It is not disputed that it is the responsibility of directors, managers, etc. to protect the business or organisation against error, fraud and defalcation; and that an auditor cannot and has never been expected to guarantee accounting and accounts. However, it seems likely that the public concept of the audit function would include an expectation that the auditor should, at least, take explicit responsibility and say that, on the basis of his examination, there is a probability (to be qualified and preferably quantified) that error, fraud and defalcation have not remained undetected.

Criticism of the audit and of auditors at the present time largely begs the question of honesty and regularity. Auditors are regarded as honest, competent and of integrity but misguided. This may well be implicitly a tribute either to the general integrity of directors, managers, etc. or to the effectiveness of the audit in that regard. Yet it is a dangerous subordination of the importance of detection of fraud and error. It fosters a complacent attitude of mind which is totally inappropriate. Another of the dicta which should be jettisoned immediately – not because it is wholly untrue but because of the attitude of mind it engenders – is again attributed to Lord Justice Lopes in the Kingston Cotton Mill[14] case.

'Auditors must not be made liable for not tracking out ingenious and carefully laid schemes of fraud where there is nothing to arouse their suspicion ...'

It is too passive. Society is entitled to expect from the auditor an imaginative, penetrating, enquiring attitude which is alert to the opportunities for irregularity in the particular circumstances; not solely waiting, however diligently, for the event which arouses suspicion.

---

[9] *Auditors: Their Duties and Responsibilities*, F. W. Pixley 7th Edition, 1896, p. 437.
[10] *Auditing*, L. R. Dicksee, 11th Edition, 1919, p. 7.
[11] *Practical Auditing*, Spicer and Pegler, 15th Edition, 1969, p. 3.
[12] 'Current Auditing Problems: Some Reflections and Queries', J. C. Stewart, *The Accountants Magazine*, Vol. LXI, 1957, p. 217.

[13] 'Auditing Methods and Responsibilities', John A. Stewart, *The Accountants Magazine*, Vol. LXIII, 1959, p. 15.
[14] In re Kingston Cotton Mill Co Ltd (1896), 2 Ch, 279.

Fairness and the public interest

However, even more demanding than this traditional responsibility is the role of the auditor as the guardian of the elusive quality of fairness in the presentation of a financial report of business. Without legislative change, society's interpretation of the application of fairness has changed over 25 years, moving with the change in what society regards as the nature of accountability of business directors and managers.

What has been insufficiently recognised is that the change in the nature of accountability obliges directors and managers to communicate not only information which demonstrates the quality of their performance, but, in addition, adequate information for the various recognised decisions of the shareholders to whom the information is addressed. However hard and conscientiously managers may try to meet this requirement, society has cast the auditor in the role of judging whether it is good enough. The auditor is the one person with sufficient knowledge of all the facts and circumstances, with the professional competence which gives an appreciation of the issues involved and an understanding of what communication can be achieved, who is required to exercise independent judgement and to say, measured against society's requirements as a report to shareholders, this financial report gives a true and fair view.

A financial report prepared by the directors with complete integrity, presenting what they believe to be a true and fair view, may not give a true and fair view, in the opinion of the auditor, not because the directors are at fault, but solely because their involvement prevents them from seeing the position dispassionately.

Perhaps the most difficult point to comprehend is that the view which is true and fair is not and cannot be defined by the statute. On its own, satisfaction of the formal requirements of the statute is not an adequate test of true and fair presentation. The directorial or managerial responsibility is to think in terms of the duty of accountability and to make the report which discharges that duty. The auditor through his skill in accounts and his knowledge of business and finance must be thinking of ways in which misunderstanding, misrepresentation or confusion could be caused not necessarily by dishonesty or error or fraud, although he obviously must consider these, but through the use or misuse of the processes of accounting. The scope for this is large in the complexities of industrial processing, of distribution and of financial relationship.

It is not sufficient for the auditor to wait for a clue. Nor is it sufficient for the auditor to act solely within what he conceives to be his legal liability. The ultimate test is the public interest – not a set of club rules which auditors may work out for themselves to make life less intolerable. It is the degree of penetration and perception which the auditor is able to and prepared to apply in his examination and in his assessment of the truth and fairness of management's report, which is at issue. The issue which is at stake is not the quantum of the disclosure but the relevance and quality of what is in fact presented.

Social responsibilities of business

A further factor which must be taken into account is that society's view as to the social responsibilities of business are changing and the emerging changes will have an impact on the pattern of financial accountability and consequently on the auditor's role. Although the legal framework of business based on the social thinking of the nineteenth century still gives prior place in accountability to the providers of capital there is now increasing acceptance that there is a major responsibility to employees and to the community – perhaps also to customers – as to how the business is managed and its policies directed. While there are inevitably financial constraints and the standards of efficient financial management are increasingly rigorous these have to be viewed in the context not solely of profitable operation for the benefit of capital but rather of efficient operation for the benefit of the several interests of employees, the community and capital – and perhaps in that order.

This is not a trend in the UK alone – employees' representation on supervisory boards in Germany and compulsory profit sharing in France are demonstrations of the same philosophy. The previous Government in this country was committed to a re-examination of 'the whole theory and purpose of the limited joint stock company, the comparative rights and obligations of shareholders, directors, creditors, employees and the community as a whole'[15] and had declared its intention to provide by legislation that trade unions could 'obtain from employers certain sorts of information that are needed for negotiations'.[16] The essential elements of the same philosophy were accepted by the present Government which stated that it considered 'that it is an essential part of the successful conduct of collective bargaining that the employer should not unnecessarily withhold information about his undertaking that the trade union representatives need in the course of negotiations' and that 'the employees of the larger employers should be entitled to some basic information about the undertaking, just as shareholders are in the case of public companies. The provision of this informa-

[15] President of the Board of Trade, House of Commons Debates, 14 February 1967, Col. 359.
[16] In Place of Strife, Command 3888, 1969.

tion to employees would recognise the interests which they have in the progress of the undertaking for which they work and would acknowledge its obligations towards them.'[17] The means of ensuring this are now included in the provisions of the Industrial Relations Act.[18]

A change in the focus of accountability does not reduce but may well enhance the importance of the auditor's role. Insofar as the change of focus is likely, if anything, to add rigour to the expectations of managerial efficiency in financial administration, the social significance of the audit function is raised in importance.

In a situation in which society has accepted that profit is one valuable yardstick of managerial performance, the next stages are not only to require norms against which to measure past performance, but to expect management to communicate on what basis and on what criteria decisions on future operations are based, which will inevitably involve saying something about future profits, however circumscribed any such figures may be.

Society is also going to expect a level of efficiency and sophistication in financial administration and in the management of business policies which will lead it to expect to be disclosed by audit not solely a fair view of the profit which has been earned as evidence of management's success, of the allocation of resources and of the prospects for the future but in addition an opinion as to the adequacy of the bases on which financial decisions were taken.

In some European countries something of this kind is already undertaken and it is significant that in current committee discussions in Europe the proposal has been made that the auditor should have the responsibility of saying when he recognises the signs of impending financial failure. In a paper in 1963 Professor Dr Willy Minz drew attention to the position in Germany 'according to a decision in the German Federal Court the auditor is obliged to issue a warning if he has formed serious doubts regarding the firm's economic state in the course of his audit, and particularly if there is a danger of some ruinous development. (This is the so called "duty to speak".)'[19]

In addition to this extended responsibility in relation to management's performance the auditor has to consider the special features of his role in relation to the report of the directors and managers to employees and to the community. The concept of fair presentation will still apply but to a different

report and to different information from that presented to shareholders. This also is a challenging role for the auditor.

It is not within the scope of this paper to deal with what is conceived as the management audit which involves examination and appraisal of the whole structure and operation of management. However, increasing social concern and increasing acceptance that management performance and accountability are matters of public concern rather than of solely private concern are likely to lead to the introduction of such an audit on some regular and recurring basis. The terms of reference can be sufficiently separately distinguished and it is not a role which should be undertaken by the financial auditor.

Social audit

If would, however, be appropriate in this paper to make brief reference to what has been described as the social audit of business. This is in connection with the social accountability of business, to the increasing recognition of which reference has been made. It is suggested that this is the way by which the public (society) may be informed of the manner in which a large business with a position bordering on monopoly is discharging its social responsibilities in the field of labour relations, pricing policies and local interests. Matters affecting the environment and pollution, which are of current concern would clearly come within this field. This is not a duty for the financial auditor but the development is a further demonstration of the important social role which society recognises for the audit function – a system of oversight and inspection to safeguard standards of conduct in the public interest.

Audit of public expenditure

What has been said of audit in the context of business enterprise carried on within the framework of a limited company is of wider application. The concepts of accountability and of audit in relation to financial affairs are of fairly universal application. It is, therefore, worth noting how the same social forces have resulted in change in another area of major importance, that of public expenditure, i.e. expenditure by central or local government, both for the execution of government and for the provision of community or social services.

As a sphere of audit this is very much older than business but the basic requirement of accountability has been essentially the same, honesty and regularity within the particular context of the government budgetary system for appropriation and control.

However, here again the concept is under radical change. The quality of financial administration is

---

[17] Industrial Relations Bill Consultative Document 1970, paras 145 and 148.
[18] Industrial Relations Act 1971, Sections 56 and 57.
[19] Record of Proceedings European Congress of Accountants, Edinburgh, 1963, p. 174.

improving; what is required of government in administrative efficiency is more rigorous. Greater appreciation of the need for efficiency in utilisation of scarce resources, greater concern about the size of the total resources administered by government, greater understanding about the impact of government expenditure on the economy and on individual living standards have all made their impact. Different considerations have to be brought to bear, because, except in State trading operations, no product is being sold, there is no market test on the value of the activity, there is no profit yardstick on the success of the operation. Accordingly, along with the adoption of more sophisticated mathematical techniques for decision making and control, study of and experimentation with cost benefit analysis and output budgeting are being undertaken in government financial administration. As the concept of accountability adjusts to embrace these changes audit must follow, ensuring for society that the quality of accountability it requires is in fact achieved. The role of the auditor in relation to central government as exercised by the Exchequer and Audit Department under the authority and direction of the Comptroller and Auditor General has already developed in this way. In Scotland, at least, this has not yet happened in local government audit and there are grounds for considering that it is overdue. The continuing concentration of external audit on honesty and regularity is out of sympathy with the trend of the times and the needs of society in relation at least to the larger authorities.[30]

Conclusion

Two significant features of modern society are the increasing concentration of economic resources in the control of national and international corporations and the increasing proportion of national income which is controlled and administered by the State. Both of these phenomena represent concentrations of power. In a democratic society power is not absolute and those who exercise it are accountable. The power must be exercised in the public interest and some system of surveillance must be operated to monitor the quality of the report on accountability. The character of accountability does not wholly lend itself to precise definition and is of an evolving nature adjusting to changes in social, political and economic thought and in the ethics and standards of society.

The audit function is a critical one in ensuring accountability in the broadest and deepest sense; to be adequate for it the auditors require to be sensitive to and to react to changes in the public concept of what accountability is. This is the area of the neglected philosophy of auditing.

---

[30] For further development of this see: 'The Audit of Local Authorities', David Flint, *Local Government Finance* (October 1971).

[2]

THE ACCOUNTING REVIEW
Vol. LVII, No. 2
April 1982

The Demand for External Auditing:
Size, Debt and Ownership Influences

Chee W. Chow

ABSTRACT: This study uses an agency theory framework to analyze firms' incentives to hire external auditing. It postulates that a major reason for firms to hire this service is to help control the conflict of interests among firm managers, shareholders, and bond-holders. Firm characteristics which affect the severity of this conflict or the marginal cost of external auditing are expected to influence a firm's demand for this service. Based on this analysis, leverage, firm size, and number of accounting-based debt covenants are predicted to increase the probability that a firm will voluntarily hire external auditing. The firm manager's ownership share is predicted to have the opposite effect. Univariate and multivariate tests were conducted on a sample of 165 NYSE and OTC firms from the year 1926. The results generally supported the hypothesized effects of leverage and accounting-based debt covenants, and moderately supported the predicted role of firm size. Manager ownership effects could not be tested due to data problems.

I. INTRODUCTION

IN recent years, large-scale auditing scandals like Continental Vending and National Student Marketing have focused public attention on auditors' incentives and ability to uphold professional standards in audits. Critics claim that firm managers control the selection of external auditors and can thus obtain auditor certification of financial statements which conform with their preferences.[1] This belief is apparently shared by accounting standard-setting bodies. The Securities and Exchange Commission (SEC) has steadily increased its disclosure requirements for auditor-client relationships.[2] Even the U.S. Congress has expressed its concern in the Moss Committee Report [1976] and the Metcalf Committee Staff Report [1976]; the latter states (p. 8):

> It appears that the "Big Eight" firms are more concerned with serving the interests of *corporate managements who select them and authorize their fees* than with protecting the interests of the public, for whose benefit Congress established the position of independent auditor (emphasis added).

Do firm managers dominate the external auditing decision? If so, can they use this power to manipulate financial reports to the detriment of investors' interests? Systematic evidence bearing

[1] Briloff [1972] and Sterling [1973] are prominent examples of this literature.

[2] Examples of SEC regulations in this area include ASR 165 [SEC, 1974] and ASR 194 [SEC, 1976].

Financial support for this study was provided by the Accounting Development Fund at the University of Washington. The author wishes to thank George Foster for his many insightful and useful suggestions, and the Editor for numerous helpful editorial comments. He also acknowledges many constructive criticisms from his advisers at the University of Oregon, and Eric Noreen and Hirokuni Tamura of the University of Washington. He is especially indebted to Ross L. Watts for crucial support and guidance in the formative stages of this project. Any remaining shortcomings of this paper, of course, are the responsibility of the author.

Chee W. Chow is Lecturer in Accounting, University of Washington.

Manuscript received October 1979.
Revisions received November 1980 and April 1981.
Accepted June 1981.

on these questions can help policymakers evaluate the need for regulation in this area. Yet, to date, few studies have addressed these issues.[3] This study attempts to contribute insights to one aspect of this inquiry by suggesting an important reason why firm managers and investors demand external auditing. Four hypotheses generated from this framework are then tested empirically.

Section II analyzes the roles played by the firm manager and investors in hiring external auditing.[4] This discussion is based on advances in agency theory by Jensen and Meckling [1976] and Fama [1980], and extensions by Watts [1977], Watts and Zimmerman [1979], and Smith and Warner [1979]. It postulates that firms demand external auditing due to the manager's and investors' efforts to control their conflict of interests. Further, regardless of who nominally makes the external auditing decision, this choice is guided by the expected effects of external auditing on the resource allocation activities of the various parties. This analysis predicts that several firm characteristics affect the expected costs and benefits from external auditing, and through this the probability a firm voluntarily hires this service.

Section III presents the empirical results. Section IV provides a summary and discussion of this study's implications for future research.

II. MANAGER-SHAREHOLDER-BONDHOLDER CONTRACTING AND FIRMS' DEMAND FOR EXTERNAL AUDITING

A. *Manager-Shareholder Conflict of Interests*

Modern firms are characterized by a separation of ownership and management.[5] Because the manager typically owns no more than a small portion of his firm's equity shares, he has incentives to

allocate the firm's resources in ways that are not necessarily consistent with the interests of non-managing shareholders.[6] The smaller the manager's ownership share, the greater are his incentives to effect such wealth transfers from external shareholders.

Jensen and Meckling [1976] and Fama [1980] point out that in a competitive market, shareholders anticipate the manager's wealth transfer activities and are able to allow for this expected cost in setting executive compensation. As a result, the manager bears the expected cost of his wealth transfer from shareholders. If a manager could guarantee to external shareholders to restrict his departure from maximizing shareholder wealth (firm value), he would receive an increase in pay equal to shareholders' reduction in expected losses. The manager, however, bears the expected cost of negotiating and executing such contracts.[7] Jensen and Meckling [1976] and Fama [1980] suggest that some managers would find such contracts desirable.

---

[3] The only exceptions of which I am aware are Watts [1977] and Watts and Zimmerman [1979]. The second study contains systematic empirical tests relating to lobbying behavior by auditors and their clients.

[4] This paper assumes that each firm has one manager. This simplification ignores the interactions among managers of various levels but does not affect the thrust of the analysis.

[5] This has been documented by Berle and Means [1932] and Larner [1970], among others.

[6] These include making investments with risk characteristics not in line with shareholders' preferences, and on-the-job consumption of perquisites like leisure, lavish offices, and the pursuit of other objectives (e.g., growth) that may not be in the shareholders' best interests. Detailed discussions of the nature of this principal-agent conflict of interests are available in Jensen and Meckling [1976], Demski and Feltham [1978] and Fama [1980].

[7] Whether the manager will bear the full expected costs and benefits of his contracts with shareholders is a contentious point. The analysis by Demski and Feltham [1978] suggests that the sharing rule would depend on the risk preferences of the manager and shareholders, the distribution of tastes for wealth transfers among potential managers, and the degree of competitiveness in the

The Accounting Review, April 1982

First, if there are significant information costs to differentiate among managers, the market would tend to adjust every manager's compensation as if he were the "average" manager. Those managers with a below "average" propensity to transfer wealth from shareholders could benefit by offering restrictive monitoring/bonding contracts to the latter. Second, much of the wealth transfer is probably job-specific. If a manager guaranteed to limit his wealth transfers from shareholders, his increase in money wages would permit a more efficient diversification of wealth.

Jensen and Meckling [1976] provide examples of monitoring/bonding contracts that mitigate the manager-shareholder conflict of interests. These include executive compensation based on financial measures of performance (such as profits) and contractual limitations on the manager's power to allocate firm resources. Watts [1977] cites numerous examples of such contracts going back hundreds of years. Lewellen [1968] and The Conference Board [1974] report that compensation schemes based on accounting measures of performance are in common use by modern firms. To the extent that accounting numbers are an essential part of such contracts, the manager has incentives to produce the requisite information at the lowest cost. Jensen and Meckling [1976, p. 338] and Watts [1977, p. 58] postulate that the manager probably already produces much of the desired information for his internal decision making purposes. If he were to provide this information to outside users, the marginal cost would likely be lower than for other alternatives. However, since the information will be used to evaluate his performance under the contracts, the manager has incentives to falsify the reports in his own favor. Thus, unless there are controls on the manager's

reporting procedures, his reports would be heavily discounted by external shareholders. In this case, the latter may desire to generate the desired accounting information on their own. Compared to this, the manager may find it less costly to agree in advance to have the accuracy of his reports testified to by an independent outside auditor. The point of this analysis is that, even if the manager nominally chooses external auditing, his choice is directed by expected investor reactions. Further, only those managers expecting to benefit more from external auditing than its cost will contract for this service. Since the degree of conflict between the manager and the firm's shareholders, and thus the amount of potential wealth transfer, increases inversely with the manager's ownership share, this hypothesis obtains:

H_1 = Ceteris paribus, the smaller is the manager's ownership share in the firm, the higher is the probability that the firm voluntarily engages external auditing.[8]

B. Shareholder-Bondholder Conflict of Interests

When a firm has risky debt outstanding, shareholders have incentives to undertake financing-investment-production activities which benefit themselves at the expense of the bondholders. These wealth-transfer mechanisms include paying liquidating dividends, changing the firm's variance of return, and diluting coverage on existing debt by issuing new

---

managerial labor market. For the purposes of the present analysis, it is sufficient that the manager and shareholders do have incentives to control their conflict of interests.

[8] This and the next two hypotheses are similar in spirit to Watts' [1977] first three hypotheses. Watts, however, is concerned with whether firms publish financial statements. Also, he does not present systematic empirical tests of his hypotheses.

debt with the same, or a higher priority than the current debt.[9]

Jensen and Meckling [1976], Myers [1977], Watts [1977], and Smith and Warner [1979] observe that, in an efficient capital market, bondholders would anticipate such shareholder behavior after the bonds have been issued. Potential bondholders would allow for these expected losses in pricing the bonds. The result is that the shareholders bear the cost of their expected wealth transfers from bondholders.

If the expected gain to the shareholders were equal to the bondholders' expected loss (i.e., if it were a zero-sum game), shareholders would be indifferent between obtaining the wealth transfer, or costlessly guaranteeing to the bondholders that the transfers would not be attempted, thus obtaining a higher price when the bonds are issued. However, the shareholder-bondholder conflict of interests is a negative-sum game. Some of the ways in which shareholders can transfer wealth from the bondholders result in a decline in firm value because they involve suboptimal investment policies. With risky debt outstanding, shareholders have incentives to reject positive net present value projects whose benefits accrue to bondholders, to accept negative net present value projects which have sufficiently high return variances to transfer wealth from the bondholders, and to pay dividends at the expense of profitable projects. As long as the wealth transferred from bondholders exceeds the decline in firm value, shareholders would benefit from such activities.

Jensen and Meckling [1976] and Myers [1977] point out that if shareholders contract to limit their own ability to transfer wealth from bondholders, they would receive a higher price for the bonds. In addition, they would benefit from an increase in firm value because

such contracts reduce the probability of suboptimal investments. Offsetting these benefits to the shareholders would be the costs of negotiating and executing their contracts with bondholders.

Smith and Warner [1979] provide an in-depth analysis of how various debt covenants help to limit the shareholder-bondholder conflict of interests. They report that accounting numbers play a central role in many of these covenants. For instance, a firm's ability to pay dividends is usually tied to its accounting earnings; its ability to invest in other businesses or to engage in new financing is often related to the accounting measure of its current or tangible assets. Rodgers [1965], Kehl [1941], and Dewing [1926] provide evidence that similar provisions were also popular in debt covenants going back hundreds of years. Because shareholders bear the cost of generating the requisite accounting numbers, they have incentives to do so at the least cost. Jensen and Meckling [1976] and Watts [1977] postulate that having the manager supply externally audited financial reports is such an alternative.

Whether the shareholders of a given firm would offer monitoring/bonding contracts to its bondholders depends on the severity of their conflict of interests. Researchers generally agree that, as the proportion of debt in a firm's capital structure increases, shareholders have a greater incentive to transfer wealth from the bondholders.[10] This, in turn, implies a greater probability of suboptimal investment policies, and a greater potential gain to shareholders from contracting with the bondholders; thus,

---

[9] Detailed discussions of these wealth-transfer mechanisms are available in Black [1976], Fama and Miller [1972], Galai and Masulis [1976], Myers [1977], and Smith and Warner [1979].

[10] See Fama and Miller [1972], Myers [1977], Jensen and Meckling [1976], Kalay [1978], Smith and Warner [1979], and Watts [1977].

H_2 = *Ceteris paribus*, the higher the proportion of debt in a firm's capital structure, the higher is the probability that the firm voluntarily engages external auditing.

This hypothesis is based on the reported importance of accounting numbers in debt covenants. But, as Smith and Warner [1979] and Foster [1980a, p. 36] observe, not all debt covenants rely on accounting numbers. For firms using more accounting-based covenants, one would expect a more important role for external auditors. Thus, I hypothesize:

H_3 = *Ceteris paribus*, the greater the number of different accounting measures in a firm's debt covenants, the higher is the probability that the firm voluntarily engages external auditing.

This hypothesis can be viewed as an extension of H_2, in that it focuses on the explicit role of accounting measures in shareholder-bondholder contracts.

Finally, firm size is predicted to affect directly the probability of external auditing. First, for a given manager ownership share and debt/equity ratio, the total amount of potential wealth transfer increases with firm size. This, in turn, implies that the benefits of monitoring/ bonding contracts to the agent are positively related to firm size. On the cost side, it appears that many costs in establishing a monitoring/bonding system are likely to be fixed. Even for a small firm, it probably takes considerable resources for the external auditor to become familiar with the firm's operations.[11] Once the monitoring/bonding system has been established, the marginal cost of its operation is likely to decrease with firm size; i.e., it does not take double the variable costs to audit a firm twice the size of another. These assumptions about

the marginal costs and benefits of monitoring/bonding contracts lead to the following hypothesis:

H_4 = *Ceteris paribus*, the larger a firm's total size, the higher is the probability that it voluntarily engages external auditing.

The next section presents empirical tests of the four stated hypotheses. It should be noted that, while these hypotheses are derived from a coherent framework, they do not include all of the major reasons for firms to hire auditors. To the extent the present analysis illustrates a major determinant of firms' external auditing decisions, it can still generate useful insights. However, it is necessary to explore the potential impacts of the omitted variables. If these are not related to the hiring of external auditing in the same systematic way as the hypothesized variables, they would add "noise" to the data in the empirical tests. More important, if they are systematically related to external auditing in the same, or opposite, direction as the included variables, leaving them out could confound the test results.

A major reason for firms to hire external auditing, aside from manager-shareholder-bondholder contracting, is institutional requirements. These may be imposed by organized stock exchanges, state "Blue Sky" laws, or institutional investors. It is also possible that firms feel obliged to engage external auditing due to "political costs."[12] If larger firms are more likely to come under these requirements, any observed impact of firm size could be due to these requirements rather

[11] Arens and Loebeckke [1976, p. 100] list three major startup costs: (1) to verify the details making up thse balance-sheet accounts that are of a permanent nature, (2) to verify the beginning balances, and (3) to become familiar with the client's operations.

[12] These are the "political costs" discussed in Watts and Zimmerman [1978].

than contracting cost considerations. In order to minimize this potential confounding impact, a time period is chosen where imposed external audit requirements were apparently rather lax.

Another reason for hiring external auditing may relate to operational efficiencies. Due to economies of scale, external auditors may be able to perform a given task more efficiently than internal auditors. External auditors may also be able to supply a wider range of services, including management consulting, to the firm. Finally, external auditors may be preferred for internal control purposes if they are considered less likely to collude with the manager's subordinates. If these expected benefits exceed the external auditing costs, the firm manager has incentives to hire external auditing. However, these operational considerations are unlikely to confound the test results. Since the manager and the shareholders share proportionally in this net benefit from external auditing, this service is desirable whenever its expected benefit exceeds its expected cost. Thus, manager ownership and leverage should not be related to the hiring of external auditing for operational reasons.

Another reason for differences in firms' hiring of external auditing may relate to industry characteristics. If an industry has very complex operations, it may be costly to audit its firms. Some industries may be very competitive, and firms may find detailed financial disclosure undesirable because it would furnish important firm-specific information to their competitors.[13] A detailed analysis is needed to predict which industries may have higher audit costs and, therefore, are less likely to engage external auditing. Such an analysis is not included in this study. However, this omitted variable would confound the test results only if firms in different industries also differ

systematically by manager ownership, leverage, number of accounting-based debt covenants, and size. Even if such differences were to exist, the sample firms in this study encompass a large number of industries and can diversify away at least part of this industry effect.

The above discussion illustrates that other factors, in addition to manager-shareholder-bondholder contracting, also affect firms' demand for external auditing. Even though these factors are not explicitly included in the present study, this study can nonetheless yield valuable insights by exploring the importance of contracting considerations to this demand.

III. DATA AND EMPIRICAL RESULTS

A. Time Period of Study

Since the hypotheses relate to firms' voluntary hiring of external auditing, it is necessary to select a time period when there were no externally imposed audit requirements. At the same time, data must be available on the variables of interest. The year 1926 was judged to satisfy both requirements reasonably well. Ripley's [1927, Ch. 6] survey of current annual reports led him to conclude that companies could select any accounting methods they desired. Similarly, Hoxsey [1930, pp. 259–261] and Littleton and Zimmerman [1962, p. 101] point to the variety of accounting alternatives available to firm managements in this period. These findings provide the basis for Benston's [1973, p. 133] and Carey's [1969, p. 182] observations that few externally imposed accounting requirements existed prior to the Securities Acts of 1933 and 1934.

In the early 1900s, some states did have corporation laws that required some

---

[13] Mautz and May [1978] and Foster [1980b] discuss the nature of this competitive disadvantage from detailed financial reporting.

financial disclosure. Hawkins [1968] surveyed these laws and concluded that seldom were the contents, much less the accounting procedures, of these reports specified. It also appears that external auditing was not a requirement, as many firms did not issue audited financial statements. External auditing was similarly not required by organized exchanges. Edwards [1960, p. 150] reports that since the early 1920s, the New York Stock Exchange (NYSE) had required listed firms to file their regular financial statements with the Exchange. However, the audit requirement was not imposed until January, 1933. The Exchange also did not regulate listed firms' accounting procedures in the 1920s, and according to Zeff [1972, p. 125], did not even require listed corporations to reveal their accounting methods. These observations are consistent with Benston's [1969, p. 519] finding that, in 1926, 18 percent of NYSE firms were not audited, 45 percent did not report sales, 55 percent did not disclose cost of goods sold, and 29 percent did not report depreciation.

Apart from its apparent lack of accounting regulation, the year 1926 was also desirable for data-availability reasons. The primary data source for this study is *Poor's Industrial Manual*. This publication did not report on the existence of an external auditor or provide details on the debt covenants until the early 1920s. Also, because there was no publicly available information on firm managers' ownership shares, a proxy had to be developed using data in a Federal Trade Commission publication. This did not appear until 1926.

B. Sample and Data Collection

The sample was restricted to over-the-counter (OTC) and NYSE firms. This focus on publicly-traded firms was based on the need for share price data to construct reasonable approximations of firm market value (firm size).

All industrial OTC and NYSE firms listed in the December 31, 1926 issue of *The Wall Street Journal* were checked for availability of financial data in the 1927 volume of *Poor's Industrial Manual*. A total of 65 OTC and 379 NYSE firms were common to both publications. *Poor's* was used to determine which of these firms was externally audited for the 1926 fiscal year. Thirty-one (48 percent) of the OTC and 300 (79 percent) of the NYSE firms were reported to be so audited.

All of the OTC firms were retained in the sample. A 100-firm random sample was selected from the 379 NYSE firms. This sample was stratified by external auditing so that 79 (79 percent) of the selected firms were audited and 21 (21 percent) were not.[14] The exchange-listing distinction was retained to allow for the potential influences of exchange requirements. Even though NYSE firms were not required to be audited, the Exchange did require financial statements to be filed. This requirement could have prompted some firms to obtain an external audit. Further, firms that obtained listing on an exchange may have done so in anticipation of new financing. This could cause exchange listing to have a positive impact on hiring external auditing independent of the four firm-specific financial variables.

For each of the 165 firms in the final sample, the following data were collected:

1. The 1926 year-end stock price per share was recorded from *The Wall Street Journal*, supplemented by the *Commercial and Financial Chronicle* where necessary. Closing prices were available for the

[14] A list of the sample firms is available from the author on request.

TABLE 1

TYPES AND FREQUENCIES OF ACCOUNTING-BASED DEBT COVENANTS

	Entire Sample		NYSE Sample		OTC Sample	
	Audited	Not Audited	Audited	Not Audited	Audited	Not Audited
Covenants Pertaining to Quick Assets[a]	15	4	10	2	5	2
Covenants Pertaining to Currents Assets[b]	16	4	11	1	5	3
Covenants Pertaining to Current Liabilities[c]	5	1	4	0	1	1
Covenants Pertaining to Tangible Assets[d]	10	1	6	0	4	1
Covenants Pertaining to Accounting Income[e]	45	9	32	1	13	8
Covenants Pertaining to Dividend Policy[f]	84[g]	31[h]	57[i]	9[j]	27[k]	22[l]
Miscellaneous	12	4	10	0	2	4
Total Number of Different Covenants	167	50	117	11	50	39
Number of Firms	110	55	79	21	31	34
Mean Number of Covenants	1.518	.909	1.481	.523	1.613	1.147

Notes to Table 1

[a] An example is: The Pneumatic Scale Corporation Ltd. agreed in its bond issue that "net quick assets must be maintained at not less than 125% of the bonds outstanding."

[b] An example is: Foote-Burt Company's debt provisions stipulated that ". . . current obligations must not be in excess of 65% of current assets."

[c] An example is: Remington Arms Company agreed that "The total combined current assets of the company and its subsidiary companies shall, upon the issuance of additional bonds, equal at least 150% of their total current liabilities."

[d] An example is: Graton and Knight Company's bond covenants required the company to "maintain at all times net tangible assets at a sum at least equal to 300% of the aggregate principal amount of bonds issued."

[e] An example is: Muller Bakeries, Incorporated consented to set aside a sinking fund "at the rate of 10% of net earnings after interest, taxes and depreciation, but before dividends."

[f] An example is: Pierce, Butler & Pierce Manufacturing Corporation contracted "not to pay dividends which would reduce its net current assets . . . below the par amount of bonds of this issue then outstanding." Because dividend constraints are often based on some of the other accounting measures reported in this table, some of the dividend constraints reported here represent double-counting, the numbers of which for each sample are reported below.

[g] This figure contains 20 cases already included in the other categories.

[h] This figure contains 4 cases already included in the other categories.

[i] This figure contains 13 cases already included in the other categories.

[j] This figure contains 2 cases already included in the other categories.

[k] This figure contains 7 cases already included in the other categories.

[l] This figure contains 2 cases already included in the other categories.

NYSE firms. For OTC firms, only bid and asked prices were available, and their arithmetic average was used as a proxy for closing price. For each firm, the total number of common shares outstanding at 1926 year-end was obtained from *Poor's*. This was multiplied by the year-end price per share to approximate the market value of owners' equity.

2. Total book value of debt was collected from *Poor's*. This was combined with the market value of owners' equity to yield two measures:

a. Firm size (SIZE) = Market value of owners' equity + book value of debt.
b. Debt/equity ratio (DE) = Book value of debt/SIZE.

TABLE 2
MEDIANS, MEANS AND STANDARD DEVIATIONS OF THE INDEPENDENT VARIABLES

		Entire Sample		NYSE Sample		OTC Sample	
		Audited (N=110)	Not Audited (N=55)	Audited (N=79)	Not Audited (N=21)	Audited (N=31)	Not Audited (N=34)
SIZE ($\times 10^6$)	Median	$ 13.80	$ 9.23	$ 27.77	$24.75	$ 6.52	$4.72
	Mean	$ 54.27	$26.35	$ 73.06	$49.69	$11.94	$6.37
	(Std. dev.)	($143.2)	($44.86)	($165.5)	($64.3)	($14.9)	($6.95)
DE	Median	.008	.000	.036	.001	.002	.000
	Mean	.136	.064	.139	.059	.128	.067
	(Std. dev.)	(.190)	(.120)	(.188)	(.101)	(.196)	(.131)
COVNUM	Median	1.237	.675	1.25	.375	1.208	.885
	Mean	1.518	.909	1.481	.524	1.613	1.147
	(Std. dev.)	(1.332)	(1.093)	(1.30)	(.68)	(1.430)	(1.234)
MGRSHR	Median	22.69%	17.45%	22.70%	11.43%	22.62%	17.83%
	Mean	25.92%	19.87%	26.12%	15.03%	25.42%	22.86%
	(Std. dev.)	(15.29%)	(14.74%)	(15.49%)	(13.07%)	(14.97%)	(15.1%)

3. *Poor's* description of the covenants for each debt issue was examined. For each firm, the total number of different accounting measures used in all of its debt issues was recorded. This measure was designated COVNUM. Table 1 reports the frequencies of different types of such accounting-based covenants. It appears that dividend constraints were the most common, followed by restrictions based on accounting income, current assets, quick assets, tangible assets and current liabilities, in that order. The notes to Table 1 provide examples of each of these constraints.

4. Information on firm manager ownership share was not available. The Appendix discusses the construction and limitations of a proxy (denoted MGRSHR) based on some Federal Trade Commission data. This proxy variable was included in some of the empirical analyses. However, serious measurement problems caution against viewing the MGRSHR results as a test of H_1.

C. Empirical Tests

Table 2 provides summary statistics on the independent variables for the entire sample and for the NYSE and OTC subsamples. Across all three samples, audited firms have higher mean and median values for SIZE, DE, COVNUM, and MGRSHR than do non-audited firms. Both univariate and multivariate tests were used to assess the statistical significance of these differences.

Univariate Tests

Univariate tests are desirable for this study because they prevent measurement errors in one independent variable from affecting test results on another. Potential measurement problems in MGRSHR are discussed in the Appendix. Another variable with this potential problem is COVNUM. First, *Poor's* provides only summaries of each firm's debt covenants and may have systematically excluded certain types of covenants. If so, COVNUM would measure the sample firms' use of accounting-based debt cove-

TABLE 3

SIMPLE PEARSON CORRELATIONS AMONG THE INDEPENDENT VARIABLES

Panel A
Entire Sample (N = 165)

	SIZE	COVNUM	DE	MGRSHR	NYSE
SIZE	1.0				
COVNUM	.018	1.0			
DE	.040	.369**	1.0		
MGRSHR	.073	.174*	.077	1.0	
NYSE	.239**	−.034	.073	−.009	1.0

Panel B
NYSE Sample (N = 100)

	SIZE	COVNUM	DE	MGRSHR
SIZE	1.0			
COVNUM	.034	1.0		
DE	.017	.255**	1.0	
MGRSHR	.098	.155	.115	1.0

Panel C
OTC Sample (N = 65)

	SIZE	COVNUM	DE	MGRSHR
SIZE	1.0			
COVNUM	.045	1.0		
DE	.17	.555**	1.0	
MGRSHR	.004	.204	.013	1.0

* Significant at .05, two-tail test.
** Significant at .005, two-tail test.

nants with error. More important, it seems likely that different accounting-based debt covenants work together as a package rather than individually. If this is true, a simple adding up of the number of such constraints may not fully capture their importance as determinants of external auditing.

In order for univariate tests to yield meaningful results, the independent variables have to be substantially uncorrelated. This is generally true for the present study. Table 3 presents the pairwise Pearson correlations among the independent variables. For the entire sample, this includes a dummy variable NYSE which is assigned a value of one for a NYSE firm, and zero otherwise. Only several of the reported correlations are significant.[15]

For the 165-firm sample, SIZE and NYSE are significantly and positively correlated. This result is not surprising since probably only the larger firms would desire access to a wider capital market through exchange listing. To control for the confounding effect of exchange listing on the observed impact of SIZE, the latter variable can be evaluated by holding NYSE constant, i.e., by focusing on NYSE and OTC firms separately.

[15] Spearman rank correlations yielded similar results and are not reported here.

TABLE 4

RESULTS OF MANN-WHITNEY U TESTS ON THE INDEPENDENT VARIABLES

Panel A
Entire Sample (N=165)

Variable	Audited Firms Average Rank	Unaudited Firms Average Rank	Z Score	2-tailed Probability
COVNUM	90.61	67.78	−3.013	.002
DE	89.66	69.67	−2.786	.005
SIZE	87.60	73.80	−1.749	.080
COVRES	88.08	72.85	−1.936	.052
MGRSHR	86.94	75.13	−1.519	.128

Panel B
NYSE Sample (N=100)

Variable	Audited Firms Average Rank	Unaudited Firms Average Rank	Z Score	2-tailed Probability
COVNUM	55.18	32.90	−3.253	.001
DE	54.41	35.79	−2.820	.004
SIZE	51.47	46.86	− .647	.517
COVRES	54.41	35.79	−2.634	.008
MGRSHR	53.45	39.40	−1.995	.046

Panel C
OTC Sample (N=65)

Variable	Audited Firms Average Rank	Unaudited Firms Average Rank	Z Score	2-tailed Probability
COVNUM	36.29	30.00	−1.40	.161
DE	37.85	28.57	−1.994	.046
SIZE	37.53	28.03	−2.002	.043
COVRES	34.63	31.51	− .676	.498
MGRSHR	34.44	31.69	− .597	.550

DE and COVNUM are significantly and positively correlated for both NYSE and OTC firms, and thus for the entire sample. This relationship also appears to be reasonable since firms with higher DE ratios probably have more debt issues, and consequently more debt provisions. In order to focus on the impact of accounting-based debt covenants, COVNUM and DE were used in the following cross-sectional regression for the NYSE and OTC samples separately:

$$COVNUM = a_0 + b_0 DE \quad (1)$$

For the NYSE sample, this regression yielded values for the coefficients of 1.057 and 1.823, respectively. The *t*-statistics were 7.10 and 2.62, the adjusted R^2 was .05 and the *F*-statistic of 6.87 was significant at the .01 level. For the OTC sample, the regression coefficients were .937 and 4.473, with *t*-statistics of 5.80 and 5.30. The adjusted R^2 was .297 and the *F*-statistic of 28.1 was significant at the .001 level. For each sample, the estimated parameters were applied to each firm to obtain a residual COVNUM, designated COVRES. For the NYSE sample, COVRES was calculated as:

$$COVRES_i = COVNUM_i - 1.057 \\ - 1.823 \; {}^*DE_i \quad (2)$$

For the OTC sample,

$$COVRES_i = COVNUM_i - .937 - 4.473 *DE_i \qquad (3)$$

Since COVRES is orthogonal to DE, it should reflect the unique impact of accounting-based debt covenants once leverage has been taken into account.

No remedial measure was taken regarding the positive correlation between COVNUM and MGRSHR for the entire sample. This correlation is not significant at conventional levels for the subsamples. More important, potential measurement errors in MGRSHR preclude firm conclusions about manager ownership impacts in any case.

The non-parametric Mann-Whitney U Test was used to compare each independent variable between the audited and non-audited portfolios. This was done both for the entire sample and at the subsample level. Table 4 reports these results. A non-parametric test was selected because there is no *a priori* reason to expect the independent variables to be normally distributed. Indeed, the reported mean and median values in Table 2 diverge so much for most of the independent variables that the normality assumption seems unlikely to hold.[16]

For the sample as a whole, H_2, H_3, and H_4 are all supported. Audited firms have significantly higher values for COVNUM, DE, SIZE, and COVRES. Because the hypotheses are directional, the significance levels are half of (i.e., higher than) those reported. Contrary to prediction, MGRSHR is higher for the audited firms relative to the non-audited ones. If MGRSHR were an adequate proxy for manager ownership, this result would not only reject H_1, but also support the opposite relationship between manager ownership and external auditing. The potential measurement errors in MGRSHR do not warrant such a firm conclusion at this stage. However, the significance level of the MGRSHR result does underscore the need to develop a more adequate proxy and to explore other factors, such as operational efficiencies and industry effects, on the external auditing choice. In view of the limitations of the MGRSHR proxy, it will not be considered in detail in the subsequent discussion.

Because exchange listing is a dichotomous variable, its effect on external auditing was tested using a Chi-square test. The obtained Chi-square, for one degree of freedom, was 17.384. This is significant at the .005 level and indicates that NYSE firms are significantly more likely to be audited.

It appears that the independent variables have different impacts across NYSE and OTC firms. In both groups, DE is significantly higher for the audited firms. However, there is less agreement on the other variables. COVNUM has the predicted effect for the NYSE subsample. This conclusion is not significantly affected by the correlation between COVNUM and DE, since COVRES is also significantly higher for audited NYSE firms. Within the OTC subsample, COVNUM is higher for the audited firms at the .085 (one-tail) level. However, even though COVRES also has the predicted effect, the one-tail significance level is only .249. Thus, accounting-based debt covenants seem to be a more important determinant of external auditing for NYSE firms than for OTC firms.

The opposite is true for firm size. Audited OTC firms have a significantly larger SIZE than do non-audited firms, but no significant size difference is observed between audited and non-audited

---

[16] Hollander and Wolfe [1973] provide an explanation of the Mann-Whitney U test. Also, Lehmann [1975] observes that even if the normality assumption would have been correct, use of an appropriate non-parametric test would only result in a five percent loss of efficiency.

NYSE firms. This result may suggest that the impact of SIZE varies with whether a firm is on an organized exchange. A more plausible explanation is that external auditing involves significant fixed startup costs. Then, only firms above some threshold size would find this service cost/beneficial. The NYSE-sample firms are significantly larger than the OTC-sample firms and may mostly be above this threshold size. This could explain the more detectable (statistically significant) effect of SIZE for the OTC sample.

The effect of MGRSHR also differs among NYSE and OTC firms. Within the former, this measure is significantly higher among audited firms. No significant difference in MGRSHR is observed between audited and non-audited OTC firms.

Multivariate Tests

Multivariate tests serve as a check on the univariate results. Significant multicollinearity and measurement errors would cause the two sets of test results to diverge. The individual impact of each independent variable was assessed by including them all in the following cross-sectional regression:

$$AUDIT = c_0 + d_0SIZE + d_1DE$$
$$+ d_2COVNUM$$
$$+ d_3MGRSHR$$
$$+ d_4NYSE \qquad (4)$$

where

AUDIT = Probability of a firm being externally audited, set equal to 1 if the firm had an external auditor, 0 otherwise.

SIZE, DE, COVNUM, MGRSHR, and NYSE are as previously defined.

The predicted signs of the coefficients are positive for d_0, d_1, and d_2 and negative for d_3. In addition, d_4, the coefficient for

NYSE listing, is expected to be positive for reasons provided earlier.

Given a dichotomous dependent variable, ordinary least squares is not appropriate for estimating the parameters.[17] Multivariate discriminant analysis was also rejected because one of the independent variables is dichotomous ("NYSE"), and because the variance-covariance matrices for the audited and non-audited portfolios are not equal.[18] Logit analysis was selected. This is a maximum likelihood estimating procedure which applies a logarithmic transformation to the dependent variable. Theil [1971] and McFadden [1973] show that given a dichotomous dependent variable, logit analysis yields estimators that are asymptotically efficient and normally distributed. This makes it feasible to construct approximate large sample confidence bounds and tests of hypotheses for parameters.[19]

Table 5 reports the logit regression results for the entire sample and for the NYSE and OTC subsamples. The NYSE dummy variable was left out of the subsample analyses. Half of the regressions excluded MGRSHR so that its measurement errors would not bias the results. Also, COVRES replaced COVNUM in half of the regressions to control for the correlation between COVNUM and DE. In addition, two regressions were run without NYSE to assess the impact of the

---

[17] Theil [1971] and Hagerman and Zmijewski [1979] illustrate the limitations of ordinary least squares when the dependent variable is dichotomous.

[18] Eisenbeis [1977] provides a detailed discussion of the assumptions underlying multivariate discriminant analysis.

[19] For an example of logit analysis in previous accounting research see Ohlson [1980]. A feasible alternative to logit analysis for this study is probit analysis, which Hagerman and Zmijewski [1979] employed in their research. I duplicated all of the logit analyses with probit analyses. The results were almost identical.

TABLE 5

PARAMETER ESTIMATES FROM MULTIPLE REGRESSIONS

(*T*-statistics in Parentheses)

Panel A
Entire Sample (N = 165)

	Constant	SIZE ($\times 10^{10}$)	DE	COVNUM	COVRES	MGRSHR	NYSE	Estimated R^2	X^2 (Significance)
Predicted Sign		+	+	+	+	−	+		
	−1.41 (−3.09)	4.86 (.21)	1.68 (1.25)	.36 (2.02)**		.027 (2.10)	1.54 (3.89)***	.263	34.69 (.005)
	−1.01 (−2.37)	4.96 (.22)	2.87 (2.28)**		.38 (2.11)**	.027 (2.07)	1.50 (3.83)***	.266	35.16 (.005)
	−.78 (−2.34)	7.60 (.37)	1.52 (1.18)	.40 (2.35)**			1.45 (3.81)***	.229	29.86 (.005)
	−.36 (−1.28)	7.85 (.37)	2.86 (2.33)**		.43 (2.45)**		1.42 (3.75)***	.234	30.51 (.005)
	−.04 (−.18)	45.52 (1.28)*	1.93 (1.52)*	.33 (2.08)**				.118	14.73 (.005)
	.29 (1.31)	44.80 (1.26)	2.89 (2.37)**		.38 (2.30)**			.127	15.94 (.005)

Panel B
NYSE Sample (N = 100)

	Constant	SIZE ($\times 10^{10}$)	DE	COVNUM	COVRES	MGRSHR	Estimated R^2	X^2 (Significance)
Predicted Sign		+	+	+	+	−		
	−.84 (−1.47)	3.36 (.12)	2.19 (1.0)	.92 (1.46)**		.05 (2.47)	.308	22.09 (.005)
	.13 (.25)	3.36 (.12)	3.87 (1.81)**		.92 (2.46)**	.05 (2.47)	.308	22.09 (.005)
	.25 (.68)	11.24 (.45)	2.25 (1.12)	.85 (2.61)**			.207	14.26 (.005)
	1.15 (3.13)	11.24 (.45)	3.80 (1.91)**		.85 (2.61)**		.207	14.26 (.005)

Panel C
OTC Sample (N = 65)

	Constant	SIZE ($\times 10^8$)	DE	COVNUM	COVRES	MGRSHR	Estimated R^2	X^2 (Significance)
Predicted Sign		+	+	+	+	−		
	−.19 (−.33)	7.02 (1.98)**	3.53 (1.57)*	.06 (.27)		.01 (.61)	.177	9.30 (.06)
	−.13 (−.22)	7.02 (1.98)**	3.82 (1.96)**		.06 (.27)	.01 (.61)	.177	9.30 (.06)
	.05 (.12)	6.97 (1.97)**	3.31 (1.50)*	.10 (.43)			.171	8.91 (.07)
	.15 (.41)	6.97 (1.97)**	3.77 (1.96)**		.10 (.43)		.171	8.91 (.07)

*** Significant at .01, one-tail test.
** Significant at .05, one-tail test.
* Significant at .1, one-tail test.

The Accounting Review, April 1982

correlation between exchange listing and firm size.

For the whole sample, the estimated R^2 ranges between .118 and .263. This by itself does not prove that the model is significant. Such a test can be constructed by multiplying -2 by the log-likelihood ratio. The resulting statistic is distributed as a Chi-square with degrees of freedom equal to the number of independent variables.[20] This statistic is reported in Table 5 and shows that the model is significant at the .005 level for the whole sample. The subsample analyses are also significant at conventional levels.

With few exceptions, the multivariate results support the univariate findings. For the whole sample, both COVNUM and COVRES have significant and positive coefficients. When both DE and COVNUM are in the equation, the former has one significant and positive coefficient out of three separate regressions. However, once the correlation between DE and COVNUM is controlled for with the use of COVRES, all the DE coefficients are positive and statistically significant.

Consistent with the Chi-square test, NYSE has significant and positive coefficients in every regression. When both NYSE and SIZE are included in the regression, the latter has a statistically insignificant, though positive coefficient. With NYSE out of the equation, however, SIZE does have a statistically significant positive coefficient in one of the two regressions. This evidence provides some support for the predicted role of firm size. Regressions at the subsample level suggest that this relatively weak result is probably due to the differential impacts of SIZE for NYSE and OTC firms.

The result on MGRSHR is unchanged from the univariate tests. This variable has a positive, rather than the predicted negative, coefficient. Further, the MGRSHR coefficient would be significant on a two-tailed test basis for the entire sample and the NYSE subsample. Also, the inclusion or exclusion of MGRSHR does not significantly affect the results for the other variables.

At the subsample level, the evidence is consistent with the independent variables having different impacts on NYSE and OTC firms. In the NYSE subsample, both COVNUM and COVRES have significant and positive coefficients. DE also has significant and positive coefficients once its correlation with COVNUM has been controlled for. SIZE, however, does not have a significant coefficient. In the OTC sample, both DE and SIZE have significant and positive coefficients, but the COVNUM and COVRES coefficients are both insignificant. These results are in general agreement with the univariate tests.

Together, the univariate and multivariate results strongly support H_2. H_3 is supported moderately to strongly, and H_4 is supported moderately. This means that leverage, number of accounting-based debt covenants, and firm size are positively related to the probability of external auditing. Exchange listing appears to influence the strength of these relationships. Measurement problems precluded an adequate test of H_1. However, the statistical significance of the MGRSHR coefficient suggests that factors other than contracting, such as operational considerations and industry effects, also could be important determinants of external auditing.

IV. SUMMARY AND CONCLUSIONS

This study uses an agency theory framework to analyze firms' incentives to hire external auditing. It postulates

[20] McKelvey and Zavoina [1975] and McFadden [1973] provide detailed discussions of this test.

TABLE 6

PERCENTAGE OWNERSHIP OF COMMON SHARES BY OFFICERS AND DIRECTORS BY INDUSTRY, 1922*

Industry	Average Percentage of Par Value of Common Stock Owned by Officers and Directors
Mining—Other	1.8
Transportation	2.1
Petroleum Mining	5.3
Manufacturing—Chemical and allied substances	6.3
Coal Mining	8.4
Manufacturing—Metal and metal products	11.4
Manufacturing—Food products	17.5
Finance	22.0
Manufacturing—Other	22.7
Manufacturing—Rubber	39.0
Manufacturing—Textile	42.9
Manufacturing—Leather	44.7
Trade	48.4
Service	49.7
Agriculture and related industries	55.9
Manufacturing—Lumber and wood products	56.9
Construction	67.6

* Source: Federal Trade Commission [1926, p. 159].

that a major reason for firms to hire this service is to help control the conflict of interests among firm managers, shareholders, and bondholders. Firm characteristics which affect the severity of this conflict or the marginal cost of external auditing are expected to influence a firm's demand for this service. Based on this analysis, leverage, firm size, and number of accounting-based debt covenants are predicted to increase the probability that a firm will voluntarily hire external auditing. The firm manager's ownership share is predicted to have the opposite effect.

Data on the selected firm characteristics were collected for 165 NYSE and OTC firms for 1926. Both univariate and multivariate tests were performed. The results generally supported the hypothesized effects of leverage and accounting-based debt covenants. There was some support for the importance of firm size. Measurement problems precluded an adequate test on manager ownership share.

Overall, these results suggest that agency cost considerations play an important role in the external auditing decision. The existence of such private incentives may imply a reduced need for auditing regulation. If policymakers do wish to influence the amount of auditing hired, these results suggest that an effective alternative would be to change the cost of manager-shareholder-bondholder contracting.

The present study can be extended in various ways. One is to develop a more continuous measure of auditing quantity. Since most large firms today are required to be audited, such a continuous measure is needed to assess their reactions to alternate regulations. Another area for study is the role of non-contracting factors such as operational considerations in the external auditing decision. While extensions like these will undoubtedly enrich this analysis, the present study has provided a useful basis for future work in this area.

The Accounting Review, April 1982

APPENDIX

DERIVATION AND LIMITATIONS OF THE
MANAGER OWNERSHIP SHARE
(MGRSHR) PROXY

The MGRSHR proxy was derived from Federal Trade Commission (FTC) statistics in its 1926 publication, *National Wealth and Income*. This report presented average percentage ownership of common stock by officers and directors for a number of industries. Table 6 summarizes part of these data.

Each sample firm was assigned to an industry class based on *Poor's* description of its operations. The FTC average percentage ownership figure for its industry class was then used as its manager ownership share.

While the above procedure was adopted for lack of a better data source, it is also recognized that the proxy measure has serious potential measurement errors. First, the FTC statistics are for both managers and directors, not managers alone. Second, the proxy necessitates a subjective assignment of firms to industry classes, though in most cases the proper assignment seemed to be rather unquestionable. Perhaps the most severe limitation of the proxy is that it may reflect industry differences rather than manager ownership differences. Indeed, if manager ownership were to vary widely among firms in a given industry, MGRSHR might reflect industry effects more than ownership effects. Since available data do not permit the separation of the two effects, the MGRSHR results presented here should be considered exploratory rather than conclusive.

In addition to the empirical tests reported in the body of the paper, an additional attempt was made to control for industry effects. The sample firms were grouped into seven MGRSHR classes, as follows:

MGRSHR Class	Industries Included	Industry MGRSHR
1	Mining—other	1.8%
	Transportation	2.1%
2	Petroleum mining	5.3%
	Manufacturing—Chemical and allied substances	6.3%
	Coal mining	8.4%
3	Manufacturing—Metal and metal products	11.4%
	Manufacturing—Food products	17.5%
4	Finance	22.0%
	Manufacturing—Other	22.7%
5	Manufacturing—Rubber	39.0%
	Manufacturing—Textile	42.9%
	Manufacturing—Leather	44.7%
	Trade	48.4%
	Service	49.7%
6	Agriculture and Related Industries	55.9%
	Manufacturing—Lumber and wood products	56.9%
7	Construction	67.6%

Since each class is relatively homogeneous with respect to MGRSHR but not industry, inter-class differences in AUDIT should reflect the impact of the former. This was tested by substituting six MGRSHR (the last six) class dummy variables for the MGRSHR variable in the logit regression. If MGRSHR is related to AUDIT, the coefficients for the dummy variables should be increasingly negative as one goes to the higher-numbered (higher MGRSHR) classes. Negative coefficients were obtained for each dummy variable. However, none even approached statistical significance. Thus, H_1 was again not supported by these tests.

As it stands, the MGRSHR result is consistent with one or more possible explanations:

a. There are industry-specific factors related to hiring external auditing.
b. Manager-shareholder conflicts do not exist, or are not costly to resolve and the agency cost consideration is overwhelmed by operational benefits from external auditing (e.g., improved internal control, management consulting services) which the manager shares in proportion to his ownership interest.
c. Manager-shareholder conflicts are better controlled by non-accounting measures.
d. Manager-shareholder conflicts are a function of other variables.
e. MGRSHR is too aggregated a measure (since all firms in the same industry are assigned the same numerical index) to permit an analysis of interfirm differences.
f. MGRSHR is not an appropriate measure of manager ownership because it includes the ownership interests of directors who may be external to the firm.

Differentiating among these alternatives will require a more reliable manager ownership measure. Such an attempt will enrich this analysis since it will introduce factors not directly related to agency contracting.

REFERENCES

Arens, A., and J. Loebbecke, *Auditing: An Integrated Approach* (Prentice-Hall, 1976).
Benston, G. J., "The Value of the SEC's Accounting Disclosure Requirements," THE ACCOUNTING REVIEW (July 1969), pp. 515–532.
———, "Required Financial Disclosure and the Stock Market: An Evaluation of the Securities and Exchange Act of 1934," *The American Economic Review* (March 1973), pp. 132–155.
Berle, A. A., Jr., and G. C. Means, *The Modern Corporation and Private Property*, (Macmillan, 1932).
Black, F., "The Dividend Puzzle," *Journal of Portfolio Management* (Winter 1976), pp. 5–8.
Briloff, A. J., *Unaccountable Accounting* (Harper & Row, 1972).
Carey, J. L., *The Rise of the Accounting Profession 1896–1936, From Technician to Professional* (AICPA, 1969).
The Conference Board, *Top Executive Compensation* (The Conference Board, Inc., 1974).
Demski, J. S., and G. A. Feltham, "Economic Incentives in Budgetary Control Systems," THE ACCOUNTING REVIEW (April 1978), pp. 336–359.
Dewing, A., *The Financial Policy of Corporations* (The Ronald Press Co., 1926).
Edwards, J. D., *History of Public Accounting in the United States* (Graduate School of Business Administration, Michigan State University, 1960).
Eisenbeis, R. A., "Pitfalls in the Application of Discriminant Analysis in Business, Finance, and Economics," *Journal of Finance* (June 1977), pp. 875–900.

Fama, E. F., "Agency Problems and the Theory of the Firm," *Journal of Political Economy* (April 1980), pp. 288–307.

———, and M. H. Miller, *The Theory of Finance* (Holt, Rinehart & Winston, 1972).

Foster, G., "Accounting Policy Decisions and Capital Market Research," *Journal of Accounting and Economics* (March 1980a), pp. 29–62.

———, "Externalities and Financial Reporting," *Journal of Finance* (May 1980b), pp. 521–533.

Galai, D., and R. W. Masulis, "The Option Pricing Model and the Risk Factor of Stock," *Journal of Financial Economics* (January/March 1976), pp. 53–81.

Hagerman, R. L., and M. E. Zmijewski, "Some Economic Determinants of Accounting Policy Choice," *Journal of Accounting and Economics* (August 1979), pp. 141–161.

Hawkins, D. F., "The Development of Modern Financial Reporting Practices Among American Manufacturing Corporations," in M. Chatfield (ed.), *Contemporary Studies in the Evolution of Accounting Thought* (Dickenson Publishing Co., 1968), pp. 247–279.

Hollander, M., and D. A. Wolfe, *Nonparametric Statistical Methods* (Wiley, 1973).

Hoxsey, J. M. B., "Accounting for Investors," *Journal of Accountancy* (October 1930), pp. 251–284.

Jensen, M. C., and W. H. Meckling, "Theory of the Firm: Managerial Behavior, Agency Costs and Ownership Structure," *Journal of Financial Economics* (October 1976), pp. 305–360.

Kalay, A., "Towards a Theory of Corporate Dividend Policy," Unpublished Paper, New York University (December 1978).

Kehl, D., *Corporate Dividends* (The Ronald Press, 1941).

Larner, R. J., *Management Control and the Large Corporation* (Dunellen Publishing, 1970).

Lehmann, E. L., *Nonparametrics: Statistical Methods Based on Ranks* (Holden-Day, 1975).

Lewellen, W. G., *Executive Compensation in the Large Industrial Corporations* (National Bureau of Economic Research, 1968).

Littleton, A. C., and V. K. Zimmerman, *Accounting Theory: Continuity and Change* (Prentice-Hall, 1962).

McFadden, D., "Conditional Logit Analysis of Qualitative Choice Behavior," Chapter 4 of Zarembka, Paul (ed.), *Frontiers in Econometrics* (Academic Press, 1973), pp. 105–142.

McKelvey, R., and W. Zavoina, "A Statistical Model for the Analysis of Ordinal Level Dependent Variables," *Journal of Mathematical Sociology* (December 1975), pp. 103–120.

Mautz, R., and W. May, *Financial Disclosure in a Competitive Economy* (Financial Executives Research Foundation, 1978).

Myers, S. C., "Determinants of Corporate Borrowing," *Journal of Financial Economics* (November 1977), pp. 147–175.

Ohlson, J. A., "Financial Ratios and the Probabilistic Prediction of Bankruptcy," *Journal of Accounting Research* (Spring 1980), pp. 109–131.

Ripley, W. Z., *Main Street and Wall Street* (Little Brown, 1927).

Rodgers, C., "The Corporate Trust Indenture Project," *Business Lawyer* (April 1965), pp. 551–571.

Securities and Exchange Commission, "Notice of Amendments to Require Increased Disclosure of Relationships Between Registrants and Their Public Independent Public Accountants," *Accounting Series Release No. 165* (Washington, D.C., December 20, 1974).

———, "Reporting Disagreements with Former Accountants—Adoption of Amendments of Requirements," *Accounting Series Release No. 194* (Washington, D.C., April 29, 1976).

Smith, C. W., Jr., and J. B. Warner, "On Financial Contracting: An Analysis of Bond Covenants," *Journal of Financial Economics* (June 1979), pp. 117–161.

Sterling, R. R., "Accounting Power," *Journal of Accountancy* (January 1973), pp. 61–67.

Theil, H., *Principles of Econometrics* (Wiley, 1971).

U.S. House of Representatives, Subcommittee on Oversight and Investigations of the Committee on Interstate and Foreign Commerce, *Federal Regulation and Regulatory Reform* (Washington, D.C., 1976).

U.S. Senate, Subcommittee on Reports, Accounting, and Management of the Committee on Government Operations, *The Accounting Establishment: A Staff Study* (Washington, D.C., 1976).

Watts, R. L., "Corporate Financial Statements, A Product of the Market and Political Processes," *Australian Journal of Management* (April 1977), pp. 53–75.

——, and J. L. Zimmerman, "Towards a Positive Theory of the Determination of Accounting Standards," THE ACCOUNTING REVIEW (January 1978), pp. 112–134.

——, "Auditors and the Determination of Accounting Standards: An Analysis of the Lack of "Independence'," Working Paper No. GPB 78-06, Graduate School of Management, University of Rochester (February 1979).

Zeff, S. A., *Forging Accounting Principles in Five Countries: A History and an Analysis of Trends* (Stipes Publishing Co., 1972).

[3]

Auditing, Directorships and the Demand for Monitoring

Don Anderson, Jere R. Francis, and Donald J. Stokes

Three monitoring mechanisms used for corporate governance are external auditing, internal auditing, and directorships. We consider the three mechanisms as endogenous to the firm and that each firm has an optimal set of monitoring mechanisms the specific mix of which is conditioned by the firm's production-investment attributes. Production-investment attributes are proxied by the degree to which firm value is determined by growth options versus assets-in-place. Empirical predictions are then made and tested concerning the total demand for monitoring from all three mechanisms, and substitutions or tradeoffs between 1) auditing and directorships and 2) external and internal auditing. The results support the hypotheses that overall monitoring expenditures decrease as the firm has relatively more assets-in-place, that relatively more auditing (compared to directorships) occurs for firms with greater assets-in-place, and that relatively more internal auditing (compared to external auditing) also occurs for firms with greater assets-in-place. Predictions are also made and tested concerning the general effect of firm size on the demand for auditing and directorships. The study helps to better understand the economic rationale for each monitoring mechanism and the role it plays in the efficient corporate governance of the firm.

1. Introduction

Accounting literature has viewed the monitoring role of the external auditors as endogenous to a contracting equilibrium in a firm (Watts and Zimmerman 1990, p. 152). It follows that in an efficient contracting equilibrium, differences in a firm's production-investment attributes will determine: 1) differences in the cross-sectional demand for auditing (and for monitoring more generally), and 2) the efficient mix of monitoring mechanisms, including conditions in which there is substitution toward or away from external auditing. The contribution of our paper is to increase

Address reprint requests to: Professor Jere R. Francis, College of Business Administration, University of Iowa, Phillips Hall, Iowa City, IA 52242.

understanding of how differences in firms' production-investment attributes affect the demand for a set of monitoring mechanisms used to achieve corporate governance.

The principal-agent approach to the demand for auditing (e.g., Jensen and Meckling 1976) is broadened by viewing external auditing within a larger set of monitoring mechanisms which include both internal auditors and directors.[1] External auditing, internal auditing, and directorships are all widely used in practice as control mechanisms and have been the subject of extensive prior research. For example, Chow (1982), Francis and Wilson (1988), and Watts and Zimmerman (1983) studied the demand for external auditing from a principal-agent perspective, while Simunic (1980), and Wallace (1984) considered the relationship between internal and external auditing. Finally, Eichenseher and Shields (1985), Pincus *et al.* (1989), and Bradbury (1990) investigated the role of audit committees in corporate monitoring.

Our paper extends the literature in line with suggestions by Watts and Zimmerman (1990) by focusing on the combined effect of monitoring provided by auditing (internal and external) and directorships to achieve corporate governance. We develop the argument that the comparative advantage of each type of monitoring in particular production-investment environments means that the substitutions among monitoring mechanisms are imperfect and that the mechanisms complement each other in the determination of an efficient mix of monitoring from these three sources.

The remainder of our paper is organized as follows. The linkage between firm production-investment attributes and the demand for monitoring from external auditing, internal auditing and directorships is developed in Section 2 as are the hypotheses concerning: 1) the relationship between the production-investment attributes and the aggregate demand for monitoring from these three sources, and 2) the efficient mix of these types of monitoring. Section 3 describes the research design, sample selection, and test variables. The research setting is the Australian corporate environment. Results are reported in Section 4 and estimation and econometric issues are discussed in Section 5. Summary and conclusions appear in Section 6.

2. The Demand for Monitoring

Coase (1937, pp 390–393) argues that firms exist because of their capacity to write efficient contracts with claimholders. We extend Coase's work to

---

[1] Although we restrict the analysis in this paper to monitoring from these three sources, this does not imply that firms face similar restrictions in their choice of monitoring mechanisms. Other monitoring mechanisms include management control systems, the services of consulting engineers, and production efficiency experts.

argue that the type and mix of claimholder contracts will vary as a function of the type of assets held by a firm because of differences in the control attributes of the asset types (see Williamson 1988, pp. 579–581). In this section we draw on a theoretical framework and existing evidence which suggests that one reason why particular types of contracts for the supply of capital emerge is that they are better able to control payoffs. The demand for claimholder control not only means that a firm's production-investment opportunity set and choice of financing are jointly determined, but also that these attributes endogenously determine a firm's investment in monitoring mechanisms to facilitate completion of these contracts (Alchian and Demsetz 1972, p. 792).

2.1 Monitoring and Asset Structure

The corporate finance literature views firm valuation as a function of expected future cash flows from two distinct sources: 1) existing investments or assets-in-place, and 2) future investment opportunities or growth options (see Weston and Copeland 1992, p. 716).[2] This framework provides a broad indicator of differences in firms' production-investment attributes, i.e., the extent to which firm value is a function of assets-in-place versus growth options. The selection of appropriate controls and governance is argued to vary systematically with these two broad categories of assets.

Assets-in-place are distinguished by their tangibility and ability to be traded in secondary markets. Growth options represent discretionary investment opportunities. Compared with assets-in-place, growth options are firm-specific and more difficult to trade in secondary markets because their value is defined relative to other firm assets (e.g., managerial skill).[3] For firms having assets-in-place, debt contracts provide explicit control over the actions of managers through periodic demands for cash, enforceable by specific provisions in contracts which rely on the firm's assets-in-place having substance (exchangeability) in the event of bankruptcy (Jensen 1986, p. 324). Long and Malitz (1985, p. 57) report empirical evidence that assets-in-place and the level of debt are positively correlated. In other words, growth options, being less liquid, are not controlled through conditions related to asset sales in contracts and are therefore less suited to use in default provisions in debt contracts. Thus firms having growth options

---

[2] The notion that firm value can be separated into these two parts goes back at least as far as the seminal work on valuation by Miller and Modigliani. See Miller and Modigliani (1961, especially pp. 415–418); Miller and Modigliani (1966); Fama and Miller (1972, especially Chapter 2). For accounting applications see Leftwich *et al.* (1981) and Bradbury (1990).

[3] Our arguments are consistent with Alchian's (1984, pp. 36–38) insights into the specific dependence of a firm on particular assets. Asset specificity defines the extent to which individual owners of factors share in a stream of quasi-rents, dependent on the continued existence of the coalition of factors which constitutes the firm.

are more likely to be equity financed, and monitoring mechanisms such as auditing and directorships will be used for control.[4]

It follows from the association among assets-in-place, debt contracts, and control enforceable through asset sales that the demand for monitoring will be lower when the proportion of assets-in-place to the total firm value is higher. Thus we hypothesize:

H1: The greater the proportion of a firm's assets-in-place relative to the market value of the firm, the lower the total dollar amount expended on monitoring from auditing and directorships, holding firm size constant.

As firm size is not constant, measures of monitoring are likely to be confounded by firm size. The reason is that outlays on monitoring of the types considered in our study (i.e., external auditors, internal auditors and directors) will all involve fixed costs. Therefore, larger firms have an opportunity for economies of scale in monitoring. Consequently, the average cost of total monitoring is expected to decline as firm size increases. That is, there are positive returns to scale from investments in monitoring which means that total monitoring increases at a decreasing rate as firm size increases. We hypothesize that:

H2: The larger the firm size, the lower the average cost of monitoring from auditing and directorships, where average cost is defined as the total cost of monitoring scaled by firm size.

2.2 Choices of Monitoring Mechanisms

This section develops hypotheses about the relative demand for monitoring from external auditing, internal auditing, and directorships.[5] We first consider the relationship between the differences in firm attributes and the choice of auditing (both internal and external) vis-a-vis directorships. We then consider the relationship between differences in firm attributes associated with the increased use of internal auditing vis-a-vis external auditing.

---

[4] Equity claims on a firm exhibit a series of attributes consistent with the supply of control in response to the existence of less vendible investments in the firm. These attributes include the equity investments existing as long-term claimholder contracts (Williamson 1985, p. 304); equity investors as holders of power with respect to appointment (and re-appointment) of directors and auditors; equity investors as risk sharers who can diversify across organizations offering such claims, and the residual claim that equity investors have to firm payoffs (Fama and Jensen 1983, p. 329.)

[5] An assumption implied in H1 is that external auditing, internal auditing, and directorships are orthogonal and therefore additive in explaining total monitoring. In other words, selection by a firm of one particular mechanism is assumed to be independent of the level of the other two monitoring mechanisms. The relationship between firm attributes and substitution among the three sources of monitoring addressed in this section necessarily depends on relaxing the assumption of orthogonality.

2.2.1 The Demand for Auditors and Directors.

Auditors. Outcomes of production-investment strategies pursued by management are important for the determination of payoffs to claimholders in a firm. The production of accounting information is one mechanism for revealing outcomes of the production-investment process.[6] Given the existence of accounting as a payoff technology to claimholders, the demand for (internal and external) auditing is derived from a demand to monitor and arbitrate on the application of accounting methods. More auditing can be acquired through either internal or external auditing as these are viewed as partial substitutes for one another. With respect to external auditing, more auditing could represent either more quantity such as an increased scope of engagement or more quality such as the use of a high-priced brand name auditor (see Francis and Simon 1987, p. 148; Francis and Wilson 1988, p. 665).

Management decides how the outcomes of production-investment decisions are to be revealed. The auditor then monitors the application of the accounting technology to reveal the outcomes. When unanticipated states arise, modification of the accounting technology may be required and the monitoring function is extended to arbitrating on the consistency of the modification with the original intentions of the contracting parties. The value of the auditor in the arbitration role is dependent on the auditor being sufficiently independent of management to report any detected discord between the intentions of the contracting parties and the revealed states (Watts and Zimmerman 1986, p. 315; Antle 1982, p. 512).

As management is interested in protecting (and enhancing) its reputation, they employ auditors as one mechanism to ensure that resources directed to and from production-investment decisions are consistent with the intent of management decisions, and that firm wealth is not deliberately expropriated by claimholders to an extent greater than the value of their claim (e.g., employees falsifying time records or suppliers short-supplying inventory).

Directors. Directors have the role of supervising the actions of management, providing advice, and vetoing, on behalf of the stockholders, poor production-investment decisions faced by the firm (Jensen 1986, p. 9). Typically, boards of directors consist of both inside and outside directors. Although outside directors are generally high-reputation members of the business community who view the directorate as a means of further developing their reputation as experts in decision control (Fama and Jensen 1983, p. 315), inside directors are included on the board (usually)

---

[6] Whether a highly specific pay-off technology will be chosen will depend on how unique a particular expected problem in contracting is. In less specific circumstances, generally accepted rules (for example, generally accepted accounting principles (GAAP)) will be adopted for payoff determination.

because of their successful association with past production and operating decisions of the firm and, as such, represent a short list of potential chief executive officers (CEOs). In addition to the role played by directors per se, outside directors serve the additional role of monitoring and replacing senior management (particularly the CEO) who are not performing well (Weisbach 1988, p. 431). Thus, though the range of actions and the incentives of inside and outside directors are different, they both fulfill the common role of monitoring the actions of top management.[7]

2.2.2 Institutional Factors Affecting the Demand for Monitoring Mechanisms.
Examination of the voluntary demand for auditing is complicated by the fact that public companies in Australia, like the United States, are required by law to appoint an external auditor. The companies legislation requires external auditors engaged by public companies in Australia be registered, and this, together with legal requirements for conduct of the external audit, establishes a minimum level of quality which the external auditor must provide. In contrast with the appointment of external auditors, companies have no statutory obligation to appoint internal auditors.[8]

As with mandatory external auditing requirements, publicly-listed firms in Australia were, in the sample data collection year, required under companies legislation to appoint a minimum of three directors (inside or outside), who had statutory obligations under the legislation. Like external auditors, directors have incentives to be diligent because of the potential deleterious effects on their human capital (Fama 1980, p. 294).

2.2.3 Mix of Auditing and Directorships.
This section of our paper develops hypotheses which link a firm's production-investment mix of assets-in-place and growth options with the demand for auditing versus directorships. High assets-in-place firms can support debt and debt contracts which use accounting numbers based on generally accepted accounting principles (GAAP) in specifying payoffs (Smith and Warner 1979; Leftwich 1983; Whittred and Zimmer 1986; Stokes and Tay 1988). In contrast, high growth option firms rely less on debt contracts and therefore less on accounting numbers, GAAP, and auditors in the determination of payoffs to claimholders.[9] In these firms, claimholders will be

---

[7] In an empirical sense it is difficult to differentiate between the monitoring and non-monitoring tasks of inside directors as inside directors are typically full-time employees of the firm. We address the effects of using measures related to total directors in Sections 4 and 5.

[8] In the United States there may be a regulation-induced demand for internal auditing due to the Foreign Corrupt Practices Act of 1977 (see Maher 1981, p. 752).

[9] GAAP provides less assistance in dealing with contingencies in the case of growth options because of the uniqueness (i.e., firm-specific value) of such assets.

more concerned with the optimal exercise of the growth options in order to maximize the value of their claim. Directors are specialized in the role of monitoring managers who develop and exercise the options. Therefore directors are likely to be more efficient in this type of monitoring than auditors. These arguments lead to hypothesis H3:

H3: The greater the proportion of a firm's assets-in-place relative to the market value of the firm, the less the relative expenditure on monitoring from directors compared to auditing (internal and external).

The size of a firm will also influence the mix of auditing and directorships. Larger firms have the opportunity to take advantage of economies of scale from investing in the fixed cost of internal auditing which include hiring and training of internal audit staff and establishing geographically-dispersed internal audit offices attached to the firms' expanded operations. The opportunity to obtain economies of scale from investing in more auditing through establishment of internal audit departments increases with firm size. This leads to the hypothesis that:

H4: The larger the firm size, the less the relative expenditure on monitoring from directors compared to auditing (internal and external).

2.2.4 Mix of External and Internal Auditing.
This section of our paper develops hypotheses which link a firm's production-investment mix of assets-in-place and growth options with the demand for internal versus external auditing. Where a greater proportion of firm value is explained by growth options, and to the extent that auditing is used as a monitoring device (H3), these firms will rely less upon internal auditors and more upon external auditors. In high growth option firms, there are greater uncertainties about the value of firms' assets and payoffs to claimholders. In these circumstances, the external auditor's ability to arbitrate (and therefore the external auditor's independence) is valued. The external auditor's value in these circumstances is dependent on his or her ability to interpret the intention of the contract (given the states which have occurred) and to be independent of the claimholders.

In contrast, with high assets-in-place firms, the assets and internal controls over the assets are more observable, and conventional accounting technologies (e.g., GAAP) are more relied upon to define claimholder payoffs than is the case with high growth option firms. As the value of auditor independence in arbitrating on accounting-based payoffs is lower in these circumstances, the external auditor can also rely more on internal accounting controls (including internal auditors) in conducting the external audit and produce cost savings to the firm.[10] This leads to hypothesis H5:

H5: The greater the proportion of a firm's assets-in-place relative to the market value of the firm, the greater the relative expenditure on monitoring from internal auditing compared to external auditing.

The size of a firm will influence the mix of internal and external auditing. It was earlier argued that the fixed costs of the external audit are sunk against the decision to operate the firm in a way that has this requirement, irrespective of firm size. By contrast, the establishment of internal audit departments is likely to be associated with other fixed costs, and the opportunity to obtain economies of scale from investing in internal audit departments will increase with firm size. Larger firms should therefore be able to (partially) substitute internal auditing for external auditing.[11] This leads to the hypothesis H6:

H6: The larger the firm size, the greater the relative expenditure on monitoring from internal auditing compared to external auditing.

3. Variables, Sample and Research Design

3.1 Variable Descriptions and Model Specification

Table 1 provides the definitions and measurements of variables used in the tests reported below. Total monitoring (MONITOR) was measured as the sum of a firm's dollar outlays on external auditing (EAUD), internal auditing (IAUD), and total directors' compensation (TDIR).[12] A maintained assumption is that the value of monitoring to claimholders is unbiasedly estimated by the dollar amount of expenditures committed to monitoring by managers.

Cross-sectional differences in firms' overall production-investment mix of assets-in-place versus growth options were approximated by the ratio total balance-sheet-assets to market value of the firm. This ratio is referred to as BVMKT. The numerator represents investments in assets-in-place

---

[10] This is consistent with institutional rules in Australia (*Auditing Guideline AUP 2: Using the Work of an Internal Auditor* (ICAA, 1992, para. 13).

[11] Internal audit is not modelled in this paper to include operational/efficiency audits directed at ex ante prevention of errors in operational decisions. However, operational/efficiency auditing also functions as part of the overall internal control system and is more likely to be of greater use where there are assets-in-place. Therefore, internal auditing, for either compliance testing or operational efficiency, increases control and should be an increasing function of assets-in-place.

[12] Our measure of directors' compensation does not include remuneration via stock options because of the lack of Australian data to quantify the value of these options. It would be expected that the greater the proportion of firm value explained by growth options the more likely that directors would be compensated with stock options. Smith and Watts (1992, pp. 271–272) provide evidence in support of this proposition. For this type of firm the measure of directors' compensation is understated and would therefore bias against the results predicted by hypotheses H1–H3.

Table 1. Variable Definitions and Measurement

Variable	Description
MONITOR	The sum of the firm's dollar outlays on 1) external audit fees of external auditors (EAUD), 2) internal auditors' salaries (IAUD), and 3) total directors' compensation (TDIR).
BVMKT	Proxy for extent of firm value represented by assets-in-place vs. growth options. Measured as the ratio of accounting book value of total assets to market value of the firm (approximated by market value of common equity plus book value of total debt and preferred stock).
DEBTMKT	Proxy for capital structure and debt intensity. Measured as the ratio of the book value of total debt to market value of the firm (approximated by market value of common equity plus book value of total debt and preferred stock).
SIZE	Proxy for firm size. Measured as total market value of common equity plus book value of total debt and preferred stock.
TDIRAUD	Proxy for substitution of directors for total auditing. Measured as ratio of total directors' compensation (TDIR) to total auditing (IAUD + EAUD).
IAUDEAUD	Proxy for substitution of internal auditing for external auditing. Measured as the ratio of internal auditors' salaries (IAUD) to external auditors' fees (EAUD).
TDIR%	TDIR divided by MONITOR.

(proxied by the accounting book values of balance sheet assets) and the denominator is the total market value of the firm which conceptually is the sum of both 1) investments in assets-in-place, and 2) future growth options. The larger the ratio, then, the greater the firm's assets-in-place relative to growth options.[13] Empirically, growth options exist to the extent firm value is not explained by assets-in-place. If BVMKT were a perfect proxy, the theoretical range would be 1.0 for an all assets-in-place firm and zero for an all growth option firm. However, because accounting rules do not perfectly measure assets-in-place, and because book values were used to measure the debt portion of firm value, BVMKT is likely to be measured with error. Implications of this are examined further in Section 5.2.

Leverage of the firm, DEBTMKT, was measured as the ratio of the book value of total debt to the market value of the firm. Leverage is expected to be positively correlated with BVMKT. The variables TDIRAUD and IAUDEAUD measure the ratio of total directors' compensation to total auditing, and internal auditing to external auditing respectively. Firm size (SIZE) was measured by the market value of the firm

---

[13] The BVMKT variable could also be viewed as a proxy for age of the firm. The older the firm the more likely it will have a larger investment in assets-in-place and therefore the larger the BVMKT variable.

(proxied by the market value of equity plus the book value of debt and preferred stock). With the exception of the IAUD and TDIR variables, and other variables based on them, all data were collected from the Australian Graduate School of Management Annual Report and Share Price Tapes, and Annual Report Microfiche Service for the 1987 fiscal year. Disclosure of the data required for IAUD and TDIR is not mandatory in Australia. A survey questionnaire was used to collect this data. This aspect of the data collection is considered further in Section 3.2.

We used three OLS regression models to test the hypotheses developed in Section 2. Model 1 tested H1 and H2, Model 2 tested H3 and H4, and Model 3 tested H5 and H6. In developing the three models, all parameters were signed as + or − in terms of theoretical predictions on the model variables.

Model 1.

Holding firm size constant, H1 hypothesizes that MONITOR is lower as BVMKT increases (i.e., relatively more assets-in-place):

$$\text{MONITOR} = a_0 - a_1 \text{BVMKT} + \varepsilon_1 \qquad (1)$$

However, firm size is not constant and H2 predicts that average costs of monitoring decreases as SIZE increases due to economies of scale in monitoring:

$$\frac{\text{MONITOR}}{\text{SIZE}} = b_0 - b_1 \text{SIZE} + \varepsilon_2 \qquad (2)$$

where MONITOR/SIZE represents a proxy for the average cost of monitoring (i.e., total monitoring scaled by firm size).

Multiplying all terms in (2) by SIZE gives:

$$\text{MONITOR} = c_0 \text{SIZE} - c_1 \text{SIZE}^2 + \varepsilon_3 \qquad (3)$$

The quadratic term SIZE^2 represents the effect of firm size on lowering the average cost of monitoring. In other words, the cost of total monitoring increases as firm size increases, but at a decreasing rate, hence the negative sign on parameter c_1.

Combining (1) and (3) we have:

$$\text{MONITOR} = d_0 - d_1 \text{BVMKT} + d_2 \text{SIZE} - d_3 \text{SIZE}^2 + \varepsilon_4 \quad \text{(Model 1)}$$

Model 1 predicts that total monitoring (MONITOR) is lower as BVMKT increases (i.e., relatively more assets-in-place), and that average monitoring costs decrease as firm size (SIZE^2) increases.

Model 2.

Combining hypotheses H3 and H4 we have the hypothesized relationships:

$$TDIRAUD = e_0 - e_1 BVMKT - e_2 SIZE + \varepsilon_5 \quad \text{(Model 2)}$$

Model 2 predicts that relatively less director's monitoring (and more auditing) is used as both BVMKT (assets-in-place) and firm size (SIZE) increase.

Model 3.

Combining hypotheses H5 and H6 we have the hypothesized relationship:

$$IAUDEAUD = f_0 + f_1 BVMKT + f_2 SIZE + f_3 TDIR\% + \varepsilon_6 \quad \text{(Model 3)}$$

Model 3 predicts that relatively more internal auditing (and less external auditing) is used as both assets-in-place (BVMKT) and firm size (SIZE) increase. We also controlled for cross-sectional differences in the percentage of monitoring from total directors' remuneration (TDIR%) in order to investigate the mix between internal auditing and external auditing. There is no predicted sign on the TDIR% control variable.

Functional forms of the models are not specified by the hypotheses nor by the theoretical arguments in Section 2. Thus, the models were initially estimated using untransformed variables. In all instances this led to serious violation of OLS regression assumptions concerning normality of residuals and homoskedasticity. As a consequence, data transformation on certain variables were undertaken to correct these problems. Specifically, the dependent variable in Model 1, MONITOR, is a natural log transformation; the dependent variables in Models 2 and 3, TDIRAUD and IAUDEAUD, are square root transformations (square root transformations were used rather than natural logs due to zero values for some observations); and the independent variable SIZE in Models 2 and 3 is specified as the natural log of SIZE. The effects of the transformations are discussed in Section 5 after presenting the results.

Models 1–3 assume that the supply of monitoring arises solely from the demand for claimholder monitoring which is endogenously derived from attributes of a firm's assets. However, this is not necessarily the case with respect to external auditors and directors as they are subject to external regulatory institutions. One possible exogenous factor affecting the supply of monitoring is the external auditors' and directors' exposure to legal liability. As the risk of litigation increases, both audit fees and directors' compensation could increase in response to expected litigation losses.

To the extent that risk of litigation is correlated with higher external audit fees and directors' compensation, and to the extent that the risk itself is an increasing function of a firm's growth options (due to increased uncertainty about asset valuation and payoffs to claimants), then a correlated omitted variable problem could exist.[14] Empirical evidence supports only a weak positive association between indirect measures of audit risk (e.g., profitability, leverage, unsystematic risk, and qualified audit reports) and the level of audit fees (for example, Firth 1985, pp. 32–33, Francis 1984, p. 143; Simunic 1980, p. 181). However, Wallace's (1989, p. 30) analysis rejected the claim that audit fees are adjusted for audit risk. One reason why audit fees might not be risk adjusted is that auditor litigation rates are very low (Palmrose 1988, p. 64). With the probability of litigation being low, there is insufficient cross-sectional differences in the expected cost of ex ante audit risk to warrant consideration by the auditor.[15] If this is the case, then the supply-side exogenity due to legal liability may not have created a correlated omitted variable problem.

3.2 Sample of Firms

A questionnaire was circulated to the Company Secretary for a sample of 396 public companies drawn from the Jobsons Year Book of Public Companies in Australia. The questionnaire asked for the total remuneration paid to the internal audit department in the 1987 fiscal year. Information was also requested on the total compensation paid to directors and the proportion of this compensation paid to outside directors. The sample was reduced to 141 companies responding to the questionnaire which had annual report information available from the data bases.[16] The sample was further reduced to 105 when firms with missing data on one or more variables were excluded.

---

[14] The effect of this exogenity would be to increase external audit fees and directors' compensation as growth options increase (i.e., a decline in the BVMKT ratio). This effect would be in the same direction as predicted in Models 1 and 3 for the variable BVMKT which means that BVMKT could proxy for an omitted correlated variable thus overstating its significance. However, the effect on Model 2 concerning the substitution of directors' monitoring for auditing is unclear. The prediction in Model 2 is that as growth options increase, directors' monitoring will be substituted for auditing, whereas the supply-side exogenity predicts more auditing and directors' monitoring as growth options increase. This would create a bias for (against) the predicted result in Model 2 if directors' compensation increased (decreased) relatively more than audit fees as growth options increased.

[15] There is no empirical evidence that we are aware of that looks at litigation risk and directors' compensation. The Australian legal system, in contrast to the U.S. system, is not characterized by contingent fees and class action suits, and we would argue that the probability of litigation against directors is also low.

[16] The total response rate on the questionnaire was approximately 76% ($n = 300$), and the usable response rate was approximately 64% ($n = 252$). As discussed in Section 4.1 a follow-up mailing occurred after three weeks.

3.3 Research Design

The research design used OLS linear regression to estimate Models 1–3. As directional effects are predicted by hypotheses H1–H6, t tests on coefficients of the independent variables in the regression models were used to test the hypotheses that the coefficients are greater or less than zero, as appropriate.

4. Results

4.1 Descriptive Statistics

Descriptive statistics are reported in Table 2 for all test variables for the sample of 105 companies. External audit costs constitute the largest component of monitoring costs with directorships and internal auditing, ranking second and third respectively. Only 36 firms (approximately 1/3) of the firms in the sample had an internal audit department. Consistent with H6, these firms were significantly larger (based on the SIZE variable) than those firms without internal audit departments ($t = 6.33$; $p < .01$, one-tailed).

The BVMKT variable had a few values outside the expected theoretical range of 0 to 1. Section 5.2 discusses potential reasons for this and the effects of the outliers. The average leverage (DEBTMKT) for the sample was 41%. Table 2 also reports descriptive statistics on market value, sales and assets for the sample firms. The average market value, sales, and total assets for the sample were $1,227 million, $463 million, and $1,122 million respectively. The average market value, sales, and total assets for the top 1000 companies (ranked on sales) in Australia were $897 million, $329

Table 2. Descriptive Statistics in Australian Dollars ($n = 105$)

Variables	Mean	Median	Std. Dev.	Minimum	Maximum
IAUD ($)*	115,503	0	455,980	0	3,500,000
EAUD ($)	341,195	91,000	725,490	2,400	4,474,000
TDIR ($)	158,481	68,000	272,215	200	2,236,000
MONITOR ($)	615,179	208,870	1,264,821	2,600	8,234,000
BVMKT	.9074	.8691	.6027	.0723	5.3812
DEBTMKT	.4085	.4121	.2298	.0023	.9488
SIZE ($000,000)	1,227	125	6,986	0.79	70,981
SALES ($000,000)	463	89	1,400	0.3484	11,370
ASSETS ($000,000)	1,122	98	6,904	2.0	70,334

* There is no mandatory requirement to have internal auditing. Of the 105 observations, 69 firms had zero expenditure on internal auditing.

million, and \$637 million respectively (in Australian dollars).[17] These figures suggest our sample may be somewhat biased towards larger Australian companies.

The Pearson product-moment correlation between the two independent variables of interest, BVMKT and SIZE, was only .002 and was insignificantly different from zero ($p = .98$). Thus there was no concern with multicollinearity between these two variables in the estimation of the models reported below in Tables 3 and 4.[18]

Tests for non-response bias in our survey data were made by comparing early and late respondents, with late respondents being used to proxy for non-respondents. Early versus late respondents were determined by whether a reply had been received within three weeks of the first mailing. As noted in footnote 16, a second mailing of the survey questionnaire was sent to non-respondents three weeks after the date of the first mailing. The results of the tests indicate that early ($n = 77$) and late respondents ($n = 28$) were not significantly different ($p \leq .10$) on the variables of interest with the exception of *ln* MONITOR.[19] As a further test for non-response bias all the models reported in Tables 3 and 4 below were re-estimated adding a dummy variable for early/late respondents. The results reported below were unaffected and in all cases the dummy variable was insignificant at $p = .05$.

4.2 Test Results: H1 and H2

A maintained hypothesis in the development of H1, H3, and H5 is that firms with increasing assets-in-place support larger amounts of debt in their capital structure. A positive correlation between DEBTMKT and BVMKT confirms this expectation (Pearson Correlation Coefficient = .279, $p < .01$; Spearman Rank Correlation = .504, $p < .01$).

Table 3 reports the OLS regressions for hypotheses H1 and H2 using Model 1. The results support both hypotheses. The adjusted R^2 of the OLS regression was .423 and the F ratio was significant at $p < .01$ level. Both test variables, BVMKT and SIZE^2, were significant in the predicted direction. The greater a firm's assets-in-place relative to total firm value, the less total monitoring by the firm ($p < .03$). The greater a firm's size,

---

[17] "Top 1000", *Business Review Weekly* (November 20, 1987, p. 98). Comparisons with the Top 1000 companies on the other variables were not possible due to data constraints in the Top 1000 survey.

[18] The Pearson correlation between BVMKT and the natural log of SIZE was $-.29$ which is significantly different from zero ($p < .01$). However, the collinearity does not appear to have degraded the regression estimate of standard error as both terms were consistently significant in the models.

[19] Late respondents had slightly lower monitoring costs ($p = .05$). Despite this, there was no evidence of differences in the proportionate mix of monitoring (i.e., relative amounts of external auditing, internal auditing, and directors' compensation).

Table 3. Ordinary Least Squares Regression Results: H1 and H2 ($n = 105$)

Variables	Predicted Sign	Parameter Estimates	t stat	(p value)*
		Model 1: Dep.Var. = *ln* MONITOR		
Intercept	$+/-$	12.420	63.333	($< .01$)
BVMKT	$-$	-0.326	-1.930	($< .03$)
SIZE	$+$	6.948×10^{-10}	7.788	($< .01$)
SIZE^2	$-$	-9.003×10^{-21}	-7.100	($< .01$)
F ratio			26.416	($< .01$)
Adj.R^2			0.423	

* For the t tests on the parameter estimates, the p values are two-tail where the predicted sign is $+/-$, and one tail for the others.

the smaller the average cost of monitoring by the firm ($p < .01$) which means that total monitoring costs increased at a decreasing rate as firm size increased.

4.3 Test Results: H3–H6

Table 4 reports the OLS regressions for hypotheses H3–H6 using Models 2 and 3. The results for Model 2 support hypotheses H3 and H4. The adjusted R^2 on Model 2 was .170 and the F ratio was significant at $p < .01$. The BVMKT variable was significant ($p < .01$) and in the predicted direction, supporting that the greater the investment in assets-in-place, the less the relative expenditure on monitoring by directors compared with auditors. The *ln* SIZE variable was also significant ($p < .01$) and in the predicted direction, i.e., the larger the firm size the less the relative expenditure on directors' monitoring compared with auditing. Separate regressions were also estimated using the ratios of TDIR to

Table 4. Ordinary Least Squares Regression Results: H3 to H6 ($n = 105$)

Variables	Predicted Sign	Parameter Estimates	t stat	(p value)*	Predicted Sign	Parameter Estimates	t stat	(p value)*
	Model 2: Dep.Var. = TDIRUD^{-5}				Model 3: Dep.Var. = IAUDEAUD^{-5}			
Intercept	$+/-$	4.439	6.155	($< .01$)	$+/-$	-2.092	-4.447	($< .01$)
BVMKT	$-$	-0.284	-2.561	($< .01$)	$+$	0.218	3.652	($< .01$)
*ln*SIZE	$-$	-0.170	-4.661	($< .01$)	$+$	0.113	5.175	($< .01$)
TDIR%					$+/-$	0.062	0.413	(.68)
F ratio			11.686	($< .01$)			12.769	($< .01$)
Adj.R^2			0.170				0.253	

* For the t tests on the parameter estimates, the p values are two tail where the predicted sign is $+/-$, and one tail for the others.

IAUD and TDIR to EAUD (see Table 1) as the dependent variables for Model 2. The same result held for both auditor groups indicating that the results reported in Table 4 were not driven by one auditor group or the other (i.e., internal or external auditing).

The adjusted R^2 on Model 3 was .253 and was significant at $p < .01$. The results for Model 3 support hypotheses H5 and H6. The BVMKT variable was significant ($p < .01$) indicating that internal auditing increases relative to external auditing in the presence of increasing investments in assets-in-place. The *ln* SIZE variable was significant ($p < .01$) and in the predicted direction, supporting that the larger the firm size the greater the relative expenditure on monitoring from internal auditing compared to external auditing. The control variable TDIR% was not significant.

5. Estimation Sensitivity and Econometric Issues

5.1 Functional Form

As noted in Section 3.1 no functional form is specified or implied by the theoretical arguments. When Model 1 was estimated using untransformed variables there was a serious heteroskedasticity problem as well as nonnormally distributed residuals. These econometric problems were corrected by using a natural log transformation on the dependent variable, MONITOR. Although the firm size variables (SIZE and SIZE^2) were significant in both model specifications, the assets-in-place variable (BVMKT) was significant only in the transformed model. Thus the results on this variable were sensitive to the functional form used to estimate Model 1.

Similar econometric problems arose in Models 2 and 3 when untransformed variables were used to estimate the models. The first solution was to use a natural log transformation on the firm size variable (*ln* SIZE) under the presumption that non-linearities (and heteroskedasticity) were introduced by the use of a raw firm size metric. This transformation on firm size eliminated the heteroskedasticity and resulted in predicted significance on both independent variables, BVMKT and *ln* SIZE. However, the residuals were still non-normally distributed so a square root transformation was made on the dependent variables in Models 2 and 3, TDI-RAUD and IAUDEAUD. This further transformation resulted in a better fit of the data in terms of the R^2 and alleviated the residual non-normality problem. In contrast to Model 1, both independent variables were significant in Models 2 and 3 even in the untransformed functional form. Overall, then, the statistical results were not sensitive to variable specification in Models 2 and 3.

5.2 Outliers on BVMKT

As noted in Section 3.1, the theoretical range of values for BVMKT (which proxies for production-investment mix of assets-in-place and growth options) is zero to one: zero when a firm has exclusively growth options and no assets-in-place, and one when all assets valued by the market are on the accounting balance sheet at market values. However, it is possible for accounting book values of assets to exceed a firm's market value, particularly in the short-run, due to accounting methods of asset valuation. Even in the long-term, values greater than one would be possible given transaction costs in liquidating a firm. [20]

There are 16 firms in the sample whose BVMKT ratio exceeded one; however, 14 of these firms ranged from only 1.03 to 1.37.[21] Only two firms had extreme outlier values of 4.37 and 5.38. Models 1–3 were re-estimated, dropping these two observations and the results reported in Tables 3 and 4 were not substantively affected. The models were also re-estimated after truncating the 16 outliers for BVMKT to a maximum value of 1.0. The results in Tables 3 and 4 were not affected; BVMKT and SIZE were significant at $p < .05$ in the predicted direction.

5.3 Industry Concentration

No control was made for industry membership on the assumption that there are no industry effects on the variables of interest. The sample is well dispersed across industries and this mitigates to some extent against an industry-related correlated omitted variables problem. As evidence of this, there are 19 different 2 digit industry categories represented in the sample out of a possible 23 categories used by the Australian Stock Exchange. Only two categories constituted more than 10% of the sample. However, as a sensitivity analysis, the results were re-estimated dropping firms in each of these two industries (one industry at a time). The results reported in Tables 3 and 4 were not affected by deleting each of these two industry groups.

---

[20] Another explanation for this result could be the disparity between book and market values of debt. Although Bowman (1980, pp. 249–250) shows that empirically in the United States, book values of debt are an efficient proxy for market values, this result is likely to be less robust when interest rates are more volatile, as is the case in Australia.

[21] Five of the sixteen outliers had ratios between 1.0 and 1.1. Ten of the sixteen outliers had ratios between 1.0 and 1.2. In other words, most of the 16 cases did not have extreme values in excess of 1.0.

5.4 Sensitivity of Proxies for Assets-In-Place and Firm Size

The proxy for assets-in-place (BVMKT) was defined as the ratio of the accounting book value of total assets to the market value of the firm (see Table 1). As a test of sensitivity, Models 1–3 were re-estimated with the independent variable BVMKT redefined as 1) accounting book value of tangible assets to market value of the firm, and 2) accounting book value of fixed assets to market value of the firm, as alternative accounting-based representations of assets-in-place. The results were not affected by these alternatives.

Firm size was defined as market value of the firm (see Table 1). Models 1–3 were re-estimated using accounting book value of total assets and sales of the firm as alternative proxies for firm size. The statistical results across all three models in Tables 3 and 4 were unaffected by the choice of proxy for firm size.

5.5 Inclusions of Non-Audit Fees in Total Auditor Fees

Total external auditor fees, EAUD, were defined to exclude remuneration for non-audit services. Some non-audit consulting work may be of a non-monitoring nature and therefore its inclusion would create noise in the measure. However, it is also possible that non-audit services represent the purchase of monitoring-related expertise such as systems consulting. Skewing may also occur between reported audit and non-audit fees (Francis 1984, p. 141). To determine the effect of broadening the measure of monitoring from external audit, EAUD was redefined to include non-audit fees and Models 1–3 re-estimated. The results reported in Tables 3 and 4 were unaffected by whether the variable EAUD included non-audit fees charged by the external auditor.

5.6 Total Versus Outside Directors' Monitoring

Following the argument in Section 2.2.1 our hypotheses were formulated in terms of monitoring provided by both inside and outside directors. However, potential confounding is introduced if compensation paid to inside directors reflects services to the firm other than monitoring. To determine the effect of combining both inside and outside director's monitoring, Models 1–3 were re-estimated using outside directors fees only. In our survey instrument we asked for both total directors' remuneration and for the percentage of remuneration related to outside directors. Respondents indicated that outside directors' remuneration expenditures averaged $1,030, or only about 1% of total directors' monitoring. Despite this data concern over the accuracy of the measure of outside directors' fees, the results in Tables 3 and 4 were unaffected by use of outside directors' instead of total directors' compensation.

5.7 *Alternative Data for Directors' Remuneration*

In addition to the disclosure of auditor remuneration, corporate annual reports in Australia also make disclosures with respect to directors' remuneration. An amount for total directors (both inside and outside) is reported. We were able to obtain this data for 80 of the 105 companies in the sample as an alternative measure of total directors' remuneration.[22] We did this given our above-mentioned concern in Section 5.6 over data reliability from our survey results.

The results in Tables 3 and 4 were re-estimated using this annual report data for the 80 observations, with the original survey data being used for the remaining 25 observations in the study. The results of this re-estimation were qualitatively the same as those reported in Tables 3 and 4. No substantive changes occurred with respect to the signs or the significance levels of the variables used in Models 1–3 to test hypotheses H1–H6.

A final point concerns the rather large variance in the directors' remuneration data. For both sets of data the dollar amounts ranged from a few hundred dollars to over a million dollars (Australian). The most likely explanation for this, apart from firm size differences, is that some companies are including the salaries of inside directors in the directors' remuneration data whereas other companies are restricting the data to compensation just in conjunction with directors' duties. In this respect both sets of data are likely to be noisy measures.

6. Summary and Conclusions

The objective of our paper was to examine how differences in firms' production-investment attributes affect the demand for a package of monitoring mechanisms which includes external auditing, internal auditing, and directorships. Following the corporate finance literature, we characterized production-investment attributes in very broad terms as the mix of investments in assets-in-place versus growth options. Controls which depend on the liquidity attributes of assets-in-place are less effective when firm value is explained by growth options characterized by uncertain cash flows. Our paper develops the argument that in these circumstances

---

[22] For these 80 observations, the Spearman correlation between the annual report data and our survey data was .74 ($p < .01$). The data were in fact identical for 23 companies, and the two amounts were within 5% for another eight companies. For these 80 companies, the mean (median) per the annual report disclosure in Australian dollars was $197,103 ($78,000) versus $149,143 ($70,000) from our survey results. Thus the annual report data, on average, were slightly larger in amount than our survey data. However, the differences do not appear to be substantial and this point is borne out by the fact that there was no material difference in the empirical tests when the annual report data were used in lieu of the survey data. The annual report disclosures did not consistently report sufficient data to make possible a partition between inside and outside directors so we were unable to undertake a further analysis of outside versus total directors' remuneration based on the annual report data.

corporate monitoring and governance is introduced in response to a reduction in claimholder capacity to sell assets. We argue that external auditing, along with internal auditing and directorships, form part of the set of monitoring mechanisms available to a firm, and that the overall level of monitoring using these mechanisms is a function of a firm's mix of assets-in-place and growth options, as is the particular mix of monitoring mechanisms.

There are three key findings concerning the effect of the mix of assets-in-place and growth options on monitoring. First, the evidence supports that total monitoring is a decreasing function of the proportion of firm value explained by assets-in-place (H1). Second, directors' monitoring decreases relative to auditing, the greater the proportion of firm value explained by assets-in-place (H3). Third, we find that internal auditing is substituted for external auditing the greater the proportion of firm value explained by assets-in-place (H5). These results held when controlling for firm size as a covariate.

Predictions are also supported with respect to the effect of firm size on monitoring. Total monitoring costs increase at a decreasing rate as firm size increases, which supports the prediction that average monitoring cost (proxied as total monitoring scaled by firm size) decreases as firm size increases due to economies of scale in monitoring (H2). It was also predicted that there are economies of scale in investments in internal auditing and this prediction is supported. Specifically directors' monitoring decreases relative to total auditing as firm size increases (H4) and internal auditing increases relative to external auditing as firm size increases (H6).

Several data limitations exist with the study in terms of potential measurement error and bias. The measure of directors' compensation excluded stock options and was dominated by inside directors. The proxy used to represent a firm's production-investment mix of assets-in-place versus growth options is imperfect as it relied on accounting book values to measure assets-in-place. Finally, a bias in the sample may also exist toward somewhat larger public companies in Australia.

These data limitations in our study may make the results suggestive rather than conclusive. Nevertheless, the findings provide insight and direction to gaining a better understanding of the economic incentives and roles of auditing and directorships in the efficient governance of a firm. The particular contribution of our paper is to use a contracting framework to theorize the role of monitoring as an endogenous function of a firm's production-investment mix of assets-in-place versus growth options, and to apply the framework to a set of monitoring mechanisms in order to understand how the demand for each mechanism is conditioned by 1) production-investment attributes, and 2) firm size and economies of scale in monitoring.

Acknowledgment

We gratefully acknowledge the financial support for this project provided by the GWA Corporation, the Australian Research Council and the McGladrey Institute for Accounting Research, University of Iowa. This paper and its earlier versions have benefited from the comments of workshop participants at the University of Chicago, the University of Michigan, the University of Rochester, Duke University, Cornell University, the Australian National University, Macquarie University, the University of Auckland, the University of Alberta, Texas Christian University, the University of Sydney, and the 1990 AAA Conference in Toronto. The research assistance and advice of John Lyon is also gratefully acknowledged.

References

Alchian, A. March 1984. Specificity, specialization, and coalitions. *Journal of Institutional and Theoretical Economics* 140(1):34–49.

Alchian, A. and Demsetz, H., December 1972. Production, information costs and economic organization. *The American Economic Review* 62(5):775–795.

Antle, R. Fall 1982. The auditor as an economic agent. *Journal of Accounting Research* 20(2):503–527.

Bowman, R. G. Spring 1980. The importance of a market-value measurement of debt in assessing leverage. *Journal of Accounting Research* 18(1):242–254.

Bradbury, M. Spring 1990. The incentives for voluntary audit committee formation. *Journal of Accounting and Public Policy* 9(1):19–36.

Coase, R. H. November 1937. The nature of the firm. *Economica* 4(16):386–405.

Chow, C. W. April 1982. The demand for external auditing: Size, debt and ownership influences. *The Accounting Review* 57(2):272–291.

Eichenseher, J. and Shields, D. Spring 1985. Corporate director liability and monitoring preferences. *Journal of Accounting and Public Policy* 4(1):13–31.

Fama, E. April 1980. Agency problems and the theory of the firm. *Journal of Political Economy* 88(2):288–307.

Fama, E. and Jensen, M. June 1983. Agency problems and residual claims. *The Journal of Law and Economics* 26(2):327–349.

Fama, E. and Miller, M. 1972. *The Theory of Finance*. New York: Holt, Rinehart and Winston.

Firth, M. Spring 1985. An analysis of audit fees and their determinants in New Zealand. *Auditing: A Journal of Practice and Theory* 4(2):23–37.

Francis, J. August 1984. The effect of audit firm size on audit prices: A study of the Australian market. *Journal of Accounting and Economics* 6(2):133–151.

Francis, J. and Simon, D. January 1987. A test of audit pricing in the small-client segment of the U.S. audit market. *The Accounting Review* 62(1):145–157.

Francis, J. and Wilson, E. October 1988. Auditor changes: A test of theories relating to agency costs and auditor differentiation. *The Accounting Review* 63(4): 663–682.

Institute of Chartered Accountants in Australia (ICAA). 1992. *Members Handbook.* Sydney: Institute of Chartered Accountants in Australia.

Jensen, M. May 1986. Agency costs of free cash flow, corporate finance, and takeovers. *The American Economic Review* 76(2):323–329.

Jensen, M. and Meckling, W. October 1976. Theory of the firm: managerial behavior, agency costs and ownership structure. *Journal of Financial Economics* 3(4):305–360.

Jobson's Yearbook of Public Companies of Australia and New Zealand (59th ed.). 1989. Melbourne: Dun and Bradstreet.

Long, M. and Malitz, I. Fall 1985. The investment-financing nexus: Some empirical evidence. *Midland Corporate Finance Journal* 3(3):53–59.

Leftwich, R. January 1983. Accounting information in private markets: Evidence from private lending agreements. *The Accounting Review* 58(1):23–42.

Leftwich, R., Watts, R. L. and Zimmerman, J. 1981. Voluntary corporate disclosure: The case of interim reporting. *Journal of Accounting Research* 19(Supplement):50–77.

Maher, M. W. October 1981. The impact of regulation on controls: Firms' response to the foreign corrupt practices act. *The Accounting Review* 66(4):751–770.

Miller, M. and Modigliani, F. October 1961. Dividend policy, growth, and the valuation of shares. *Journal of Business* 34(4):411–433.

Miller, M. and Modigliani, F. June 1966. Some estimates of the cost of capital to the electric utility industry, 1954–1957. *The American Economic Review* 56(3): 333–391.

Palmrose, Z. V. January 1988. An analysis of auditor litigation and audit service quality. *The Accounting Review* 63(1):55–73.

Pincus, K., Rusbarsky, M. and Wong, J. Winter 1989. Voluntary formation of corporate audit committees among NASDAQ firms. *Journal of Accounting and Public Policy* 8(4):239–265.

Simunic, D. A. Spring 1980. The pricing of audit services: Theory and evidence. *Journal of Accounting Research* 18(1):161–190.

Smith, C. W. and Warner, J. B. June 1979. On financial contracting: An analysis of bond covenants. *Journal of Financial Economics* 7(2):117–161.

Smith, C. W. and Watts, R. L. December 1992. The investment opportunity set and corporate financing, dividend and compensation policies. *Journal of Financial Economics* 32(3):263–292.

Stokes, D. J. and Leong, T. K. May 1988. Restrictive covenants and accounting information in the market for convertible notes. *Accounting and Finance* 28(1): 57–73.

Top 1000. November 20, 1987. Insert to *Business Review Weekly.*

Wallace, W. A. 1989. Are audit fees sufficiently risk adjusted in *Advances in Accounting* Supplement 1 (J. Gangolly, Ed.) Greenwich, CT: JAI Press Inc. pp. 3–38.

Wallace, W. A. March-April 1984. Internal auditors can cut outside CPA costs. *Harvard Business Review* 62(2):16–20.

Watts, R. L. and Zimmerman, J. October 1983. Agency problems, auditing, and the theory of the firm: Some evidence. *Journal of Law and Economics* 26(3): 613–634.

Watts, R. L. and Zimmerman, J. 1986. *Postive Accounting Theory*. Englewood Cliffs: Prentice-Hall.

Watts, R. L. and Zimmerman, J. January 1990. Positive accounting theory: A ten-year perspective. *The Accounting Review*, 65(1):131–156.

Weisbach, M. S. January-March 1988. Outside directors and CEO turnover. *Journal of Financial Economics* 20(1–2):431–460.

Weston, J. F. and Copeland, T. 1992. *Managerial Finance* (9th ed.). Chicago: Dryden Press.

Whittred, G. and Zimmer, I. November 1986. Accounting information in the market for debt. *Accounting and Finance* 26(2):19–33.

Williamson, O. 1985. *The Economic Institutions of Capitalism: Firms, Markets, Relational Contracting*. New York: Free Press.

Williamson, O. July 1988. Corporate finance and corporate governance. *The Journal of Finance* 43(3):567–591.

[4]

Accounting, Organizations and Society, Vol. 18, No. 7/8, pp. 605–620, 1993.
Printed in Great Britain

0361–3682/93 $6.00+.00

GETTING COMFORTABLE WITH THE NUMBERS: AUDITING AND THE MICRO-PRODUCTION OF MACRO-ORDER

BRIAN T. PENTLAND

University of California, Los Angeles

Abstract

Field observations of two audit engagements are used to interpret auditing as a ritual which transforms the financial statements of corporate management from an inherently untrustworthy state into a form that the auditors and the public can be comfortable with. The analysis draws on Collins' theory of interaction ritual chains (*American Journal of Sociology*, 1981, pp. 984–1014) to create an interpretative theory of auditing which offers insights into both the micro-level interactions within the audit team and the macro-level role of auditing in the economic order.

What do auditors really do when they are on site with a client? What kind of model will be most helpful in understanding and explaining auditor behavior and the formation of audit opinions? Given their unique and critical role as *public* accountants, these are important questions. Given the immense complexity and proprietary nature of the audit process, these are also very hard questions. We know that auditors generally work in teams, not individually, and that they work in cluttered, crowded conference rooms, not laboratories. We know that auditors on the job are situated in the context of intensive, on-going interactions with other members of their engagement team, their firm, their client's organization, and their profession. But we have yet to explore the implications of these facts for the conduct of audit work, the formation of audit opinions, or the larger phenomenon of auditing in general.

The present paper offers an interpretive approach to understanding auditor behavior that emphasizes the social and contextual aspects of the work. In particular, I will analyze the behavior of two audit teams as examples of interaction ritual (Goffman, 1967; Collins, 1981). While one could select among various theoretical perspectives on audit team behavior, the micro-sociological concept of interaction

ritual is particularly appropriate because it draws our attention to the collective nature of the setting and to the process of the work, rather than to the content. In doing so, it offers a vehicle for exploring the relationship between the micro-level behavior of the engagement team and macro-level context in which they work.

The interpretation of auditing as a ritual is not new in itself. Gambling (1977, 1987) describes a remarkable diversity of rituals in finance and accounting, both primitive and modern. While Gambling opens the door, he does not go far enough in asking what functions these rituals serve. From a sociological or anthropological perspective, to note that a particular secular profession engages in ritual behavior merely states the obvious. This paper contributes to our understanding of audit ritual on both empirical and theoretical grounds. Empirically, it uses observational data of audit teams in the field, as well as interview and verbal protocol data, to describe the details of audit work. There have been interview based studies of audit planning (Humphrey & Moizer, 1990), and generalized descriptive studies of audit firms (Stevens, 1981), but little in the way of field observation of actual engagement teams. Observational data are essential to provide an empirical basis for an interpretative, contextual theory.

Theoretically, the micro-sociological perspective offers a fundamentally different way of understanding the formation of audit opinion, and offers some insight into the social construction of auditing as a whole, including such things as "professionalism", "independence", and "trust". The concept of interaction ritual provides an explanation of how these macro-constructions are accomplished in the details of day-to-day work.

AUDIT RITUAL AND THE ECONOMIC ORDER

The world is fraught with uncertainties and dangers that individuals cannot know. Against this background, we perform rituals which offer a sense of order and safety (Moore & Myerhoff, 1977). Within the realm of modern economics and investment, it is easy to lose sight of the chaotic, uninterpreted world which precedes (ontologically, if not historically) our current worldview. As an exercise, try to imagine what business would be like without accounting or auditing. In particular, how would it feel to own stock in a corporation whose annual financial statements were never audited? The reader who seriously engages in this thought experiment will no doubt feel a distinct sense of discomfort. The relative absence of this feeling in the normal conduct of affairs demonstrates how effectively the audit ritual has succeeded in transforming chaos into order.

Accounting, in general, is an institutionalized means of making sense out of the world. The extent to which accounting procedures shape our understanding of economic life is well documented elsewhere (Burchell *et al.*, 1980; Boland & Pondy, 1983; Tinker, 1985; Meyer, 1986; Morgan, 1988; Hines, 1989). But auditing plays a somewhat different and more specialized role in the economic order. Auditors judge and attest to the validity of corporate financial statements, which contain a stylized interpretation of the fiscal health of a corporation. Accountants construct these interpretations, but auditors reassure the public and other interested parties that the interpretations are trustworthy. In what is perhaps the paradigmatic example for agency theory (Eisenhardt, 1989), auditors are used by investors (the principals) to monitor the activities of management (the agents).

But while the example is paradigmatic of agency theory, the conceptual framework and analysis presented here are not. In the spirit of Armstrong's (1991) critique of existing agency theory, I will focus not on contracts and monitoring, but on the social production and distribution of cultural and emotional resources, such as trust. Armstrong's (1991) remarks are relevant to this research for both methodological and substantive reasons. Methodologically, he suggests an interpretative framework for the analysis of meaningful social action. Substantively, auditors are centrally implicated in the social production of trust in financial markets. Auditors give "comfort" to people who are vulnerable to erroneous, self-interested, and possibly fraudulent statements from corporate management. The interpretation offered here is that micro-interactions within the engagement team create comfort, which makes the macro-order of capital markets and other financial institutions possible.

Interaction ritual

Contrary to common usage, the sociological sense of the term "ritual" does not necessarily imply "irrational". Rather, the term ritual refers to any collective activity that has the effect of maintaining social order, no matter how commonplace or mundane it may seem (Goffman, 1967; Collins, 1981, 1987). Greetings, conversations, and other routine interactions are rituals to the extent that they draw our attention to important ideas or feelings, such as group affiliation, property or authority (Lukes, 1975; Collins, 1981). Rituals may be carefully calculated and highly rationalized, as is the case with many accounting practices. The critical insight, however, is that these practices have significance beyond their manifest purpose and that this significance operates at an emotional level for the participants.

Goffman (1967) used interaction ritual as a framework in which to examine the routine structures of daily life. Collins (1981, 1987) introduced the concept of interaction ritual chains as a way of understanding macro-level phenomena in terms of micro-level interaction. In Collins' view, "sociological concepts can only be made fully empirical by grounding them in a sample of the typical micro-events that make them up" (1981, p. 988). There are several aspects of Collins' theory that are relevant to the analysis of audit ritual. Above all, Collins argues that emotion, not rational calculation, is the fundamental process through which social order is constructed. The idea that auditing is an emotional process will figure prominently in the argument here, as well. Collins also argues that interaction rituals increase or decrease the emotional energy of the participants automatically, depending on whether the rituals were successfully negotiated or not. Interaction ritual encompasses all kinds of conversation, including task-oriented interactions, shop-talk, gossip, and general discussion. Each conversational topic invokes a different group. Taken together over time, chains of interaction rituals have the effect of generating (or destroying) the cultural and emotional resources of a group.

Layers of ritual interpretation

The analysis of rituals is always a question of interpretation, where the job of the analyst is to unpack carefully the layers of meaning which may be present. Moore & Myerhoff (1977) note at least five such layers in secular ritual, each of which can be easily seen in audit work: (1) explicit purpose (to verify financial statements); (2) explicit symbols and messages (the signature in the annual report); (3) implicit statements (that the auditor is a competent professional); (4) social relationships affected (within the audit team and with the client organization); and (5) culture versus chaos (transforming the chaos of the "raw numbers" into a sanctified, culturally accepted form). Auditing research and professional ideology have traditionally been limited to the explicit, rational purpose of the work: verifying financial

statements. The reason for invoking the concept of ritual as an analytical device is to examine the deeper, more ambiguous levels of meaning associated with the work.

Collins (1981, 1987) emphasizes group affiliation on the societal level, providing a theory which is compelling but rather abstract. In order to apply the theory of interaction ritual chains to the empirical example of auditing, some accommodations are necessary. In particular, Collins (1981, 1987) limits his view of interaction ritual to the creation of group affiliation and solidarity. The anthropological and sociological literature has identified other aspects of ritual, including purification, social control, and impression management, which are equally relevant to an understanding of audit work, if not more so.

Purification. Purification is a central function of audit ritual and of rituals in general. Douglas (1966) shows that in all kinds of settings, both religious and secular, rituals reinforce and recreate our distinctions between the pure and the impure, the clean and the unclean. Using examples for historical and contemporary anthropology, Douglas shows how ritual purification transforms its object into something which is symbolically "clean". Moore & Myerhoff's (1977) analysis of secular ritual frames the concept of purification in terms of the opposition between order and chaos, between form and indeterminacy: "Ritual is a declaration of form *against* indeterminacy, therefore indeterminacy is always present in the background of any analysis of ritual" (Moore & Myerhoff, 1977, p. 17, emphasis in original). To the extent that the indeterminacy of financial records is a fundamental issue in auditing, we can expect the process of purification to have considerable significance in audit ritual.

Social control. Organizational theorists have recognized culture in general and ritual in particular as mechanisms of managerial control (Van Maanen & Kunda, 1988; Kunda, 1992). Anthropologists have also argued that "collective ritual can be seen as an especially dramatic attempt to bring some particular part of life firmly and definitely into orderly control"

Governance and Auditing

B. T. PENTLAND

(Moore & Myerhoff, 1977, p. 3). Lukes (1975) injects a critical interpretation into this assertion by pointing out that ritual is often an instrument of social control of one group by another. In applying this perspective to audit ritual, we would expect to observe patterns of behavior which enforce compliance to norms and expectations about the manner in which the work is performed.

Social cohesion. The view that ritual is an instrument of social cohesion can be traced to Durkheim's (1933) *Elementary Forms of Religious Life*. Collins (1981, 1987) emphasizes this aspect of ritual almost exclusively in his theory. Through participation in ritual, group identification is created and maintained, values are transmitted, and group cohesion is built. We would expect auditors to be an extremely cohesive social group, since they engage in the intensive performance of collective rituals on a daily basis.

Impression management. Rituals preserve order by helping maintain and manage our public selves. Goffman's (1959, 1967) analysis of ritual action in daily life reveals how we routinely enact a suitable "front" for others, create a sense of regularity and predictability, and repair difficulties when they crop up. The behavior in question is mundane and often apparently off-handed or unmotivated. But the effect is essential to the preservation of our sense of order in the social world. One immediate implication of this perspective is that in order to be an auditor, you have to act like one; displaying the appropriate behavior is critical to the creation of the "audit professional".

In a sense, the preceding observations consitute hypotheses about the kinds of things one would expect to see among members of an audit team. They are the layers of interpretation that we should expect when examining ritual action. Analytically, we can separate out these layers, but in practice, they operate simultaneously to create what Goffman (1967) calls the ritual order. After briefly describing the field sites and the research methodology, I will examine the field data in light of these theoretical expectations. Throughout the analysis, the emphasis will be on the very things which are typically omitted from research on auditor behavior; the process of the work, the collective way it is accomplished, and the feelings that these collective processes engender. By focusing on what has traditionally been considered noise, the micro-sociological perspective offers the possibility of uncovering a new signal.

RESEARCH SITES AND DATA COLLECTION

The data reported here were collected as part of a study of how auditors in a large public accounting firm create and use working papers. Working papers are the central cultural artifact of professional auditors. Working papers document the work done during the audit and support the conclusions; nearly everything that auditors do on the job involves creating or using these documents. By studying working papers, one learns a great deal about auditors.

Three methods were used to collect data for this study: observation, interviews, and verbal protocols of working paper reviews. This combination of methods was chosen to provide as much data as possible about two specific audits without interfering excessively in the conduct of the work. The two audit engagements were selected for observation based on the criteria that they be "moderate" in size (between 1000 and 2000 hours of staff time budgeted) and have a team of a least four people on-site at the time of observation. In addition, the sites were selected to reflect different kinds of clients and different phases in the audit cycle. Table 1 outlines some important features of each site. The team at Engagement 2 had a particularly experienced staff because it was a relatively new client and issues they expected to encounter were particularly difficult.

I was permitted to observe and interact with the members of the audit team for five days at each engagement. Although a substantial part of each day was spent observing the team at work, I occasionally interrupted members of the team to get explanations of what they were working

TABLE 1. Two audit engagements observed

	Engagement 1	Engagement 2
Phase of audit	Year end	Interim
Sector	Manufacturing	Financial services
Size of team	1 Partner	2 Partners
	1 Manager	2 Managers
	1 Senior	6 Seniors
	4 Staff	3 Staff
Entities audited	One	Three
Years as client	More than ten	One

on. Ten days of observation resulted in about 200 pages of handwritten notes. This methodology allowed me to collect detailed data on audit practices, but with the exception of a few quotations that I wrote down, these notes consist of narratives in my own voice. In many cases, it could hardly be otherwise, because the participants themselves were silent. The use of narrative is unusual in auditing research, but it is fairly common in ethnographic writing in general (Van Maanen, 1988), and provides data that are not available any other way.

Verbal protocols (where the subject "thinks aloud" while performing some task) are a more common technique in auditing research (Klersey & Mock, 1989). At the first engagement, I recorded verbal protocols of actual working paper reviews from the senior, the manager, and the partner. No protocols were obtained from the second engagement because there were no reviews being done during the week I was there. The 32 pages of transcribed protocols provide a verbatim record of what auditors at each level were looking for when they reviewed working papers.

Ten individuals not involved in the two audit engagements were also interviewed. These individuals included all levels of seniority and were selected to reflect diverse backgrounds and experience. Two of them specialized in audits of financial service institutions, while several specialized in audits of smaller clients. These interviews lasted about one hour each and were tape recorded and transcribed, providing a source of longer verbatim quotations.

GETTING COMFORTABLE: AUDITING AS RITUAL PURIFICATION

The basic problem in auditing is that numbers don't speak for thesmelves. Numbers may reflect management self-interest rather than reality, or they may simply be wrong. In Douglas' (1966) terms, they are unclean, disorderly, and dangerous. Professional auditing standards discuss this problem in terms of "risk" and provide detailed procedures for reducing the "risk of misstatement" to obtain "assurance" or "satisfaction" (AICPA, 1987). But on the job and in interviews, auditors at all levels talked about "comfort". As one staff auditor commented, "You're not going to finish that job until the senior's comfortable, the manager's comfortable, and the partner's comfortable".

The use of emotional language to describe an ostensibly rational decision process signals an important layer of meaning that auditors attach to their work. Objectively, unaudited numbers may be risky or uncertain, but subjectively, they make auditors feel uncomfortable. Audit rituals make them "comfortable" by transforming and purifying the inherently "unclean" client data. One of the interviewees (a senior) explained how she decided whether the work was complete:

> You try to get as comfortable as you can with those numbers and feel that you're comfortable with the work you told somebody to do. Then pull back from it and say am I comfortable with the balance sheet and the income statement. When you are then you give it to somebody else to review . . .

The focus on comfort was echoed in the behavior of the partner in charge of Engagement

1, as well. I observed a meeting of the partner, the manager, and the senior as they sat down to review a draft of "net effects schedule" for the audit. For each of about a dozen items, the partner asked about the "comfort level" of the item. For example, "What's your comfort level with these workmen's compensation accruals?" In some cases, his questioning linked comfort to the way in which the audit work was accomplished: "Do you have adequate coverage in these receivables to be comfortable?" Apparently, it was through a process of questioning the members of the audit team about their comfort that the partner himself became comfortable.

From the perspective of audit judgement or decision-making, these observations raise some provocative questions. First, what is the role of affect in the formation of an audit opinion? Team members consistently used emotional language in their deliberations about what items to include in the net effects schedule. This schedule contains adjustments to the client's balance sheet that will go into the financial statement. The language of comfort suggests a process which, if taken literally, is more descriptive of "gut feel" than of rational thought. The primacy of gut feel over formal, rational procedure was a critical finding in Humphrey & Moizer's (1990) research on the audit planning process. The prevalence of emotional language in the conduct of audit work tends to confirm their finding. Another question that arises concerns the role of social interaction in the creation of these emotional states. How does an auditor get comfortable in a real audit situation? The partner did not get comfortable by simply reading the working papers or dispassionately searching audit evidence. Rather, it would appear that he got comfortable through a series of repeated interactions with the members of the team. These task-oriented conversations are exactly the kind of rituals that Collins (1981, p. 1002) refers to as a "marketplace for cultural and emotional resources". In the case of auditing, the emotional resource being created and distributed is comfort.

Comfort as a commodity

In conversations and interviews, comfort was implicitly treated as a commodity that could be passed on from person to person or group to group. In this sense, comfort is reminiscent of Armstrong's (1991) concept of trust as a social product. There are three levels at which this comfort was produced and exchanged; within the engagement team, within the audit firm, and between the audit firm and the public. As we move to progressively higher levels of analysis, the concept of comfort shifts from being an emotional state of an individual or a group to being an objectified, institutionalized fact.

Within the engagement team, comfort is passed up the chain of command, from the staff to the partner. The partner who renders an opinion is forced to rely on the work of others, because there is no way that he or she could personally conduct the detailed audit work. This reliance exists at all levels in the chain of command. One senior explained it this way:

> Everybody is relying on somebody else's work all the way down to staff. The partner is the one signing the firm's name on the opinion on the assumption that the manager did a good job. The manager is relying on the work of the senior that they did everything they were supposed to do.

This principle was illustrated by the behavior of the partner at Engagement 1, described above, who questioned the manager and the senior about their comfort in order to get comfortable. No individual conducts the entire audit, yet in the end, every member of the team is comfortable. At this level, comfort has what Collins (1981) would call a "fully empirical" referent in the feelings of the team.

A similar principle seems to operate between branches of the audit firm as a whole. At Engagement 2, one of the entities being audited maintained a data processing center in another part of the country. As a result, the engagement team was forced to delegate the compliance testing for those systems to auditors from another office. One of the staff at Engagement 2 was unaware of this arrangement and asked her senior if she would rely on numbers from those systems. The senior explained the arrangement and said, "as long as they are comfortable with the system, then we can rely on it, too". In this way, the engagement team used the work of auditors in another office as a source of comfort. The term comfort still has a micro-empirical referent.

The most important sense in which comfort becomes a commodity is when it is given to others outside the audit firm. The audit opinion found in every annual report constitutes the paradigm example of comfort as a commodity. The objective of every audit engagement is to render some opinion on the financial statements of the entity being audited. At this level, the empirical reference is less clearly tied to particular individuals. The audit opinion objectifies comfort into a culturally defined resource available to anyone who needs to make decisions based on the financial statements of the entity being audited. Collins (1981) would argue that in order to understand this macro-level phenomenon, we need to translate it into some sample of micro-level experiences, a question we will return to below.

Auditors deliver comfort in other ways, as well. Consider the practice of issuing occasional "comfort letters", as described by a senior at Engagement 2:

> We give comfort on the prospectus. We do certain detailed procedures on the prospectus and on the deal in general. Clients need that kind of on-going service from us because the worst thing in the world is for them to have big adjustments at year end. They lose all their credibility on the street.

In this context, the language of comfort has become institutionalized as part of the Generally Accepted Auditing Practices. Comfort letters are a standard document that accompanies the issuance of debt and certain other kinds of securities. The significant thing about audit opinions and comfort letters is that they objectify comfort as a resource that can be "given" to clients and investors. The "background of indeterminacy" (Moore & Myerhoff, 1977) in economic affairs creates a societal need for comfort, and audit ritual fills this need.

If this formulation seems artificial or even a bit melodramatic, consider the situation faced by the audit team at Engagement 2. One of the entities being audited was a savings and loan association that was quite close to the statutory limit on capital reserves. As a result, small changes on their balance sheet would be critical to their solvency. The significance of this problem was heightened by the alarming number of failures in this industry[1] and by the fact that the client had just switched auditors. Everything about the structure of their business, their assets, their organization, and their accounting system, was unfamiliar. To make matters worse, the client had a substantial percentage of their assets in high-risk mortgage-backed securities, which one member of the team described as "worse than junk bonds". The Generally Accepted Auditing Practices (and associated FASB technical memoranda) offered no specific rules on how to value these kinds of securities, but their value was extremely sensitive to changes in long term interest rates and the turnover rate in home mortgages. The senior responsible for valuing these securities was clearly very anxious about it: "It's really difficult to get comfortable with this kind of situation. Just really, really difficult". While this is admittedly an unusual situation, the difference is in degree, not in kind. For example, the auditors at Engagement 1 encountered a similar problem is deciding the appropriate level of accruals for workmen's compensation claims: "It's all guess-work at this point. It'll be five years at least before this all settles out ..." Fundamentally, auditing involves the certification of the unknowable and the reduction of continuous variables into dichotomous categories of "comfort" and, implicitly, "discomfort".

---

[1] The magnitude of the "savings and loan crisis" in the U.S. was just beginning to surface when this research was conducted. This particular institution, although pushed to the limit, managed to weather the storm.

The procedure used by the senior at Engagement 2 to value the mortgage-backed securities further illustrates the concept of purification in audit ritual. Several binders filled with alternative scenarios computed by a well-known New York financial consulting firm had been purchased for this job. These projections were to be used to compute the value of the securities held by the client. Since there were several different scenarios for each kind of security, the question of which ones to use and how they should be weighted was entirely a matter of "professional judgement". The senior spent several days pouring over the scenarios in the binders, selectively copying numbers onto a computer spreadsheet. To produce the financial statement, the current value (a reasonably well-known number) would be adjusted using the projections from the consultants (which in spite of their high cost are essentially speculative) to create a new, "audited" number. Through the ritual of copying numbers from one place to another and arithmetically combining them with other numbers, the underlying indeterminacy of the United States mortgage market was transformed into something the auditors could be comfortable with.

Rituals and priests

As Gambling (1987, p. 326) points out, "for the magic to work, the rituals have to be seen to be validly performed". Most audit rituals are only valid when performed by certain individuals. In particular, only the professionals of the audit firm can be trusted to perform the steps of the audit ritual. The distinction between the auditor and the client begins with the assumption that management acts opportunistically and may be motivated in some cases to deceive the auditor. The distinction is reinforced continuously throughout the engagement by interaction rituals which include team members in task-oriented conversation and informal gossip, and exclude client personnel from these conversations. But the distinction has much greater significance than simply marking who is and is not "on the team", as can be seen in the following two examples.

At Engagement 1, I observed the assembly of the consolidated financial statements which form the basis for the client's annual report. The client's internal audit department was given a copy of last year's consolidation working papers and instructions on how to re-create the working papers in their entirety using this year's data. They did so faithfully and produced a complete set of working papers conforming perfectly to the firm's format, including all the appropriate cross-references. The pages were even corner-punched and ready for insertion into the audit firm's standard binders. In a physical sense, the work was "done". In spite of this, the staff assigned to complete the consolidation still had to go through the dozens of pages of schedules, foot them again, and write over each and every one of those references in red pen, checking them in the process, and sign off on each page. Until the references and tick marks were done by a member of the audit team, the ritual wasn't complete.

At Engagement 2, an auditor told a story about taking a late night physical inventory and then accidently leaving the inventory sheets with the client until the next morning. The sheets had to be discarded; the risk of alteration by the client meant they could not be trusted. This example is also interesting because the auditor observing the inventory did not actually count anything herself. Rather, she observed the client doing the counting. The distinction may seem trivial if one believes that the client cannot (or will not) deliberately miscount while being watched. But it is important because it underscores the way that members of the audit team symbolically overcome the opportunism which is assumed to motivate the client. The client still does the counting but the auditor provides the comfort.

These two examples share an underlying similarity concerning the role of the auditor in ritual purification. In each case, the "work" was performed by someone else, but the "audit" was accomplished by the mere presence of the auditor. This general pattern occurs throughout the audit process, because auditors cannot personally observe all of the systems, procedures and accounts of the firms they audit. Rather, they must rely on the client to explain how the business works, what accounts are used for, how they are updated, etc. When an auditor listens to an explanation and deems it "reasonable", they write it up in a tick mark and then sign off on it. In signing off, they transform the client's inherently untrustworthy explanation into an inherently trustworthy one. The explanation is identical; only the person giving it changes.

The sacred signature

"Signing off" is perhaps the key to understanding audit ritual. One's signature, however minutely inscribed, gives comfort to those who see it, establishes one's participation in the audit team and one's commitment to the profession. It is important to note that auditors sign off constantly throughout the audit process. Staff sign off on every tick mark and audit step. Seniors have to agree and sign off on every conclusion that the staff makes (e.g. whether an item is immaterial), on every page of working papers, on every audit step and every audit file. Managers also sign off on major conclusions, and on every audit file. Partners sign off on every file and on the overall conclusions and footnotes associated with the financial statements. The importance of the initials that accompany literally every tick mark and audit step arises partly from their sheer frequency, but mostly from what they signify to the members of the audit team.

Since comfort depends on the completion of rituals by others, "signing off" is a necessary part of "getting comfortable". Someone can test a number, tie it in and put a tick mark, but until he or she signs off, it's not "done". This is true of trivial things like cross-referencing and footing, as well as whole audit steps. Conversely, when a step is signed off, it is assumed to be done, as this senior explained in an interview:

What I'm taught and what everyone is taught is that you don't sign off until you've done the step ... Even if you

think you're going to do it an hour from now. I might make a reference like, "See page A10", but I won't sign off on that step until it's done. ... The assumption is if you see someone's initials on something you know it's done.

The manifest purpose of signing off is to indicate the completion of audit work. But a deeper level of significance arises from the fact that signing one's name to an opinion involves putting one's professional reputation on the line.

That's all we have, our ethics, our reputation. By signing off you put your job on the line. That's all they have to hang over your head. Otherwise our financial statements that we give to the bank that [the firm signs] would be meaningless if the bank didn't believe in that signature.

In this sense, the signature is a sacred symbol for the auditor. It is like the talisman that, when attached to a conclusion at any level of detail, signifies the purity of the conclusion. The sanctity of the signature can be seen by considering what happens to people who sign off carelessly or deceitfully, thereby defiling the symbol. These two quotations are from two different staff auditors:

There are people who do things like "powerticking". You're supposed to agree this number to this number, without exception. But you can just check it off and draw the line and never really look at all the information. That's called powerticking. ... As soon as you find out that somebody has been powerticking, they go very fast. That's definite grounds for immediate dismissal.

If somebody was irresponsible I would tell the manager in a second no matter if I was best friends with the guy or whatever because you could be in court sometime. That's our support for our financial statements. That's very serious no matter how immaterial it is. Say you said you did something that you didn't do no matter how small the step is. To me that's the same level of responsibility. I haven't really heard of that happening [around here]. If it did, I think that that person would probably be let go if they found out who did it. Who would want that person working with them? Nobody. There would be no place for him or her. That would be sad.

The second quotation is especially striking because it suggests that the sanctity of the signature carries more weight in this individual's mind than protecting a friend from certain dismissal, no matter how small the transgression. These comments underscore the significance attached to the signature. Given that staff sign off hundreds of times in the course of a single audit, we can begin to appreciate its significance in the overall audit ritual.

CONTROL AND COHESION: AUDIT MACHINES IN ACTION

Control and cohesion are closely intertwined in the conduct of audit ritual. A cohesive, tightly knit audit team is essential to the creation of a coherent set of working papers and a successful engagement. In the sections that follow, we will consider the broader context of an audit engagement, including some aspects of auditor behavior that are not directly concerned with auditing. What emerges is a picture of the auditor as a "audit machine".

"Audit machine" is a term that was used by the auditors (mainly the seniors and staff) at both sites to register their impressions of each other's work habits: "You're finished with that schedule already? You're a regular audit machine". The prevalence of this mechanistic metaphor in the lingo of the auditors is interesting because it implies both a kind of infallibility and also a selflessness which, in terms of the professional ideology, represent positive things about auditors. But in actual practice, life as an audit machine can be a difficult and dehumanizing experience.

Review notes and social control

The practice of reviewing the work of staff auditors (and team members at all levels up to and including partners) is the most obvious control mechanism in audit work. Reviewing has a sound basis in rational principles of error avoidance and correction, and as a way of training and evaluating staff. But at the same time, the practice of writing review notes (called "to-dos" by the members of the engagement teams I observed) reveals something more. For example, the first "to-do" note on

nearly every audit file tells the staff to "clear open points". Open points are audit steps that the staff working on the file has indicated remain to be complete. Telling staff to "clear open points" is completely redundant, since they themselves have indicated that the point is still open. Although unnecessary, this kind of "to-do" signals the authority of the person writing it.

Subsequent review notes were more substantive, but still had value in terms of signalling authority. Consider the following quotations from the verbal protocol of the senior at Engagement 1 reviewing a file. When an audit step was apparently completed but no initials appeared on the audit program, the senior would write a "to-do":

> I noted that the staff had done the audit step, but just had not signed off on the audit program. So I wrote a "to do" to sign off on the audit program.

> The staff did not sign off the note on the bottom of the page, so I will write a review note to do so.

> I see that there are more pages that he neglected to include in his sign-off, so write him a review note to change his page references in the audit program.

Since the senior knows who did the work and that it is done, why doesn't she "sign off" on it for the staff? Or simply skip that formality and "sign off" herself? At other points in the same review, the same senior executed certain mechanical aspects of working papers herself, such as completing cross-references, rather than writing a "to-do". This difference points to the sanctity of the signature, but also to the way that review notes are used to communicate that sanctity. By selectively writing to-dos for sign-off and not for cross-references (although they would require a roughly equivalent amount of work on her part), the senior is signalling the importance of the sign-off.

Verbal protocols from the manager and the partner were qualitatively different. Direct comparisons are impossible, because they were not reviewing the same file. However, some general observations can be made. The manager relies on the senior to take care of the mechanics, as he explained in a kind of preamble to his verbal protocol.[2]

At the time that I'm looking at this file, the senior has already gone through and done her review. As manager, I rely upon her to make sure that the fundamental workpaper requirements that we have, cross-referencing, executing the program, and these types of things, I rely upon her to make sure that all those attributes, etc., are already documented well in the files.

In contrast to the senior's review, which was filled with references to footing, tick marks, cross-references, and sign-offs, the manager hardly mentioned these details. Instead, the manager's review notes focused on more substantive issues, as in these examples:

One particular accrual has gone from $958,000 down to zero. There is not much explanation for the change, so I've written a "to do" to the Staff person to explain to me why no such accrual is needed this year, and maybe to explain why so much was needed last year.

I can see the Staff person has done some detail testing agreeing to the schedules, and subsequent liquidation, etc. . . . I've given her a comment to quantify the coverage she got of this account through her basis of selection. It just can't be determined too easily by looking at the schedule itself.

The Staff just said "See Net Effect entry on the Net Effect Schedule". Typically I like to see a Net Effect entry in the workpapers itself, and then also again on the Net Effect Schedule, so I asked her to add it to the workpapers here.

These examples span a range of different kinds of to-dos. The first to-do is a request for an explanation of a rather large substantive variance in accruals from year to year. Depending on what the explanation is, the manager may decide that the issue requires further investigation. In the second example, the manager isn't asking the staff to change the basis of selection, but merely to explain more clearly what it was. The explanation won't change the outcome, but it will have the effect of making

the outcome more defensible should the need arise (for example, in the case of audit failure). The third to-do seems to be a matter of personal preference, having no bearing on either the substantive outcome or its defensibility. These examples show that the manager guides the substantive outcome of the audit through review notes. But at the same time, the manager guides the process of the audit, including details of style and presentation in the working papers.

The partner's verbal protocol was somewhat cursory because the file he chose to review for the purposes of this study was incomplete. Like the manager, the partner focused on "fluctuations" from last year's data, taking the mechanics of the working papers for granted. His review notes concerned incomplete or missing explanations of the differences from last year, as in these examples:

. . . the margins in 89 are more than double those that existed in 1988. I've made a review note, since there's no explanation in the workpapers, with respect to that increase in margins . . .

. . . there's a balance of other receivables [this year] which is approximately $216,000. There was no comparable balance [last year]. Accordingly, I've asked a question as to why there were no other receivables [last year] and what is included in the $216,000 [this year].

What the partner is asking for in these to-dos are explanations from the staff which would be signed off by the staff, the senior and the manager. The process of getting explanations from subordinates via review notes echoes the face-to-face interactions described above. For the partner to be comfortable with the fluctuations in these accounts, he needs comfort from the members of the team. Of course, review notes are not the only vehicle for comfort, nor are they the only mechanism of control, as the following examples demonstrate.

Long hours

While review notes enforce the details of audit mechanics, the process of auditing

---

[2] I was not present while this protocol was recorded, but the manager obviously framed the situation and made these comments as though someone unfamiliar with the review process was present.

involves other layers of control that operate in more subtle and generalized ways. Consider the fact that auditors often work extremely long hours. Sixteen-hour days are not unusual for a job at year end, where deadlines are pressing in. But auditors put in long hours even when there are no deadlines. For example, at Engagement 2, one of the seniors had evening plans that he cancelled because his manager worked until 9:00 p.m. that night: *"He* was staying, so I didn't even *think* about not staying". What is at stake in this situation is the high degree of loyalty that staff must demonstrate in order to be seen as truly professional and worthy of promotion. That loyalty extends beyond what most people would accept as reasonable, as another senior explained:

> I don't assume that I'm actually going to make my weekend plans until my foot is actually out the door. I'm not free until 5:00 on Friday. ... Sometimes I just want to tell them, "Keep the money, take it back, I just don't want to break my weekend plans again!" Plans just don't matter. If you say, "I can't stay, I've got a plane ticket", they'll say, "We've got a reimbursement check". The bottom line is, they own your time.

Although everyone objects to the hours, there is a great deal of respect among auditors for the people who put in the most. Putting in long hours of overtime is an important way to earn your badge of honor as an audit machine. The rationale for long hours is based in the economics of how jobs are budgeted and scheduled, and the assumption that members of the team will put in enormous amounts of time is essentially built-in. The audit firm has institutionalized these kinds of schedules, and in doing so, has forced members to become machines.

No breaks

In addition to working long hours, audit machines keep working under almost any circumstances. Based on my observations, auditors take few if any breaks while on the job. In general, interruptions are tolerated to the extent necessary to remain polite, but then work continues. The intense work norms build group

cohesion within the audit team at the same time that they reflect the exercise of social control over members of the team. While it could be argued that the norms simply encourage hard work and are a natural reaction to the pressure to bring the job in under budget, this explanation is not sufficient to explain the observed behavior. The peculiar strength of the audit ritual and the way it extends beyond what is strictly needed to accomplish the work was demonstrated by an incident at Engagement 2.

The auditors worked year-round for the client at Engagement 2. They had their own permanently assigned room with an impeccably mounted plexiglass sign outside the door with the firm's name on it. At the time of my observations, the floor on which this room was located was being remodeled. New walls were being constructed, old walls were being taken down, light fixtures were being replaced, ceilings were being re-hung. In short, with the exception of the audit room itself, it was a disaster area. The contractor seemed to vacuum the hallway constantly, but everything outside the audit room was covered in plaster dust and dirt. Nail guns pounded and vacuum cleaners whined, but the audit team kept on working.

Early one afternoon, a workman came in and said, "I need to take the ceiling down at that end of the room. If you guys can just slide everything down about six feet, I think that'll do it." The team members clearly were not pleased; their haven had been violated. But with only minimal objections they stopped working just long enough to move their audit cases, their trunks, their tables, their file cabinets, and themselves the necessary distance. After about 15 minutes of rearranging things, they sat back down to work. As they did, the workmen brought in a ladder and began removing a strip of ceiling along one end of the room, section by section, practically over the auditors' heads. Fluorescent light fixtures were detached and dangled down, metal cross-members were wrestled free, panels laden with years of accumulated dirt were tipped and slid free. But the audit team kept on working.

This incident is revealing because of two

things the team did *not* do that they could have. First, they did not put up a fight to defend their work from interruption. There were six people working in the room when the ceiling came down. Although they could have made a good case based the value of their collective time, they did not. My interpretation is that objecting too strongly might be seen as uncooperative or unprofessional. Auditors take whatever space the client gives them. In fact, auditors seem to take pride in working under these conditions. When I commented that these seemed like pretty adverse conditions, they all chimed in with stories about audits where things were *much worse.* They all knew it was ridiculous to be working like that, but they didn't stop. It seems to be a badge of honor to have dusty bits of ceiling tile rain down on your working papers.

Second, the team did not leave the room while the work was being done. It is plausible that they could have taken a break for 20 minutes while the ceiling was being removed, but they did not. Naturally, you have to keep working to earn your "badge", but there is more here than this. During ten days with audit teams in the field, I observed no breaks from work that involved getting up and leaving the immediate work setting which were not part of eating lunch. An "audit machine" doesn't need breaks.

How can we interpret the virtual taboo on taking breaks? The subject came up explicitly among the team at Engagement 2 when one of the staff asked, "Why *do* we work so hard?" A variety of fairly rational answers were offered in response. Personal motivation and sheer volume of work were two of the explanations offered. "We have to work this hard because there's so much to do, and besides, I want to do a good job". Another explanation had to do with the fact that personnel at higher levels didn't seem to take breaks. This observation led one staff to comment that she was afraid that taking breaks would be seen as evidence of a lack of commitment or lack of professionalism. This comment linked adherence to a machine-like work ethic to the ideals of commitment and professionalism, both of which are highly valued

in the professional ideology. To "take a break" would be to put oneself outside the flow of audit ritual, to be apart from the team, to distance oneself from the work, the firm, and the profession.

Lunch with the team

Lunch time seems to offer no respite from interaction with the team. On the two engagements I observed, the audit teams almost always ate lunch together. There were occasional stragglers, but only with good, work-related reasons. The norm on these engagements was that someone would signal lunch at around 12:00. When this happened, the entire team would simply drop whatever they were doing, right there. If necessary, the team would wait for members working in other rooms to be contacted and assemble together. Then the entire team would head for the client's company cafeteria for lunch. There was never any suggestion of anyone splitting off, and nobody brought their own lunch. One senior mentioned that she had considered bringing her own lunch for dietary reasons, but had been told that it would be unprofessional. In general, the entire team sat at the table until the last person finished eating his or her last bite. One day at Engagement 1, the manager started to leave while one of the staff was still eating an apple. When he noticed she wasn't done, he sat back down and implored her to please finish it so people could get back to work. When she did, everyone jumped up and left. Their veneer of politeness was apparently stretched rather thinly over the drive to get back to work.

Only once did the idea of going out for lunch come up. When it did, it revealed an interesting aspect of how fear of authority serves to enforce the work norms. The audit at Engagement 2 was at interim, so there were no deadlines pressing down. Team members were limiting their work schedule to "office hours": 8:00 a.m to 6:00 p.m. So it seemed natural when one of the seniors proposed going out to lunch one day. Everyone wanted to go, but they were afraid of how it might look to their superiors. A long discussion ensued among the four team members present. The following excerpts capture the gist of their dilemma:

Staff 1: We can't go out; [partner] and [senior manager] are here today! What will they think?

Senior 3: You're right, I didn't know they were going to be here today. What are we going to do? Do you think we should just go anyway?

Senior 1: We should ask [Senior 2], he knows them better. Or maybe we should just wait until tomorrow. They won't be here tomorrow.

Staff 1: Don't they [the partner and manager] go out to lunch sometimes? I mean, it's only fair that we should be able to go out if we want to, right? It's only going to take an hour . . .

Senior 1: Yeah, we oughta be able to go out, but I don't think we should. They usually eat here in the cafeteria when they're on site.

Senior 3: I guess you're right. We'll wait.

[*Just then, Senior 2 returns from a meeting with the partner and the senior manager. Senior 1 asks him:*] Would they care if we went out to lunch?

Senior 2: Hell no, why should they care? They're taking the afternoon off to play golf!

This revelation shocked the group. How could they have been so reluctant to take an hour for lunch when the very people whose sanction they feared were taking the whole afternoon off? It seemed for a moment like the chains were broken and the momentum had shifted back towards going out, until it was discovered that one of them had only 20 minutes for lunch. Then the group lunch norm became relevant and rather than going out, which now seemed perfectly justifiable to everyone, the team stayed in.

The point of examining lunchtime and breaks is that these events (or non-events) reflect *how* the work is done more than *what* is done. There is very little in the preceding examples that is specific to auditing; the occupational group in question could just as well be teachers or ditch-diggers. Work schedules, breaks and lunchtime routines are interesting data because they reveal

a striking lack of discretion or individuality among members of the team. In some respects, these examples suggest a social context that is anything but professional. There are no time cards, but there is also no discretion: In other examples of professional work (e.g. Kunda, 1992), long hours are common, but so is the freedom to work these hours in a somewhat flexible manner. Even this brief examination of the social context and the process of the work suggests an image that is rather different from the accounting professional dispassionately evaluating the audit evidence. In the field, auditors are so highly socialized, and the degree of control over their behavior is so stringent, that they are more aptly characterized as machines.

The metaphor of the machine suggests not only the kind of non-stop peformances described above, it connotes infallibility. If the ritual were conducted in a less mechanistic fashion, it might be less convincing, less capable of producing the right impression. One . is tempted to conclude that the production of comfort in audit work rests not so much on the careful exercise of judgement as on the relentless application of effort. That effort, manifested in the on-going interactions of the audit team, gives the audit ritual its enormous power and significance for the participants, and for observers, as well.

In great measure, auditing is a display, an effort on the part of auditors to maintain a professional front (Goffman, 1959). Professionalism is symbolized by the comportment of the auditor on the job, including language and dress. For example, auditors on the job wear impeccable clothing, and while they may take their jackets off while working in the audit room, they generally put them back on before going out frontstage. These kinds of details are not unlike the kind of impression management carried on by other occupational groups. Dressing well, carrying the right kind of briefcase, not bringing one's lunch, and otherwise "looking the part" are essential basics of the professional front. One of the conditions of my entry into the field to conduct this research was that I had to dress "appropriately", so that I would look like a member of the audit team.

The working routines of auditors are an important way to symbolize and establish their legitimacy. The qualities of the audit machine (long hours of uninterrupted work) symbolize an intense level of commitment to the audit process. They also symbolize a machine-like infallibility on the part of the auditor. An auditor who fails to conform to the rituals would very likely be labeled as incompetent or unreliable. It is somewhat ironic that the very qualities that create the impression of professionalism and commitment when viewed from frontstage seem to remove individual discretion when viewed from backstage. Either way, the intensive, mechanistic quality of audit ritual plays an important part in managing impressions and therefore, in the success of the ritual in producing comfort.

DISCUSSION AND CONCLUSION

The interpretation of auditing as a ritual draws our attention to the social context of the work, the process of the work, the meanings that participants and others attach to the work, and to the emotional aspects of those meanings. This interpretation has important implications for our understanding of auditor judgement and the formation of audit opinion. Audit judgement research conceptualizes auditing as a primarily cognitive process (Johnson *et al.*, 1989). Within this paradigm, there is no way to account for the influence of "gut feel" in the formation of audit opinion. Humphrey & Moizer (1990) identify gut feel as a significant factor in audit planning, and the findings here suggest that gut feel is critical throughout the entire engagement. The essential point is that auditors need to achieve an emotional state with respect to their work, not just a cognitive one. Johnson *et al.* (1989, p. 88) correctly point to the need to understand the meaning that auditors attach to their work, but they seem to conceive of "meaning" in a rather limited, psycho-linguistic sense. The ritual perspective suggests that a fuller sense of meaning that includes affect as well as cognition is critical to an understanding of auditor judgement.

There is good reason to expect that no amount of rationalistic analysis will ever produce a sufficient explanation of auditor judgement. The difficulty hinges on a fundamental problem in social theory, namely the insufficiency of rule-following as an explanation of social order (for the sociological argument, see Heritage, 1984, pp. 120–129; or Giddens, 1984, pp. 16–23; for the philosophical argument, see Wittgenstein, 1958). The thrust of the argument can be stated quite simply. For any given rule, one must decide when to apply it, which requires more rules, each of which requires more rules. In principle, any attempt to construct a purely rational explanation of auditor behavior (in the form of rules or other abstract representations) must ultimately fail in the face of an infinite regress. In practice, of course, rules fail us almost immediately. Recall the situation at Engagement 2 where the auditors were attempting to establish the value of a large portfolio of mortgage-backed securities. There were no rules for this procedure, yet the auditors were able to reach a conclusion. To reach a conclusion (even a qualified one) in the face of an essentially unknowable situation, auditors must rely on the emotional resources generated by the audit ritual: *gut feel*. The ritual perspective offers a sufficient explanation for a problem that, as a matter or principle, cannot be addressed through rationalist means and has been systematically excluded from current research.

In summary, audit rituals produce comfort, which is treated like a commodity within the engagement team, the audit firm, and the investment community at large. For the rituals to be effective, they must be performed by the right people. In particular, only members of the audit team can perform the work, or if the work is performed by others (as in the case of physical inventory or procedural explanations), it must be signed off on by a member of the engagement team. To members of the team, and the auditing profession in general, the signature is sacred. It signifies completion, purity, and comfort. To society at large, the sanctity of the audit ritual is largely taken for granted, presupposed as a shared cultural resource. And therein lies the myth: as long as the audit machines are working, we can all be comfortable with the numbers.

BIBLIOGRAPHY

American Institute of Certified Public Accountants, *AICPA Professional Standards, US Auditing Standards* (Chicago, IL; Commerce Clearing House, 1987).

Armstrong, P., Contradiction and Social Dynamics in the Capitalist Agency Relationship, *Accounting, Organizations and Society* (1991) 1–25.

Boland, R. J. & Pondy, L. R., Accounting in Organizations: a Union of Natural and Rational Perspectives, *Accounting, Organizations and Society* (1983) pp. 223–234.

Burchell, S., Clubb, C. & Hopwood, A. G., The Roles of Accounting in Organizations and Society, *Accounting, Organizations and Society* (1980) pp. 5–27.

Collins, R., On the Microfoundations of Macrosociology, *American Journal of Sociology* (1981) pp. 984–1014.

Collins, R., Interaction Ritual Chains, Power and Property: the Micro–Macro Connection as an Empirically Based Theoretical Problem, in Alexander, J. C., Giesen, B., Munch, R. & Smelser, N. J. (eds), *The Micro–Macro Link*, pp. 193–206 (Berkeley, CA: University of California Press, 1987).

Douglas, M., *Purity and Danger: an Analysis of the Concepts of Pollution and Taboo* (New York: Praeger, 1966).

Durkheim, E., *The Division of Labor in Society* (New York: Free Press, 1933).

Eisenhardt, K. M., Agency Theory: an Assessment and Review, *Academy of Management Review* (1989) pp. 57–74.

Gambling, T. E., Magic, Accounting, and Morale, *Accounting, Organizations and Society* (1977) pp. 141–151.

Gambling, T. E., Accounting for Rituals, *Accounting, Organizations and Society* (1987) pp. 319–329.

Giddens, A., *The Constitution of Society* (Berkeley, CA: University of California Press, 1984).

Goffman, E., *The Presentation of Self in Everyday Life* (Garden City, New York: Anchor, 1959).

Goffman, E., *Interaction Ritual: Essays on Face-to-Face Behavior* (New York: Doubleday, 1967).

Heritage, J., *Garfinkel and Ethnomethodology* (Cambridge: Polity Press, 1984).

Hines, R. D., Financial Accounting Knowledge, Conceptual Framework Projects, and the Social Construction of the Accounting Profession, *Accounting, Auditing, and Accountability* (1989) pp. 72–92.

Humphrey, C. & Moizer, P., From Techniques to Ideologies: an Alternative Perspective on the Audit Function, *Critical Perspectives on Accounting* (1990) pp. 217–238.

Johnson, P. E., Jamal, K. & Berryman, R. G., Audit Judgement Research, *Accounting, Organizations and Society* (1989) pp. 89–99.

Klersey, G. F. & Mock, T. J., Verbal Protocol Research in Auditing, *Accounting, Organizations and Society* (1989) pp. 133–151.

Kunda, G., *Engineering Culture: Culture and Control in a High-Tech Organization* (Philadelphia: Temple University Press, 1992).

Lukes, S., Political Ritual and Social Integration, *Sociology* (1975) pp. 289–308.

Meyer, J. W., Social Environments and Organizational Accounting, *Accounting, Organizations and Society* (1986) pp. 345–356.

Moore, S. F. & Myerhoff, B. G., *Secular Ritual* (Amsterdam: Van Gorcum, Assen, 1977).

Morgan, G., Accounting as Reality Construction: Towards a New Epistemology for Accounting Practice, *Accounting, Organizations and Society* (1988) pp. 477–485.

Stevens, M., *The Big Eight* (New York: Macmillan, 1981).

Tinker, T., *Paper Prophets: a Social Critique or Accounting* (New York: Praeger, 1985).

Van Maanen, J., *Tales of the Field: On Writing Ethnography* (Chicago: University of Chicago Press, 1988).

Van Maanen, J. & Kunda, G., "Real Feelings": Emotional Expression and Organizational Culture, in Staw, B. & Cummings L. L. (eds), *Research in Organizational Behavior*, Vol. 11 (Greenwich, CT: JAI Press, 1988).

Wittgenstein, L., *Philosophical Investigations* (New York: MacMillan, 1958).

[5]

Pergamon

Accounting, Organizations and Society, Vol. 21, No. 2/3, pp. 289-315, 1996
Copyright © 1996 Elsevier Science Ltd
Printed in Great Britain. All rights reserved
0361-3682/96 $15.00+0.00

0361-3682(95)00004-6

MAKING THINGS AUDITABLE*

MICHAEL POWER

The London School of Economics and Political Science

Abstract

In contrast to official images of audit as a derived and neutral activity, this essay argues that audit is an active process of "making things auditable" which has two components: the negotiation of a legitimate and institutionally acceptable knowledge base; the creation of environments which are receptive to this knowledge base. These two components are explored and clarified in relation to three areas where the concept of auditability has been officially invoked: making public sector research auditable, and hence accountable; making quality auditable; making brand valuations auditable. The choice of these apparently marginal practices is deliberate. They provide an opportunity to observe a "logic of auditability" which is hidden in more established contexts. In the three cases auditability is accomplished by: auditable measures of performance; systems of control; reliance on other experts. After considering each of these areas in turn, their general implications for a "constructivist" understanding of the concept of auditability are developed. The challenges that this may pose for more established frameworks of audit research are considered briefly. Copyright © 1996 Elsevier Science Ltd.

Unless financial data are verifiable, auditing has no reason for existence (Mautz & Sharaf, 1961, p. 43)

Attempts to develop "philosophies" of audit have emphasized the importance of verifiability. And yet, in contrast to debates about the "representational faithfulness" of financial reporting, the concept of "verifiability" has been relatively immune from controversy and discussion. Mautz & Sharaf (1961, p. 43) argue that "whatever word is selected to carry the connotation of 'auditability', there must be something that auditors do to give them a basis for expressing an opinion on the reliability of the financial statements they examine". Flint (1988) echoes this claim by postulating that the "subject matter of audit ... is susceptible to verification by evidence" and Wolnizer's

(1987) extensive discussion ties both "verifiability" and "auditability" to the idea of "independent testability" in which statements can be tested by reference to independent evidence (see also Flemming-Ruud, 1989, pp. 58-5, 117). Wolnizer argues that the independence which really matters in auditing is not so much that of an ethical "state of mind" but that of "independent authentication" which has the virtues of objectivity, publicity and replicability. In making this claim, Wolnizer, like Mautz and Sharaf, explicates auditing as a quasi-scientific practice[1] with roots in the "common human need" to remove doubt and alleviate anxiety (Lee, 1993, pp. 19-20).

The concepts of "verifiability" and "auditability" are widely regarded as synonymous

---

* Earlier versions of this essay were presented at the Maastricht Auditing Research Symposium, October 1993, and the Universities of Sheffield and Aberdeen. The author is grateful for the comments of Richard Laughlin, Christopher Napier, Miklos Vasarhelyi, Joni Young and two anonymous reviewers.

[1] One obvious problem with this view is the extent to which it relies on a model of scientific inquiry which has been largely discredited by philosophers of science.

and it is through this identity that conceptual linkages between financial reporting and auditing exist (Lee, 1993, pp. 23–24). It has been said that "Verifiability is that attribute of information which allows qualified individuals working independently of one another to develop essentially similar measures or conclusions from an examination of the same evidence, data or records" and financial statements embody "rules and procedures" which "leave a trail of evidence and procedures that can be verified" (American Accounting Association, 1966, p. 10). Verifiability is also "The ability through consensus among measurers to ensure that information represents what it purports to represent or that the chosen method of measurement has been used without error or bias" (FASB, 1980, p. xvi). As Solomons (1986, p. 91) observes, these definitions indicate the close connection between the idea of verification and agreement among observers of measurements. However, the FASB linkage between verification and measurement is much looser than that postulated by earlier theorists of accounting (Lee, 1993, p. 168) and generally reinforces the conceptual priority of decision relevant measurement practices over verificatory practices (FASB, 1980, para. 81). The official relationship between reporting and auditing is based on this: auditing is fundamentally a *derived* activity which *adds* credibility to financial statements.

This official image of the "external" audit is well established in professional literature. This externality, independence by another name, is one of the fundamental concepts which gives audit its value. The notion of externality also implies a certain technical neutrality in the manner of intervention in the auditee organization: the auditor is a temporary visitor to an organization charged with monitoring the relevant activities of the organization. The technologies of audit may be a transient nuisance but they do not disrupt or transform the operations of the audited organization other than to make recommendations for control improvements or to push for adjustments to the financial statements. Auditors make these recommendations on the basis of their claimed expertise in risk assessment procedures, in internal control technologies and in the rules and regulations governing financial reporting. In this way, audits are supposed to "add value".

From the point of view of these official rhetorics, it seems almost self-evident that financial reporting pre-exists and is independent of the audit process. However, even if it is plausible to argue that, for any particular financial audit, the financial accounting rules are independent of, and prior to, the audit process, particular accounts are nevertheless negotiated *within* the audit process; accounts and audits get co-produced (see Pentland, 1994). The supposed priority of financial accounting is even less clear when the systems of financial reporting and auditing are considered as a whole. A brief glance at history indicates how these systems have co-evolved and how, in many cases, auditing values have played a constitutive role for financial reporting rather than simply "adding credibility". For example, a history of accounting policy could be written in terms of the impact of claims for the legal objectivity *and auditability* of the historic cost measurement convention; a rhetoric of "objectivity" has often played a decisive role in blocking the development of current value measurement practices.

Thus, in contrast to conceptual accounts of their relationship, it could be argued that financial reporting is simply a sub-system in the larger system of auditing.[2] In this essay I argue

---

[2] Flemming-Ruud (1989, p. 126) argues for a new conceptual integration between financial reporting and auditing. Like Wolnizer and Chambers, he argues that auditing can be reformed only if financial reporting "reflects reality". Accordingly, he is critical of Mautz and Sharaf's identification of verifiability and auditability and argues that auditing rarely *verifies* accounting numbers but merely examines allocations and calculations. While he may be correct that verification is a more robust concept than mere inspection, the actual conceptual slippage between concepts of auditability, testability and verification is an important feature of "making things auditable".

that audit evidence is not just "out there" but must be constructed to count as evidence within this system of audit knowledge. Auditability is not just a natural property of economic transactions, not simply a function of the "quality" of evidence which exists in the environment within which auditing operates. Rather, auditing actively constructs the legitimacy of its own knowledge base and seeks to create the environments in which this knowledge base will be successful. Auditing knowledge in this systemic sense does not emerge from the experimentally isolated cognitive judgements of practitioners in relation to sets of cues in the outside world, as the tradition of audit judgement research would have it (Felix & Kinney, 1982; Power, forthcoming). Audit plays a decisive role in constituting the environment of cues itself (Kirkham, 1992, p. 296) and its techniques are part of a system of knowledge which is driven by the imperative of "making things auditable".

In the next section this idea of a "system of audit knowledge" is elaborated. This is followed by an exploration of the motif of "making things auditable" in three areas where the concept of auditability has been officially invoked; accountability in public sector research; quality assurance and environmental management systems; brand accounting. In the case of research, the theme of making a new domain auditable by creating an environment of "measurable facts" is emphasized. In the case of quality assurance and environmental management, the issue is primarily one of creating a legitimate surface of auditable facts in the form of a management system. In the case of brands, it is less a case of *creating* an auditable environment so much as *negotiating* auditability in terms of the credibility of valuation experts. This ordering of the cases provides a development from a more conventional exploration of the auditability-measurability nexus through to a consideration of the socially negotiated nature of audit knowledge. After considering each of these cases and their dominant auditability strategies in turn, the more general implications of the

analysis are explored. In particular, the prospects for a "sociology of audit knowledge", and the challenges that this may pose for the more established framework of audit judgement research, are considered.

THE SYSTEM OF AUDIT KNOWLEDGE

A great deal has been written recently in North America, the U.K. and elsewhere on the "crisis" of financial audit. Problems of legitimacy have been generated by publicly visible scandals and questions of independence, of reporting responsibilities and of the burden of litigation preoccupy both academics and practitioners. In the face of these difficulties, which have a longer history than is commonly imagined, accountants have been determined to defend their jurisdiction (Sikka & Willmott, forthcoming). And despite the problems confronting financial audit practice, audit as a regulatory model seems to be remarkably durable and has developed in many new areas. As Beneviste (1973, p. 137) puts it, "In every policy making environment there is a culture that affects the style of discussion and intervention." The recent "explosion" of auditing (Power, 1994a) reflects a decisive shift in regulatory style and is due in part to the success and power of the large accounting firms to promote their claims to expertise in new areas, particularly as advisors to and agents of government. Audit has become important to a new style of public administration. While it has become fashionable to emphasize the decentralizing and market oriented tendencies of "rethinking government" (Osborne & Gaebler, 1992), centralist anxieties of control nevertheless persist and it is here that audit plays a vital role. As Van Gunsterten (1976, p. 142) has noted, "the anxious ruler tries to make his phantasies come true by way of a mixture of minute controls and rigorous isolation". In the face of regulatory anxiety, audit institutionalizes the production of comfort (Pentland, 1993, p. 610), something which is particularly evident in the rise of quality assurance programmes.

To understand the institutional significance of auditing and auditors (not all of whom are necessarily accountants) requires a more detailed consideration of auditing as a system of knowledge, its core values and the manner in which it reproduces those values in existing and new settings. The notion of a "system" of knowledge is not to be read too strictly; one could equally talk of a "field" in Bourdieu's (1990) sense.[3] The argument attempts to draw attention to the self-constituting nature of auditing knowledge rather than to make theoretically doctrinal claims. Furthermore, this exploration of how things are made auditable complements but adopts a different focus from that of a political economy of auditing in which the interests and behaviour of accounting firms would be relevant. To put the point in Abbott's (1988) terms, the argument emphasizes the task dimension of audit rather than the jurisdictional struggles (Sikka & Willmott, forthcoming) and regulatory games (Willmott, 1991) which are conducted by accounting firms. With this somewhat artificial division of intellectual labour in mind, the broad structure of the system of auditing knowledge can be considered.

One can identify at least four principle elements or levels in the system represented in Fig. 1. Firstly, one can talk of the official knowledge structures of audit practice. This is the public face of audit, its codified rules and regulations on appropriate procedure and behaviour which have evolved over time (Preston *et al.*, forthcoming). Such rules may subsist in the technical publications of firms or they may be documented at the level of professional institutes and regulatory bodies. These rules constitute auditing "best practice" and have the widely claimed virtue of being credible in a court of law. Accordingly, auditing working papers seek to reproduce the public face of auditing with contingent legal and regulatory audiences in mind (Cushing &

Fig. 1. The system of auditing knowledge.

Loebbecke, 1986; Francis, 1994, p. 260; Van Maanen & Pentland, 1994). In this way, as Pentland (1993, p. 610) has argued, the production of regulatory comfort flows out of the audit process in an institutionalized form because practitioners have incentives to replicate this form in their representations of what they do.

Second, there are the many mechanisms of knowledge dissemination which involve varying degrees of formal and informal, on- and off-site, education (Power, 1991), training and socialization (Harper, 1991; Coffey, 1994). It is here that certain styles of behaviour, speech and recording of practice are learned and the audit practitioner is constructed. It is also here that formal examination systems contribute to the institutionalization of audit knowledge by connecting idiosyncratic procedures to legitimate forms of abstract knowledge (Abbott, 1988; Carpenter & Dirsmith, 1993). In this way, credentializing mechanisms which, from one point of view, function as barriers to entry also reproduce the internal "technical" culture within which audit practitioners can be judged by their peers.

Third is the level of practice itself. At this level of the system, particular audit judgements are made and written up. Here the pub-

---

[3] On this occasion, I prefer the idiom of system, as it is used by theorists such as Luhmann, since the theme of the *self-reproduction* of knowledge is useful in the auditing context.

lic production of comfort by the audit process is the product of elaborate internal interactions within the audit process itself, in particular to shape representations of audit knowledge consistent with economic constraints, and of strategic games between auditor and auditee in which accounting "facts" are negotiated (Pentland, 1994). It is also here that vague intuitions about assurance levels must be rationalized for public consumption (Humphrey & Moizer, 1990) and where emotional responses about comfort must be re-presented as cognitive in an "essentially unknowable situation" (Pentland, 1993). This level of practice reproduces and depends on official and legitimate myths of practice (Boland, 1982) such as sampling and risk analysis. However, the process is not without conflict between practitioner values and the institutional demand for acceptable representations of practice. The eternal dialectic between structure and judgement in audit knowledge is an example of this. The struggle is between formal, public and supposedly replicable forms of knowledge and local craft cultures of situated "expert" practice (see Francis, 1994, pp. 251–257). Within this dialectic there is a constant "cognitive reinvention of the audit" in which cost reduction and audit quality can be reconciled and represented (Fischer, 1996). It could be said that the structure vs judgement issue, which is common to most professionalized fields, is less concerned with how audits are actually done than with how they are represented. But, as Francis (1994) and Van Maanen & Pentland (1994) suggest, the distinction between doing an audit and writing an audit is not sharp: "at the limit, the audit becomes a pure simulacrum, an institutionally driven discourse about auditing that is its own reality. Audits become centred solely on the production of working papers for the purpose (reality) of producing working papers ... audit has become its own sign with the focus on the production of the sign (working papers)" (Francis, 1994, p. 261). The publication of audit opinions circulates signs with aesthetic (comfort), rather than informational, value

(Lash & Urry, 1994, p. 15).

The "writing" of auditing is also important for the fourth element of the system of audit knowledge: the various feedback mechanisms by which the practice and official knowledge structures mediate ideals of quality control. Here we can identify institutionalized mechanisms of peer review which provide comfort about comfort production. As Fogarty (1996) notes, this process is itself dependent on the production of working papers. The quality audit expresses a manner of *writing* the audit. In addition there are those in-house processes whereby attempts are made to amend audit procedures and to construct new forms of "value adding" proprietorial audit practice. The benefits of these changes become benefits only when new technologies are accepted (Fischer, forthcoming) and the public face of the reconstructed audit knowledge is that of efficiency gains and technical improvement. In this writing of audit quality, there is a circuit of conformation and reproduction of the tasks which constitute the system of audit knowledge. Quality control procedures may function less to make quality observable and more to construct and define quality itself.

This preliminary sketch of a system of knowledge composed of four interacting but distinguishable elements is directly relevant to the present theme of "making things auditable". On one interpretation of the theme, it is a rather trivial matter. Making things auditable is what practitioners do when they audit organizations and processes. This is not to say that techniques cannot be "improved"; this is going on all the time. Nor is it to say that practitioners never make mistakes; quality control procedures exist for that very purpose. On such a view "making things auditable" is largely a matter of common sense and audit judgement research examines the operation of this common sense in experimentally controlled settings. The image is one of auditors as cognitive agents confronted with "cue rich" environments. On the basis of personal factors and a tried and tested kit of techniques they can conduct a reasonable audit.

In what follows I wish to explore a different interpretation of what might be meant by "making things auditable", one that builds on the constructivist reading of the system of auditing knowledge provided above. Common sense suggests that the forms of audit knowledge are relatively stable and accepted and it is their implementation and, from the point of view of audit judgement research, the consensus supporting that implementation, which is the interesting research problem. But from a constructivist standpoint, consensus at the level of application is less interesting than the consensus which supports, albeit temporarily, the system of audit knowledge as a whole. The contrast can be put like this: whereas the common sense view of "making things auditable" would argue that techniques are accepted by practitioners because they "work", this essay is concerned with how techniques and procedures are perceived to "work" because they are institutionally acceptable. Making things auditable in this specialized sense is not simply a technical matter and the variability of how auditability is accomplished *and claimed* cannot simply be attributed to improvements in audit technique, as the common sense view might argue. What it is for an audit technique to work or not work itself depends on what gets accepted as common (legitimate) sense within the system and to address the production of legitimate knowledge emphasizes the institutionalizing process which inform all four levels of the system of audit knowledge in Fig. 1. It is the *production* rather than the *presumption* of the common sense of auditability which concerns us here. This production has two related themes which are often run together in the concept of "social construction": negotiation and creation.

NEGOTIATING AUDIT KNOWLEDGE AND CREATING AUDITABLE ENVIRONMENTS

The negotiation of knowledge involves the processes of closure which render knowledge acceptable and stable. Particular procedures and techniques come to be accepted or not accepted as constituting reliable knowledge, either at the public level through specific codification or more informally in terms of acceptable practice. This is evident for those procedures where practitioner consensus is not automatic and where there is "interpretive flexibility" (Pinch & Bijker, 1987, p. 40). One such area of flexibility is the auditability of charity income which is "made auditable" in specific cases not necessarily because an objectively superior technique exists but because of practitioner determination to make it auditable by "taking a view" that controls over, say, collecting tins are a reliable guarantee of the completeness of income. The particular audit can then be written in such a way as to connect this determintion with institutionally acceptable and defendable forms of reasoning. As Pentland (1993, pp. 611–612) puts it: "Fundamentally auditing involves the certification of the unknowable ... Rituals of copying numbers allowed the underlying indeterminacy of the U.S. mortgage market to be auditable i.e. something auditors can be comfortable with." Of course, events like the crisis in the U.S. Savings and Loans industry show that society can choose to withdraw its trust in auditors' certification of the unknowable. And, as the emerging debate on the regulation of derivatives suggests, it may also push auditors into new "unknowable" areas.

Another example of flexibility concerns the impact of the information technology environment on auditor conceptions of evidence. Yates's (1993) study of the U.S. life insurance industry demonstrates the longstanding resistance, particularly by auditors, to records in magnetic form. Auditors are only just beginning to overcome this resistance and auditability or non-auditability in such cases as these reflect the ability to write the audit in such a way as to conform to official bodies of knowledge produced by auditing standard setters and to accepted standards of evidence. In turn standard setters will grant official recognition to forms of audit knowledge which have become acceptable (as cost-efficient solutions) to practitioners. Hence, the closure of what counts as knowledge depends not so much on solving "problems in the common sense of that word but on whether the relevant social groups *see* the problem as being solved" (Pinch & Bijker, 1987, p. 44). This process reflects a cycle of externalization from specific practices, objectivication as knowledge in official documents and then the reinternalization of this institutionalized knowledge at the level of practice (Fischer, 1996).[4]

The *negotiation* of acceptable audit knowledge can be contrasted with the manner in which the system of auditing makes itself possible by actively *creating* the external organizational environment in which it operates. Though it would be implausible to suggest that organizations are literally created by audit processes, it can nevertheless be said that a significant "auditable sub-organization" is constructed and partly (often) or wholly (rarely) exists to correspond to the audit process.[5] The question is whether controls, measurement systems and their associated forms of documentation pre-exist the audit process or have been created with a view to making the organization auditable. Where organizations have already been "legalized" (Scott, 1994) bureaucratic media, systems, documents and

so on act as a surface upon which audit can "work". In general, audit procedures, like any technique, demand the environments in which they can be perceived to succeed; problems and their technical solutions are tightly coupled (Pinch & Bijker, 1987, p. 30). Clearly, primary forms of documentation such as invoices play many roles and it would be absurd to suggest that they have been constructed solely relative to the audit process. But in other cases it may be less clear cut. There is evidence in complaints about the bureaucracy of quality assurance mechanisms that systems have been created for the purpose of being audited and little else. This complaint has also been levelled at the regulatory system for financial auditing in the U.K. Auditing may demand the creation of measurement and control systems which are explicitly designed to affect auditee behaviour. The empirical question is the extent to which audit "trusts, and make use of, order which is there and which is constantly being recreated" (Van Gunsterten, 1976) or whether audit "colonizes" the organization and creates auditees to make its own processes possible.[6]

The negotiation of audit knowledge and the creation of auditable environments are linked themes in the project of making things auditable. The greater the institutional reliance on the system of audit knowledge by regulators and others, the greater the potential for forms of audit knowledge to be supported by active transformations in the auditee organization. Financial auditing would not be possible with-

---

[4] To take another example, sampling emerged as an officially acceptable technique because practitioners could not cost effectively test in detail large volumes of transactions. Non-100% testing was externalized by practice and projected on to a public stage of debate where it was objectified as legitimate technique. Subsequently it was reinternalized by practice in the form of statistical sampling (Power, 1992a; Carpenter & Dirsmith, 1993).

[5] In this respect auditing can be regarded as an autopoietic system of knowledge in Luhmann's sense which constructs the environment-system distinction for itself internally. It is a system which builds for itself the facts which are relevant to its continued functioning.

[6] In other words, is audit in some sense an autopoietic system which "productively misunderstands" (Teubner, 1992) its environments but does not substantively interact with them? Or, as Armstrong (1991) and Johnson & Kaplan (1987) have suggested, is financial auditing responsible for disseminating a distinctive financial control culture at the expense of other possibilities?

out a data base of books, records and internal controls but equally it reinforces this control environment in order to maintain auditability. According to theorists such as Flint (1988, p. 32), audit is not possible without clear standards of auditee performance. But it would be more correct to say that audit is not possible without "auditable" standards of performance. This is not quite a tautology since the negotiation of audit knowledge and the creation of auditable environments are not free from conflict and resistance. What counts as auditable may be fundamentally contested and agents may resist attempts to transform them into auditees. In this sense the system of audit knowledge is powerful but not monolithic, a point which will become evident from a more detailed consideration of how things are made auditable in three different contexts.

MAKING RESEARCH AUDITABLE

Following widespread national and international initiatives in public sector management and control, the need to demonstrate "economy, efficiency and effectiveness" is now ubiquitous and value-for-money auditing practices have grown rapidly. The wave of "new public management" (Hood, 1991) has created remunerative opportunities for the consultancy arms of the large accountancy firms[7] and it has been suggested that consultants are now the new policy makers.[8]

In the U.K. and elsewhere, the reorganization of health care continues to occupy considerable public attention and there is resistance amongst medical practitioners to many of the market based changes to their working environment (Broadbent *et al.*, 1992). These changes are also visible in many other areas of public service provision, such as education. As far as higher education is concerned, a number of funding related reforms has taken place (Puxty *et al.*, 1994, pp. 155–158) and the financing of research has been a particular area for change. Public sector funded research is increasingly under pressure to provide a return on investment (Sherman, 1994; White Paper, 1993) and greater accountability for the use of public funds has been demanded. The task of making research auditable is the responsibility of the Higher Education Funding Council (HEFC) who commissioned a report from accountants Coopers & Lybrand to address ways in which this might be achieved (Coopers & Lybrand, 1993). It will be argued that the analysis and recommendations of this report are shaped by a conception of auditability which reflects a particular style of making things auditable and which demonstrates the close links between auditability and measurability.

The HEFC provides funding to universities by way of a block grant. In the past this has been calculated and notionally split between teaching and research. The purpose of the Coopers Report was to explore mechanisms of accountability for the research element of this funding. The HEFC consultation paper (HEFC, 1993), which was produced to accompany the Coopers Report, stresses the requirement of public accountability for the use of research funds and the need to establish arrangements which are "auditable" at an "*appropriate* level of detail" (emphasis added) in order to show that the research element of the HEFC block grant has been "properly used". The HEFC was concerned with the precise nature of the mechanisms in question and whether a ("top down") allocative method of demonstrating accountability would be "appropriate" in the required sense or whether

---

[7] The role of accountants in these changes is complex: they are cause and effect, shaping and being shaped by their institutional environment: "The nature and language of expertise i.e. the fact that certain kinds of problems, measurements, and concerns are highlighted by technical language, favours some implementers and beneficiaries and does not affect others" (Beneviste, 1973, p. 131).

[8] See "Commentary: Auditing the Accountants", *The Political Quarterly* (1993) pp. 269-271.

there would be a need to account in more detail for expenditure ("bottom up").

The Coopers Report addresses possible interpretations of the concept of accountability and argues that, for each Higher Education Institution (HEI), accountability could be publicly demonstrated by reference to seven possible modes of audit as follows:

(a) The audit of research output via the mechanism of Research Assessment Exercise (RAE) results.

(b) The audit of projects conducted by research centres in HEIs.

(c) The verification of the percentage of research outcomes funded by the HEFC.

(d) The verification of the percentage of research outcomes per Academic Subject Category (ASC) funded by the HEFC.

(e) The audit of resource allocation where block grants have been allocated to research and teaching activities.

(f) The audit of expenditure of research funds in relation to analyses of actual patterns of expenditure.

(g) The audit of income sources allocated to different expenditure categories.

These possible "methods" of operationalizing accountability embody different levels of aggregation and detail at which reporting and auditing would occur. Options (a) and (b) lend themselves to non-financial measures of research output, such as intellectual judgements about its quality.[9] Options (c) and (d) quantify the percentage of these outcomes funded by the HEFC at two different levels of aggregation. However, the Coopers Report states that the arrangements under (a), (b), (c) and (d) are not really "auditable" and argues that the only serious candidates for mechanisms of accountability are those which are auditable at the level of detail of (e), (f) and (g). The Report goes on to elaborate the difficulties inherent in operationalizing these three

options: many central costs in higher education institutions are deducted from income sources before they are attributed to individual units or cost centres (the grant is "top sliced") and any exercise to allocate "lumpy" forms of income (block grants) and expenditure to discrete activities is subject to the classical difficulties of choosing an allocation base. In the end Coopers & Lybrand favour option (f) above, for which the biggest difficulty is the allocation of salary costs. To overcome this problem a system of time recording is proposed under the following categories of activity:

T: Teaching
R: Research,
Ra: Allowable research for HEFC
      purposes
Rb: Other research organization grants
Rc: Explicitly subsidized research
C: Consulting
S: Savings
A: Administration

In making this proposal, Coopers & Lybrand acknowledge HEFC demands for sensitivity in the design of a non-intrusive system (in this way both Coopers and the HEFC seek to preserve the ideal of audit neutrality: audits are intended to "colonize" only to the extent of intended improvements of accountability mechanisms). The Report proposes an allocation system for the seven expenditure categories which operates in terms of "notional week" units of time. Academic time would be reported on a quarterly basis, usually compiled by the head of department. It also proposes (para. C11) that time spent on administration should be re-allocated to the other categories.

The Report frequently appeals to the concept of auditability although it is never defined directly. For example, in defending its choice of option (f) above, it says, "to be auditable, an institution would have to adopt a mechanism for analysing expenditure ... we doubt that

---

[9] Although the rise of patentable output as an assessment category for REAs suggests a more commercial orientation at this level too (Sherman, 1994).

anything much less could be described as auditable in the normal sense of the word" (para. 708). And in the context of the attribution of income under option (g) it is stated that, "... all that would be being audited would be that the assumptions had in fact been followed — not the validity of the assumptions themselves" (para. 720). Indeed, even though the Report never defines auditability directly, a number of possibilities for demonstrating accountability are dismissed as being "unauditable" in the sense of being "too dependent on assumptions" and "merely mathematical". However, when the proposed time sheet system is looked at in detail *it is also unauditable in these terms*: it operates with such highly aggregated categories that it is heavily dependent upon assumptions and allocations itself and must therefore fail the concept of auditability implicit in the Report's assumptions even though it is intended to satisfy them.

At one level this internal contradiction in the appeal to auditability suggests technical problems in the specific design of the time sheet system. One could address these problems by refining the reporting categories, the periodicity of reporting and so on. For example, one specific concern in the context of academic research is the problem of cross-subsidization of non-research activities. However, even in very "precise" systems of time recording, such as those used by firms of accountants and solicitors, there is still scope for "creative" time recording. It is well known that certain jobs can bear the allocation of fictitious time. Furthermore, cross-subsidization across different tasks occurs because billing has only a very loose relationship to recorded time, especially where there is also unrecorded time (McNair, 1991). Accordingly, the prospects are poor for a relatively crude time reporting system to address the problem of cross-subsidization. However, the issues are not simply technical in this operational sense.

The very fact that there are different possibilities for research accountability suggests that auditability is variable in meaning (on this point see also Sikka *et al.*, 1994). The concept of

auditability implicit in the Coopers Report expresses a level and style of calculative elaboration which the drafters of the report believe will be an *institutionally acceptable* (to the HEFC and the government) operationalization of the demand for accountability. This is evident from the fact that the Coopers Report is not concerned with measuring and representing the time spent by academics as accurately as possible, but only "sufficiently accurate as to be meaningful . . . (and) auditable" (para. 112). Of a "more accurate time recording system ... we doubt that it would be acceptable to the generality of the academic community" (para. 606). And one purpose of the measurement system is to "reassure" the HEFC (para. 110). Hence, far from being an objective and neutral property of information systems, auditability is largely a product of a consensus about the nature *and detail* of evidence required by those whom the audit is intended to serve. This consensus about the "appropriate level of detail" reflects a certain *style of verification*, a style which is not necessarily natural or objective but which serves institutionally legitimate "rituals of inspection".

In the Coopers Report, concepts of accountability, auditability and time recording mutually define one another and cannot be independently settled. The auditable measurement system which makes research accountable is worked out as a compromise between different perceived pressures and constituencies. Even though the rejection of options (a)–(d) above may reflect an "accounting" bias, the report stops short of recommending a more elaborate time sheet system with multiple codes. Indeed, doubts about the technical efficacy of the proposed time sheet system and its lack of apparent precision and elaboration demonstrates how there is nothing "natural" about the level of calculative detail in a measurement system. One cannot say that arrangements which have it are "auditable" and those which don't are not. Rather, "measurabiity" and "auditability" are negotiable practices which are determined by an institutional need or an anxiety (Van Gunsterten, 1976) for a style of control which reaffirms core values of accountability and efficiency. This institutional need has its genesis in broader transformations in public service provision as we saw above. It generates a regulatory style caught between "disciplinary" values which require appropriate images of rigour (on this point see also Fogarty, 1996) and a more facilitative emphasis consistent with the values of the auditee domain. It follows that operationalizations of the concept of auditability express a contingent mixture of trust and distrust and a distinctive regulatory demand for comfort.

Making research auditable demonstrates the close relation between auditing and measurement. Indeed, making things auditable is also making things measurable. Auditing requires a "reality" against which its verificatory procedures can operate and in the research context audit must literally *create* the environment in which it operates. This case also demonstrates a very direct coupling between what I call above the *negotiation* of audit knowledge and the *creation* of the audit environment. The former concerns those processes of exploration of a style of measurement which corresponds to institutionally stabilized conceptions of what is auditable. The latter concerns the explicit transformations in the auditee domain that this proposal would bring about. Accounting measurement systems, such as the proposed time recording technology considered here, make possible certain ways of thinking and acting. In so doing they inhibit other ways of thinking and acting. Already some of the data produced by the Research Assessment Exercise in the U.K. has reinforced tendencies to talk in terms of "high" and "low" earning subjects. High earning departments and subjects may now wish to bargain on the basis of their new found economic "strength". Equally, a time recording sytem which separates research and teaching would make it possible to think in a binary fashion and to change organizations, contracts and working

habits on that basis. Making research auditable, even in the technically crude manner proposed, embodies a potential for forms of discourse and for research strategies which were not formerly conceivable but which subsequently become "rational" (Puxty *et al.*, 1994).

The research context shows how audit knowledge is negotiated as auditing is extended into new areas. The Coopers Report extends into a new domain presuppositions about auditability which are relatively stable within the system of financial audit knowledge. Indeed, the stability of this knowledge base is one of the sources of the accountant-consultant's authority in new domains; it is difficult for outsiders to question concepts of accountability and auditability as accountants formulate them. However, in this case the discussion has focused on a discourse of intention rather than outcome. In fact the proposed time recording system is on ice and the proposals met considerable resistance, not least from the HEFC itself. This demonstrates that the project of making things auditable is also a precarious one, requiring not simply a stability *within* the expert system of knowledge about appropriate procedure but also a level of operational consensus among sponsoring institutions and auditees themselves.

MAKING QUALITY AUDITABLE

Quality certification has become big business. Today quality has become an explicit organizing concept for a wide variety of institutions and there has been an explosion of conferences and publications on the subject geared to industry-specific audiences. New institutions, such as the Higher Education Quality Council, and new institutional roles, such as Quality Assessors and Directors of Quality Enhancement, have been created with the explicit aim of defining, encouraging, managing and monitoring quality. And on the back of these developments there has even been a reflexive application of quality ideas to the quality assurance process itself.[10] The concept of quality is at the heart of an elaborate process of image management which invokes and demands a tight coupling between quality performance, however that is to be defined, and processes to ensure that this performance is visible to a wider audience. "Making quality auditable" is therefore an essential element of this quality impression management. Without audit and the certification that follows from audit, quality remains too private an affair. It is as if there is no quality without quality *assurance*.

The discourse of quality has its origins in very specific engineering preoccupations with controlling the "fitness of use" of products and processes (Wolnizer, 1987). This involved forms of verification which were directly linked to production processes and product inspection practices became organized around measures of statistical control. In other words, quality was originally a "production" based concept (Bowbrick, 1992, p. 7) with relatively well-defined measurement parameters, such as defect rates.[11] In recent years there has been an important transformation and generalization of this engineering based conception of quality. Quality has been extracted from the specificities of engineering discourse and has been expressed in more abstract terms.[12] In short, quality has been transformed from an engineering concept to a management concept, a "managerial turn" (Power, 1994b) which has

provided opportunities for quality experts to sell their services. And it has recently been suggested that "the quality audit represents a new market offering growth opportunities for the public accounting profession" (AAA, 1993).

Quality management and assurance has itself become a product to be priced like the commodities whose quality it is intended to promote. At the centre of this "commodification" of quality is the quality management *system* whose role is not merely to monitor and control product and process standards for local use but also to be externally auditable. Performance and the visibility of performance are tightly coupled in the idea of a management system; the system is the "hinge" between internal operations and the external audience. Accordingly, the auditability of quality is not a subordinate matter, it is almost the essence of quality itself. Quality is an empty concept without accreditability and hence auditability. In this way audit processes have the potential to become constitutive of quality.

If product or service quality is well defined by reference to standards of performance which have a high degree of consensus, then systems of control can be regarded merely as secondary monitoring of compliance with these standards.[13] For example, where products or activities have public, readily visible "non-expert" criteria of success and failure (such as light bulbs and plumbing services) certification of quality concerns itself directly

---

[10] For example, in September 1994 a conference was organized by the South Bank University, London, and the British Standards Institute on the theme of "Quality *in* Auditing" (emphasis added).

[11] Of course, it can be argued that notions of "defect" are not very well defined at all. Furthermore, as the sociology of technology informs us, there is nothing "natural" about product design and concepts of "fitness for use". So ideas of quality itself are profoundly social in character. Notwithstanding such doubts, I merely wish to work with the contrast between a technical standards orientation towards quality and a systems approach.

[12] One should not overstate this point. In parallel with this generalization of the quality concept, there has also been an explosion of product-specific standards in areas such as safety. Such standards have emerged in the so-called "self-regulatory" space between the state and industry and organizations such as the British Standards Institute have acquired the multiple roles of quasi-regulator, industry mouthpiece, lobbyist and technical advisor.

[13] Flemming-Rudd (1989, p. 127) makes a similar point when he argues that auditing would in principle be very simple if financial accounting was a bona fide measurement system.

with compliance with these standards as well as indirectly with the systems of control for assuring quality. In such cases the auditability and certifiability of quality is a secondary process; it would be an exaggeration to claim a constitutive role for it. Just as financial auditors may rely on internal controls within the auditee organization, so it would appear that management systems pre-exist the audit of their quality. However, where standards are ill-defined and controversial or even where they don't exist at all, the certification of quality assurance systems may take on a life of its own.

The "technical" elements of these systems, such as sampling and other statistically based controls, have been common currency for many years. The idea of such a system plays an increasingly influential institutional role, formalized in general quality standards such as BS 5750 (now BS EN ISO 9000). This point can be illustrated in the context of recent initiatives for the audit of environmental management systems. In the U.K., the British Standards Institute (BSI) issued BS 7750, *Environmental Management Systems* (BSI, 1992) which is an adaptation and application of the general quality assurance principles of BS 5750. In March 1993, the European Commission issued a Regulation on *Eco-Management and Auditing* (EMA) which is similar in orientation (CEC, 1993). Both schemes focus on the quality of internal management *systems* rather than the quality of the product or service itself as specified in standards. Both schemes emphasize a system structure which can be verified and approved by independent outsiders. Furthermore "environmental audit" is conceived primarily as a "management tool" within the environmental management system more generally (Hillary, 1993).[14] Both are voluntary schemes and, at the time of writing, it is not yet clear to what extent organizations will register with either or both of them. Both schemes provide for external accreditation

arrangements in order that compliance can be publicly signalled and the discourse of environmental management has made much of the "competitive advantage" that this will bring for registrants under these schemes. BS 7750 provides for a structured and integrated environmental management system. The elements of this system are derived from the common principles embodied in earlier quality documents (BSI, 1992, p. 2). Indeed, BS 5750 and 7750 constitute a kind of conceptual framework for management systems and hence abstraction is necessary for their applicability to "all types and sizes of organization". Thus, the shift in quality assurance from standards to systems is also a shift from the specific to the abstract. And of course, as Abbott (1988) reminds us, abstract bodies of knowledge provide opportunities for claims to occupational monopoly; professionalization projects in the environmental management field have been conspicuous (Power, 1994b).

For both EMA and BS 7750, quality is conceived as compliance with to-be-specified standards of performance. The justification for splitting form and substance in this way is that the setting of any standards is considered to be better than none at all and may be a stimulus for year-on-year improvements. The idea of performance benchmarking has emerged from this division of intellectual labour between documents such as BS 7750 and standard setting processes. BS 7750 initially de-prioritizes and abstracts from the substance of performance in favour of system values and their auditability. Performance is simply an abstract and formal reference point which is subsumed under the goal of verifiability. However, BS 7750 insists that once an environmental management system is established, then companies will have a benchmark against which they can attempt to improve performance. In other words, an environmental management system is

---

[14] Strictly speaking there are two levels of audit: one which is an internal management affair and one which is an external assurance function. This distinction, which resembles closely that between internal and external financial auditors, is not crucial to the argument being advanced.

claimed to make substantive change thinkable and possible.[15]

An unintended consequence of this division of labour is that environmental performance has come to be closely identified with having an (auditable) system (see Shaylor *et al.*, 1994). In addition to abstracting from all specific knowledges, such as engineering and accounting, EMA and BS 7750 embody arrangements by which the system performance can be made externally visible. Indeed, it is essential that the system structure embodies the capacity to be verified externally. While a quality assurance system may (or may not) have any perceived *technical* benefits for the organization, it will not give them any perceived *institutional* benefits without certification. Hence, demonstrability, auditability and verifiability are fundamental properties of the system structure and the environmental management system can be understood as a "surface" which makes them possible. Far from being a by-product of management systems structures, "auditability" becomes, in the absence of specific standards of performance, their constitutive ideal. In other words, for BS 7750 and EMA auditability is central to their status as self-regulatory "products". They would have no institutional value, although they may have technical value, without systems elements which are in large part designed to be "made auditable".

The commodification of quality assurance in general, and environmental performance in particular, is evident in the BS 7750 emphasis upon the role of the external consumer. For example, it is stated that a goal of compliance

with the standard is to "achieve and demonstrate sound environmental performance" (p. 3). The role of demonstration in the form of audit is central because the "standard is intended to support certification schemes". The basic elements of the scheme provide for review of the environmentally relevant performance of the entity, the development of a policy in relation to these performances and then the development of a system with the capability of assuring *and demonstrating* compliance with the policy. Accordingly, "the organisation shall establish and maintain a system of records in order to demonstrate compliance with the requirements of the management system" (BSI, 1992, p. 7). The systems elements will include registers and other documents, such as manuals specifying procedures, and then arrangements for audit and feedback; "environmental performance" itself is not specified beyond the requirement that entities will formulate environmental policy relative to legal requirements, perceptions of pressures from the community and their own "culture".

This silence on the content of environmental policy is taken for granted by the emphasis on formal systems values. It gives the environmental audit and assurance process a certain abstract indifference to the substance of performance which reflects a broad shift in regulatory orientation from performance standards to systems, or what Fogarty (1996) and others describe as a shift from substance to process. Another important shift is also implied here: from the *inspection* of processes to the *audit* of systems compliance.

[15] Initial German resistance to the EC Regulation is instructive (Hillary, 1993). German companies regard themselves as leaders on the question of standards of environmental performance in industry-specific settings. In addition, German environmental laws are among the most demanding in Europe. Accordingly, the EC Regulation, with its emphasis upon systems entirely abstracted from first-order performance, was viewed as permitting and legitimating the lower standards of other member states and of eclipsing the "superior" performance of German companies. This perception reflects a difference in philosophy in which there is greater resistance to subsuming standards of performance under an abstract systems concept. The German regulatory style favours "uniform emissions standards and technical expertise" (Weale, 1992, p. 179). Implicit in the German concern about EMA is the risk that performance becomes too closely identified with the ideal of auditability itself. If the role of an environmental management system is to make itself visible, and hence auditable, for accreditation purposes, then the management system effectively becomes an artifact for the purpose of external persuasion and legitimacy.

Whatever the outcome of the almost theological deliberations about the meaning of environmental and quality audits, it is the material traces of the management system and its associated forms of documentation which are the conditions of possibility for audit protocols, checklists and questionnaires.[16] The audit process is constituted by a "rhetoric of records" which couples the auditee and auditor. The environmental management system effectively mediates the "front (public) regions of an organization and its back (private) regions" (Van Maanen & Pentland, 1994, p. 54). Accordingly, "making quality auditable" is essentially a process of constructing a particular kind of auditable front region for an organization and it is here that impression management and management are tightly coupled through the audit process. For example, an emphasis on the demonstrability and *defendability* of compliance to accreditation organizations is evident in BS 7750: "organisations may find it beneficial to establish self-assessment procedures carried out by the responsible line management to assess audit readiness" (BSI, 1992, p. 14). Here we have an explicit suggestion of a *pre-audit audit*, a quality check to see whether the system is suitable to be checked for quality. Although this suggestion is made only in an appendix of the standard, it nevertheless expresses the ideal of auditability in its purest form where actions must always be conducted with a view to their auditability at a later date by different parties.

The manner in which quality is made auditable emphasizes both the negotiation of audit knowledge, with selective borrowings from the financial audit tradition, and the creation of auditable environment by institutionalizing internal elements of the organization. The idea of a management system and its control structures is both an essential component of a form of audit knowledge which can justify the abandonment of direct inspection and also an institutionally legitimate practice for an auditee. A close analysis of the official documents in this area reveals much about how a "logic of auditability" gives priority to the accreditation of systems of control, rather than standards, an emphasis with obvious cost implications. BS 7750 and EMA operate in an institutional space in which companies place an economic value on demonstratable compliance for legal purposes and for marketing advantage with a newly conscious public. This "certification explosion" corresponds to a specific style of control through the production of symbols of comfort (Pentland, 1993). It would be wrong to suggest that there has been no resistance to the systems emphasis of documents such as BS 5750 and 7750.[17] There is widespread concern that they have become ends in themselves and have constructed a mentality of "abstract compliance" regardless of the substance of quality standards.[18] And there are concerns that environmental audit will become a simulacrum in which "there no longer *is* an audit, only a discourse *about* an audit" (Francis, 1994, p. 261).

---

[16] A great deal of effort and expense has been expended on defining audit in the environmental area. While there has been agreement about its role as a "management tool" (ICC, 1991), the relation between reviews and verifiction, internal and external audits, and the nature of external reporting have been the subject of considerable discussion. BS 7750 differentiates between verification and audit in terms of their temporal proximity to the process being controlled. Audit appears to be more of an *ex post* and independent function than verification which seems closer to a kind of self-checking but "in all cases ... the objectives should be to control the activity in question in accordance with specified requirements ... and to verify the outcome".

[17] See, for example, "Concern at Pointless Quality Rules", *Times Higher Education Supplement* (9 April 1993).

[18] See, "Quality Under Fire", *Financial Times* (21 June 1994), which raises the problem of the quality of quality assessors; "Bitten by the Bug", *Financial Times* (20 September 1994), which reports the use of BS 5750 in controlling supplier quality.

The institutional origins of the demand for environmental audits is a complex admixture of influences (Power, 1994a). A general shift in regulatory style, publicly articulated concerns about the environment, a critical mass of consulting practitioners operating in related areas, the threat of litigation and a history of more general quality initiatives have all shaped the regulatory space within which environmental auditing initiatives have and are being formulated. But, above all, environmental audit must be possible and cost effective. The audit of environmental management systems represents a particular style of dealing with and processing environmental risk which reaffirms the possibility of a cost-effective assurance function. It is a style which focuses on management process, which emphasizes the compatibility of commercial and environmental imperatives and whose object is the "production of comfort" for varied constituencies. The auditability and certifiability of BS 7750 and EMA are essential to these diverse public roles and, more generally, to the status of quality assurance as a product worth paying for.

MAKING BRANDS AUDITABLE

The 1980s was a period of intense merger and acquisitions activity in the U.K. As companies became commodities to be bought and sold (Espeland & Hirsch, 1990), targets and predators sought increasingly to account "creatively" both to resist or enhance the chances of takeover and, where successful, to enhance post-acquisition performance. Consequently, the accounting rules for business combinations and the enforcement of these rules by financial auditors evoked a stream of critical commentary (e.g. Smith, 1992). The use of "non-subsidiary subsidiaries", of merger relief in combination with acquisition accounting and of pre-acquisition provisions deliberately under-

mined the intention of existing guidance. More generally, the pressure to perform according to the perceived criteria of capital markets (such as earnings per share) coupled with indeterminate accounting rules (e.g. about income recogniton) fuelled this process.

The U.K. brand accounting debate has its origins in this ferment of takeover activity.[19] Acquirors with large amounts of goodwill in their consolidated balance sheets were faced with two unpalatable options under the existing, somewhat lax, rules in the U.K.: immediate write-off to reserves or capitalization and amortization. For a complex mixture of reasons a number of U.K. companies (notably Grand Metropolitan plc and Ranks Hovis MacDougall plc) sought to value and capitalize their brands. RHM's policy was particularly controversial because it involved the valuation of internally generated brands as well as those purchased as part of an acquisition.

At the centre of the accounting debate is the question: can brands be measured with *sufficient reliability* to be recognized on the "balance sheet". The FASB and IASC conceptual frameworks guide us to this question, as the essential hurdle condition for the recognition of an asset, but not to its answer. If the answer is that brands can be measured reliably then the related question as to whether brand-names are separable (from goodwill and other intangibles) will be affirmative. In other words, in the case of brands, and intangibles more generally, it is impossible to distinguish clearly between measurement, recognition and "element" issues; the problem of separability cannot be disentangled from that of the reliability of the technology of measurement (Napier & Power, 1992). Hence a linkage between the question of measurability and that auditability, which was explored above in the case of research, is also relevant here.

Opposition to brand accounting in the U.K. crystallized around the London Business School

---

[19] The background to this debate has been documented extensively elsewhere (see Barwise *et al.*, 1989; Napier & Power, 1992).

(LBS) report (Barwise *et al.*, 1989). This report argued that many of the claimed rationales for capitalizing brands were doubtful. It argued that, despite the assertions of valuers such as Interbrand plc, there was no general agreement about the validity of their valuation methodology. The report claimed that this methodology was neither "totally theoretically valid nor empirically verifiable" (p. 7). Indeed, the LBS report explicitly links the question of verifiability to that of accounting recognition: "Verifiability . . . has implications for 'auditability' since it is a necessary condition for recognition that asset valuations should be auditable" (p. 16). The recognition test for status as an asset seems to be that putative assets be measured *and verified* with reasonable certainty. Here then we see another version of the claim for a tight link between the credibility of economic measurement for accounting recognition purposes and auditability.

The LBS report also argues that brand valuations give rise to auditability problems because all the "auditors can really check is the process, not the book values". In other words, auditors can check any calculation to agreed procedures but cannot check the procedures themselves since they are "not experts and cannot make such judgements" (p. 74). In contrast to the LBS, Sherwood (1990, pp. 82–84), whose firm were the auditors of RHM, is less doubtful about the limits of auditor expertise. He suggests that the auditor can "verify the underlying facts" on which valuation is based; brand valuation is not an "exact science" and it is "better to be broadly right than precisely wrong". On the face of it, the question seems to be whether the auditor is restricted to retraversing accounting calculations or whether s/he can inspect directly any "inputs" into this calculative process, especially since the form of the calculation is a matter of convention.[20] But, on closer inspection, much of the

controversy about verifiability and auditability hangs on the expertise of those whose calculations are being revisited by the auditor. In other words verifiability and auditability are less properties of things in themselves and more a function of the institutional credibility of experts. Auditability on this view is a function of agreement about the limits of auditor expertise and the credibility of other specialists. There are at least three levels to this issue:

(1) If the measurement/calculation is widely regarded as a matter of accounting "common sense", there is no need for other expertise.

(2) If the measurement/calculation is regarded as depending on a particular body of knowledge, the auditor may choose to endorse and rely upon that expertise.

(3) If the measurement/calculation is regarded as *beyond expertise*, it is unverifiable.

The difference between each level is not absolute and may reflect different jurisdictions of professional knowledge. For example, verifying the valuation of commercial vehicles might be something that falls firmly within the province of accounting expertise. Verifying the valuation of land and buildings seems to fall within the jurisdiction of chartered surveyors, although their expertise is not immune from doubt.[21] Verifying the value of a healthy working environment may be regarded, from the point of view of accountants at least, as beyond expertise. However, the relation between levels 1, 2 and 3 is dynamic and, for any particular accounting issue, potentially contestable. A shift from position 3 to 2 reflects a shift in consensus about the credibility of non-accounting expertise. For example, in the case of environmental liabilities accounting necessarily overlaps with legal and scientific bodies of knowledge; matters which were formerly unaccountable and unauditable become so by virtue of the institutionalized credibility of "other" experts. In the transition from level 2 to 1 external expertise is internalized and

---

[20] This is probably true of all auditing (cf. Flemming-Ruud, 1989, p. 117).

[21] See "A Revamped Red Book", *Financial Times* (4 November 1994), which suggests that the credibility of land and building valuation practice suffered during the recession in the property markets in the early 1990s.

appropriated as part of the accountant's knowledge system. This is highly unlikely in the case of science and law but less implausible in the case of valuation work, hence the tensions between accountants and actuaries regarding pension scheme accounting.

The interesting threshold for the question of brand accounting is between levels 3 and 2, the point at which a body of knowledge is sufficiently credible for its practitioners to be reliable for accounting purposes. In a technical release on this matter, the former Accounting Standards Committee stated that "A valuation may be regarded as verifiable if different independent valuers using the same information would be likely to arrive at a similar valuation" (ASC, 1990a, para. 3.2, echoed in ASC, 1990b, para. 27).[22] Given that such a consensus between valuers is an *empirical* matter of the acutal standard deviation among measurers (Ijiri & Jaedicke, 1966), then there are no *a priori* grounds for saying that brand valuation is unreliable and hence unauditable. The logic of the ASC view is that questions of auditability cannot be settled only by looking at the technical detail of the valuation method. They are a matter of what becomes generally accepted.

By locating "auditability" as a function not of things themselves but of agreement within a specialist community which learns to observe and "verify" in a certain way with certain instruments (Hacking, 1983), features of the brand accounting debate which might appear to be marginal begin to assume considerable importance. The debate in the U.K. was initiated in part by the decision of Ranks Hovis MacDougall to capitalize its acquired and home grown brands using the valuation expertise of its consultants Interbrand. The valuation methodology was opposed by appealing to its technical failings ("too subjective") but underlying this claim were doubts about the credibility of Interbrand (Power, 1992b). Brands were regarded as unauditable largely because Inter-

brand were not trusted. However, as accounting firms began to declare their commercial interest in and support for valuation methodologies in a technical sense, it became increasingly obvious that this marginalization of Interbrand could be sustained only at the level of doubts about their specific methodology, which they claimed to be robust and auditable, not brand valuation as such.

As paradoxical as it sounds, the case of brand valuation strongly suggests that the more the practice is accepted, the more "true" its claims become. Arnold *et al.* (1992) have argued that, "in order to include intangibles as assets, managers will have to *persuade* the company's auditors that the amount at which they are included is reasonable" (pp. 76-77, emphasis added). The more widespread the acceptance of brand valuations the easier will this persuasive process become. The realist about accounting measurement will want to argue that any reduction in the standard deviation of measurement across individual valuers arises because the measures are becoming more objective. In contrast to this line of reasoning, the brand valuation case suggests that the standard deviation of measurement practice decreases because of a consensus that the valuation method is "objective" and this arises when a critical mass of practitioners follows an increasingly institutionalized methodology.

The involvement of accounting with "alien" bodies of expertise is not peculiar to brand accounting. For a number of years it has been permitted in the U.K. for companies to revalue their land and buildings. These revaluations are performed by "expert" valuers — usually chartered surveyors — and among the disclosures relating to the valuation which are required are its basis and, in the period in which it is carried out, the names of the valuers and the details of their qualifications. In addition, auditors rely upon the work of actuaries in a number of

---

[22] If all valuers use a method such as NPV then they may differ only in their assumptions about cash flows and discount rate. These assumptions are verifiable in Sherwood's sense to the extent that they are based on extrapolations from "existing facts" and agreed methods of extrapolation.

different contexts — a relationship for which guidance has been supplied by the Auditing Practices Committee in the U.K. (APC, 1990).[23] This means that verification takes place against the background of a network of trusted experts. The list of such specialists is expanding and now includes environmental consultants for some purposes. Substantiating the credibility of that expertise, rather than any detail about what has been done, is becoming a fundamental auditing and disclosure requirement.

This explicitly sanctioned reliance on non-accounting professional expertise in the U.K. is addressed more generally in the auditing guideline *Reliance On Other Specialists*, (APC, 1986), to be replaced by Statement of Auditing Standard (SAS) 520, *Using the Work of a Specialist*.[24] It is stated that the auditor, like the accountant, cannot be expected to have detailed knowledge and experience of specialists in other disciplines but he/she must nevertheless form an opinion of *inter alia* the need for specialist evidence and the *competence and objectivity of the specialist*. The guideline states that the latter is normally "indicated by technical qualifications or membership of an appropriate professional body. Exceptionally, in the absence of any such indications of his competence, the specialists's experience and established reputation may be taken into account" (para. 9). It is clear that institutional legitimacy in the form of established professional status is regarded as strong evidence for such credibility and hence for the acceptability of the related practices. In addition, the auditor must consider the relationship between the specialist and the client

and whether the specialist has a significant financial interest in the client.

At the extreme, auditors will audit brand valuations in the same way many other items are audited: by relying primarily on other expertise. In this way the auditability of problematic things is ultimately accomplished by an *externalization and proceduralization of the evidence process*, a specific style of delegation to credible experts which is a mixture of trust and verification. It is not verification in the pure and probably unrealizable sense of unmediated contact with the thing to be verified but it makes claims to auditability possible.[25] Brand valuation is not simply a body of techniques and operations. Rather, it represents a body of knowledge in which the relevant experts must seek a certain level of social credibility and trust.[26] Expertise is in general a peculiar mixture of internal (epistemic) and external (institutional) validity in which the "how" and the "who" of that expertise are deeply interrelated. The question of the auditability of brand valuations is therefore inextricably linked to territorial sensitivities and doubts about credibility couched in the seemingly neutral and disinterested language of "asset measurement". Where measurement is controverisal, the credibility of measures assumes considerable importance. From this point of view the distinction between measurement and calculation which preoccupies the normative-realist school of accounting theory is not an absolute one. Collins (1985, p. 145) has argued that knowledge claims become more certain the further they are from their point of origin; reliability of measurement becomes a function of this distance and trust enables

---

[23] The APC was replaced by the Auditing Practices Board (APB) during 1991.

[24] Similar guidance exists in the U.S.A.

[25] See Lee's (1993, pp. 21–22) examples of different situations where third party reliance may be necessary to alleviate doubt.

[26] It is notable that in Australia there are fewer inhibitions about relying upon non-auditor expertise provided that there is sufficient disclosure (Australian Accounting Research Foundation, 1989).

knowledge to become "black boxed" in Latour's (1987) sense.

How are we to explain the fact that in the U.K. in 1988 there was widespread scepticism about the auditability of brands whereas by 1994 this position seems to have softened? Nothing has changed in the underlying measurement technology to make it more "reliable". What has changed is the climate of acceptability for the practice. Indeed, in a very important sense brand valuations *are* auditable because auditors have given clean audit reports and in this way they have acquired a *de facto* institutional legitimacy. Since 1988 the consensus about the credibility of brand accounting has widened and resistance has tailed off. In contrast to the previous cases, making brands auditable emphasizes the *negotiated* nature of audit knowledge construction and of consensus formation in relation to bodies of expertise, rather than the creation of an audit environment.[27] Brand valuations have become auditable because large numbers of people who matter regard them as reliable. Indeed, accountants themselves are providing a brand valuation service so there has been a slide from level 3 to 2 to 1 in the analysis above. The auditor can now rely on the "who" of the independent expert rather than examine the substance of the valuation itself, especially where the who is another accountant. The normalization of the measurement of brand values is co-extensive with making them auditable.

CONSTRUCTING AUDITABILITY

In the preceding sections three cases have been considered where the concept of auditability has played a key role in shaping policy deliberations. One could say that in all these cases it is a concept which is appealed to more than it is understood. When questions of auditability are invoked it is usually in the form of vague claims to expert common sense. Each of these different examples shares another common characteristic: they are contexts of practice which are or have been negotiable and in which audit practices, either proposed or actual, have been resisted and remain controversial. Pressures for greater accountability for academic research funds are recent and continuing. Markets for environmental auditing and environmental management systems have also recently been stimulated by regulatory initiatives in Europe, though they have a longer history in North America, and the regulatory arrangements are still in their infancy. Brand accounting is far from being an entirely legitimate practice in the U.K. and, while it is likely to become so, the accounting and auditing controversy is not yet over. In other words, each of the three cases has not yet been subject to closure. Accordingly, assumptions sustaining the "logic of auditability" are readily visible in these unstable contexts. In each case, it has been suggested that questions of "auditability", far from being obvious, are the product of active strategies of "making things auditable".

It was suggested that the commercial strategies of individual auditors or firms take place against the backdrop of a system or field of

---

[27] Naturally there is a link between the themes of negotiation and creation here in so far as brand valuers will need to base their work on data supported by a system which controls and records it. Whether they would do this anyway regardless of financial reporting and auditing is unclear. Napier (1994, p. 95) has argued that, "In Britain companies are permitted to capitalise the costs of developing new products and processes. Although market research is explicitly excluded from the definition of development costs, there are clear parallels between product development and brand establishment (indeed, in consumer goods industries, the distinction between them is artificial). Brand oriented companies might wish to design their internal management accounting systems in order to identify the cost of establishing and developing new brands, with a view to using the ASC's own logic in the case of product development costs as a justification for capitalising the costs of creating and establishing new brands".

knowledge which is both the condition of possibility for these stragegies and is reproduced by them. Such a system requires, above all, both a stable and legitimate knowledge base and an "auditable environment" to which this can be applied. What is at stake in this co-production of stable knowledge and auditable environments for audit practice is to a large extent a project of "fact building" (Latour, 1987, p. 104). At first glance such an idea is counterintuitive since facts are facts, they are not created. However, once these facts have been built, audit knowledge can be regarded as common sense and the audit environment assumes a "natural" externality to the audit process. Once facts are "built" the context of their construction is effaced and one is left with practitioner common sense and routine practice, until that practice fails, in which case new processes of fact building (and blame avoidance) are set in motion and new audit techniques and responsibilities are created.

In making academic research auditable, the measurement technology of the time recording system creates a layer of facts which make the auditability of research activity possible. Of particular significance here is a conception of auditability imported into the research context by consultants who recommend a particular level of detailed elaboration in this layer of facts. The building of these auditable facts consists in creating a sufficiently atomized and elaborate domain for the purpose of making research accountable, a ritual of precision which has little to do with accurate representation of research activity and more to do with producing a legitimate style of regulatory control. Rhetorics of auditability, measurability and accountability are tangled up in this context.

In the second case of making quality auditable, environmental management systems and environmental performance illustrate how auditability is linked to the creation of a system which establishes a bureaucratic surface upon which the audit process can work, independently of substantive performance. By emptying the system of content the ideal of auditability can emerge unencumbered by idiosyncratic specificities. The environmental management system specifies the construction of a domain of facts capable of external certification. In this way the management system is not only a technological construct; its elements have an essential public face which is offered for the purpose of accreditation.

In the third case of brand accounting, it was argued that the auditability of these valuations depends in large part upon the credibility of the expert valuers. Once experts are credible, the substance of what they know need not become a direct object of the audit process. In this manner things are made auditable by constructing networks of trust which can be proceduralized. Hence, a thing which was unauditable at one time may become auditable later by virtue of a shift in the network of trust. Practices which were once soft, subjective and unauditable can become hard, objective and auditable. There is therefore nothing intrinsic about the objectivity of certain facts over others; this is relative to the position of a fact within a field or system of knowledge. For example, the more entrenched a measurement/auditing procedure (low standard deviation of measures/auditors) has become, the more it is likely to be regarded as a matter of common sense. Auditability is therefore a distinctive form of administrative objectivity (Porter, 1994), one in which certain routines and procedures have acquired an accepted role in facilitating audit practice.

Table 1 summarizes the conclusions of the paper. While making research auditable stressed the creation of a measurable environment, the brand context concentrated on the construction of trust in expertise. The audit of quality illustrates both the construction of audit knowledge around the idea of a management system and the creation of an auditable environment through the implementation of this system. The dimensions of this matrix are not intended to be exhaustive and could be extended in both dimensions. For example, the columns could be extended into, say, financial services audits (Power, 1993a), or even into more traditional and institutionally stable

TABLE 1. Making things auditable

| | Context of fact building Audit of: | | |
Method of fact building	Research	Quality	Brands
Credibility of other experts	Low	Low	High
Abstract management systems	Low	High	Low
Detailed measurement	High	Low	Low

contexts such as the audit of debtors. The rows could be extended to embrace other forms of fact building, such as sampling (Power, 1992a; Carpenter & Dirsmith, 1993). While a particular form of "fact building" for audit purposes has been emphasized in each of the three cases, this is not intended to exclude the others. Thus, the audit of brand valuations also depends on systems which capture marketing data. Environmental audits involve reliance upon various specialists. And the audit of research activity seems likely also to involve abstract quality assurance systems.

Fact building, whether for science or auditing, is an expensive process. Recent studies which draw attention to the socially negotiated nature of the audit process emphasize the interpenetration of economic and epistemic dimensions of audit practice. What gets accepted and stabilized as evidence and technique is always affected and limited by economic factors. In this sense the construction of auditable environments and the building of audit-relevant facts must be registered constantly in relation to a need to maintain a cost-assurance equation for the auditor, not only directly incurred and knowable costs but also the possible costs arising from litigation processes. Making academic research auditable imposes costs on the auditee and leaves the external auditor unburdened by the more time-consuming and costly audit of research output. In the case of environmental audit, the audit of systems is less costly than the audit of transactions and procedures. This might require the auditor to invest in alien bodies of knowledge either directly or by the use of specialists. In the case of brands, the audit

process relies on valuation experts whose costs are borne by the auditee.

One problem in these and many other cases is that it is relatively easy to know the cost element of the audit process. The assurance function is much more difficult to specify. This is something that audit has in common with a number of activities where it is difficult to measure benefits: policing, teaching and so on (Power, 1993b). Making things auditable is in large part to do with maintaining institutionalized images of assurance which are externally legitimate and which are consistent with the claimed practicalities of cost. This is a precarious task, and gaps, and hence legitimacy problems, can emerge when the demand for assurance is out of step with the supply for a given cost. All three cases considered suggest how the building of auditable facts involves an "exacerbated concern with documentation" (Fogarty, 1996) and procedure: timesheets, system documents, working papers to support the reliance on experts. Making things auditable is the construction of the visible signs of "reasonable practice" for consumption by markets, regulators, courts of law, the state and others whose programmes depend on the production of comfort. Audit reports are a symbol of legitimacy which do not so much communicate as "give off" information by virtue of a rhetoric of "neutrality, objectivity, dispassion, expertise" (Van Maanen & Pentland, 1994, p. 54).

The production of auditable facts is therefore not a simple question of writing up what has been done. The process of writing up is a strategic act which brings the fact of auditability into being and has consequences for the "professional" identity of the auditor. By editing out elements which might raise questions, audit documentation is also a way of socializing staff, a form of "institutionalized purification" which produces the administrative objectivity which corresponds to auditability. Facts have no reality for audit purposes until they are organizationally inscribed in some way: "To provide an account in ... the auditing world ... means adhering to descriptive devices (numerical and narrative) that are by and large conventional and arbitrary. They are neither right nor wrong but stand as coding or reporting standards that are "generally accepted" as adequate for the task. They can be regarded as strategic representations, collectively validated by members, designed to put the organization's best foot forward" (Van Maanen & Pentland, 1994, p. 81).

Finally, the three cases considered above challenge the idea of independent verifiability. For example, Wolnizer (1987) argues that the concept of "independent testability" should characterize audit. However, at crucial junctures in his argument, the social and consensually grounded aspects of testability become evident. Thus, in arguing that the past states of phenomena may be reliably authenticated "if reliably documented" (p. 15), the dependence of testability upon a domain of testable documented facts is clear. For Wolnizer, and other auditing "realists", these facts are somehow independent of relatively trivial documentation processes. In addition, Wolnizer argues that the testability of statements consists "in their openness to critical scrutiny by any skilled tester" (p. 16). But who is skilled in this context? Much depends upon the social allocation of trust and hence the concept of auditability is already loaded with problems of whose scrutiny is to count. Wolnizer argues that replication "is the nub of independent testability: that skilled inquirers may repeatedly test hypotheses and that their results may, in turn, be corroborated or refuted by others. Capacity for replication is essential ..." (p. 20). However, Collins' (1985) study of scientific replication suggests that the production of public knowledge depends crucially

upon the credibility of the agents producing it. An enormous amount of consensus *precedes* any process of replication because an event will count as replication, and hence as an instance of possible refutation, only if it is conducted by reputable experts. In other words, replication requires as much a consensus about *whose* judgement is to count as it does a consensus in the judgements themselves.

Attempts to describe auditing in a manner which stresses cognitive accomplishments such as verification and replication systematically disattend to, but cannot entirely abstract from, the social support for these accomplishments. This is most evident within the audit judgement tradition of research which is concerned very broadly with the forms of consensus, or lack of them, which emerge from the judgements of individual auditors in response to experimentally constructed environments. Broadly speaking, this tradition attempts to understand on a systematic basis the nature of auditor responses to environmental cues, their processing of information and its biases, and the nature and stability of the judgements they make. This paradigm of inquiry is interested primarily in the consensus of specific groups of auditors as a *product* of audit technologies in conjunction with "human information processing" structures. What is necessarily invisible within this tradition of research is the manner in which audit knowledge is an institutionalized system of knowledge. In the three cases I have tried to show that, for environments to be auditable, a consensus about the form of audit knowledge and about a domain of facts relevant for audit purposes must exist or must be created, since all techniques demand the environments in which they "work".

CONCLUSION

Like any practice, auditing has a "front" and "back" stage in Goffman's terms. The back stage practice works hard to produce, for institutional consumption, the front stage as a "natural" outcome.[28] Audit judgement research focuses on the production of consensus on the front stage as the contingent product of individual cognitive judgements. But, from the point of view of the institutional construction of auditability, cognition itself emerges from a more fundamental consensus produced in back stage arenas. Processes of consensus formation about evidence and relevant facts precede and make possible the "cognitive judgements" of individual auditors which may or may not deviate from one another. Audit judgement research makes sense when the system of knowledge is stable and where the judgements of auditors in relation to this background stability are the interesting variable. In this respect, audit judgement research can be regarded as a "normal science" of audit practice. Lack of consensus at the individual level may indicate poor training, and so on, but the system of knowledge is not usually directly at issue. However, lack of individual auditor consensus may also indicate more systematic instabilities in the system of knowledge. When the system of knowledge is unstable, as it is in the three cases considered above, what is of interest is less the process of consensus formation at the level of the individual auditor but those processes by which procedures and routines, paradigms of auditability, become institutionalized as the public face of practice.

To conclude, a sociology of audit technique (Power, forthcoming) which takes on the "back stage" of audit knowledge production provides an alternative to the cognitive tradition. Such a sociology takes the cognitive claims of audit practice as *explanandum* rather than *explanans* (Pinch & Bijker, 1987, p. 24). As recent themes in the sociology of science suggest, concepts of evidence, observation, experiment, testability and replication are far from being stable elements which can be utilized to explicate audit practice. They are themselves the product of processes which mark out the, often competitive, jurisdictions of knowledge-producing communities. Making things auditable is a constant and precarious project of a system of knowledge which must reproduce itself and sustain its institutional role from a diverse assemblage of routines, practices and economic constraints. It is when this knowledge system extends its reach into new areas that this project, and the logic of auditability which requires facts for its procedures, is most apparent. It is a logic in which the demand for things to be auditable and for things to be seen to be auditable are almost identical:

> the more we are concerned with the ... financial health of our institutions, the more we must rely on appearances created by organizations whose very success is judged by the appearances they create (Van Maanen & Pentland, 1994, p. 60).

BIBLIOGRAPHY

AAA, *A Statement of Basic Accounting Theory* (Sarasota, Florida: American Accounting Association, 1966).

AAA, *The Auditor's Report* (1993).

AARF, *Exposure Draft 49: Accounting for Identifiable Intangible Assets* (Sydney: Australian Accounting Research Foundation, 1989).

Abbott, A., *The System of Professions: an Essay on the Division of Expert Labour* (Chicago: University of Chicago Press, 1988).

---

[28] Latour (1987) makes very similar claims for natural science but with a different metaphor: the two faces of Janus. One face corresponds to "science in the making" and the other represents "ready made science" with its context and process effaced for public consumption.

APC, *Reliance on Other Specialists* (London: Auditing Practices Committee, 1986).

APC, *Practice Note 2: Accounting for Pension Costs under SSAP 24, Liaison Between the Actuary and the Auditor* (London: Auditing Practices Committee, 1990).

Armstrong, P., Contradiction and Social Dynamics in the Capitalist Agency Relationship, *Accounting, Organizations and Society* (1991) pp. 1–26.

Arnold, J., Egginton, D., Kirkham, L., Macve, R. & Peasnell, K., *Goodwill and Other Intangibles* (London: Institute of Chartered Accountants in England and Wales, 1992).

ASC, *Technical Release 780, Accounting for Intangible Fixed Assets* (London: Accounting Standards Committee, 1990a).

ASC, *Exposure Draft 52, Accounting for Intangible Fixed Assets* (London: Accounting Standards Committee, 1990b).

Barwise, P., Higson, C., Likierman, A. & Marsh, P., *Accounting for Brands* (London: London Business School/ICAEW, 1989).

Beneviste, G., *The Politics of Expertise* (London: Croom Helm, 1973).

Boland, R., Myth and Technology in the American Accounting Profession, *Journal of Management Studies* (1982) pp. 109–127.

Bourdieu, P., *In Other Words: Essays Towards a Reflexive Sociology*, Adamson, M. (transl.) (Cambridge: Polity Press, 1990).

Bowbrick, P., *The Economics of Quality, Grades and Brands* (London: Routledge, 1992).

Broadbent, J., Laughlin, R. & Shearn, D., Recent Financial and Administrative Changes in General Practice: an Unhealthy Intrusion into Medical Autonomy, *Financial Accountability and Management* (1992) pp. 129–148.

BSI, *Environmental Management Systems* (London: British Standards Institute, 1992).

Carpenter, B. & Dirsmith, M., Sampling and the Abstraction of Knowledge in the Auditing Profession: an Extended Institutional Theory Perspective, *Accounting, Organizations and Society* (1993) pp. 41–63.

CEC, Council Regulation (EEC) No. 1836/93 of 29 June 1993, Allowing Voluntary Participation by Companies in the Industrial Sector in a Community Eco-management and Audit Scheme, *Official Journal* (June 1993).

Coffey, A., Timing is Everything: Graduate Accountants, Time and Organisational Commitment, *Sociology* (1994) pp. 943–956.

Collins, H., *Changing Order: Replication and Induction in Scientific Practice* (London: Sage, 1985).

Coopers & Lybrand, *Research Accountability* (London: Coopers & Lybrand, 1993).

Cushing, B. E. & Loebbecke, J. K., *Comparison of Audit Methodologies of Large Accounting Firms* (Sarasota, Florida: American Accounting Association, 1986).

Espeland, W. & Hirsch, P., Ownership Changes, Accounting Practice and the Redefinition of the Corporation, *Accounting, Organizations and Society* (1990) pp. 77–96.

FASB, *Statement of Financial Accounting Concepts No. 2, Qualitative Characteristics of Accounting Information* (Stamford, Connecticut: Financial Accounting Standards Board, 1980).

Felix, W. L. & Kinney, W. R., Research in the Auditor's Opinion Formulation Process: State of the Art, *The Accounting Review* (1982) pp. 245–271.

Fischer, M. J., "Real-izing" the Benefits of New Technologies as a Source of Audit Evidence: an Interpretive Field Study, *Accounting, Organizations and Society* (1996) pp. 219–242.

Flemming-Ruud, T., *Auditing as Verification of Financial Information* (Oslo: Norwegian University Press, 1989).

Flint, D., *Philosophy and Principles of Auditing* (London: Macmillan Education, 1988).

Fogarty, T., The Imagery and Reality of Peer Review in the U.S.: Insights from Institutional Theory, *Accounting, Organizations and Society* (1996) pp. 243–267.

Francis, J., Auditing, Hermeneutics and Subjectivity, *Accounting, Organizations and Society* (1994) pp. 235–269.

Hacking, I., *Representing and Intervening* (Cambridge: Cambridge University Press, 1983).

Harper, R., Notes on the Accounting Character: an Ethnography of Auditing, Unpublished manuscript, University of Lancaster (1991).

HEFC, *Accountability for Research Funds* (Higher Education Funding Council, 1993).

Hillary, R., *The Eco-management and Audit Scheme: a Practical Guide* (Letchworth: Technical Communications, 1993).

Hood, C., A Public Management for all Seasons, *Public Administration* (1991) pp. 3–19.

Humphrey, C. & Moizer, P., From Techniques to Ideologies: an Alternative Perspective on the Audit Function, *Critical Perspectives on Accounting* (1990) pp. 217-238.

ICC, *Effective Environmental Auditing* (Paris: ICC Publishing, 1991).

Ijiri, Y. & Jaedicke, R. K., Reliability and Objectivity of Accounting Measurement, *The Accounting Review* (1966) pp. 474-483.

Johnson, K. T. & Kaplan, R. S., *Relevance Lost — the Rise and Fall of Management Accounting* (Cambridge, Massachusetts: Harvard Business School Press, 1987).

Kirkham, L., Putting Auditing Practices in Context: Deciphering the Message in Auditor Responses to Selected Environmental Cues, *Critical Perspectives on Accounting* (1992) pp. 291-314.

Lash, S. & Urry, J., *Economies of Signs and Space* (London: Sage, 1994).

Latour, B., *Science in Action* (Milton Keynes: Open University Press, 1987).

Lee, T., *Corporate Audit Theory* (London: Chapman & Hall, 1993).

McNair, C. J., Proper Compromises: the Management Control Dilemma in Public Accounting and its Impact on Auditor Behaviour, *Accounting, Organizations and Society* (1991) pp. 635-654.

Mautz, R. K. & Sharaf, H. A., *The Philosophy of Auditing* (Sarasota, Flordia: AAA, 1961).

Napier, C., Brand Accounting in the United Kingdom, in Jones, G. & Morgan, N. (eds), *Adding Value: Brands and Marketing in the Food and Drink Industries* (London: Routledge, 1994) pp. 76-100.

Napier, C. & Power, M., Professional Research, Lobbying and Intangibles: a Review Essay, *Accounting and Business Research* (Winter 1992) pp. 85-95.

Osborne, D. & Gaebler, T., *Reinventing Government* (Reading, Massachusetts: Addison Wesley, 1992).

Pentland, B., Getting Comfortable with the Numbers: Auditing and the Micro Production of Macro Order, *Accounting, Organizations and Society* (1993) pp. 605-620.

Pentland, B., Audit the Taxpayer, not the Return: Tax Auditing as an Expression Game, Working paper, John E. Anderson School of Management, UCLA (1994).

Pinch, T. & Bijker, W. E., The Social Construction of Facts and Artifacts: Or How the Sociology of Science and the Sociology of Knowledge Might Benefit Each Other, in Bijker, W., Hughes, T. & Pinch, T. (eds), *The Social Construction of Technological Systems*, pp. 17-50 (Cambridge, Massachusetts: MIT Press, 1987).

Porter, T., Making Things Quantitative, *Science in Context* (1994) pp. 389-407.

Power, M., Educating Accountants: Towards a Critical Ethnography, *Accounting, Organizations and Society* (1991) pp. 333-353.

Power, M., From Common Sense to Expertise: Reflections on the Pre-history of Audit Sampling, *Accounting, Organizations and Society* (1992a) pp. 37-62.

Power, M., The Politics of Brand Accounting in the United Kingdom, *European Accounting Review* (1992b) pp. 39-68.

Power, M., Auditing and the Politics of Regulatory Control in the U.K. Financial Services Sector, in McCahery, J., Picciotto, S. & Scott, C. (eds), *Corporate Control and Accountability*, pp. 187-202 (Oxford: Oxford University Press, 1993a).

Power, M., The Politics of Financial Auditing, *The Political Quarterly* (1993b) pp. 272-284.

Power, M., *The Audit Explosion* (London: Demos, 1994a).

Power, M., Expertise and the Construction of Relevance: Accountants, Science and Environmental Audit, in *Proceedings of the Interdisciplinary Perspectives in Accounting Conference*, Department of Accounting and Finance, University of Manchester, (July 1994b).

Power, M., Auditing, Expertise and the Sociology of Technique, *Critical Perspectives on Accounting* (forthcoming).

Preston, A., Cooper, D. J., Scarbrough, D. P. & Chilton, R. C., Changes in the Code of Ethics of the US Accounting Profession, 1917 and 1988: the Continual Quest for Legitimation, *Accounting, Organizations and Society* (1995) pp. 507-546.

Puxty, A., Sikka, P. & Willmott, H., Systems of Surveillance and the Silencing of Academic Labour, *British Accounting Review* (1994) pp. 137-171.

Scott, W. R., Law and Organizations, in Sitkin, S. B. & Bies, R. J. (eds), *The Legalistic Organization*, pp. 3-18 (Thousand Oaks, California: Sage, 1994).

Shaylor, M., Welford, R. & Shaylor, G., BS7750: Panacea or Palliative?, *Eco-management and Auditing* (1994) pp. 26-30.

Sherman, B., Governing Science: Patents and Public Sector Research, *Science in Context* (1994) pp. 515-537.

Sherwood, K., An Auditor's Approach to Brands, in Power, M. (ed.), *Brand and Goodwill Accounting Strategies*, pp. 78-86 (Cambridge: Woodhead Faulkner, 1990).

Sikka, P., Puxty, A., Willmott, H. & Cooper, C., The Impossibility of Eliminating the Expectations Gap: Some Theory and Evidence, Working paper, East London Business School (1994).

Sikka, P. & Willmott, H., The Power of Independence: Defending and Extending the Jurisdiction of Accounting in the U.K., *Accounting, Organizations and Society* (1995) pp. 547-581.

Smith, T., *Accounting for Growth* (London: Century Business, 1992).

Solomons, D., *Making Accounting Policy* (New York: Oxford University Press, 1986).

Teubner, G., The Two Faces of Janus: Rethinking Legal Pluralism, *Cardozo Law Review* (1992) pp. 1443-1462.

Van Gunsterten, H. R., *The Quest for Control: a Critique of the Rational-central-rule Approach in Public Affairs* (Chichester: John Wiley, 1976).

Van Maanen, J. & Pentland, B., Cops and Auditors: the Rhetoric of Records, in Sitkin, S. & Bies, R. (eds), *The Legalistic Organization* pp. 53-90 (Thousand Oaks, California: Sage, 1994).

Weale, A., Vorsprung durch Technik? The Politics of German Environmental Regulation, in Dyson, K. (ed.), *The Politics of German Regulation*, pp. 159-183 (Aldershot: Dartmouth, 1992).

White Paper, *Realizing Our Potential: a Strategy for Science, Engineering and Technology* (London: HMSO Cm 2250, 1993).

Willmott, H., The Auditing Game: a Question of Ownership and Control, *Critical Perspectives on Accounting* (1991) pp. 109-121.

Wolnizer, P. W., *Auditing as Independent Authentication* (Sydney: Sydney University Press, 1987).

Yates, J., From Tabulators to Early Computers in the U.S. Life Insurance Industry: Co-evolution and Continuities, Working paper 3618-93, Sloan School of Management, MIT (1993).

[6]

Critical Perspectives on Accounting (1992) **3**, 137–161

THE AUDIT EXPECTATIONS GAP—PLUS CA CHANGE, PLUS C'EST LA MEME CHOSE?

CHRISTOPHER HUMPHREY,* PETER MOIZER† AND STUART TURLEY*

* Department of Accounting and Finance, University of Manchester and
† School of Business and Economic Studies, University of Leeds

This paper explores the response of the accounting profession to the audit expectations gap, with primary reference to the profession's behaviour in the United Kingdom during the period of the last 20 years. Starting from a brief examination of the history of expectation concerns over a somewhat longer period, it is argued that both the existence of a gap and the specific aspects of audit performance it comprises have shown considerable continuity and resilience against solution. The profession's response to the expectations gap are then discussed, considering them as interrelated with, rather than independent of, the nature of professional interests. Two main strategies of response are identified: a defensive approach focusing on education and reassurance of the public; and a constructive approach, seeking to convey a willingness to change audit activities to meet public concern. The paper evaluates these responses, and their likelihood of success in reducing expectations problems, in the context of the inherent conflicts in the structure of auditing as a self-regulated activity,

The history of the statutory audit of the annual financial statements of corporate entities has been characterized by a seemingly ever present uncertainty over its purpose, content and effect. During the last 20 years or so, this uncertainty has become known as the "audit expectations gap", suggesting that auditors are performing in a manner which is in some way at variance with the wishes of those for whose benefit the audit is being carried out. The 1970s and 1980s have seen a growing literature on audit expectations, with doubts and uncertainties being expressed about the role and value of auditing (for summaries, see Humphrey, 1991; Humphrey & Moizer, 1990; Porter, 1991).

Two basic views appear to be advanced by the accounting profession as to the causes of this expectations gap. One is that the nature of auditing, the various roles and responsibilities of auditors and, in particular, the probabilistic foundations of audit practice are poorly understood by non-auditors. Critics of auditing are deemed to be unfairly using the benefit of knowledge after the event to argue that auditors are not performing adequately. As the editorial comment in the September 1990 issue of Accountancy (the journal of the Institute of Chartered Accountants in England and Wales) stressed, business failures have "nothing to do with the standards of auditing. The press should recognise this, and stop blaming auditors for the economic facts

Address for correspondence: Professor Christopher Humphrey, University of Manchester, Department of Accounting, Roscoe Building, Oxford Road, Manchester M13 9PL, UK.

Received 7 June 1990; revised 31 July 1991; accepted 22 November 1991.

of life" (p. 1). For some, such attributions of blame, albeit misplaced and regrettable, are even regarded as an inevitable, unavoidable condition for the auditing profession. For example, Olson (1973), executive vice-president of the AICPA stated:

> "As long as investors suffer losses from a sudden and drastic drop in earnings or the bankruptcy of a corporation which was widely regarded as a good investment, our profession is going to be criticized in the news media. And since such situations are not likely to disappear completely, we ought to become more mature in our reactions to criticisms and recognise that this is an inescapable part of our life".

The second view propounded by the profession regards the expectations gap as a symptom of the evolutionary development of audit responsibilities; a direct consequence of the understandable time lags between the accounting profession identifying and responding to continually changing and expanding public expectations. For example, Tricker (1982) argued that corporate crises (defined broadly to include corporate collapse, undetected major frauds or even social disquiet at any abuse of corporate power) lead to new expectations of and requirements for accountability, which lead in turn to new demands on the audit function and eventually to changes in auditing standards and practice. In support of this, he noted how periods of high activity in audit standard setting exactly mirror the periods of major crisis in the corporate sector. This view implies a profession gradually and constructively responding to the changing expectations of society.

Both these approaches portray the existence of an expectations gap as being somewhat autonomous of the auditing profession, dependent on public misconceptions or changing demands of auditing. In contrast, such implicitly passive perspectives on the nature and influence of professional action would be challenged by an emerging body of literature that has questioned the extent to which the type of self-regulatory monopoly granted to the audit profession in Anglo–Western countries operates in the public interest (see Willmott, 1986, 1989; Sikka *et al.*, 1989; Booth & Cocks, 1989; Robson & Cooper, 1989; Hines, 1989*a,b*; Humphrey & Moizer, 1990; Hopwood, 1990; Tinker, 1985). Here, the audit profession is not regarded as a selfless, neutral body, responding diligently to the changing dictates and expectations of society. Rather, it is seen in a more proactive, economically interested light, needing to maintain the appearance of independent, highly technically competent individuals in order to defend and advance its members' interests. Symbolic traits of independence, trustworthiness, altruism and expertize are viewed as professional mystiques that together with the existence of a professional monopoly of labour and a mutually dependent relationship with the state serve to enhance the remuneration of members of the profession (Humphrey & Moizer, 1990, p. 222). As argued by Hines (1989*b*, p. 85), in relation to accountants, auditors compete for work not only on the basis of a body of auditing knowledge, but on *claims* to an auditing knowledge, or at least the *appearance* of auditing knowledge. Given such alternative viewpoints, it becomes very difficult to see how the audit expectations gap, with all its potential questioning of the nature and standard of audit performance, can be studied in virtual isolation of the actions of the audit profession. Indeed, it can be argued that the profession retains a considerable interest in seeking to capture the debate on audit expectations and hence to have some control over its outcome.

This paper seeks to examine the nature of the response of the audit profession to expectations questions. The starting point for our investigation is a historical review of the relationship between auditors and their critics. The purpose of this review is to establish that concern over the ambiguities in the role and responsibilities of the auditor is not a new phenomenon, but has existed for over 100 years. Further, despite the fact that it is the same basic aspects of auditor performance which give rise to concern at different points during that period and in differential national environments (although the terms in which the debate is conducted have varied), the expectations gap has proved resilient against solution and shows little sign of reducing. These observations give considerable justification for looking at the contribution of the accounting profession's response to the removal or continuation of expectations questions. The remaining sections of the paper focus on the responses of the accounting profession to the expectations gap, and the possibilities of change in auditing during the period of the last 20 years. Greatest attention is given to the situation in the United Kingdom, although reference is also made to other environments. The paper highlights a number of identifiable strands in the nature of the profession's responses, comprising defensive strategies focusing on "educating" the public about auditor responsibilities, and reassuring them as to the standards of audit performance, and strategies based on attempts to convey a willingness to extend the scope of the audit. The paper concludes by suggesting that the longevity and resilience of the audit expectations gap are largely a consequence of the structure of auditing in Anglo–Western countries, and the inherent conflicts and contradictions in a self-regulated audit function.

A Brief History of the Last 100 Years of the Expectations Gap

Within the United Kingdom context the appointment of the professional accountant as an independent auditor dates from the 1840s, and in common with many other British accounting developments was closely connected with the growth of the railways (Edwards, 1989, p. 266). Auditors helped with the form of the published accounts as well as providing an audit service. Eventually, the process became enshrined in statute law. The Companies Act of 1862 and the Banking and Joint-Stock Companies Act of 1879 required company auditors to report to shareholders on whether or not in their opinion a company's balance sheet was full and fair and properly drawn up so as to exhibit a true and fair view of the state of the company's affairs as shown by the books of the company. Despite such legal stipulations, the role and responsibilities of company auditors had not gained universal acceptance, and remained very much open to debate. As Littleton commented, the statutes did not pass without criticism, with some clauses being open to an interpretation that:

> "little need be done by the auditor except a formal examination of vouchers and a comparison of the items in the statement with the ledger. Such a perfunctory examination would of course leave the possibilities of irregularities very largely uninvestigated and the 'audit' would therefore be of little value" (Littleton, 1966, pp. 313–314).

The Institute of Chartered Accountants of England and Wales (ICAEW) was formed in 1880 and soon found itself having to respond to public concern about the work of auditors. Indeed, the 1880s and 1890s provided early evidence of what was to become a regular event, when the auditing profession debates its role in public amidst the fallout of a celebrated court case or series of cases. Towards the end of the nineteenth century there had been a number of cases which were perceived by non-auditors to involve an element of audit failure. These included, in 1878, the spectacular failure of the incorporated City of Glasgow Bank. By overvaluing assets, undervaluing debts and misdescribing balance sheet items, the bank's directors had for years hidden its insolvency while continuing to pay dividends (see Chatfield, 1977).

The City of Glasgow Bank failure generated a lively discussion in the main accounting periodical, *The Accountant* (established in 1874), about the expectations that were held about the work of auditors. Whilst the term "expectations gap" was not used, the content of some of the speeches and articles would not have looked out of place in more recent debates on the topic. The editorial of *The Accountant* of 3 November 1883, for instance, made an ironic attack on the misconceptions of shareholders:

> "We would suggest that in future the auditors' certificates should, in accordance with the defence now made for them, run thus: We have been allowed to audit not from month to month, but only once a year; having had too little time to make an exhaustive report, because the documents are required for the printer; knowing that shareholders are generally impatient to get through the business; being paid a fee out of all proportion to the work required to be done; and being aware that the voting power is in the absolute control of the Board—certify that, so far as we, under these disabilities, can ascertain and dare disclose the facts, it is all right. This would at any rate let shareholders know from the certificate, as we know from the general chorus of certifiers, what the true meaning and value of the certificate really amounts to. Our complaint was and is that at present they do not know this, but are led and are meant to imagine that bladders are lanterns and auditors' certificates proofs of all excellences and complete solvency and security...." (quoted by Brief, 1975, p. 289–290).

In a similar vein, in an address to the Students' Society of London in 1885, the president of the ICAEW stressed the need for the profession to educate an unenlightened public:

> "It appears to me to be the rooted opinion of an unenlightened public and of the ignorant portion of the press that an auditor must have failed in his duty if a fraud has been effected, whether it is eventually discovered or not... The result of this ignorance has been that in cases where such frauds have been discovered, an immediate outcry is raised for the dismissal of the auditor. Without any careful investigation or enquiry into the facts, his utter ruin is decreed, and the whole profession is attacked and menaced. Audits performed by us are described as useless, wasteful and dangerous; as deceitful and fraudulent pretences, and as traps laid to catch fees and deceive confiding clients and the public.... In my experience I have found men of ordinary business ability holding the most ridiculous opinions as to the power of a professional accountant to detect fraud and error.... Let us be open and frank with the public and our clients, endeavour to create a true public opinion of the value of our services, and the scope and limits of our capacity" (Griffiths, 1885, p. 27).

The audit expectations gap   **141**

The story remains strikingly similar throughout the twentieth century. Whilst the phrase "audit expectation gap" first appeared in the terms of reference of the Cohen Commission (AICPA, 1978), set up in 1974 by the American Institute of Certified Public Accountants (AICPA), the issues it incorporates have a far deeper rooted history. For example, it is possible to identify the existence of such a gap in the US in the 1930s. The cases of Ultramares Corporation vs. Touche, Niven and Company (1931) and McKesson and Robbins (1939) both highlighted dramatic failings on the part of auditors. Although Ultramares is principally remembered now for its consideration of the rights of third parties, it was not disputed that the auditors had failed to discover that the management of a rubber importer, Fred Stern and Company, had falsified entries in order to overstate accounts receivable. The court criticized Touche Niven for not clearly indicating the scope of their examination and particularly for failing to distinguish their statement of the audit's scope from their statement of opinion. The profession responded defensively by eliminating the word "certify" from the audit report to emphasize that the auditor's certificate was an opinion, not a guarantee. As Chatfield reflected:

> "His [the auditor's] examination of the books was not intended to prove anything, but simply to put his mind in contact with the company's affairs. His knowledge and his skill in applying audit techniques then allowed him to express a professional opinion of management's financial statements". (1977, p. 132).

The McKesson and Robbins case produced a comprehensive overhaul of audit priorities. The SEC committee investigating the case concluded that existing audit standards were inadequate and that the type of audit being performed was not serving even its ostensible purpose (Chatfield, 1977). As in the 1890s in the UK, the response of the accounting profession was tinged with educative tones, to reassure the public as to the profession's desire to operate in the public interest and to ensure that they held more realistic expectations of what auditors could deliver. The AICPA secretary at the time noted (see Miller, 1986, p. 35):

> "We find that the public has believed that the certified public accountant was an infallible superman; that the signature of a CPA invariably meant that everything was perfect; that it was unnecessary to read the accountant's certificate or the financial statements to which it was appended as long as the three major letters were in evidence... Whether through its own fault or not, the accounting profession seems to have been oversold. Its limitations have been overlooked, whilst its abilities have been emphasized. Now the public has been somewhat shocked to find that even auditors can be fooled by clever criminals".

Comparable tones were prominent in the comments of the distinguished professional accountant Carman G. Blough 1940, writing in 1940:

> "If there occurs any event which tends to shake the public confidence, and if it gains sufficient attention, sooner or later the Government is likely to turn its attention to the problem. Such an unfortunate event occurred during the past year which has resulted in some critical comment regarding auditing procedures. Financial writers, congressmen, reformers, and others, some informed, and some uninformed, some friendly to accountants some unfriendly, have been free with their suggestions and with their criticisms

of the public accountants.... The best way that I can imagine to prevent unwise public action is for us to work more energetically in the public interest and at the same time to educate the public to an understanding of what we are doing" (p. 40 and p. 42).

In the more recent past in the UK, the 1970s were characterized by a number of Department of Trade investigations which often included critical comments on auditing matters.[1] For example, auditors were criticized for failure to detect error, failure to collect specific pieces of evidence, not acting on evidence which had been collected, inadequate reporting and forming erroneous judgements on accounting treatments adopted by companies (Russell, 1991). The concern about auditor performance produced two investigations (the Cross Report, 1977 and the Grenside Report, 1978), which in turn generated the establishment of a Joint Disciplinary Scheme to investigate cases of public interest concerning auditors. The increased pressure on the auditing profession led to the setting up of the Auditing Practices Committee (APC) which developed the first set of Auditing Standards, published in 1980.[2] In 1978, there was also an attempt to pass a private members bill which would have had the effect of introducing a State Auditing Board with the responsibility for licensing and appointing corporate auditors, but the bill never made it into legislation (Sherer and Kent, 1988).

Despite these changes, however, in the 1980s the expectation gap has increasingly come to the fore in debates about auditing. The working party on the "Future of the Audit" (ICAEW, 1986) concluded that "there appears to be a considerable gap between the public's perception of the role of the audit and auditors' perception of that role". According to Tweedie (1987), the need for the profession to address this issue was the prime reason for the APC establishing its "Emerging Issues Task Force" in early 1987. The APC also set up a working party charged specifically with developing proposals to deal with the expectations gap. Rather than the gap reducing as a result of past changes and responses, it obstinately remains unbridged and appears to be as large in the 1990s as it was in the 1880s.

Further evidence of the unresolved problem of expectations is provided by the rise (somewhat more recent in the United Kingdom than in the United States) in litigation involving auditors, and also situations which, while they may not have resulted in litigation, have attracted considerable public exposure in the financial press and other media. Cases have arisen in which fraud has been found to exist but not reported by the auditors. Current *cause celebre* such as Ferranti, Barlow Clowes, Polly Peck and the Levitt Group have provided ammunition for a large amount of unfavourable press comment and a series of 436 parliamentary questions in the 2 years to February 1991 from two back-bench Members of Parliament about the role and regulation of auditors (see Accountancy, March 1991, p. 9).

The experience of other countries also tends to lead to the conclusion that the expectations gap is a continuing problem. In the US, several government and professional investigations have commented on aspects of audit expectations. In early 1974, the Commission on Auditor's Responsibilities (the Cohen Commission) was set up by the AICPA with the specific task of making recommendations on the appropriate responsibilities of auditors. In so doing, the Commission's terms of reference stated that it was to consider "whether a

gap exists between what the public expects or needs and what auditors can
and should reasonably expect to accomplish" (AICPA, 1978, p. 92). The AICPA
had been prompted to establish the Cohen Commission by the growing public
concern about the criticisms of the quality of auditor's performance. The
failure of auditors to detect or disclose failures or wrong doings by publicly
owned corporations (such as Equity Funding) was also officially stated as the
reason for the US government establishing a Senate Subcommittee on
Reports, Accounting and Management (the Metcalf Committee) in the Autumn
of 1975 to investigate and suggest ways of improving the accountability of
publicly owned corporations and their auditors (see Metcalf Report, 1978, p.
89). This was followed in 1976 by the setting up of the House (of Representatives) Subcommittee on Oversight and Investigations of the House Commerce
Committee (the Moss Committee) which was also concerned with standards
of corporate accountability. In Canada similar concerns led the Canadian
Institute of Chartered Accountants (CICA) to establish, in 1977, a "Special
Committee to Examine the Role of the Auditor" (the Adams Committee). This
group reported in 1978, soon after the Cohen Commission (see Johnston *et
al.*, 1980, for a discussion of the respective findings of the Adams and Cohen
investigations).

A feature common to all these studies was the finding that a gap between
performance and expectation did exist, and that this was not just due to
ignorance on the part of users of accounting information. According to the
Cohen Commission, generally users had reasonable expectations of auditor's
abilities and of the assurances they can give. It attributed the expectation gap
more to the public accounting profession's failure to react and evolve rapidly
enough to keep pace with changing business and social environment. Whilst
reaching different overall conclusions, the Metcalf Committee also called for
more visible regulatory procedures, noting that "the public is not willing to
accept things on faith today. Government and business leaders must demonstrate that they are worthy of the trust they ask of the public" (Metcalf,
1978, p. 90).

The Congressional findings that an expectation gap existed and that
auditors were underperforming were challenged (see Milne and Weber, 1981;
Benston, 1985). Benston (1985) undertook a detailed analysis of the Congressional recommendations and came to the conclusion that:

> "There is little evidence of collusion and other anticompetitive actions by
> CPA firms. Audit failures appear to be fewer than the optimal amount as a
> consequence of enforced minimum standards. Therefore, there would
> seem to be few valid arguments for additional regulation in the public
> interest. In fact, the arguments made in the Moss Report (1976) and in the
> Metcalf Committee's Staff Report (1976) are almost completely devoid of
> empirical or logical support. If enacted, they would increase auditing and
> regulatory costs and reduce competition. In any event, a principal aspect of
> the demand for regulation by legislators, journalists, academicians, and
> public interest activists appears to have been fulfilled. The legislators have
> had publicity, journalists have gotten copy, academicians received data and
> the opportunity of writing papers like this, and some public interest activists
> have had a shot at authority" (p. 74).

Nevertheless, the expectations gap continued to remain at the forefront of
debate in the 1980s. In 1985, the US accountancy profession was again put

under the spotlight of government investigation with the establishment of two Congressional committees. The Brooks Committee (officially, the Legislation and National Security Subcommittee of the House Committee on Government Operations) was concerned with the quality of CPA audits of federal expenditure, which had been reported as being substandard (with frequent non-compliance with professional auditing standards), while the Dingell Committee (officially the Subcommittee on Oversight and Investigations of the House Committee on Energy and Commerce) was established to investigate the "effectiveness of independent accountants who audit publicly owned corporations and the effectiveness of the SEC who audits those accountants". Again, the setting up of this committee came after a number of notable corporate failures where the role of the auditor had been called into doubt (for example, the cases of ESM Government Securities Inc., and Beverly Hills Savings and Loans Association).

In the course of the Dingell Committee's hearings, the "National Commission on Fraudulent Financial Reporting" (the Treadway Commission) was established. This commission reported in October 1987 with a number of recommendations including restatements of the auditor's responsibility for fraud detection and quarterly reporting (see AICPA, 1987). At the same time as the Treadway Commission was conducting its investigations, the profession's Auditing Standards Boards (ASB) launched a number of projects with the aim of reducing the expectation gap. These produced a series of new Statements on Auditing Standards (known as the expectation gap standards), covering such issues as the detection of fraud and illegal acts, the assessment of internal controls and audit reporting (see Journal of Accountancy, July, 1988, pp. 144–197).

The audit expectations gap has also continued to figure prominently in the 1980s in Canada. In 1986, the CICA established the Macdonald Commission (where the majority of members were not chartered accountants) with the specific task of investigating the "public's expectations of audits". This found considerable divergence between the public's expectations of auditors and auditor performance (CICA, 1988). As with the earlier 1970s studies it concluded that for the most part public expectations of auditors are reasonable and achievable. In the Commission's view "expectation gaps will only be narrowed by the profession's acceptance of the need for change and improvement" (p. 4) and its detailed report contained 50 recommendations as to ways by which the expectation gap could be narrowed. Similarly, in Australia, the president of the Institute of Chartered Accountants called on the profession to respond to public concern about the role of the auditor and to seek ways of narrowing the expectations gap, and in New Zealand research has been undertaken to investigate the nature of any expectation gap that may exist (Porter, 1988, 1991).

In addition to the above professional and governmental investigations, there have, during the last 2 decades, been numerous attitude surveys of auditors, preparers and users of financial statements, which have in effect tried to "measure" the expectations gap. These have provided striking evidence of the differing perceptions of auditors and non-auditors as to the functions performed by the present statutory external corporate audit (see, for example, Lee, 1970; Beck, 1973; Arthur Andersen, 1974; Baron *et al.*, 1977; Arrington *et al.*, 1983; Porter, 1988; Steen, 1990). Such studies have sometimes been criticized for methodological weakness (see Davidson, 1975) but they have produced a consistent picture of users of financial statements perceiving a broader function than that performed, or regarded as legitimate, by auditors or that required by legislation. The list of areas in which higher standards are perceived by users include the extent of testing, the accuracy of financial statements, the quality of management control and the financial status of the audited enterprise (for summaries, see CICA, 1988; Turley, 1985; Gwilliam, 1987; Holt & Moizer, 1990).

The overall conclusion from this review of the last 100 years is that the expectations gap appears to be a perennial problem. In addition, whilst it is possible to point to changes in the auditing environment prompting expectations questions, many issues have remained consistently on the expectations agenda, including the question of fraud detection arising from those occasions when a fraud came to light undetected by the auditor. It is of interest to ask why this should be the case, and why, despite the successive committees and inquiries which have investigated the gap and made recommendations for its reduction, the problem has not been resolved. Such questions have, however, persistently been subordinated to attempts to either define, identify and/or provide means to close the gap. In the remainder of this paper, questions concerning the enduring, static nature of the expectations gap are addressed, principally through an analysis of the responses of the UK auditing profession to expectations problems.

The Responses of the UK Auditing Profession to the Expectations Gap

The responses of the auditing profession in the United Kingdom to the expectations gap can be seen to have two apparently contrasting, but ultimately compatible, forms: a defensive response, stressing the misconceived nature of public expectations and perceptions regarding the role and performance of auditors; and a constructive response, seeking to convey a willingness to widen the scope of the audit. Both forms, and their interrelationship, will now be considered in turn.

Education and Reassurance. . . The Art of Protection

The predominant response of the UK profession to concerns about the audit function has been of a defensive, protective nature. This protective spirit has been reflected in two complementary arguments. At one level, the profession has emphasized the "unreasonable" nature of the investing (and wider) public's expectations of auditors. At another level, it has sought to reassure the public and regulators that, despite appearances to the contrary, all is well with the state of professional auditing and that corporate collapses and notable audit failures do not signify any deterioration in the general level of audit quality and performance.

Educating the Public In highlighting the need for the public to be better educated as to the "true" responsibilities of auditors, much emphasis has been placed upon the manner in which the profession informs the public of its responsibilities and duties. In this respect, changes to the wording of the audit report, and the publication of a number of professional statements describing in general terms what auditors do, have both been favoured as ways of closing the expectations gap.

Changing the Wording of the Audit Report Making changes to the wording of the audit report relies on a perception that users are being misled by the particularly arcane phraseology appearing in audit reports. Thus, the expectations gap is framed as a codification problem—that if users better understood the code being used by auditors in reporting their opinions, they would more accurately perceive the messages being given by the various forms of audit report. Research findings have frequently been seen to lend support to the need for changes in the form and content of audit reports. Divergences between the intended message of an audit report and the impression/meanings attributed to them by users have persistently been revealed in studies of both unqualified and qualified audit reports (for summaries, see Craswell, 1985; Holt & Moizer, 1990; CICA, 1988; Tweedie, 1987).

In the late 1970s, short form, standardized reporting was typically in favour, in the hope that it would reduce the inconsistency and complexity of audit reports and generate at-a-glance understanding (Holt & Moizer, 1990). The continuance of the expectations gap in the 1980s has somewhat discredited this exception-based approach to audit reporting and longer-form reporting has come back into favour (albeit in many cases in a standardized form). Typical of this movement was the ICAEWs (1986) report which called for more consideration of positive reporting and the inclusion in the audit report of explicit statements of assurance regarding each aspect of the auditor's responsibilities. The stylized, short form reports were seen as employing a rather complex codification system and emphasis was now placed on the adoption of a language more understandable to non-expert readers of reports. This latter form of reporting has recently been adopted in the US as a part of the AICPA's expectation gap standards—a change also recommended by the final report of the Treadway Commission (AICPA, 1987). The CICA (1988) also concluded that short form reports were being misinterpreted and recommended that the Canadian audit report be changed more closely to reflect the new US format. It saw consistency of format across nations as particularly important in the light of the increasingly global nature of capital markets. Given such developments, it is of little surprise to find the APC's working party on audit expectations publicly indicating that it plans to recommend lengthening the present UK audit report (Accountancy Age, November, 1989). However, longer does not always mean better and the new US audit report has been the subject of criticism from those who believe it has added to the confusion surrounding the audit process (see, for example, Financial Times, 17 August 1989).

Such strugglings and about-turns in attempts to "educate the public" via the audit report are by no means peculiar to the 1970s and 1980s. Indeed, our earlier historical survey was sprinkled with repeated calls for improved communication between auditors and users of audited financial statements.[3] That auditors have been tinkering with the wording of the audit report for the last 100 years does little to inspire confidence that the most recent, or even further, changes to the audit report are likely to provide a resolution of the expectation gap. Such observations, however, do help to pinpoint the particular problems facing educative initiatives. If, underneath all the apparent confusion regarding the work of auditors, there was one all embracing definition of the audit function, the outcome of an educative initiative (such as changing the wording of the audit report) could be expected to be far less contentious. However, such unanimity does not exist. Far from there being an agreed underlying conceptual base for auditing, theoretical studies of auditing continue to offer quite sharp contrasts in the possible interpretations of the role and purpose of auditing. Most notable is the distinction between the view that auditing is a socially-oriented function in which auditors are portrayed as ethical, socially responsible individuals (Mautz & Sharaf, 1961; Flint, 1988) and the view of auditing as a monopolistic business with auditors hiding behind the profitable mystique of professional judgement (see Willmott, 1986; Robson & Cooper, 1989).

Given divergent theoretical, and indeed legal (see Gwilliam, 1991), views as to the role and responsibilities of auditors, it would seem more appropriate to visualize the audit expectations gap debate as resembling a struggle between the various parties to the audit process, in which each seeks to ensure that a particular view of the audit remains in the ascendancy. In such a context, educational initiatives can be seen as a possible mechanism by which certain preferred positions are protected. In this respect, it is notable how profession-led educational exercises and discussions are usually framed in terms of a lack of understanding on the part of non-auditors as to the role of auditing, and how rarely they extend to a debate as to what the role of the auditor should be, or provide more information on the nature and quality of audit performance. This is well reflected in the move towards longer-form audit reporting, where the dominant emphasis has been on providing information on generalized audit responsibilities rather than the detailing of specific considerations and findings affecting the enterprise which has been audited. The intention, therefore, appears to be to give to readers more information about auditing, rather than more information about the results of the audit. As such, it is not surprising to find some commentators noting that the recent changes in the American audit report will not be seen as unselfish, socially-orientated concessions on the part of the auditor, but rather as a self-serving retreat from responsibility by the audit profession (Neebes & Roost, 1987).

Publication of Professional Auditing Statements   Similar protective themes are evident in other published professional auditing statements. The Auditing Practices Committee (APC), since its formulation in 1976, has issued a series of Auditing Standards and Guidelines, and a variety of *ad hoc,* specially commissioned reports, known as Audit Briefs (see APC, 1986, for a summary of the first 10 years of the APC). Not surprisingly from a committee which was set up in the face of a growing public and governmental questioning of audit performance to "satisfy our critics and political circles outside" (APC, 1978, p.

50), much of its output has been regarded in a protective, legitimating spirit. As such, it is seen as having done little either to expand the boundaries of audit practice or to provide clearer depictions of the precise nature of auditing performance (see Booth & Cocks, 1989; Sikka *et al.*, 1989; Davison, 1981). Reflections of this spirit can be found in the APC's publication of an audit brief on the role of the audit. Entitled "What is an Audit" (Buckley, 1980), the document provided minimal discussion, or even acknowledgement, of the varying possibilities as to what an audit could comprise, focusing instead on descriptions of audit responsibilities derived from companies legislation, as interpreted by the profession, and the favoured approach to satisfying those responsibilities. With regard to Auditing Standards and Guidelines, the general acknowledgement within the profession that they amount to little more than codifications of the established practices of the largest audit firms (APC, 1986; Moizer *et al.*, 1987) points again to a concern with legitimacy and the maintenance of an appearance, rather than the active pursuit, of high professional standards and the protection of the public interest. Indeed, some have severely questioned the efficacy of Auditing Standards and Guidelines in even ensuring compliance with minimum standards, citing the lack of disciplinary action by the professional accounting institutes for inadequate audit performance (Sikka *et al.*, 1990), and the vague, general nature of some of the audit guidance. As Davison (1981, p. 63) commented:

> "The publications to date of the APC lack depth and give no more than obvious facts representing the lowest common ground: they in no sense form a comprehensive framework against which the effectiveness of an audit can be judged".

Booth and Cocks (1989) spoke of such professional practice rules as repre-senting practice in auditors' interests rather than the provision of a rigid codification of acceptable performance. In this vein, it can be argued that the predominant influence underlying the publication of Auditing Standards and Guidelines has been the desire to give an appearance of standardization and a rationalistic basis to audit expertize, without necessarily providing sufficient details by which the nature of audit expertise and audit performance can be gauged. As Hopwood (1990) noted, the profession's regulatory and standard-ization institutions have tended to become:

> "rhetorical bodies whose activities might have even reinforced and in-creased the gap which already existed between the generality of accounting concepts and the operational procedures of the craft. Responding to practical affairs in a piecemeal way, they have rarely adopted either a consistent or a proactive stance. They have also tended to avoid too close an involvement with the detailed functioning of the auditing craft" (p. 84).

In this regard, the questionable operational influence of Auditing Standards and Guidelines on audit practice is merely reinforced by the way such statements are littered with subjective terms such as reasonable, materiality,[4] adequacy, relevance, reliability, sufficiency and judgement, and by the fact that compliance with the more specific of the two types of publication (Auditing Guidelines) is not deemed to be mandatory by the professional accountancy bodies.

Whilst these observations may, as with the changes to the wording of the audit report, suggest a rather narrow "educational" process (in a sense of facilitating a varied, informed debate on the varying roles and performance of auditors), they offer the potential benefit to the auditing profession of both giving an impression of responding to public concern and of serving to reinforce the claimed validity of the profession's perspective. By repeatedly propounding favoured professional views on the role and responsibilities of auditors, they offer a potential closure of the expectations gap without any movement by the profession. In short, the more one is told by professional "experts" what an audit comprises, without the availability of views to the contrary, the more one is likely to accept such pronouncements.

Nevertheless, there remain limitations as to what such communications can, and have, achieved. Codifications of audit practice and professional pronouncements on the audit function retain a double-edged status in that the more specific they become, the more they undermine the mystical qualities of professional behaviour and judgement (a frequently noted critical factor underlying the power base of a profession—see Robson & Cooper, 1989; Hopwood, 1990). This raises the interesting paradox that, if the general public really knew the full extent of the work performed by auditors, then it may conclude that the audit service is rather overrated, which presumably is the last impression the auditors want to give. As stated by the CICA report, in commenting on market research showing favourable impressions of public accountants:

> "it may be of little comfort to the profession to know that a vast majority of the general and reader/investor publics are satisfied with the performance of auditors, if the profession concludes that the views of a substantial portion of both publics are based on a misperception of the role of the auditor" (CICA, 1988, p. 149).

Professional auditing pronouncements, and even annual corporate audit reports also have a limited circulation and readership, and the publicity attached to them is frequently far outweighed by that given to a dramatic corporate failure or the unearthing of a major fraud missed by the auditors. The deeply ingrained, heartfelt nature of such public and governmental expectations of the audit as an early warning system of impending financial failure (Tweedie, 1987) has been persistently reflected in investigations of the performance of the audit profession. The Macdonald Commission (CICA, 1988), for instance, concluded that better communication of the respective roles of auditors and management could have only a limited effect in reducing the expectations gap and saw a need for the audit to be more adaptive and receptive to change

Reassuring the Public

Consideration of a publicly perceived need for auditors to change brings into focus a second mode of response to the audit expectations gap, namely, one of reassurance, wherein the profession seeks to counter public concern over its performance by stressing that little, if anything, is wrong with the auditing profession and reasserting its claim of best serving the public interest. Much of this response has seen the profession attempting to maintain the image of the selfless, disinterested auditor; to reassure financial statement users and regulators that, despite, perceptions to the contrary, auditors remain independent, and are not being brow beaten by, or acting as the paid handservants of, corporate management.

The importance of auditors performing, and being seen to perform, in an unbiased, impartial manner has been highlighted repeatedly in the governmental and professional investigations reviewed earlier. Indeed, the Metcalf (1978) Report regarded independence as the auditor's single most valuable attribute. In terms of the expectation gap, the concern has been that auditors have not been operating in a sufficiently independent fashion, with competitive pressures adversely affecting audit quality.

The profession's defence against these concerns has rested on appeals to professional ideals and the need to trust professionals to behave in an appropriate, responsible manner. Economic arguments have also been invoked to support assertions as to the effectiveness of a self regulatory system, stressing that auditors will have an incentive to act in an independent way because of the effects on reputation of doing otherwise (see Moizer, 1991). In this respect, the often repeated view is that no audit firm could afford to stay in practice, given today's litigious environment, if it was not committed to high quality audit performance. The US-based chairman of (the then firm of) Deloitte, Haskins and Sells even went so far as to state that companies are now more concerned with audit quality than with audit fees (Financial Times, 6 October 1988) and that his firm saw a positive marketing advantage in publicising the fact that they had received fewer large writs for negligence than other large audit firms.

This type of reassurance can be found throughout the history of the expectations gap, serving to dampen down debate on audit performance, at least until auditing is implicated in the next major corporate scandal (Humphrey & Moizer, 1990). Their ability to alleviate and negate concerns about auditors' performance has much to do with the auditing profession's powerful role and position in society, its particularly favoured relationship with the state, and its continuing capacity to portray its practices as being rooted in a coherent, unbiased body of knowledge and expertize (Willmott, 1986; Robson & Cooper, 1989; Hines, 1989b; Hopwood *et al.* 1990). In this regard, it has been argued that concerns with the performance of the audit profession, have paradoxically served to strengthen it. By failing to challenge seriously the nature of the prevailing economic system, and the role, and claimed neutrality, of accounting and auditing within it, such debates are subsequently seen as offering the profession the opportunity to reaffirm its independent and selfless image (Willmott, 1989, p. 327). Acknowledged audit failures become classified as "one-offs", attributable to the failings of errant individuals. Rather than pointing to any inherent weaknesses or contradictions in the provision and regulation of audit services (Kaplan, 1987), such instances more often are dominated by restatements of the profession's commitment to quality and its pursuit of the public interest. As Willmott (1986) concluded:

> "the historical and contemporary response of the profession to market and state pressure for reform has been to re-affirm its technical, politically-neutral role and to represent its defensive and disorganised responses as

necessary adjustments, made in the public interest to further improve the quality and value of professional service" (p. 576).

Change may be inhibited because it is invariably the proposed changes, rather than the status quo, which are scrutinized and usually ultimately rejected for their questionable contribution to the public interest; for adding merely to the costs of regulation without producing any noticeable benefit. Reflections of the profession's ability to resist and dismiss what it regards as unsuitable change are readily apparent. In the last 20 years a whole host of recommendations have been put forward as ways of bolstering audit independence.[5] Yet there remains a remarkable similarity, for instance, between the recommendations of the Cohen and Metcalf investigations in the 1970s and those of the Treadway and Dingell investigations of the late 1980s. More recently, the development of legislation to implement the European Community (EC) Eighth Company Law Directive concerned with audit regulation, provided an opportunity to observe the approach of the UK profession to the prospect of changes in its regulatory environment.

The Eighth Directive affects UK auditors in a number of ways, including, for example, the educational requirements for qualification, recognition of UK qualifications in other EC states and vice versa, and the ability of audit firms to adopt corporate status. It is not possible to go into detail on all aspects of the Directive here (see Cooper *et al.*, 1989 for a discussion of its development and implementation), but in the context of this paper the most important aspects are those concerning the regulatory system for auditors and the possibility of the imposition of statutory controls related to auditor independence.

Briefly, three regulatory regimes were considered possible: (a) to give statutory powers to the professional bodies; (b) to allow the Secretary of State to recognize professional bodies for the purposes of both qualification and supervision, such recognition being revocable; and (c) to create a new tier of regulatory control involving representatives of the profession and the state in some form of supervisory council. Whichever alternative was adopted, the intention of the Directive was that the regulation of auditors should be legally enforceable in the sense that the rules governing auditors should be matters of public law (Cooper *et al.*, 1989). The options contrasted with the prior position where the members of certain professional bodies were recognized as suitable for appointment as auditors, but the rules and standards of those bodies were esentially matters of "private" or "self" regulation. In the area of independence, the consultative document issued by the UK government on implementation of the Directive (DTI, 1986) raised a variety of possible rules. These included compulsory rotation of audit appointments and the prohibition of the provision of audit and non-audit services to the same client. These suggestions, whether they were intended as serious possibilities or simply to give warning to the audit profession of the dangers of failure in their own regulatory approach, came as a shock to the profession, which had hoped that most of the threats of EC legislation had been averted in the drafting of the Directive (Cooper *et al.*, 1989).

The status of the Eighth Directive meant that some regulatory change was inevitable. With some exceptions, the UK profession favoured option (b), which was the system most akin to the existing system of audit regulation. However, it continued to resist the idea that independence should be subject to statutory control. Repeated assertions appeared in the accountancy press and submissions to government stressing both the quality of independence as an attitude of mind and the efficacy of the professional bodies in ensuring high ethical standards. In the event, the 1989 Companies Act implemented the professionally favoured regulatory alternative and did not introduce any further statutory controls on independence other than certain disclosure rules.

Professional resistance to change could be regarded as a consequence of ill-thought out proposals for reform; proposals with which a public spirited profession, given its greater knowledge of the regulatory system, could do little else but reject. Whilst the pursuit of the greater public good may well be the way that the profession would characterize its responses, it remains naive, however, not to acknowledge a degree of self-interest in the profession's actions. Indeed, in the case of the UK profession, interested influences can be detected in its responses to proposed regulatory change. Willmott (1989), for instance, noted how the profession at varying times had dismissed changes rooted in opposite ends of the regulatory spectrum—from the efficient markets view of regulation to a statutory, legislative approach. The spirit of the profession's response to the implementation of the Eighth Directive generally was one of damage limitation, with increased regulation tending to be viewed more from the perspective of an increased cost to the auditing profession than in terms of its potential benefit for the public interest activity of auditing.

Support for the profession's general defensiveness towards criticisms emanating from the expectations gap has come from some writers who have explicitly pointed to the lack of evidence of cases where it can be demonstrated that independence was compromised. Such writers have in turn criticized governmental committees for making recommendations for change based resultingly on little more than heresay and invention (see Hall, 1988; Benston, 1985; Milne & Weber, 1981). Nevertheless, whilst rigorous, statistical evidence on auditors' lack of independence remains understandably hard to document given its claimed status as an attitude of mind, anecdotal evidence of commercial pressure on auditor behaviour continues to abound (Stevens, 1988; Zeff, 1987; Kaplan, 1987). Further, both case-based research and historical analysis are starting to provide practice-based support for concerns regarding the audit function by revealing the extent of the difference between the acclaimed public-spiritedness of the auditing profession and the commercial, business-orientated nature of day-to-day audit practice (e.g. see Humphrey & Moizer, 1990; Power, 1990; Hopwood *et al.*, 1990; Willmott, 1989; Preston *et al.*, 1990).

Acting Creatively?: Accepting Additional Duties and Responsibilities

Increasingly, the continuing concern regarding audit performance would appear to have stimulated a third professional response to the expectations gap—an apparently creative response wherein the auditing profession puts itself forward as willing to accept additional duties and to consider the need for extending auditing to include areas not currently covered, e.g. reporting on interim financial statements (not currently required in the United Kingdom) and assessing aspects of financial management. It is important to recognize that in this shopping list approach to audit responsibilities the possible duties are seen as additional, as added extras to what is a currently valid set of activities, rather than necessary adjustments to a defective product. In this way, the developments are put forward as a way of "adding value" to the basic audit (Steen, 1989; Davis, 1990) and characterized as a positive approach to enhancing audit service. For example, a number of senior audit partners have suggested that more responsibility could be accepted in the area of fraud, but as an extra to the current audit, and at a price.

In a subtle way, therefore, the profession's response has been to try to change the character of the debate from one where the focus is on the possibility that auditing as it is practised is not fulfilling desired objectives to one which is concerned with new possibilities for enhancing an already acceptable product. The apparently constructive offer of new services is therefore consistent with the more traditional, protective defence of the status quo. Indeed, whilst the profession continues to stress its commitment to the public interest, its actions in respect of the acceptance of additional duties portrays a rather narrow, self-interested, commercially-orientated depiction of the public interest—both in terms of the manner in which the additional duties are specified and the precise nature of the duties being suggested.

In itself, the emphasis on the audit as a package of services is indicative of an approach which regards auditing as a commodity, or a set of commodities, to be sold at the appropriate price, rather than a service performed, at least partially, for reasons of the public interest. The predominant direction in which offers of enhanced service possibilities are made also questions the broadness of auditors' perceived public interest duties. Such services are not directed principally at shareholders, or other users of corporate financial reports, but to the preparers of financial information (and ultimately, the audit paymasters)—corporate management. Suggestions for adding value to the audit normally involve the provision of certain consultancy type services, such as evaluating aspects of financial management and reviewing information systems, but with a view to reporting internally to management, not externally. Even additional fraud reviews are discussed in terms of the auditor's report to management. Audit firms' manuals, which set out their philosophy and approach to the conduct of audits, frequently refer to the need to identify opportunities for giving constructive advice to management, to offer consultancy services and to increase the scope of work to meet additional objectives. There is a marked tendency for the major firms' methodologies to stress the benefits of an audit not in terms of any societal role and contribution to decision making, but as a commercial service to the management of the company being audited (Turley & Cooper, 1991).

Examination of the nature of some of the "additional" duties being subscribed to also casts doubt on any public-spirited motives underlying the actions of the audit profession. This is well illustrated by considering the nature of the auditor's responsibility for fraud detection—a persistently fundamental element of the expectations gap debate. In the UK, according to the relevant Auditing Guideline (APC, 1990), the primary responsibility for the prevention and detection of irregularities and fraud rests with an enterprise's management. The auditor's principal responsibility is seen as reporting on the truth and fairness of the enterprise's financial statements, and any duty for fraud detection is restricted to any resultant distortion of that true and fair view. Recent developments, involving auditing firms offering additional fraud reviews and systems evaluations, give an impression of the auditing profession lending its expertize to help management execute its due responsibilities for the prevention and detection of fraud. Such a tone is evident in publications emanating from the large accounting firms:

> "We are conscious that this subject is one of considerable concern to management, and to non-executive directors, and that in dealing with it you will most naturally turn to your accountancy and financial advisors. Ernst & Young has therefore invested in developing a systematic approach to combating the threat of fraud" (Ernst & Young, 1991, p. 8).

However, such an impression belies the rather more controversial history attached to the construction of fraud detection responsibilities of auditors. Indeed, uptil the 1940s the detection of fraud was still seen by auditors as the primary objective of the audit (Brown, 1962). Since that time, pronouncements of the professional auditing bodies throughout the world have tended to displace it with the broader objective of reporting on the fairness of a company's financial statements. Lee (1986, p. 23) asserted that such a switch reflected the growing concern of users with the quality of financial information and the tendency of company management to assume more responsibility for fraud prevention and detection, and the belief that the cost of searching out fraud and error by external audit had become uneconomic.

Other writers, however, attribute a much more proactive and self-interested role for the audit profession in bringing about such a change. Brown (1962) suggested that the profession's down playing of this responsibility was largely a response to the massive undetected fraud revealed in the McKesson and Robbins case referred to earlier. As Willingham (1975) notes:

> "perhaps the discussion of the auditor's responsibility for the detection of fraud has not yet diminished because it was a stated audit objective for over 400 years and was removed as an objective by the profession rather than by a change in the demand of clients of accounting firms. A solicitous consuming public could reinstate it" (p. 19).

Gwilliam (1987) expressed concern at the lack of explanation for the changed emphasis with regard to fraud detection, particularly when it was clear that courts or regulatory bodies have continually stressed the importance of the auditors' responsibility in this respect.

The pressure concerning auditors' responsibility for fraud detection has continued in the 1980s. The UK government, in response to a serious questioning of the role of the auditor in such scandals as DeLorean and Johnson Matthey Bank[6] and to a growing concern as to levels of corporate fraud "invited" the auditing profession to rethink its role regarding fraud detection (Accountancy Age, 25 October 1985, p. 4). A number of working parties were set up and the opinions of auditors surveyed. The outcome of these activities was that the profession reported a great reluctance amongst auditors to accept any extension in their responsibility for the detection of fraud (Allen & fforde, 1986). The issue of the auditor's duty in respect of fraud has continued to remain on the agenda, however, with further corporate scandals and developments in financial services legislation (see Humphrey *et al.,* 1991).

An Auditing Guideline on fraud was eventually finalized and issued by the APC in 1990, some 5 years after its initial draft guideline was published (APC, 1990). Whilst giving some recognition to a duty for auditors in relation to certain illegal acts apart from fraud, the main focus of attention and debate in the development of professional guidance in the 1980s has been the reporting of fraud by auditors to various regulatory bodies. On the basic issue of fraud detection, the profession has conceded little, if anything. In fact, the lack of expansion in this respect remains one of the few consistencies amongst all the proposals put forward by a variety of professional reports issued in the mid 1980s on the subject of auditors and fraud (Humphrey *et al.,* 1991). As such, the professional response has been quite consistent with the general defensive pattern outlined above. First, it has been argued that the auditor's role is misunderstood; that the odd undetected fraud and ensuing corporate collapse is not a serious indictment of the standard of professional audit practice; and that education regarding the responsibilities of management is what is required to resolve expectations differences. Second, the audit profession has creatively shifted the focus of debate, partly with the aid of financial services legislation, from issues of underperformance on fraud detection, to issues of extra performance on reporting to regulators and to the voluntary provision of much needed, but additional, fraud prevention and detection services. In the latter respect, it is illuminating that a brochure produced by Ernst & Young (1991) explaining the services offered to help corporate management in their fight against fraud fails to make any mention of the contribution of the annual external audit, choosing instead to stress such remunerating extras as compliance reviews, information systems security services and discovery action. Further, whilst citing findings from the "Fraud '89" survey (Ernst & Young, 1989) regarding the extent of fraud, the brochure rather conveniently fails to mention that the survey had also revealed strong support amongst corporate management for auditors assuming a greater responsibility in the detection of fraud![7]

It remains to be seen what impact such efforts on the part of the profession will have on expectations of the auditor and fraud. The historical precedents in the self-regulatory audit environment, however, do little to contradict views reported from within the Department of Trade and Industry, which may continue to retain a certain appropriateness:

> "management and shareholders see an important role for auditors generally, and the prevention and detection of fraud in particular and there is a wide gap between these expectations and the view of the auditors' responsibilities offered in the proposed guidelines" (Department of Trade and Industry spokesperson, reported in Accountancy Age, 9 March 1989, p. 3).

The Expectations Gap: an Inevitable Feature of a Self-regulated Audit Function?

The writing of this paper was in a large part stimulated by the lack of consideration given in the literature on audit expectations to the static nature of the expectations gap. As the paper shows, the issues covered by the expectations gap have remained strikingly similar since the emergence of the term nearly 25 years ago. Further, issues such as the fraud detection responsibilities of auditors, concerns about auditors' independence, public interest reporting and the meaning of audit reports have a history far outliving that of the phrase "expectations gap". Neither is it just in terms of the subject matter of the expectations gap that historical similarities occur. The recommendations of various committees and professional/governmental investigations as to how to close an expectations gap have repeatedly borne a considerable likeness. The pattern which thus emerges from a historical analysis of the audit expectations gap is far less convenient for the audit profession than Tricker's (1982) thesis that corporate crisis places enhanced demands on processes of regulation and accountability, which in turn produces changes in the nature and standards of audit practice. What appears more appropriate is evidence of a wealth of concern and investigation following a notable corporate (audit) failure, followed by reflection and reconsideration on the part of the audit profession and appropriate governmental regulatory agencies, leading to some, albeit minor, change but also a watering down of controversial reforms and a gradual settling down of the audit services market—at least until the next major crisis or scandal when the same issues are addressed and similar recommendations for change put forward (see Humphrey, 1991).

The great difference between the above two depictions is the active consideration that the latter gives to the interested nature of the activities of the audit profession in both framing the content of the expectations gap and in making and implementing recommendations and strategies designed to close the gap. Indeed, not giving explicit attention to such aspects of the audit profession, or promoting rather one-dimensional, public-serving perspectives on professionalism, would appear to be a general failing of much of the existing literature attempting to explain the expectations gap, resulting in solutions being proposed without adequate consideration of their historical significance or the context in which they are to be implemented. Debates on audit expectations and the ways to close any gap continue to be characterized with a high degree of hope—seemingly unable to recognize the tinges of *deja vu*, with (failed) solutions propounded 20 years ago being re-invented, re-implemented and subsequently returned to the shelf to await the next search for a "new" solution to the expectations gap.

This paper has sought to focus explicitly on the responses of the auditing profession, principally in the United Kingdom, to the expectations gap. Through historical analysis informed by emerging perspectives questioning the nature of professionalism and serving the public interest, it has been argued that the continued perpetuation of the expectations gap is, at least in part, a consequence of the profession's responses to the gap. Whether through attempts to "better educate" the public as to what the profession regards as the appropriate responsibilities of auditors, or to reassure the public and relevant government agencies as to the standards of audit performance, or in conveying a willingness to widen the scope of the audit, the profession's responses have been of a largely protective, defensive nature. The expectations gap has thus been classified by the profession as a problem caused by the public's misunderstanding of the audit function (the "blame the victim" thesis—Kaplan, 1987), by over-exaggerated responses to the isolated failings of individual auditors, and by mis-appreciation of the extent to which the profession is actively responding to public interest demands and enhancing the quality of the audit service.

Such responses reflect the threat to the nature of a profession's operations and its claims to expertize. In this respect, the paper has argued that the audit profession has had, and still retains, a considerable interest in seeking to capture the expectations gap debate and thereby ensure that it has some control over its outcome. Indeed, the expectations gap debate may have served to enable the profession, given its existing powerful role and position in society, to convey an impression of responding to public concern; to reaffirm its independent and selfless image; to assert the validity of its own perspectives on the nature of the audit function; and to direct questioning away from the existing audit system to the limitations of proposed reforms and solutions for closing the expectations gap. As such, there are some grounds for arguing that the nature, and continuing existence, of the expectations gap debate provides an important legitimating and strategic role in enabling the profession to promote its commitment, and engender aspirations, to the development of a desired, all satisfying audit function. Such a practice can be seen as facilitating the profession's maintenance of the status quo and helping to stave off competition from state auditors or other forms of government intervention such as increased regulation.

If history can be taken as any precedent, the prospects for a major shift in professional perspectives on the expectations gap remain dim. The recurrent defensiveness of the audit profession would appear to be a reflection of a number of potentially inherent conflicts within a self-regulated auditing system. Conflict is engendered in the audit process at the level of operational structure because auditors are placed in positions where their appointment and the nature of their work is capable of being, or at least being seen to be, influenced significantly by those (corporate management) on whom they are reporting. Conflict, however, goes beyond a management–public interest dichotomy, for behind such socially constructed terms as "serving the public interest", there are a variety of parties with different interests in, and demands on, the audit function—from creditors to shareholders and potential investors to government and associated regulatory agencies and, not least, to the private-sector audit firms themselves. With respect to the latter, there exists basic tensions between levels of audit quality and the profitability of audits, particularly given the relative unobservability of audit work (see Moizer, 1991). Such conflict is merely compounded when it comes to communicating the results of an audit. Where at one level, the lack of visibility of audit work can cause professional concern about audit quality, any communications which seek to place such work, and its characteristics, more clearly in the public gaze can serve, in turn, to undermine audit profitability by clarifying the probabilistic nature of a product sold on its risk-education characteristics.

Acknowledgement of such conflicts go some way to helping to understand the defensive nature of the profession's responses to the expectations gap—by pointing to its inability to act in any other manner given the institutional pressures and diversity of interests to be served by the audit function. How much more comfortable, and less costly, to seek to preserve the status quo, by falling behind claims of public ignorance and misconception, persuasive reassurances and the qualities of public-serving professionalism. The analysis in this paper, with the resultant recognition of the inherent conflicts in the auditing system, however, does not provide a mandate for excusing further action on the part of the auditing profession and relevant government regulatory bodies. Nor, at the other extreme, does it provide specific and definitive solutions to the expectations gap. Rather, the principal benefit rests in the spirit of the messages coming from the analysis, and particularly the view that the expectations gap is unlikely to be reduced if responses to it are left solely in the hands of the auditing profession. In this respect, we draw close parallels to the conclusions of Hopwood (1990) on the efficacy of self-regulation:

"Both accounting and auditing are subject to highly charged and interested pressures on the exercising of the very considerable discretion which presently exists. And in both arenas the active participants in managerial and auditing circles adopt a most cautious stance towards the delimitation of that discretion by any form of regulatory intervention. Equally, however, none of the parties is prepared to engage in an open and explicit discussion of the interested and political nature of what they do. Appeals are still made to the myths and conventional wisdoms of the past, however distant these might be from the practicalities of today, and I cannot see that changing. Unfortunately that is most likely to mean that we will continue to have accounting and auditing policy making institutions that have an ambiguous relationship to practical affairs and still engage in an stylised form of double-talk, knowing what is going on but being unable to say so".

Acknowledgements

The Financial Support of the Auditing Research Foundation of the Institute of Chartered Accountants in England and Wales facilitated the preparation of this paper and is gratefully acknowledged.

Notes

1. The Department of Trade and Industry (previously the Department of Trade) is the UK government department with responsibility for business and commercial affairs, including corporate governance and regulation. It has the power (and in some circumstances the duty) to appoint inspectors to investigate company affairs to establish the facts regarding any alleged irregularities in the way a company has been run.
2. In April 1991, the UK professional accountancy bodies agreed to replace the Auditing Practices Committee with the Auditing Practices Board (APB). The main changes from APC to APB concern membership and selection for membership, which is now to include more representation from outside the profession, and authority to issue standards and guidelines, which moves to APB whereas previously APC developed these statements but they were issued by the individual bodies. It is as yet too early to comment on the significance and effect of this change. To begin with, APB will adopt the work programme of APC providing continuity with the previous system, which is the basis of the comments in this paper.
3. An early example of the debate can be found in 1894 following the presentation of a paper by J. S. Harmood Banner which the chairman of the meeting summed up in the following terms: "Whether the certificate should be long or short, whether it should say absolutely what has been done, or simply, as some speaker indicated, what had not been done, must depend very much on the judgement and discretion of individual members" (Harmood Banner, 1894, p. 91).
4. Lee (1984) noted that the term materiality appears 126 times in Auditing Standards and Guidelines published at that time.

5. These have included peer review systems, the development and strengthening of audit committees, the rotation of audit appointments, the prohibition of auditors performing non-audit services for a company they also audit, the declaration in company financial statements of non-audit fees paid to the auditor, and the establishment of state auditing boards (see Moizer, 1991).
6. The latter resulting in its auditors paying a reported £49 million to Johnson Mathey and the Bank of England in out of court settlements.
7. Of 200 large corporations surveyed in the UK, more than two-thirds agreed that external auditors should be expected to detect substantial frauds (Ernst & Young, 1989, p. 8).

References

American Institute of Certified Public Accountants (AICPA), *Report Conclusions and Recommendations of the Commission on Auditor's Responsibilities* (Cohen Commission) (New York: AICPA, 1978). Re-printed in *The Journal of Accountancy,* April, 1978, pp. 92–102.

American Institute of Certified Public Accountants (AICPA), *Report of the National Commission on Fraudulent Financial Reporting* (Treadway Commission) (New York: AICPA, 1987).

Allen, R. & fforde, W., *The Auditor and Fraud,* Audit Brief (London: APC, 1986).

Arrington, C. E., Hillson, W. A. & Williams, P. F., "The Psychology of Expectations Gaps: Why is there so much Dispute about Auditor Responsibility", *Accounting and Business Research,* Autumn, 1983, pp. 243–250.

Arthur Andersen & Co., *Public Accounting in Transition: American Shareholders View the Role of Independent Accountants and the Corporate Reporting Controversy* (Chicago: Arthur Andersen & Co., 1974).

Auditing Practices Committee (APC), *True & Fair, No. 7,* Spring, 1978.

Auditing Practices Committee (APC), *APC: The First Ten Years* (London: APC, 1986).

Auditing Practices Committee (APC), *"The Auditor's Responsibility in Relation to Fraud, Other Irregularities and Error"* (London: APC, 1990).

Baron, C. D., Johnson, D. A., Searfoss, D. G. & Smith, C. H., "Uncovering Corporate Irregularities: Are We Closing the Expectations Gap?", *The Journal of Accountancy,* October, 1977, pp. 14–24.

Beck, G. W., "The Role of the Auditor in Modern Society: An Empirical Appraisal", *Accounting and Business Research,* Spring, 1973, pp. 117–22.

Benston, G. J., "The Market for Public Accounting Services—Demand, Supply and Regulation", *Journal of Accounting and Public Policy,* Vol. 4, 1985, pp. 33–80.

Blough, C. G., "The Auditor's Responsibility to the Investor", a 1940 Article Reprinted in W. G. Shenkir (ed.), *Carman G. Blough—His Professional Career and Accounting Thought* (New York, Arno Press, 1978).

Booth, P. & Cocks, N., "Power and the Study of the Accounting Profession", in D. J. Cooper and T. M. Hopper (eds), *Critical Accounts* (Basingstoke: MacMillan, 1989).

Brief, R. P., "The Accountant's Responsibility in Historical Perspective", *Accounting Review,* April 1975, pp. 285–97.

Brown, R. G., "Changing Audit Objectives and Techniques", *Accounting Review,* October, 1962, pp. 696–703.

Buckley, R., *What is an Audit?,* Audit Brief (London: APC, 1980).

CICA, *Report of the Commission to Study the Public's Expectation of Audits, Macdonald Commission* (Toronto: CICA, 1988).

Chatfield, M., *A History of Accounting Thought* (Huntington, New York: Robert E. Krieger, 1977).

Cooper, D., Puxty, A., Lowe, A., Robson, K. & Willmott, H., "(In)stalling European Standards in the UK: The Case of the Eighth Directive on the Regulation of Auditors", Paper Presented at the European Institute for Advanced Studies in Management Workshop on the Eighth Directive, Brussels, September, 1989.

Craswell, A., "Studies of the Information Content of Qualified Audit Reports", *Journal of Business Finance and Accounting,* Spring, 1985, pp. 93–116.

Gross Report, "Report of a Committee under the Chairmanship of the Rt Hon the Lord Cross of Chelsea", *Accountancy,* December, 1977, pp. 80–86.

Davidson, L., "The Role and Responsibilities of the Auditor: Perspectives, Expectations and Analysis", Unpublished Background Paper for the AICPA Commission on Auditors' Responsibilities, 1975.

Davis, R., *Added Value to the External Audit,* Audit Brief (London: APC, 1990).

Davison, J., "Accountancy's Golden Goose", *Management Today,* May, 1981, pp. 60–65.

Department of Trade and Industry, *Regulation of Auditors—Implementation of the EC Eighth Company Law Directive,* Consultative Document, 1986.

Edwards, J. R., *A History of Financial Accounting* (London: Routledge, 1989).

160 **C. Humphrey** *et al.*

Ernst & Young, *Fraud, '89: The Extent of Fraud Against Large Companies and Executive Views on What Should be Done About it* (London: Ernst & Young, 1989).

Ernst & Young, *Fraud: How to Fight it!* (London: Ernst & Young, 1991).

Flint, D., *Philosophy and Principles of Auditing—An Introduction* (Basingstoke: MacMillan, 1988).

Grenside Report, "Report on the Joint Committee Appointed to consider the Cross Report and Related Matters", *Accountancy*, June, 1979, pp. 124–32.

Griffiths, J. G., "Accountants and the Public", *The Accountant*, 26 December, 1885. Re-printed in M. Chatfield (ed.), *The English View of Accountant's Duties and Responsibilities 1881–1902*, pp. 25–29 (New York, Arno Press, 1978).

Gwilliam, D., *A Survey of Auditing Research* (London: Prentice Hall/ICAEW, 1987).

Gwilliam, D., "The Auditor's Liability to Third Parties", in W. S. Turley and M. J. Sherer (eds), *Current Issues in Auditing*, 2nd Edition, pp. 60–75 (Paul Chapman Publishing, 1991).

Hall, W. D., "An Acceptable Scope of Practice", *The CPA Journal*, February, 1988, pp. 24–33.

Harmood Banner, J. S., "The True Meaning of an Audit Certificate", *The Accountant*, 27 October 1894. Re-printed in M. Chatfield (ed.), *The English View of Accountant's Duties and Responsibilities 1881–1902* (New York: Arno Press, 1978, pp. 82–91).

Hines, R. D., "The Sociopolitical Paradigm in Financial Accounting Research", *Accounting, Auditing and Accountability*, Vol. 2, 1989a, pp. 52–76.

Hines, R. D., "Financial Accounting Knowledge, Conceptual Framework Projects and the Social Construction of the Accounting Profession", *Accounting, Auditing and Accountability*, Vol. 2, 1989b, pp. 72–92.

Holt, G. & Moizer, P., "The Meaning of Audit Reports", *Accounting and Business Research*, Spring, 1990, pp. 111–122.

Hopwood, A. G., "Ambiguity, Knowledge and Territorial Claims: Some Observations on the Doctrine of Substance Over Form: A Review Essay", *British Accounting Review*, Vol. 22, 1990, pp. 79–88.

Hopwood, A., Page, M. & Turley, S., *Understanding Accounting in a Changing Environment* (Prentice Hall/ICAEW, 1990).

Humphrey, C. G., "Audit Expectations", in W. S. Turley and M. J. Sherer (eds), *Current Issues in Auditing*, 2nd Edition, pp. 3–21 (Paul Chapman Publishing, 1991).

Humphrey, C. G. & Moizer, P., "From Techniques to Ideologies: an Alternative Perspective on the Audit Function", *Critical Perspectives on Accounting*, Vol. 1, 1990, pp. 217–238.

Humphrey, C. G., Turley, W. S. & Moizer, P., "Protecting Against Detection: The Case of Auditors and Fraud?", Paper Presented at the Third Inter-Disciplinary Perspectives on Accounting, University of Manchester, July, 1991.

Institute of Chartered Accountants in England and Wales (ICAEW), *Report of the Working Party on the Future of the Audit* (London: ICAEW, 1986).

Johnson, D. J., Morley Lemon, W. & Neumann, F. L., "The Canadian Study of the Role of the Auditor", *Journal of Accounting, Auditing and Finance*, Vol. 3, 1980, pp. 251–263.

Kaplan, R. L., "Accountants' Liability and Audit Failures: When the Umpire Strikes Out", *Journal of Accounting and Public Policy*, Vol. 6, 1987, pp. 1–8.

Lee, T. A., "The Nature of Auditing and its Objectives", *Accountancy*, April, 1970, pp. 292–296.

Lee, T. A., *Materiality: A Review and Analysis of its Reporting Significance and Auditing Implications*, Audit Brief (APC, 1984).

Lee, T. A., *Company Auditing*, 3rd Edition (Wokingham: Van Nostrand Reinhold, 1986).

Littleton, A. C., *Accounting Evolution to 1900*, 2nd Edition (New York: Russell & Russell, 1966).

Mautz, R. K. & Sharaf, H. A., *The Philosophy of Auditing* (New York: American Accounting Association, 1961).

Metcalf Staff Study Report, Prepared by the Subcommittee on Reports, Accounting and Management of the Committee on Governmental Affairs, United States Senate, Washington, D.C., U.S. Government Printing Office, December, 1976. Re-printed in *The Journal of Accountancy*, March, 1977, pp. 104–120.

Metcalf Report, "Improving the Accountability of Publicly Owned Corporations and Their Auditors", *Report of the Subcommittee on Reports, Accounting and Management of the Committee on Governmental Affairs* (Washington: United States Senate, 1978). Re-printed in *The Journal of Accountancy*, January, 1978, pp. 88–96.

Miller, R. D., "Governmental Oversight of the Role of Auditors", *The CPA Journal*, September, 1986, pp. 20–36.

Milne, F. & Weber, R., "Regulation and the Auditing Profession in the USA: The Metcalf Subcommittee's Recommendations Re-examined", *Accounting and Business Research*, Summer, 1981, pp. 197–205.

Moizer, P., "Independence", in W. S. Turley and M. J. Sherer (eds), *Current Issues in Auditing*, 2nd Edition (Paul Chapman Publishing, 1991, pp. 34–46).

Moizer, P., Turley, S. & Walker, D., "Reliance on Other Auditors: A U.K. Study", *Accounting and Business Research*, Autumn, 1987, pp. 343–352.

Neebes, D. L. & Roost, W. G., "ASB's Ten "Expectation Gap" Proposals—Will they do the Job?", *The CPA Journal*, October, 1987, pp. 23–25.

Olson, W. E., "Whither the Auditors", Speech to the Annual Meeting of the New York State Society of CPA's Bermuda, Reported in *The Journal of Accountancy*, August, 1973, pp. 9–10.

Porter, B. A., "Towards a Theory of the Role of the External Auditor in Society", Research Monograph, Massey University, 1988.

Porter, B. A., "The Audit-Expectation-Performance Gap—A Contemporary Approach", *Pacific Accounting Review*, Vol. 3, 1991, forthcoming.

Power, M., "From Common Sense to Expertise: Reflections on the Prehistory of Audit Sampling", Unpublished Working Paper, Department of Accounting and Finance, London School of Economics and Political Science, 1990.

Preston, A. M., Scarborough, D. P. & Chilton, R. C., "Transformations in the Moral Code and Ethics of the U.S. Accounting Profession, 1960–1988: A Tale of Changing Narratives of Legitimation", Working Paper No. 90-01, Institute for Accounting Research and Education, Boston University, January, 1990.

Robson, K. & Cooper, D. J., "Understanding the Development of the Accountancy Profession in the United Kingdom", in D. J. Cooper and T. M. Hopper (eds), *Critical Accounts* (Basingstoke: MacMillan, 1989).

Russell, P., "Department of Trade Investigations", in M. Sherer and S. Turley (eds), *Current Issues in Auditing*, 2nd Edition, pp. 76–98 (Paul Chapman Publishing, 1991).

Sherer, M. & Kent, D., *Auditing and Accountability* (London: Paul Chapman Publishing, 1988).

Sikka, P., Willmott, H. C. & Lowe, E. A., "Guardians of Knowledge and Public Interest: Evidence and Issues of Accountability in the U.K. Accountancy Profession", *Accounting, Auditing and Accountability Journal*, Vol. 2, 1989, pp. 47–71.

Stevens, M., "No More White Shoes", *Business Month*, April, 1988, pp. 39–42.

Steen, D. M. C. E., "Adding Value to the Audit", in *Auditing and the Future—Proceedings of an Auditing Research Conference* (Edinburgh, ICAS/ICAEW, 1989).

Steen, D. M. C. E., *Audits and Auditors—What the Public Thinks* (London: Peat Marwick McLintock, 1990).

Tinker, T., *Paper Prophets* (New York: Praeger, 1985).

Tricker, R. I., "Corporate Accountability and the Role of the Audit Function", in A. G. Hopwood, M. Bromwich and J. Shaw (eds), *Auditing Research: Issues and Opportunities* (London, Pitman Books, 1982).

Turley, W. S., "Empirical Research in Auditing", in D. Kent, M. J. Sherer and W. S. Turley (eds), *Current Issues in Auditing*, pp. 248–266 (Harper & Row Publishers Ltd., 1985).

Turley, W. S. & Cooper, M., *Auditing in the UK: Developments in the Audit Methodologies of Large Accounting Firms* (London: Prentice Hall/ICAEW, 1991).

Tweedie, D., "Challenges Facing the Auditor; Professional Fouls and the Expectation Gap", The Deloitte, Haskins and Sells lecture, University College, Cardiff, 30 April 1987.

Willingham, J. J., "Discussant's Response to Relationship of Auditing Standards to Detection of Fraud", *The CPA Journal*, April, 1975, pp. 18–21.

Willmott, H. C., "Organizing the Profession; A Theoretical and Historical Examination of the Development of the Major Accounting Bodies in the UK", *Accounting, Organizations and Society*, Vol. 11, 1986, pp. 555–82.

Willmott, H. C., "Serving the Public Interest? A Critical Analysis of a Professional Claim", in D. J. Cooper and T. M. Hopper (eds), *Critical Accounts* (Basingstoke: Macmillan, 1989).

Zeff, S. A., "Does the CPA Belong to a Profession?", *Accounting Horizons*, June, 1987, pp. 65–8.

Part II
Audit Quality and Auditor Reputation

[7]

Journal of Accounting and Economics 3 (1981) 113–127. North-Holland Publishing Company

AUDITOR INDEPENDENCE, 'LOW BALLING', AND DISCLOSURE REGULATION

Linda Elizabeth DeANGELO*

The Wharton School, University of Pennsylvania, Philadelphia, PA 19104, USA

Received August 1980, final version received January 1981

This paper investigates the allegations of the Commission on Auditors' Responsibilities and the Securities and Exchange Commission that 'low balling' on initial audit engagements impairs auditor independence. We demonstrate that, contrary to these claims, 'low balling' does not impair independence; rather it is a competitive response to the expectation of future quasi-rents to incumbent auditors (due, e.g., to technological advantages of incumbency). 'Low balling' in the initial period is the process by which auditors compete for these advantages. Critically, initial fee reductions are sunk in future periods and therefore do not impair auditor independence. The implications for current regulation governing changes of auditor (Accounting Series Release No. 165 et al.) and audit fees (Accounting Series Release No. 250) are also discussed.

1. Introduction

The practice of 'low balling' (setting audit fees below total current costs on initial audit engagements) has been cited by both the Securities and Exchange Commission and the Commission on Auditors' Responsibilities (Cohen Commission) as impairing auditor independence. While both parties have expressed concern about 'low balling', neither has established a causal link from this pricing practice to impaired independence. In other words, policy-makers lack a positive theory which ties the intertemporal fee structure of audit services to auditor independence. The purpose of this paper is to provide that link. We argue that the existence of client-specific quasi-rents to incumbent auditors both lowers the optimal amount of auditor independence and leads to 'low balling' in the initial period. Importantly, while these two effects are associated, 'low balling' does *not* itself impair auditor independence.

The expressed regulatory and professional view, however, is just the opposite. For example, the Report of the Commission on Auditors'

---

*The author wishes to thank the members of her dissertation committee: Y. Barzel, W.L. Felix (Chairman), E. Noreen, and E.M. Rice. Helpful comments were provided by H. DeAngelo, R. Adelsman, R. Leftwich, J. Zimmerman, R. Watts, N. Gonedes, W. Lanen, and the participants in the Accounting Workshop at the University of Rochester. Substantial improvements were made by incorporating the suggestions of the referee, G. Jarrell. The author retains the property rights to any remaining errors.

Responsibilities (Cohen Report) claims that 'low-balling' *itself* impairs auditor independence by generating a receivable from the client similar to an unpaid audit fee. Outstanding audit fees are proscribed by both the American Institute of Certified Public Accountants and the SEC because of their perceived negative impact on auditor independence. According to the Cohen Report (p. 121, emphasis added): 'We believe that accepting an audit engagement with the expectation of offsetting early losses or lower revenues with fees to be charged in future audits *creates* the same threat to independence' (as an unpaid audit fee). The allegation that 'low balling' impairs auditor independence has led the Cohen Commission to suggest that the Ethics Division of the AICPA should devote resources to the study of this 'problem'.[1]

The SEC has also expressed concern that 'low balling', i.e., price competition among auditors, may lead to an overproduction of dishonest reporting. In particular, the SEC is concerned that 'situations where the auditor agrees to a fee significantly less than is normal in order to obtain the client' may constitute a lessening of independence (Securities Act Release No. 33-5869). Accordingly, Accounting Series Release No. 250 requires disclosure of 'fee arrangements where the accountant has agreed to a fee significantly less than a fee that would cover expected direct costs in order to obtain the client'.

Despite professional and regulatory concern, 'low balling' on initial audit engagements appears to be a common practice.[2] Furthermore, 'low balling' is

---

[1]Others have argued that 'low balling' is also 'anticompetitive' and 'unfair' to small firms [see, e.g., the discussions in Causey (1979, pp. 185–186), Arnett and Danos (1979, pp. 5–7), and in the Metcalf Report (1976, pp. 1729–1730)]. The concern of the present paper is not the alleged predatory effects of 'low balling', but its alleged negative impact on auditor independence. For a discussion of why predatory price tactics in general are likely to be a dominated strategy, see McGee (1958).

[2]Casual evidence gathered by the Cohen Commission supports the prevalence of 'low balling' to obtain initial audit engagements:

> . . . the experiences of some members of the Commission and staff indicate that fee competition is common and increasing.

> Discussions with a few companies that have recently negotiated with new auditors indicated readiness on the part of public accounting firms to offer competitive prices, to make bids with fees guaranteed for several years, to renegotiate prices after receipt of competitive offers, and to set billing rates at as much as 50 percent below normal (p. 110)'

A recent article in the New Orleans newspaper, *The Times-Picayune* (March 23, 1979), reports on the practice of 'low balling' in conjunction with the audit of the city of Slidell:

> Leonard Brook of Deloitte, Haskins and Sells said his firm expected just to break even on the first city audit at a charge of $16,000. 'I'd be amazed if it can be done for $25,000', said Brook, who admitted his firm was submitting a low proposal the first year in order to do business with the city in succeeding years. . . .

> A fee of $15,000 — lowest of the four — was proposed by Wally Giles and Eugene Fremaux of Price–Waterhouse. 'In reality, that fee does not constitute what our full rate would be if we didn't absorb the first year's start-up cost', said Giles (sec. 1, p. 6).

not confined to auditing; rather, it is observed in such diverse environments as bidding for franchise contracts [see, e.g., Goldberg (1976, p. 437)], bidding for cable television monopolies [Williamson (1976)], bidding for input contracts [Williamson (1975, p. 93)], and initial payments for future franchise rights [Rubin (1978, p. 226)]. For example, Williamson (1975, p. 93) discusses the initial competition to become the supplier of spark plugs to Ford Motor Company. Apparently this contract gave the winner significant advantages in the replacement market and 'Ford was able to purchase plugs at much less than cost on this account'.

A non-auditing example of 'low balling' commonly observed today is the distribution of free samples when a manufacturer brings out a new product. Clearly, the price of these samples (zero) is less than their total current cost to manufacture, and yet these inducements apparently are of little concern to regulators. What then is different about auditing?

The crucial difference between 'low balling' in general and 'low balling' by auditors lies in its alleged negative impact on auditor independence. In order to analyze the link between this fee structure and independence, we first provide a definition of auditor independence which is equivalent to one offered by Watts and Zimmerman (1980) (section 2).

When contracting is costly, certain aspects of the audit environment (e.g., technological advantages to incumbent auditors and significant transactions costs of changing auditors) enable incumbent auditors to earn quasi-rents on future audits of a given client (section 3). These expected future quasi-rents induce 'low balling'. The reason is that competition among auditors for the right to become the incumbent (and capture the quasi-rents) drives fees below total costs in the initial period. Critically, initial fee reductions are sunk in future periods and therefore do not impair auditor independence. The implications for current regulation governing audit fees (Accounting Series Release No. 250) and auditor changes (Accounting Series Release No. 165 et al.) are also developed (section 4). Conclusions and a brief summary are provided (section 5).

2. The economic benefits of auditor independence

The ex ante value of an audit to consumers of audit services (which include current and potential owners, managers, consumers of the firm's products, etc.) depends on the auditor's perceived ability to

(1) discover errors or breaches in the accounting system, and

(2) withstand client pressures to disclose selectively in the event a breach is discovered.

In order to concentrate on independence (rather than on an auditor's technical capabilities), we assume that the probability of discovering a breach is positive and fixed. The level of auditor independence is defined as the conditional probability that, given a breach has been discovered, the auditor will report the breach.[3]

For his opinion to have value in the capital market, the auditor must have *some* incentive to tell the 'truth' when the truth is 'bad news' from the client's perspective. This analysis does not imply that the audit opinion is valueless unless the auditor always tells the truth. Rather, the greater the incentive for the auditor to tell the truth, the greater the value of the auditor's opinion. If the capital market expected the auditor never to deviate from management's position, then it would assess the value of the auditor's opinion as zero. Therefore, in at least some cases, the capital market must expect the auditor to oppose management.

On the other hand, as Watts and Zimmerman have argued, it is unlikely that auditors are perfectly independent from their clients. By definition, there is perfect independence when the conditional probability that the auditor will report a discovered breach is one. A necessary condition for the optimal amount of independence to be less than perfect independence is the expectation by the author of future quasi-rents specific to a given client relationship.

A given period's client-specific quasi-rent equals the excess of revenues over *avoidable* costs, including the opportunity cost of auditing the next-best alternative client. Quasi-rents arise naturally in a multiperiod world when agents invest in the current period with the expectation of return in future periods. With a positive initial investment, future revenues must exceed future (avoidable and unavoidable) costs in order that the project be undertaken. The expectation of future quasi-rents does not imply that auditors earn monopoly rents. A future quasi-rent stream constitutes a monopoly rent only when the net present value of the investment is positive.[4] When the net present value of the investment is zero, the quasi-rent stream yields a normal rate of return on an initial outlay.

If no client-specific quasi-rents are expected from a given client relationship, an auditor is indifferent to termination of that relationship; consequently he has no economic incentive to conceal a discovered breach. In this case, the auditor is perfectly independent with respect to that particular client. The existence of perfect substitutes for a given client (with zero transactions costs of switching) implies the absence of client-specific

---

[3]In reality, these two probabilities are unlikely to be separable, e.g., how thoroughly an auditor searches for a breach depends on his expectations about subsequent disclosure. For simplicity, we treat them here as separable. This definition of auditor independence is equivalent to one put forth by Watts and Zimmerman (1980, p. 8).

[4]For a more extensive discussion of the distinction between quasi-rents and monopoly rents, see Klein, Crawford and Alchian (1978, p. 299).

quasi-rents,[5] and therefore also implies perfect auditor independence.[6]

Thus, as the accounting profession has long argued, 'future economic interest' in a given client lessens auditor independence with respect to that client.[7] And ceteris paribus, the greater the client-specific quasi-rent stream (the more the auditor stands to lose by client termination), the lower the conditional probability that he will report a discovered breach. It follows that the greater the observed economic interest (e.g., the greater the auditor's ownership interest in the client firm), the lower the perceived probability that the auditor will report a breach.

In an efficient capital market, rational agents forecast that auditors who possess a known economic interest in their clients have increased incentives for misrepresentation; the expected costs resulting from these incentives are reflected in the client's share price. Since auditor independence has potential benefits to clients (through its impact on firm value) and to auditors (through the fees they can charge for audit services), both parties have incentives to voluntarily choose contractual arrangements which enable them to capture the expected net benefits of auditor independence.

If contracting among agents were costless, auditors would always be perfectly independent[8] from their clients. Perfect independence would result from an exhaustively specified and perfectly enforced contract negotiated (at zero cost) in the initial period. In other words, auditors and clients could capture the benefits to perfect independence at zero cost. However, in an important sense it is internally inconsistent to assume costless contracting in an auditing context. After all, costless contracting also enables firm owners and managers to remove conflicts of interest, and therefore implies a zero demand for (costly) auditing and other monitoring technologies. It follows that a necessary condition for both (1) a positive demand for costly auditing, and (2) less than perfect auditor independence is that contracting among agents be costly. Therefore, we shall maintain the costly contracting assumption throughout the paper.

---

[5]Recall that the costs of auditing a given client are appropriately defined to include the opportunity cost of auditing the next-best alternative client.

[6]Conversely, the absence of (costlessly available) perfect substitute clients implies less than perfect auditor independence. An auditor who expects to earn client-specific quasi-rents from a given relationship is *not* indifferent to client termination, and is therefore not perfectly independent with respect to that client. This statement is subject to the caveat set forth in footnote 7.

[7]Future economic interest is necessary but not sufficient for misrepresentation. In addition, the auditor must perceive the expected gains from 'cheating' exceed the expected costs. These expected costs will incorporate the present value of the loss in future audit fees resulting from the loss of reputation, should the auditor be caught 'cheating', and the probability of being caught.

[8]It is important to note that perfect independence is a 'Nirvana-type' construct useful only as a benchmark. The observation that the optimal amount of auditor independence is not perfect independence has no normative implications; rather it is to be expected in a world of costly contracting.

3. 'Low balling' and auditor independence

When contracting is costly, incumbent auditors who possess a comparative advantage over competitors in future periods expect to earn quasi-rents. For example, when client-specific start-up costs are significant, the incumbent auditor enjoys a technological advantage on future audits of a given client.[9] Transactions costs of changing auditors (e.g., disclosure requirements) also create advantages to incumbents. Incumbent auditors can capture future benefits from technological and transaction cost advantages by setting future audit fees above the avoidable costs of producing audits. Therefore, these advantages represent assets to incumbents which are specialized to both the auditor and a particular client.[10]

The specialized nature of these shared assets implies that the future relationship between client and incumbent auditor is a bilateral monopoly. Each party can impose real costs on the other by termination; each can potentially gain, therefore, from the threat of termination. Clients can potentially gain concessions such as selective disclosure. Auditors can potentially raise audit fees. Rational clients and auditors anticipate the future bilateral monopoly when contracting for initial audit engagements and their expectations are reflected in the equilibrium fee structure.[11]

In particular, when incumbent auditors earn quasi-rents, competition among auditors for the initial engagement, i.e., for the property rights to incumbency, results in 'low balling' (setting initial audit fees less than current total costs). A simplified model which illustrates this process is presented below. It is important to note at the outset that 'low balling' is a general result which in no sense depends on the assumptions of this simple model. Rather, 'low balling' occurs in settings where

---

[9]It is well recognized in the literature that initial audit engagements entail significant start-up costs. Arens and Loebbecke (1976, p. 100) provide three reasons for this phenomenon:

(1) It is necessary to verify the details making up those balance sheet accounts that are of a permanent nature, such as fixed assets, patents, and retained earnings.

(2) It is necessary to verify the beginning balances in the balance sheet accounts on an initial engagement.

(3) The auditor is less familiar with the client's operations in an initial audit.

[10]To the extent that start-up costs are not client-specific (e.g., some portion is marketable to other auditors or transferable to the auditor's other clients), client-specific quasi-rents to incumbents are reduced. The advantages to incumbency with which we are concerned here are those which are completely client-specific, i.e., whose value in alternative uses is zero.

[11]When information is costly, *unanticipated* broken agreements (opportunism) can still occur. For example, auditors may promise a given fee structure, and then opportunistically renege, perhaps claiming 'cost overruns'. It is, of course, costly for clients to determine whether costs have actually increased or whether the auditor is 'gouging' him. On the other hand, clients may initially promise to retain the auditor., encouraging him to bear some of the start-up costs, and then opportunistically terminate him to take advantage of unanticipated future events. This behavior occurs when it is costly for outsiders to determine (and perhaps verify) that the auditor was fired opportunistically rather than for cause. Potential costs to loss of reputation (e.g., clients who are shown to 'cheat' auditors must pay higher audit fees, auditors who are shown to 'cheat' clients may lose other clients) govern the extent to which opportunism will occur.

(a) incumbent auditors earn quasi-rents, due, e.g., to transactions costs or technological advantages, and

(b) the initial market for audit services is competitive.

Conditions (a) and (b) are obviously met in many more complex environments than the simple one which follows.

Consider a multiperiod ($t=1,2,...,\infty$) model in which the market for initial audit engagements at time $t=1$ is perfectly competitive insofar as all potential auditors have identical technological capabilities. The market for subsequent audits (in future periods $t=2,...,\infty$) is not perfectly competitive because incumbent auditors possess cost advantages over potential new auditors. The incumbent's advantage arises because new auditors must bear

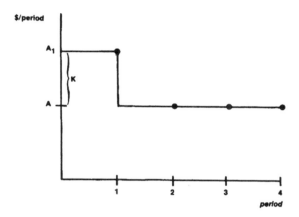

Fig. 1. Audit costs per period (A is audit cost, K is the start-up cost in period 1, $A_1 = A + K$ is audit cost in period 1).

technological start-up costs (which are sunk costs to incumbents) and because of the transactions costs of switching auditors. Consequently, incumbent auditors expect to earn quasi-rents on subsequent audits and 'low balling' in the initial period is the competitive response required to capture the quasi-rents.

Formally, let A_t represent the cost of producing an audit in time period t. Thus, A_1 represents the cost of producing the initial audit, and A_2, A_3, and so on represent the production costs of subsequent audits. For analytical simplicity only, assume that all subsequent audits are produced at the same cost each period, $A = A_2 = A_3 = ... = A_\infty$. The initial audit requires a start-up cost of K which dictates total production costs of $A_1 \equiv A + K$ for initial audits. This simple intertemporal cost structure is illustrated in fig. 1 for the special case of four time periods.

In each time period t, the client contracts to pay the auditor a fee, F_t, to produce that period's audit. Thus, F_1 represents the auditor's fee on the initial engagement and $F = F_2 = F_3 = \ldots = F_\infty$ represents fees on subsequent audits, assumed for simplicity to be equal in periods $t = 2, \ldots, \infty$.

With this preparation, we can characterize the endogenously determined intertemporal fee structure. In particular, we will show that competition for the initial audit engagement among auditors with rational expectations leads to a market equilibrium in which 'low balling' obtains. In symbolic terms, the equilibrium price structure requires that initial fees be set below costs: $F_1 < A_1 \equiv A + K$.

Viewed at time $t = 1$, the present value of each potential auditor's profit from obtaining the initial engagement for a given client is

$$\pi = (F_1 - A_1) + (F - A)/r. \tag{1}$$

The first term of eq. (1) is the profit on the initial engagement and the second term is the discounted (at rate r) profit or quasi-rent stream from subsequent audits of this client.[12] The equilibrium initial audit fee, denoted F_1^*, depends on current costs, A_1, and on the present value of future quasi-rents, $(F - A)/r$.

Importantly, future audit fees exceed the avoidable costs of production $(F - A > 0)$ so that the incumbent auditor earns quasi-rents on subsequent audits of this client. To see why, first recognize that $(F - A)$ must be non-negative because the incumbent auditor can (and will) withdraw from the engagement if total costs exceed total revenues on any subsequent audit. While any start-up costs incurred in the initial period are sunk, the incumbent auditor will not supply future audit services if audit fees are insufficient to cover the avoidable costs of producing audits. Thus, in each future period, the incumbent auditor's avoidable costs, A, constitute a lower bound on audit fees.

The upper bound on the incumbent's future fees depends on both the alternative supply price and the transactions costs of changing auditors. In this model, each time a client switches auditors, he incurs a transactions cost, denoted CS, in the period of the switch. Therefore, clients will change auditors only if they perceive that the present value of the incumbent's fees exceeds the present value of a new auditor's fees plus the transactions cost of changing auditors.[13] Formally, the client's switching decision is

---

[12]Eq. (1) implicitly assumes that the initial auditor retains the engagement in perpetuity. This condition is derived below assuming that incumbent auditors always set future fees to be entry preventing (see footnote 14).

[13]This statement is strictly correct only when audit quality is held constant. When audit quality varies inversely with rents to incumbents, clients will change auditors when they perceive that the present value of the incumbent's fees plus the (negative) impact on client firm value of retaining the incumbent exceeds the present value of a new auditor's fees plus the costs of changing auditors. Allowing audit quality to vary complicates the analysis without altering the 'low balling' result.

straightforward in this simplified setting: retain the incumbent auditor in every future period as long as

$$F < A + r(CS + K)/(1 + r). \tag{2}$$

To see why eq. (2) is entry preventing, note that new auditors hired at $t=2$ incur start-up costs on the initial audit so that $A_2 \equiv A + K$ and $A = A_3 = A_4$ and so on. Competition among new auditors at time $t=2$ assures that they earn zero profits. Therefore the discounted present value of a new auditor's fees equals the discounted present value of his total costs, $A_2 + A/r$. The present value of the incumbent's fees at time $t=2$ is $F + F/r$. The incumbent's entry preventing fee must therefore satisfy

$$F + F/r < A_2 + A/r + CS,$$

where $A_2 \equiv A + K$ which simplifies to eq. (2). The same logic applies to periods $3, 4, \ldots, \infty$.

Thus, the incumbent auditor's future fees lie in the range

$$A \leq F < A + r(CS + K)/(1 + r). \tag{3}$$

The equilibrium fee depends, in general, on the bilateral negotiation process in future periods. By inspection of (3), one can easily see that when both $CS = 0$ and $K = 0$, audit fees equal avoidable production costs in every future time period. In this case, the market for subsequent audits is perfectly competitive because all auditors possess identical technologies with zero adjustment costs: perfect competition in each future period drives the quasi-rents to zero. It follows that 'low balling' does not occur because incumbents possess no advantages.

Under the assumptions of the current model, the winner of the initial bidding at $t=1$ can prevent entry in each future period[14] by setting future fees such that (2) is satisfied. For simplicity only, assume that the incumbent auditor sets F in order to extract the maximum entry-preventing quasi-rent. Formally, the auditor sets future fees such that

$$F^* = A + r(CS + K)/(1 + r) - \varepsilon,$$

where asterisks denote equilibrium values and ε is some arbitrarily small positive number. When $CS > 0$, $K > 0$, future fees are set such that $F^* - A > 0$, i.e., incumbents extract positive future quasi-rents.

[14] Because the incumbent auditor always sets future audit fees to prevent entry, clients will not change auditors in this model. In a more general model, clients change auditors when audit quality varies (see footnote 13) and/or competitors' fees are stochastic. With future quasi-rents reinterpreted in expected value terms, 'low balling' still obtains in market equilibrium.

Auditors bidding for the initial engagement hold rational expectations about the future advantages to incumbency and submit initial bids based on these expectations. Competition for the initial audit (i.e., for the property rights to incumbency) will force auditors to lower their initial bids until zero profits are expected (in net present value terms).[15] In other words, auditors bidding for the initial engagement will 'low ball' until the expected rate of return on the foregone fees in the initial period is a normal one. Thus, in market equilibrium, eq. (1) becomes

$$\pi^* = (F_1^* - A_1) + (F^* - A)/r = 0. \tag{4}$$

As demonstrated above, the second term of (4) is positive. By the competitively-enforced zero profit condition, the first term is negative, and 'low balling' is established, i.e., market equilibrium requires that initial fees be less than production costs,

$$F_1^* - A_1 < 0.$$

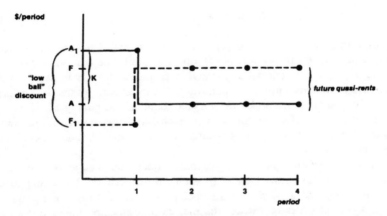

Fig. 2. Audit fees and audit costs per period (A is audit cost, K is the start-up cost in period 1, $A_1 = A + K$ is audit cost in period 1, F is the future audit fee, F_1 is the audit fee in period 1).

Fig. 2 illustrates the equilibrium intertemporal fee structure in the special case of a four-period model. Note that the discounted value of the area labelled 'future quasi-rents' equals the area labelled 'low ball' discount when auditors earn zero profits at equilibrium. By inspection of fig. 2 [and of eq. (4)], one can also see that the greater the expected future rents, ceteris paribus, the greater the 'low balling' for the property rights to those rents.

---

[15]This effect of bidding 'for the market' has been previously analyzed by Demsetz (1968, p. 65), Williamson (1971, p. 116), and Posner (1976).

A number of factors have been ignored in the simplified model. In particular, potential benefits to independence (section 2) provide the parties with incentives to devise contracts which reduce client-specific quasi-rents to incumbent auditors (and thereby raise the level of auditor independence). Negotiated contracts may be implicit (e.g., client and auditor reputation) or explicit (e.g., engagement letters which typically specify the scope of the engagement, audit fees, responsibility for inputs, etc.).[16] In addition, both auditors and clients have incentives to refrain from explicit vertical integration,[17] contingent fee structures, auditor ownership of client firm securities, and other practices that are expected to affect negatively the perceived independence of the auditor.

When considering contractual responses, one might be tempted to argue that the level of independence can be increased by an agreement to set F_1^* $= A_1$, i.e., to preclude 'low balling' in the initial period.[18] In fact, this solution is ineffective in reducing quasi-rents (and raising the level of independence). To see why, note that the line of causation runs from anticipated future rents to 'low balling' in the initial period, *not* vice versa as regulators as the Cohen Commission have suggested. 'Low balling' for the initial audit is a competitive response to future rents to incumbents; 'low balling' does not *cause* future rents to occur. Because initial fee reductions are sunk in future periods they have no effect on either (i) the magnitude of future rents, or (ii) auditor independence.

By parallel reasoning, agreements to refrain from 'low balling' in the initial period are *also* sunk, i.e., irrelevant in future periods, and thus do not prevent incumbent auditors from raising future fees above avoidable production costs. In other words, the incumbent's future fee-raising potential is unchanged by these initial agreements. Rational clients recognize this fact and are unwilling to agree to contracts whose sole purpose is to reduce 'low balling' in the initial period. While contracts which reduce client-specific quasi-rents increase the level of auditor independence, those which simply reduce 'low balling' in the initial period have no effect on independence. Thus, potential benefits to independence provide joint incentives to negotiate the former, but not the latter type of contractual agreement.

4. Implications for current disclosure regulation

The logical framework developed in earlier sections can be used to evaluate the effects of current regulation intended to increase the level of

---

[16]See Macaulay (1963) for discussion of the use of explicit and implicit contracts in business relationships.

[17]While explicit vertical integration (i.e., client ownership of the audit firm, as with internal auditors) is not feasible for auditor–client contracting, the length of the relationship is endogenous. Obviously, the longer the relationship, the more it approaches vertical integration.

[18]In fact, this may have been the SEC's reason for imposing sanctions on 'low balling' in ASR-250, as discussed in the next section.

auditor independence. Two sets of rules are considered: ASR-165 et al. governing auditor changes[19] and ASR-250 governing auditor-client fee relationships.[20] The expressed intent of both sets of rules was to increase auditor independence by increased disclosure of the circumstances surrounding a change of auditor (ASR-165 et al.) and the contractual, in particular, the fee relationship between clients and auditors (ASR-250).

The logic underlying ASR-165 et al. is that increased disclosure of auditor changes reduces the client's ability to extract accounting concessions from the auditor by threatening to terminate the relationship. The Cohen Commission supports the SEC's position on auditor changes because 'measures that increase the outside scrutiny of a change in independent auditors are likely to inhibit the tendency to apply pressure to the independent auditor by threatening dismissal' (Cohen Report, p. 107).

While it is true that increased outside scrutiny renders client threats of termination less effective, the Cohen Report's analysis is overly simplistic. Both the Cohen Commission and the SEC overlooked an important offsetting effect of ASR-165 et al. By raising the costs of changing auditors (raising CS in the model), ASR-165 et al. raises client-specific quasi-rents to incumbent auditors, which, ceteris paribus, reduces the optimal level of independence.[21] Thus, contrary to accepted doctrine, the net effect of ASR-165 et al. on auditor independence is indeterminate.

Despite the ambiguous net impact on auditor independence, the effect of ASR-165 et al. on audit pricing is straightforward: by raising the costs of switching auditors, this regulation raises future quasi-rents to incumbent auditors. When competition among auditors for the rights to the increased future quasi-rents occurs on price dimensions, initial audit fees are lowered, i.e., more 'low balling' occurs. While ASR-165 et al. is predicted to increase

---

[19]Four rules are relevant to auditor changes: Securities Release No. 34-9344 (effective October 31, 1971), ASR-165 (effective January 1, 1975), ASR-194 (effective August 31, 1976), and ASR-247 (effective July 31, 1978). The principal reporting requirements under ASR-165 et al. are disclosure of both the resignation of the prior accountant and the engagement of the new accountant, and the existence of any significant disagreement with the prior accountant within the two most recent fiscal years. The client must request that the prior accountant respond to the filing, and his response is appended as an exhibit. In addition, financial statement disclosure of the effect of the disagreement, if material, is required.

[20]ASR-250 requires disclosure of the services provided by the principal accountant and the percentage relationship of non-audit fees (if material) to audit fees. Any limits on audit fees (current or future) that are not subject to renegotiation if unanticipated difficulties develop require disclosure as well. While Securities Act Release No. 33-5869 proposed that the dollar amount of audit fees be disclosed, ASR-250 does not require disclosure of the magnitude of audit fees.

[21]Furthermore, ASR-165 et al. may have enabled existing incumbent auditors to earn monopoly rents by causing an unanticipated increase in the future rent stream. As such, this regulation represents a wealth transfer from clients to extant incumbent auditors. Auditors bidding for incumbency subsequent to the regulation do not benefit to the extent that competition dissipates any gains.

'low balling', ASR-250 attempts to reduce it and therefore these two rules appear to be inconsistent.

The apparent inconsistency between ASR-165 et al. and ASR-250 raises the question of intent: if there is no causal relationship between 'low balling' and impaired independence, why the professional and regulatory concern over 'low balling'? One potential explanation is that these parties fail to recognize the sunk cost nature of initial fee reductions and mistakenly believe that imposing sanctions on 'low balling' raises the level of auditor independence. An alternative hypothesis is that the expressed concern over 'low balling' is an 'excuse' for an attempt to preserve monopoly rents to auditors.[22]

To show why the second explanation is plausible, we draw on the audit pricing model to predict the joint economic consequences of ASR-165 et al. and ASR-250. Recall that an auditor's profit from a given client can be expressed as eq. (1),

$$\pi = (F_1 - A_1) + (F - A)/r,$$

where future fees, F, are an increasing function of the transactions costs of switching auditors.

By raising these costs, ASR-165 et al. raises the second term in (1), which represents the present value of the auditor's quasi-rent stream from future audits of this client. At equilibrium, fee competition among auditors for the initial audit assures that the first term adjusts to maintain the equilibrium zero profit condition.

However, if sanctions against 'low balling' (as, e.g., in ASR-250) can effectively prevent the first term of (1) from adjusting via initial price competition, auditors earn monopoly rents, $\pi^* > 0$, at least initially. In effect, regulation lowers the cost of monitoring (explicit or implicit) price-fixing agreements which would aid a cartel of auditors in sustaining monopoly pricing. However, it is unlikely that monopoly rents can be sustained in the long run because innovative auditors will substitute into non-price competition (e.g., more brochures on accounting issues, more attractive personnel) to obtain the initial engagement. This substitution occurs because incumbent auditors continue to earn future quasi-rents subsequent to regulation. Thus, auditors will 'low ball' (on non-price dimensions) to obtain

---

[22]For a positive theory of the demand for accounting 'excuses', see Watts and Zimmerman (1979). It should be noted that regulation governing audit fees is potentially a means of raising independence by lowering *future* client-specific quasi-rents. In other words, government-enforced limits on future fees may be the minimum cost contractual response to these quasi-rents. However, ASR-250 makes no attempt to limit future fees, and therefore is not of this genre of contractual response.

the initial engagement and thereby dissipate the monopoly rents.[23] Furthermore, to the extent that client-specific quasi-rents are unchanged by the regulation, auditor independence is unaffected by ASR-250.

5. Conclusions

This paper develops a model of intertemporal audit pricing when incumbent auditors possess cost advantages over competitors in future audits of a given client. These advantages occur due to significant start-up costs in audit technology and transactions costs of switching auditors. When incumbent auditors possess these advantages, they can raise future audit fees above the avoidable costs of producing audits, i.e., incumbent auditors earn client-specific quasi-rents.

The expectation of client-specific quasi-rents to incumbent auditors has two effects. First, it implies that the optimal level of auditor independence is less than perfect independence. In fact, client-specific quasi-rents to incumbency are a necessary condition for lessened independence. Second, competition for the property rights to incumbency forces auditors to 'low ball' in the initial period.

Regulators and the profession have claimed that 'low balling' impairs auditor independence by itself creating a future economic interest in clients. Contrary to these assertions, the current paper demonstrates that 'low balling' is a competitive response to the expectation of future quasi-rents, and does not itself impair independence. Regulation which attempts to curtail 'low balling' (without altering the client-specific quasi-rent stream) is predited to have no effect on auditor independence.

[23]To the extent that the regulation of price competition causes auditors to supply services whose costs are greater than their value to clients, it induces a misallocation of resources as monopoly rents are dissipated.

References

Arens, A. and J. Loebbecke, 1976, Auditing: An integrated approach (Prentice-Hall, Englewood Cliffs, NJ).
Arnett, H. and P. Danos, 1979, CPA firm viability (University of Michigan, Ann Arbor, MI).
Causey, D., 1979, Duties and liabilities of public accountants (Dow Jones–Irwin, Homewood, IL).
Ciko, L., 1979, Finance director defends Slidell accounting system, The Times–Picayune, March 23, sec. 1,b.
Commission on Auditors' Responsibilities, 1978, Report, conclusions, and recommendations (Commission on Auditors' Responsibilities, New York).
Demsetz, H., 1968, Why regulate utilities?, Journal of Law and Economics, 55–65.
Goldberg, V., 1976, Regulation and administered contracts, Bell Journal of Economics, 426–448.
Klein, B., R. Crawford and A. Alchian, 1978, Vertical integration, appropriable rents, and the competitive contracting process, Journal of Law and Economics, 297–321.

Macaulay, S., 1963, Non-contractual relations in business: A preliminary study, American Sociological Review, 55–67.

McGee, J., 1958, Predatory price cutting: The Standard Oil (N.J.) case, Journal of Law and Economics, 137–169.

Posner, R., 1976, Antitrust law: An economic perspective (University of Chicago Press, Chicago, IL).

Rubin, P., 1978, The theory of the firm and the structure of the franchise contract, Journal of Law and Economics, 233–234.

Securities and Exchange Commission, 1971, Securities Exchange Act of 1934, Release no. 9344.

Securities and Exchange Commission, 1977, Securities Act of 1933, Release no. 5869.

Securities and Exchange Commission, 1978, Accounting Series Release no. 250.

United States Senate, 1976, The accounting establishment, Prepared by the Subcommittee on Reports, Accounting and Management of the Committee on Governmental Affairs (U.S. Government Printing Office, Washington, DC).

Watts, R. and J. Zimmerman, 1979, The demand for and supply of accounting theories: The market for excuses, The Accounting Review, 273–305.

Watts, R. and J. Zimmerman, 1980, The markets for independence and independent auditors, Unpublished manuscript (University of Rochester, Rochester, NY).

Williamson, O., 1971, The vertical integration of production: Market failure considerations, American Economic Review, 112–123.

Williamson, O., 1975, Markets and hierarchies: Analysis and antitrust implications (Free Press, New York).

Williamson, O., 1976, Franchise bidding for natural monopolies — In general and with respect to CATV, Bell Journal of Economics, 73–104.

[8]

Journal of Accounting and Economics 3 (1981) 183–199. North-Holland Publishing Company

AUDITOR SIZE AND AUDIT QUALITY

Linda Elizabeth DeANGELO*

University of Pennsylvania, Philadelphia, PA 19104, USA

Received May 1981, final version received July 1981

Regulators and small audit firms allege that audit firm size does not affect audit quality and therefore should be irrelevant in the selection of an auditor. Contrary to this view, the current paper argues that audit quality is not independent of audit firm size, even when auditors initially possess identical technological capabilities. In particular, when incumbent auditors earn client-specific quasi-rents, auditors with a greater number of clients have 'more to lose' by failing to report a discovered breach in a particular client's records. This collateral aspect increases the audit quality supplied by larger audit firms. The implications for some recent recommendations of the AICPA Special Committee on Small and Medium Sized Firms are developed.

1. Introduction

Large audit firms are increasingly criticized on the basis of size alone both by regulators and by smaller firms within the accounting profession.[1] The allegation underlying these criticisms is that professional standards impart a homogeneity across different sized audit firms such that audit quality is independent of audit firm size. For example, employing the assumption that audit quality is relatively homogeneous across audit firms, Arnett and Danos (1979) argue that size alone '*should* not be a prime determinant of future success' (p. 8, emphasis added). Furthermore, they argue that 'as long as professional standards and qualifications were maintained, it is *unfair* to arbitrarily distinguish between the largest eight and all other CPA firms' (p. 56, emphasis added).

Because of the alleged discriminatory impact on smaller audit firms, eighteen small-to-medium sized audit firms filed suit in 1978 to block the division of the American Institute of Certified Public Accountants into two practice sections. One section now consists of audit firms whose clients are required to file reports with the Securities and Exchange Commission, the

*The author wishes to express her gratitude to Y. Barzel, H. DeAngelo, W.L. Felix, W. Kinney, B. Klein, E. Noreen, E.M. Rice, R. Watts, J. Zimmerman, and the referee, M.C. Jensen.

[1]See the Report of the Subcommittee on Reports, Accounting, and Management of the Committee on Government Operations (U.S. Senate, 1977) (Metcalf Report), Arnett and Danos (1979), and the Report of the Special Committee on Small and Medium Sized Firms (AICPA, 1980) (Derieux Committee Report).

other of firms whose clients are not. According to Public Accounting Report (February 1978), the grounds for suit were that 'this seemingly innocuous proposal is part of a calculated design...to further concentrate power in the hands of the largest accounting firms'. While the suit was later dismissed, the AICPA considered the size issue sufficiently important to appoint a special committee (the Derieux Committee) to study it in more depth.

The Derieux Committee Report stresses the 'concern that smaller firms may be replaced simply because they are less well known, even though the smaller firms may well be providing as high or higher quality services' (p. 5). The Committee articulates this 'problem' and the recommended solution as follows:

> *Problem:* Auditors are sometimes chosen on the basis of *arbitrary* factors such as size of their firm.

> *Recommendation:* An information booklet should be published stressing that the selection of a CPA firm *should* be based not on size, but on the ability to provide service. (p. 18, emphasis added)

In other words, the Derieux Committee's position is that auditor size should be irrelevant in the selection of an auditor. Justification for this position is provided by the assumption that auditor size does not affect the quality of audit services supplied.

Contrary to this view, the current paper argues that size alone alters auditors' incentives such that, ceteris paribus, larger audit firms supply a higher level of audit quality. When audit technology is characterized by significant start-up costs, incumbent auditors earn client-specific quasi-rents. These quasi-rents, when subject to loss from discovery of a lower quality audit than promised, serve as collateral against such opportunistic behavior. This implies that, ceteris paribus, the larger the auditor as measured by number of clients,[2] the less incentive the auditor has to behave opportunistically and the higher the perceived quality of the audit.[3]

In order to demonstrate this relationship between audit quality and auditor size, we first provide an operational definition of audit quality (section 2). When quality is costly to evaluate, self-interested individuals who

---

[2]This size measure is appropriate when client-specific quasi-rents do not vary across clients of a given auditor. When quasi-rents vary across clients, the relationship between the quasi-rents specific to a given client and the auditor's total quasi-rents becomes important. Besides altering the magnitude of the collateral bond aspect of the quasi-rents, size also affects the incentives of the partners within the audit firm. We hold these incentives constant in order to concentrate on the collateral aspect of client-specific quasi-rents. Thus, the current analysis isolates one previously unrecognized benefit of auditor size, but does not attempt to characterize the optimal size audit firm. These issues are discussed further in sections 3 and 4 of the paper.

[3]Watts and Zimmerman (1981) develop an alternative theory that predicts that auditor size is a surrogate for audit quality. Their argument is that large audit firms supply higher quality audits because they possess a comparative advantage in monitoring individual auditor behavior.

potentially benefit from the exchange of quality-differentiated audits have incentives to devise surrogates for quality. When larger audit firms have 'more to lose' from supplying a lower-than-promised level of audit quality, consumers properly use size as a quality surrogate[4] (section 3). The theory supports conventional wisdom that perceived auditor independence is inversely related to the percentage of total audit fees dependent on retaining any one client. Large audit firms are a means of lowering this percentage, as are alternative quality enforcing arrangements (section 4). Implications for some recommendations of the Derieux Committee which would subsidize smaller audit firms at the expense of larger audit firms and clients are developed (section 5). Conclusions and a brief summary are provided in section 6.

2. The quality of audit services

Audit services are demanded as monitoring devices because of the potential conflicts of interest between owners and managers as well as those among different classes of security holders [see Watts (1977), Watts and Zimmerman (1981), and Benston (1980) for elaboration]. In at least some cases, the provision of audited financial statements is the least-cost contractual response to owner-manager and intra-owner conflicts of interest, i.e., agency costs. Agency costs vary across potential client firms and perhaps over time for a given client. For example, it is well known that client firms going public often switch to Big Eight auditors [Carpenter and Strawser (1971)].[5] Differential agency costs across firms and over time for a given firm imply a heterogeneous demand for audit services, i.e., differing 'levels' of auditing are demanded.

How are different 'levels' of auditing exchanged? In order to address this question, we define the production of audits in terms of inputs and outputs supplied by the auditor alone, and ignore client inputs.[6] With this simplification, audit output can be characterized as independent verification of management-prepared financial data, and consists of a stated opinion (e.g.,

---

[4]Our argument differs from other arguments for auditor size found in the literature, such as economies of scale in the production of audit services [Arnett and Danos (1979), Benston (1980), Dopuch and Simunic (1979)], greater partner personal wealth (Benston), and benefits to specialization combined with the risk of industry-specific business cycle fluctuations (Arnett and Danos). The current argument is that client-specific quasi-rents create an advantage to large audit firms because of their collateral properties.

[5]Of course, other reasons besides a demand for 'more' auditing may also motivate these switches. For example, Big Eight firms may possess more expertise in preparing SEC documents, auditing large clients, and/or greater industry-specific knowledge.

[6]Defining audit inputs and output in this manner simplifies the analysis at the cost of bypassing some interesting auditor-client interactions caused by the jointness of the production process. See Alchian and Demsetz (1972) for an analysis of the incentives faced by input owners when the production process is joint. For a model which explicitly recognizes auditor–client interactions, see Demski and Swieringa (1974).

an unqualified opinion) with an associated quality dimension. The type of opinion constant, changes in the level of auditing are equivalent to changes in audit quality.

The quality of audit services is defined to be the market-assessed joint probability that a given auditor will *both* (a) discover a breach in the client's accounting system, and (b) report the breach. The probability that a given auditor will discover a breach depends on the auditor's technological capabilities, the audit procedures employed on a given audit, the extent of sampling, etc. The conditional probability of reporting a discovered breach is a measure of an auditor's independence from a given client. This definition of auditor independence is used in DeAngelo (1981) and Watts and Zimmerman (1981), who argue that the ex ante value of an audit depends on the auditor's incentives to disclose selectively ex post.

Consumers incur costs of evaluating audit quality, i.e., of assessing the joint probability that a given auditor will both discover and report a breach on a given client's audit.[7] First, the actual procedures employed on a given audit engagement are generally not directly observed by consumers.[8] Second, consumers have little information about the incentives induced by the form of a given auditor–client contract which affect the probability of reporting a discovered breach. For these reasons, audit quality evaluation costs are likely to be significant.[9]

When audit quality is costly to evaluate, self-interested individuals have incentives to devise alternative arrangements which enable quality-differentiated audits to be exchanged. Furthermore, competitive forces dictate that the arrangement chosen will be the one which minimizes the total costs of exchange (including the costs of differentiating quality). This cogent observation was first made in a more general setting by Barzel (1977). One potential response is for consumers to develop surrogates for audit quality, i.e., to rely on some other (less costly to observe) variable which is (imperfectly) correlated with quality. The argument of the current paper is that auditor size serves as a surrogate for audit quality.[10]

---

[7]Consumers of audit services include current and potential owners (both shareholders and bondholders), managers, consumers of the firm's products, employees, government agencies, etc.

[8]Certification and audit standards aid consumers in assessing a lower bound on the probability a given auditor discovers a breach. These standards enforce a minimum level of audit quality by (typically) constraining auditor inputs. Standardization of auditor inputs serves other functions besides assuring output quality. First, it provides a defense for the auditor in litigation. Second, standardization also economizes on contracting costs, much in the same way as do 'boiler plates' in standardized contracts. Parties desiring to exchange higher than minimum quality audits must rely on private contracts.

[9]It cannot be the case, however, as several authors have claimed [e.g. Baiman (1979), Dopuch and Simunic (1979), Kaplan (1978), Magee (1979), and Ng (1978)] that audit quality is unobservable, i.e., infinitely costly to evaluate. In this case, no audits would be exchanged, i.e., the market for audit services would 'collapse' as in Akerlof (1970).

[10]See next page.

Another potential response to consumer quality evaluation costs is for auditors to specialize in a uniform level of audit quality, both across clients and over time. If auditors substantially vary the level of audit quality supplied from period to period, consumers would have to re-evaluate quality over time. If auditors substantially vary the level of quality from client to client, each audit engagement would require separate evaluation by consumers.

Because quality evaluation is costly, consumers will compensate auditors who enable them to avoid these costs by maintaining a relatively uniform quality level. Auditors have incentives to specialize in a uniform quality level because they can capture higher fees by doing so. However, when differential agency costs across clients imply a heterogeneous demand for audit quality, different auditors will specialize in different (albeit uniform) quality levels.[11] When auditors specialize in a given quality level, clients wishing to change the level of audit quality purchased will find it necessary to change auditors.

A distinction should be made between differing levels of audit quality voluntarily exchanged and opportunistic (unanticipated) changes in audit quality. A different level of audit quality is supplied when the market-assessed joint probability that an auditor will both discover and report a breach in a client's records changes. Significant costs of quality evaluation provide auditors with the opportunity to promise a given level of audit quality ex ante and to opportunistically lower it ex post by, e.g., reporting fewer discovered breaches than promised. This opportunity occurs because it is costly to discover auditor 'cheating' (the probability of being caught is less than one).

We argue below that certain aspects of audit technology provide auditors with incentives to opportunistically lower audit quality in order to retain a particular client. However, disincentives to 'cheat' are also provided by audit technology, and these disincentives increase as auditor size increases. Because larger auditors have reduced incentives to lower audit quality opportunistically, consumers rationally use auditor size as a surrogate for audit quality.

3. The relationship between auditor size and audit quality

When audit technology is characterized by significant client-specific start-up costs, incumbent auditors possess cost advantages over potential

[10]Of course, in order for auditor size to serve as a surrogate for audit quality, it must be the case that, on average, larger audit firms supply higher quality audits. The relationship between auditor size and audit quality is developed in section 3. It is also important to note that auditor size cannot be a *perfect* surrogate for audit quality or other quality-assuring arrangements would not be observed in the market for audit services. These other arrangements are discussed in section 4.

[11]Supply side competition ensures that, while auditors specialize in a uniform level of audit quality, audit fees adjust so that marginal auditors are indifferent to the quality 'class' to which they belong.

competitors in future audits of a given client. Even when the initial market for audit services is perfectly competitive insofar as all auditors possess identical technological capabilities, these advantages to incumbency imply the absence of perfect substitute auditors in future periods. The absence of perfect substitutes enables incumbent auditors to set future audit fees above the avoidable costs of producing audits, i.e., incumbent auditors earn client-specific quasi-rents.[12] Transactions costs of changing auditors also enable incumbents to raise future fees without making it profitable for clients to switch. In the presence of start-up and transactions costs, the relationship between clients and incumbent auditors is a bilateral monopoly [see DeAngelo (1981)].

In a bilateral monopoly, both parties have incentives to continue an established relationship because of the absence of costlessly available perfect substitute auditors (clients). In other words, termination of the relationship imposes costs on both parties. If terminated, incumbent auditors will lose the wealth equivalent of the client-specific quasi-rent stream. Clients will be forced to bear transactions costs of switching and the duplication of start-up costs associated with training a new auditor.[13] The theory therefore predicts an inverse relationship between the magnitude of start-up/transactions costs (and hence client-specific quasi-rents) and auditor turnover.[14] Consequently, observation of the rate at which client firms change auditors provides indirect evidence on the magnitude of these start-up/transactions costs.

Extant empirical evidence is consistent with the existence of significant start-up/transactions costs in the exchange of audit services. In particular, the uniform finding of extant studies [Burton and Roberts (1967), Bedingfield and Loeb (1974), Carpenter and Strawser (1971), Bolton and Crockett (1979), Hobgood and Sciarrino (1972), Financial Executives' Institute (1978), and Coe and Palmon (1979)] is that the rate at which client firms change auditors is low. For example, Burton and Roberts found a change rate of approximately one percent per annum for a sample of Fortune 500 firms for the time period 1955–1963, while Coe and Palmon found a change rate of approximately 2 percent per annum for a random sample of firms listed on the COMPUSTAT tape from 1952–1975. For smaller firms, the auditor

[12]A client-specific quasi-rent is the excess of a given period's revenues over the avoidable costs incurred in that period, including the opportunity cost of auditing the next-best alternative client. Whether a given quasi-rent stream constitutes a monopoly rent depends on whether the net present value of the stream is positive. For a more extensive discussion of the distinction between quasi-rents and monopoly rents, see Klein, Crawford and Alchian (1978, p. 299).

[13]This logic apparently underlies the position of the Commission on Auditors' Responsibilities (Cohen Commission) that mandatory auditor rotation would 'considerably increase the cost of audits because of the frequent duplication of the start-up and learning time necessary to gain familiarity with the company...' [Cohen Report (1978, pp. 108–109)].

[14]Similar logic can be found in Becker (1975) for the case of employee training that is specific to the training employer. The prediction in this case is that, ceteris paribus, firms characterized by larger (smaller) amounts of specific training experience lower (higher) employee turnover.

change rate is generally higher, but does not exceed five percent per annum. This evidence is consistent with the assumption that client-specific start-up/transactions costs (and therefore quasi-rents to incumbent auditors) are material.

The anticipation of future technological and transactions cost advantages to incumbent auditors has at least two effects. First, auditors bidding for the initial audit engagement, i.e., for the property rights to become the incumbent and capture the quasi-rents, will 'low ball' (set audit fees below total costs on the initial audit) to obtain the client [DeAngelo (1981)]. Second, because these quasi-rents are client-specific (i.e., they have no alternative use to this auditor and are not marketable to other auditors), incumbent auditors have some incentive to lower quality opportunistically in order to retain the client in future periods.[15]

This incentive occurs because clients can impose real costs on auditors by termination (loss of the wealth equivalent of the client-specific quasi-rent stream). Therefore clients can potentially extract accounting concessions from incumbent auditors by a credible threat of termination. In particular, incumbent auditors have a lessened incentive to report a discovered breach in the client's records, i.e., incumbent auditors are not perfectly independent from clients.[16]

Rational consumers recognize that incumbent auditors are not perfectly independent from clients. Consequently, they lower the price they are willing to pay for securities of firms that retain incumbents. In other words, the lower expected level of independence is reflected in reduced client firm value. Rational clients recognize the negative valuation consequences of retaining incumbent auditors. Therefore, they have incentives to reduce this wealth impact by choosing incumbent auditors perceived by the market as being more independent, i.e., as having fewer incentives to 'cheat' in order to retain this particular client.

When auditors earn client-specific quasi-rents, auditors with a greater number of current clients have reduced incentives to 'cheat' in order to retain

---

[15]To the extent that these quasi-rents are not client-specific, e.g., they are marketable to other auditors or have value in alternative uses to the current auditor, they do not provide an incentive to 'cheat'. The quasi-rents with which we are concerned here are those whose alternative use value is zero.

[16]By perfect independence, we mean that the conditional probability the auditor reports a discovered breach is one. Of course, if contracting among individuals were costless, perfect auditor independence could be exchanged via an exhaustively specified and perfectly enforced explicit contract. Unfortunately, costless contracting also enables owners and managers to eliminate the conflicts of interest which underlie the monitoring demand for (costly) auditing. Because auditing models which assume costless contracting are internally inconsistent in this sense, the assumption maintained throughout this paper is that explicit contracts which guarantee perfect independence are prohibitively costly to negotiate and enforce.

any one client. Intuitively, client-specific quasi-rents lower auditor independence with respect to a particular client because they provide an incentive to 'cheat' in order to retain the client in future periods. On the other hand, the quasi-rents specific to other current clients of a given auditor provide a disincentive to 'cheat', i.e., act as a collateral bond against such opportunistic behavior.

To see this collateral effect, consider an individual auditor's decision to 'cheat' in some future period when, due to technological and transactions cost advantages, the auditor earns client-specific quasi-rents. For the moment, we assume that alternative quality-enforcing arrangements (.e.g., explicit contracts, collateral bonds, auditor brand name expenditures) are prohibitively costly. We also assume that the magnitude of a given auditor's client-specific quasi-rents does not vary across clients.[17] Both of these assumptions are relaxed in section 4.

Suppose that, at some future date, a given incumbent auditor discovers a breach in a particular client's records.[18] The client can attempt to dissuade the auditor from reporting the breach, perhaps by threats of termination. Indeed, the client has a credible threat of termination, should the auditor report the discovered breach.[19] The auditor's incentive to 'cheat' is provided by the present value of the quasi-rents specific to this client, which are lost if the auditor reports truthfully and is terminated by the client.

A countervailing disincentive is provided by the present value of the quasi-rents specific to other current clients of the auditor. If the auditor 'cheats' and is caught, he stands to lose some portion of this value both through termination by other clients and through reduced fees from those that continue to retain him.[20] The amount the auditor stands to lose depends on

---

[17]This assumption is a reasonable one when auditors specialize in a uniform level of audit quality across clients in response to consumer quality evaluation costs. This assumption is not necessary for our conclusions to hold and, in fact, is relaxed in the following section.

[18]No other breaches are simultaneously discovered by the auditor, by assumption. The analysis would become considerably more complex if the auditor had the incentive to 'cheat' simultaneously on several clients. However, the result that a larger number of current clients lowers the probability of misrepresentation still obtains.

[19]Although termination is not costless to clients, such termination is rationally assessed to be a positive probability event. This is the case because a discovered breach (which the incumbent auditor intends to disclose) increases the potential benefits of termination to the client. Specifically, when it is costly for outsiders to discover and verify why termination occurred, opportunistic clients can 'blame' the auditor and perhaps avoid or at least mitigate the negative valuation associated with disclosure of the breach. This possibility apparently underlies the SEC and Cohen Commission positions that auditor changes should receive increased scrutiny through mandated disclosure requirements.

[20]The tradeoff which these other clients face (the negative impact on firm value of retaining an auditor who has been shown to 'cheat' versus the costs of switching auditors) has changed, and thus the other clients are more likely to change auditors. The costs of switching properly include not only transactions costs but also any duplication of start-up costs borne by the client.

both the value of this client-specific collateral and on the probability of being caught lowering audit quality.[21,22]

As a general proposition, auditors with a greater number of audit clients have reduced incentives to 'cheat' in order to retain any one client, ceteris paribus. When client-specific quasi-rents are identical across clients of a given auditor, auditors with a greater number of current clients supply a higher level of audit quality, because their total collateral is greater. Thus, significant start-up/transactions costs create a benefit to large audit firms.

In order to concentrate on the collateral properties of auditor size, we have ignored other potential costs and benefits to large audit firms.[23] In particular, we have implicitly held constant internal organizational structure and incentives (i.e., agency costs within the audit firm). In reality, these agency costs can be expected to vary with auditor size. The introduction of internal organizational issues may either strengthen or weaken the association between auditor size and audit quality. Three possibilities deserve brief mention here. First, if large audit firms possess a comparative advantage in monitoring individual auditor behavior, as argued by Watts and Zimmerman (1981), the benefits to auditor size are greater than specified here. On the other hand, as pointed out by Alchian and Demsetz (1972), the greater the number of partners, the greater an individual partner's incentive to shirk. This effect would act to weaken the association between auditor size and audit quality.

Finally, the collateral properties to size argument can also be applied on the individual auditor level.[24] When partners share proportionately in audit firm profits, the greater the number of clients, the less the wealth of the partner-in-charge of a given client depends on retaining that client. Therefore, the greater is the probability that he will report a discovered

[21]Of course, if the probability of being caught were zero, the auditor's expected net gain from 'cheating' in order to retain a troubled client is always positive. One function of professional organizations like the AICPA may be to curtail auditor opportunism by raising the probability of getting caught. Measures such as mandatory peer review or mandatory audit committees composed of outside directors, for example, serve this function. While it may not be in one individual auditor's narrow self-interest to raise this probability, it may be in the collective interest of auditors to do so. Thus, institutional arrangements (or regulation) may be an efficient means of accomplishing this goal.

[22]In this analysis, only the quasi-rents specific to *current* clients of the auditor serve as collateral when the initial market for audit services is perfectly competitive. Because auditors expect to earn zero profits on *new* clients in future periods (competition for new clients dissipates any monopoly rents), auditors are indifferent to losing potential new clients. Therefore, in the absence of monopoly rents, potential new clients have no impact on an auditor's decision to lower audit quality.

[23]The observation that auditors of various sizes exist indicates that there are offsetting costs to auditor size, e.g., of monitoring individual auditors, of maintaining uniformity, or of coordinating audit engagements. We have not attempted to specify these costs. Nor have we addressed the issue of how internal organizational structure and incentives change with auditor size. For these reasons, our analysis is properly viewed as isolating an important benefit to auditor size, but not as deriving the optimal size audit firm. This task is left for future research.

[24]Eric Noreen deserves credit for pointing out this implication.

breach. In effect, the impact of his audit decisions on his personal wealth is reduced. While these other effects are potentially important to a positive theory of audit firm size, we continue to ignore them in order to focus on the collateral properties to size associated with client-specific quasi-rents.

4. Generalizations and alternative arrangements

The general proposition that client-specific quasi-rents create a benefit to auditor size continues to hold when these quasi-rents vary across clients. However, another factor becomes important: the percentage of the auditor's total quasi-rent stream which is specific to any one client. In particular, clients for which client-specific quasi-rents are relatively large in a given auditor's portfolio pose special independence problems not captured by the analysis so far. When quasi-rents are not identical across clients, the variable of interest to consumers is the relationship between the value of an auditor's quasi-rents specific to a particular client and the value of the auditor's total quasi-rent stream.

When client-specific quasi-rents vary across clients, auditor size (as measured by the number of current clients) continue to serve as a surrogate for audit quality because larger auditors possess greater total collateral. However, size alone does not inform consumers about the relationship between the quasi-rents specific to one (potentially large) client and the auditor's total quasi-rent stream. Therefore, when client-specific quasi-rents vary across clients of a given auditor, consumers can be expected to develop other quality surrogates in addition to auditor size.

One potential surrogate is the percentage of total audit fees dependent on retaining any one client. For example, the Cohen Report (pp. 113–114) notes that:

> When one or a few large clients supply a significant portion of the total fees of a public accounting firm, the firm will have greater difficulty in maintaining its independence. The staff study of the Subcommittee on Reports, Accounts and Management (the Metcalf Report), for example, cites the case of a relatively small firm with a single client that represented 30 percent of the firm's total fees in the year 1973. In the celebrated Equity Funding case, that company represented more than 40 percent of the fees of the Wolfson, Weiner firm that audited the parent company.

Strictly speaking, this statement is incorrect because a client could 'supply a significant portion of the total fees of a public accounting firm' and future client-specific quasi-rents be zero. However, when the percentage of total fees dependent on one client is viewed as surrogate for the relative magnitude of client-specific quasi-rents, this fee relationship also serves as a surrogate for audit quality.

An interesting example of disclosure of the percentage of total fees dependent on retaining one client is the 1977 annual report of Peat, Marwick, Mitchell, which states that the single largest audit fee comprises only $\frac{1}{2}\%$ of total revenues. Moreover, a requirement of the new SEC practice section of the AICPA is that members of the section disclose the existence of clients whose fees comprise more than five percent of total audit fees. The Accountant's International Study Group (1976) recommends that auditors be prevented from accepting clients whose fees are expected to exceed ten percent of total income from clients.

When consumers use the percentage of total fees dependent on one client as a quality surrogate, and this percentage is perceived to be 'high' for a given auditor-client pair, the market expects auditor independence to be reduced with respect to that client. This will affect the auditor through the fees he is able to charge. Because of these costs of reduced independence, auditors have incentives to devise arrangements which reduce the percentage of the total fees observed to depend on retaining any one client. Large audit firms are one potential response to these costs.

Large audit firms, however, are not the only potential response to costs of reduced independence. Auditors can also increase perceived independence by increasing their investment in collateral which is not client-specific. Of course, in order to serve as a deterrent to auditor 'cheating', all collateral must be *auditor*-specific. However, it need not be *client*-specific. For example, it could be an established reputation for uniform quality audits or other brand name-type collateral.[25] To the extent that brand name expenditures are not dependent on retaining a particular client, they increase an auditor's total collateral and therefore decrease the percentage of total quasi-rents specific to any one client. Consumers are likely to view brand name collateral as a substitute for client-specific collateral, i.e., consumers view auditors with established reputations as having 'more to lose' from misrepresentation.[26]

The client-specific collateral analyzed here, however, has an important advantage over brand name collateral. When client-specific start-up costs are viewed as an unavoidable (sunk) cost of producing audits, their use as collateral may be less costly than incurring additional brand name-type expenditures. This point is made by Klein and Leffler (1981, p. 628) with

---

[25]As noted in footnote 10, auditor size cannot be a perfect surrogate for audit quality or these other arrangements would not be observed.

[26]For discussion of the brand name mechanism in general, see Barzel (1977, 1980), Darby and Karni (1973), Klein, Crawford, and Alchian (1978), and Klein and Leffler (1981).

respect to productive assets in general:

> One potentially efficient alternative or supplement to the pure price pre-
> mium method of guaranteeing quality may be the use of nonsalvageable
> productive assets rather than brand name (selling) assets...In particular,
> if the firm uses a production process that has a non-salvageable capital
> element, the normal rate of return (quasi-rent stream) on this element of
> production capital effectively serves as a quality assuring premium.

In other words, technological sunk costs which generate future quasi-rents
serve as collateral because they provide auditors with 'something to lose' if
caught 'cheating'. Client-specific start-up costs are of this genre, as are other
technological sunk costs such as investments in SEC expertise or industry
specialization.

Another advantage of the surrogates analyzed here over brand name
explanations for quality-differentiated audits [as in, e.g., Benston (1975,
1980), Dopuch and Simunic (1979), and Simunic (1980)], is that our analysis
is conditioned on a more easily measured choice variable, auditor size. In
addition, the percentage of total fees dependent on retaining any one client is
subject to empirical estimation, e.g., by using relationships developed in Simunic
(1980). Predictions that auditors supply more or less 'brand name' in
response to some parameter shift are more difficult to operationalize. For
example, how does one determine that 'more' brand name is supplied?[27] The
next section develops the implications of our collateral properties to auditor
size argument for some recent recommendations of the Derieux Committee.

5. 'Discrimination' against small audit firms

It is well recognized that client firms tend to change to Big Eight auditors
when going public [Carpenter and Strawser (1971)]. According to Arnett
and Danos (1979, p. 8), this displacement occurs in part because 'underwriters
frequently recommend that one of the largest eight accounting firms be used
because securities will sell at higher prices as a result'. The Derieux
Committee Report labels this the 'bigness syndrome' and asserts that 'in the
selection of a CPA firm, size is important only to the extent that it indicates
sufficient staff to carry out the engagement' (p. 21).

The Report goes on to attack 'discriminatory clauses' in both underwriting
and loan agreements which stipulate the client firm will engage a Big Eight
or 'nationally recognized' accounting firm. In the words of the Committee

---

[27]As an empirical proposition, it is difficult to identify material brand name expenditures by
auditors. In particular, given the profession's long-standing ban on advertising (removed in
1978), auditor brand name expenditures do not appear significant relative to the probable
magnitude of consumer quality evaluation costs.

Report (p. 21):

> Failure to oppose such discriminatory agreements leads to a further concentration of auditing services in an increasingly smaller group of the largest firms. This is not in the public interest since companies and other entities should be offered a choice from among firms of various sizes and characteristics.

It is difficult to see how imposing sanctions on parties who voluntarily contract with large audit firms preserves choice. If implemented and effective, these sanctions decrease the choice set by restricting the ability to engage large audit firms.

The Arnett and Danos (1979) study also opposes agreements which stipulate large or nationally known audit firms. Their argument rests on an explicit assumption that audit quality is independent of audit firm size (p. 9, emphasis added):

> *If we assume that the quality of the audit is the same regardless of the size of the firm performing it,* the banker would be supplied with the same information on which to base his decision; in this way the size of the firm should not necessarily be a consideration.

Provided that consumer perceptions of audit quality are also independent of auditor size, this statement is correct.

However, the collateral properties of auditor size identified in the current paper suggest that this assumption is not justified. Rather, our result that auditor size is a surrogate for audit quality provides economic justification both for displacement and for the alleged discriminatory contracts. It seems reasonable to assume that clients going public are those which have experienced a great deal of growth. In turn, growing clients are likely to have become a significant factor in a small auditor's portfolio. In other words, the value of quasi-rents specific to this client may have come to constitute a significant portion of the total value of the prior auditor's quasi-rent stream. In addition, a standard agency costs argument dictates that publicly held clients demand more monitoring, on average, than do privately held clients.

A change to a larger audit firm raises the level of audit quality exchanged when the client constitutes a smaller portion of the new auditor's total quasi-rents (that he did of the prior auditor's). Furthermore, as argued in section 2, when quality-evaluation costs lead auditors to specialize in a relatively uniform level of audit quality, a change of auditor may be required in order to increase the audit quality exchanged. Changing to a larger auditor with an established reputation when going public is consistent with an increase in audit quality at that time.[28]

Finally, when evaluating whether underwriters' and lenders' agreements are 'discriminatory', one should consider these parties' incentives. Competition among underwriters (and among bankers) ensures that the most efficient, i.e., those which are consistently able to get the highest prices for securities (able to evaluate loan applicants most accurately) survive. When consumers use auditor size as a quality surrogate, bankers and underwriters rationally request large audit firms.

If sanctions are successfully imposed against this choice (as advocated by the Derieux Committee), bankers and potential purchasers of firm securities will charge client firms which continue to contract with smaller, less well known auditors through lower security prices (higher interest rates). To the extent that the bilateral monopoly between client and incumbent auditor implies a sharing of these costs, audit fees do not fully adjust to shift these costs to incumbent auditors. In this case, successful prevention of 'discrimination' (that is, of competition from large audit firms) represents a windfall gain to smaller auditors at client expense. The allegation that these voluntary contracts discriminate against smaller firms, therefore, serves as an excuse,[29] i.e., a justification to effect a wealth transfer from clients to smaller audit firms.

The incentive to develop these justifications is provided by the existence of quasi-rents to larger audit firms. When quality evaluation costs are significant, smaller audit firms must incur costs to convince consumers that they supply a uniform level of high quality audits. Larger audit firms with an established clientele do not bear these costs currently. By alleging that this is 'unfair', smaller audit firms may avoid these costs and convert these quality related quasi-rents to monopoly profits. One strategy to effect this transformation is to impose sanctions on underwriters and bankers who voluntarily contract with large audit firms.

Another strategy is to shift these costs to professional bodies like the AICPA. In this case, quality related costs are borne by audit firms of all sizes, while the benefits accrue primarily to smaller, less well known audit firms. For example, one could argue, as do Arnett and Danos (p. 9, emphasis

---

[28]A more traditional technological economies of scale argument is also consistent with displacement. However, there is no apparent *technological* advantage, in this case, to a large audit firm over a consortium of smaller audit firms. Ultimately, as explained by Coase (1937), differences in organizational structure rely on differences in transactions costs, and not on differences in technology. In the current case, as elaborated in footnote 16, costly contracting prevents firms from contracting away client-specific quasi-rents. For more on this point, see DeAngelo (1981).

[29]For an extensive development of the use of public interest-type excuses for self-interested behavior, see Watts and Zimmerman (1979).

added) that:

> Bankers, lawyers, audit committee members, and others who affect selection of CPA firms *should* make an effort to evaluate the quality of the professional service offered as opposed to the package in which it is delivered...The bigness syndrome *should* not be permitted to govern the selection of auditors. We feel that without a major educational drive aimed at third parties, the current economic and legal environment unfortunately tends to favor selection of larger firms.

This argument commits the Nirvana fallacy of prescribing behavior as though audit quality evaluation costs are, or *should* be zero.

Perhaps more importantly, it serves as justification for policy recommendations, as in the Derieux Report, that the AICPA underwrite a national public relations program to 'educate' consumers and to 'bring about a more objective process of selection of a CPA firm' (p. 19). If implemented and effective, this recommendation represents a subsidy of smaller, less well known audit firms by larger, more well known audit firms. However, such a program will be ineffective to the extent that consumers continue to recognize the association between auditor size and audit quality discussed here.

6. Summary and conclusions

By asserting that audit quality is independent of auditor size, smaller audit firms have justified proposed wealth transfers from clients and from larger audit firms. This paper has shown that, when incumbent auditors earn client-specific quasi-rents, audit quality is not independent of auditor firm size. These quasi-rents, when subject to loss from discovery of a lower-than-promised audit quality, serve as collateral against such opportunistic behavior. This implies that, ceteris paribus, the larger the auditor as measured by the number of current clients and the smaller the client as a fraction of the auditor's total quasi-rents, the less incentive the auditor has to behave opportunistically, and the higher the perceived quality of the audit.

This collateral property of auditor size both creates a benefit to large audit firms and provides auditors with incentives to design their client portfolios so that the percentage of quasi-rents dependent on retaining any one client is low. Alternative means of reducing this percentage were discussed, and it was argued that technological sunk costs are likely to dominate brand name-type expenditures as a quality-assuring mechanism in the market for audit services.

Finally, some recent allegations of discrimination against smaller audit firms by bankers and underwriters were analyzed in the current framework.

It was argued that these allegations rest on an assumption that audit quality is independent of auditor size, and that the analysis of this paper casts serious doubt on the validity of that assumption.

References

Akerlof, G.A., 1970, The market for 'lemons': Quality uncertainty and the market mechanism, Quarterly Journal of Economics, Aug., 488–500.

Alchian, A. and H. Demsetz, 1972, Production, information costs, and economic organization, American Economic Review, Dec., 777–795.

American Institute of Certified Public Accountants, 1978, Report, conclusions, and recommendations of the Commission on Auditors' Responsibilities.

American Institute of Certified Public Accountants, 1980, Report of the Special Committee on Small and Medium Sized Firms.

Arnett, H. and P. Danos, 1979, CPA firm viability (University of Michigan, Ann Arbor, MI).

Baiman, S., 1979, Discussion of auditing: Incentives and truthful reporting, Studies on Auditing — Selections from the Research Opportunities in Auditing Program, 25–29.

Barzel, Y., 1977, Some fallacies in the interpretation of information costs, Journal of Law and Economics, 291–307.

Barzel, Y., 1980, Measurement cost and the organization of markets, Unpublished manuscript (University of Washington, Seattle, WA).

Becker, G., 1975, Human capital, second edition (The University of Chicago Press, Chicago, IL).

Bedingfield, J. and S. Loeb, 1974, Auditor changes — An examination, Journal of Accountancy, March, 66–69.

Benston, G., 1975, Accountants' integrity and financial reporting, Financial Executive, Aug., 10–14.

Benston, G., 1980, The market for public accounting services: Demand, supply, and regulation, Accounting Journal, forthcoming.

Bolton, S. and J. Crockett, 1979, How independent are the independent auditors?, Financial Analysts' Journal, Nov.–Dec., 76–78.

Burton, J. and W. Roberts, 1967, A study of auditor changes, Journal of Accountancy, April, 31–36.

Carpenter, C. and R. Strawser, 1971, Displacement of auditors when clients go public, Journal of Accountancy, June, 55–58.

Coase, R., 1937, The nature of the firm, Economica 4, 386–405.

Coe, T. and D. Palmon, 1979, Some evidence of the magnitude of auditor turnover, Unpublished manuscript (New York University, New York).

Darby, M. and E. Karni, 1973, Free competition and the optimal amount of fraud, Journal of Law and Economics, April, 67–88.

DeAngelo, L., 1981, Auditor independence, 'low balling', and disclosure regulation, Journal of Accounting and Economics, Aug., 113–127.

Demski, J. and R. Swieringa, 1974, A cooperative formulation of the audit choice problem, Accounting Review, July, 506–513.

Dopuch, N. and D. Simunic, 1979, The nature of competition in the auditing profession: A descriptive and normative view, Presented at the Conference on Regulation and the Accounting Profession (University of California, Los Angeles, CA).

Financial Executives' Institute, 1978, The annual audit revisted, Financial Executive, March, 38–44.

Hobgood, G. and J. Sciarrino, 1972, Management looks at audit services, Financial Executive, April, 26–32.

Kaplan, R., 1978, Supply and demand for auditing services and the nature of regulation in auditing: A critique, Arthur Young Professors' Roundtable Conference Proceedings, 125–131.

Klein, B., R. Crawford and A. Alchian, 1978, Vertical integration, appropriable rents, and the competitive contracting process, Journal of Law and Economics, Oct., 297–321.

Klein, B. and K. Leffler, 1981, The role of market forces in assuring contractual performance, Journal of Political Economy, Aug., 615–641.

Magee, R., 1979, Regulation and the cost-effectiveness of independent audits by CPAs, Presented at the Conference on Regulation and the Accounting Profession (University of California, Los Angeles, CA).

Ng, D., 1978, Supply and demand of auditing services and the nature of regulation in auditing, Arthur Young Professors' Roundtable Conference Proceedings, 99–124.

Simunic, D., 1980, The pricing of audit services: Theory and evidence, Journal of Accounting Research, Spring, 161–190.

Suit launched by '3 magic words' charges big 8 domination of AICPA, 1978, Public Accounting Report, Feb., 1–2.

United States Senate, 1977, Report of the Subcommittee on Reports, Accounting, and Management of the Committee on Government Operations (U.S. Government Printing Office, Washington, DC).

Watts, R., 1977, Corporate financial statements, a product of the market and political processes, Australian Journal of Management, April, 53–75.

Watts, R. and J. Zimmerman, 1978, Towards a positive theory of the determination of accounting standards, Accounting Review, Jan., 112–134.

Watts, R. and J. Zimmerman, 1979, The demand for and supply of accounting theories: The market for excuses, Accounting Review, 273–305.

Watts, R. and J. Zimmerman, 1981, The markets for independence and independent auditors, Unpublished manuscript (University of Rochester, Rochester, NY).

[9]

THE ACCOUNTING REVIEW
Vol. LXIV, No. 4
October 1989

Notes

Auditor Reputation and the Pricing of Initial Public Offerings

Randolph P. Beatty

ABSTRACT: It is hypothesized that an inverse relation exists between the reputation of the auditor of an initial public offering and the initial return earned by an investor. Specifically, clients that hire more reputable CPA firms should exhibit lower initial returns than clients that choose to hire CPA firms with less reputation capital at stake. Two proxies for auditor reputation are used to test this hypothesis. The first reputation proxy uses indicator variables for auditor size. Results indicate that the widely used Big Eight/non-Big Eight classification may measure CPA firm reputation capital with error particularly for the smaller Big Eight and larger non-Big Eight firms. A second reputation proxy is developed by regressing compensation paid to the auditing firms on measures of marginal cost of performing the audit. The initial return to the IPO investors is regressed on the residual from the compensation regression to provide evidence of the reputation hypothesis. Results indicate that clients that pay a premium for their registration audit exhibit lower initial returns for their investors. Thus, the results of both tests provide support for the hypothesized inverse relation between auditor reputation and initial public offering initial return.

A COMPANY "going public" must provide a prospectus that includes a description of its present and future operations and *audited* financial statements. Since privately held firms face limited disclosure requirements, the market usually possesses less publicly available data from them than from comparable publicly traded firms. This difference in regulatory environment provides a potentially fruitful setting in which to consider the role of the public accountant.

Since switching auditor just prior to going public is widely alleged, it is natural to investigate management's motivation for such a change (see "Small

The author would like to thank Linda DeAngelo, Victor Defeo, Nick Gonedes, Pat Hughes, Prem Jain, Rick Lambert, Bill Kinney, David Larcker, Laurentius Marais, Jay Ritter, Rex Thompson, Ivo Welch, and workshop participants at the Wharton School, Indiana University, Northwestern, New York University, University of Southern California, Temple, Columbia, and University of Pittsburgh for providing comments and suggestions. I'm particularly indebted to Jay Ritter for the construction of the database used in this project. Financial support was provided by the Fishman-Davidson Center for the Study of the Service Sector at the Wharton School.

Randolph P. Beatty, Graduate School of Business, University of Chicago.

Manuscript received June 1987.
Revisions received August 1988 and March 1989.
Accepted April 1989.

694   The Accounting Review, October 1989

CPA Concern Sues an Underwriter Over Loss of Client," *The Wall Street Journal* [July 18, 1983, p. 1]). Carpenter and Strawser [1971] describe the results of a survey of AICPA members concerning the displacement issue as follows:

> Almost universally, the reason expressed [for the change in auditors] was that the underwriters informed the client that a "nationally known firm" was necessary to sell their offering at the highest possible price [p. 55].

This widely held view suggests that the employment of a "nationally known" audit firm will increase the price (reduce the initial return) received by the initial public offering (IPO) client.

This paper presents and tests the hypothesis that audit firm reputation is inversely related to the initial return earned by an IPO investor. The evidence is consistent with an inverse relation between auditor reputation and the initial return to the IPO investor. First, tests of linear restrictions of indicator variable coefficients are interpreted within the traditional Big Eight/non-Big Eight framework to suggest a negative relation between auditor reputation and initial return. A second partition (Largest-Five, Middle-Six, and Smallest-Nine audit firms) is introduced to provide evidence that *ad hoc* classification schemes may only crudely separate the set of audit firms by reputation capital. In particular, it appears that smaller Big Eight and larger non-Big Eight firms exhibit similar reputations in the IPO market. To test the reputation hypothesis without relying on an *ad hoc* classification, reputation capital is inferred from the observation of auditor compensation. These tests use a measure of the residual compensation paid to the IPO auditing firm and provide the first direct evidence of the hypothesized reputation relation.

Section I draws from the previous empirical and theoretical literature to suggest testable assertions relating auditor reputation and the initial return to an IPO investor. Section II describes the data used in the empirical tests and provides a number of descriptive statistics. Results of regression tests of the reputation hypothesis are presented in Section III and, finally, Section IV concludes with a summary.

I. UNDERPRICING AND THE ROLE OF THE AUDITING FIRM

Previous studies of the IPO market have focused on an empirical phenomenon that has been described as "underpricing" of the firm's equity securities.[1,2] The term "underpricing" is used to describe the difference between the offering price and the market clearing price at issuance. Numerous empirical papers have demonstrated this persistent underpricing of equity securities [Ibbotson, 1975; Ibbotson and Jaffee, 1975; and Ritter, 1984].

Various asymmetric information models have been proposed to explain this phenomenon. In one model, the investment banker is "better informed" than the issuing firm as to the demand for the issuing firm's securities [Baron, 1982]. In another, two classes of IPO investors, informed and uninformed, are assumed to exist [Rock, 1982 and 1986; Beatty and Ritter, 1986]. In each of these models, the investment banker or the uninformed investors face uncertainty concerning the IPO firm value. The precision

---

[1] For a review of the literature on the IPO market, see Smith [1986].

[2] Underpricing translates directly into the initial return, defined as the return earned by an investor buying at the offering price and selling at the first-day closing price. These terms will be used interchangeably in the remainder of this paper.

of the distribution of uncertainty of firm value has been described as *ex ante* uncertainty [Beatty and Ritter, 1986]. Both of these models imply that there is a positive relation between *ex ante* uncertainty and the underpricing of the IPO.

Some investigators have argued in the agency literature that auditing services are demanded to reduce costs arising from conflicts of interests between owners and managers [Jensen and Meckling, 1976; Watts and Zimmerman, 1983]. Since the nature and extent of agency costs vary across firms that attempt to minimize these costs, the auditing services demanded will be heterogeneous. This heterogeneity may lead CPA firms to differentiate themselves on the basis of investment in reputation capital to facilitate the attestation function [Kinney, 1988].

Simunic and Stein [1987] suggest that auditor product differentiation on the dimensions of control, credibility, and product line motivates management's auditor choice in the IPO market. They conclude that the form of the underwriter agreement, the proportion of common stocks held by outsiders after the IPO, and a measure of uncertainty are related to the choice of auditing firm. Beatty [1989] provides evidence consistent with Simunic and Stein [1987] that larger and less risky IPO clients tend to hire Big Eight audit firms. As in this study, preliminary evidence from indicator variable regressions suggested that auditor reputation might be related to underpricing.

Titman and Trueman [1986] present a signalling model that results in auditor quality providing information useful to investors in assessing the value of the IPO firm. Two features of their model lead to signalling of the IPO firm's value. First, high quality auditors (or investment bankers) are those individuals with a comparative advantage in establishing the reported information variable that is related to the firm value. Second, the firm is required to pay a "price premium" for this higher quality audit.[3] These two expected costs of hiring the high quality auditor exceed the expected benefits of misclassification for the low firm value IPOs. This cost-benefit relation leads the entrepreneur to choose an audit firm that "signals" firm value to the market. Although this model does not consider the underpricing phenomenon, a similar signalling environment is used here to hypothesize a relation between auditor reputation and the underpricing of an IPO.

The firm's existing owners have an incentive to minimize underpricing since it transfers wealth from them to the new investors.[4] The literature suggests a direct relation between *ex ante* uncertainty and underpricing of the IPO [Baron, 1982; Rock, 1982 and 1986; and Beatty and Ritter, 1986]. All firms (existing owners) have an incentive to disclose "low" *ex ante* uncertainty, giving rise to the classic "lemons" problem [Akerlof, 1970]. However, firms whose *ex ante* uncertainty is in fact "high" have a greater incentive to misrepresent.

One means of reducing the misrepresentation problem is to hire an agent who can credibly attest to the assertions contained in the audited financial statements [Kinney, 1988]. Auditors have an incentive to investigate and report deviations in application of accounting principles since their reputation capital is

---

[3] Klein and Leffler [1981] present a model of product quality variation that requires a price premium for the high quality product to assure its production.

[4] The "amount of money left on the table," the difference between the offering price and the market clearing price multiplied by the number of shares in the IPO, is a measure of the wealth transferred from existing owners to new investors.

reduced by *ex post* revelation of errors or misstatements [Palmrose, 1988]. Since auditing firms that have invested more in reputation capital have greater incentives to reduce application errors, the information disclosed in the accounting reports audited by these firms will be more precise, *ceteris paribus*. This reduction in measurement error will allow uninformed investors to estimate more precisely the distribution of firm value. Since the high reputation auditor attests to a report that reduces uninformed investors' *ex ante* uncertainty, this comparative advantage will be priced in the market for audit services. Value-maximizing owners of the IPO firm will choose the auditing firm with reputation capital that equates the marginal benefit of less underpricing with the marginal cost of a higher quality audit.

The preceding arguments have two implications. First, the initial return of an IPO will be inversely related to the reputation of the auditing firm attesting to the accounting reports. Second, the premium paid for a high quality auditing firm will be inversely related to the initial return of the IPO client.

II. DATA AND DESCRIPTIVE STATISTICS

The data used in the empirical tests are drawn from the population of 2,567 IPOs from 1975–1984. The final sample was reduced to 2,215.[5] The main data sources for the variables are the IPO's registration statement and amendments and *Going Public: The IPO Reporter* (published weekly).

The initial return for a firm going public is defined as the first day gross return to an investor who acquires a share and sells at the closing bid price on the first day of public trading.[6] For 1975–1984, the average initial return is 22.1 percent.

A test of the compensation premium

implication of the reputation hypothesis requires a measure of the fee paid to the auditor. A proxy for this fee that is available for the entire sample is the cash compensation. This measure includes auditing, printing, legal, and other miscellaneous fees (such as "Blue Sky" registration fees). The average cash compensation for 1975–1984 is $218,929.

Aftermarket standard deviation is presented as an *ex post* proxy for *ex ante* uncertainty to assess cross-sectional differences in *ex ante* uncertainty for the sample. The aftermarket standard deviation is computed as the standard deviation of returns for the first 20 trading days excluding the initial return using bid prices. This measure is available for only 1,807 firms since the remaining firms were not listed on NASDAQ or another exchange. The average aftermarket standard deviation in the sample is .033.

---

[5] Each IPO included in the final sample had initial return, age, type of offering, gross proceeds, sales, book value of equity, and cash expenses (auditor fees, legal fees, and miscellaneous fees) available in their S1 or S18 registration statement or other publicly available sources. Regulation A registrations, small public offerings, were not included in this study due to data limitations. An initial public offering that is registered under Regulation A is significantly smaller than the average offering in this sample. Prior to 1978, the maximum amount raised in a Regulation A offer was $500,000. After 1978, the limit was raised to $1,500,000. Missing registration statements and the lack of an observable bid price (firms trading in the "pink sheets") account for the reduction in observations from 2,567 to 2,215.

[6] The first day closing price is not always available. The closing bid price is available for 1,499 of the IPOs within one day of the closing date. An additional 412 bid prices are available within one week of the closing date. Bid prices are available for 236 IPOs within a month of the closing date of the IPO. The remaining 68 firms' bid price is obtained within one year of the offering. For IPOs listed on NASDAQ (82.6 percent), the first available closing bid price from the *Daily Stock Price Record* has been used to construct the initial return. Finally, 12.4 percent of the IPOs in this study were not listed on NASDAQ. These firms required the use of other data sources to estimate the initial returns for these securities [Ritter, 1984].

Table 1 presents selected descriptive statistics for audit firm IPO clients. The identified firms audited at least ten IPOs during the 1975–1984 period and the Big Eight firms audited 58 percent of the IPO clients.[7] The statistical tests suggest a number of differences in IPO clients by Big Eight/non-Big Eight distinction. First, larger clients generally are audited by Big Eight firms.[8] However, the traditional Big Eight/non-Big Eight distinction does not completely capture differences in client size. In particular, Peat Marwick, Touche Ross, and Coopers & Lybrand clients exhibit similar magnitudes of median sales revenue as Laventhol Horwath, Seidman & Seidman, and Alexander Grant clients.

Panels A and B of Table 1 suggest that auditor compensation is larger for Big Eight audit firms relative to competing non-Big Eight firms.[9] Aftermarket standard deviation is smaller for Big Eight compared to non-Big Eight clients. Finally, initial return is significantly smaller for Big Eight compared to non-Big Eight clients. These differences in risk and return suggest that clients of particular subsets of CPA firms may not be homogeneous with respect to *ex ante* uncertainty.

III. Underpricing, *Ex Ante* Uncertainty, and Auditing Firm Reputation

In this section, an indicator variable approach is used to test for a relation between auditing firm reputation and the underpricing of initial public offerings. The regression model controls for *ex ante* uncertainty (client age, type of underwriting contract, and percentage ownership offered in the IPO), industry affiliation (oil and gas indicator variable), and other reputation effects (underwriter indicator variable). The marginal impact of a particular CPA

firm is tested with an indicator variable for each of the 20 CPA firms auditing more than ten IPOs in the 1975–1984 period, and the reputation hypothesis is evaluated by testing linear restrictions on the estimated coefficients of the Big Eight/non-Big Eight indicator variables.[10] Finally, sensitivity of the results to the traditional Big Eight/non-Big Eight grouping is considered by alternative groupings based on client size.

The estimated model is:

$$\begin{aligned}
\text{Initial Return}_i \\
= a + b \,(\text{Age of Client}_i) \\
+ c \,(\text{Type of Underwriting Contract}_i) \\
+ d \,(\text{Percentage of Ownership Offered}_i) \\
+ e \,(\text{Oil \& Gas Indicator}_i) \\
+ f \,(\text{Underwriter Reputation Indicator}_i) \\
+ r \,(\text{Auditing Firm (1-20) Indicator}_i). \qquad (1)
\end{aligned}$$

Indicator Variable Regression

Client age is used as a control variable in the regression model (panel A of Table 2) since a longer operating history may provide market participants with in-

---

[7] This percentage is consistent with the 59 percent, 68 percent, and 62 percent concentration ratios for publicly traded clients reported in Simunic [1980], Palmrose [1986], and Francis and Simon [1987].

[8] Book value of equity, age, gross proceeds, and net proceeds provide additional support for the notion that larger clients tend to be audited by Big Eight firms [Beatty, 1989].

[9] For a subsample of 1,276 IPOs (1981–1984), auditor fees for preparation of the registration document were collected from Part II of the registration statement. Typically, this involves obtaining amendments to the registration statement since the auditing fees are rarely submitted with the final prospectus. The correlation between reported accounting fees (Part 2 of the prospectus) and cash compensation is .771, suggesting that the cash compensation (available for the entire sample) provides a reasonable proxy for the auditor's compensation for reviewing the prospectus.

[10] Testing linear restrictions on estimated coefficients is described in Judge et al. [1980, pp. 61–62].

TABLE 1

DESCRIPTIVE STATISTICS (1975–1984)
CLIENT SIZE, RETURN, AND *Ex Ante* UNCERTAINTY MEASURES
MEDIAN SALES REVENUE, AUDITOR COMPENSATION, INITIAL RETURN,
AND STANDARD DEVIATION BY AUDITOR

Auditor	Sales (000's)	Cash Compensation[1] (000's)	Initial Return	Aftermarket Standard Deviation[2]	Number of Clients[3] (N_1, N_2)
Panel A. Big Eight Audit Firm Clients:					
Ernst & Whinney (EW)	$10,423	$219	.025	.027	141, 125
Deloitte Haskins & Sells (DHS)	6,437	241	.023	.034	122, 102
Price Waterhouse (PW)	5,939	240	.021	.030	141, 128
Arthur Young & Co. (AY)	6,404	252	.038	.031	163, 149
Arthur Andersen & Co. (AA)	5,695	230	.053	.034	225, 207
Peat, Marwick, Mitchell & Co. (PMM)	4,110	210	.028	.026	191, 171
Touche Ross & Co. (TR)	3,220	199	.050	.030	153, 139
Coopers & Lybrand (CL)	2,246	185	.018	.033	146, 133
Big Eight	4,926	220	.031	.031	1282, 1154
Panel B. Non-Big Eight Audit Firm Clients:					
Laventhol Horwath (LH)	$ 4,321	$180	.050	.034	59, 49
Seidman & Seidman (SS)	3,668	175	.042	.037	27, 25
Alexander Grant (AG)	2,300	175	.042	.035	55, 45
Main Hurdman (MH)	1,755	188	.033	.033	78, 67
Mann Judd Landau (MJL)	1,631	112	.044	.033	16, 12
McGladrey Hendrickson (MHD)	778	108	.250	.034	18, 16
Oppenheim, Appel (OAD)	307	147	.150	.040	10, 7
All Others	87	90	.068	.040	577, 372
Fox, Fox & Co. (FOX)	96	85	.125	.038	37, 33
Hein & Sikora (HS)	6	75	.375	.062	13, 12
Newman & Co. (NEW)	3	58	.188	.037	12, 10
Lehman, Butterwick (LB)	1	56	.125	.034	10, 4
Roth (R)	0	50	.600	.073	21, 1
Non-Big Eight	154	101	.067	.038	933, 653

Panel C. Non-Parametric Statistical Comparisons of Big Eight and Non-Big Eight Clients:

Statistic	Sales	Cash Compensation	Initial Return	Aftermarket Standard Deviation
Big Eight, non-Big Eight Comparison				
Mann-Whitney *U*-Test	−15.390	−15.452	2.435	−6.100
(Probability)	.000	.000	.015	.000
Median Test Chi-Square	159.608	191.257	7.610	27.374
(Probability)	.000	.000	.006	.000

[1] Cash Compensation = Auditor fees + Legal fees + Printing fees + Miscellaneous fees.

[2] Aftermarket Standard Deviation = standard deviation of return 2 through 21.

[3] Panels A and B present medians for selected variables by individual audit firm and Big Eight/non-Big Eight distinction. In the final column of panels A and B N_1 = the number of IPO clients and N_2 = the number of clients available to compute aftermarket standard deviation. Panel C presents the Mann-Whitney *U*-test and Median test for differences in the selected variables by Big Eight/non-Big Eight.

TABLE 2

INDICATOR REGRESSION RESULTS WITH DEPENDENT VARIABLE = INITIAL RETURN AND INDEPENDENT VARIABLES = AGE, TYPE OF OFFERING, PERCENT RETAINED BY OWNERS, OIL AND GAS, UNDERWRITER, AND AUDITING FIRM INDICATORS

1975–1984

($n = 2,215$)

$$\text{Initial Return}_i = a + b\,(\text{Age of Client}_i) + c\,(\text{Type of Underwriting Contract}_i) + d\,(\text{Percentage of Ownership Offered}_i) + e\,(\text{Oil and Gas Indicator}_i) + f\,(\text{Underwriter Reputation Indicator}_i) + r\,(\text{Audit Firm (1–20) Indicator}_i)$$

Panel A. Control Variable Coefficient Estimates:

	Constant	Age	Type of Offering (0, 1)	Percent by Owners	Oil and Gas Indicator (0, 1)	Underwriter Indicator (0, 1)
	.29829	−.00182	−.21432	.15384	.13985	−.06997
	(.03830)	(.00095)	(.02720)	(.07313)	(.03720)	(.03153)
	$t = 7.79$	$t = -1.91$	$t = -7.88$	$t = 2.10$	$t = 3.76$	$t = -2.22$

Panel B. Indicator Variable Coefficient Estimates:

Big Eight Firms

AA	AY	CL	DHS	EW	PM	PW	TR
.01113	.02305	.03156	−.01340	.01514	.06304	−.04721	.02402
(.04143)	(.04647)	(.04812)	(.05181)	(.04936)	(.04367)	(.04902)	(.04725)
$t = .27$	$t = .50$	$t = .66$	$t = -.26$	$t = .31$	$t = 1.44$	$t = -.96$	$t = .43$

Non-Big Eight Firms

AG	FOX	HS	LB	LH	MH	MHD	MJL	NEW	OAD	R	SS
.02590	.16427	.41680	−.27260	−.00981	.02303	.62291	−.03848	−.02625	.00283	.73832	−.05193
(.07251)	(.08684)	(.14364)	(.16328)	(.07034)	(.06219)	(.12250)	(.12991)	(.15094)	(.16308)	(.11443)	(.10126)
$t = .36$	$t = 1.89$	$t = 2.90$	$t = -1.67$	$t = -.14$	$t = .37$	$t = 5.09$	$t = -.30$	$t = -.18$	$t = .02$	$t = 6.45$	$t = -.51$

$R^2 = .116$ $F\text{-statistic} = 11.523^*$

continued overleaf

TABLE 2—Continued

Panel C. Tests of Hypothesis that Linear Combinations of Audit Firm Coefficients Equal Zero—$\underline{Lr}=0^{**}$:

	F-statistic	Probability
Big Eight—non-Big Eight Comparisons		
Sum of the Big Eight Coefficients Equal Zero	$F_{1,2109}=.222$	.638
Sum of the non-Big Eight Coefficients Equal Zero	$F_{1,2109}=10.897$	.001
Big Eight Minus non-Big Eight Coefficients Equal Zero	$F_{1,2109}=11.581$	.001
Largest-Five, Middle-Six, and Smallest-Nine Comparisons Classification by Client Sales Revenue (Table 1)		
Sum of the Largest-Five Coefficients Equal Zero	$F_{1,2109}=.006$	.940
Sum of the Middle-Six Coefficients Equal Zero	$F_{1,2109}=.146$	.702
Sum of the Smallest-Nine Coefficients Equal Zero	$F_{1,2109}=14.318$	.001
Largest-Five Minus Middle-Six Coefficients Equal Zero	$F_{1,2109}=.247$	.619
Middle-Six Minus Smallest-Nine Coefficients Equal Zero	$F_{1,2109}=13.378$	.001
Largest-Five Minus Smallest-Nine Coefficients Equal Zero	$F_{1,2109}=16.053$	.001

Note: Standard errors are in parentheses. The sample is composed of 2,215 SEC-registered initial public offerings from 1975–1984. The mean of the initial return is 22.1 percent. The mean of the age of the clients is 7.359 years. There were 1,484 firm commitment offerings in the 2,215 IPOs. The average percentage offered by owners is .338. There were 233 oil and gas firms going public from 1975–1984. Major bracket underwriters were associated as lead underwriter or co-managing an IPO in 390 cases out of the 2,215. The remaining variables (AA through SS) are indicator variables (0, 1) for firms listed in Table 1. The t-statistics are presented below each coefficient in panels A and B.

* Significant at the .0001 level.

** $\underline{L}$ is a 1 by 20 vector with 0's, 1's, or −1's to create the appropriate restriction of interest. $\underline{r}$ is a 20 by 1 vector of the estimated indicator variable coefficients.

formation concerning managerial production-investment decisions. This additional information may allow investors
to marginally reduce their estimate of *ex
ante* uncertainty. The estimated coefficient is negative and statistically significant at the .06 probability level. This
result suggests that larger client age indicates lower *ex ante* uncertainty.[11]

The second control variable is the type
of underwriting contract, firm commitment or best efforts.[12] The type of
underwriter agreement may provide a
proxy for the underwriter's assessment
of the price uncertainty for an IPO. The
type of offering (best efforts=0, firm
commitment=1) is inversely related to
the initial return for the IPO at the .0001
probability level. This result is consistent
with lower *ex ante* uncertainty for firm
commitment underwriting contracts.

Research by Leland and Pyle [1977]
and Downes and Heinkel [1982] suggests
that the percent ownership retained by
insiders signals private information
possessed by the owner/manager to investors. The percentage offered by
owners in the IPO is positively related to
the initial return at the .04 level consistent with Leland and Pyle's model.

Table 2 reports two final indicator
variable coefficients for each regression.
The oil and gas indicator variable (oil
and gas=1, others=0) is considered
since Ritter [1984] observes a significant
association between industry affiliation
and initial return during the "Hot Issue"
market of 1980. Panel A of Table 2
shows that, as in the previous study, oil
and gas IPOs exhibit significant positive
initial returns.[13] The underwriter indicator variable controls for underwriter
reputation. Beatty and Ritter [1986]
argue that underwriter reputation is related to the level of underpricing of an
initial public offering. This study uses an
indicator variable (top 18=1, others=0)

for the 18 largest underwriters by total
capital that are members of the Securities Industry Association.[14] The underwriter indicator variable regression coefficient is significant at the .03 level.

Panel B of Table 2 summarizes the indicator variables for the 20 identified
CPA firms. Four CPA firm indicator
variables are positive and significant at
the .05 level. They are Fox, Fox & Co.;
Hein & Sikora; McGladrey, Hendrickson
& Co.; and Allen Roth. Clients of these
four non-Big Eight firms exhibited significantly higher initial returns than
those of other auditors.

Two sets of tests of linear combinations of the coefficients of the CPA firm
indicator variables are presented in panel
C of Table 2. First, the traditional Big
Eight/non-Big Eight dichotomy is investigated. The second is partitioned based
upon the largest-five, middle-six, and

---

[11] It has been suggested in Manegold [1987] that distinguishing between startup and operating firms may
control for client risk. In unreported regressions, a
startup/operating indicator variable replaced the age
variable. The results were consistent with the reported
results and the startup/operating variable was not
significant.

[12] A "firm commitment" underwriting agreement
specifies that the underwriter purchases the shares from
the client to be offered for resale. In a "best efforts"
underwriting arrangement, an underwriter agrees to
place as many securities as a "best effort" permits.

[13] Elimination of the oil and gas firms from the sample
does not alter any of the inferences of the tests. Also, an
indicator variable for "high tech" firm was considered
with insignificant results.

[14] The Securities Industry Association is an organization that lobbies for members' interests. Membership is
restricted to "reputable" securities industry members.
As with other voluntary organizations, the definition of
reputable member of the securities industry is not well-
defined. The SIA has summarized the capital ranks for
their membership in an annual publication, *Securities
Industry Yearbook*. The top 18 underwriters have been
assigned to the "highly" reputable category for purposes of the underwriter indicator variable. The top 18
underwriters capital as of January 1, 1985 exceeded
$200,000,000. Alternative classifications of underwriter
reputation by capital rank did not appreciably change the
qualitative results.

smallest-nine audit firm median client sales revenue.

Panel C reports tests of the linear restrictions on the coefficients of the Big Eight and non-Big Eight indicator variables. The results indicate significant differences in initial return based upon the Big Eight/non-Big Eight distinction. The trichotomous partition tests indicate that the middle-six CPA firms are more similar to the largest-five CPA firms than to the smallest-nine CPA firms. This sensitivity analysis suggests that the traditional Big Eight/non-Big Eight distinction may measure reputation with error since the smallest Big Eight and largest non-Big Eight appear to exhibit substantial similarities. Finally, the correlation matrix (not reported) indicates that correlations across covariates are small (all less than .32) and, thus, multicollinearity is not expected to affect the results.

These results provide evidence of a relation between auditor classification and the initial return. However, interpreting these results as consistent with a relation between reputation and initial return requires the maintained hypothesis that a particular partition, such as the traditional Big Eight/non-Big Eight distinction, captures differences in firm reputation capital. Since choice of an appropriate partition is rather *ad hoc*, an alternative approach that does not rely on arbitrary classifications to test the reputation hypothesis is considered in the next subsection.

Two-Stage Regression Approach

There are two salient features of the reputation hypothesis that suggest the use of an omitted variables technique to establish a proxy for reputation. First, a firm's reputation capital is unobservable. Second, the reputation hypothesis implies that the IPO client is charged a premium for employing the auditor's

reputation capital. A two-stage approach estimates an auditor compensation regression with observable independent variables. Then the residuals from the first regression are used as a proxy for the unobservable variable, reputation capital. The relation between the residual of the estimated auditor compensation regression and the unobservable reputation variable is illustrated and then the "omitted variables" formulation is applied to test the reputation hypothesis.

A compensation regression model that does not include the omitted variable can be estimated as follows:

$$\begin{aligned}
\text{Cash Comp}_i \\
= a_1 + b_1 \text{ (Gross Proceeds}_i) \\
+ c_1 \text{ (Sales}_i) \\
+ d_1 \text{ (Equity}_i) + u_i.[15]
\end{aligned} \quad (2)$$

However, the reputation hypothesis asserts that the correct specification of the regression equation is:

$$\begin{aligned}
\text{Cash Comp}_i \\
= a_1{}^* + b_1{}^* \text{ (Gross Proceeds}_i) \\
+ c_1{}^* \text{ (Sales}_i) \\
+ d_1{}^* \text{ (Equity}_i) \\
+ e_1{}^* (R_i) + v_i.
\end{aligned} \quad (3)$$

If one assumes that the omitted variable, R (a firm's reputation capital), is uncorrelated with the other independent variables, the sign of the correlation between the estimated residual and the omitted variable is directly related to the sign of $e_1{}^*$. Formally, this correlation is:

$$\begin{aligned}
\text{corr}(u_i, R_i) \\
= e_1{}^* E\{(R_i - E(R))^2\} \\
/(\text{std. dev}_u)(\text{std. dev}_R).
\end{aligned} \quad (4)$$

Since we assume that the IPO client is

---

[15] The chosen independent variables in the compensation regression are intended to proxy for the marginal cost of the audit. Omitted variables analysis is discussed in Kmenta [1986], pp. 392–395.

charged a premium for the auditor's reputation, the sign of the omitted variable coefficient, e_1^*, is positive. Thus, u_i from equation (2) provides a measure that is positively correlated with the variable of interest. The second-stage regression relates the initial return to the control variables and the residual from the compensation regression as follows:

$$\text{Initial Return}_i$$
$$= a_2 + b_2 \text{ (Age of Client}_i)$$
$$+ c_2 \text{ (Type of Underwriting Contract}_i)$$
$$+ d_2 \text{ (Percentage of Ownership Offered}_i)$$
$$+ e_2 \text{ (Oil \& Gas Indicator}_i)$$
$$+ f_2 \text{ (Underwriter Reputation Indicator}_i)$$
$$+ r_2 (u_i). \tag{5}$$

A negative coefficient on the unexpected cash compensation, u_i, is consistent with the reputation hypothesis.

Table 3 presents results of the two-stage least squares approach used to assesss the relation between audit firm reputation and initial return. In the first stage, auditor compensation is regressed on three size variables, gross proceeds, sales revenue, and book value of equity. The residual from the regression should be interpreted as the price paid to a particular audit firm above or below the average price paid for auditor reputation. The average price paid for reputation is imbedded in the constant term in equation (2). From the analysis in Section II, as the price paid for the CPA firm's reputation capital is increased, less "money is left on the table" in the form of underpricing, which suggests an inverse relation with initial return. The reputation hypothesis predicts that the coefficient on the residual auditor compensation variable will be negative in the second stage regression.

Sales revenue, book value of equity,

and gross proceeds provide proxies for the size variables that have been found by previous studies to be related to auditor compensation. Although these three measures are different from the independent variables suggested by previous researchers of auditor compensation [Simunic, 1980; Mayer et al., 1985; and Francis and Simon, 1987], they provide similar control for the marginal cost of performing an audit. For instance, increased sales revenue can be expected to be directly related to increased inventories and accounts receivable. In addition, one would expect that larger firms (measured by book value of equity and gross proceeds) would more likely exhibit more consolidated subsidiaries, two-digit SIC codes, and foreign operations. It should be noted that the R-squared for equation (2) of Table 3 is .18, which is comparable to Simunic's less-than-$125,000,000 regression results of .28. However, the results of this analysis rest on the assumption that any missing variables are uncorrelated with the initial return of the IPO.

The coefficients for gross proceeds and sales revenue in panel A of Table 3 are positive and significantly related to cash compensation,[16] suggesting that as the size of the IPO client increases the total payment to auditor, lawyer, and printing fees increases (see Simunic [1980] and Mayer et al. [1985]).

Panel C of Table 3 provides average and median residuals from equation (2) that suggest Big Eight firms are being

---

[16] Panel B of Table 3 discloses relatively higher correlations between sales, book value of equity, and gross proceeds than any other correlations of other independent variables. Thus, the estimated coefficients in equation (2) should be viewed with caution. This high level of multicollinearity may explain the negative and significant coefficient on stockholders' equity. The purpose of this regression is merely to filter out the size related costs of performing an audit, not to emphasize the magnitudes of the coefficients in equation (2).

TABLE 3
TWO-STAGE REGRESSION ESTIMATES:
EQUATION (2) = CASH COMPENSATION PREDICTION MODEL
EQUATION (5) = UNDERPRICING MODEL WITH DEPENDENT VARIABLE = INITIAL RETURN AND
INDEPENDENT VARIABLES = AGE, TYPE OF OFFERING, PERCENT RETAINED BY OWNERS,
OIL AND GAS INDICATOR, UNDERWRITER INDICATOR, AND
UNEXPECTED CASH COMPENSATION
($n = 2,215$)

Panel A. Regression Results:

Dependent Variable—Cash Expenses for Audit, Legal, Printing, and Miscellaneous Fees

$$\text{Cash Comp}_i = a_1 + b_1 \text{ (Gross Proceeds}_i) + c_1 \text{ (Sales}_i)$$
$$+ d_1 \text{ (Equity}_i) \qquad + u_i \qquad (2)$$

	Constant	Gross Proceeds	Sales	Book Value of Equity
Equation (2)	178.90638	.003632	.00036	−.00011
	(4.40544)	(.000233)	(.00006)	(.00003)
	$t = 40.61$	$t = 15.61$	$t = 5.88$	$t = -3.22$

$R^2 = .183$ F-statistic = 165.293*

Dependent Variable—Initial Return

$$\text{Initial Return}_i = a_2 + b_2 \text{ (Age of Client}_i) + c_2 \text{ (Type of Underwriting Contract}_i)$$
$$+ d_2 \text{ (Percentage of Ownership Offered}_i)$$
$$+ e_2 \text{ (Oil and Gas Indicator}_i)$$
$$+ f_2 \text{ (Underwriter Reputation Indicator}_i)$$
$$+ r_2 \text{ (}u_i) \qquad (5)$$

	Constant	Age	Type of Offering	Percent by Owner	Oil and Gas	Underwriter Indicator	Residual from Equation (2)
Equation (5)	.34275	−.00204	−.21628	.10011	.13753	−.05873	−.00018
	(.03586)	(.00096)	(.02720)	(.07378)	(.03712)	(.03191)	(.00006)
	$t = 9.56$	$t = -2.13$	$t = -7.95$	$t = 1.36$	$t = 3.71$	$t = -1.84$	$t = -2.74$

$R^2 = .085$ F-statistic = 34.116*

   Standard errors are in parentheses. The mean of the dependent variable (audit fees, legal fees, and miscellaneous expenses) for equation (2) is $218,929. The means of the independent variables, gross proceeds, sales, and book value of equity, are $9,173,808, $20,825,369, and $7,409,655, respectively. The final variable (residual from eq. (2)) represents the difference between the OLS estimate of auditor, legal, and printing fees and the actual observed fees by IPO client.
   * Significant at the .01 level.

paid relatively more than non-Big Eight firms after controlling for client size differences. The residuals for the audit firms that were statistically significant in the indicator variable regressions (Fox, Fox & Co.; Hein & Sikora; McGladrey Hendrickson; and Roth) tend to have the largest negative residuals.

Panel D of Table 3 partitions the CPA firms based on the largest-five, middle-six, and smallest-nine audit firms by client sales revenue from Table 1. These results indicate that the auditor compensation premium is significantly larger for the largest-five firms than for the two remaining groups. In addition, the fee

TABLE 3—Continued

Panel B. Pearson Product-Moment Correlation:

	Age	Type of Offering	Percent by Owners	Oil and Gas	Underwriter	Gross Proceeds	Sales	Book Value of Equity
Gross Proceeds	.236*	.209*	−.124*	−.063	.375*			
Sales	.328*	.160*	−.122*	−.053	.321*	.538*		
Book Value of Equity	.084*	.035	−.065*	−.072*	.089*	.336*	.525*	
Residual from Equation (2)	.142*	.368*	−.222*	−.060	.279*	.000	.000	.000

  * Significant at the .01 level.

Panel C. Average Residual from Equation (2) Panel A by Audit Firm and Big Eight/Non-Big Eight Classification:

		Average Residual	Median Residual	Big Eight Average Residual	Median Residual
(1) AA	(225)	29.258	2.769		
(2) AY	(163)	26.901	11.068		
(3) CL	(146)	9.081	−34.347		
(4) DHS	(122)	24.377	22.288	23.867	−2.231
(5) EW	(141)	28.824	−17.952		
(6) PMM	(191)	34.964	−6.217		
(7) PW	(141)	21.309	7.297		
(8) TR	(153)	10.349	−14.796		

				Non-Big Eight Average Residual	Median Residual
(9) AG	(55)	−18.877	−31.567		
(10) FOX	(37)	−69.082	−106.279		
(11) HS	(13)	−105.641	−114.743		
(12) LB	(10)	−124.984	−129.163		
(13) LH	(59)	3.298	−30.437		
(14) MH	(78)	20.577	−24.392		
(15) MHD	(18)	−73.237	−83.854	−32.795	−86.003
(16) MJL	(16)	36.502	−76.752		
(17) NEW	(12)	−116.726	−127.294		
(18) OAD	(10)	30.847	−40.083		
(19) SS	(27)	23.831	−20.503		
(20) R	(21)	−112.410	−130.719		
(21) Oths	(718)	−27.343	−84.363		

	Mann-Whitney U-Test	Probability (two-tailed)
	−12.744	.0000
	Chi-Square Median Test	Probability (two-tailed)
	140.636	.0000

The number of CPA firm clients during the 1975–1984 period is listed in column 2. Columns 3 and 4 present the average and median residual from the regression model of Table 3 for each of 20 CPA firms and the other category. These residuals are the result of relating cash compensation (audit fees, legal fees, and miscellaneous fees) to gross proceeds, sales revenue, and book value of equity. Columns 4 and 5 summarize the average and median residuals by the Big Eight/non-Big Eight classification.

continued overleaf

TABLE 3—*Continued*

Panel D. *Average Residual from Equation (2) Panel A by Audit Firm and Largest-Five, Middle-Six, and Smallest-Nine Audit Firm Clients by Median Sales Revenue Classification:*

		Average Residual	Median Residual	Largest-Five	
				Average Residual	Median Residual
(1) EW	(141)	28.824	−17.952		
(2) DHS	(122)	24.377	22.288		
(3) PW	(141)	21.309	7.297	26.529	6.216
(4) AY	(163)	26.901	11.068		
(5) AA	(225)	29.258	2.769		

				Middle-Six	
				Average Residual	Median Residual
(6) PMM	(191)	34.964	−6.217		
(7) TR	(153)	10.349	−14.796		
(8) CL	(146)	9.081	−34.347		
(9) LH	(59)	3.298	−30.437	14.877	−15.375
(10) SS	(27)	23.831	−20.503		
(11) AG	(55)	−18.877	−31.567		

				Smallest-Nine	
				Average Residual	Median Residual
(12) MH	(78)	20.577	−24.392		
(13) MJL	(16)	36.502	−76.752		
(14) MHD	(18)	−73.237	−83.854		
(15) OAD	(10)	30.847	−40.083		
(16) Oths	(718)	−27.343	−84.363		
(17) FOX	(37)	−69.082	−106.279	−38.381	−92.363
(18) HS	(13)	−105.641	−114.743		
(19) NEW	(12)	−116.726	−127.294		
(20) LB	(10)	−124.984	−129.163		
(21) R	(21)	−112.410	−130.719		

	Mann-Whitney U-Test	Probability (two-tailed)
Largest-Five, Middle-Six	−2.379	.0174
Middle-Six, Smallest-Nine	−10.383	.0000

	Chi-Square Median Test	Probability (two-tailed)
Largest-Five, Middle-Six	8.789	.0030
Middle-Six, Smallest-Nine	105.453	.0000

Column 1 lists the 20 CPA firms by Largest-Five, Middle-Six, and Smallest-Nine firms by client sales revenue classification from Table 1. The firms are listed by median client sales revenue. The number of firm clients during the 1975–1984 period is listed in column 2. Columns 3 and 4 present the average and median residual from the equation (2) for Table 3 for each of 20 firms and the other category. These residuals are the result of relating cash compensation (audit fees, legal fees, and miscellaneous fees) to gross proceeds, sales revenue, and book value of equity.

premium is significantly larger for the middle-six than for the smallest-nine audit firms. This substantial variation in premiums suggests that, within the historical Big Eight/non-Big Eight classification, audit firms may not be homogeneous [Kinney, 1986]. Again, these results suggest that the traditional Big Eight/non-Big Eight distinction for reputation capital may suffer from substantial measurement error.

In the second stage regression, the residuals from equation (2) and the control variables are regressed on the initial return.[17] Table 3 results are similar to the indicator variable regression results for each of the control variables. The coefficient on the residuals from equation (2) is significantly negatively related to the initial return at the .003 level (one-tailed). For payments to the auditor above that predicted by equation (2), the initial return will be lower, *ceteris paribus*.[18] These results provide direct evidence of a positive relation between the compensation paid to an auditor and the wealth of the incumbent owners of a client. This evidence is consistent with the proposition that an IPO client hires the reputation capital of an auditing firm to "signal" its *ex ante* uncertainty to IPO investors.

Signalling models (e.g., Downes and Heinkel [1982] and Titman and Trueman [1986]) rely on the firm signalling information to the market by undertaking a costly activity that cannot be duplicated by firms not possessing the signalled characteristic. In the market for IPOs, firms appear to signal their *ex ante* uncertainty by hiring a "nationally known" CPA firm to perform the registration audit. This "signal" is credible to the market since auditor compensation is higher *ceteris paribus* for those firms that are commonly viewed as exhibiting firm-specific reputation capital.

The two-stage least squares method provides a direct test of the relation between the cost (auditor fees) and the benefit (lower initial return) of this signal.

IV. CONCLUSIONS

It has been argued that the auditor performs the role of attesting to the level of *ex ante* uncertainty faced by the IPO investor. Since owners of the IPO firm choose an auditor from a set of competing CPA firms, value-maximizing owners will choose to employ a particular CPA firm's reputation capital when the marginal benefit equates to the marginal cost.

It was conjectured that a marginal benefit of employing a more reputable audit firm is an increase in the price obtained by the firm that offers the IPO *ceteris paribus*. The descriptive results suggest that the assumption of homogeneity in *ex ante* uncertainty does not hold for particular subsets of IPOs. Larger and less risky clients were audited by Big Eight firms. Although this result is not new [Simunic and Stein, 1987; Beatty, 1989], the cross-sectional tests of the reputation hypothesis necessitate control for differences in client *ex ante* uncertainty there are unrelated to auditor reputation.

Two separate methods of considering auditor reputation were considered. First, a positive relation between four non-Big Eight firm indicator variables and the IPO's initial return was documented. The analysis of linear restric-

---

[17] An unreported two-stage least squares model using reported auditor fees from Part II of the registration statement for the 1982–1984 subperiod is consistent with the Table 3 model results. These results are available on request.

[18] The second stage of the two-stage least squares model was analyzed employing a bootstrap technique [Marais, 1984]. Inferences from the probability levels of observing the OLS coefficients with this resampling technique are unchanged.

tions implies that there are significant differences in the relation between the initial return and various subsets of audit firms. With the maintained hypothesis that the Big Eight/non-Big Eight dichotomy or largest-five/middle-six/smallest-nine firm trichotomy proxy for differences in firm-specific reputation capital, the results are consistent with the reputation hypothesis. An omitted variables method that measures reputation as the amount of auditor compensation unexplained by measures of the marginal cost of performing the audit was applied. It shows that the residual from the auditor compensation regression is positively correlated with the unobservable auditing firm reputation capital. The results of the two-stage least squares approach provide stronger and more direct evidence of a relation between auditor reputation and the initial return than the traditional indicator variable approach.

In both approaches, an omitted vari-

ables problem may produce errors in inference. For the indicator variable approach, an omitted variable may explain the relation between the four firms and the initial return. The two-stage regression approach is based upon the notion that the residual from the first regression captures the unobservable reputation variable. An omitted variable in the underpricing regression that is positively related to both the auditor's unexplained compensation and the underpricing of the IPO may explain the observed relation. This omitted variables problem should temper the interpretation of the results of this test of reputation. Despite this limitation, the relation observed in the indicator variable approach and the results provided by the residual approach suggest that hiring of a "nationally known" audit firm is related to less underpricing of an initial public offering of equity securities.

REFERENCES

Akerlof, G. A., "The Market for 'Lemons': Quality, Uncertainty, and the Market Mechanism," *Quarterly Journal of Economics* (August 1970), pp. 488–500.

Baron, D. P., "A Model of the Demand for Investment Banking Advising and Distribution Services for New Issues," *Journal of Finance* (September 1982), pp. 955–976.

Beatty, R. P., and J. R. Ritter, "Investment Banking, Reputation, and the Underpricing of Initial Public Offerings," *Journal of Financial Economics* (January/February 1986), pp. 213–232.

——, "The Initial Public Offerings Market for Auditing Services," *Auditing Research Symposium 1986* (University of Illinois, in press).

Carpenter, C. G., and R. H. Strawser, "Displacement of Auditors When Clients Go Public," *Journal of Accountancy* (June 1971), pp. 55–58.

Downes, D. H., and R. Heinkel, "Signalling and the Valuation of Unseasoned New Issues," *Journal of Finance* (March 1982), pp. 1–10.

Francis, J. R., and D. T. Simon, "A Test of Auditing Pricing in the Small-Client Segment of the U.S. Audit Market," THE ACCOUNTING REVIEW (January 1987), pp. 145–157.

Ibbotson, R. G., "Price Performance of Common Stock New Issues," *Journal of Financial Economics* (September 1975), pp. 235–272.

——, and J. F. Jaffee, " 'Hot Issue' Markets," *Journal of Finance* (September 1975), pp. 1027–1042.

Judge, G. G., W. E. Griffiths, R. C. Hill, and T. C. Lee, *The Theory and Practice of Econometrics* (Wiley, 1980).

Jensen, M. C., and W. H. Meckling, "Theory of the Firm: Managerial Behavior, Agency Costs and Ownership Structure," *Journal of Financial Economics* (October 1976), pp. 305–360.

Kinney, W. R., Jr., "Audit Technology and Preferences for Auditing Standards," *Journal of Accounting and Economics* (March 1986), pp. 73–89.

————, "Attestation Research Opportunities: 1987," *Contemporary Accounting Research* (Spring 1988), pp. 416–425.

Klein, B., and K. B. Leffler, "The Role of Market Forces in Assuring Contractual Performance," *Journal of Political Economy* (August 1981), pp. 615–641.

Kmenta, J., *Elements of Econometrics*, Second Edition (MacMillan, 1986).

Leland, H. E., and D. H. Pyle, "Informational Asymmetries, Financial Structure, and Financial Intermediation," *Journal of Finance* (May 1977), pp. 371–387.

Manegold, J. G., "An Empirical Analysis of the New Issues Securities Markets: The Effects of the Form S-18 Registration Statement," *Research Report Series No. 2 for the SEC and Financial Reporting Institute* (January 1987).

Marais, M. L., "An Application of the Bootstrap Method to the Analysis of Squared, Standardized Market Model Prediction Errors," *Journal of Accounting Research* (Supplement 1984), pp. 34–54.

Mayer, M. W., A. J. Broman, R. Colson, and P. Tiessen, "Pricing of Audit Services: Additional Evidence," Unpublished manuscript (1985).

Palmrose, Z., "Audit Fees and Auditor Size: Further Evidence," *Journal of Accounting Research* (Spring 1986), pp. 97–110.

————, "An Analysis of Auditor Litigation and Audit Service Quality," THE ACCOUNTING REVIEW (January 1988), pp. 55–73.

Ritter, J. R., "The 'Hot Issue' Market of 1980," *Journal of Business* (April 1984), pp. 215–240.

Rock, K., "Why New Issues Are Underpriced," Unpublished Ph.D. dissertation (University of Chicago, 1982).

————, "Why New Issues Are Underpriced," *Journal of Financial Economics* (January/February 1986), pp. 187–212.

Simunic, D. A., "The Pricing of Audit Services: Theory and Evidence," *Journal of Accounting Research* (Spring 1980), pp. 161–190.

————, and Michael Stein, "Product Differentiation in Auditing: Auditor Choice in the Market for Unseasoned New Issues," *Monograph Prepared for the Canadian Certified General Accountant Research Foundation* (June 1987).

Smith, C. W., Jr., "Investment Banking and the Capital Acquisition Process," *Journal of Financial Economics* (January/February 1986), pp. 3–29.

Titman, S., and B. Trueman, "Information Quality and the Valuation of New Issues," *Journal of Accounting and Economics* (June 1986), pp. 159–172.

Watts, R. L., and J. L. Zimmerman, "Agency Problems, Auditing, and the Theory of the Firm: Some Empirical Evidence," *The Journal of Law & Economics* (October 1983), pp. 613–633.

[10]

ELSEVIER Journal of Accounting and Economics 20 (1995) 297–322

JOURNAL OF
Accounting
& Economics

Auditor brand name reputations and industry specializations

Allen T. Craswell[a], Jere R. Francis[*,b], Stephen L. Taylor[a]

[a]*Department of Accounting, University of Sydney, Sydney, NSW 2006, Australia*
[b]*School of Accountancy, University of Missouri, Columbia, MO 65211, USA*

(Received October 1993; final version received August 1995)

Abstract

The development of both brand name reputation and industry specialization by Big 8 auditors is argued to be costly and therefore to increase audit fees. For a sample of 1484 Australian publicly listed companies we estimate audit fee premia for Big 8 auditors. On average, industry specialist Big 8 auditors earn a 34% premium over *nonspecialist* Big 8 auditors, and the Big 8 brand name premium over non-Big 8 auditors averages around 30%. These results support that industry expertise is a dimension of the demand for higher quality Big 8 audits and a basis for *within* Big 8 product differentiation.

Key words: Auditor reputation; Industry specialization; Auditor choice

JEL classification: L84; M40

1. Introduction

Prior research indicates that the large international Big 6 (formerly Big 8) accounting firms earn systematically higher audit fees.[1] Based on economic

---

*Corresponding author.

We thank workshop participants at the following universities: Auckland, Iowa, Limburg, Michigan, Missouri, New England, Sydney, and Western Australia. We also appreciate helpful comments from Ross Watts (the editor) and Dan Simunic (the referee) who was also discussant on the paper when presented at the American Accounting Association's 1993 annual meeting.

[1]Simon and Francis (1988) estimate a Big 8 premium of approximately 18% across a number of studies (Baber et al., 1987; Ettredge and Greenberg, 1990; Francis, 1984; Francis and Simon, 1987; Francis and Stokes, 1986; Palmrose, 1986a; Rubin, 1988).

298   *A.T. Craswell et al. | Journal of Accounting and Economics 20 (1995) 297–322*

theories of product differentiation (Klein and Leffler, 1981; Shapiro, 1983), higher observed Big 8 audit fees in competitive markets are consistent with positive returns to Big 8 investments in brand name reputation for higher quality audits.[2] Demand for quality-differentiated audits has been explained in terms of agency/contracting costs (Simunic and Stein, 1987; Watts and Zimmerman, 1986).[3]

The purpose of this study is two-fold. First, using a much larger sample than in prior studies the findings of a Big 8 fee premium are replicated. Second, and more importantly, the study posits that prior evidence of a Big 8 premium has confounded two separate components of audit pricing: (1) a general brand name premium, representing positive returns to brand name development and maintenance, and (2) an industry-specific premium, representing positive returns to investment in industry specialization by subsets of Big 8 accounting firms, above and beyond general brand name investments.[4]

Reputation development with respect to both brand name and industry specialization is argued to be costly and to result in higher audit fees. Three levels of increasingly costly audit quality are posited and supported by the tests: non-Big 8 audits, brand name Big 8 audits, and in certain industries a further within Big 8 differentiation based on industry specialization. The models in the study estimate the Big 8 brand name premium to average in the range of 28%–39%. For industries deemed to have specialists, specialist Big 8 auditors earn on average a 34% premium over nonspecialist Big 8 auditors. In dollar magnitudes, industry specialization is as important as general brand name in explaining Big 8 fee premia. These results add to our understanding of auditor choice and support that within Big 8 industry specialization is an additional dimension of the quality-differentiated character of Big 8 audits.

The remainder of the paper is organized as follows. The next section discusses the demand for and supply of quality-differentiated audits and develops three

---

[2]Other studies claim that the larger Big 8 accounting firms are brand name suppliers of higher-quality audits. See Davidson and Neu (1993), DeAngelo (1981), Defond (1992), Dopuch and Simunic (1982), Francis and Wilson (1988), Palmrose (1988), Simunic and Stein (1987), Slovin et al. (1990), Teoh and Wong (1993). The claim that the Big 8 have brand name reputations is also supported by research on initial public offerings (Balvers et al., 1988; Beatty, 1989; Datar et al., 1991; Feltham et al., 1991; Menon and Williams, 1991; Simunic and Stein, 1987; Titman and Trueman, 1986).

[3]The argument about higher Big 8 qualilty is not pejorative to non-Big 8 accounting firms. What the brand name argument means is that some accounting firms voluntarily invest in higher levels of expertise beyond the minimum required by professional standards and therefore have incentives to maintain their reputations by producing higher-quality audits.

[4]Palmrose (1986a) reports no evidence of an industry specialization premium though she specifically notes a possible confounding effect between brand name reputation and industry specialization which is the focus of our study. In related research Pearson and Trompeter (1994) and Ettredge and Greenberg (1990) find that initial engagement pricing may be affected by industry specialization.

A.T. Craswell et al. / Journal of Accounting and Economics 20 (1995) 297–322   299

hypotheses about the effects of brand name reputation and industry specialization on audit fee premia. Research design, sample selection and data collection are then discussed followed by the empirical results, sensitivity analyses, and conclusions.

2. Background and hypothesis development

Prior research has differentiated auditor quality in terms of non-Big 8 and brand name Big 8 accounting firms. This study investigates an additional dimension of audit quality based on within Big 8 industry specialization and uses Craswell and Taylor's (1991) classification of Big 8 industry specialists. Our primary test determines if audit fees of Big 8 industry specialists are systematically higher than those of nonspecialist Big 8 auditors.[5] If auditees voluntarily contract with higher-priced industry specialists even though any licensed auditor can legally perform audits, then this is evidence that quality-differentiated audits based on industry expertise are economically demanded.[6]

2.1. Agency costs and quality-differentiated audits

Research on the demand for quality-differentiated audits has drawn on agency and contracting literature. The argument is that as agency costs increase there is a demand for higher-quality audits, either voluntarily undertaken by managers as a bonding mechanism or externally imposed as a monitoring mechanism by stockholders and/or debtholders (see Watts and Zimmerman, 1986). The demand for auditing in general and for quality-differentiated auditing in particular is thus assumed to be the efficient resolution of costly contracting problems where the auditee's accounting technology is an important component of the firm's contracting system. Auditors provide assurance of the integrity of accounting numbers produced by the auditee's accounting technology and used for contracting. Empirical studies offer at least qualified support for this agency cost/audit quality linkage (e.g., Defond, 1992; Francis and Wilson, 1988; Palmrose, 1984).

Agency/contracting theory can be extended to explain both brand name audits and industry specialization as a function of increasing agency costs. There

---

[5]Copley et al. (1994) report evidence of a voluntary demand for higher-priced specialist audits in the U.S. market for governmental audits. Consistent with economic theory, they also find that the demand for higher-quality audits is decreasing in price which would explain why all companies do not necessarily purchase higher-quality but costlier audits.

[6]Assuming of course that the audit market is competitive. If the market is not competitive, then one could not distinguish between monopoly pricing and normal returns to investment in industry specialization. This issue is examined further in Section 5.1.

is an interplay of firm-specific factors (such as financing and ownership structure) as well as more general industry-wide factors (such as industry-specific transactions and contracts) which determine a company's agency cost structure and corresponding monitoring needs. For each company, a cost–benefit analysis would derive the optimal choice of audit quality as well as the mix of auditing versus other monitoring mechanisms (see Anderson et al., 1993).

Prior research has shown there is cross-sectional variation in firm-specific factors affecting agency costs. Industry-wide factors affecting agency costs could also be expected to vary across industries. In addition, industry characteristics may affect some companies more than others in which case there might also be within-industry variation in the demand for auditor specialists.[7] Thus, the combination of firm-specific and industry-wide factors results in cross-sectional variation in the demand for monitoring and, consequently, for different levels of audit quality. Differential demand for auditing allows multiple types of audit quality to co-exist in the same industry and leads to within Big 8 product differentiation through industry specialization. This is consistent with the data in our study. In industries having specialist auditors, 22% of companies voluntarily contract with a specialist Big 8 firm, 34% with nonspecialist Big 8 firms, and 44% with non-Big 8 firms.

The term 'accounting technology' as used above refers to a firm's accounting system, and to the selection and application of accounting policies for reporting the firm's economic activity. Crucial accounting policy issues concern the recognition and measurement of assets, liabilities, and income arising from the firm's economic activity. To the extent accounting technology is industry-specific rather than generic, the firm's agency/contracting problems and their method of resolution via accounting will also have unique industry features.[8] For example, certain types of complex contracts such as forward sales contracts, long-term leases, joint ventures, and other off-balance-sheet financing arrangements are more common in some industries. Other industries such as natural resources and financial services have specialized accounting rules and reporting requirements, and some industries such as financial services have sophisticated EDP technology and internal control systems.

Demand for industry specialization drives audit firm investments in specialization and leads to industry-based clienteles (which is the rationale for using market share data to infer specialization). For industries having specialized contracts and accounting technologies, auditor industry specialization (as

---

[7] In neoclassical economic theory of the firm, industry is well-defined and all firms within an industry are identical. However, in reality, industries are less well-defined and there is considerable within-industry variation.

[8] Additional support for this argument can be found in the AICPAs annual audit risk alerts which highlight special accounting and audit problems in particular industries (*Audit Risk Alert – 1994*, American Institute of Certified Public Accountants, 1994).

A.T. Craswell et al. / Journal of Accounting and Economics 20 (1995) 297–322   301

evidenced by significant clienteles) will lead to a higher level of audit assurance compared to audits performed in those industries by nonspecialist auditors.[9] Specialized industry knowledge is thus a component of auditor expertise in addition to the general knowledge base required for all audits (Shockley and Holt, 1983; Palmrose, 1984).[10]

In this study we do not directly identify and measure industry attributes leading to the demand for industry audit specialists. Instead we infer their existence based on auditor clienteles. The Australian industry groups identified by Craswell and Taylor (1991) as having specialist auditors (based on market shares equal to or greater than 10%) are: (1) natural resources, which have unique accounting problems with respect to the valuation of mineral/oil reserves, income determination, and complex forward sales and hedging contracts; (2) building suppliers and engineering firms, both of which are involved in multi-period contracting which creates special accounting problems relating to cost capitalization and income recognition; (3) retailers, which have elaborate inventory systems and special revenue recognition issues associated with sales returns and various types of customer financing; and (4) investment and financial services, which have complex contracts for financial instruments and derivatives, large-scale EDP systems, and special regulatory accounting requirements.

2.2. Hypotheses regarding brand name and industry specialization

Audit firms acquire a reputation as industry specialists by developing industry-specific skills and expertise over and above normal auditor expertise. To the extent Big 8 auditors invest in industry expertise they require a normal return on their investment and, *ceteris paribus*, would be expected to charge higher fees compared to nonspecialists for audits in these industries. However, because auditors develop industry specialization by increasing their clienteles, specialists could also achieve production economies and become more efficient, lower-cost producers of audits.[11] We predict that the required return on investment in industry expertise will dominate potential production economies and lead to higher audit fees. Ultimately, though, this an empirical question to be tested.

---

[9]Studies by Bonner and Lewis (1990) and Ashton (1991) offer evidence on the linkage between the quality of auditor task-level performance and the auditor's industry knowledge. Accounting firms also promote industry specializations and cite their clienteles as evidence of their expertise.

[10]A recent study by Carcello et al. (1992) supports this claim. The most important perceived attribute of audit qualilty after the audit team's direct experience with the client is the audit team's prior experience in the industry. O'Keefe et al. (1994) also report that auditor industry specializaion is positively related to audit quality, as measured by an assessment of auditor compliance with GAAS.

[11]We thank the referee and editor for clarifying this point. See also Danos and Eichenseher (1986) and Eichenseher and Danos (1981) for a discussion of auditor production economies.

The following hypotheses are formulated to separate the confounding effects of brand name reputation and industry specialization. Hypotheses H1 and H2 test for audit fee premia representing positive returns to brand name investments by Big 8 auditors:

H1: In those industries not having specialist auditors, Big 8 auditors will have higher audit fees than non-Big 8 auditors.

H2: In industries having specialist auditors, *nonspecialist* Big 8 auditors will have higher audit fees than non-Big 8 auditors.

In hypothesis H1 the confounding of brand name and industry specialization effects is avoided by restricting the brand name test to those industries not having specialist auditors. Thus any differences in observed audit fees can be attributed solely to the effect of brand name, all other factors held constant.

Hypothesis H2 tests for a brand name effect in industries having specialist auditors. However, the confounding effect of industry specialization is avoided by eliminating Big 8 specialists from the sample and thus restricting the comparison to nonspecialist Big 8 auditors and non-Big 8 auditors (who are also nonspecialists). Since the test is restricted to nonspecialists, any observed fee differences can be attributed solely to the effect of brand name, all other factors held constant.

Hypothesis H3 tests for an audit fee premium representing positive returns to Big 8 investments in industry specialization *in addition* to a brand name reputation:

H3: In those industries having auditor specialists, specialist Big 8 auditors will have higher audit fees than nonspecialist Big 8 auditors.

Hypothesis H3 restricts the sample to industries having auditor specialists. The confounding effect of brand name (Big 8 versus non-Big 8) is controlled by an additional restriction of the sample to Big 8 audited companies. Differences in audit fees are attributable to the Big 8 auditor being an industry specialist, all other factors held constant. While we predict higher fees, the opposite would occur if there are production economies from specialization and these dominate the return on investment in industry expertise. For this reason two-tail *p*-values are reported in the test of H3 to reflect both possibilities.

3. Data and model specification

3.1. Auditor industry specialization

As indicated in Section 2, we use Craswell and Taylor's (1991) analysis of auditor industry specializations for all 23 Australian Stock Exchange industry

A.T. Craswell et al. / Journal of Accounting and Economics 20 (1995) 297–322   303

Table 1
Australian industries with specialist auditors (with specialist auditors defined by Craswell and Taylor, 1991)

Australian Stock Exchange industry code	Specialist audit firms
01 Mining – Gold	Arthur Young, Coopers & Lybrand, Peat Marwick
02 Mining – Other metals	Coopers & Lybrand, Price Waterhouse
03 Solid fuels	Coopers & Lybrand, Peat Marwick
04 Oil and gas	Peat Marwick
07 Building materials	Arthur Young, Coopers & Lybrand, Peat Marwick
09 Food & household goods	Deloitte Haskins & Sells, Price Waterhouse
11 Engineering	Coopers & Lybrand, Peat Marwick
13 Retail	Arthur Young, Deloitte Haskins & Sells, Price Waterhouse, Touche Ross
19 Investment & financial services	Touche Ross

The Australian Stock Exchange has 23 industry classifications. Craswell and Taylor (1991) defined industries as having specialist auditors if the industry had 30 or more observations, and if one or more individual accounting firm had a market share greater than or equal to 10%.

classifications. Results of their analysis are summarized in Table 1. They determined auditor specialization by first considering the overall number of companies in an industry and then examining each accounting firm's industry market share using two measures: (1) the percentage of companies audited, which is an unweighted measure of market share, and (2) the accounting firm's share of total industry audit fees, which represents a size-weighted measure of market share (weighted by audit fees). A minimum of 30 companies per industry (averaged over the period 1982–87) was a precondition for industry specialization.[12] This reduced the number of eligible industries from 23 to 14. As in prior studies (Defond, 1992; Palmrose, 1984, 1986a), a threshold of 10% of market share based on either the number of clients in the industry or the percentage of total audit fees in the industry was required in these 14 industries for a specific accounting firm to be designated an industry specialist.[13] If an accounting firm

---

[12]Craswell and Taylor (1991) also investigated industries with less than 30 companies but concluded that the number of companies was too small to provide a reliable indicator of auditor specialization. However, all industries are included for testing the Big 8 brand name premium hypotheses (H1 and H2).

[13]The 10% market share rule is arbitrary and therefore could misclassify some Big 8 auditors as specialists. See further discussion in Section 5.6.

met the 10% threshold test in *any* year (1982–87), it was then classified as an industry specialist. This resulted in nine industries having specialist auditors.

Craswell and Taylor's analysis indicates that only Big 8 accounting firms had industry specializations.[14] Specializations occurred in natural resources-related industries (01, 02, 03, 04), building materials (07), food and household goods (09), engineering (11), retailing (13), and investment and financial services (19). Two industries had only one specialist (04, 19), four industries had two specialists (02, 03, 09, 11), two industries had three specialists (01, 07), and one industry had four specialists (13). Coopers & Lybrand and Peat Marwick each had five specialist industries, Price Waterhouse and Arthur Young each had three specializations, and Deloitte Haskins & Sells and Touche Ross each had two specializations. Two Big 8 accounting firms, Arthur Andersen and Ernst & Whinney, did not have industry specializations for the period analyzed based on the definition used in this study.

3.2. Sample and data

The 1987 fiscal-year auditor remuneration data used to estimate the audit fee models were obtained from *Who Audits Australia?* (Craswell, 1988) and data on other variables hand-collected from annual reports.[15] The final sample consists of 1484 publicly listed companies after eliminating 85 unusable observations.[16]

Table 2 reports the distribution of the 1484 companies across the 23 Australian Stock Exchange industry codes. Overall, 911 companies are in the nine industries designated as having industry specialists. This represents 61% of the total of 1484 companies. Of these 911 companies, 204 companies (22%) contracted with a specialist Big 8 auditor. Table 2 also classifies the full sample into the number of companies audited by Big 8 auditors ($n = 862$) and non-Big 8 auditors ($n = 622$), making the Big 8 market share 58%. Of the 862 companies

---

[14]A possible concern noted by the editor is that the industry specialists in Table 1 might be a proxy for the bigger or more well-known of the Big 8 firms in Australia. However, based on our data, audit clients are reasonably evenly distributed across the Big 8 ranging from a low market share of 9% to a high of 16% (with the total Big 8 share being 58%). In addition, a Spearman rank correlation shows that there is no significant correlation ($p = 0.10$) between a Big 8 firm's overall size (total number of audits) and the number of industry specialist audits it performs, which demonstrates that Big 8 firm size per se is not driving the classification of within Big 8 industry specialists.

[15]The study uses total audit fees reported by the consolidated group of companies. As a sensitivity analysis, tests were also performed using audit fees attributable just to the auditor of record for the parent (holding) company thus excluding fees of other auditors (e.g., an auditor of a subsidiary company). There were no substantive differences between the two sets of results.

[16]Companies were deleted for the following reasons: 8 were not publicly listed companies, 31 had overseas auditors, 13 had unusual reporting periods exceeding 12 months, and 33 had incomplete data.

A.T. Craswell et al. / Journal of Accounting and Economics 20 (1995) 297–322   305

Table 2
Distribution of sample of 1484 Australian publicly listed companies across industries and auditors in fiscal 1987

Australian Stock Exchange industry code	All Big 8 auditors	Specialist Big 8 auditors	Non-Big 8 auditors	Total sample (columns 1 + 3)
01 Mining – Gold	165	78	147	312
02 Mining – Other metals	45	15	23	68
03 Solid fuels	11	9	5	16
04 Oil and gas	45	15	29	74
05 Diversified resources	6	0	1	7
06 Developers & contractors	26	0	31	57
07 Building materials	24	12	20	44
08 Alcohol & tobacco	2	0	4	6
09 Food & household goods	26	16	18	44
10 Chemicals	14	0	5	19
11 Engineering	39	22	24	63
12 Paper & packaging	5	0	3	8
13 Retail	27	16	14	41
14 Transport	7	0	4	11
15 Media	12	0	23	35
16 Banks	9	0	5	14
17 Insurance	11	0	1	12
18 Entrepreneurial investors	11	0	7	18
19 Investment & financial services	131	21	118	249
20 Property trusts	15	0	8	23
21 Miscellaneous services	89	0	59	148
22 Miscellaneous industrials	118	0	58	176
23 Diversified industrials	24	0	15	39
Total	862	204	622	1484

audited by the Big 8, 204 companies are in specialist industries and are audited by a Big 8 industry specialist which means that 24% of the Big 8's total clientele are industry specializations.

3.3. Research design and model specification

A cross-sectional audit fee regression model based on prior Australian audit fee research (Francis, 1984; Francis and Stokes, 1986) is used to test H1–H3. Audit fee models use a set of variables to control for cross-sectional differences in factors that affect fees such as auditee size, audit complexity, and auditor–auditee risk sharing (Simunic, 1980). These empirical models have demonstrated good explanatory power (r-squares of 0.70 and higher) and have been robust across different samples, different time periods, different countries, and to sensitivity analysis for model misspecification (Francis and Simon, 1987; Chan et al., 1993).

To test for differential audit pricing by different classes of audit firms, an auditor indicator variable, which is the experimental variable of interest, is added to the audit fee model. This provides a statistical test of differences in mean audit fees across the two subsets of companies audited by each of the two auditor groups after controlling for other factors in the model. Formally the test determines if there is a significant intercept shift in the fitted regression model.[17]

The OLS regression model to be estimated is

$$LAF = b_0 + b_1 LTA + b_2 Sub + b_3 Current + b_4 Quick + b_5 DE$$

$$+ b_6 ROI + b_7 Foreign + b_8 Opin + b_9 YE + b_{10} Loss$$

$$+ b_{11} Auditor + e,$$

where

LAF	= natural log of total audit fees,
LTA	= natural log of total assets ($000),
Sub	= square root of the number of subsidiaries,
$Current$	= ratio of current assets to total assets,
$Quick$	= ratio of current assets, less inventories, to current liabilities,
DE	= ratio of long-term debt to total assets,
ROI	= ratio of earnings before interest and tax to total assets,
$Foreign$	= proportion of subsidiaries that represent foreign operations,
$Opin$	= indicator variable, 1 = qualified audit report,
YE	= indicator variable, 1 = non-June 30th yearend,
$Loss$	= indicator variable, 1 = loss in past three years,
$Auditor$	= indicator variable, either 1 = Big 8 or 1 = Specialist.

The error term, e, is assumed to have the normal OLS regression properties. Econometric and estimation issues are examined in Section 5.

Two different auditor indicator variables are used for the tests of H1–H3. For tests of the Big 8 brand name premium (H1 and H2), the auditor indicator variable is Big 8 versus non-Big 8 auditors. For the test of industry specialization (H3), the auditor indicator variable is specialist versus nonspecialist Big 8 auditors.

The percentage shift in audit fees in the fitted regression model is estimated to infer the magnitude of changes in audit prices attributable to brand name

---

[17]Cross-sectional differences in observed audit fees are used to infer the presence of audit pricing diffrences attributable to Big 8 brand name and industry specialization. However, audit prices are not directly observable; rather, pricing implications are inferred by observing changes in audit fees, after controlling for other factors that may affect pricing (see Simunic, 1980; O'Keefe et al., 1994).

A.T. Craswell et al. / Journal of Accounting and Economics 20 (1995) 297–322   307

reputation and to industry specialization. Therefore, in addition to the statistical tests of parameter b_{11} to determine whether or not there is a significant intercept shift across the two subsets of observations, the magnitude of the intercept shift can be calculated using the procedure described in Simon and Francis (1988, p. 263, fn. 7). The shift in the intercept term affects audit fees in the fitted model in the following manner:

$$(e^{(x+z)} - e^x)/e^x,$$

where

e^x $\quad$ = audit fees of non-Big 8 or nonspecialist auditors,

$e^{(x+z)}$ = audit fees of Big 8 or specialist auditors, where z *is the* upward shift in the intercept term due to the *Auditor* variable.

The above equation simplifies to $e^z - 1$, which is solved using the mean parameter value (z) of the *Auditor* variable in the fitted regression model. This expresses the mean shift in Big 8 audit fees as a percentage of non-Big 8 fees, and the mean shift in specialist Big 8 audit fees as a percentage of nonspecialist Big 8 fees. For all of the subsequent tests reported below in Section 4, the percentage increase in audit fees due to brand name or industry specialization is based on the above formula.

3.4. Descriptive statistics

Descriptive statistics are reported in Table 3. Three sets of data are reported: the full sample of 1484 companies, the subsample of 573 companies in industries not having auditor specialists, and the subsample of 911 companies in the 9 industries in Table 1 designated as having one or more auditor industry specialist.

Univariate statistics (available from the authors on request) indicate that the 911 companies in specialist industries had proportionally fewer foreign subsidiaries (*Foreign*), fewer qualified audit reports (*Opin*), were more likely to have a non-June 30th yearend (*YE*), and were more likely to have reported a loss in any of the three most recent years (*Loss*). There were no significant differences ($p = 0.05$) for the other variables in Table 3 (*LTA, Sub, Current, Quick, DE*, and *ROI*).

4. Test results

Tests of hypotheses H1–H3 are reported in Tables 4 and 5. The auditor indicator variables are significant at $p < 0.03$ (two-tail) in all tests reported in Tables 4 and 5. Therefore the hypotheses are supported. In addition the magnitudes of audit fee premia are economically large as discussed below.

308   A.T. Craswell et al. / Journal of Accounting and Economics 20 (1995) 297–322

Table 3
Descriptive statistics from fiscal 1987 for the sample of 1484 Australian publicly listed companies
(June 30, 1987 exchange rate was $1 Aus = 72c U.S.)

Variables	Total sample (n = 1484)		Industries without auditor specialists (n = 573)		Industries having specialist auditors (n = 911)	
	Mean	Std. dev.	Mean	Std. dev.	Mean	Std. dev.
LAF	3.150	1.495	3.650	1.528	2.836	1.385
LTA	10.023	1.825	10.420	1.962	9.773	1.687
Sub	2.313	2.491	2.844	3.041	1.979	2.004
Current	0.393	0.251	0.382	0.237	0.399	0.259
Quick	5.828	17.597	3.657	15.517	7.194	18.666
DE	0.085	0.177	0.102	0.200	0.075	0.160
ROI	0.017	0.227	0.029	0.253	0.010	0.208
Foreign	0.482	1.235	0.682	1.662	0.356	0.842
Opin(= 1)	27%		32%		24%	
YE(= 1)	16%		13%		18%	
Loss(= 1)	27%		16%		35%	
Big 8(= 1)	58%		61%		56%	
Specialist (= 1)	14%		0%		22%	

LAF	= log$_e$ total audit fees;
LTA	= log$_e$ total assets ($000);
Sub	= square root of the number of subsidiaries;
Current	= ratio of current assets to total assets;
Quick	= ratio of current assets less inventories to current liabilities;
DE	= ratio of long-term debt to total assets;
ROI	= ratio of earnings before interest and tax to total assets;
Foreign	= proportion of subsidiaries that are foreign operations;
Opin	= dummy variable, qualified = 1;
YE	= dummy variable, non-30th June balance date = 1;
Loss	= dummy variable, reported loss in prior three years = 1;
Big 8	= dummy variable, Big 8 auditor = 1;
Specialist	= dummy variable, auditor is Big 8 industry specialist = 1.

4.1. Benchmark test with prior studies

The first set of results, reported on the left side of Table 4, does not test hypotheses H1 and H2, per se, but is reported for the purpose of a benchmark comparison to prior audit pricing studies. It replicates Francis (1984) and Francis and Stokes (1986) using the full sample of 1484 firms to test if Big 8 audit fees are higher than non-Big 8 fees. The model is significant at $p < 0.01$ and has an adjusted r-square of 0.74.

As expected, the Big 8 auditor indicator variable is positive and significant at $p < 0.01$. The Big 8 coefficient is 0.27 which means that on average Big 8 fees are

Table 4

Audit fee regression models: estimation of Big 8 brand name premia for (1) the full sample of 1484 Australian publicly listed companies, (2) the subsample of 573 companies in nonspecialist industries, and (3) the subsample of 707 companies in specialist industries having nonspecialist auditors; dependent variable is natural logarithm of audit fee

Independent variables	Total sample			Test of H1 Firms in nonspecialist industries			Test of H2 Firms in specialist industries (having nonspecialist auditors)		
	Estimate	t-value	Prob. (2-tail)	Estimate	t-value	Prob. (2-tail)	Estimate	t-value	Prob. (2-tail)
Control variables									
Intercept	-1.823	-11.70	0.0001	-1.413	-6.146	0.0001	-1.766	-7.437	0.0001
LTA	0.405	24.58	0.0001	0.368	15.300	0.0001	0.389	15.353	0.0001
Sub	0.224	16.40	0.0001	0.210	11.222	0.0001	0.222	10.311	0.0001
Current	0.589	7.23	0.0001	0.933	7.419	0.0001	0.389	3.355	0.0008
Quick	-0.010	-8.44	0.0001	-0.008	-4.335	0.0001	-0.008	-5.228	0.0001
DE	0.444	3.86	0.0001	0.284	1.899	0.0581	0.727	3.909	0.0001
ROI	-0.250	-2.72	0.0066	-0.167	-1.383	0.1674	-0.256	-1.780	0.0756
Foreign	0.014	0.63	0.5299	0.009	0.340	0.7343	0.070	1.640	0.1014
Opin	0.217	4.92	0.0001	0.179	2.885	0.0041	0.229	3.343	0.0009
YE	0.032	0.58	0.5637	0.279	3.087	0.0021	-0.002	-0.031	0.9754
Loss	-0.129	-2.92	0.0035	0.004	0.046	0.9631	-0.058	-0.866	0.3870
Experimental variable									
Big 8	0.269	6.77	0.0001	0.291	4.904	0.0001	0.195	3.289	0.0011
Sample size	1484			573			707		
Big 8/Non-Big 8	862/622			349/224			309/398		
F-statistic	195.78			213.99			124.22		
Adjusted R^2	0.74			0.80			0.66		

LTA   = $\log_e$ total assets ($000);
Sub   = square root of the number of subsidiaries;
Current = ratio of current assets to total assets;
Quick   = ratio of current assets less inventories to current liabilities;
DE   = ratio of long-term debt to total assets;
ROI   = ratio of earnings before interest and tax to total assets;
Foreign = proportion of subsidiaries that are foreign operations;
Opin   = dummy variable, qualified = 1;
YE   = dummy variable, non-30th June balance date = 1;
Loss   = dummy variable, reported loss in prior three years = 1;
Big 8   = dummy variable, Big 8 auditor = 1.

310   A.T. Craswell et al. / Journal of Accounting and Economics 20 (1995) 297–322

31% higher than non-Big 8 audit fees. This is larger than reported in prior Australian studies. However, as stated above such an approach potentially misestimates the Big 8 brand name premium because it fails to separate the premium related to industry specialization.

4.2. Test of brand name (H1 and H2)

Hypothesis H1 is tested using the subset of 573 companies in industries without auditor specializations. This result is reported in the middle section of Table 4. The model is significant at $p < 0.01$ and the adjusted r-square is 0.80. As predicted by H1, Big 8 fees are significantly higher at $p < 0.01$. The parameter value is 0.29 which means that Big 8 audit fees are, on average, 34% higher than audit fees of non-Big 8 auditors.

The brand name test in hypothesis H2 uses the subset of companies in specialist industries not audited by specialist Big 8 auditors ($n = 707$).[18] This result is reported on the right side of Table 4. The model is significant at $p < 0.01$ and the adjusted R-square is 0.66. As predicted by H2, nonspecialist Big 8 audit fees are significantly higher than non-Big 8 fees at $p < 0.01$. The parameter value is 0.195 which means that, on average, nonspecialist Big 8 audit fees are 22% higher than those of non-Big 8 auditors.

4.3. Test of industry specialization (H3)

The test of hypothesis H3 is reported in Table 5. Specialist Big 8 fees are compared with nonspecialist Big 8 fees for 513 companies in specialist industries, 204 of which are audited by specialists and 309 by nonspecialist Big 8 auditors. The model is significant at $p < 0.01$ and the adjusted R-square is 0.73.

As predicted, specialist Big 8 fees are significantly higher at $p < 0.03$ (two-tail). The parameter value is 0.15 which indicates that specialist Big 8 auditors have an average fee premium of 16% over nonspecialist Big 8 auditors.

4.4. Discussion of tests

The tests of H1–H3 support the study's two predictions: (1) after controlling for industry specializations, Big 8 fees are greater than non-Big 8 fees, consistent with the presence of positive returns to auditor investments in brand name reputations (H1 and H2), and (2) specialist Big 8 fees are greater than nonspecialist Big 8 fees, which is consistent with the presence of positive returns to

---

[18]The reduced sample of 707 is derived from the 911 companies in industries having auditor specialists, less the 204 companies using an industry specialist auditor (see Table 1).

A.T. Craswell et al. / Journal of Accounting and Economics 20 (1995) 297–322   311

Table 5
Audit fee regression model: estimation of industry specialist premium for the subsample of 513 Australian publicly listed companies in industries having auditor specialists and which are audited by Big 8 accounting firms; dependent variable is natural logarithm of audit fee

Independent variables	Test of H3 Specialists versus Big 8 nonspecialists		
	Estimate	t-value	Prob. (2-tail)
Control variables			
Intercept	− 1.622	− 6.094	0.0001
LTA	0.395	14.373	0.0001
Sub	0.207	9.561	0.0001
Current	0.582	4.277	0.0001
Quick	− 0.012	− 5.824	0.0001
DE	0.833	3.766	0.0002
ROI	− 0.387	− 1.932	0.0539
Foreign	0.102	2.255	0.0246
Opin	0.153	1.983	0.0479
YE	0.032	0.386	0.6998
Loss	− 0.130	− 1.871	0.0620
Experimental variable			
Specialist	0.146	2.185	0.0294
Sample size		513	
Specialists/Nonspecialists		204/309	
F-statistic		124.05	
Adjusted R^2		0.73	

LTA   = $\log_e$ total assets ($000);
Sub   = square root of the number of subsidiaries;
Current   = ratio of current assets to total assets;
Quick   = ratio of current assets less inventories to current liabilities;
DE   = ratio of long-term debt to total assets;
ROI   = ratio of earnings before interest and tax to total assets;
Foreign   = proportion of subsidiaries that are foreign operations;
Opin   = dummy variable, qualified = 1;
YE   = dummy variable, non-30th June balance date = 1;
Loss   = dummy variable, reported loss in prior three years = 1;
Specialist = dummy variable, auditor is Big 8 industry specialist = 1.

auditor investments in industry specializations (H3). These results support the existence of two distinct elements of Big 8 audit fee premia: a brand name component and an industry specialization component.

The Big 8 brand name audit fee premium is somewhat larger in nonspecialist industries (34%) than in specialist industries (22%) which suggests that brand name reputation of Big 8 auditors may be less valued in those industries where Big 8 auditor specializations also occur. An explanation for this phenomenon is that in industries having specialist auditors, nonspecialist Big 8 auditors are perceived to be more like the non-Big 8 firms who are also nonspecialists, hence nonspecialist Big 8 firms are unable to command the same level of brand name premium. In other words, the presence of industry specialists undermines the value of the brand name for nonspecialist Big 8 auditors who must compete more directly on price with non-Big 8 firms. Additional results in Section 5.2 support this conjecture.

5. Econometric and estimation issues

All of the OLS models estimated in Tables 4 and 5 are statistically significant and are well-specified in terms of standard OLS assumptions. Explanatory power is good as adjusted R-squares range from 0.66 to 0.80. Residuals are normally distributed and there is no evidence of heteroskedasticity. Using the White (1980) correction process for heteroskedasticity the adjusted p-values for the auditor indicator variables are not different from those reported in Tables 4 and 5.

5.1. Market competitiveness

Interpretation of audit fee premia as returns to brand name or industry specialization relies on the assumption that audit markets are competitive. It is widely accepted that the audit market is competitive for smaller companies due to the large number of suppliers. But for larger companies Big 8 domination does raise a question about market competitiveness (Simunic, 1980).

This is of less concern in the Australian context, however. Overall the Big 8 market share is only 58% and companies are not especially large making the Australian market more like the U.S. over-the-counter market (Francis and Stokes, 1986). For the full sample of 1484 companies, company size measured by total assets ranges from $107,000 to $70.3 billion (Australian dollars). The mean size is $290.3 million; however, the median is only $18.2 million. The 742 companies in the upper half of size (based on median total assets of $18.2 million) have median total assets of only $63.8 million and the Big 8 market share of audits is still only 64%. The 742 companies in the lower half of size have median total assets of $6.3 million and the Big 8 market share drops only slightly to 52%. Table 3 shows that the 911 companies in specialist industries are slightly smaller on average and the Big 8 share is also smaller compared to the 573 companies in nonspecialist industries (56% vs. 61%). As can be seen from this data Big 8 market shares are hardly dominant even for the larger-sized companies in the sample.[19]

5.2. Model specification and company size

Prior audit fee research has found that model specification is sensitive to company size (Francis and Stokes, 1986; Palmrose, 1986a; Simunic, 1980). This potential specification problem is evaluated using a Chow test (Chow, 1960). Structural consistency of the models in Tables 4 and 5 is tested across the upper/lower halves of company size based on median total assets of 18.2 million for the full sample. All of the Chow tests are significant at $p < 0.05$, which indicates that model parameters are not consistent across the upper/lower halves of company size. However, the Chow test is a test of all parameters in a model. What is of particular interest is how the parameters on each of the auditor indicator variables behave across the size partitions. This is summarized in Table 6.

Table 6 reveals the following about the general brand name premium. For the test of H1 (industries without auditor specialists), the Big 8 premium is significant in both the upper/lowers halves, though it is somewhat greater for larger auditees than for smaller auditees (39% versus 28%). For the test of H2 (industries having auditor specialists but dropping the specialist auditors), the Big 8 premium is significant only for smaller auditees in the sample. The premium is 33%. In Section 4.4 it was suggested that where Big 8 industry specializations occur, the Big 8 brand name effect is diminished for nonspecialist Big 8 auditors who must compete on price with non-Big 8 auditors. This appears to be the case for larger auditees in specialist industries and is consistent with the

---

[19]Larger-sized companies in specialist industries, because of their size and industry, might have to choose from a smaller set of audit firms in which case the fee premium might be an economic rent rather than a specialist premium. However, if the audit market were characterized by a monopoly supplier situation, Big 8 specialists would be expected to have a dominant market share, especially in the upper half of auditee size. This does not occur. For the sample used to test H3, specialist Big 8 firms audited 39% of companies in the lower half of auditee size and 40% of companies in the upper half of auditee size. In other words, the proportion of specialist audits is virtually constant across the lower/upper halves of auditee size and is not a dominant market share since it is less than 50% of the Big 8 total.

Another point is that there are alternative monitoring mechanisms such as boards of directors and internal auditors (Anderson et al., 1993). Auditors are not monopoly suppliers of monitoring and there will be competition from alternative mechanisms. Nor are there obvious barriers to entry to industry specialization. There are two or more specialists in seven of the nine specialist industries which suggests the presence of competition. However, to extend the analysis the two idustries having only one auditor specialist (04, 19) are deleted to be sure the specialist premium is not driven by a possible monopoly supplier situation. In this test specialist auditors still have a significant premium of comparable magnitude to that reported in Table 5.

314   A.T. Craswell et al. / Journal of Accounting and Economics 20 (1995) 297-322

Table 6
Regression parameter estimates for auditor indicator variables when the samples used for estimations in Tables 4 and 5 are partitioned into upper/lower halves of auditee size based on median value
($18.2 million) of total balance sheet assets for the full sample of 1484 Australian publicly listed
companies

Tables 4 and 5 samples	Auditor indicator variable, parameter estimate, p-value, sample size	
	Partition on observations in upper half of auditee size	Partition on observations in lower half of auditee size
Table 4, Test of H1 ($n = 573$)	Big 8, $+0.322$, $p < 0.01$, $n = 329$	Big 8, $+0.245$, $p < 0.01$, $n = 244$
Table 4, Test of H2 ($n = 707$)	Big 8, $+0.082$, $p = 0.37$, $n = 309$	Big 8, $+0.285$, $p < 0.01$, $n = 398$
Table 5, Test of H3 ($n = 513$)	Specialist, $+0.295$, $p < 0.01$, $n = 258$	Specialist, -0.035, $p = 0.67$, $n = 255$

results described below which show that the industry specialist premium only
occurs for larger auditees.

The results summarized in Table 6 reveal the following about industry
specialization. For smaller-sized companies in our sample, specialist Big 8 audit
fees are not significantly different from the fees of nonspecialist Big 8 auditors.
The premium for industry specialization, and by implication the underlying
demand, is significant *only* for the upper half of auditee size in the sample. The
magnitude of the premium is also much larger than estimated in Table 5. The
parameter value is 0.295 indicating a specialist premium of 34% over nonspecialist Big 8 auditors. This result is not surprising. Fama and Jensen (1983)
argue that larger-sized companies in general have greater agency problems and
hence are more likely to benefit from the additional audit quality of a Big 8
industry specialist. The corollary is that, on average, smaller-sized companies do
not.

To sum up, for larger auditees in specialist industries there is a specialist Big
8 premium but no brand name premium for nonspecialist Big 8 auditors. For
smaller auditees in specialist industries there is a brand name Big 8 premium but
no specialist premium.

5.3. Individual Big 8 firms and specialist industries

To determine if one or more individual Big 8 accounting firm is driving the
results, the models in Tables 4 and 5 were re-estimated dropping each Big
8 auditor one at a time. These additional results are qualitatively the same and
indicate that the results reported in Tables 4 and 5 are not dominated by or
driven by individual Big 8 accounting firms.

A.T. Craswell et al. / Journal of Accounting and Economics 20 (1995) 297–322   315

To determine if the industry specialization results in Table 5 are driven by one or more individual industries, the models in Table 5 were re-estimated dropping each of the nine specialist industries one at a time. Again, these additional results are qualitatively the same and indicate that the results reported in Table 5 are not dominated by one or a few industry groups.

5.4. Potential confounding of audit risk

The 10 control variables in the audit fee regression model are intended to control for the effects of auditee size, audit complexity, and auditor–auditee risk-sharing (see Francis, 1984; Simunic, 1980). However, there is a possibility that the premium for industry specialization might simply represent a risk-related fee premium not fully captured by the audit fee model.[20] In other words, if an audit is systematically 'riskier' in the nine industries identified as having specialists, and if this riskiness is not adequately captured by the 10 variables in the audit fee model, there could be a correlated omitted variables problem.

While audit risk is different in concept from financial risk, there is likely to be correlation between the two, and this provides one way of evaluating whether there is a risk-related correlated omitted variables problem. Two measures of financial risk, systematic risk (beta) and total risk measured as the standard deviation of daily stock returns, are reported in Table 7 for each of the 23 industries in the study.[21] Industries having auditor specialists are higher in both systematic risk and total risk. The primary source of difference is in mining/oil companies (industry codes 01–04) which are considerably riskier than industrial companies.

Therefore, to assure that the results in Table 5 are not driven by the mining/oil industry, the sample used to test H3 (Table 5) is partitioned into mining/oil (industry codes 01–04) and industrial (all other codes). These results are reported in Table 8 and show that the auditor specialist variable is significant at about the same level in both samples and that the parameter estimates are comparable. Based on this analysis there is no reason to believe that the industry specialist premium reported in Table 5 is driven by underlying audit risk differences not controlled for in the audit fee model.

---

[20] This may not even be a concern since Wallace (1989) reports that audit fees are not risk-sensitive or risk-adjusted. Anderson et al. (1993) suggest that this is because very few audits result in litigation and that it is difficult to assess accurately cross-sectional differences in *ex ante* audit risk.

[21] Industry averages are published by the Centre for Finance Research, Australian Graduate School of Management, and the underlying data reported in Table 7 are based on four years of daily returns ending December 31, 1987.

316   A.T. Craswell et al. / Journal of Accounting and Economics 20 (1995) 297–322

Table 7
Industry-level measures of systematic risk (beta) and total risk (standard deviation of returns) for Australian publicly listed companies

Industry	Industry beta	Std. dev. of returns
Industries with specialists		
01 Mining – Gold	1.38	15.2
02 Mining – Other metals	1.36	13.3
03 Solid fuels	0.63	7.2
04 Oil and gas	1.07	10.8
07 Building materials	0.99	9.2
09 Food & household goods	0.76	7.8
11 Engineering	0.59	6.3
13 Retail	0.90	8.7
19 Investment & financial services	0.67	7.1
Unweighted averages	0.93	9.5
Industries without specialists		
05 Diversified resources	1.03	9.8
06 Developers & contractors	0.90	8.1
08 Alcohol & tobacco	0.87	9.0
10 Chemicals	0.80	8.2
12 Paper & packaging	0.74	7.2
14 Transport	1.20	11.4
15 Media	1.08	10.9
16 Banks	0.72	7.8
17 Insurance	0.23	7.2
18 Entrepreneurial investors	1.53	14.3
20 Property trusts	0.50	5.1
21 Miscellaneous services	0.62	6.1
22 Miscellaneous industrials	0.70	8.4
23 Diversified industrials	0.92	8.5
Unweighted averages	0.85	8.7

Source: Risk Estimation Service, Centre for Research in Finance, Australian Graduate School of Management. Estimations are based on four years of daily stock returns ending December 31, 1987.

5.5. Jointness of audit and nonaudit fees

Another concern is that the fee model used in this study does not take into consideration the possibility of cross-elasticity between audit and nonaudit fees. Simunic (1984), Palmrose (1986b), and Davis et al. (1993) report a positive association between audit and nonaudit fees. It is possible that either the brand name premium (Table 4) or the industry specialist premium (Table 5) could be driven by the level of nonaudit fees, a variable which is omitted from the models.

Table 8
Specialists versus Big 8 nonspecialists: partition of the Table 5 sample of 513 Australian publicly listed companies in industries having specialist auditors into the mining sector ($n = 266$) and industrial sector ($n = 247$); dependent variable is natural logarithm of audit fees

Independent variables	Mining auditees			Industrial auditees		
	Estimate	t-value	Prob. (2-tail)	Estimate	t-value	Prob. (2-tail)
Control variables						
Intercept	− 1.352	− 3.83	0.0002	− 1.735	− 4.36	0.0001
LTA	0.376	10.72	0.0001	0.410	9.56	0.0001
Sub	0.131	4.77	0.0001	0.248	7.14	0.0001
Current	0.276	1.37	0.1735	0.432	2.17	0.0312
Quick	− 0.009	− 3.51	0.0005	− 0.012	− 3.59	0.0004
DE	0.547	1.98	0.0490	0.953	2.73	0.0069
ROI	− 0.449	− 1.88	0.0609	− 0.311	− 0.92	0.3574
Foreign	0.209	2.84	0.0049	0.034	0.59	0.5565
Opin	0.068	0.67	0.5063	0.179	1.53	0.1266
YE	0.062	0.61	0.5437	0.063	0.47	0.6377
Loss	− 0.054	− 0.63	0.5279	0.014	0.10	0.9197
Experimental variable						
Specialist	0.132	1.55	0.1222	0.163	1.53	0.1274
Sample size		266			247	
Specialists/ Nonspecialists		117/149			87/160	
F-statistic		47.38			67.92	
Adjusted R^2		0.66			0.75	

LTA	= $\log_e$ total assets ($000);
Sub	= square root of the number of subsidiaries;
Current	= ratio of current assets to total assets;
Quick	= ratio of current assets less inventories to current liabilities;
DE	= ratio of long-term debt to total assets;
ROI	= ratio of earnings before interest and tax to total assets;
Foreign	= proportion of subsidiaries that are foreign operations;
Opin	= dummy variable, qualified = 1;
YE	= dummy variable, non-30th June balance date = 1;
Loss	= dummy variable, reported loss in prior three years = 1;
Specialist	= dummy variable, auditor is Big 8 industry specialist = 1.

The models in Tables 4 and 5 are re-estimated in two ways to evaluate this concern. First the dependent variable is redefined as total auditor remuneration (for both audit and nonaudit work). This has no significant effect on the auditor variables or on the tests of H1–H3. Second the natural logarithm of nonaudit fees is added to the models as an additional independent variable. The parameter is positive and significant at $p < 0.01$ which is consistent with other studies but it has no effect on the auditor indicator variables or on the tests of

H1–H3. There is no indication that the audit fee premia reported in Tables 4–5 are in any way confounded by the presence of nonaudit fees.[22]

5.6. Alternative definition of industry specialization

Because the 10% market share rule used by Craswell and Taylor (1991) is arbitrary, we obtained access to their source data and redefined auditor industry specialization using a much larger 20% market share rule. The purpose was to evaluate the sensitivity of our results to the 10% rule. This alternative procedure results in fewer specialist industries, six rather than nine, and only 67 companies (compared to 204 using the 10% rule). Five of the six industries have only one specialist auditor, and the remaining industry has two specialist auditors. Using this more restrictive definition the auditor specialist variable is not significant. This indicates that the results reported here are sensitive to the definition of industry specialization. Given the arbitrariness of any market share rule, we cannot rule out the possibility of spurious results in our study when using a 10% rule to define auditor industry specialists.

5.7. Number of specialist audits performed by specialists

An auditor can be classified as a specialist with as few as three audits using Craswell and Taylor's (1991) results: a 10% market share rule times the required minimum of 30 companies per industry. This is arguably a small number to warrant such a classification. In further analyzing the data we find that the mean (median) number of audits for the 20 auditor specialists in Table 1 is 10.2 (6.5), with a range from 3 to 31.

---

[22]Another aspect of nonaudit fees concerns the question of whether the level of nonaudit fees is related to auditor type. To investigate this we compared the mean level of nonaudit fees (deflated by total assets of auditees) between Big 8 and non-Big 8 auditors in the sample of companies used to test H1. We find, not surprisingly, that the level of Big 8 nonaudit fees (scaled by auditee size) is significantly higher. This is consistent with the argument by Simunic and Stein (1987) that the Big 8 supply a larger bundle of audit and nonaudit services.

We also compared the level of nonaudit fees (scaled by total assets) between specialist and nonspecialist Big 8 auditors in the sample of companies used to test H3. However, there was no significant difference between the two groups. Our speculation was that industry specialization might lead to greater levels of nonaudit services based on the accounting firm's industry expertise. Parkash and Venable (1993) report such an association using U.S. data.

As a further test we regressed the natural log of total assets, plus an auditor indicator variable for 'specialists', on the natural log of nonaudit fees (for those observations having positive nonaudit fees). This test resulted in a weakly positive t-statistic on the auditor 'specialist' variable ($p = 0.06$, one-tail) which suggests that specialist Big 8 auditors, on average, may provide somewhat more nonaudit services, holding all other factors constant and controlling for auditee size differences.

A.T. Craswell et al. / Journal of Accounting and Economics 20 (1995) 297–322   319

Larger values are concentrated in five industries (01, 04, 09, 11, 19) having nine of the 20 auditor specialists. The mean number of audits for specialist auditors in these industries is 16.9 audits with a range from seven to 31. The other four industries (02, 03, 07, 13) have 11 specialist auditors with an average of only 5.6 audits and a range from three to nine. As a sensitivity analysis, these latter observations were dropped from the sample, and the industry specialist premium re-estimated only for the former five industries having a larger number of audits per specialist. This reduced the sample to 406 observations (152 specialist and 254 nonspecialist audits). The parameter estimate for auditor specialist (*Spec*) was 0.161, and the t-statistic 2.02, which is significant at $p < 0.05$ (two-tail). This result is consistent with that reported in Table 5 and indicates that the estimations are robust across the number of specialist audits and are not driven by those industries in which the number of audits per specialist is relatively small.

6. Summary and conclusions

The purpose of this study has been to use empirical audit fee models to infer the existence of Big 8 reputations for both industry specialization and general brand name. Agency/contracting theory is used to explain the economic demand for costlier quality-differentiated Big 8 audits. We argue that industry specialization will increase a Big 8 auditor's reputation (within that industry), but will require development of expertise beyond the general expertise of the audit firm. Additional investments in expertise will require a positive return resulting in an audit fee premium, all other factors held constant.

Our empirical results, based on a large sample of Australian companies, are supportive that the audit fees of Big 8 auditors contain premia relating to both general brand name and industry specialization.[23] While specialization may lead to auditor production economies, the evidence here is that positive returns to investment in specialization dominate potential production economies and lead to higher average audit fees. Based on these results future auditing research should be careful to control for industry specialization since it appears to be an important dimension of quality-differentiated Big 8 audits above and beyond brand name reputation.

---

[23]There is a question about the generality of these results using Australian data to the U.S. or other audit markets. The Australian accounting profession and audit market closely resemble the U.S. Apart from smaller companies and a smaller Big 8 market share there are no obvious differences. The Australian market was deregulated in the early 1980s similar to that which occurred in the U.S. in the late 1970s. Competitive tendering for audits is commonplace as is auditor switching. Thus we are unaware of reasons why the results reported here would not be applicable to the U.S. and other comparable audit markets.

There are three important limitations to the study. First, the definition of auditor industry specialization is arbitrarily based on a 10% market share rule and the results are sensitive to this definition (see Section 5.6). Second, we do not know why auditor specializations occur in some industries but not others. Craswell and Taylor (1991) identified specialists in nine of 23 Australian industry groups. What are the industry-wide factors which make audits in some industries generic while others give rise to auditor specialists? Industry size limits the opportunity for auditor specialization but we do not understand the fundamental industry characteristics leading to the supply of and demand for auditor specialization. Third, and relatedly, we do not know what causes some companies within an industry to contract with specialist auditors while others do not. The sample in this study indicated that 22% of eligible companies elected to hire the more costly industry specialist.

Demand for auditor specialization has not been clearly linked to either industry-wide factors or to company-specific factors within industries. Subsequent research is needed to explore the linkages between the demand for quality-differentiated audits and the industry-wide and company-specific factors such as ownership and financing structure, and production–investment attributes that affect agency costs. Absent these linkages the empirical results reported here, while consistent with the presence of such a demand, are not directly indicative.

References

Anderson, D., J. Francis, and D. Stokes, 1993, Auditing, directorships and the demand for monitoring, Journal of Accounting and Public Policy 12, 353–375.

Ashton, A., 1991, Experience and error frequency knowledge as potential determinants of auditor expertise, The Accounting Review 66, 216–239.

Baber, W., E. Brooks, and W. Ricks, 1987, An empirical investigation of the market for audit services in the public sector, Journal of Accounting Research 25, 293–305.

Balvers, R., B. McDonald, and R.Miller, 1988, Underpricing of new issues and the choice of auditors as a signal of investment banker reputation, The Accounting Review 63, 605–622.

Beatty, R., 1989, Auditor reputation and the pricing of initial public offerings, The Accounting Review 64, 693–709.

Bonner, S. and B. Lewis, 1990, Determinants of auditor expertise, Journal of Accounting Research, Suppl., 28, 1–28.

Carcello, J., R. Hermanson, and N. McGrath, 1992, Audit quality attributes: The perceptions of audit partners, preparers, and financial statement users, Auditing: A Journal of Practice and Theory 11, 1–15.

Chan, P., M. Ezzamel, and D. Gwilliam, 1993, Determinants of audit fees for quoted UK companies, Journal of Business Finance and Accounting 20, 765–786.

Chow, G., 1960, Tests of equality between sets of coefficients in two linear regressions, Econometrica 28, 591–605.

Copley, P., M. Doucet, and K. Gaver, 1994, A simultaneous equations analysis of quality control review outcomes and engagement fees for audits of recipients of federal financial assistance, The Accounting Review 69, 244–256.

Craswell, A., 1988, Who audits Australia? (Accounting and Finance Foundation, University of Sydney, Sydney).

Craswell, A. and S.Taylor, 1991, The market structure of auditing in Australia: The role of industry specialization, Research in Accounting Regulation 5, 55–77.

Danos, P. and J. Eichenseher, 1986, Long-term trends toward seller concentration in the U.S. audit market, The Accounting Review 61, 633–650.

Datar, S., G. Feltham, and J. Hughes, 1991, The role of audits and audit quality in valuing new issues, Journal of Accounting and Economics 14, 3–49.

Davidson, R. and D. Neu, 1993, A note on the association between audit firm size and audit quality, Contemporary Accounting Research 9, 479–488.

Davis, L., D. Ricchiute, and G. Trompeter, 1993, Audit effort, audit fees, and the provision of nonaudit services to audit clients, The Accounting Review 68, 135–150.

DeAngelo, L., 1981, Auditor size and auditor quality, Journal of Accounting and Economics 1, 113–127.

Defond, M., 1992, The association between changes in client firm agency costs and auditor switching, Auditing: A Journal of Practice and Theory 11, 16–31.

Dopuch, N. and D. Simunic, 1982, Competition in auditing: An assessment, Fourth auditing research symposium (University of Illinois, Champaign, IL).

Eichenseher, J. and P. Danos, 1981, The analysis of industry specific concentration: Toward an explanatory model, The Accounting Review 56, 479–492.

Ettredge, M. and R. Greenberg, 1990, Determinants of fee cutting on initial audit engagements, Journal of Accounting Research 28, 198–210.

Fama, E. and M. Jensen, 1983, Separation of ownership and control, Journal of Law and Economics 26, 301–326.

Feltham, G., J. Hughes, and D. Simunic, Empirical assessment of the impact of auditor quality on the valuation of new issues, Journal of Accounting and Economics 14, 375–399.

Francis, J., 1984, The effect of audit firm size on audit prices: A study of the Australian market, Journal of Accounting and Economics 6, 133–151.

Francis, J. and D. Simon, 1987, A test of audit pricing in the small-client segment of the U.S. audit market, The Accounting Review 62, 145–157.

Francis, J. and D. Stokes, 1986, Audit prices, product differentiation, and scale economies: Further evidence from the Australian audit market, Journal of Accounting Research 24, 383–393.

Francis, J. and E. Wilson, 1988, Auditor changes: A joint test of theories relating to agency costs and auditor differentiation, The Accounting Review 63, 663–682.

Klein, B. and K. Leffler, 1981, The role of market forces in assuring contractual performance, Journal of Political Economy 89, 615–641.

Menon, K. and D. Williams, 1991, Auditor credibility and initial public offerings, The Accounting Review 66, 313–332.

O'Keefe, T., R. King, and K. Gaver, 1994, Audit fees, industry specialization, and compliance with GAAS reporting standards, Auditing: A Journal of Practice and Theory 13, 40–55.

O'Keefe, T., D. Simunic, and M. Stein, 1994, The production of audit services: Evidence from a major public accounting firm, Journal of Accounting Research 32, 241–261.

Palmrose, Z., 1984, The demand for differentiated audit services in an agency-cost setting: An empirical examination, Fifth auditing research symposium (University of Illinois, Champaign, IL).

Palmrose, Z., 1986a, Audit fees and auditor size: Further evidence, Journal of Accounting Research 24, 97–110.

Palmrose, Z., 1986b, The effect of nonaudit services on the pricing of audit services: Further evidence, Journal of Accounting Research 24, 405–411.

Palmrose, Z., 1988, An analysis of auditor litigation and audit service quality, The Accounting Review 63, 55–73.

Parkash, M. and C. Venable, 1993, Auditee incentives for auditor independence: The case of nonaudit services, The Accounting Review 68, 113–133.

Pearson, T. and G. Trompeter, 1994, Competition in the market for audit services: The effect of supplier concentration on audit fees, Contemporary Accounting Research 11, 115–135.

Rubin, M., 1988, Municipal audit fee determinants, The Accounting Review 63, 219–236.

Shapiro, C., 1983, Premiums for high quality products as returns to reputations, Quarterly Journal of Economics 98, 659–679.

Shockley, R. and R. Holt, 1983, A behavioral investigation of supplier differentiation in the market for audit services, Journal of Accounting Research 21, 545–564.

Simon, D. and J. Francis, 1988, The effects of auditor change on audit fees: Tests of price cutting and price recovery, The Accounting Review 63, 255–269.

Simunic, D., 1980, The pricing of audit services: theory and evidence, Journal of Accounting Research 18, 161–190.

Simunic, D., 1984, Auditing, consulting, and auditor independence, Journal of Accounting Research 22, 679–702.

Simunic, D. and M. Stein, 1987, Product differentiation in auditing: Auditor choice in the market for unseasoned new issues (Canadian Certified General Accountants' Research Foundation, Vancouver).

Slovin, M., M. Sushka, and C. Hudson, 1990, External monitoring and its effect on seasoned common stock issues, Journal of Accounting and Economics 12, 397–417.

Teoh, S. and T. Wong, 1993, Perceived auditor quality and the earnings response coefficient, The Accounting Review 68, 346–366.

Titman, S. and B. Trueman, 1986, Information quality and the valuation of new issues, Journal of Accounting and Economics 8, 159–172.

Wallace, W., 1989, Are audit fees sufficiently risk adjusted?, Advances in Accounting, Suppl. 1, 9, 3–38.

Watts, R. and J. Zimmerman, 1986, Positive accounting theory (Prentice-Hall, Englewood Cliffs, NJ).

White, H., 1980, A heteroskedasticity-consistent covariance matrix estimator and a direct test for heteroskedasticity, Econometrica 48, 817–838.

[11]

THE ACCOUNTING REVIEW
Vol. LXIII, No. 1
January 1988

An Analysis of Auditor Litigation and Audit Service Quality

Zoe-Vonna Palmrose

ABSTRACT: This study compares litigation activities of independent auditors to assess litigation as a means for making quality distinctions among auditors. The study provides a framework suggesting auditors with relatively low (high) litigation activity represent higher (lower) quality suppliers. The empirical analysis examines a sample of legal cases ($n = 472$) and resolutions for these cases (if available, $n = 183$). The cases involve audit-related litigation against both Big Eight and large non-Big Eight firms during 1960–1985. The results indicate that non-Big Eight firms as a group have higher litigation activity than Big Eight firms. This result is consistent with existing research supporting the Big Eight as quality-differentiated auditors. Comparisons among Big Eight firms reveal some significant differences. However, identification of particular Big Eight firms as low (high) litigation activity auditors appears sensitive to the type of analysis.

THIS study compares litigation activities among the largest U.S. independent audit firms. Litigation against auditors typically involves a process, from initial discovery of potentially false or misleading financial statements, to filing of lawsuits, and eventual resolution of such suits. In investigating differences in litigation among auditors, the study utilizes data on both litigation occurrences and resolutions.

The primary objective of the comparisons is to assess litigation as a means for making quality distinctions among independent audit firms. Previous empirical research on auditor litigation (Kellogg [1984]; Palmrose [1987]; and St. Pierre and Anderson [1984])[1] and on audit quality (Francis and Simon [1987]; Nichols and Smith [1983]; Palmrose

Financial assistance of the University of California at Berkeley Professional Accounting Program and the research assistance of Hay Young Chung, Changyong Ham, and Richard Taylor are gratefully acknowledged. I would like to thank Mike Duffy and Robert Kellogg for contributions during the data-gathering process. In addition, I would like to acknowledge the helpful comments of various individuals and groups including, William L. Felix, Jr., Marcia Niles, Kent St. Pierre, participants in workshops at the University of Washington and the University of Arizona, and especially William R. Kinney, Jr.

Zoe-Vonna Palmrose is Assistant Professor at the School of Business Administration, University of California at Berkeley.

Manuscript received February 1987.
Revision received July 1987.
Accepted August 1987.

*Editor's Note: "Taxes and Off-Balance-Sheet Financing: Research and Development Limited Partnerships" by Terry Shevlin that appeared in the July 1987 issue of

[1986]; and Shockley and Holt [1983]) has not provided evidence on this issue. However, the potential usefulness of litigation in judging audit quality has been recognized (Dopuch and Simunic [1982]; Simunic and Stein [1987]).

An inverse expected relation between auditor quality and litigation is developed. Briefly, the value of external audits derives from users' expectations auditors will detect and correct/reveal any material omissions or misstatements of financial information. Failure to do so, termed an audit failure,[2] typically results in litigation when clients/users incur losses in conjunction with materially false or misleading financial information. This suggests that (under *ceteris paribus* conditions) users can view auditors with relatively low (high) litigation activity as higher (lower) quality suppliers.

This study examines auditor litigation to determine if firms differ, and if so, which ones represent low (high) activity firms. The evidence constitutes a first step in assessing the usefulness of litigation in making quality distinctions among independent audit firms. In examining auditors' litigation activities, the study also considers non-qualitative factors that may influence auditors' litigation.

As a secondary objective, the study provides unique descriptive data on litigation activities for each Big Eight firm and a group of the largest non-Big Eight firms. A sample of 472 cases relating to audits performed from 1960 through 1985 serves as a basis for analyses.

The remainder of the study is organized as follows. The next section develops a framework using litigation to make quality distinctions among auditors. The remaining sections describe sample selection criteria; discuss analyses of litigation occurrences and litigation resolutions, and concluding remarks.

I. CONCEPTUAL FRAMEWORK

This section develops possible associations among audit quality, audit failures, and litigation. While a three-part characterization is somewhat complicated, it is necessitated by users' inability to directly observe either audit quality (see DeAngelo [1981]; Palmrose [1986]) or audit failures. In essence, litigation helps identify audit failures, so that litigation potentially represents the most observable component of the three. However, litigation is not perfectly associated with audit quality and this section discusses considerations that may affect the association. A definition of audit quality serves as a starting point for these developments.

Audit "quality" is defined in terms of the level of assurances—the probability financial statements contain no material omissions or misstatements.[3] Higher levels of assurances correspond to higher

THE ACCOUNTING REVIEW is also a Co-Winner of the 1987 Competitive Manuscript Contest. Announcement of Shevlin's award was received too late for designation at publication.

[1] Kellogg [1984] analyzed associations between stock prices and accounting announcements for 10b-5 class action suits; Palmrose [1987] examined the role of business failures and management fraud in auditor litigation; and St. Pierre and Anderson [1984] investigated factors associated with litigation against public accountants. The Kellogg and St. Pierre studies relied on smaller sample sizes ($n = 56$ and $n = 129$, respectively) and did not limit sample observations to audit-related lawsuits or lawsuits with auditors as one of the defendants. None of the studies presented comparisons of individual audit firm litigation.

[2] Here, audit failures include financial statements with material omissions/misstatements whether or not auditors have obtained adequate audit evidence.

[3] This definition is consistent with both DeAngelo's [1981] definition of audit quality and the professional literature that describes audit quality in terms of audit risk, with higher quality services reflecting lower audit risk. Audit risk is defined as the risk that "the auditor may unknowingly fail to appropriately modify his opinion on financial statements that are materially mis-

quality services. An important implication of this definition is that audit failures (financial statements with material
omissions/misstatements) become less
likely with higher quality services.

In discussing litigation as a consequence of audit failures, we assume that
litigation is costly and that litigation
costs provide additional incentives to
higher quality auditors for avoiding
audit failures. Auditors face unlimited
liability in connection with civil actions
against them which accounts, in part, for
litigation costs.[4] However, other costs
accompany litigation, including costs associated with professional and regulatory (e.g., SEC) sanctions and with reduced reputations for quality of service.
While insurance may help reduce impacts from civil penalties, insurance does
not cover criminal actions against individuals, professional and regulatory
sanctions against firms and individuals,
or losses from reputation diminishment.[5]
The latter becomes particularly relevant
to high quality auditors, since they have
more to lose [DeAngelo, 1981]. Thus,
high quality auditors, with reputations
for detecting and correcting/revealing
material omissions or misstatements,
have greater incentives to minimize audit
failures to maintain this reputation.

Figure 1 shows the presumed links between client/user losses and audit litigation outcomes. As denoted in Figure
1, when clients and/or users (such as
creditors or investors) incur losses, these
losses may or may not entail material
omissions/misstatements of financial
statements, i.e., audit failures.[6] An example of circumstances when user losses
occur without audit failures would be client bankruptcies not involving false or
misleading financial statements.[7] As
illustrated in Figure 1, litigation helps
reveal which loss situations also involve
audit failures. Lawsuits against auditors
(or threatened lawsuits) represent the

most likely (probable) action with an
audit failure. Furthermore, payments by
auditors to plaintiffs represent the most
likely outcome from audit failure litigation. Auditor payments include both
court imposed judgments and out of
court settlements. Out of court settlements may come from actual or merely
threatened lawsuits. Conversely, when
client/user losses occur without audit
failures, the most likely outcome is no
litigation against auditors and no payments by auditors.

These two links reflecting most likely
actions and outcomes, audit failure-liti-
gation-payments versus no audit failure-
no litigation-no payments, suggest both
litigation occurrences and resolutions
should be associated with audit failures.
However, each of these measures have
ambiguities of interpretation that require
some discussion.

First, Figure 1 recognizes the possibility clients/users may undertake legal actions against auditors when no audit failure exists. Auditors as persons having

---

stated" (AICPA (SAS No. 47) [1985]). Because auditing
is costly, a positive, albeit "low" level of audit risk is
allowed under auditing standards. Thus, some "audit
failures" would be expected for even high quality
auditors.

[4] This study assumes "keeping auditors honest"
rather than insuring clients/users against losses serves as
the role of litigation in the audit services market.

[5] In addition, insurance costs partly depend on audit
firms' litigation experience. Other litigation-related costs
that larger firms usually absorb include: legal fees, staff
costs associated with case preparation and defense, settlement payments below insurance deductibles, and set-
tlements/judgments in excess of insurance policy limits.

[6] St. Pierre and Anderson [1984] suggest losses as a
major factor in initiating searches for audit failures.
Plaintiffs must allege losses to meet one requirement for
filing lawsuits.

[7] Palmrose [1987] found nearly 80 percent of 458 companies declaring bankruptcy (identified via the *WSJ
Index* [1970–1985]), that also used auditors listed in
Table 1, had no indication of litigation against the
auditors.

FIGURE 1

LIKELIHOOD OF AUDITOR LITIGATION OCCURRENCES/OUTCOMES GIVEN CLIENT/USER LOSSES[a]

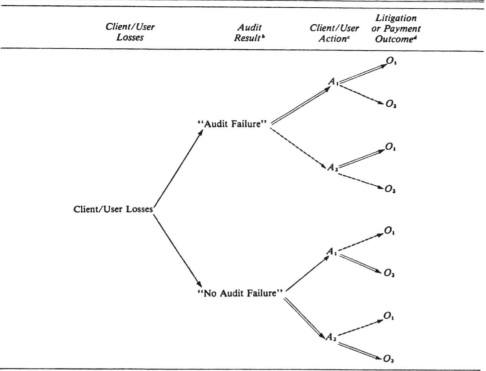

Client/User Losses	Audit Result[b]	Client/User Action[c]	Litigation or Payment Outcome[d]

* ═══▶ Probable (Most Likely)
  ───▶ Possible
  -------▶ Remote

[b] "Audit Failure" includes material misstatements whether or not the auditor has obtained adequate audit evidence.

[c] A_1 Lawsuit Against Auditor
   A_2 No Lawsuit Against Auditor

[d] O_1 Auditor Payments (Including Out-Of-Court Settlements, Court Imposed Judgments, and Payments to Avoid Litigation)
   O_2 No Auditor Payments (Including Court Dismissals of Claims Against Auditors)

"deep pockets" characterizes one motivation for such suits. Since these cases allege audit failures, users can find it difficult to distinguish these cases from audit failures at initiation of lawsuits against auditors. In addition, estimates of audit failure rates based on litigation occurrences would be overstated because of these cases.

To some extent, litigation outcome data help resolve this difficulty. Assuming the litigation process (including discovery and court hearings) reveals merits of claims, lawsuits without audit failures would most likely result in court dismissals of claims against auditors and/or out of court settlements without any payments by auditors. Empirically this means litigation occurrences as a measure of audit quality might be reduced by cases with lawsuit dismissals/no auditor payments when comparing litigation among auditors, as discussed in section IV.

However, a second issue arises when utilizing resolution data and assuming auditor payments represent remote outcomes from litigation not involving audit failures. In settling litigation out of court, auditors frequently state that payments were made to avoid expenses of protracted litigation and such payments do not indicate an inadequate audit. Although auditors do not necessarily confine these statements to situations involving small (token) payments, relatively small payments may signify circumstances in which users view such statements as credible.[8] While the study classifies cases with any auditor payments as meritorious and cases without auditor payments as non-meritorious, additional analyses consider payment size, in part, to provide insight into this issue (see section IV).

A third issue requiring discussion relates to auditors negotiating settlement payments to avoid litigation in the face of audit failures. As shown in Figure 1, in these instances payments by auditors describe the most likely outcome (audit failure but no lawsuit against auditor). In selecting the sample, cases of auditor payments without litigation are included in both litigation occurrences and resolutions (as meritorious cases) consistent with an underlying assumption that these cases represent audit failures (see section II).

Finally, resolution data entail weaknesses not necessarily evident in Figure 1. One of the foremost problems with users relying on resolution data in assessing audit quality relates to long time horizons, including appeals, from inception of litigation to full and complete case resolution. Settlements several (or many) years after initiation of suits may be too delayed to allow meaningful revisions in users' assessments of audit quality. Other problems with resolution data involve the degree of expertise attributed to the court process in correctly specifying cases (as audit failure/not audit failure) and reflecting this correct specification in litigation outcomes. For example, favorable resolutions for auditors based on an inability of plaintiffs to meet class-action requirements might still involve audit failures. Furthermore, there may be (un)favorable resolutions because of changing interpretations of laws, jurisdictional differences, or randomness of juries. All of these considerations may reduce associations among audit quality, audit failures, and litigation outcomes.

Thus, this framework proposes an inverse relation between audit quality and litigation rates. Briefly, with higher quality services, audit failures become less likely. When audit failures occur in conjunction with client/user losses, clients/users file lawsuits against independent auditors. Accepting both audit failures as less likely with higher quality services and litigation as a primary consequence of audit failures, yields a basic proposition that higher quality auditors have relatively lower litigation rates than lower quality auditors. Because litigation helps reveal audit failures, this framework suggests users can observe differences in litigation occurrences among auditors and infer relative audit quality.

Figure 1 also shows that litigation against independent auditors can occur without audit failures. Therefore, making inferences regarding auditor quality using observed differences in litigation requires considering merits of plaintiffs'

---

[8] To protect reputations, some auditors may avoid even token payments to settle non-meritorious suits. Thus, users may perceive even token payments as admissions of audit failures.

claims. If non-meritorious lawsuits (i.e., those not involving audit failures) get resolved favorably for auditors (auditor dismissals/no auditor payments), while audit failures that involve inadequate audit evidence require payments by auditors, then resolution data can supplement litigation occurrence data in identifying audit failures and assessing auditor quality. Note, the framework also includes as audit failures instances of auditor payments to avoid litigation.

In summary, the framework suggests the potential usefulness of litigation rates to distinguish among auditors on the basis of quality. To provide preliminary insights into this potential, we examine data on litigation occurrences and resolutions for differences among auditors. The next section describes selection of the sample.

II. SAMPLE SELECTION

This section summarizes criteria used to acquire a sample of legal cases involving independent auditors. Cases encompass audit services[9] rendered for the 26-year-period from 1960 through 1985. This time period includes the major concentration of lawsuits against independent auditors.[10] The (approximately) 15 largest audit firms were selected for the study. Table 1 lists and classifies firms as Big Eight and non-Big Eight. While some firms have international operations, the sample is confined to cases involving audits in the U.S. market. During 1960–1985, many audit firms engaged in mergers and an attempt was made to include cases for primary components of present firms. Table 1 notes these components.

Firms in Table 1 comprise a major portion of the audit services market. For example, these firms audit over 90 percent of public companies (see *Who*

Audits America (WAA) [1984]). In addition, limiting the sample to large firms recognizes that audit firms may differ in their attractiveness as litigation targets. As previously discussed, suits against auditors may be filed without an audit failure, partly because auditors represent potential "deep pockets." In this regard, larger audit firms may present more desirable targets than smaller firms because of greater resources and insurance coverage. However, the Big Eight and largest non-Big Eight firms appear relatively homogeneous on this dimension.[11]

Cases were identified using the following sources:

(1) *The Wall Street Journal Index (WSJ)* listing for each firm in Table 1 [January 1960–November 1986].

(2) Litigation news in the *Public Accounting Report (PAR)* [January 1978 (first issue)–November 1986].

(3) Litigation news in the *International Accounting Bulletin (IAB)* [July 1983 (first issue)–November 1986].

(4) Securities and Exchange Commission (SEC) Accounting Series Re-

---

[9] While nearly all cases involve audit services, several cases entail less than a full scope audit (e.g., review or compilation services). By focusing on audit services supplied to specific clients, the study excludes a variety of litigation against public accounting firms (e.g., litigation regarding employment practices and employee activities, anti-competitive practices, and non-audit services).

[10] For example, *Forbes* noted "as recently as 1962 there were perhaps two lawsuits pending against major CPA firms" (Minard and Wilson [1980], p. 14).

[11] There are other possible dimensions to the attractiveness of audit firms as litigation targets. For example, Kinney [forthcoming] models the probability of suits against auditors as follows:

P(suit) $= f$ (actual user losses, amount of misstatement in audited financial statements, reputation of auditor for audit quality (i.e., low detection risk), auditor legal posture, and user's and client's costs to sue).

Audit firm litigation posture is discussed in section IV.

Palmrose   61

TABLE 1

AUDIT FIRMS INCLUDED IN THE SAMPLE

Big Eight	
(AA)	Arthur Andersen & Co.
(AY)	Arthur Young & Co.
(CL)	Coopers & Lybrand (Lybrand, Ross Bros. & Montgomery)
(DHS)	Deloitte Haskins & Sells (Haskins & Sells)
(EW)	Ernst & Whinney (Ernst and Ernst)
(PMM)	Peat, Marwick, Mitchell & Co.
(PW)	Price Waterhouse
(TR)	Touche Ross & Co. (Touche, Ross, Bailey & Smart)
Non-Big Eight	
(AG)	Grant Thornton
	Alexander Grant & Company
	Fox & Company
	Including: Elmer Fox & Co.
	Westheimer, Fine, Berger & Co.
	Elmer Fox, Westheimer & Co.
(MH)	KMG Main Hurdman
	Including: Main Lafrentz & Co.
	Hurdman & Cranstoun
	Hurdman & Cranstoun, Penney
	Main, Hurdman & Cranstoun
	L. H. Penney & Co.
	John F. Forbes & Co.
(LH)	Laventhol & Horwath (Laventhol, Krekstein, Horwath, and Horwath)
(JKL)	J. K. Lasser & Co.[a]
(SDL)	S. D. Leidesdorf & Co.[b]
(McHP)	McGladrey, Hendrickson, Pullen & Co.
	Including: McGladrey Hendrickson & Co.
	Broeker, Hendrickson & Co.
	McGladrey, Hansen, Dunn & Co.
	A. M. Pullen & Co.
(PKF)	Pannell Kerr Forster (Harris Kerr Forster)
(SS)	Seidman & Seidman
	Including: Wolfson, Weiner, Ratoff & Lapin

[a] Included as non-Big Eight prior to merger with TR.
[b] Included as non-Big Eight prior to merger with EW.

leases (ASR) and Accounting and Auditing Enforcement Releases (AAER).

(5) Cases reported on Mead Data's LEXIS system in the general federal file [January 1960–April 1986] where firms in Table 1 were named as either plaintiff/defendant or appellee/appellant.

(6) Cases reported on Mead Data's LEXIS system in the California and New York state files [January 1975–April 1986] where firms in Table 1 were named as either plaintiff/defendant or appellee/appellant.

(7) Cases disclosed in Mead Data's NAARS system in files for general annual reports and proxy statements [December 1985].

(8) Lawsuits mentioned in prior studies of accountants' liability/litigation (e.g., Kellogg [1984]; St. Pierre and Anderson [1984]).

(9) Miscellaneous sources, including auditing texts (e.g., Arens and Loebbecke [1984]; Carmichael and Willingham [1979]) and books

62

The Accounting Review, January 1988

on accountants' liability (e.g., Causey [1982]; Davies [1983]; and Jaenicke [1977]).

From these sources a total of 472 cases were identified. A client/audit firm combination counts as one case. This means multiple actions (both criminal and civil; by investors, creditors, regulators, or bankruptcy trustees) regarding similar services and issues count as one case. Nearly all cases entail lawsuits filed in federal or state courts. The few remaining cases involve auditor payments to avoid litigation over allegations of audit failure.[12] Finally, some actions included more than one audit firm as defendant, primarily due to related companies with different auditors or companies changing auditors. Since allegations of audit failure were made against all auditors, these situations were counted as a case for each audit firm.

Section III uses the full sample of 472 cases to examine differences in litigation occurrences among auditors—without regard to case outcomes. Section IV considers resolution data for a reduced sample of 183 cases.[13] The resolution sample is smaller because some cases are not yet resolved. Also, sources reviewed for information on auditor litigation did not necessarily reveal all resolved cases. Thus, 183 cases do not capture all resolved cases in the 472, just resolved cases for which resolution data were available in the sources previously outlined.

III. RESULTS: LITIGATION OCCURRENCES

Overall Sample Comparisons

Table 2 presents total number of cases ($n = 472$) for each Big Eight firm and the group of non-Big Eight firms. These cases comprise public companies, closely-held companies, municipalities, chari-

ties, and other non-public entities, along with a few companies of indeterminable ownership. However, most of the sample consists of public companies ($n = 343$) and Table 2 provides the number of public company cases for each Big Eight firm and the group of non-Big Eight firms.

Before comparing among auditors, numbers in Table 2 require scaling because of differences among sample firms in numbers of audit clients served. The study uses two methods of scaling litigation occurrences. First, from data on audit clients and changes in clients (see *PAR, WAA*, McConnell [1984], etc.), an estimate of number of audit clients served during 1960–1985 is computed for each firm and grouping of firms.[14] As this estimate encompasses only public clients, it is used to scale public company litigation cases. Table 3 (column 1) shows the resulting 26-year litigation occurrence rates for each Big Eight firm and Big Eight/non-Big Eight groupings.[15]

As a second method of scaling, the study uses estimated annual U.S. audit-

---

[12] For public companies, auditor settlements to avoid litigation may be disclosed in proxy statements or 8-K's. For both public and closely-held companies, some such payments receive press disclosure (*PAR, WSJ*).

[13] Resolution data pertain to auditors' litigation. In all but a few cases auditors comprise just one of a number of defendants. Although auditors' resolutions may not be independent of resolutions by other parties, resolutions for non-auditor defendants are not considered in the study.

[14] The number of clients for each firm and grouping of firms are as follows: AA (1,665); AY (807); CL (1,345); DHS (1,053); EW (1,228); PMM (1,456); PW (1,024); TR (1,024); Big Eight (9,602); and non-Big Eight (1,100).

[15] Big Eight rates and rankings are sensitive to the denominator computation. For example, using numbers from *WAA* [1976] (viewed as an average of 1960–1985 client base) results in the following ranking: TR, PMM, AA, AY, PW, CL, DHS, and EW. Using *WAA* [1976–1985] to compute an average number of public clients produces the following ranking: PMM, PW, AY, AA, TR, CL, DHS, and EW. However, each of these two rankings is significantly associated with the ranking in Table 3 (column 1), based on Spearman correlation coefficients of .67 and .95, respectively.

TABLE 2

NUMBER OF CASES CLASSIFIED BY AUDIT FIRM AND TIME-PERIOD
(1960–1985)

	All Cases			Public Company Cases		
	Total	1960–1972	1973–1985	Total	1960–1972	1973–1985
Big Eight						
AA	64	25	39	56	23	33
AY	35	14	21	26	11	15
CL	45	11	34	34	9	25
DHS	31	14	17	23	9	14
EW	39	17	22	29	12	17
PMM	72	29	43	53	21	32
PW	45	13	32	36	12	24
TR	50	18	32	30	13	17
Subtotal	381	141	240	287	110	177
Non-Big Eight	91	40	51	56	25	31
Total	472	181	291	343	135	208

related revenue for 1984 and 1985 from *PAR*.[16] Since this estimate consists of both public and non-public clients, it serves as a denominator with total cases as a numerator. Computed litigation occurrence rates (per $MM of revenue) are shown in Table 3 (column 2).

Although rankings in Table 3 (columns 1 and 2) are significantly associated (Spearman correlation coefficient = .71), the two methods of computing litigation occurrence rates result in slightly different positions for some Big Eight firms. Perhaps the most notable shift in rank occurs with TR's movement from fifth (column 1) to first (column 2). Otherwise, PMM and AA tend to rank near the top (higher activity) and CL, DHS, and EW tend to rank near the bottom (lower activity) under both computations.

To address a central question—are litigation occurrences independent of Big Eight firm identity?—an 8 × 2 contingency table and chi-square statistic is used. For each Big Eight auditor, public clients served during 1960–1985 (see footnote 14) are classified into two categories, clients with/without auditor litigation. A computed chi-square (9.0) is not significant at the .10 level. While litigation frequencies differ among Big Eight firms, differences are not statistically significant.

A similar test using a 2 × 2 contingency table, comparing Big Eight and non-Big Eight public clients with/without litigation (see footnote 14) is significant (at the .005 level). A computed chi-square (14.5) reflects a greater number of cases than expected for non-Big Eight firms. This result appears consistent with prior research supporting Big Eight firms as quality-differentiated auditors (Francis and Simon [1987]; Palmrose [1986]).

[16] Big Eight rankings were not altered with a denominator based on an average of U.S. audit revenues from 1971–1972, 1977, 1982, 1983, 1984, and 1985 collected from various sources.

TABLE 3

AUDIT FIRM LITIGATION RATES

(26 YEAR RATES 1960–1985)

	Using Cases Filed				Using Meritorious Cases			
	PCC/ENPC (1)		TC/EAR (2)		EMCPC/ENPC (3)		EMC/EAR (4)	
Big Eight								
	PMM	3.6%	TR	17.7%	TR	2.4%	TR	12.4%
	PW	3.5%	PMM	13.4%	AA	2.3%	PMM	8.4%
	AA	3.4%	AA	11.8%	PMM	2.2%	AA	8.3%
	AY	3.2%	PW	11.7%	CL	2.1%	CL	7.7%
	TR	2.9%	AY	11.4%	DHS	1.9%	DHS	6.8%
	CL	2.5%	CL	9.3%	EW	1.8%	PW	4.7%
	EW	2.4%	DHS	9.1%	PW	1.3%	EW	4.0%
	DHS	2.2%	EW	8.3%	AY	0.4%	AY	2.3%
Big Eight	3.0%		11.4%		1.9%		6.9%	
Non-Big Eight	5.1%		16.7%		3.8%		10.6%	

PCC = Public Company Cases Filed
ENPC = Estimated Number of Public Clients (1960–1985)
TC = Total Cases Filed
EAR = Estimated Annual U.S. Audit-Related Revenue (MM)
EMCPC = Estimated Meritorious Cases for Public Companies
EMC = Estimated Meritorious Cases

This comparison of auditor litigation rates does not consider differences in auditors' client portfolios (other than portfolio size) that may affect likelihood of auditor litigation irrespective of audit quality supplied, including differences in client industry affiliations. Furthermore, comparisons aggregating data over 1960–1985 do not consider time-series variations in auditor litigation occurrences. These two issues are discussed below.

In interpreting results of this section, it should be noted that litigation represents a rare occurrence relative to numbers of clients served by auditors. The low rates may inhibit users' attempts to distinguish among auditors.[17] In addition, a small numbers problem becomes magnified when comparing litigation occurrences intra-industry and/or across time.

Intra-Industry Comparisons

This section compares auditor litigation occurrences within the context of client industries. There are several reasons for making comparisons intra-industry. First, auditors differ in their client industry concentrations (Palmrose [1986]). Second, studies of auditor litigation (Palmrose [1987]; St. Pierre and Anderson [1984]) found severe financial distress, including bankruptcy, to be a factor in auditor litigation.[18] Third, pro-

[17] From a perspective of users' awareness of auditor litigation, an even smaller number of occurrences should be considered "observable," therefore, available to users in making comparisons among auditors. For example, only a portion of the cases (approximately 50 percent) received widespread public disclosure (as evidenced by inclusion in the *WSJ*).

[18] Auditor litigation involving clients with financial difficulties cannot be viewed as simply users with losses looking for deep pockets. Palmrose [1987] found that legal cases involving financial difficulties frequently occur in conjunction with management fraud.

files of business failures reveal differences in frequencies of company failures on an industry basis (*WSJ* [December 15, 1986], p. 29).[19] Together, these three considerations suggest propensity for auditor litigation may be influenced by business risks as captured through client industry affiliations. In essence, examining auditor litigation intra-industry may yield different insights than those from overall comparisons.

Tables 4 and 5 profile client industry affiliations for the 472 cases in the sample. Table 4 presents percentage of cases in each industry for the total sample, each Big Eight firm, and non-Big Eight firms as a group. Supplementing data in Table 4, Table 5 presents a percentage breakdown of cases in each industry by auditor (each Big Eight auditor and non-Big Eight firms as a group).

Focusing on percentages for the total sample in Table 4, some industries have higher (lower) incidences of litigation than expected given relative numbers of companies. Computers and electronics (SIC codes 357 and 366) provides an illustration. Computers and electronics represents eight percent of total legal cases in the sample. Yet, companies from this industry comprise only about five percent (445 of about 9,000 companies) in *WAA* [1980].[20]

To develop implications of client industry on auditor litigation rate comparisons, again consider computers and electronics. For each Big Eight firm, litigation rates within this industry are computed. The number of public company legal cases in computers and electronics (37 cases in Table 5 reduced by one non-public case (AY)) is used as the numerator and the number of public clients in the industry, based on data from *WAA* [1980], serves as a denominator. Computed litigation rates for each Big Eight firm are as follows:

(1)	AA	16.4%	(5) TR	9.5%
(2)	DHS	15.4%	(6) PMM	7.0%
(3)	CL	14.7%	(7) AY	6.1%
(4)	PW	10.3%	(8) EW	2.1%

This ranking of Big Eight firms appears quite different from the ranking in Table 3 (column 1). Furthermore, the two rankings are not significantly associated, based on a computed Spearman correlation coefficient of $-.05$. Using computers and electronics as an illustrative industry, intra-industry assessments of auditors with low (high) litigation activities differs from assessments made using data aggregated across industries.

However, it should be emphasized that, intra-industry, a paucity of cases for individual audit firms, presents an underlying problem. Because of small numbers of cases, slight differences in numbers can have large effects on occurrence rates and rank-orderings. From the users' perspective, this problem may undermine any usefulness of litigation in comparing among auditors. Small numbers would make it difficult to estimate true industry litigation rates from observed auditor litigation, thus making it difficult to distinguish meaningfully among auditors.

Time-Period Comparisons

Using the timeframe of the alleged audit failure, Table 2 provides a breakdown of cases into two time-periods— (1) 1960–1972 and (2) 1973–1985. Table 2

---

[19] Industry analysis is also consistent with the more general issue of assessing audit quality intra-industry. For example, industry-specific regulations and accounting can translate into unique audit considerations. Thus, litigation activities involving an auditor in one industry, say banking, may not provide meaningful information on quality supplied by that auditor in a quite different industry, say utilities.

[20] Using a 2×2 contingency table and a chi-square statistic, a computed chi-square of 9.5 is significant (at the .005 level), with a greater number of legal cases than expected in computers/electronics given the relative number of companies in the industry.

TABLE 4
AUDIT FIRM CASES CLASSIFIED BY INDUSTRY (AS A PERCENTAGE OF TOTAL FOR FIRM)
(1960–1985)

	Total	AA	AY	CL	DHS	EW	PMM	PW	TR	NB8*
Agriculture	2%	2%			3%	5%	4%	2%		2%
Mining and Construction (Including Oil and Gas)	7%	11%	8%	13%	3%	5%	6%	11%	8%	1%
Manufacturing										
Computers and Electronics	8%	16%	8%	11%	13%	3%	4%	9%	4%	6%
Other	20%	28%	26%	18%	23%	31%	14%	16%	16%	19%
Transportation, Communications, Electric, Gas, and Sanitary Services	6%	8%	3%			3%	6%	20%	4%	5%
Retail and Wholesale Trade	6%	3%	3%	7%	3%	8%	8%	9%	10%	4%
Finance, Insurance, and RE										
Brokers and Dealers	4%	2%	6%	2%	10%	5%	1%		6%	8%
REIT's	3%	3%	6%	5%	3%	3%	7%	9%	2%	1%
RE Development	4%	3%	6%	2%	6%	2%	3%		4%	8%
Mutual Funds	2%	3%	3%	2%	13%	18%	1%	2%		2%
Banks and Savings & Loans	9%	9%	6%	13%	3%	5%	15%	5%	10%	6%
Insurance	5%	6%		5%	7%	3%	6%	2%	6%	3%
Other	3%		3%	5%		3%	4%	2%		2%
Subtotal	30%	23%	30%	31%	42%	36%	37%	18%	28%	30%
Services										
Computer and Data Processing	3%		3%			2%	6%	2%	4%	3%
Other	6%	6%	8%	4%	7%	5%	4%	7%	6%	9%
Miscellaneous (Including Charities and Municipalities)	2%		8%	5%		2%		2%	2%	2%
Unknown	10%	3%	3%	11%	6%	5%	11%	4%	18%	19%
Total (Percent)	100%	100%	100%	100%	100%	100%	100%	100%	100%	100%
Total (Number of Cases)	472	64	35	45	31	39	72	45	50	91

* NB8=Non-Big Eight

TABLE 5

INDUSTRY CASES CLASSIFIED BY AUDITOR (AS A PERCENTAGE OF TOTAL FOR INDUSTRY)
(1960–1985)

	Number of Cases	Percentage									
		Total	AA	AY	CL	DHS	EW	PMM	PW	TR	NB8
Agriculture	8	100%	13%			12%		38%	12%		25%
Mining and Construction (Including Oil and Gas)	33	100%	21%	9%	19%	3%	6%	12%	15%	12%	3%
Manufacturing											
Computers and Electronics	37	100%	27%	8%	14%	11%	3%	8%	11%	5%	13%
Other	96	100%	19%	9%	8%	7%	13%	11%	7%	8%	18%
Transportation, Communications, Electric, Gas, and Sanitary Services	27	100%	19%	4%			4%	15%	33%	7%	18%
Retail and Wholesale Trade	29	100%	7%	4%	10%	3%	10%	21%	14%	17%	14%
Finance, Insurance, and RE											
Brokers and Dealers	20	100%	5%	10%	5%	15%	10%	5%		15%	35%
REIT's	15	100%		13%	13%			33%	27%	7%	7%
RE Development	18	100%	17%	11%	6%	9%	8%	11%			38%
Mutual Funds	11	100%	19%	5%	9%	18%	17%	9%	5%		18%
Banks and Savings & Loans	43	100%	14%		2%	17%	9%	26%	8%	13%	11%
Insurance	23	100%		9%	26%	6%	9%	17%	9%	11%	13%
Other	12	100%	11%	8%	17%	5%	6%	25%		11%	17%
Subtotal	142										
Services											
Computer and Data Processing	14	100%		7%	14%		7%	29%	7%	14%	22%
Other	28	100%	14%	11%		7%	7%	11%	11%	11%	28%
Miscellaneous (Including Charities and Municipalities)	10	100%		30%	20%		10%		10%	10%	20%
Unknown	48	100%	4%	2%	10%	4%	4%	17%	4%	19%	36%
Total	472										

68

reveals that the latter period has a greater number of legal cases. Also, the relative litigation activity of each firm is not necessarily similar across time. For example, based on litigation occurrence rates for public companies, Big Eight firm rankings in each (arbitrarily selected) period, 1960–1972 and 1973–1985, are as follows:

1960–1972		1973–1985	
TR	2.7%	PW	3.7%
AY	2.2%	PMM	3.4%
AA	2.1%	CL	3.3%
PMM	1.9%	AY	3.2%
PW	1.6%	AA	3.1%
DHS	1.6%	TR	2.8%
EW	1.5%	DHS	2.5%
CL	1.4%	EW	2.1%

Rankings for these two periods are not significantly associated (Spearman correlation coefficient = .05).[21] All firms shift positions between periods, notably TR (from first to sixth), CL (from eighth to third), and PW (from fifth to first). To the extent shifts in firms' relative litigation activities do not reflect fundamental changes (improvements or reductions) in audit quality, any usefulness of litigation in distinguishing among auditors on the basis of quality diminishes.

IV. Results: Litigation Resolutions

The prior section analyzed litigation against independent auditors based on allegations of audit failures without regard to outcomes of the litigation process. Since outcomes can yield insights on merits of allegations, resolution data can supplement litigation occurrences in assessing auditor quality. This section examines litigation resolutions and compares resolutions with litigation occurrences.

As previously noted, resolution infor-

mation was located for 183 of the 472 cases in the sample (of the 183 cases 137 involve public companies). Table 6 classifies resolution information in two categories, (1) case dismissed and/or no auditor payments and (2) auditor payments (including payments under out of court settlements, court imposed judgments, and agreements to avoid litigation). Table 6 presents the number of cases in these two resolution categories for each Big Eight firm and Big Eight/ non-Big Eight groupings. Information is provided for both the 183 cases and the subset of 137 public company cases.

With a few exceptions, all cases involve full and complete settlement of all actions and claims against auditors. Because exceptions consist of partial settlements requiring large (over $1 million) auditor payments, it seems reasonable to include these "not fully settled" cases in the analysis. Finally, settlement amounts do not consider any subsequent recovery by auditors from other defendants, as this information tends not to be available.

The association between type of resolution (payments/no payments) and auditor identity is assessed using a chi-square statistic and a 2 × 2 contingency table for Big Eight/non-Big Eight groupings. Computed chi-squares are not significant (at the .10 level) using either all cases (.16) or only public company cases (1.03). However, within the Big Eight (using an 8 × 2 contingency table) computed chi-squares (of 17.55 for all cases and 23.92 for public company cases) are significant (at less than the .05 level). In both computations, AY and PW have

---

[21] Comparing rankings for each subperiod with aggregate rate rankings (Table 3 column 1) reveals a significant association between aggregate and subperiod 2 rankings but not between aggregate and subperiod 1 rankings (Spearman correlation coefficients are .45 and .79, respectively).

TABLE 6

RESOLUTION DATA
NUMBER OF CASES CLASSIFIED BY AUDIT FIRM
(1960–1985)

	All Cases			Public Company Cases		
	Total	Dismissed or No Payments by Audit Firm	Payments by Audit Firm	Total	Dismissed or No Payments by Audit Firm	Payments by Audit Firm
Big Eight						
AA	26	8	18	23	7	16
AY	14	11	3	10	9	1
CL	23	4	19	17	3	14
DHS	11	3	8	7	1	6
EW	12	6	6	8	2	6
PMM	29	11	18	23	8	15
PW	20	12	8	17	11	6
TR	17	5	12	12	2	10
Subtotal	152	60	92	117	43	74
Non-Big Eight	31	11	20	20	5	15
Total	183	71	112	137	48	89

more cases dismissed (and fewer cases with payments) than expected.

The statistically significant association between auditor and type of resolution suggests resolution data may alter the interpretation of low (high) activity auditors based on litigation occurrence data. Litigation rates were recalculated for each Big Eight firm using only estimated meritorious cases. Meritorious cases are estimated by deleting non-meritorious cases from numbers in Table 2 using each firms' relevant dismissal percentage (based on numbers in Table 6 for either all cases or only public company cases). Note, this recomputation assumes cases with auditor payments represent meritorious allegations (i.e., audit failures) and cases with auditor dismissals/no payments represent non-meritorious allegations.

Table 3 presents these adjusted rates for meritorious public company cases

scaled by estimated public clients (column 3) and all meritorious cases scaled by estimated annual audit revenue (column 4). Firm rankings appear only slightly sensitive to the scaling procedure and rankings in columns 3 and 4 are significantly associated (Spearman correlation coefficient = .95).

Using Table 3 and comparing Big Eight rankings from public company *occurrence* rates (column 1) versus public company *meritorious* litigation rates (column 3), reveals that resolution data cause each Big Eight firms' position to shift. Notable shifts include, AY (fourth to eighth), PW (second to seventh), and TR (fifth to first). Ranks in columns 1 and 3 of Table 3 are not significantly associated (Spearman correlation coefficient = .09).

Under the alternate scaling procedure (estimated annual audit-related revenues), Big Eight firm rankings appear slightly affected when using estimated meritorious cases (column 4) rather than all cases filed (column 2). Firm rankings in columns 2 and 4 of Table 3 are significantly associated (Spearman correlation coefficient = .74). However, assessments of individual firms may still be altered. In particular, AY moves to a low activity firm with the use of resolution data (i.e., from fifth to eighth position).

Finally, using resolution data and considering only meritorious public company cases shows significant differences in litigation rates among Big Eight auditors. An 8 × 2 contingency table in which each Big Eight firms' estimated public clients during 1960–1985 (see footnote 14) are classified into those with meritorious litigation and those with either no litigation or non-meritorious litigation yields a chi-square statistic of 16.63. The null hypothesis of no association between auditor identity and "true" public company audit failure frequencies can be rejected at less than the .05 level.

In summary, while assessments of Big Eight/non-Big Eight groupings remain unaffected when considering litigation outcomes, assessments of firms within the Big Eight are altered. Adjusting Big Eight litigation rates using resolution data does change identities of low (high) activity Big Eight firms. Furthermore, comparisons of public client audit failure frequencies reveal significant differences among Big Eight firms.

Size of Auditor Payments

This section provides a disaggregation of auditor payments to discuss several issues related to payment size. Classifying auditor payments of all amounts into one category of meritorious litigation does not recognize that small auditor payments may be regarded as reasonable actions to avoid the expenses of protracted litigation and not as indications

of low quality audits. In addition to reducing litigation costs, small out of court settlements may minimize adverse publicity from litigation, and, therefore, minimize reputation effects. Certainly this issue is not clear-cut as alternate arguments exist for avoiding even token payments to settle non-meritorious allegations (see footnote 8). The study does not attempt to resolve this controversy, rather, small payments are reclassified as non-meritorious litigation to determine any effects on assessments of low (high) activity Big Eight firms.

To provide insight into the prevalence of small versus large auditor payments, Table 7 presents a breakdown of all resolved cases into percentages in each of three categories: (1) auditor dismissed/ no auditor payments, (2) auditor payments of less than $1 million, and (3) auditor payments in excess of $1 million. The two categories of payments under and over $1 million represent somewhat gross categorizations for small and large payments. For example, payments were described in data sources as "small" or "minor" contributions to settlement funds rather than specified amounts. This lack of precise specification precludes a finer partitioning of resolution data.

AY has the highest percentage of cases dismissed (79 percent), DHS has the highest percentage of cases with payments under $1 million (55 percent), and TR has the highest percentage of cases with payments over $1 million (53 percent). These percentages can be compared with percentages for Big Eight firms as a group of 40 percent, 31 percent, and 29 percent, respectively.

DHS appears as the Big Eight firm most affected by classifying smaller payments along with dismissals/no payments as non-meritorious cases, leaving only payments in excess of $1 million as

Palmrose

TABLE 7

AUDIT FIRM RESOLUTION DATA CLASSIFIED BY TYPE OF RESOLUTION
AS A PERCENTAGE OF TOTAL BY FIRM
(1960–1985)

	Number of Cases	Percentage of Cases		
		Dismissed or No Payments by Audit Firm	Audit Firm Payments Under $1 million	Audit Firm Payments $1 million and Over
Big Eight				
AA	26	30%	35%	35%
AY	14	79%	14%	7%
CL	23	17%	48%	35%
DHS	11	27%	55%	18%
EW	12	50%	25%	25%
PMM	29	38%	34%	28%
PW	20	60%	20%	20%
TR	17	29%	18%	53%
Subtotal	152	40%	31%	29%
Non-Big Eight	31	36%	32%	32%
Total	183	39%	31%	30%

audit failures. Recomputing meritorious litigation rates under this approach and ranking the Big Eight, shifts DHS's position to eighth with the following rank-order: TR, AA, PMM, CL, EW, PW, AY, and DHS (as compared to the ranks in Table 3 column 3).

It is tempting to argue AY's high dismissal/no payment rate (79 percent in Table 7) represents a consequence of fighting all litigation [Liggio, 1978]. Likewise, DHS's settlement rate (55 percent) for payments under $1 million may reflect a posture of making minimal payments to avoid further expense of litigation. However, the nature of the claims cannot be ignored. For example, Palmrose [1987] provides evidence that management fraud cases are more likely to entail auditor payments rather than dismissals/no auditor payments. DHS has the highest percentage of cases with management fraud (58 percent) and AY has the lowest (23 percent) for Big Eight firms.

Furthermore, resolution data in Table 7 suggest inconsistencies with AA's reported posture of settling even non-meritorious cases [Klott, 1984]. While AA's percentage of cases dismissed/no payments appears somewhat lower than Big Eight firms as a group, AA's percentage is not among the lowest. Also, percentages for both large and small payments are not dramatically above percentages for Big Eight firms as a group.

V. SUMMARY AND CONCLUDING REMARKS

This study compared litigation activities among the largest U.S. independent audit firms. The primary objective was to assess litigation as a means for making quality distinctions among auditors using an inverse relation—auditors with relatively low (high) litigation activity represent higher (lower) quality suppliers. Litigation activity included both occurrences and resolutions of actions against auditors involving allegations of audit failure. Resolution data were included to help determine the merits of claims against auditors. Using resolutions assumed that courts dismiss (auditors avoid payments of) non-meritorious allegations while meritorious allegations require auditor payments.

The empirical analysis examined a sample of legal cases ($n = 472$) and resolutions, if available ($n = 183$), involving both Big Eight and large non-Big Eight firms during 1960–1985. Results indicate that non-Big Eight firms as a group had higher litigation occurrence rates than the Big Eight. This result was not altered by considering the merits of claims from resolution data. In essence, this result is consistent with existing research supporting the Big Eight as quality-differentiated auditors.

Comparing within the Big Eight, the study found some significant differences in litigation activity, particularly when focusing on meritorious litigation. However, these classifications were not unambiguous as results appeared sensitive to the type of analysis. Furthermore, identities of low (high) activity firms changed when conducting comparisons intra-industry and across time. This inability to consistently identify the same firms as low (high) activity tends to weaken litigation as a basis for quality-differentiating among auditors. In addition, litigation against auditors is a rare occurrence. This leaves small numbers of cases from which to reasonably estimate auditors' relative litigation activities, thereby increasing the difficulty in distinguishing among firms.

REFERENCES

American Institute of Certified Public Accountants, *Professional Standards Volume 1* (New York: AICPA, 1985).

Arens, Alvin A., and James K. Loebbecke, *Auditing: An Integrated Approach* (Englewood Cliffs, NJ: Prentice-Hall, Inc., 1984).

Carmichael, D. R., and J. J. Willingham, Eds., *Perspectives in Auditing* (New York: McGraw-Hill Book Company, 1979).

Causey, D. Y., Jr., *Duties and Liabilities of Public Accountants* (Homewood, IL: Dow Jones-Irwin, 1982).

Davies, J. J., *CPA Liability: A Manual for Practitioners* (New York: John Wiley & Sons, 1983).

DeAngelo, Linda E., "Auditor Size and Audit Quality," *Journal of Accounting and Economics* (December 1981), pp. 183–199.

Dopuch, N., and Dan Simunic, "Competition in Auditing: An Assessment," in *Fourth Symposium on Auditing Research* (Urbana: Office of Accounting Research, 1982), pp. 401–450.

Francis, Jere R., and Daniel T. Simon, "A Test of Audit Pricing in the Small-Client Segment of the U.S. Audit Market," THE ACCOUNTING REVIEW (January 1987), pp. 145–157.

Harris, S., Ed., *Who Audits America* (Menlo Park, CA: The Data Financial Press).

Jaenicke, H. R., *The Effect of Litigation on Independent Auditors* (New York: The Commission on Auditors' Responsibilities, 1977).

Kellogg, Robert L., "Accounting Activities, Security Prices, and Class Action Lawsuits," *Journal of Accounting and Economics* (December 1984), pp. 185–204.

Kinney, William R., Jr., *Contemporary Financial Auditing* (Englewood Cliffs, NJ: Prentice-Hall, Inc., Forthcoming).

Klott, Gary, "Uneasy Period for Andersen: Suits Besiege Big 8 Firm," *New York Times* (November 23, 1984), pp. D1 and D3.

Liggio, Carl D., Litigation and the Accounting Profession Conference (Arthur Young & Co.), Speech, Chicago, IL (September 10, 1978).

McConnell, Donald K., Jr., "Auditor Changes and Related Disagreements," *Auditing: A Journal of Practice & Theory* (Spring 1984), pp. 44–56.

Minard, Lawrence, and David A. Wilson, Eds., *Forbes Numbers Game* (Englewood Cliffs, NJ: Prentice-Hall, Inc., 1980).

Nichols, Donald R., and David B. Smith, "Auditor Credibility and Auditor Changes," *Journal of Accounting Research* (Autumn 1983), pp. 534–544.

Palmrose, Zoe-Vonna, "Audit Fees and Auditor Size: Further Evidence," *Journal of Accounting Research* (Spring 1986), pp. 97–110.

———, "Litigation and Independent Auditors: The Role of Business Failures and Management Fraud," *Auditing: A Journal of Practice & Theory* (Spring 1987), pp. 90–103.

St. Pierre, K., and J. Anderson, "An Analysis of the Factors Associated with Lawsuits Against Public Accountants," THE ACCOUNTING REVIEW (April 1984), pp. 242–263.

Shockley, R. A., and R. N. Holt, "A Behavioral Investigation of Supplier Differentiation in the Market for Audit Services," *Journal of Accounting Research* (Autumn 1983), pp. 545–564.

Simunic, Dan, and M. Stein, *Product Differentiation in Auditing: A Study of Auditor Choice in the Market for New Issues* (Canadian Certified General Accountants' Research Foundation, 1987).

The Wall Street Journal, "By the Numbers," (December 15, 1986), p. 29.

[12]

Journal of Business Finance & Accounting, 26(7) & (8), Sept./Oct. 1999, 0306-686X

Audit Quality and Auditor Size: An Evaluation of Reputation and Deep Pockets Hypotheses

CLIVE S. LENNOX*

1. INTRODUCTION

There is now a great deal of evidence that large audit firms provide higher quality audits and offer greater credibility to clients' financial statements than small audit firms. The stock market reacts more favourably when a company switches to a large auditor rather than to a small auditor (Nichols and Smith, 1983; and Eichenseher et al., 1989); large audit firms give more accurate signals of financial distress in their audit opinions (Lennox, 1999); companies with higher agency costs are more likely to hire large audit firms (Francis and Wilson, 1988; Johnson and Lys, 1990; DeFond, 1992; and Firth and Smith, 1992); large audit firms charge higher fees than small audit firms (Simunic and Stein, 1987; Beatty, 1989; Chan et al., 1993; and Craswell et al., 1995); and companies involved in IPOs experience less under-pricing when they hire large audit firms (Balvers et al., 1988; and Firth and Smith, 1992). Two explanations for the positive correlation between auditor size and audit quality have been provided by theoretical research – these relate to auditors' reputations and the depth of auditors'

* The author is a lecturer in Accounting and Economics at Bristol University. This paper is based on his doctoral dissertation completed at Oxford University. He would like to thank Anindya Banerjee and Steve Bond for helpful comments. Financial assistance from the ESRC is gratefully acknowledged. (Paper received December 1997, revised and accepted February 1999)

Address for correspondence: Clive S. Lennox, Department of Economics, Bristol University, 8 Woodland Road, Bristol BS8 1TN, UK.
e-mail: c.lennox@bristol.ac.uk

pockets.[1] This paper's contribution is to provide empirical evidence that distinguishes between these hypotheses.

DeAngelo (1981) has argued that large auditors have more incentive to issue accurate reports because they have more valuable reputations. When it becomes known that an auditor has negligently issued an inaccurate report, the auditor could suffer a loss of rent through fewer clients or lower fees. If large auditors have higher client-specific rents than small auditors, the loss of rent is greater for a criticised large auditor than a criticised small auditor. Therefore, large auditors should have more incentive to issue accurate reports. An alternative hypothesis is that auditors with more wealth at risk from litigation have more incentive to issue accurate reports (Dye, 1993). Since large auditors have deeper pockets, they should have more incentive to be accurate.

This paper empirically tests the predictions of these two hypotheses. In the absence of a deep pockets effect, the reputation hypothesis implies that large auditors are more accurate because they have more incentive to avoid reputation-damaging criticism. Therefore, one should find that large auditors receive less criticism (and litigation) than small auditors and that criticised auditors suffer reductions in demand compared to similar uncriticised auditors. In contrast, the findings suggest that large auditors are more prone to litigation and that criticised auditors do not suffer reductions in demand. This casts significant doubt on the empirical validity of the reputation hypothesis.

In contrast, the deep pockets hypothesis is consistent with litigation being positively correlated with auditor size. Intuitively, large auditors' deep pockets give them more incentive to issue accurate reports and increase the likelihood of litigation, conditional on an audit failure occurring. Moreover, the deep pockets hypothesis explains why there is little evidence for reputation effects. The reputation hypothesis presumes that there is some reliable signal of auditor accuracy, such as litigation. In the deep pockets model, litigation is a poor signal of accuracy for two reasons. First, auditors are only sued for issuing reports that are insufficiently conservative (type I errors); they are never sued for being too conservative (type II errors). Therefore, litigation does not signal auditors' type II error rates. Secondly, large auditors are more accurate than small auditors but are also more likely to be sued when a type I error occurs because they are more prone to deep pockets court actions. Therefore, litigation is a poor signal of auditors' type I error rates.

Section 2 sets out a deep pockets model which examines the relationships between auditors' wealths, audit accuracy and litigation. The model illustrates important differences between the predictions of the deep pockets and reputation hypotheses. Section 3 then tests these differences empirically.

2. THE DEEP POCKETS MODEL

This section presents a model in which auditors have different wealth levels. The framework is similar to Dye (1993) where wealthier auditors have more incentive to issue accurate reports because they suffer larger litigation penalties. Auditor j has wealth, W_j ($j \, \varepsilon (L, S)$, L denotes a large auditor and S a small auditor). The assumption that large auditors have more wealth at risk from litigation ($W_L > W_S$) reflects the joint and several liability regime for audit firms, and means that large auditors have more incentive to issue accurate reports.

The model differs from previous deep pockets research by endogenising the litigation decision. Auditors' wealths affect not only the size of the litigation penalty, but also the probability that an inaccurate report results in a litigation suit. As in the reputation hypothesis, the deep pockets model predicts a positive relationship between auditor size and auditor accuracy. However, in contrast to the reputation hypothesis the deep pockets hypothesis allows a positive relationship between auditor size and litigation.

The time line of the model is shown in Figure 1. First, nature determines the company's future cashflows which are only observed after an investment costing I. The company has cashflows of Π_N with probability p, and Π_F with probability $1 - p$, where $0 < p < 1$ and $\Pi_N > I > \Pi_F$. N denotes a non-failing company (a company with positive going-concern value), whilst F denotes a failing company (negative going-concern value). Prior to the investment, the company is offered for sale to outside investors who do not observe the company's type but do observe

Figure 1

$t = 1$	$t = 2$	$t = 3$	$t = 4$	$t = 5$
Nature determines the company's future cashflows	The initial owner hires a large or small auditor	The auditor sets a fee and decides how much effort to exert	The company is sold to the new owner	Nature determines the new owner's litigation costs, and the new owner decides whether to sue the auditor

the audit report and the auditor's wealth.[2] Perfect competition is assumed amongst potential new investors so that the company's selling price is equal to expected cashflows minus the required investment, I.

After the initial move by nature, the incumbent owner decides whether to hire a large or small auditor. It is assumed that the owner does not observe the company's type although the probability of corporate failure (p) is common knowledge. The fee agreed between the incumbent owner and the profit-maximising auditor is determined by perfect competition in the audit market.[3]

Following the auditor hiring decision, auditor j chooses effort e_j, where $e^* \leq e_j \leq 1$. By definition, the minimum effort choice (e^*) occurs when the audit report does not signal information about the company's type. It is assumed that the auditor does not observe the company's type prior to the effort decision, otherwise there would be no need for the auditor to exert effort. Exerting effort imposes a non-pecuniary cost $C(e_j)$ on the auditor, where $C'(e_j) > 0$, $C''(e_j) > 0$, $C(e^*) = 0$ and $C(1) = +\infty$.[4] The assumption that effort is privately observable and costly to the auditor introduces a moral hazard problem – the threat of litigation (rather than loss of reputation) is what deters the auditor from shirking. Audit quality is measured in terms of type I and II errors. A type I error occurs if a failing company (F) is given a report of 'N'; a type II error occurs if a non-failing company (N) is given a report of 'F'. The audit report is assumed to be accurate with probability e_j:

$$\text{Prob} ['F' \mid F, e_j] = \text{Prob} ['N' \mid N, e_j] = e_j.$$

Consistent with empirical evidence, it is assumed that auditors can only be sued for committing type I errors (see Table 1 and St. Pierre and Andersen, 1984).[5]

After the auditor's effort decision (and audit report), the company is sold by the incumbent owner to a new investor. The company's selling price depends on the audit opinion ('F' or 'N'), auditor effort (e_j), and the cost of the investment, I.[6] Given a report of 'N' by auditor j, the company's selling price is zero if the investment cost exceeds the company's expected cashflow; otherwise, the selling price is equal to the difference between expected cashflow and the cost of the investment. Given a report of 'N' by auditor j, the company's selling price is therefore equal to:

$$\max\left\{0, \frac{pe_j\Pi_N + (1-p)(1-e_j)\Pi_F}{pe_j + (1-p)(1-e_j)} - I\right\}. \tag{1}$$

Given a report of 'F' by auditor j, the company's selling price is equal to:

$$\max\left\{0, \frac{p(1-e_j)\Pi_N + (1-p)e_j\Pi_F}{p(1-e_j) + (1-p)e_j} - I\right\}. \tag{2}$$

It is easily shown that the company's selling price is weakly increasing (decreasing) in e_j given a report of 'N' ('F'). Intuitively, audit reports are more accurate signals of financial health, the more effort that auditors exert.

Definition
The minimum level of audit effort (e^*) occurs when the audit report has no information value – that is, e^* satisfies:

$$\frac{pe^*\Pi_N + (1-p)(1-e^*)\Pi_F}{pe^* + (1-p)(1-e^*)} = \frac{p(1-e^*)\Pi_N + (1-p)e^*\Pi_F}{p(1-e^*) + (1-p)e^*}.$$

Solving the above equation gives $e^* = 0.5(= 1 - e^*)$. When the report has no information value, the company's expected selling price is:

$$\max\{0, p\Pi_N + (1-p)\Pi_F - I\}.$$

Assumption 1

$$\frac{pe_j\Pi_N + (1-p)(1-e_j)\Pi_F}{pe_j + (1-p)(1-e_j)} > \frac{p(1-e_j)\Pi_N + (1-p)e_j\Pi_F}{p(1-e_j) + (1-p)e_j}.$$

Assumption 1 means that attention is confined to equilibria where audit reports signal information about the company's type ($e_j > e^*$, $j = L, S$).

After the company is sold to the new owner, the investment (I) is made and cashflows are realised. Having observed the company's cashflows, the new owner decides whether to sue the auditor – this assumption is realistic since most litigation claims occur following liquidation or take-over. It is assumed that there are two types of new owner and the types are only observed privately. A new owner with low litigation costs (K_L) is more likely to sue and therefore poses a high litigation risk to the auditor; a new owner poses a low litigation risk if litigation costs are high (K_H), where $K_H > K_L > 0$. The assumption of different litigation costs captures the fact that client characteristics other than financial health help to explain the amount of litigation incurred by auditors (Stice, 1991; Stice, 1993; and Hall and Renner, 1988). The new owner has low litigation costs with probability h, where h is determined by nature and both cost types exist in the population ($0 < h < 1$).

Perfect competition in the audit market implies that the audit fee (F_j) is equal to the cost of exerting effort ($C(e_j)$) plus the auditor's expected litigation cost. The expected litigation cost depends on auditor wealth (W_j) and the probability that the new owner chooses to sue. The probability of a litigation suit depends on the probability of corporate failure ($1 - p$), auditor effort (e_j), the new owner's litigation costs (K_H or K_L), and wealth (W_j).

The analysis begins by describing four mutually exclusive cases for the new owner's litigation costs and auditor wealth:

(a) $K_H > K_L > W_L > W_S$,
(b) $W_L > K_H > K_L > W_S$,
(c) $W_L > W_S > K_H > K_L$,
(d) $W_L > K_L > W_S > K_L$.

Proposition 1 considers cases (a) and (b).[7]

Proposition 1

The set of equilibria in which $K_H > K_L > W_L > W_S$, or $W_L > K_H > K_L > W_S$ violates Assumption 1.

The proof to Proposition 1 is very straightforward. When litigation costs exceed auditors' wealths $(K_H > K_L > W_L > W_S)$, neither the large nor small auditor face the threat of litigation and both types of auditor choose the minimum level of effort $(e_L = e_S = e^*)$. When litigation costs exceed the small auditor's wealth $(W_L > K_H > K_L > W_S)$, the small auditor faces no litigation threat and chooses the minimum level of effort $(e_S = e^*)$. Both cases violate Assumption 1, which requires the reports of large and small auditors to have some information value.

Previous deep pockets models have analysed equilibria in which auditors are always sued for committing type I errors (Dye, 1993; and Schwartz, 1997). Proposition 2 demonstrates that this is true in case (c) where litigation costs are less than auditor wealth.

Proposition 2

When $W_L > W_S > K_H > K_L$:

- *Large auditors exert more effort than small auditors $(e_L > e_S)$ and issue more accurate reports.*
- *Large auditors are less likely to be sued than small auditors.*
- *Audit fees are $F_j = C(e_j) + (1 - p)(1 - e_j)W_j$ $(j = L, S)$*
- *There exist equilibria in which only large auditors, only small auditors, or both types of auditor are hired.*

To explain Proposition 2, consider auditor j's profit-maximisation problem:

$$\max_{e_j} \pi_j = F_j - C(e_j) - (1 - p)(1 - e_j)W_j \quad (j = L, S). \tag{3}$$

Since the fee is set before the auditor's effort choice, the auditor takes the fee as given in (3), resulting in the first order condition, $C'(e_j) = (1 - p)W_j$. Since $W_L > W_S$ and $C''(e_j) > 0$, it must be true that $e_L > e_S$. Therefore, large auditors' reports are more accurate than small auditors' reports and large auditors are less likely to be sued. In Proposition 2, the predictions of the reputation and deep pockets hypotheses are identical – large auditors are more accurate and incur less litigation than small auditors.

There are three factors affecting the difference between large and small auditors' fees (F_L and F_S).

$$F_L = C(e_L) + (1 - p)(1 - e_L)W_L,$$
$$F_S = C(e_S) + (1 - p)(1 - e_S)W_S.$$

First, large auditors exert more effort and therefore have higher costs ($C(e_L) > C(e_s)$). Secondly, large auditors have more wealth at risk ($W_L > W_S$) and may therefore charge a higher insurance premium. These two effects mean that large auditors' fees tend to be higher than small auditors' fees. However, a third effect works in the opposite direction – since large auditors exert more effort, they are less likely to incur litigation and may therefore charge a lower insurance premium.

To explain why the audit market can consist of only large, only small or both types of auditor, it is necessary to consider the auditor hiring decision. When deciding whom to hire, the incumbent owner's expected payoff depends on the company's expected selling price minus the audit fee. The owner would prefer to hire the large auditor if he knew that the report would be 'N' since the large auditor's report is more credible and has a greater effect on the company's selling price. The owner would prefer to hire the small auditor if he knew that the report would be 'F', since the small auditor's report is less credible. When deciding who to hire, the initial owner does not know what the audit report will be and so is unsure whether to hire the large or small auditor. The initial owner's choice of auditor depends on the values for the exogenous parameters (p, h, I, Π_F, Π_N, W_L, W_S, K_L, K_S) and the functional form of the cost function $C(e_j)$. In numerical examples, the Appendix describes three equilibria where only large auditors are hired, only small auditors are hired, or both types are hired.

Proposition 3 considers case (d) where, conditional on a type I error occurring, the large auditor is always sued whilst the small auditor is only sued by new owners who have low litigation costs.

Proposition 3
When $W_L > K_H > W_S > K_L$:

- *Large auditors exert more effort than small auditors ($e_L > e_S$) and issue more accurate reports.*

- *Large auditors' fees are $F_L = C(e_L) + (1 - p)(1 - e_L)W_L$.*
- *Small auditors' fees are $F_S = C(e_S) + (1 - p)h(1 - e_S)W_S$.*
- *Equilibria exist in which only large auditors, only small auditors, or both types of auditor are hired.*
- *There is an ambiguous relationship between auditor size and litigation.*

The intuitions for the relationships between auditor size, auditor accuracy, audit fees and auditor hiring are exactly the same as in Proposition 2. The profit maximisation problems for large and small auditors are:

$$\max_{e_L} \pi_L = F_L - C(e_L) - (1 - p)(1 - e_L)W_L$$

$$\max_{e_s} \pi_S = F_S - C(e_s) - (1 - p)h(1 - e_S)W_S e_S.$$

The large auditor exerts effort such that $C'(e_L) = (1 - p)W_L$, whilst the small auditor exerts effort such that $C'(e_S) = h(1 - p)W_S$. The large auditor chooses to exert more effort $(e_L > e_S)$ and large auditors' reports are more accurate.

The key insight of Proposition 3 is that the relationship between auditor size and litigation is ambiguous despite the superior accuracy of large auditors. In Proposition 2, large auditors are less likely to be sued because they are more accurate, $(1 - p)(1 - e_L) < (1 - p)(1 - e_S)$. In Proposition 3, there is a second effect – large auditors are more prone to deep pockets actions. Given that a type I error occurs, large auditors are always sued whilst small auditors are only sued with probability h. Therefore, the large auditor is sued with probability $(1 - p)(1 - e_L)$ whilst the small auditor is sued with probability $h(1 - p)(1 - e_S)$. The Appendix provides two numerical examples where large auditors are less likely to be sued because of their superior accuracy $((1 - p)(1 - e_L) < h(1 - p)(1 - e_S))$, and where large auditors are more likely to be sued because they are more prone to deep pockets actions $((1 - p)(1 - e_L) > h(1 - p)(1 - e_S))$.

The deep pockets model is important because it identifies two differences between the predictions of the reputation and deep pockets hypotheses. First, the reputation hypothesis predicts that large auditors are less likely to be sued because of their superior accuracy. In contrast, the deep pockets hypothesis predicts that large auditors may be more prone to litigation. Secondly, the reputation hypothesis predicts that signals of auditor accuracy, such as litigation and auditor criticism, affect the demand for audit services. The validity of this prediction depends on whether these signals are strongly correlated with auditor accuracy. The deep pockets hypothesis predicts that litigation against audit firms is not a strong signal of accuracy for two reasons. First, auditors are only sued for type I errors and so litigation does not signal auditors' type II error rates. Secondly, deep pockets make a large auditor more prone to litigation conditional on a type I error occurring – therefore, litigation is a poor signal of auditors' type I error rates. The next section tests the predictions of the reputation and deep pockets hypotheses by examining the relationship between auditor size and litigation, and by comparing the market shares of criticised and uncriticised auditors.

3. THE EMPIRICAL EVIDENCE

There are two key findings in this section. First, large auditors are more likely to be sued (and criticised) – this contradicts the reputation hypothesis but is consistent with the deep pockets hypothesis. Secondly, the evidence does not suggest that auditors suffered falls in demand as a result of criticism – this is also contrary to the reputation hypothesis, but is consistent with the deep pockets hypothesis.

The population consists of all UK publicly quoted companies between 1987–94. Data were collected on each company's auditor, audit report, audit fee, shareholdings and assets from annual reports kept on microfiche at Warwick University. The sample was selected on the basis of microfiche availability and consists of 1,036 companies.[8] There were 123 companies in the sample that entered administration, liquidation or receivership – the frequency of failure averaged 1.3% per annum which was approximately equal to the population frequency (Morris, 1997).

Next, a search was made of the *Financial Times,* the *Economist, Accountancy Age* magazine and Department of Trade and Industry (DTI) investigations for news items in which auditors received criticism. These criticisms are listed in Table 1. Auditors were most susceptible to criticism when one of two events occurred.

REPUTATION VERSUS DEEP POCKETS   789

Table 1

Criticisms of UK Audit Firms (1988–94)

Auditor	Date	News
Stoy Hayward	19:02:90	The bankrupt AT Trust served Stoy with writ for audit.
	23:12:90	ICAEW announced investigation into audit of bankrupt Levitt Group.
	22:11:90	Stoy criticised by shareholders for its audits of Polly Peck and Astra Holdings.
	10:01:91	Labour Party criticised Stoy for its audit of the Levitt Group.
	08:04:91	Amber Day decided not to retain Stoy as its auditor because of concern shown by some City institutions over Stoy's audits of Polly Peck, Sock Shop, Levitt Group and Homes Assured.
	29:04:93	Stoy served with writ for its audit of Polly Peck.
	18:06:93	Stoy criticised in DTI investigation of Astra Holdings.
	21:06:93	Stoy served with writ in connection with audit of Beverley Group (formerly known as Petrocon).
	30:11:93	Financial Reporting Review Panel criticised the accounts of Chrysalis which were unqualified.
	14:05:94	Stoy served with writ for audit of Astra Holdings.
Ernst and Young	27:07:88	Ruberoid served writ for £8.9m against Ernst and Whinney for audit of Camrex.
	22:10:88	Arthur Young paid £12m in settlement to the Bank of England for its audit of Johnson Matthey Bank.
	27:10:88	Arthur Young criticised by DTI over audit of Milbury Plc.
	30:06:89	Stoddard Sekers considered legal action against Arthur Young for its audit of Sekers International, with which it had merged.
	02:03:89	Arthur Young criticised by shareholders and creditors over its audit of Sound Diffusion.
	04:08:89	Arthur Young admitted that two sets of accounts for Budgens (1986 and 1987) which it had audited were incorrect.
	19:10:89	Ernst and Young faced legal action from a Lloyd's syndicate for its audit of Warrilow.
	30:11:89	Arthur Young and Ernst and Whinney received a writ for their work on Sound Diffusion.
	29:08:90	Arthur Young criticised by DTI for its audit of Alexander Howden Holdings.
	01:05:91	Arthur Young and Ernst and Whinney criticised by DTI for its audit of Sound Diffusion.
	06:07:91	BCCI was liquidated – speculation begins over the role of Ernst and Young.
	24:07:91	Arthur Young criticised by DTI for its audit of Rotaprint.
	12:09:91	Arthur Young served with writ for its audit of Magnet.
	18:02:92	Arthur Young fined £100,000 by Joint Disciplinary Scheme for its work on Milbury.
	07:03:92	Ernst and Young (and Price Waterhouse) received writ from the liquidators of BCCI for £7.5 bn.
	25:04:92	Joint Disciplinary Scheme announced investigation into Ernst and Young for its audit of BCCI.
	01:10:92	Claim made by Walker Greenbank for £15m against Arthur Young regarding the acquisition of Alkar.
	18:02:93	Ernst and Young criticised by DTI regarding its work on Edencorp Leisure.
	19:06:94	Magnet made a claim against its auditor Arthur Young for £50m.

                    continued overleaf

790   LENNOX

Table 1 (Continued)

Auditor	Date	News
Price Waterhouse	07:04:88	UniChem made official complaint over a report PW prepared for its audit client Macarthy in its bid for UniChem.
	02:05:90	PW accused in court of misleading Guiness directors.
	12:04:91	PW reached out of court settlement with Pifco for negligence in its audit of Salton – amount undisclosed.
	06:07:91	BCCI was liquidated – speculation begins over the role of Price Waterhouse.
	07:03:92	Price Waterhouse (and Ernst and Young) received writ from the liquidators of BCCI for £7.5bn.
	29:01:94	Financial Reporting Review Panel criticised the accounts of Intercare which were not qualified by Price Waterhouse.
	01:02:94	Joint Disciplinary Scheme reprimanded Price Waterhouse for failing to reveal a fraud it had uncovered 14 years previously during an audit of Bryanston Finance.
Touche Ross	25:10:88	ICAEW started investigation into Touche Ross's work on Barlow Clowes.
	19:10:89	Spicer and Oppenheim faced legal action from a Lloyd's syndicate for its audit of Warrilow.
	20:03:91	Spicer and Pegler criticised by DTI for its work on Aldermanbury Trust.
	25:02:92	Joint Disciplinary Scheme re-opened Barlow Clowes investigation (the previous investigation was suspended following a request from the Serious Fraud Office).
	16:10:92	Financial Reporting Review Panel forced Trafalgar House to amend its 1991 accounts which were not qualified by Touche Ross.
	03:11:92	The Treasury and liquidators issued a writ against Touche Ross for Barlow Clowes.
	21:07:94	Spicers criticised by DTI over its work on Atlantic Computers.
KPMG Peat Marwick	18:11:89	Ferranti served writ against Peat Marwick.
	13:09:90	Peat Marwick criticised for its audit of the N.U.M.'s accounts.
	10:04:91	Riva Group sued KPMG for negligence over its acquisition of Hugin Sweda.
	13:08:91	Peat Marwick paid out £40m in settlement to Ferranti.
	17:09:92	KPMG served with writ for its audits of HS Weavers.
	22:12:92	Adam & Co. announced they are considering legal action against KPMG.
	23:09:93	KPMG criticised by DTI for its work on London United Investments.
	30:11:93	Financial Reporting Review Panel argued that Chrysalis' accounts audited by KPMG in 1992 were contrary to *SSAP1*.
	23:12:93	KPMG sued over its valuation of Medway Ports.
Coopers & Lybrand	26:01:89	Coopers issued with a writ for 1.96m pounds for its audit of Espley Trust.
	08:04:89	Laird Group dismissed Coopers after finding errors in the accounts of Metro-Cammell Weymann.
	18:05:89	Deloitte Haskins criticised following its overvaluation of stocks and work-in-progress held by E&L Instruments.

Table 1 (Continued)

Auditor	Date	News
	08:05:91	TGI dismissed Coopers following incorrect profit figures in the accounts of Tannoy Audix which were audited by Coopers.
	12:12:91	Coopers criticised for its role as auditor in Maxwell Communications.
	04:01:93	Guardian Royal Exchange issued a writ against Coopers in relation to its 1986–8 audits.
	11:08:93	Financial Reporting Review Panel criticised accounts of Royal Bank which were not qualified by Coopers.
	27:09:93	Financial Reporting Review Panel criticised accounts of Control Techniques which were not qualified by Coopers.
	21:07:94	Deloittes criticised by DTI for work on Atlantic Computers.
Arthur Anderson	11:03:88	UK government sued Arthur Anderson in US courts over its audit of DeLorean Motor Company.
	12:09:91	Arthur Anderson served with writ for its audit of Magnet.
	23:02:93	Financial Reporting Review Panel criticised the accounts of Eurotherm which were not qualified by Arthur Anderson.
Pannell Kerr Forster	11:07:91	Pannell Kerr Forster paid £1.63m in settlement to Beaverco Kerr for its audit of Body Sculpture.
	29:01:92	Financial Reporting Review Panel criticised the annual report of Williams Holdings, which contravened *SSAP3* yet Pannell Kerr Forster gave no qualification.
Binder Hamlyn	29:07:92	ADT issued a writ for £146m against Binder in connection with the takeover of Britannic Security.
Grant Thornton	01:02:90	Platignum served a writ against Grant Thornton for its profit forecast.
Moores Rowland	31:07:91	SEET issued a writ against Moores Rowland in connection with past acquisition of Homemaker Shops.

First, auditors were criticised for not giving adequate warnings of bankruptcy. Secondly, auditors were criticised following take-overs – the auditors of target companies were sometimes criticised by acquirers who believed they had paid too much as a result of over-stated accounts.

Table 2 summarises the criticisms, the number of clients, average client size, and the number of failing clients by audit firm. The evidence shows that large auditors received much more criticism and litigation than small auditors. Large auditors also audited larger companies than small auditors and audited more companies. This suggests that it is important to control for client numbers and client size when investigating the relationship between auditor size and litigation. Ernst and Young and Stoy Hayward were the most heavily criticised audit firms. Whilst a

Table 2

Number of Criticisms, Number of Clients, Average Client Size and
Number of Corporate Failures

AUDITOR	CRITICISMS			CLIENTS	ASSETS	FAILURES
	TOTAL	DTI	WRITS			
KPMG Peat Marwick	9	1	5	238	305,308	17
Coopers and Lybrand	9	1	2	185	724,530	20
Ernst and Young	13	4	7	127	669,603	9
Price Waterhouse	6	0	2	116	465,768	13
Touche Ross	5	2	2	104	191,718	11
Arthur Anderson	3	0	2	58	158,138	8
Binder Hamlyn	1	0	1	70	90,254	11
Stoy Hayward	7	1	4	40	53,579	9
Grant Thornton	1	0	1	38	44,486	6
Pannell Kerr Forster	2	0	1	29	75,656	0
Robson Rhodes	0	0	0	23	28,720	1
Kidsons Impey	0	0	0	13	194,816	1
Hacker Young	0	0	0	13	23,649	3
Moores Rowland	1	0	1	11	25,119	1
Clark Whitehill	0	0	0	10	496,273	0
Neville Russell	0	0	0	9	18,211	0
Baker Tilly	0	0	0	5	152,494	0
Very small audit firms[1]	0	0	0	1.25	28,925	0.11

Notes:
CRITICISMS ≡ Number of criticisms cited in Table 1 for each auditor.
TOTAL   ≡ Total number of criticisms (cases mentioned in more than one news item
             were only counted once).
DTI   ≡ Number of criticisms by DTI.
WRITS   ≡ Number of writs and liability settlements.
ASSETS   ≡ Average asset size of clients.
CLIENTS   ≡ Number of clients audited between 1987-94.
FAILURES   ≡ Number of clients that entered liquidation, administration or
             receivership between 1987–94.

[1] An audit firm falls into this category if it audited fewer than five of the quoted companies
in the data – there are 122 such audit firms. The CLIENTS, ASSETS and FAILURES values
are averaged over these 122 firms.

relatively large proportion of Stoy Hayward's clients (22.5%) were
failing companies, the same was not true for Ernst and Young
(7.1%). Thus, there does not appear to be a straightforward
relationship between client portfolios and the amount of
criticism incurred by auditors.

If the reputation hypothesis is valid, one would expect to find a
negative relationship between auditor size and litigation. If the
deep pockets hypothesis is important, the relationship between

auditor size and litigation is ambiguous. Unfortunately, it is difficult to investigate the relationship between auditor size and litigation, because many disputes appear to be settled in undisclosed out-of-court agreements. To address this problem, two dependent variables are used as proxies for litigation. In Table 3, models 1 and 2 use the number of disclosed writs and litigation settlements ($WRIT_j$); models 3 and 4 use the total number of criticisms ($CRIT_j$) as a proxy for disclosed and undisclosed litigation.[9] Client size is controlled for by including a variable equal to the average asset size of auditor j's clients ($ASSETS_j$). Differences in client portfolios might also explain the amount of litigation – in particular, audit firms with aggressive marketing strategies may be less likely to suffer falls in demand, but may also have clients that are more likely to sue. Hence, the number of failing companies as a proportion of total audited clients ($FAILS_j$) is included to capture differences in litigation risk across auditors' client portfolios. Finally, dummy variables (SH_j and EY_j) are included to capture the fact that Stoy Hayward and Ernst and Young were most heavily criticised.

The results show a highly significant positive association between auditor size ($BIGSIX_j$) and both measures of litigation ($WRIT_j$ and $CRIT_j$) – this result was found to be robust for different model specifications.[10] The strong positive relationship between auditor size and litigation shows that large auditors were more prone to litigation despite their superior accuracy.[11] This is consistent with the deep pockets hypothesis, but inconsistent with the reputation hypothesis. The coefficients on average client size ($ASSETS_j$) were insignificant indicating that it is auditor size rather than company size that determines the amount of litigation. The insignificant coefficients on $FAILS_j$ show that differences in client portfolios do not explain the amount of litigation incurred. Finally, models 1 and 3 confirm that Stoy Hayward (SH_j) and Ernst and Young (EY_j) were much more likely to receive criticism than other audit firms.

If the reputation hypothesis is valid, one would expect to find that criticised auditors suffered declines in demand.[12] Arguably, the most serious criticisms involved Polly Peck, Astra Holdings (both audited by Stoy Hayward) and BCCI (audited by Price Waterhouse and Ernst and Young).[13] Taking into account the number, severity and timing of these criticisms, one can make

Table 3

Model Explaining the Amount of Litigation Incurred by Auditors
(*t*-statistics in parentheses)

	Model 1	Model 2	Model 3	Model 4
Dependent Variable	WRIT$_j$	WRIT$_j$	CRIT$_j$	CRIT$_j$
Explanatory Variables				
FAILS$_j$	0.012e-02	0.232e-02	0.006e-02	0.382e-02
	(0.157)	(0.932)	(0.064)	(0.925)
ASSETS$_j$	−0.571e-08	0.827e-08	0.377e-08	2.200e-08
	(−1.128)	(0.670)	(0.854)	(1.428)
BIGSIX$_j$	0.021	0.022	0.045	0.045
	(5.435)	(4.495)	(13.702)	(6.815)
SH$_j$	0.099	−	0.173	−
	(122.568)	−	(191.359)	−
EY$_j$	0.044	−	0.054	−
	(13.810)	−	(22.166)	−
CONSTANT	0.001	0.002	0.001	0.002
	(1.802)	(1.498)	(1.557)	(1.312)
R^2	0.590	0.152	0.781	0.274

Notes:
Number of observations = 139.

$$\text{WRIT}_j = \frac{\text{Number of Writs and Liability Settlements}}{\text{Number of Clients}}$$

$$\text{CRIT}_j = \frac{\text{Number of Individual Criticisms}}{\text{Number of Clients}}$$

$$\text{FAILS}_j = \frac{\text{Number of Failing Clients}}{\text{Number of Clients}}$$

ASSETS$_j$ = Average asset size of clients for auditor *j*.

BIGSIX$_j$ = 1 if auditor *j* was one of the Big Six; = 0 otherwise.

SH$_j$ = 1 if auditor *j* was Stoy Hayward; = 0 otherwise.

EY$_j$ = 1 if auditor *j* was Ernst and Young; = 0 otherwise.

A standard regression model was found to suffer from heteroscedasticity and outlier problems – therefore, robust regression was used to estimate consistent standard errors.

three predictions which relate to the market shares of criticised and uncriticised auditors.[14]

1. Stoy Hayward received more criticism than other medium-sized auditors between 1990–94. One therefore expects that Stoy Hayward lost more clients than similar uncriticised auditors and/ or suffered lower growth in audit fees between 1990–94.

Moreover, Stoy Hayward received much more criticism after 1990 than it did before 1990. One therefore expects that Stoy Hayward lost more clients and/or had lower growth in audit fees between 1991–94 than between 1988–90.

2. Ernst and Young received more criticism than other large auditors between 1988–94. One therefore expects that Ernst and Young lost more clients and/or had lower growth in audit fees compared to other large auditors.

3. The BCCI affair created serious criticism of Ernst and Young and Price Waterhouse between 1991–93. One therefore expects that Ernst and Young and Price Waterhouse lost more clients and/or had lower growth in audit fees between 1991–93 than between 1988–90. One also expects that between 1991–93, Ernst and Young and Price Waterhouse lost more clients and/or had lower growth in audit fees compared to other large auditors.

Table 4 shows average audit fees and auditors' net gains (+) and losses (−) of clients. The evidence indicates that large auditors gained more quoted clients than small auditors. This is consistent with the view that large auditors were believed to be more accurate despite being more prone to criticism. In addition, the early 1990s witnessed a slowdown in the growth of audit fees, particularly for small and medium-sized audit firms.

The evidence does not support the first prediction – Stoy Hayward did not suffer greater losses compared to similar uncriticised auditors. Stoy Hayward had a net loss of 1 client (2.5% of its clients) between 1990–94, whilst other medium-sized auditors had average losses of 1.7 clients (6.9% of their clients). Between 1990–94, audit fees fell by 23.0% for Stoy Hayward – for other medium-sized auditors fees rose by 3% (excluding Kidsons Impey, audit fees for other medium-sized auditors fell by 11.6%).[15] Thus, Stoy Hayward did not suffer as many client losses as similar uncriticised auditors but did suffer a greater decline in fees. Stoy Hayward did not appear to suffer larger losses between 1991–94 as a result of criticisms received after 1990. Stoy Hayward's client loss was worse between 1991–94 than it had been between 1988–89 – however, the same was true for four of the other seven medium-sized auditors (Grant Thornton, Panell Kerr Forster, Kidsons Impey and Hacker Young). Between 1988–89, Stoy Hayward gained two clients (5% of its clients) and had a 26.1% increase in fees – between 1991–94 Stoy Hayward

Table 4

Changes in Clients (+/−) and Average Audit Fees (£000's) (1988–94)

Big-Six Auditors	1988	1989	1990	1991	1992	1993	1994
KPMG Peat Marwick: Clients	+3	−1	+2	+2	+4	+3	+3
Average audit fees	255.6	284.8	308.8	315.8	346.5	373.5	350.9
Coopers & Lybrand: Clients	+3	+4	+1	0	+5	+5	−1
Average audit fees	383.9	430.0	450.0	444.8	464.1	452.0	462.3
Ernst & Young: Clients	+1	+3	−3	+2	−1	−2	+8
Average audit fees	407.6	426.1	475.5	490.7	526.5	558.4	546.3
Price Waterhouse: Clients	+4	+3	+6	0	0	+4	+1
Average audit fees	292.9	327.5	322.6	348.6	391.7	379.6	370.8
Touche Ross: Clients	+4	0	−2	−1	+1	+2	+1
Average audit fees	214.5	231.9	254.3	249.1	241.0	199.3	203.5
Arthur Anderson: Clients	+5	+1	+1	+1	+1	+1	+1
Average audit fees	197.2	223.7	263.6	251.0	273.2	263.3	266.3
Total: Clients	+20	+10	+5	+4	+10	+13	+13
Average audit fees	304.6	334.4	358.4	364.4	388.8	391.3	385.8

Medium-Sized Auditors	1988	1989	1990	1991	1992	1993	1994
Binder Hamlyn: Clients	−3	−3	+3	0	+2	−2	0
Average audit fees	93.6	108.1	118.0	138.6	123.4	133.4	138.6
Stoy Hayward: Clients	+1	+1	+1	0	−2	+1	−1
Average audit fees	83.6	105.4	94.6	93.1	78.7	78.3	72.8
Grant Thornton: Clients	0	+1	0	+1	−2	−2	−2
Average audit fees	70.8	88.0	102.4	94.5	91.7	91.7	78.6
Pannell Kerr Forster: Clients	+1	+1	−2	+2	0	−2	−2
Average audit fees	156.0	187.9	209.7	202.0	167.5	167.3	133.7
Robson Rhodes: Clients	0	−1	0	0	0	−1	0
Average audit fees	49.9	51.3	61.2	63.3	61.4	61.1	62.8
Kidsons Impey: Clients	−1	+1	+1	−2	0	0	−1
Average audit fees	238.1	282.8	271.0	410.0	456.8	544.7	707.7
Hacker Young: Clients	−1	+1	−1	0	0	−2	0
Average audit fees	107.6	122.9	69.0	70.9	61.0	37.6	37.0
Moores Rowland: Clients	0	0	0	0	+1	0	0
Average audit fees	54.5	69.5	81.8	84.4	63.4	61.1	65.2
Total: Clients	−3	+1	+2	+1	−1	−8	−6
Average audit fees	99.7	119.7	123.9	132.4	121.7	126.8	123.7

Small Auditors	1988	1989	1990	1991	1992	1993	1994
All other auditors: Clients	−17	−11	−7	−5	−9	−5	−7
Average audit fees	61.7	73.6	74.8	80.3	80.1	72.4	79.9

lost three clients (7.5% of its clients) and suffered a 21.2%% fall in fees. Whilst Stoy Hayward's market share performance was much worse between 1991–94 than between 1988–89, the same was also true for other medium-sized auditors. Between 1988–89, other medium-sized auditors lost five clients (2.5% of their clients) and had a 19.0% increase in fees – between 1991–94 these auditors lost 13 clients (6.6%) and suffered a 3.9% fall in fees (excluding Kidsons Impey, other medium-sized auditors suffered a 15.7% fall in fees). Overall, the evidence does not indicate that Stoy Hayward experienced a larger fall in demand compared to similar uncriticised auditors.

The evidence is less clear for the second prediction – that Ernst and Young suffered greater losses than other large auditors. Between 1988–94, Ernst & Young gained eight clients (6.3% of its clients) whilst other large auditors had average gains of 13.4 clients (9.6% of their clients). Over the same period, fees rose 34.0% for Ernst & Young and 24.7% for other large auditors. This suggests that Ernst & Young did not gain as many clients as other large auditors because of an increase in fees.

Finally, the evidence does not support the third prediction – that Price Waterhouse and Ernst and Young suffered falls in demand as a result of the BCCI affair. Between 1991–93, Ernst & Young lost one client (0.8% of its clients) and had a 13.8% increase in fees, while Price Waterhouse gained four clients (3.4% of its clients) and experienced an 8.9% increase in fees. Over the same period, other large auditors gained an average of six clients (4.1% of their clients) whilst fees increased by 5.8%. The worse performance of Ernst & Young and Price Waterhouse in terms of client gains appears to have been offset by a relative increase in fees.[16]

To examine further the effects of criticism, a reputation variable (REP_{it}) was included in a model of auditor switching. The most heavily criticised audit firms were Stoy Hayward (1990–94), Ernst & Young (1987–94) and Price Waterhouse (1991–93). For companies audited by these auditors in these time periods, $REP_{it} = 1$; for other observations $REP_{it} = 0$.

Previous research indicates that companies are more likely to switch following qualified reports and that failing companies are more likely to switch (Chow and Rice, 1982; and Menon and Schwartz, 1985). Therefore, lagged audit reports (Q_{it-1}) and

Table 5

Probit Model of Auditor Switching (1988–94)
(SW$_{it}$ is the dependent variable – z-statistics in parentheses)

Explanatory Variables	Model 1	Model 2	Model 3	Model 4
Q$_{it-1}$	0.734	0.718	0.716	–
	(5.414)	(5.386)	(5.480)	–
FAILS$_{it}$	0.457	0.556	0.571	–
	(2.689)	(3.547)	(3.755)	–
MGTSH$_{it}$	0.342e-02	0.485e-02	–	–
	(2.202)	(3.405)	–	–
MAJSH$_{it}$	0.552e-02	0.812e-02	–	–
	(2.666)	(4.274)	–	–
ASSETS$_{it}$	−0.216e-06	–	–	–
	(−1.852)	–	–	–
REP$_{it}$	−0.003	0.001	−0.022	−0.036
	(−0.031)	(0.013)	(−0.268)	(−0.451)
CONSTANT	−1.939	−2.024	−1.820	−1.771
	(−30.824)	(−35.942)	(−53.614)	(−55.072)

Notes:
Number of observations = 6,052.

SW$_{it}$ = 1 if company i experienced a change in auditor in year t; = 0 otherwise.
Q$_{t-1}$ = 1 if company i received a qualified report in year $t - 1$; = 0 otherwise.
FAILS$_{it}$ = 1 if company i received its final audit report in year t prior to entering bankruptcy; = 0 otherwise.
MGTSH$_{it}$ = The percentage of ordinary shareholdings held by the directors.
MAJSH$_{it}$ = The percentage of ordinary shareholdings held by other large shareholders.
ASSETS$_{it}$ = Asset size of company i in year t.
REP$_{it}$ = 1 if company i hired Stoy Hayward (1990–94), Ernst & Young (1987–94), or Price Waterhouse (1991–93) in year t; = 0 otherwise.

Directors' ordinary shareholdings are expressed as a percentage of issued ordinary share capital. Shareholding data were not collected for all observations because of the high cost of collecting this information. For companies that did not switch auditor over the study period, shareholding information was only collected for 1990 and is used as a proxy for the missing observations in other years. In practice, this is unlikely to cause measurement error problems since ownership patterns typically exhibit little variation over time. For companies that did switch, shareholding data were collected for all years because ownership patterns may be less stable for such companies.

Large shareholdings held by individuals, companies and trust funds were only disclosed in the accounts if they exceeded 5%. For each company, the sum of these excess shareholdings was calculated. For example, suppose that company i had the following large shareholders in year t:
Individual A: 8%   Individual B: 10%   Individual C: 5.5%.
For this observation, MAJSH$_{it}$ would be calculated as follows:
MAJSH$_{it}$ = (8−5) + (10−5) + (5.5−5) = 8.5.
This measure avoided putting undue weight on observations with a lot of shareholdings only slightly in excess of 5%.

financial health (FAILS$_{it}$) are included in the switching model. Event study evidence indicates that a switch may signal un- favourable news to investors (Fried and Schiff, 1981; and Eichen- seher et al., 1989). Agency theory implies that companies have more incentive to avoid signalling unfavourable news when agency costs are high (when there is a high degree of separation of ownership from control). Therefore, the shareholdings of directors (MGTSH$_{it}$) and large investors (MAJSH$_{it}$) are hypothe- sised to have a positive effect on auditor switching. The effect of company size is controlled for using companies' assets (ASSETS$_{it}$).

Consistent with previous research, models 1–3 show that lagged reports (Q$_{it-1}$) and financial health (FAILS$_{it}$) were significant determinants of auditor switching. Failing companies were more likely to switch auditor than non-failing companies, and companies were more likely to switch after receiving qualified reports. The significant positive coefficients on the shareholding variables (MGTSH$_{it}$ and MAJSH$_{it}$) indicate that companies had more incentive to switch when directors' and other large share- holdings were high (when agency costs were low). Consistent with the analysis of Table 4, the coefficients on the reputation variable (REP$_{it}$) were completely insignificant – the evidence does not support the view that there were significant reputation effects.[17]

4. CONCLUSION

Analytical studies have developed reputation and deep pockets hypotheses to explain why large auditors are more accurate than small auditors. To try to distinguish between these hypotheses, this paper investigated the effects of criticism on the demand for audit services and the relationship between auditor size and litigation. The evidence appears to give stronger support to the deep pockets hypothesis in two ways. First, large auditors were more prone to litigation despite their superior accuracy – this is contrary to the reputation hypothesis, but is consistent with the deep pockets hypothesis. The main limitation of this finding is that most litigation cases are resolved privately, which makes it difficult to accurately test the relationship between auditor size and litigation. Secondly, criticised auditors did not suffer client losses or lower fees compared to similar uncriticised auditors. This suggests that reputation does not explain the superior accuracy of large auditors.

The lack of evidence for reputation effects is unsurprising if the deep pockets hypothesis is valid, because the reputation hypothesis relies upon there being a reliable signal of auditor accuracy. In the deep pockets model, litigation is an unreliable signal of accuracy for two reasons. First, litigation does not signal auditors' type II error rates because auditors are never sued for issuing reports that are too conservative. Secondly, large auditors are more likely to incur litigation despite their superior accuracy – therefore, litigation is a noisy signal of auditors' type I error rates.

This paper's conclusion does not contradict the widely-held view that large audit firms have reputations for higher quality audits. If investors know that large auditors have deeper pockets, they would know that large auditors have more incentive to issue accurate reports – in this sense, large auditors have better reputations. However, it appears to be the threat of litigation rather than the loss of client-specific rents that drives the superior accuracy of large auditors.

APPENDIX

The Incumbent Owner's Auditor Hiring Decision

From (1) and (2), the incumbent owner's expected payoff from hiring auditor j is the company's expected selling price minus the audit fee:

$$\max\{0, pe_j\Pi_N + (1 - p)(1 - e_j)\Pi_F - I[pe_j + (1 - p)(1 - e_j)]\}+$$
$$\max\{0, p(1 - e_j)\Pi_N + (1 - p)e_j\Pi_F - I[p(1 - e_j) + (1 - p)e_j]\} - F_j.$$

For Propositions 2 and 3, it is easy to find numerical examples in which the incumbent owner always hires the large auditor, always hires the small auditor, or is indifferent between hiring the small and large auditor. For example, consider the following cost function:

$$C(e_j) = (0.5 - e_j)/\ln(e_j).$$

It is easy to verify that for $0.5 \le e_j \le 1$, this cost function satisfies the assumptions $C'(e_j) > 0$, $C''(e_j) > 0$, $C(0.5) = 0$ and $C(1) = +\infty$.

Consider case (c) where $W_L > W_S > K_H > K_L$.

In example (1), the incumbent owner's expected payoff is greater when the large auditor is hired.

Example (1):

$$p = 0.9 \quad e_L = 0.9 \quad e_S = 0.6 \quad C(e_L) = 3.8 \quad C(e_S) = 0.2$$
$$F_L = 8.9 \quad F_S = 1.8 \quad W_L = 505.8 \quad W_S = 39.0 \quad K_H = 20.0 \quad K_L = 15.0$$
$$I = 900 \quad \Pi_N = 1000 \quad \Pi_F = 500.$$

In example (2), the incumbent owner's expected payoff is greater when the small auditor is hired.
Example (2):

$$p = 0.9 \quad e_L = 0.9 \quad e_S = 0.6 \quad C(e_L) = 3.8 \quad C(e_S) = 0.2$$
$$F_L = 8.9 \quad F_S = 1.8 \quad W_L = 505.8 \quad W_S = 39.0 \quad K_H = 20.0 \quad K_L = 15.0$$
$$I = 700 \quad \Pi_N = 1000 \quad \Pi_F = 500.$$

In example (3), the incumbent owner is indifferent between hiring the large and small auditor:
Example (3):

$$p = 0.9 \quad e_L = 0.9 \quad e_S = 0.6 \quad C(e_L) = 3.8 \quad C(e_S) = 0.2$$
$$F_L = 8.9 \quad F_S = 1.8 \quad W_L = 505.8 \quad W_S = 39.0 \quad K_H = 20.0 \quad K_L = 15.0$$
$$I = 789.5 \quad \Pi_N = 1000 \quad \Pi_F = 500.$$

The Relationship Between Auditor Size and Litigation in Proposition 3

Using the above cost function, it is easy to find numerical examples in which the large (small) auditor incurs more litigation. In example (4), the incumbent owner is indifferent between hiring the large and small auditor and the large auditor incurs more litigation than the small auditor $(1 - p)(1 - e_L) > h(1 - p)(1 - e_S)$:
Example (4):

$$p = 0.9 \quad e_L = 0.9 \quad e_S = 0.6 \quad C(e_L) = 3.8 \quad C(e_S) = 0.2$$
$$F_L = 8.9 \quad F_S = 1.8 \quad W_L = 505.8 \quad W_S = 195.0 \quad K_H = 200 \quad K_L = 20$$
$$I = 789.5 \quad \Pi_N = 1000 \quad \Pi_F = 500 \quad h = 0.2$$

Example (5):
In example (5), the incumbent owner is indifferent between hiring the large and small auditor and the large auditor incurs less litigation than the small auditor $(1 - p)(1 - e_L) < h(1 - p)(1 - e_S)$:

$$p = 0.9 \quad e_L = 0.9 \quad e_S = 0.6 \quad C(e_L) = 3.8 \quad C(e_S) = 0.2$$
$$F_L = 8.9 \quad F_S = 1.8 \quad W_L = 505.8 \quad W_S = 43.3 \quad K_H = 200 \quad K_L = 20$$
$$I = 789.5 \quad \Pi_N = 1000 \quad \Pi_F = 500 \quad h = 0.9.$$

NOTES

1 *The Economist* writes (7 October, 1995), 'As partnerships, the large accountancies operate under the legal principle of joint and several liability. This means that when a company collapses, its auditors who not only have deep pockets, but cannot abscond, may be hit for the entire bill if they were negligent, even if other parties were careless too. Moreover, if the claim amounts to more than an auditing firm's capital, all of the firm's partners are liable right down to their bootstraps for the bill – even if they had nothing to do with the error.' Similarly, the *Financial Times* writes (4 July, 1996), 'The big audit firms can find themselves targeted for lawsuits because of their "deep pockets" – including their statutory insurance cover.'

2 If the company's type were perfectly observable, the investor would not wish to buy a failing company $(I > \Pi_F)$, but would wish to buy a non-failing company $(I < \Pi_N)$.

3 The key insights of the model are robust to relaxing this assumption.

4 Assuming that the cost of effort is non-pecuniary simplifies the analysis as it implies that effort does not affect auditor wealth.

5 This assumption raises the question why auditors would not choose to always shirk and report 'F'. Following previous studies, there are two justifications for assuming that such behaviour does not occur (Dye, 1993; and Acemoglu and Gietzmann, 1997). First, if auditors always shirk, audit reports would be completely uninformative and there would be no voluntary demand for audits. Secondly, an auditor might face a threat of litigation for reporting 'F' when the company is N and this would deter the auditor from always shirking (Dye, 1993). Finally, empirical evidence indicates that a company is more likely to switch its auditor after receiving an unfavourable report (Chow and Rice, 1982; Craswell, 1988; Citron and Taffler, 1992; and Krishnan and Stephens, 1995). This suggests that auditors have incentives to avoid always reporting 'F' because a low report could trigger a switch of auditor and a loss of rent.

6 Although audit effort is not directly observable, auditors' objective functions are common knowledge and therefore the equilibrium choices of audit effort can be inferred by potential investors.

7 The solution concept is that of a strategically stable sequential equilibrium (Fudenberg and Tirole, 1993). The equilibrium is strategically stable since all weakly and strongly dominated strategies are eliminated. The assessments of players are required to be sequentially rational and consistent which implies that beliefs and strategies can be regarded as limits of totally mixed strategies and beliefs. Updating of beliefs is carried out using Bayes' rule.

8 Using this sample, Lennox (1999) has shown that large auditors give more accurate signals of financial distress compared to small auditors. This finding is consistent with both the reputation and deep pockets hypotheses.

9 Microfiche copies of annual reports were unavailable for most of the companies cited in Table 1. This prevented a more detailed investigation of the causes of criticism.

10 Alternative definitions for the dependent variable gave very similar results – for example, the criticism variable ($CRIT_j$) was re-weighted to take account of the possibility that DTI criticisms were more serious and more likely to result in litigation.

11 In contrast, Palmrose (1988) found a negative relationship between auditor size and litigation using US data for 1960–85. More recently, Stice (1991) found no significant relationship between auditor size and litigation for the US.

12 Two studies have tested the reputation hypothesis by investigating the effects of criticism on auditors' market shares (Firth, 1990; and Wilson and Grimlund (WG), 1990). Firth investigated the effect of criticisms by Department of Trade investigators against UK audit firms. However, there are reasons to believe that Firth's claims – that criticised auditors lost market share compared to uncriticised auditors – may be misleading. First, whilst criticised auditors lost more clients compared to 'control groups' of similar uncriticised auditors, there was no net loss of clients for the group of criticised auditors. The criticised auditors lost 11 clients but also gained 11 clients over the three year period following each criticism. Although the control groups of uncriticised auditors experienced net client gains, the uncriticised auditors left out of the control groups must have lost clients. Therefore, Firth's results may be sensitive to which uncriticised auditors were included in the control groups. Secondly, Firth did not find that criticised auditors received lower fees. Using US data, WG found that large and small audit firms lost market share following disciplinary actions carried out by the Securities and Exchange Commission (SEC). However, no comparison was made between criticised and uncriticised large auditors because of a lack of data. Although WG found that the market share performance of small criticised auditors was worse than that of small uncriticised auditors, it is unclear how robust these results were for different control groups and time periods. In contrast, this paper shows the number of clients gained/lost and audit fees received by each auditor in each year. Thus, one can be confident that the conclusions are not sensitive to control groups or time periods. Moreover, this study takes into account more sources of criticism and the severity of criticisms.

13 The allegations of audit failure in the case of BCCI were particularly serious, as shown by the size of the writ and the news coverage that the case created (occupying many more column inches than any other story).

14 This analysis is subject to the caveat that many factors may influence the effects of criticism – for example, the nature of the case, visibility, whether the criticism is perceived as being justified, etc.

15 Average audit fees for Kidsons Impey were higher and more volatile compared to other medium-sized auditors because of two outliers. In particular, Kidsons Impey audited BSG International and RMC Group between 1988–94 – audit fees for these two clients averaged more than £1,000,000 per year.

16 These results relate to the contemporaneous effects of criticism on the demand for auditors. No evidence was found for reputation effects when criticism was allowed to have lagged effects on auditor switching and audit fees – Table 4 shows that the conclusions are robust to alternative time horizons.

17 This conclusion is robust to alternative definitions of the reputation variable (i.e. to definitions which consider a subset of Stoy Hayward, Ernst and Young and Price Waterhouse and which consider alternative time periods).

804   LENNOX

REFERENCES

Acemoglu, D. and M. Gietzmann (1997), 'Auditor Independence, Incomplete Contracts and the Role of Legal Liability', *The European Accounting Review*, Vol. 6, pp. 355–76.

Balvers, R., B. McDonald and R. Miller (1988), 'Underpricing of New Issues and the Choice of Auditor as a Signal of Investment Banker Reputation', *The Accounting Review*, Vol. 63, pp. 605–21.

Beatty, R. (1989), 'Auditor Reputation and the Pricing of Initial Public Offerings', *The Accounting Review*, Vol. 64, pp. 693–709.

Chan, P., M. Ezzamel and D. Gwilliam, (1993), 'Determinants of Audit Fees for Quoted UK Companies', *Journal of Business, Finance & Accounting*, Vol. 20, No. 6 (November), pp. 765–86.

Chow, C. and S. Rice (1982), 'Qualified Audit Opinions and Auditor Switching', *The Accounting Review*, Vol. 57, pp. 326–35.

Citron, D. and R. Taffler (1992), 'The Audit Report under Going-Concern Uncertainties: An Empirical Analysis', *Accounting and Business Research*, Vol. 22, pp. 337–45.

Craswell, A. (1988), 'The Association between Qualified Opinions and Auditor Switches', *Accounting and Business Research*, Vol. 19, pp. 23–31.

_____ J. Francis and S. Taylor (1995), 'Auditor Brand Name Reputations and Industry Specialisations', *Journal of Accounting and Economics*, Vol. 20, pp. 297–322.

DeAngelo, L. (1981), 'Auditor Size and Audit Quality', *Journal of Accounting and Economics*, Vol. 3, pp. 183–99.

DeFond, M. (1992), 'The Association between Changes in Client Firm Agency Costs and Auditor Switching', *Auditing: A Journal of Practice and Theory*, Vol. 11, pp. 16–31.

Dye, R, (1993), 'Auditing Standards, Legal Liability and Auditor Wealth', *Journal of Political Economy*, Vol. 101, pp. 887–914.

Eichenseher, J., M. Hagigi and D. Shields (1989), 'Market Reaction to Auditor Changes by OTC Companies', *Auditing: A Journal of Practice and Theory*, Vol. 9, pp. 29–40.

Firth, M. (1990), 'Auditor Reputation: The Impact of Critical Reports Issued by Government Inspectors', *Rand Journal of Economics*, Vol. 21, pp. 374–88.

_____ and A. Smith (1992), 'Selection of Auditor Firms by Companies in the New Issue Market', *Applied Economics*, Vol. 24, pp. 247–55.

Francis, J. and E. Wilson (1988), 'Auditor Changes: A Joint Test of Theories Relating to Agency Costs and Auditor Differentiation', *The Accounting Review*, Vol. 63, pp. 663–82.

Fried, D. and A. Schiff (1981), 'CPA Switches and Associated Market Reactions', *The Accounting Review*, pp. 347–74.

Fudenberg, D. and J. Tirole (1993), *Game Theory* (Massachusetts Institute of Technology).

Hall, W. and A. Renner (1988), 'Lessons that Auditors Ignore at their Own Risk', *Journal of Accountancy*, Vol. 166, pp. 50–58.

Johnson, W. and T. Lys (1990), 'The Market for Audit Services: Evidence from Voluntary Auditor Changes', *Journal of Accounting and Economics*, Vol. 12, pp. 281–308.

Krishnan, J. and R. Stephens (1995), 'Evidence on Opinion Shopping from Audit Opinion Conservatism', *Journal of Accounting and Public Policy*, Vol. 14, pp. 179–201.

Lennox, C. (1999), 'Are Large Auditors More Accurate than Small Auditors?' *Accounting and Business Research* (forthcoming).

Menon, K. and K. Schwartz (1985), 'Auditor Switches by Failing Firms', *The Accounting Review*, Vol. 60, pp. 248–61.

Morris, R. (1997), *Early Warning Indicators of Corporate Failure: A Critical Review of Previous Research and Further Empirical Evidence* (Ashgate Publishing).

Nichols, D. and D. Smith (1983), 'Auditor Credibility and Auditor Changes', *Journal of Accounting Research*, Vol. 21, pp. 534–44.

Palmrose, Z. (1988), 'An Analysis of Auditor Litigation and Audit Service Quality', *The Accounting Review*, Vol. 63, pp. 55–73.

Schwartz, R. (1997), 'Legal Regimes, Audit Quality and Investment', *The Accounting Review*, Vol. 72, pp. 385–406.

Simunic, D. and M. Stein (1987), 'Production Differentiation in Auditing: A Study of Auditor Choice in the Market for New Issues' (Canadian Certified General Accountants' Research Foundation).

St. Pierre, K. and J. Anderson (1984), 'An Analysis of the Factors Associated with Lawsuits against Public Accountants', *The Accounting Review*, Vol. 59, pp. 242–63.

Stice, J. (1991), 'Using Financial and Market Information to Identify Pre-Engagement Factors Associated with Lawsuits Against Auditors', *The Accounting Review*, Vol. 66, pp. 516–33.

_____ (1993), 'Reading the Warning Signs: Assessing the Risk of Litigation in Audit Engagements', *The National Public Accountant* (March), pp. 22–25.

Wilson, T. and R. Grimlund (1990), 'An Examination of the Importance of an Auditor's Reputation', *Auditing: A Journal of Practice and Theory*, Vol. 9, pp. 43–59.

[13]

THE ACCOUNTING REVIEW
Vol. LXIII, No. 4
October 1988

Auditor Changes: A Joint Test of Theories Relating to Agency Costs and Auditor Differentiation

Jere R. Francis and Earl R. Wilson

ABSTRACT: This study tests whether there is a positive association between a firm's agency costs and its demand for a quality-differentiated audit. Audit firm quality is represented in two ways: a continuous size model in which a direct association is posited between auditor size (measured by clients' sales) and audit quality, and a "brand name" model in which the Big Eight group of auditors is defined as higher quality suppliers. The tests are supportive of the brand name model of audit quality: agency cost proxies are significant as a group, after controlling for client size and growth, only in the brand name model. The results are also supportive (albeit weakly in some instances) of the following individual agency-related incentives for higher quality audits: monitoring of incentive performance contracts, diffusion of ownership, owner-debtholder conflict, and the subsequent issue of public securities after the auditor change. However, the explanatory power of the models tested is low, after controlling for client size and growth.

THIS paper tests whether the demand for quality-differentiated audits is, in part, associated with variables that proxy for the firm's agency costs (after controlling for client size and growth). Auditing is widely viewed as a means of reducing agency costs [Jensen and Meckling, 1976; Ng, 1978; Simunic and Stein, 1987; Watts, 1977; and Watts and Zimmerman, 1983]. It follows that when agency costs are greater there is increased demand for higher-level audit quality.

To test the hypothesis that higher-quality audits are demanded as a function of increasing agency costs, a sample of firms is selected that changed auditors. The framework adopted for testing can be described as follows: given that a change in auditor has occurred, is the choice of the new auditor associated with the firm's agency costs? Audit quality is measured in each of two different ways to correspond to the two general theories of audit quality: (1) a continuous auditor size metric based on combined sales of all public companies audited (a proxy for client-specific quasi-rents) and (2) an ordinal categorical variable representing either the brand name Big Eight or non-Big Eight accounting firms. Two repre-

Jere R. Francis is an Associate Professor at University of Iowa, and Earl R. Wilson is an Assistant Professor at University of Missouri–Columbia.

Manuscript received June 1986.
Revisions received March 1987, September 1987, and April 1988.
Accepted May 1988.

The Accounting Review, October 1988

sentations of agency costs are tested: (1) the "level" of agency cost proxies in the year preceding the auditor change and (2) the "change" in the level of agency cost proxies over the three-year period prior to auditor change. The agency cost proxies tested are (1) managerial stock ownership, (2) presence of accounting-based bonus plans, (3) largest individual percentage of stock ownership (diffusion of ownership), and (4) ratio of long-term debt to total assets (leverage). An agency cost-related variable, the future issuance of public securities, is also tested.

This study constitutes a joint test of audit quality differentiation and the demand for higher-quality audits as a function of agency costs. If an association exists, it may be evidence of an agency-driven demand for higher-quality audits as well as evidence that the proxies used in the study represent differentiated audit quality. However, in any empirical study, there is the possibility that variables may proxy for something other than the underlying construct being assumed in the test. Of particular concern with respect to auditor changes is the possible confounding effects of client size and growth on the choice of the new auditor. Simply put, larger or growing companies may require a larger audit firm if the auditor is to be technically *capable* to conduct the audit. In most prior related research, client size and/or growth is significant in explaining auditor choice. Thus, in order to control for the possible confounding effects of client size or growth, these variables are included in the empirical models and tested.

The remainder of the paper is organized as follows. The next section summarizes the audit quality literature and the two models of audit firm quality differentiation. Agency cost proxies are defined in the following section and related

empirical research is reviewed. The research design and sample are described next followed by a discussion of the results. The final section summarizes the study and its principal conclusions.

TWO THEORIES OF AUDIT FIRM QUALITY DIFFERENTIATION

DeAngelo [1981] defines audit quality as the joint probability of detecting and reporting material financial statement errors and concludes that larger audit firms have incentives to supply a higher level of audit quality. The argument relies on the assumption that client-specific quasi-rents, the cost advantages of incumbency due to auditor startup and client switching costs, accrue to incumbent auditors. Since larger audit firms have more clients, they have more aggregate client-specific quasi-rents at stake if a lack of independence or a low-quality audit becomes known. It is assumed that an audit firm will lose clients if such a breach occurs. DeAngelo argues that these quasi-rents serve as "collateral" or a "bond" on independence and audit quality, and that, *ceteris paribus*, auditor size is a surrogate for unobservable audit quality.[1]

Taken literally, DeAngelo's argument suggests that a cardinal ordering of auditor size can be used to proxy for audit quality. We adopt such a metric as one representation of audit quality. Specifically, an auditor size metric is developed based on the combined sales of publicly-listed companies audited by an auditor in the year of auditor change as indicated in *Who Audits America*. Companies listed in *Who Audits America* approximate the population of SEC registrants and, thus,

---

[1] DeAngelo [1981, fn. 9, p. 186] argues that audit quality is costly to directly observe (though not unobservable in the limit), and for this reason there are incentives to find less costly surrogates of audit quality.

serve as a proxy for the aggregate client-specific quasi-rents of public companies for each audit firm.

In DeAngelo's formulation, differential audit quality is a passive by-product of client-specific quasi-rents. This contrasts with the brand name (reputation) investment model of Klein et al. [1978] and Klein and Leffler [1981] in which firms are explicitly motivated to develop and maintain brand name reputations for quality in order to secure and protect quasi-rents arising from the brand name. In other words, the brand-name development comes first and this in turn leads to a quality-assuring price that is higher than the minimum-quality price. There is a disincentive to shirk on delivering the higher-quality product because of the potential loss of brand name (i.e., loss of the present value of future quasi-rents).[2] Klein and Leffler [1981, p. 634] conclude "Our analysis implies that consumers can successfully use price as an indicator of quality."

In the auditing industry the Big Eight firms appear to be brand name producers in the U.S. audit market.[3] Support for this can be found in the popular financial press [Stevens, 1981], in Congressional hearings [U.S. Senate, 1977], in AICPA-sponsored studies [AICPA, 1978 and 1980], and in the scholarly literature [Dopuch and Simunic, 1980 and 1982; Libby, 1979; Palmrose, 1988; Shockley, 1981; and Simunic and Stein, 1987]. There is also evidence that the Big Eight firms command price premiums [Francis and Simon, 1987; Palmrose, 1986; Rubin, 1988; Simon and Francis, 1988; for the Australian market see Francis, 1984; and Francis and Stokes, 1986]. Simon and Francis [1988] report that Big Eight fees have been consistently estimated at 16 percent to 19 percent higher than non-Big Eight audit fees across several independent studies. Big

Eight price premiums are consistent with Klein and Leffler's [1981] claim that price is an indicator of quality. Further, Francis and Simon [1987] report that the Big Eight price premium holds with respect to *both* other national firms and local-regional firms and that non-Big Eight national firms do *not* command a price premium over local-regional firms.[4] Based on these studies, a two-category representation of audit quality is used with the Big Eight firms defined as brand name higher-quality suppliers.

The preceding two models can be viewed, in a sense, as competing hypotheses about audit firm quality. If audit firm size can be used to rank-order audit firm quality while holding technology constant, then agency costs should be systematically associated with changes in auditor size across the continuum of auditor size. On the other hand, if the Big Eight are brand name firms that perform higher-quality audits, then agency costs should be systematically associated with changes to or from the Big Eight group of firms. Tests are designed to determine if either (or both) of these hypotheses is supported by the data.

AGENCY COSTS AND THE DEMAND FOR HIGHER QUALITY AUDITS

Agency theory posits an inherent moral hazard problem in principal-agent (owner-manager) relations that gives rise

---

[2] DeAngelo [1981, p. 193] points out that in both the brand name model and her model of client-specific quasi-rents that the collateral is auditor-specific. The brand name model, however, substitutes *non-client-specific* collateral (investments in the brand name) for the *client-specific* collateral in her model.

[3] The Big Eight are: Arthur Andersen, Arthur Young, Coopers & Lybrand, Deloitte Haskins and Sells, Ernst and Whinney, Peat Marwick Main, Price Waterhouse, and Touche Ross.

[4] Francis and Simon [1987] restrict their analysis to the small public company market segment which mitigates against the Big Eight premium being confounded by auditor technology differences across market segments.

The Accounting Review, October 1988

to agency costs. While audited financial statements are widely viewed as a means of mitigating agency costs, the arguments linking auditing with reduced agency costs are informal and rely on the fact that auditing has survived in a competitive setting and presumably is cost-effective [Dopuch and Simunic, 1982; and Dopuch, 1984]. Jensen and Meckling [1976] identify two classes of agency conflict, owner-manager and owner-debtholder, and these two classes are the basis for the agency cost proxies used in the study.

Owner-Manager Conflict

If there are no debt contracts, the agency problem reduces to the moral hazard between managers and owners.[5] Jensen and Meckling [1976] argue that this basic agency problem can be mitigated by making managers owners of the firm. Since owner-managers have an opportunity for entrepreneurial gains, they have incentives to increase the value of the firm rather than shirk. In the absence of manager ownership, the moral hazard problem leads owners to discount the value of their initial investments and lower management compensation. Managers then have an incentive to choose a higher-quality audit as a means of increasing their compensation. It follows from this argument that firms with higher levels of manager ownership would have less need for higher-quality audits than would firms with lower levels of manager ownership assuming a "convergence of interests" as manager ownership increases.

More recently, Demsetz [1983] and Fama and Jensen [1983a, 1983b] point out that high levels of manager ownership can lead to management "entrenchment" because control challenges are difficult to mount by nonmanager stockholders. Following this line of reasoning,

Morck et al. [1986] hypothesize a non-linear relation between manager ownership and corporate performance. Their results show that firms with 5 to 20 percent manager ownership perform better than firms *either* below 5 percent or greater than 20 percent. Thus, manager ownership is tested both as a continuous variable and as a nonlinear variable coded one if outside the 5 to 20 percent range and zero if in the 5 to 20 percent range. Data on manager ownership is found in the firm's annual proxy statement and represents the proportion of issued stock owned by officers and directors of the firm.

Another means of reducing agency costs is the use of incentive performance contracts for managers. While incentive contracting may improve managerial performance compared with pure wage contracts, the use of incentive compensation contracts also results in additional monitoring costs. Watts and Zimmerman [1983, pp. 614–615] state "Corporate managers or promoters write contracts (by-laws, charters, indenture agreements, compensation plans) that reduce their opportunism. Enforcement of the contract requires monitoring of management's activities and it is hypothesized by Jensen and Meckling that this is a role of auditing." In other words, the creation of an additional contract that relies on accounting-based performance measurement creates a demand for more or higher-quality monitoring. Firms having incentive perfor-

---

[5] Jensen and Meckling [1976] argue that divergent interests and inability of the principal to directly observe the agent's actions lead directly to a "moral hazard" or inherent conflict of interests between principals and agents. Agency costs can be offset to some extent by writing contract provisions for bonding and monitoring to guarantee that the agent will act in the principal's interest. The sum of bonding, monitoring, and residual costs of agent's actions are collectively referred to as agency costs.

mance plans are hypothesized to be more likely to use a higher-quality auditor than firms without such plans. The existence of accounting-based incentive performance (bonus) contracts is reported in the firm's annual proxy statement.

A third variable affecting the extent of owner-manager conflict is diffusion of ownership. Alchian and Demsetz [1972, p. 788] argue that the operative aspect of diffusion is its effect on the probability that management will be removed. Greater diffusion of ownership increases the cost and effort required to obtain proxy transfers necessary to affect management policy and, in particular, to force a change in management. Thus, owner constraints on management actions are inversely proportional to the degree of diffusion. Fama and Jensen [1983a, 1983b] contend that large organizations with diffuse ownership resolve the agency cost problem by separating internal decision management and control. Hierarchical separation of decision management and control reduces the ability of individual agents to expropriate residual claimants' wealth. Empirical tests of Demsetz and Lehn [1985] are supportive of Fama and Jensen's argument because no difference in corporate performance is found as a function of ownership diffusion.

These arguments suggest that a higher-quality audit can be considered as part of the complex control system that mitigates the relative inability of diffused ownership to directly monitor and control management action. Diffusion is measured as the percentage of common stock owned by the largest single shareholder as reported in proxy statements. A ten percent reporting threshold exists for pre-1982 proxy disclosures. Thus, the variable is coded one if the largest individual owner has ten percent or more of outstanding stock, and zero if the largest

individual holding is less than ten percent. Dhaliwal et al. [1982] and Palmrose [1984] use the same coding rule. The hypothesis is that firms with more diffuse ownership are more likely to use a higher-quality auditor.

Owner-Debtholder Conflict

Agency theory posits that debtholders are concerned about possible wealth transfers to stockholders [Smith and Warner, 1979]. Managers favor the interests of stockholders to the detriment of debtholders and, for this reason, restrictive covenants are written into debt contracts. Thus, it has been hypothesized [Eichenseher and Shields, 1986; Palmrose, 1984; and Simunic and Stein, 1987] that the presence of long-term debt contracts creates a demand for higher-quality audits. However, Healy and Lys [1986] and Johnson and Lys [1986] draw a distinction between *existing* debtholders at the time of an auditor change, and incentives with respect to *future* debt issues after an auditor change. If a firm switches to a lower-quality auditor, the value of existing debt claims is expected to drop, thus, increasing the value of stockholders' residual claims. Based on this reasoning, it is hypothesized that firms with higher debt levels are more likely to switch to a lower-quality auditor. The ratio of long-term debt (excluding deferred credits) to total assets is used to proxy for debt. The effect of *future* debt issues after an auditor change is treated as a separate variable as discussed below.

Firms may change auditors (especially from a non-Big Eight firm to a brand name Big Eight firm) to increase the marketability of the new securities [Carpenter and Strawser, 1971]. Thus, issuance of new securities could be either an incentive to change auditors or an indication of the nature of the change itself.

A variable is used indicating the firm's publicly issued new stock or debt within two fiscal years after the year of auditor change. An auditor change is argued to have signalling value regarding the firm and information about the firm *vis-a-vis* accounting data [Titman and Trueman, 1986]. While this argument relates to signalling and asymmetric information, the underlying condition that gives rise to it is a principal-agent problem in which there is asymmetric information between the owner (or would-be owner) and the agent. Johnson and Lys [1986] also point out that *existing* stockholders at the time of an auditor change "capture" the benefits of this reduced information risk *vis-a-vis subsequent* stock or debt issues, thus creating the incentive for switching to a higher-quality auditor.

Related Empirical Research

Several studies have investigated the association of agency cost proxies and auditor choice. Results of these five studies with respect to the specific variables tested here are as follows.

Managerial Ownership. Manager stock ownership was tested in Eichenseher and Shields [1986] and was significant but positively associated with the change to a Big Eight auditor, contrary to predictions. Simunic and Stein [1987], on the other hand, found that lower levels of manager ownership were associated with the choice of a Big Eight auditor in initial public offerings as predicted.

Bonus Plans. The presence of accounting-based plans was only tested in Palmrose [1984] and was not significant.

Diffusion of Ownership. Diffusion of ownership was only tested by Palmrose [1984] and was not significant.

Leverage. Leverage was hypothesized to be positively associated with the choice of a Big Eight auditor by Palmrose [1984], Eichenseher and Shields

[1986], and Simunic and Stein [1987], and negatively associated with Big Eight audit firms whose clients underwent mergers [Healy and Lys, 1986] and larger firms changing auditors [Johnson and Lys, 1986]. A positive association was reported by Eichenseher and Shields [1986], a negative association found by Simunic and Stein [1987], with insignificant results were reported by Palmrose [1984], Healy and Lys [1986], and Johnson and Lys [1986].

New Issues. New debt/stock, post auditor change, was tested by Healy and Lys [1986] and was not significant. Johnson and Lys [1986] report a positive and significant association with the choice of a larger auditor.

In sum, the research in this area exhibits a wide range of designs. At best, only a very weak association has been demonstrated to exist between agency cost proxies and audit firm choice with little interstudy consistency.

RESEARCH DESIGN

While agency costs alone may sometimes lead to the decision to change auditors, the evidence suggests that auditor changes are frequently motivated by other factors [Carpenter and Strawser, 1971; Bedingfield and Loeb 1974; and Eichenseher and Shields, 1983].[6] Thus, the auditor change decision is characterized as a two-step process: first, a decision is made to change auditors (which may or may not be motivated by agency costs) and, second, a new auditor is chosen. If agency costs influence *both*

---

[6] Some reasons identified for voluntary auditor changes include: (1) change in top management, (2) corporate mergers, (3) need for additional services, (4) dissatisfaction with old auditor, (5) ability to raise new capital, (6) disputes over accounting principles, (7) regular rotation policy, (8) audit partner switched to another accounting firm, (9) retirement of audit partner, and (10) audit fee disputes.

the decision to change as well as the choice of a new auditor, then "changes" in agency costs preceding the auditor change should be associated with the new auditor size. However, even if "changes" in agency costs are insufficient, in themselves, to motivate a costly auditor switch, it is still possible that the existing "levels" of agency costs could be an important factor in the choice of the new auditor, given that a decision to change has been made for other reasons. Agency costs are, thus, tested as both "changes" and "levels" in the models to be estimated.

Since client size and/or growth is significantly associated with auditor choice in other studies [Healy and Lys, 1986; Johnson and Lys, 1986; Palmrose, 1984; and Simunic and Stein, 1987], it is incorporated here as a covariate. Client size, measured by total assets the year prior to change, is included in the "levels" model and growth, measured as the percentage change in client size over the three years prior to auditor change, is included in the "changes" model. Two additional tests are conducted to determine the effect of client size and/or growth on the results. First, a Chow test is used to determine if the empirical models are consistent across the upper/ lower halves of the samples partitioned by median client size or growth as appropriate. Second, the explanatory power of the models is evaluated *with* and *without* client size/growth in order to assess the marginal contribution of the agency variables over and above client size/growth variables.

A final point concerns the meaning of client size and growth with respect to auditor choice. Fama and Jensen [1983a, 1983b] argue that, in general, as firm size increases so does its agency costs. From this perspective, client size/growth could be argued to proxy (albeit in-

directly) for agency costs in which case a positive association would exist between client size or growth and the demand for audit quality. Alternatively, Johnson and Lys [1986, p. 10] argue that fixed investments in the auditor's error-detection technology leads to specialization in market segments and the "differences in technologies and cost functions across market segments are likely to be reflected by differences in audit firm size, with each segment dominated by audit firms of approximately the same size." In the Johnson and Lys framework, client size or growth is likely to be associated with larger sized auditors primarily due to technology or audit efficiency rather than agency costs. We make no attempt to interpret what client size and growth may mean with respect to auditor changes. Instead, we estimate the effect of the more specific agency proxies after controlling for client size and growth. This approach implicitly assumes that there is no relation between client size/ growth and agency costs.

Specification of the Model

To test the hypothesized relation between audit firm choice and agency costs, three model specifications are used: a pre-change *levels* of agency cost model, a *changes* in agency cost model, and, for completeness, a composite model of both *levels* and *changes* in agency cost variables. Each of the three model specifications is estimated using two alternative measures of audit firm quality. The first is a dichotomous measure based on the Big Eight and non-Big Eight categories. An "upgrade" in quality from a non-Big Eight to a Big Eight audit firm is assigned a value of one and a "downgrade" is assigned a value of zero. The second measure is a continuous size measure defined as the natural logarithm of the ratio of total dollar sales audited by the new auditor to that of the old auditor at the time of the auditor change.[7] Table 1 defines all variables and the predicted direction of association with audit firm size.

Since a dichotomous dependent variable violates OLS regression assumptions, probit is used to estimate the "brand name" models using the categorical Big Eight vs. non-Big Eight dependent variable.[8,9] OLS regression is used for the continuous size models.

Sample Selection and Data Sources

Auditor changes were identified using the 4th to 13th editions of *Who Audits America* [Data Financial Press, 1979–1985]. The sample included auditor changes occurring from June 1978 through April 1985. A total of 3,264 auditor changes were listed. From this total, 676 auditor changes were selected which represented companies for which data were available for the year of the auditor change from both COMPUSTAT and *Q-DATA* microfiche (proxy statements and 10-K annual reports). However, prior years' data needed to compute changes in agency costs were missing in many cases and many of the companies were not publicly traded three years prior to the auditor change. In addition, the client sales audited data were missing for many of the audit firms, particularly in the earlier volumes of *Who Audits America*. Since the COMPUSTAT sample tends to be biased toward larger companies that are more likely to change to or from another Big Eight audit firm, 129 smaller, non-COMPUSTAT companies that changed from a non-Big Eight to another non-Big Eight firm were added to the sample. Financial data for these firms were obtained from *Q-DATA* annual reports and the *Moody's Industrial Manual* or *Moody's Over The Counter Manual*. The final sample, after deleting the com-

panies with missing data, consisted of 196 companies.[10,11] Of these 196 com-

[7] Since ratios close to one might suggest little preference for a different size auditor, the models were also estimated on a reduced sample in which the middle one third of the distribution was excluded. However, since the results were similar to the full model, only the full model results are reported.

[8] The probit procedure relies on maximum likelihood estimators rather than ordinary least squares estimators. The sampling properties of maximum likelihood estimators are described by McKelvey and Zavoina [1975]. Under fairly general conditions, the MLE's are asymptotically normally distributed and are consistent and efficient. Hypotheses on individual variables can, thus, be tested using a Chi-square statistic with one degree of freedom. Alternatively, the significance of individual coefficients can be tested by using a test statistic defined as the ratio of the maximum likelihood estimate to its standard error. This statistic is asymptotically distributed as a t-statistic with $n-k$ degrees of freedom where n is the number of observations and k is the number of parameters being tested.

[9] Logit and OLS were also used to test whether the results were sensitive to the statistical procedure used. The significance levels and signs of all coefficients were very similar to the probit results. Probit was used since the procedure specifically utilizes the ordinality of the dependent variable and it is not clear that this is the case for logit when the dependent variable is dichotomous.

[10] To ensure that the change was not due to an audit firm merger or liquidation, we checked *Who Audits America* to determine whether the old auditor continued to exist under the same name for two years following each auditor change. No changes due to auditor merger were detected. However, six changes were associated with one audit firm that liquidated. Of these changes, two involved a change to a Big Eight firm and four to another regional or national firm. All models were run with these changes deleted and the results are not materially affected by the inclusion of these changes. Although there may have been some instances of client mergers, that would not mean that a related auditor change was involuntary. That is, the decision to change auditors in light of a corporate merger is still a voluntary auditor change.

[11] Four firms reflecting nonrepresentative asset growth (in two cases greater than 1100 percent) over the three years preceding the change were eliminated from the sample as the skewness of the distribution for this sample was clearly distorting the association between GROWTH and choice of auditor. The large asset growth for the firms discarded were not due to data errors; they were simply very small firms that experienced extraordinary growth. Logarithmic or other transformation was not considered appropriate given the extreme skewness and the fact that negative change values also occur. Results for the agency variables were not substantially different, however, whether the full sample of 200 firms was used or the 196-firm final sample for which the results are reported.

TABLE 1
DESCRIPTION OF VARIABLES

Variable Name	Expected Sign	Description
Dependent:		
Brand Name Model		Dependent variable based on either a change from a non-Big Eight to a Big Eight audit firm (=1) or from a Big Eight to a non-Big Eight audit firm (=0).
Continuous Size Model		Dependent variable defined as the natural logarithm of the ratio of combined sales of public companies audited by the new auditor to that by the old auditor in the year of the auditor change as reported in *Who Audits America*.
Independent:		
MGRSK	+	Indicator variable indicating the amount of a company's outstanding common stock owned by management (officers and directors) the year preceding auditor change (0=five to 20 percent, 1=less than five percent or greater than 20 percent).
MGRSKCHG	+	Change in MGRSK for the three years prior to auditor change. If manager stock ownership was in the range of five to 20 percent in year preceding auditor change but outside this range three years prior, MGRSKCHG was coded "1," if the opposite was the case a "−1" was assigned, and if there was no change in status, a "0" was assigned.
BONUS	+	Indicator variable indicating the existence of an accounting-based incentive bonus plan for top executives in year preceding auditor change (0=no, 1=yes).
BONUSCHG	+	A three-level variable indicating whether a bonus plan was implemented during the three years preceding the auditor change (1=yes), there was no change in the existence of the bonus plan during the preceding three years (=0), or a bonus plan was terminated during the preceding three years (=−1).
LGOWN	−	Diffusion of ownership, proxied for by the percentage of outstanding shares owned by the largest single shareholder. (1 if greater than ten percent, 0 if less.)
LGOWNCHG	−	A three-level variable indicating change in LGOWN prior to the auditor change. If largest ownership four years prior to change was less than ten percent but was more than ten percent the year prior to change, LGOWNCHG was coded "1," if the opposite was the case it was coded "−1," and if there was no change it was coded "0."
LTDBT	−	Ratio of long-term debt (excluding deferred income taxes) to total assets for the year preceding the auditor change.
LTDBTCHG	−	The ratio of long-term debt to assets for year preceding the auditor change minus the same ratio three years earlier.

TABLE 1—*Continued*

Variable Name	Expected Sign	Description
NEWISSUE	+	Total dollar amount of publicly issued stock and debt for two fiscal years after year of new auditor's initial engagement, deflated by total assets in year preceding auditor change.
SIZE	+	Natural logarithm of total assets at end of the year preceding auditor change.
GROWTH	+	Total assets year preceding the auditor change minus total assets three years earlier deflated by total assets three years earlier, expressed as a percentage change, where total assets are in raw (not logarithmic) form.

panies, 194 were used in the "continuous size" OLS models. Since only the upgrades and downgrades were used in the "brand name" probit models, 118 same-size group changes (i.e., Big Eight to Big Eight or non-Big Eight to non-Big Eight) were excluded leaving 78 firms for testing, 57 upgrades, and 21 downgrades. Details of the sample are summarized in Table 2.

RESULTS

Table 3 reports descriptive statistics for all variables for the "brand name" sample of 78 auditor changes. These descriptive statistics are comparable to those for the "continuous size" sample. Therefore, descriptive statistics for the continuous size model are not reported. LGOWN and LTDBTCHG have opposite than expected associations with auditor changes. Otherwise, the differences in means for upgrades vs. downgrades are in the predicted directions.

The "brand name" probit estimates are reported in Table 4 for the three model specifications. Table 5 reports the same three model specifications for the "continuous size" OLS estimations. Spearman bivariate correlations among independent variables are reported in

Table 6 for the "continuous size" sample. These are similar to those for the "brand name" sample which are not reported.

The brand name model (Table 4) is not significant when using "levels" of agency variables; however, both the "changes" in agency variables model and the composite variables model are significant at the .05 level. Since the "levels" model is not significant, it will not be discussed further. The composite model has slightly greater explanatory power than the "changes" model as indicated by the probit (psuedo) R-square and classification accuracy; however, an incremental Chi-square test indicated that the "levels" variables were not significant (as a group) when added to the "changes" variables.[12] In the "changes"

---

[12] McKelvey and Zavoina [1975] describe the probit estimated R-square as an indication of how well the data fit the presumed underlying theoretical distribution. This measure should not be interpreted in the conventional manner since OLS regressions indicated R-squares ranging from about .03 for the "levels" model to .11 for the "changes" model, though the coefficient significance levels and overall model significance were very similar to the probit results. Considering the probable poor fit in the OLS models due to violation of underlying regression assumptions, the actual goodness of fit is probably somewhere between the OLS and probit estimates.

TABLE 2

DESCRIPTION OF SAMPLE SELECTION

Panel A: Sample Selection Procedures

Total auditor changes listed in *Who Audits America* (June 1978 through June 1985)	3,264
Auditor changes for which COMPUSTAT data, proxy statements, and 10-K reports were available for year of change.	676
Added 129 non-Big Eight to non-Big Eight changes for which *Q-DATA* annual reports and *Moody's Industrial Manual* (or other Moody's manuals, as appropriate) were available, but not COMPUSTAT.	129
Total preliminary sample	805
Eliminated due to missing data for three years preceding auditor change and data on total dollar sales audited.	609
Final sample	196*

Panel B: Classification of Auditor Changes

Non-Big Eight auditor to Big Eight auditor	57
Big Eight auditor to non-Big Eight auditor	21
Changed to same-size auditor group	118
Total	196*

* For two of these 196 audit firms no details were available in *Who Audits America* to calculate total dollar sales audited which resulted in a sample of 194 for the "continuous size" sample. However, these two observations are included in the "brand name" sample.

model BONUSCHG, LGOWNCHG, and GROWTH are individually significant at the .05 level, and NEWISSUE is nearly significant at the .10 level. In the composite model BONUSCHG, LGOWN-CHG, LTDBT, LTDBTCHG, SIZE, and GROWTH are all significant at the .10 level or less, and NEWISSUE is nearly significant. Of the significant variables only LTDBTCHG has an unexpected sign, and, overall, three of the agency cost proxies are significant in the predicted direction.

The continuous size model (Table 5) broadly parallels the brand name model. Using "levels" of agency variables the model is not significant, but the "changes" in agency variables model

and the composite variables model are both significant at the .10 level. The individually significant variables are two agency proxies, BONUSCHG and NEW-ISSUE, along with GROWTH. There is little difference in explanatory power between the "changes" and composite models, thus, it appears that the composite model is driven entirely by the "changes" in agency variables. An incremental F-test for the "levels" variables was not significant when they were added as a group to the "changes" variables.

Collinearity is not a serious problem among the independent variables. Table 6 indicates that among the "level" variables, bivariate Spearman correlations

TABLE 3

DESCRIPTIVE STATISTICS FOR "BRAND NAME" SAMPLE (1978–1985)
("LEVELS" OF VARIABLES FOR YEAR PRECEDING AUDITOR CHANGE AND "CHANGES"
IN VARIABLES OVER THREE YEARS PRECEDING AUDITOR CHANGE)

Variables*	Full Sample (N=78)				Non-Big Eight to Big Eight (N=57)				Big Eight to Non-Big Eight (N=21)			
	Mean	S.D.	Min.	Max.	Mean	S.D.	Min.	Max.	Mean	S.D.	Min.	Max.
MGRSK	.744	.439	.000	1.000	.772	.423	.000	1.000	.667	.483	.000	1.00
MGRSKCHG	-.013	.470	-1.000	1.000	.035	.421	-1.000	1.000	-.143	.573	-1.000	1.00
BONUS	.423	.497	.000	1.000	.456	.503	.000	1.000	.333	.483	.000	1.00
BONUSCHG	.154	.512	-1.000	1.000	.211	.526	-1.000	1.000	.000	.447	-1.000	1.00
LGOWN	.859	.350	.000	1.000	.877	.331	.000	1.000	.810	.402	.000	1.00
LGOWNCHG	.038	.340	-1.000	1.000	.000	.327	-1.000	1.000	.143	.359	.000	1.00
LTDBT	.180	.139	.000	.530	.163	.123	.000	.432	.228	.169	.002	.53
LTDBTCHG	.000	.127	-.279	.413	.005	.126	-.279	.286	-.011	.131	-.214	.41
NEWISSUE	.071	.292	.000	2.132	.094	.339	.000	2.132	.011	.049	.000	.22
SIZE	65.219	112.640	1.523	696.824	68.567	116.345	1.523	696.824	56.132	104.058	2.208	472.93
GROWTH	66.472	90.475	-77.489	342.515	79.969	92.312	-76.188	342.515	29.836	75.672	-77.489	206.86

* Definition of variables: (See Table 1 for complete description)

MGRSK = Percentage of stock owned by managers and directors, 0 = five to 20 percent ownership; 1 = less than five percent or greater than 20 percent

MGRSKCHG = Change in stock owned by managers and directors, 1 indicates a change from outside the 5-20 percent range into the range; -1 indicates a change from within the 5-20 percent to outside the range; 0 indicates no change across ranges

BONUS = Existence of a bonus incentive compensation plan (0 = no, 1 = yes)

BONUSCHG = Change in existence of bonus plan (1 = initiation of a new plan, 0 = no change in status of bonus plan; -1 = termination of plan)

LGOWN = Percentage of stock ownership by largest single owner (1 if greater than ten percent; 0 if less than ten percent)

LGOWNCHG = Change in stock ownership by largest single owner (1 indicates a change from less than ten percent to greater than ten percent; -1 is the opposite change; 0 is no change in the ten percent value).

LTDBT = Leverage, debt divided by total assets

LTDBTCHG = Change in leverage ratio

NEWISSUE = New security issues after auditor change deflated by total assets

SIZE = Total assets (logarithmic form)

GROWTH = Percentage change in total assets

TABLE 4

PROBIT REGRESSION ESTIMATES FOR "BRAND NAME" MODELS ($N=78$)
(DEPENDENT VARIABLE IS CHANGE FROM A NON-BIG EIGHT FIRM TO A BIG EIGHT FIRM (1)
OR CHANGE FROM A BIG EIGHT TO A NON—BIG EIGHT FIRM (0))

Variables	Predicted Sign	Model One Pre-change Levels of Independent Variables		Model Two Three-year Changes in Independent Variables		Model Three Composite Model	
		Coefficient	Asymptotic t-statistics	Coefficient	Asymptotic t-statistics	Coefficient	Asymptotic t-statistics
CONSTANT		.170	.28	.329	1.64	−.284	−.35
MGRSK	+	.304	.76			−.150	−.26
MGRSKCHG	+			.244	.65	.074	.15
BONUS	+	.313	0.89			.134	.29
BONUSCHG	+			.683	1.85**	.648	1.35*
LGOWN	−	.063	.13			.692	1.06
LGOWNCHG	−			−1.018	−1.80**	−1.166	−1.85**
LTDBT	−	−2.633	−2.13**			−3.338	−2.20**
LTDBTCHG	−			1.394	.94	2.743	1.59*
NEWISSUE	+	2.518	1.05	2.885	1.23	3.853	1.21
SIZE	+	.150	1.12			.213	1.32*
GROWTH	+			.004	1.83**	.005	2.10**
Probit psuedo R^2		.397		.517		.658	
Model Chi-Square statistic (two-tailed test)		9.59 (6 df)		15.54** (6 df)		23.02** (11 df)	
Percent Correctly Predicted:							
Overall		71.8		73.1		75.6	
Non-Big Eight to Big Eight		91.2		93.0		89.5	
Big Eight to non-Big Eight		19.0		19.0		38.1	

Note: Definition of independent variables: (See Table 1 for complete description)
　　　　MGRSK = Percentage of stock owned by managers and directors
　　MGRSKCHG = Change in stock owned by managers and directors
　　　　BONUS = Existence of a bonus incentive compensation plan
　　BONUSCHG = Change in existence of bonus plan
　　　　LGOWN = Percentage of stock ownership by largest single owner
　LGOWNCHG = Change in stock ownership by largest single owner
　　　　LTDBT = Leverage, debt divided by total assets
　　LTDBTCHG = Change in leverage
　　NEWISSUE = New security issues after auditor change
　　　　SIZE = Total assets (logarithmic form)
　　GROWTH = Percentage change in total assets
Levels of significance (one-tailed tests):
　* $p < .10$
　** $p < .05$
　*** $p < .01$

are no greater than $\bar{r} = .30$, and among the "change" variables the correlations are no greater than $\bar{r} = .19$. As might be expected, there is a larger correlation between the level of a variable and the related change in the variable.[13] For

example, MGRSK and MGRSKCHG, BONUS and BONUSCHG, and LGOWN

[13] If a firm's agency costs have changed over a three-year period, it follows *ceteris paribus* that the level of agency costs at the end of the three-year period will be correlated with the change (in a cross-section of firms).

and LGOWNCHG are all fairly highly correlated ($r > .47$). However, examination of the collinearity diagnostics suggested by Belsley et al. [1980] indicates that there is no serious degradation of the regressions due to collinearity among the data and, also, that the results are not being driven by outliers, after deletion of the four firms with nonrepresentative asset growth as discussed in fn. 11.

Effects of Client Size and Growth

As discussed above, it is possible that client size and/or growth could confound the empirical tests of the agency variables. For this reason, the "levels" model in Tables 4 and 5 is tested for consistency across client size and the "changes" model in Tables 4 and 5 is tested for consistency across client growth. A Chow test [Chow, 1960] is used to determine if the model parameters are consistent across the upper/lower halves of client size and growth.[14] Median SIZE and GROWTH are used to divide the sample for testing. None of the F-statistics from the Chow tests are significant at the .10 level. Thus, one cannot reject the hypothesis that parameters are equal across client size in the "levels" model and across client growth in the "changes" model. The Chow tests provide evidence that agency-related variables are associated with auditor choice independently of client size and growth.

A further analysis determines the relative explanatory power of the agency-related variables *alone* compared with client size and growth *alone*, as well as the incremental explanatory power of the agency-related variables over and above client size and growth. The composite models in Tables 4 and 5 are used for these analyses.

Results of reestimating the probit models (Table 4) are as follows: The

agency variables *alone* had a probit R-square of .595 and classification accuracy of 75.6 percent; SIZE and GROWTH *alone* had a probit R-square of .142 and an overall classification accuracy of 74.4 percent. The incremental effect of adding the agency variables was significant at the .05 level (Chi-square of 17.23, nine degrees of freedom) and the probit R-square increased from .142 to .658. The overall classification accuracy only increased from 74.4 percent to 75.6 percent, but there was a marked improvement in downgrade classification as SIZE and GROWTH alone classified only 4.8 percent of downgrades compared with 38.1 percent for the full model that included agency-related variables. That is, the incremental effect of the agency variables did not improve classification of upgrades but substantially improved the classification of downgrades.

Results of reestimating the OLS continuous size models (Table 5) are as follows: the agency variables *alone* had an adjusted R-square of .01; SIZE and GROWTH *alone* had an adjusted R-square of .036; the incremental effect of adding the agency variables was not significant even at the .10 level, and the adjusted R-square only increased from .036 to .040. In the continuous size model, then, the agency variables are not incrementally significant when added to size and growth.

In sum, these additional tests indicate that the agency-related variables *alone* explain auditor changes about the same as SIZE and GROWTH *alone*. Because of the ambiguity in interpreting client size and growth, a conservative approach is taken by assuming *no* relation

[14] For the Chow test, the brand name model had to be estimated using OLS regression rather than probit in order to derive the standard errors required for the test.

Francis and Wilson

TABLE 5

OLS REGRESSION ESTIMATES FOR "CONTINUOUS SIZE" MODELS ($N=194$)
(DEPENDENT VARIABLE IS NATURAL LOG OF THE RATIO OF DOLLAR SALES
AUDITED BY NEW AUDITOR TO THAT BY THE OLD AUDITOR)

Variables	Predicted Sign	Model One Pre-change Levels of Independent Variables		Model Two Three-year Changes in Independent Variables		Model Three Composite Model	
		Coefficient	t-statistic	Coefficient	t-statistic	Coefficient	t-statistic
CONSTANT		.650	.61	.547	1.54	.375	.33
MGRSK	+	.491	.74			.224	.28
MGRSKCHG	+			.555	.94	.350	.48
BONUS	+	.520	.87			−.384	−.54
BONUSCHG	+			1.131	2.00**	1.361	1.91**
LGOWN	−	.565	.77			.879	1.03
LGOWNCHG	−			−.352	−.46	−.763	−.85
LTDBT	−	−1.268	−0.93			−1.131	−.83
LTDBTCHG	−			.018	.28	.013	.20
NEWISSUE	+	1.118	1.33*	1.104	1.33*	.932	1.11
SIZE	+	−.049	−.26			−.084	−.45
GROWTH	+			.009	2.63***	.009	2.76***
R^2 (adj.)		−.004		.045		.040	
Model F-statistic (two-tailed test)		0.89 (6,187 df)		2.52** (6,187 df)		1.73* (11,182 df)	

Note: Definition of independent variables: (See Table 1 for complete description)
    MGRSK = Percentage of stock owned by managers and directors
    MGRSKCHG = Change in stock owned by managers and directors
    BONUS = Existence of a bonus incentive compensation plan
    BONUSCHG = Change in existence of bonus plan
    LGOWN = Percentage of stock ownership by largest single owner
    LGOWNCHG = Change in stock ownership by largest single owner
    LTDBT = Leverage, debt divided by total assets
    LTDBTCHG = Change in leverage
    NEWISSUE = New security issues after auditor change
    SIZE = Total assets (logarithmic form)
    GROWTH = Percentage change in total assets
Levels of significance (one-tailed tests)
  * $p < .10$
  ** $p < .05$
  *** $p < .01$

between client size/growth and agency costs. Using this framework, the agency variables have explanatory power (above and beyond SIZE and GROWTH) but only in the brand name model. As noted above, the agency proxies are incrementally useful primarily in classifying downgrades.

Discussion

Four matters are of primary interest: (1) comparison of the brand name versus continuous size models, (2) overall importance of the agency variables, (3) individually significant agency variables, and (4) comparison of the "levels" and "changes" variables.

TABLE 6

SPEARMAN CORRELATION COEFFICIENTS
CONTINUOUS SIZE SAMPLE ($N=194$)

Variables		X1	X2	X3	X4	X5	X6	X7	X8	X9	X10
MGRSK	(X1)										
MGRSKCHG	(X2)	.55*									
BONUS	(X3)	-.05	-.05								
BONUSCHG	(X4)	-.07	.07	.57*							
LGOWN	(X5)	.30*	.02	.01	.02						
LGOWNCHG	(X6)	-.00	-.05	.08	.02	.48*					
LTDBT	(X7)	-.12*	-.03	.11	-.01	-.16*	.08				
LTDBTCHG	(X8)	.06	.11	-.04	-.03	.07	.08	.37*			
NEWISSUE	(X9)	-.01	-.06	-.06	-.03	.02	.02	-.01	-.04		
SIZE	(X10)	-.14*	-.02	.18*	.15*	-.20*	.03	.29*	.00	.06	
GROWTH	(X11)	.04	-.02	.06	.07	.03	.01	.14*	.19*	.17*	.10

* Significant at the .10 level (two-tail)
Definition of variables: (See Table 1 for complete description)
    MGRSK = Percentage of stock owned by managers and directors
MGRSKCHG = Change in stock owned by managers and directors
    BONUS = Existence of a bonus incentive compensation plan
BONUSCHG = Change in existence of bonus plan
    LGOWN = Percentage of stock ownership by largest single owner
LGOWNCHG = Change in stock ownership by largest single owner
    LTDBT = Leverage, debt divided by total assets
 LTDBTCHG = Change in leverage
 NEWISSUE = New security issues after auditor change
     SIZE = Total assets (logarithmic form)
  GROWTH = Percentage change in total assets

Brand Name vs. Continuous Size Models. The tests consistently support the brand name model of auditor quality differentiation but not the continuous size model. While the agency variables as a group are significant in both models, they are significant after including client size/growth *only* in the brand name model. In the brand name composite model, four individual agency variables are significant at the .10 level (and NEWISSUE is nearly significant), whereas, only one agency variable is significant in the continuous size composite model. It also appears that the brand name model has substantially greater explanatory power, though a direct comparison of the brand name versus continuous size models cannot be based on *R*-square statistics since each model uses a different dependent variable. [15]

Agency Variables. The agency variables, as a group, are significant and explain about the same amount of cross-sectional variance in the models as do client size and growth by themselves. However, the agency variables as a group are incrementally significant after client size and growth, only in the brand name model. Therefore, assessment of the individual variables will be confined to the brand name model. The number of individually significant agency proxies is greater than in prior studies. Five agency-related variables in Table 4 are either significant or nearly significant at the .10 level: BONUSCHG, LGOWN-CHG, LTDBT, LTDBTCHG, and NEWISSUE. [16] All of the model variables have the expected sign with the exception of LTDBTCHG. Contrary to predictions, there is a significant positive association between a change in the firm's leverage level and the demand for a Big Eight brand name auditor. Yet the level of leverage (LTDBT) at the time of the auditor change is consistent with

theoretical predictions. Apart from this anomaly, the individual variables are at least weakly supportive of the individual agency arguments except for managerial stock ownership. As indicated earlier, managerial ownership is tested as both a continuous variable and as a nonlinear indicator variable based on the work of Morck et al. [1986], and there is no indication that managerial ownership (measured either way) affects the demand for a quality-differentiated auditor.

Levels vs. Changes in Agency Variables. In both the brand name and continuous size models, the specification using "levels" of agency variables is not significant while the specification using

[15] Table 4 evidences that changes to or from brand name Big Eight auditors (upgrades/downgrades) are associated with agency cost variables. We reestimated the brand name sample of auditor changes using the continuous size measure as the dependent variable and obtained results broadly consistent with those reported in Table 4. We then deleted the "brand-name-switches" from the continuous size model to see if the continuous size model was significant for auditor changes *other than* brand-name upgrades/downgrades. The reestimated model was not significant which suggests that the results in Table 5 are dominated by the effect of brand name upgrades/downgrades. This is further evidence that the brand name model is significant and that the continuous size model is not significant.

[16] The alternative use of an indicator variable for a new issue within two years after the auditor change was consistently significant across models and the overall performance of the models was similar to those reported. In addition, a variable indicating the post-change vs. pre-change difference in issue magnitude was not significant in any model. However, one would not necessarily expect pre-change issues followed by no post-change issues to influence the choice of auditor. To further assess the effects of pre- vs. post-change issues, nonparametric tests were performed on the magnitudes of issues before and after the auditor changes. A Mann-Whitney *U*-test indicated no significant difference in pre-change issues between the lower one third and upper one third groups based on continuous auditor size. The same test for post-change issues between the two groups revealed a significant difference at the .05 level. In a second test, Wilcoxon Signed Rank tests conducted on the full sample ($N = 196$) found significant differences between pre-change and post-change issues. Thus, these univariate tests suggest that the timing and relative magnitudes of new security issues may have more influence on auditor choice than the multiple regression models indicate.

"changes" in agency variables is significant at the .05 level for both models. Consistent with this is the fact that the composite model (which includes both "levels" and "changes" in agency variables) is not significantly different from the "changes" model in either Table 4 or Table 5. In the auditor change framework set out earlier in the paper (where the decision is first made to change auditors and then the new auditor is chosen) the significant results using "changes" in agency variables is consistent with agency costs *both* motivating the auditor change *and* affecting the choice of a new auditor. However, the incremental effect of the agency variables above client size and growth is fairly small and is confined to explaining downgrades.

SUMMARY AND CONCLUSIONS

This study examined the possible linkage between agency costs and demand for quality-differentiated audits. Audit firm quality was defined as a categoric variable, the brand name Big Eight vs. non-Big Eight auditors, and as a continuous size variable based on total client sales audited by the audit firm. The tests provided support for the hypothesized association between agency cost proxies and the choice of a brand name Big Eight auditor after controlling for the effects of client size and growth; however, no consistent association was evident using the "continuous size" proxy for audit quality. The individual agency cost proxies that were at least weakly significant were the presence of accounting-based incentive bonus plans, diffusion of ownership, leverage, and new issues of securities following the auditor change.

A final *caveat* concerns the overall explanatory power of the models (including the incremental effect of agency variables). Holding aside possible measurement error problems, the results indicate that *neither* client size/growth *nor* agency costs explain a large portion of the demand for larger-sized or Big Eight auditors. While agency costs appear, at the margin, to affect auditor choice above and beyond client size/growth, the auditor selection process seems to be more complex than modelled in this and related studies.

REFERENCES

Alchian, A., and H. Demsetz, "Production, Information Costs, and Economic Organization," *American Economic Review* (December 1972), pp. 777–795.
American Institute of Certified Public Accountants, *Commission on Auditors' Responsibilities: Report, Conclusions, and Recommendations* (AICPA, 1978).
———, *Report of the Special Committee on Small and Medium Sized Firms* (AICPA, 1980).
Bedingfield, J., and S. Loeb, "Auditor Changes—An Examination," *Journal of Accountancy* (March 1974), pp. 66–69.
Belsley, D., E. Kuh, and R. Welsch, *Regression Diagnostics: Identifying Influential Data and Sources of Collinearity* (John Wiley, 1980).
Carpenter, C. G., and R. H. Strawser, "Displacement of Auditors When Clients Go Public," *Journal of Accountancy* (June 1971), pp. 55–58.
Chow, G., "Tests of Equality Between Sets of Coefficients in Two Linear Regressions," *Econometrica* (July 1960), pp. 591–605.
DeAngelo, L. E., "Auditor Size and Audit Quality," *Journal of Accounting and Economics* (December 1981), pp. 183–199.
Demsetz, H., "The Structure of Ownership and the Theory of the Firm," *Journal of Law and Economics* (June 1983), pp. 375–390.
———, and K. Lehn, "The Structure of Corporate Ownership: Causes and Consequences," *Journal of Political Economy* (December 1985), pp. 1155–1177.

Dhaliwal, D., G. Salamon, and E. Smith, "The Effect of Owner Versus Management Control on the Choice of Accounting Methods," *Journal of Accounting and Economics* (July 1982), pp. 41–53.

Dopuch, N., "The Demand for Quality-Differentiated Audit Services in an Agency Cost Setting: An Empirical Investigation, Discussion Comments," *Auditing Research Symposium* (University of Illinois, 1984), pp. 253–263.

———, and D. Simunic, "The Nature of Competition in the Auditing Profession: A Descriptive and Normative View," in J. W. Buckley and J. F. Weston, Eds., *Regulation and the Accounting Profession* (Lifetime Learning, 1980), pp. 77–94.

———, "Competition in Auditing: An Assessment," *Symposium on Auditing Research IV* (University of Illinois, 1982), pp. 401–450.

Eichenseher, J. W., and D. Shields, "Corporate Capital Structure and Auditor 'Fit,'" Working paper (University of Wisconsin, 1986).

———, "The Correlates of CPA Firm Changes for Publicly-Held Corporations," *Auditing: A Journal of Practice and Theory* (Spring 1983), pp. 23–37.

Fama, E. F., and M. C. Jensen, "Separation of Ownership and Control," *Journal of Law and Economics* (June 1983a), pp. 301–326.

———, "Agency Problems and Residual Claims," *Journal of Law and Economics* (June 1983b), pp. 327–349.

Francis, J. R., "The Effect of Audit Firm Size on Audit Prices: A Study of the Australian Market," *Journal of Accounting and Economics* (August 1984), pp. 133–151.

———, and D. T. Simon, "A Test of Audit Pricing in the Small-Client Segment of the U.S. Audit Market," THE ACCOUNTING REVIEW (January 1987), pp. 145–157.

———, and D. J. Stokes, "Audit Prices, Product Differentiation, and Scale Economies: Further Evidence from the Australian Market," *Journal of Accounting Research* (Autumn 1986), pp. 383–393.

Healy, P., and T. Lys, "Auditor Changes Following Big Eight Takeovers of Non-Big Eight Audit Firms," *Journal of Accounting and Public Policy* (Winter 1986), pp. 251–265.

Jensen, M. C., and W. H., Meckling, "Theory of the Firm: Managerial Behavior, Agency Costs, and Ownership Structure," *Journal of Financial Economics* (October 1976), pp. 305–360.

Johnson, W. B., and T. Lys, "The Market for Audit Services: Evidence From Voluntary Auditor Changes," Working paper (Northwestern University, 1986).

Klein, B., R. Crawford, and A. Alchian, "Vertical Integration, Appropriable Rents, and the Competitive Contracting Process," *Journal of Law and Economics* (October 1978), pp. 297–326.

———, and K. Leffler, "The Role of Market Forces in Assuring Contractual Performance," *Journal of Political Economy* (August 1981), pp. 615–641.

Libby, R., "Bankers' and Auditors' Perceptions of the Message Communicated by the Audit Report," *Journal of Accounting Research* (Spring 1979), pp. 99–122.

McKelvey, R. D., and W. Zavoina, "A Statistical Model for the Analysis of Ordinal Level Dependent Variables," *Journal of Mathematical Sociology* (No. 1, 1975), pp. 103–120.

Morck, R., A. Shleifer, and R. W. Vishny, "Management Ownership and Corporate Performance: An Empirical Analysis," Working paper (University of Chicago, 1986).

Ng, D., "An Information Economics Analysis of Financial Reporting and External Auditing," THE ACCOUNTING REVIEW (October 1978), pp. 910–920.

Palmrose, Z., "The Demand for Quality-Differentiated Audit Services in an Agency-Cost Setting: An Empirical Investigation," *Auditing Research Symposium* (University of Illinois, 1984), pp. 229–252.

———, "Audit Fees and Auditor Size: Further Evidence," *Journal of Accounting Research* (Spring 1986), pp. 97–110.

———, "An Analysis of Auditor Litigation and Audit Service Quality," THE ACCOUNTING REVIEW (January 1988), pp. 55–73.

Rubin, M., "Municipal Audit Fee Determinants," THE ACCOUNTING REVIEW (April 1988), pp. 219–236.

Shockley, R., "Perceptions of Auditors' Independence: An Empirical Analysis," THE ACCOUNTING REVIEW (October 1981), pp. 785–800.

Simon, D. T., and J. R. Francis, "The Effects of Auditor Change on Audit Fees: Tests of Price Cutting and Price Recovery," THE ACCOUNTING REVIEW (April 1988), pp. 255–269.

Simunic, D., and M. Stein, *Product Differentiation in Auditing: A Study of Auditor Effects in the Market for New Issues* (The Canadian Certified General Accountants' Research Foundation, 1987).

Smith, C. W., and J. B. Warner, "On Financial Contracting: An Analysis of Bond Covenants," *Journal of Financial Economics* (June 1979), pp. 159–172.

Stevens, M., *The Big Eight* (MacMillan, 1981).

Titman, S., and B. Trueman, "Information Quality and the Valuation of New Issues," *Journal of Accounting and Economics* (June 1986), pp. 159–172.

United States Senate, "Improving the Accountability of Publicly Owned Corporations and Their Auditors," *Report of the Subcommittee on Reports, Accounting, and Management of the Committee on Governmental Affairs* (U.S. Government Printing Office, November, 1977).

Watts, R. L., "Corporate Financial Statements: A Product of the Market and Political Processes," *Australian Journal of Management* (April 1977), pp. 52–75.

———, and J. L. Zimmerman, "Agency Problems, Auditing, and the Theory of the Firm: Some Evidence," *Journal of Law and Economics* (October 1983), pp. 613–633.

[14]

Journal of Accounting and Economics 12 (1990) 281-308. North-Holland

THE MARKET FOR AUDIT SERVICES
Evidence from Voluntary Auditor Changes*

W. Bruce JOHNSON and Thomas LYS

Northwestern University, Evanston, IL 60208, USA

Received October 1987, final version received March 1989

This paper argues that audit firms achieve competitive advantages through specialization, and that clients purchase audit services from the least cost supplier. Client–auditor realignments thus represent efficient responses to changes in client operations and activities over time. Results obtained from analyzing the financial characteristics and share price performance of corporations that changed auditors between 1973 and 1982 support the view that realignments can generally be attributed to cross-temporal changes in client characteristics and differences in audit firm cost structures.

1. Introduction

This paper examines whether changes in clients' financing, investing, and operating characteristics are related to voluntary auditor realignments. We argue that economic considerations affect client–auditor alignments: individual audit firms obtain competitive advantages through specialization, and clients purchase audit services from the least costly supplier. The incumbent auditor's competitive advantage for an existing client can be eroded over time by changes in the client's operations and activities. Voluntary auditor realignment is a natural consequence of these market forces: when the incumbent's competitive advantage is lost, the client will change to a less costly supplier.

A sample of roughly 600 realignments occurring from 1973 through 1982 indicates that a voluntary auditor realignment is not an isolated event but occurs in conjunction with shifts in clients' financing and operating characteristics. The data are consistent with the notion that realignment decisions are

*The authors would like to thank Ray Ball, Paul Healy, Robert Magee, Terry Shevlin, and particularly Richard Lambert, Chee Chow (the referee), and Ross Watts (the editor), and workshop participants at the University of Chicago, Massachusetts Institute of Technology, University of Michigan, and Washington University for providing insightful comments and suggestions. The financial support provided by the Accounting Research Center of the Kellogg Graduate School of Management is gratefully acknowledged.

related to an erosion of the incumbent's competitive advantage. In addition, realignment clients exhibit lower share price and profit performance prior to changing auditors when compared to nonrealignment companies, but we find no contemporaneous abnormal daily stock price reaction to auditor realignment announcements. Nor do we find evidence of changes in clients' accounting policies following realignment.

The remainder of the paper is organized into five sections. Section 2 describes the economics of client–auditor realignment decisions and identifies client factors that determine the incumbent auditor's competitive advantage. Section 3 describes the sample selection procedures. Section 4 documents the influence of client and auditor characteristics on realignment decisions. Section 5 examines the daily stock price response to realignment announcements and the long-term share price performance of realignment clients. The major findings of the study are summarized and conclusions are drawn in section 6.

2. The economics of client–auditor realignment

External audits function as part of the efficient technology for organizing business enterprises [Jensen and Meckling (1976), Benston (1979), Watts and Zimmerman (1986)], and standard economic considerations presumably dictate the alignment of clients and audit firms. More than 400 accounting firms currently supply audit services to publicly-traded domestic corporations [AICPA (1986)], and it may seem that a given client could satisfy its demand by hiring any one of these firms.

Two explanations dominate the literature on differences among audit firms. One perspective focuses on specialization in audit technology [Dopuch and Simunic (1980), Danos and Eichenseher (1982), Eichenseher (1984)], while the other perspective emphasizes audit quality and reputation [DeAngelo (1981), Chow and Rice (1982), Schwartz and Menon (1985)]. These two perspectives differ in several important respects, but share a common view of audit engagement decisions: clients purchase audit services from the least cost supplier and change auditors in response to changes in the amount or type of services required.

Audit firm investments in specialized resources (e.g., employee recruiting and training, branch offices, statistical software, and decision aids) yield economies of scale and scope for services rendered to particular market segments.[1] These resources must often be acquired in combination if the

---

[1] For example, 'branch office' investments reduce the incremental cost of auditing clients with geographically dispersed division, but fixed audit costs are increased because of the need to coordinate and monitor multi-office activities.

economies available from any single investment are to be fully utilized.[2] Cost structure variations also occur because of differences in auditor's 'brand name' resulting from investments in expertise and quality control mechanisms. These investments serve as a collateral bond: accounting firms that supply levels of expertise or independence below the market's expectation dissipate the value of their reputation [Klein and Leffler (1981)].

Market competition induces clients and audit firms to align themselves to achieve efficient utilization of specialized resources and 'brand name' investments. Accounting firms that normally audit small, unregulated clients may be unable to offer their services at competitive prices to large, geographically dispersed corporations because they lack the economies available to firms already serving this market segment. Conversely, firms that typically audit large geographically dispersed clients will be unwilling to allocate productive resources to small localized corporations (at competitive prices) unless this reduces the cost of resources that would otherwise remain idle. Auditors of comparable size and clientele mix can thus be expected to have similar cost structures.

Changes in the client's operations and activities over time can erode the incumbent auditor's competitive advantage. Rapid growth, for example, typically entails substantial increases in transaction volume and accounting complexity, in the geographical dispersion of activities, and in the decentralization of financial reporting and control systems, and rapid growth is often achieved through acquisitions of existing businesses using funds obtained from capital markets. These factors can disrupt the economies previously available to the incumbent, enabling the client to obtain fee reductions (or increased service for the same fee) through realignment.[3] Conversely, when the level and scope of activities undergo significant contraction, clients can achieve audit fee reductions by changing to audit firms with relatively few specialized resources.

Changes in client financial and operating characteristics provide one explanation for auditor realignment. Clients that replace their incumbent auditor with a substantially larger (smaller) firm are predicted to exhibit systematic growth (contraction) in their activities around the time of realignment. On the

---

[2] For example, public accounting firms can (in principle) acquire the technical skills needed to efficiently audit the voluminous transactions and complex accounting practices of large corporations without committing resources to branch offices, SEC compliance expertise, or other specialized resources. As a practical matter, however, large corporations are likely to register with the SEC, access capital markets on a regular basis, and have geographically dispersed operations.

[3] Auditor realignment imposes transaction costs on both the client and the incumbent auditor [DeAngelo (1981), Magee and Tseng (1987)]. Clients lose the opportunity cost of resources (including managerial time) devoted to familiarizing new auditors with enterprise reporting systems and operations. Clients will therefore voluntarily change auditors when the incremental benefit of hiring a new audit firm (reduced fees for a given level of services rendered) outweighs the cost of realignment.

other hand, clients that replace an incumbent with an audit firm of similar size are predicted to be responding to rotation policies or other forces.[4]

Our analysis also has implications for the behavior of security prices around announcements of voluntary auditor changes. Because audit fees are small relative to equity values, any contemporaneous share price reaction to realignment is likely to be attributable to factors other than fee savings.[5] One possibility is that realignment decisions convey information about future changes in corporate production, investment, and financing activities.

3. Sample selection

A preliminary sample of 3,751 auditor changes was compiled from corporate 8-K filings reported by *Disclosure Journal* (January 1973 through April 1975) and *Who Audits America* (January 1976 through December 1982). Auditor realignments were excluded from the final sample if:

(i) The client was not among the companies contained in the 1984 Compustat Annual Industrial, Over-the-Counter, or Research data files (2,797 cases or 74.6%).

(ii) The client was a public utility or was primarily engaged in banking, insurance or diversified financial services (74 cases or 2.0%).

(iii) The client was acquired by another company in the fiscal year of realignment and the new auditor was the auditor of record of the acquirer (43 cases or 1.1%).

(iv) The realignment involved auditors of the client's subsidiaries but not the client's auditor of record (52 cases or 1.4%).

(v) The realignment occurred in conjunction with the acquisition (merger) of the former auditor into another public accounting firm, bankruptcy court or trustee intervention, or incumbent withdrawal precipitated by a fee arrearage (87 cases or 2.3%).

These selection criteria reduced the preliminary sample to 698 realignments.

---

[4] For example, the incumbent auditor can also be outbid by a firm that adopts an innovative (less costly) audit technology or by a firm with idle capacity and thus with lower opportunity costs. In such cases, however, realignment would not be associated with changes in the client's activities. Similarly, periodic auditor rotation presumably reduces client agency costs because previously undetected or nonreported accounting irregularities are likely to be discovered during intensive initial audits. The accounting literature has yet to identify the circumstances that cause certain clients to adopt explicit mandatory auditor rotation policies.

[5] Francis and Simon (1987), for example, report that annual audit fees average 0.2% of clients' asset book values; hence, the capitalized value of even the largest realignment-induced audit fee reduction is likely to be quite small in comparison to the market value of equity.

Table 1

Composition of the auditor realignment sample by Big Eight membership and relative audit firm size: 603 cases occurring in 1973–1982.

(A) *Sample frequency of changes by audit firm 'Big Eight' membership*

Percent changing from 'Big Eight' to 'Big Eight'	52.9%
Percent changing from 'Other' to 'Big Eight'	26.2%
Percent changing from 'Big Eight' to 'Other'	12.9%
Percent changing from 'Other' to 'Other'	8.0%

(B) *Sample frequency of changes by relative audit firm size (RS)[a]*

Percent where	$RS \leq 0.01$	7.0%
Percent where	$0.01 < RS \leq 0.10$	7.4%
Percent where	$0.10 < RS \leq 0.50$	4.5%
Percent where	$0.50 < RS \leq 1.00$	22.7%
Percent where	$1.00 < RS \leq 2.00$	23.4%
Percent where	$2.00 < RS \leq 10.00$	6.0%
Percent where	$10.00 < RS \leq 100.00$	9.8%
Percent where	$100.00 < RS$	19.2%

[a] Relative audit firm size is defined as the ratio of successor to predecessor firm size measured by total sales audited as reported in *Who Audits America*. Values less (greater) than 1.00 denote sample events where the client changed to a smaller (larger) audit firm.

An additional 95 cases (2.5%) were deleted because they failed to satisfy minimum Compustat data requirements (availability of financial data for the year prior to and the year following realignment). The tests described in section 4 therefore rely on a maximum sample of 603 auditor changes involving 568 clients and 139 different audit firms (127 predecessors and 65 successors).

Some characteristics of the final sample are reported in table 1. Panel A describes the composition of the sample by auditor membership in the Big Eight. Realignments from one Big Eight audit firm to another Big Eight firm comprised 52.9% of the sample. A non-Big Eight firm was replaced by a Big Eight firm in 26.2% of the cases. The remaining cases involved Big Eight incumbents replaced by non-Big Eight successors (12.9%), and movements within the non-Big Eight segment of the market (8.0%).

Panel B reports the composition of the sample according to the relative size of successor and predecessor auditors, defined as the ratio of realignment-year total client sales audited by the successor to that of the predecessor (RS). The successor firm was smaller than the former incumbent ($RS \leq 1.0$) in 41.6% of the cases, and larger ($RS > 1.0$) in 58.4% of the sample. Realignments where the successor firm was more than twice as large as the former incumbent ($RS > 2.00$) occur in 35.0% of the sample, and 18.9% of the sample involves successor firms less than half the size of the former incumbent ($RS \leq 0.50$). Substantial variations in relative audit firm size thus occur in the sample even though Big Eight accounting firms tend to dominate.

4. Cross-sectional tests and results

4.1. Specification of variables

Because the production functions of audit firms are not observable, we rely on relative audit firm size (RS) as a proxy for cost structure variations. This proxy is motivated by the discussion in section 2, which argues that audit firms with similar production technologies will attract a similar clientele and will therefore be of comparable size.[6]

Audit services pricing studies [e.g., Simunic (1980), Francis and Simon (1987)] and audit firm differentiation studies [Dopuch and Simunic (1980), Danos and Eichenseher (1982), Eichenseher (1984), DeAngelo (1981), Chow and Rice (1982), Schwartz and Menon (1985), Francis and Wilson (1988)] were used to identify client characteristics that influence supplier costs. Jointly, the variables identified from these studies can be classified into four broad categories: expansion, financing, profitability, and audit risk.[7]

Expansion entails increases in the scope, geographical dispersion, and volume of the client's activities. The corresponding increases in the quantity and complexity of accounting transactions result in economies for larger auditors. Alternatively, if large audit firms supply a higher quality audit [DeAngelo (1981)] and if client agency costs increase with client size, changes in client size are likely to be associated with realignments. Independent of whether competitive advantages are achieved through investments in production technologies or through brand name investments, rapidly growing clients are predicted to replace small incumbents with larger accounting firms that have production economies in these areas. Conversely, clients undergoing contraction are predicted to realign with comparatively smaller audit firms. However, it is unclear whether realignment will occur prior to or following periods of abnormal expansion and contraction.[8] In certain instances, the benefit of the successor's competitive advantage can only be obtained if realignment occurs before the client's policies are fully implemented (e.g.,

---

[6]Several alternative measures of cost structure differentials were considered but rejected. For example, information pertaining to other manifestations of audit cost differentials (e.g., reliance on computerized audit procedures) could not be obtained for the sample (139 audit firms over a 10-year period). Moreover, although differences in cost structures are ultimately reflected in audit fees, the relevant fee-based proxy for our purposes would involve a comparison between the successor's fee and 'bids' submitted by alternative suppliers (including the former incumbent), and such data are unavailable.

[7]Unless noted otherwise, data corresponding to the five fiscal years before realignment were used to compute variables relating to the pre-realignment period, and data corresponding to the fiscal year of and the four fiscal years following realignment were used to construct variables relating to the post-realignment period (subject to data availability).

[8]In cases of extreme client contraction, the (large) incumbent auditor may retain a competitive advantage because of expertise in bankruptcy and liquidation proceedings.

expertise in merger and acquisition activities). In other instances, realignment may occur following the change in client characteristics (e.g., when internal growth results from factors outside the client's control). Two variables were used as proxies for pre-realignment and post-realignment expansion: annualized growth in total assets and average expenditures for acquisitions (deflated by total assets).

Large audit firms have incentives to develop economies in SEC compliance and to establish ongoing relations with underwriters and investment bankers. Therefore, clients of small incumbents can benefit from hiring large firms in advance of major security offerings [Titman and Trueman (1986), Simunic and Stein (1986)]. However, realignment must occur before the financing change if the client is to take full advantage of the successor's expertise and reputation. Consequently clients that change to large audit firms are predicted to exhibit higher levels of post-realignment financing when compared to clients that change to small audit firms.[9] External financing before and after realignment is measured by the proceeds from newly issued debt and equity securities, divided by asset book value.

Two measures' of profitability before and after realignment were examined: average annual return on assets and average operating cash flows to assets.[10] If poor earnings and cash flow performance are symptomatic of enterprise decline, these variables serve as lead indicators for contraction, and client profitability prior to the realignment should be positively correlated *RS*. On the other hand, it is often alleged that realignment occurs because clients seek to employ accounting firms that are more 'accommodating' than their incumbents [Chow and Rice (1982)]. If realignment decisions are governed by accounting policy consideration rather than audit costs, accounting profits should increase following realignment and this increase should exceed the level implied by the change in cash flow performance.

Variables proxying for audit risk comprise the final category of enterprise characteristics examined. The variables used are: client size (total assets in 1982 dollars), financial risk (average leverage and times-interest-earned before and after realignment), recent audit qualifications; and client–auditor reporting disagreements.[11] Clients expose public accounting firms to varying degrees of audit failure risk. Large accounting firms can better achieve efficient

---

[9]A similar line of argument is found in Francis and Wilson (1988).

[10]Working capital from continuing operations was adjusted for changes in noncash current assets and current liabilities.

[11]Information about audit qualifications issued by the incumbent during the preceding two years, and about client–auditor reporting disagreements at the time of realignment (both dichotomous variables) was obtained from *Disclosure Journal* or the client's 8-K filing; however, these data were not readily available for auditor changes occurring between mid-1975 and December 1978. Tests employing these two variables are accordingly performed over a reduced sample of realignments. Consistency exceptions arising from mandatory accounting changes were ignored in constructing the qualifications variable.

diversification of audit risk, and can therefore render services to risky clients at a lower fee than would be charged by firms with limited diversification opportunities [Eichenseher and Shields (1983)]. This line of argument implies that, ceteris paribus, our measures of audit risk should exhibit a positive correlation with RS.

4.2. Auditor realignment and changes in client characteristics

Table 2 provides a univariate analysis of the relation between individual client characteristics and RS using two complementary approaches. First, we compute Spearman (rank-order) correlation coefficients between each variable and RS. This approach assumes that RS provides a relatively continuous measure of cost structure differentials among audit firms. Second, we adopt a less stringent view of RS and focus on subsample comparisons involving audit firms of substantially dissimilar size. Using t-tests (Mann–Whitney tests), we compare means (medians) for realignments where the successor was at least 50% larger than the incumbent (Increase) to those where the successor was at least 50% smaller than the incumbent (Decrease).

The results in table 2 are consistent with our predictions about the relation between client expansion and realignment. Asset growth rates and post-realignment acquisition expenditures exhibit a significant positive correlation with RS ($p \leq 0.01$), and these results are confirmed by the subsample comparisons. The correlation between pre-realignment acquisition expenditures and RS is not statistically significant.

As predicted, post-realignment new financing exhibits a significant positive correlation ($p \leq 0.01$) with RS although the subsample differences are not significant at conventional levels. Pre-realignment new financing also exhibits a positive (though less significant) correlation with RS, and the subsample comparisons are again not significant.

Pre-realignment profit performance (return on assets) exhibits a significant positive correlation with RS ($p \leq 0.01$), and this result is confirmed by the subsample comparison tests. The remaining profitability variables are statistically unrelated with RS.

Client size is negatively correlated with RS ($p \leq 0.05$). Increase subsample clients are slightly larger (on average) than are their Decrease counterparts although the size differential is statistically insignificant. Debt risk before the auditor change is also negatively correlated with RS ($p \leq 0.01$). Increase clients exhibit significantly lower leverage and higher times-interest-earned than do Decrease clients. Leverage after realignment is negatively correlated with RS ($p \leq 0.01$) but times-interest-earned is not, and we do not detect differences in leverage and times-interest-earned between Increase and Decrease clients after the realignment. Audit qualifications and reporting disagreements are more common among Decrease clients (31% and 11%, respectively) than they are among Increase clients (19% and 2%); however, the subsample comparison of qualification frequency is not significant.

Interpretation of the univariate results is hampered by the possibility of cross-sectional or inter-temporal dependence among the individual client characteristics. For example, contrary to our predictions, table 2 reports a significant correlation between *RS* and pre-realignment new financing. However, because new financing and asset growth are likely to be correlated, this result could be due to the statistically higher pre-realignment growth exhibited by Increase clients. The multivariate tests described below address this concern.

The joint relation between client characteristics and *RS* is investigated by estimating (i) a multiple regression with the natural logarithm of RS as the dependent variable and (ii) a logit regression with the dependent variable coded as 1 for clients that changed to a larger audit firm and 0 for clients that changed to a smaller auditor.[12] These two approaches correspond to the continuous and less stringent dichotomous view of *RS* used in the univariate tests. The multivariate analysis also uses each client as its own control: except as noted below, the explanatory variables are constructed by subtracting the pre-realignment value from the post-realignment value for each client. The multivariate analysis thus provides a test of the association between changes in client characteristics and auditor realignment.

Six client attributes in table 2 were retained in the analysis: compound asset growth rates before and after realignment (*GROWb* and *GROWa*); the change in external financing, acquisitions, cash flow performance, and average times-interest-earned ($\Delta FIN, \Delta ACQN, \Delta CFO, \Delta TIE$). Positive coefficient estimates are predicted for variables that proxy for enterprise expansion (*GROWb*, *GROWa*, and $\Delta ACQN$), increased external financing activity (ΔFIN), and cash flow performance (ΔCFO), and a negative coefficient is predicted for reduced audit risk (ΔTIE). Two variables in table 2 (return on assets and leverage) were discarded because they were highly collinear with one or more retained variables. The influence of accounting policy considerations on realignment (e.g., qualifications and auditor–client disagreements, and changes in accounting profits) are described in section 4.3. This approach was adopted because data on auditor qualifications and reporting disagreements were available for only 36.3% of the sample.

Table 3 reports correlation coefficients for the variables retained in the analysis. Changes in acquisition activity ($\Delta ACQN$) are positively correlated with post-realignment asset growth (*GROWa*, $\rho = 0.46$) and with changes in

---

[12] The natural logarithm of *RS* is used to reduce potential heteroskedasticity caused by extreme values for *RS*. Subsequent specification tests, however, revealed pronounced heteroskedasticity, with the variance of ln(*RS*) inversely correlated with client *SIZE* (total client assets in the realignment year). Accordingly, weighted-least-squares (*WLS*) procedures, with *SIZE*-deflated values of ln(*RS*) and the remaining explanatory variables, were used to correct for this problem.

Table 2

Selected characteristics of companies that changed principal auditors in 1973–1982.

Characteristic[a]	Full sample				Sample 'major' realignments[d]			
	Sample[b] size	Mean	Standard deviation	Correlation with RS[c]	Increase mean	Decrease mean	Significance levels[e]	
							t-test	mw-test
Expansion								
1. Asset growth (before)	581	1.20	0.32	0.22**	1.25	1.14	0.00	0.00
2. Asset growth (after)	570	1.13	0.27	0.12**	1.17	1.08	0.00	0.03
3. New acquisitions (before)	560	0.01	0.03	−0.01	0.01	0.02	0.09	0.47
4. New acquisitions (after)	544	0.01	0.04	0.11**	0.02	0.01	0.08	0.03
Financing								
5. New financing (before)	561	0.11	0.14	0.07*	0.12	0.11	0.45	0.17
6. New financing (after)	540	0.10	0.11	0.12**	0.11	0.09	0.14	0.11
Profitability								
7. Return on assets (before)	598	0.03	0.08	0.18**	0.05	0.02	0.00	0.00
8. Return on assets (after)	565	0.02	0.13	−0.01	0.02	0.01	0.59	0.95
9. Operating cash flows to assets (before)	521	0.06	0.11	0.03	0.06	0.05	0.50	0.30
10. Operating cash flows to assets (after)	522	0.08	0.14	−0.05	0.07	0.07	0.93	0.61

continued overleaf

Table 2 (continued)

Characteristic[a]	Full sample				Sample 'major' realignments[d]		Significance levels[e]	
	Sample[b] size	Mean	Standard deviation	Correlation with RS[c]	Increase mean	Decrease mean	t-test	mw-test
Audit Risk								
11. Client size	603	3.88	1.66	-0.07^*	3.74	3.63	0.46	0.78
12. Leverage (before)	603	0.53	0.31	-0.10^{**}	0.50	0.60	0.06	0.04
13. Leverage (after)	569	0.53	0.25	-0.11^{**}	0.52	0.54	0.39	0.45
14. Times-interest-earned (before)	599	1.72	2.18	0.15^{**}	1.97	1.42	0.01	0.00
15. Times-interest-earned (after)	568	1.42	1.94	0.03	1.41	1.68	0.30	0.40
16. Qualifications (before)	195	0.26	0.44	—	0.19	0.31	0.13	0.11
17. Auditor disagreement	208	0.06	0.23	—	0.02	0.11	0.06	0.03

[a] The following definitions were employed: Asset growth rates are continuously compounded, annual rates of change for the five years prior (before) and four years following (after) auditor realignment; acquisition, financing, and profitability variables are annual averages for the five years prior (before) and four years following (after) auditor realignment; size (natural log of assets); leverage (total debt/assets); times-interest-earned (earnings from operations/interest expense); new financing (new long-term debt plus equity/assets); new acquisitions (funds used for acquisitions/assets); audit qualifications (consistency exceptions excluded).

[b] Variation in sample size are caused by missing data on Compustat for characteristics 1 through 13 and unavailability of 8-K information for qualifications and auditor disagreement.

[c] The rank-order (Spearman) correlation coefficient between the client characteristic and relative audit firm size (RS), defined as the ratio of incumbent to successor firm size using total sales audited. Significant correlation coefficient ($p \leq 0.05$ and $p \leq 0.01$) are denoted by * and **, respectively. Correlation coefficients were not computed for dichotomous characteristics (denoted by —).

[d] 'Major' realignments involved successors at least 50% larger (Increase subsample) or 50% smaller (Decrease subsample) than incumbents.

[e] The two-sample t-test (Mann–Whitney test) compares the null hypothesis of equal subsample means (medians) against a two-tailed alternative. Chi-square tests replaced the Mann–Whitney procedure for dichotomous characteristics.

Table 3

Correlation coefficients for variables included in the cross-sectional model of auditor realignment for 490 client companies that replaced their principal auditor in 1973–1982.[a]

	SIZE	GROWb	GROWa	ΔCFO	ΔFIN	ΔACQN
GROWb	0.03					
GROWa	−0.18	0.24				
ΔCFO	0.00	0.02	0.13			
ΔFIN	−0.07	−0.25	0.21	−0.25		
ΔACQN	−0.11	−0.08	0.46	0.05	0.38	
ΔTIE	−0.07	−0.16	0.15	−0.13	−0.03	0.01

[a] The following definitions were employed: $SIZE$ = natural logarithm of total assets (in 1982 dollars) one year before realignment; $GROWb$ ($GROWa$) = continuously compounded, annual rate of growth in total assets over the five years before (four years following) realignment; ΔCFO = change in average cash flow performance (operating cash flows/total assets); ΔFIN = change in average new financing (debt plus equity issued/total assets); $\Delta ACQN$ = change in average acquisitions (acquisition expenditures/total assets), ΔTIE = change in average times-interest-earned (earnings from operations/interest expense), where Δ denotes instances where pre-realignment values were subtracted from post-realignment values. Correlation coefficients were computed using all cases with complete data ($N = 490$).

external financing (ΔFIN, $\rho = 0.38$); the remaining bivariate correlations are not larger than 0.25 in absolute value.

Table 4 summarizes the results obtained from estimating the cross-sectional model. The results indicate that RS exhibits a significant positive association with the change in external financing (ΔFIN), cash flow performance (ΔCFO), pre-realignment asset growth ($GROWb$), and a significant negative association with the change in times-interest-earned (ΔTIE).[13] The regression explained 20.1% of the cross-sectional variation in RS ($F = 18.64$, $p \leq 0.05$). The null hypothesis that the logit coefficients were jointly equal to zero was rejected ($\chi^2 = 35.97$, $p \leq 0.05$), and the model correctly classified 59.0% of the realignments ($p \leq 0.05$). The logit coefficient estimates were consistent with the regression coefficients reported in table 4, although significance levels were generally reduced.[14]

[13] Eichenseher and Danos (1981), among others, have found a moderate degree of industry specialization by individual audit firms. Therefore, expansion may be correlated with the omitted variable 'industry specialization', resulting in biased regression coefficients. However, changes in the industry classification of realignment clients were not prevalent in our sample. Using SIC code histories provided on the CRSP tape, we found that only 9.0% of our realignment clients changed industry classifications over the ten-year period centered on the realignment year. Roughly two-thirds of the SIC reclassifications involved 'related' industries (e.g., from 'Radio TV Receiving Sets' to 'Wholesale-Electronic Parts and Equipment') or revisions in the fourth digit of the SIC code.

[14] A variety of tests were conducted to assess the sensitivity of the results in table 4 to outliers and to gauge the impact of alternative measures of expansion and debt risk (e.g., $GROWa$ was replaced by the change in average asset growth). These tests indicate that the model is reasonably well-specified and the results in table 4 are robust, although the residuals are characterized by moderate kurtosis. Details regarding the sensitivity tests are available from the authors.

Table 4

Results obtained from cross-sectional regression and logit analyses of the relation between relative audit firm size and realignment client characteristics for companies that replaced their principal auditor in 1973–1982.[a]

	Predicted sign	All auditor realignments ($N = 490$)
(A) *WLS regression results*[b]		
Intercept	NA	−3.35 (−3.50)**
GROWb	+	4.99 (7.46)**
GROWa	+	−0.98 (−1.16)
ΔCFO	+	3.68 (2.84)**
ΔFIN	+	7.73 (4.14)**
ΔACQN	+	1.71 (0.29)
ΔTIE	−	−0.22 (−1.88)*
Adjusted R^2		20.1%
F-statistic		18.64**
(B) *Logit classification results*		
Larger auditor		70.9%
Smaller auditor		50.5%
Overall		59.0%
Expected accuracy		51.4%

[a] The dependent variable was defined as the natural logarithm of relative audit firm size (RS), the ratio of successor size to predecessor size. The independent variables are $GROWb$ ($GROWa$) = continuously compounded, annual rate of change in total assets over the five years before (four years following) realignment; ΔCFO = change in average cash flow performance (operating cash flows/total assets); ΔFIN = change in average new financing (debt plus equity issued/total assets); $\Delta ACQN$ = change in average acquisitions (acquisition expenditures/total assets), ΔTIE = change in average times-interest-earned (earnings from operations/interest expense), where Δ denotes instances where pre-realignment values were subtracted from post-realignment values. Significance levels are denoted by * ($p \leq 0.10$) and ** ($p \leq 0.05$).

[b] The weighted least square results are based on deflation by ($1/SIZE$) to correct for heteroscedasticity. Size deflation was unnecessary in logit analysis, because heteroscedasticity was not present when RS was transformed into a $(0,1)$ variable. $SIZE$ was added into the model as a control variable. Classification results are based on proportional prior probabilities (without jack-knifing), and the statistical significance of overall classification accuracy is evaluated using a binomial test.

Earlier studies of auditor changes have produced mixed results on the association between client characteristics and the direction of realignment. Eichenseher and Shields (1986), for example, document a positive association between client leverage and changes to Big Eight audit firms, whereas leverage effects were not found by Palmrose (1984) or Healy and Lys (1986), and a negative association was documented by Francis and Wilson (1988). Healy and Lys (1986) found no relation between the direction of realignment and subsequent offerings of debt or equity securities, whereas Francis and Wilson (1988) document a positive relation implying that clients change to larger auditors in advance of issuing additional securities.[15] Eichenseher and Shields (1986) found a positive association between managers' stock ownership and changes to Big Eight auditors but this result was not corroborated by Francis and Wilson (1988). Palmrose (1984) found no evidence to support a relation between auditor realignment and the presence of accounting-based bonus plans, whereas Francis and Wilson (1988) found that bonus plan adoption (termination) was positively (negatively) associated with changes to larger audit firms. However, these four prior studies have produced two consistent results that are consistent with our findings: client size and asset growth both exhibit significant positive associations with changes to larger audit firms.

4.3. Auditor realignment and changes in accounting policies

The possibility that accounting policy considerations also influence realignment decisions was not specifically addressed by the preceding analysis. This issue is investigated by examining the incremental explanatory power of variables thought to be associated with policy-induced auditor changes: reporting disagreements or opinion qualifications involving the former incumbent, and abnormal increases in post-realignment accounting profits.

Realignments precipitated by current or impending accounting disputes involve a tradeoff between realignment costs and the benefits derived from an increased likelihood of auditor acquiescence (i.e., the probability that client–auditor disputes will be favorably resolved from the client's perspective). Replacing a large incumbent with a smaller audit firm is commonly thought to increase the likelihood of acquiescence because the client's value is comparatively greater for the small successor.[16] Lateral realignments or changes to comparatively large audit firms, on the other hand, would presumably have

---

[15] Beatty (1986) and Balvers, McDonald, and Miller (1988) have found that the degree of underpricing associated with unseasoned equity issues is reduced by employing a large audit firm prior to the equity offering.

[16] Large audit firms have numerous clients, and the rents specific to any individual client comprise a small fraction of the firm's total rents from incumbency; hence, the benefits of client retention through acquiescence are likely to be comparatively small.

Table 5

Results obtained from tests of the relation between accounting policy disputes and auditor realignment decisions for companies that replaced their principal auditor in 1973–1982.

Characteristic	Client subsamples[a]		
	Disagreement or qualification ($N = 55$)	No dispute ($N = 139$)	t-statistic for[b] difference in sample means
(A) *Subsample proportions by direction of realignment*[c]			
Decrease: to smaller firm	30.9%	24.5%	—
Lateral : to similar firm	40.0%	29.5%	—
Increase: to larger firm	29.1%	46.0%	—
(B) *Earnings performance before realignment*			
Average return on assets (*ROA*)	−0.006	0.054	−6.29**
ROA in year −1	−0.042	0.043	−5.00**
Fraction reporting a loss in year −1	0.407	0.130	4.44**
(C) *Earnings performance following realignment*[d]			
Average return on assets	−0.019	0.024	−1.81*
Change in average profitability	−0.010	−0.031	0.90
Incremental profit performance	0.023	−0.054	2.27**
Fraction reporting positive incremental profits	0.478	0.285	2.40**

[a]Information about audit qualifications issued by the incumbent auditor during the two years preceding switch and about client–auditor disagreements were not available for auditor changes occurring between mid-1975 and December 1978. Accordingly, the sample size was reduced to 194 auditor displacements with available Compustat data.
[b]Statistically significant t-statistics (two-tailed test) are denoted by * ($p \leq 0.10$) and ** ($p \leq 0.05$). T-statistics were not computed for the difference in means for panel A because rows and columns are not independent (denoted by —). The χ-squared statistic for independence is 4.71 (2 degrees of freedom); $p \leq 0.10$.
[c]The realignment subsamples were defined as Decrease (Increase) when the successor firm was at least 50 smaller (larger) than the former incumbent, or Lateral (all remaining cases).
[d]Average return on assets is computed in the five years prior to the auditor change and change in average profitability is computed as the difference between the average returns on assets in the four years subsequent to the auditor change minus the average return on assets in the five years prior to the auditor change. Incremental profit performance for each client was defined as the change in average profitability (return on assets) minus the corresponding change in average cash flow performance.

minimal impact on acquiescence because the client's value to the incumbent is equal to or larger than the value to the successor firm.

Table 5 compares the direction of realignment and earnings performance of clients involved in potential policy disputes (disagreement or qualification) to that of other realignment clients. The data in panel A indicate that dispute clients favor lateral realignment or a smaller successor firm more frequently than do nondispute clients ($\chi^2 = 4.71$, $p \leq 0.10$). Only 29.1% of the dispute clients changed to a comparatively large audit firm, while 46.0% of the nondispute clients changed to a larger audit firm. Panel B indicates that clients involved in potential accounting disputes are characterized by significantly lower return on assets over the five years prior to realignment and in the year immediately preceding the auditor change when compared to the nondispute clients. Moreover, 40.7% of the dispute clients reported a net loss in the year before realignment compared to only 13.0% of the nondispute clients.

Both client subsamples exhibit moderate decreases in earnings performance following realignment (panel C), although the difference in earnings decline and post-realignment average profitability of the two subsamples is not significant. This result is inconsistent with the acquiescence hypothesis because auditor changes precipitated by accounting disputes are generally thought to yield enhanced earnings following realignment.[17]

A more powerful test is provided by the panel C comparison of clients' incremental profit performance, defined as the post-realignment change in accounting profitability (ΔROA) minus the corresponding change in cash flow performance (ΔCFO). Clients involved in accounting disputes exhibit positive incremental profits following realignment, whereas the remaining clients exhibit negative incremental profits, and the between-group difference in incremental profits is statistically significant ($t = 2.27$; $p < 0.05$). Furthermore, 47.8% of the presumably dispute-induced auditor changes were followed by profit increases that exceeded the corresponding increase in cash flow performance; only 28.5% of the remaining clients exhibit increased incremental profit performance. These results are thus consistent with the implications of the acquiescence hypothesis.

To gain further insights about auditor realignment and accounting policies, the incremental profits variable ($PROFIT$) was incorporated into the regression in table 4. The coefficient estimate for $PROFIT$ was negative but not statistically significant (t-statistic of -1.14). A similar pattern of coefficient estimates (and significance levels) was obtained in a second regression where incremental profitability was conditioned by the presence of qualifications or disagreements.[18] There was no significant association between relative auditor size (RS) and the interaction term representing the profit performance of clients with disagreements or qualifications (t-statistics of -0.62). These results thus fail to document a consistent association between relative auditor size and variables that proxy for policy-induced realignments.

---

[17]Consistent with the general tenor of the literature, we assume that clients (on average) favor implementation of earnings-enhancing accounting policies although we readily acknowledge that some clients may in fact prefer earnings-decreasing procedures under certain circumstances [see Healy (1985) and Watts and Zimmerman (1986)].

[18]Coefficient estimates for this second model are based on the reduced realignment sample of 194 cases where information about qualifications and disagreements was available.

4.4. Control sample validation tests

If auditor realignments occur when the incumbent's competitive advantage is eroded over time by changes in financing and operating activities of the client, comparable shifts in activity levels should not be observed among companies that maintain existing client–auditor pairings. The control sample validation tests address this question by investigating whether our explanatory variables differentiate realignment clients from companies that do not change auditors over the ten-year test period.

The nonrealignment (control) samples were selected by ranking the 490 realignment clients by RS and matching every third client with two comparison companies according to auditor, industry membership (three-digit SIC code), and, to a lesser extent, audit firm size (total client sales audited in the year of realignment).[19] One comparison firm was chosen from among the companies audited by the realignment client's former incumbent, and the second comparison firm was drawn from among those firms audited by the successor. Potential comparison firms were discarded if they changed auditors during the 1973–1982 period. The final validation sample contained 147 triplets (a realignment client, an incumbent client, and a successor client) after discarding cases where suitable comparison firms could not be identified or where sufficient Compustat data were not available.

The validation sample was then partitioned into four subsamples according to the direction of realignment ($RS < 1.0$ or $RS > 1.0$) and the type of comparison firm (client of former incumbent or client of eventual successor). A logit model was estimated for each subsample with the dependent variable assigned a value of 1 for realignment clients and a value of 0 for nonrealignment clients.

The null hypothesis that the logit coefficient estimates were jointly equal to zero was rejected for each subsample (chi-square tests, $p \le 0.05$).[20] The subsample classification success rates ranged from 60.9% to 68.5%, and ex-

---

[19] Realignment clients from the Compustat Research File were matched with comparison firms that also appeared on that file to partially control for bankruptcy, merger, and liquidation possibilities. Strict adherence to industry and Compustat file criteria proved difficult when the audit firm was relatively small and therefore had few clients. To avoid the sample-selection bias introduced by systematic deletion of these cases, we either resorted to a two-digit SIC classification match or chose a comparison firm from among the clients audited by a comparable (small) accounting firm. These departures involved less than 10% of the sample.

[20] Clients that changed to comparatively large auditors were growing more rapidly ($GROWb$ and $\Delta ACQN$) and more active in financial markets (ΔFIN) than were their nonrealignment counterparts. Clients that changed to comparatively small audit firms exhibited significantly less asset growth following realignments ($GROWb$) than did their comparison companies. Lateral realignment clients were indistinguishable from their nonrealignment counterparts. Realignment clients were significantly less profitable before and after changing auditors than were their matched comparison companies. Details regarding the logit results and related univariate paired-comparison tests are available from the authors.

ceeded chance expectations in each case (binomial tests, $p \leq 0.01$). The correct classification rates for realignment clients ranged from 58.2% to 65.0% across subsamples and nonrealignment classification rates ranged from 62.5% to 72.2%.

Collectively, the evidence presented is consistent with the hypothesis that audit firms specialize through investments in production technologies and quality assurance mechanisms, and that changes in enterprise characteristics are important determinants of optimal client–auditor alignment. Moreover, although our data indicates that realignment clients are less profitable than comparison firms, we are unable to detect evidence that opinion shopping is, on average, an important determinant of auditor realignments.

Two aspects of the results obtained here and in earlier studies of auditor realignment warrant mention. First, the overall explanatory power of the various cross-sectional models that have been used to isolate correlates of realignment is generally quite modest. Second, these models often exhibit a systematic prediction bias in that logit or probit classification success rates tend to be highest for clients that change to larger auditors and lowest for clients that realign with comparatively smaller auditors. Of course, clients may change auditors for reasons other than those examined here, and thus omitted variables may account partially for the modest explanatory power of the cross-sectional models used to date.[21]

5. Common stock returns and auditor realignment

This section investigates two related questions. First, the information content of auditor realignment announcements is investigated by examining the distribution of daily excess returns coincident with 8-K filings that disclose the auditor change. Second, monthly excess returns are examined for evidence of systematic differences in the long-term share price performance of selected client subsamples.

5.1. The share price implications of auditor realignment

The discussion in section 2 argued that auditor realignment can have potentially large common stock price implications to the extent that realignments provide information about (unanticipated) changes in future corporate activities. Definitive predictions regarding the sign of these price adjustments are, however, difficult to derive.

---

[21]Among the other reasons for voluntary auditor realignment cited by Carpenter and Strawser (1971) and Bedingfield and Loeb (1974) are: changes in senior management, dissatisfaction with the former incumbent's performance, audit fee disputes, retirement of audit partner assigned to client, and audit partner was hired by another accounting firm.

For example, clients anticipating pronounced expansion were predicted to benefit from realignments that replace small incumbents with comparatively large audit firms. Similarly, clients anticipating substantial reductions in the level and scope of their activities were predicted to benefit from realignments that replace large incumbents with comparatively smaller successors. However, the stock price implications of corporate growth and contraction seem to depend on a variety of factors that render general predictions somewhat tenuous.[22] Consequently, although we investigate the average price response to realignment for various client portfolios, daily excess returns are also examined for evidence of increased dispersion.

5.2. Sample selection

The preliminary sample described in section 3 was further reduced by discarding cases where (i) the client was not included on the CRSP daily stock return file or (ii) definitive 8-K filing dates were not available through *Disclosure Journal* (events occurring prior to June 1975) or the Chicago regional office of the Securities Exchange Commission (events occurring after December 1978).[23] Imposition of these additional restrictions produced a final sample of 194 auditor realignments, and this subsample was indistinguishable from the full realignment sample except for the systematic exclusion of auditor changes announced between late 1975 through 1978.

5.3. Common stock returns test procedures

Common stock excess returns were computed using the single-factor market model [Fama (1976)]. The announcement date (day 0) was defined as the trading day on which the 8-K filing of a change in auditors was received by the

---

[22]Although increases in capital investments are associated with significant positive abnormal stock returns [McConnel and Muscarella (1985)], the sign of bidder-firm abnormal returns to merger and acquisition announcements are influenced by a number of factors [see Halpern (1983) or Jensen and Ruback (1983)]. Moreover, the share price adjustments associated with corporate contraction (including divestitures and spin-offs) can be negative [McConnel and Muscarella (1985)] or positive [Miles and Rosenfeld (1983), Schipper and Smith (1983, 1986)] depending on the specific circumstances surrounding the restructuring. Related studies also document both positive and negative share price adjustments to corporate financial structure changes, with the sign of abnormal returns influenced by the specific mode and stated purpose of the financing [see Smith (1986)].

[23]In contrast to the approach typically adopted in event studies, we have purposely not controlled for the presence of contemporaneous 8-K disclosures (e.g., technical defaults, election of directors, changes in exchange listing, etc.) because these events are unlikely to be independent of the auditor change. Consequently, the excess returns reported here capture the combined effects of auditor realignment and concurrent events.

SEC.[24] Daily returns and the value-weighted market index series were collected for a 121 trading-day test period centered on day 0, a 200-day pre-announcement period ending on day -61, and a 200-day post-announcement period begining on day $+61$. Scholes–Williams (1977) coefficient estimates were obtained from separate regressions over the pre-announcement and post-announcement periods.

A similar approach was used to estimate monthly excess common stock returns for a 48-month test period beginning 36 months prior to the 8-K filing date. Monthly returns and a value-weighted composite of the monthly NYSE and AMEX market index series were collected for the test period, a 60-month pre-announcement estimation period ending on month -37, and a 60-month post-announcement estimation period beginning on month $+12$.

5.4. Daily excess returns

Table 6 presents a time series of average daily excess returns over the 21 days centered on day zero. Average daily excess returns were examined for statistical significance using standard test procedures.[25] The results indicate that auditor realignments are not (on average) associated with significant share price adjustments during trading periods coincident with the 8-K filing. The average day 0 excess return for the full sample was -0.43%, and the three-day cumulative average excess return for day -1 to day $+1$ was -0.05%. Clients that changed to comparatively large (small) audit firms experienced a three-day average excess return of $+0.49\%$ ($+0.79\%$). By contrast, realignments that involved audit forms of similar size (Lateral subsample) were associated with a three-day average excess return of -1.30%. None of the average daily excess returns or three-day average excess returns around the 8-K filing date were statistically different from zero.[26]

[24] For each sample company, the *Wall Street Journal Index* citations covering a six-month period around the 8-K filing date were examined to identify alternative public announcement dates. Definitive *Wall Street Journal* announcements were identified in less than 5 percent of the sample, and in each case publication of the news release occurred one or more trading days after the 8-K stamp date.

[25] Following Ruback (1982), the test statistic is $t = CPE_t/(\sigma + c)$, where CPE_t denotes the average excess return on day t, σ is the estimated standard deviation of daily average excess returns over a 48-day (24-month) base period ending on day -61 (month -37), and c is a correction factor reflecting the autocorrelation of base-period excess returns. Test statistics for cumulative excess returns are constructed in a similar manner with σ and c adjusted to compensate for cumulation over time. The results in table 6 are robust with respect to alternative specifications of the returns generating process: raw returns and market-adjusted returns exhibited patterns of behavior qualitatively identical to the excess returns series reported in table 6.

[26] Eighty-two percent of the 8-K filings contained information pertaining to other corporate events. A partition of the sample based on the presence or absence of concurrent disclosures revealed no difference in three-day excess returns or dispersion for 'clean' and 'contaminated' 8-K filings. However, the 'contaminated' portfolio exhibited a significant negative excess return (-2.1% over the 10 trading days following realignment; the 'clean' portfolio return for this 10-day period (-0.7%) was not statistically different from zero.

Table 6

Average daily common stock excess returns and cumulative average excess returns around the announcement of a change in principal auditor for clients that replaced their principal auditors in 1973–1982.[a]

Trading day	Full sample (N = 194) (%)	Subsamples formed on the relative size of incumbent and successor audit firm[b]		
		Decrease subsample (N = 65) (%)	Lateral subsample (N = 65) (%)	Increase subsample (N = 64) (%)
(A) Daily excess returns				
− 10	− 0.03	− 0.38	0.08	− 0.18
− 9	− 0.34	− 0.90	− 1.30	1.21
− 8	0.43	0.55	0.37	0.39
− 7	0.59	0.80	0.40	0.59
− 6	− 0.07	− 0.58	− 0.14	0.48
− 5	− 0.48	− 0.14	− 1.10	− 0.13
− 4	0.09	− 0.06	0.39	− 0.08
− 3	0.20	0.48	0.04	0.11
− 2	− 0.32	− 0.51	− 0.30	− 0.15
− 1	0.21	0.49	− 0.30	0.63
0	− 0.43	− 0.09	− 0.84	− 0.32
1	0.12	0.39	− 0.16	0.18
2	− 0.21	− 0.63	− 0.07	− 0.12
3	− 0.02	− 0.65	− 0.03	0.58
4	− 0.46	− 0.09	− 0.41	− 0.84
5	− 0.01	− 0.57	− 0.10	0.60
6	0.01	0.11	− 0.09	0.03
7	− 0.22	0.36	− 0.60	− 0.38
8	− 0.22	− 0.26	− 0.37	− 0.04
9	0.16	0.26	0.37	− 0.17
10	0.23	0.20	0.10	0.40
(B) Cumulative excess returns				
− 60 to − 11	− 0.74	− 6.51**	0.54	3.81**
− 10 to − 1	0.34	− 0.23	− 1.87	3.24**
− 1 to + 1	− 0.05	0.79	− 1.30	0.49
+ 1 to + 10	− 0.67	− 0.89	− 1.35	0.25
+ 11 to + 60	− 3.24**	− 5.15**	− 0.42	− 4.16**

[a] Information about audit qualifications issued by the incumbent auditor during the two years preceding switch and about client–auditor disagreements were not available for auditor changes occurring between mid-1975 and December 1978. Accordingly, the sample size was reduced to 194 auditor displacements with available return data. Day 0 corresponds to the trading day on which the 8-K filing that announced the change in principal auditor was received by the SEC. Daily excess returns or cumulative average excess returns statistically different from zero are denoted by * ($p \leq 0.10$) or ** ($p \leq 0.05$).

[b] The three subsamples correspond to the lower third (Decrease), middle third (Lateral), and upper third (Increase) of sample companies rank-ordered according to the relative size of predecessor and successor auditor. Clients in the Increase subsample changed from relatively small to relatively large audit firms.

Average daily excess returns for portfolios based on audit firm membership in the 'Big Eight', and on the presence or absence of accounting disagreements reported concurrently with the auditor change were also examined. These portfolios follow the sample partitions used previously [Fried and Schiff (1981), Smith and Nichols (1982), Nichols and Smith (1983)]. None of the portfolios formed by auditor classification exhibited three-day excess returns statistically different from zero, although significant negative excess returns of about −2.5% were documented over the ten days following the 8-K filing for portfolios where the former incumbent was replaced by a Big Eight audit firm.[27] The presence or absence of client–auditor disagreements had no discernible impact on announcement-period excess returns or on excess returns for the ten days following realignment.[28]

One explanation for the absence of a significant average price reaction to realignment announcements is the possibility that offsetting positive and negative excess returns occur within the sample. To investigate this possibility, excess returns for the three-day announcement period were examined for evidence of abnormal dispersion using procedures described in McNichols and Manegold (1983). This approach compares the firm-specific variance of excess returns to the variance of market model residuals observed over some base period (in our case, days −108 to −61).[29] A significant increase in excess return variance was found for clients that changed to comparatively small audit firms ($Z = 2.09$), and this effect was concentrated on day +1 ($Z = 3.52$). The remaining two subsamples (Increase and Lateral) did not exhibit abnormal announcement-period dispersion.[30]

A second possibility is that auditor realignment was a predictable consequence of readily observed changes in client characteristics (e.g., rapid historical growth) or previously announced plans for future financing, investing, and operating activities.[31] To investigate this possibility, the cross-sectional model

---

[27] The average excess return over days 0 and +1 for each auditor portfolio was: −0.78% (Big Eight to Big Eight), +0.23% (Big Eight to non-Big Eight), +0.32% (non-Big Eight to Big Eight), and −1.20% (non-Big Eight to non-Big Eight).

[28] The average excess return over days 0 and +1 for realignments preceded by disagreements or qualifications was −0.91%. The average excess return for auditor changes without prior disagreements or qualification was −0.07%.

[29] Squared residual tests tend to overreject the null hypothesis of no abnormal dispersion [Marais (1984)] and our test results should be interpreted with caution.

[30] A significant increase in excess return variance for the Decrease subsample was also detected on day +2 ($Z = 7.97$).

[31] One other possibility is that explicit information regarding the (impending) auditor change became available to market participants prior to the 8-K filing date. Leakage may have occurred because realignment required shareholder ratification and the proposed auditor change was described in proxy materials distributed prior to the 8-K filing date, or because a news release describing the realignment was issued prior to the 8-K filing. Several instances of prior disclosure of proposed auditor changes were discovered; however, the magnitude of this problem remains unclear because clients' proxy statements were not systematically examined. Examination of *Wall Street Journal Index* citations failed to reveal instances where leakage of the second type occurred.

of section 4 was used as a proxy for the market's expectations about realignment, and three equally-sized portfolios were formed by rank-ordering clients according to the standardized prediction errors from that regression.[32] This procedure groups clients according to whether the successor audit firm was larger, smaller, or roughly equivalent in size to that predicted by the cross-sectional model.

Two results were obtained. First, clients that changed to larger than predicted successor firms exhibited a significant, positive three-day excess return of $+1.63\%$ ($t = 2.02$). The mean three-day excess return for clients that changed to smaller than predicted successors was $+1.06\%$ ($t = 1.38$) and the mean three-day return for the remaining portfolio was -0.70% ($t = -1.18$). Second, clients that changed to smaller than predicted successors exhibited significantly increased excess return variance over the three-day period ($Z = 4.32$). No significant increase in the dispersion of excess returns was found for the other two client portfolios.

Although the common stocks of clients that voluntarily changed audit firms do not exhibit systematic excess returns at the 8-K filing date, statistically significant abnormal stock price changes before and after realignment are indicated in table 6. For example, the sixty-day pre-announcement excess return for clients that changed to a comparatively large (small) audit firm was $+7.05\%$ (-6.74%). Lateral clients also experienced a negative pre-announcement excess return of -1.33%; although this share price adjustment is not statistically different from zero. Both Increase and Decrease subsamples exhibit significant negative excess returns of roughly -5.0% over days $+11$ through $+60$.

The security market reaction around auditor changes is analyzed in two prior studies. Smith and Nichols (1982) compared the weekly share price performance of clients that changed auditors and disclosed the existence of a client–auditor dispute over accounting practices to the share price performance of clients that changed auditors where no accounting policy disputes surfaced. Clients involved in accounting disputes experienced a statistically significant average price decline during the announcement week whereas the mean announcement week abnormal return for nondispute-related clients was not statistically different from zero. In a related study, Nichols and Smith (1983) found that clients changing from non-Big Eight to Big Eight auditors experienced a share price increase during the announcement week whereas clients that changed from Big Eight to non-Big Eight auditors experienced a share price decline during the announcement week. However, in both cases the average announcement-week abnormal return was not significantly different

---

[32] Forty-six realignments were discarded from this analysis because of missing COMPUSTAT data, and the mean three-day excess return associated with these discarded events was -2.61% ($t = -2.74$). We were unable to detect systematic differences in the distribution of relative auditor size (RS) between discarded and retained clients, and cannot explain why these discarded events exhibit significant negative excess returns.

from zero at conventional levels. Moreover, the samples used in these two studies were quite small (less than 30 realignments per group).

In summary, our evidence indicates that auditor realignment announcements are not associated with a contemporaneous shift in average share prices. There is a modest increase in excess return variance at the announcement date. Clients that shift to larger (smaller) auditors exhibit significant share price increases (declines) over the 60-day trading period before the realignment announcement. These findings indicate that realignment announcements have little information content, perhaps because realignment is a predictable consequence of earlier changes in the client's operations and activities. However, we are unable to document systematic abnormal returns when the model developed in section 4 is used to control for changes in client characteristics.

5.5. Monthly excess returns and auditor turnover

Table 7 describes the behavior of monthly common stock returns around the announced auditor change for the entire sample and three relative audit firm size portfolios (Decrease, Lateral, and Increase). Table 7 also describes the behavior of monthly common stock returns for a matched sample of comparison companies selected on the basis of four-digit SIC classification, availability of CRSP monthly returns data, and incumbent auditor.[33]

As table 7 indicates, voluntary auditor changes are (on average) preceded by a three-year period of negative share price performance. The mean excess return for realignment clients was -27.58% over the two-year period beginning in month -36, and each realignment subsample exhibits significant share price decline over this period. The Lateral and Decrease subsamples exhibit significant negative excess returns of -12.67% and -15.52% over the 12-months period ending in month zero. The average excess return over this 12-month period for Increase subsample clients was not statistically different from zero. The excess return for comparison corporations that remained with the incumbent audit firm was -2.17% and 7.94% over these same two periods.

These results are consistent with Fried and Schiff (1981), who document a negative security market reaction in the 21-week period centered on the 8-K receipt date. The differential share price performance of realignment and nonrealignment clients during months -36 to -1 is partially attributable to the superior profitability of nonrealignment clients: realignment clients exhibit significantly ($p \le 0.05$) lower average returns on assets before changing audi-

---

[33] In the absence of an exact audit firm match, a less stringent criterion was utilized and the comparison company was required to be audited by an accounting firm of approximately the same size as the (former) incumbent of the realignment client. *Who Audits America* and various *Moody's* manuals were consulted to insure that comparison companies did not change audit firms during the four years from month -35 to month $+11$, where month 0 denotes the month in which the realignment client reported the auditor change to the SEC.

Table 7

Cumulative average monthly common stock returns and excess returns around the announcement of an auditor change for clients that replaced their principal auditor in 1973–1982.

Clients that changed auditors[b]	Sample size	Cumulation period[a]				
		−36 to −13	−12 to −1	−1 to +1	0 to +11	−36 to +11
(A) *Monthly excess returns* (%)						
Full sample	142	−27.58**	−9.69*	−2.57	6.76	−30.51**
Increase subsample	42	−27.17**	−0.42	−1.56	−4.66	−32.25*
Lateral subsample	51	−29.09**	−12.67*	−1.64	0.53	−41.22**
Decrease subsample	49	−26.86**	−15.52*	−5.31	20.19**	−22.20
Comparison sample[c]	91	−2.17	−7.94*	−4.98	−2.77	−12.87
(B) *Monthly raw returns* (%)						
Full sample	142	−5.96	−16.28**	−7.48*	6.44	−15.79*
Increase subsample	42	−6.72	−6.03	−8.61	−4.11	−16.86
Lateral subsample	51	−3.84	−16.59**	−4.84	3.70	−16.72*
Decrease subsample	49	−7.30	−24.05**	−9.25	17.72**	−13.63
Comparison sample	91	19.78*	−5.44	−7.12	4.17	18.51*

[a] Month 0 corresponds to the month in which the SEC received the 8-K filing that announced the auditor change. Cumulative average excess returns (panel A) and cumulative average unadjusted returns (panel B) statistically different from zero are denoted by * ($p \leq 0.10$) and ** ($p \leq 0.05$).

[b] The three subsamples correspond to the lower third (Decrease), middle third (Lateral), and upper third (Increase) of sample companies rank-ordered according to the relative size of predecessor and successor auditor. Clients in the Increase subsample changed to comparatively large audit firms.

[c] Comparison clients were matched in event time according to four-digit SIC classification and the realignment client's former incumbent audit firm. A suitable match was found for 101 realignment clients; however, 10 comparison clients were discarded because of missing return data.

tors than do nonrealignment clients. The difference in accounting profits is not statistically significant following realignment.

The common stocks of clients that replaced incumbent auditors with smaller accounting firms (Decrease subsample) exhibit significant positive excess returns of +20.19% during the year following realignment. This result was attributable to a small number of cases where realignment was followed by takeover activity.[34] The post-announcement excess returns for the remaining

[34] Nine instances of potential takeover activity (18.4% of the subsample) were identified from *Wall Street Journal Index* citations covering the 12 months following realignment. Six citations described explicit takeover attempts or rumored takeover activities, and three cases involved 13-D filings of large stock purchases. After deleting these cases, neither the average excess return nor the average unadjusted return for the subsample was statistically different from zero over the year following realignment.

realignment subsamples and for the comparison sample were not statistically different from zero.

In summary, monthly excess returns indicate that voluntary realignment clients experience negative abnormal performance in the three-year period preceding the auditor change. This result is consistent with our finding that realignment clients had smaller returns on assets when compared to a nonrealignment matched sample. Jointly these results imply that, while clients that change to larger auditors outperform clients that change to smaller firms, audit realignment clients as a group, independent of the direction of the auditor change, are less profitable than clients not replacing their audit firm. Therefore, the results indicate that realignments are part of restructuring plans by underperforming clients.

6. Concluding remarks

This paper has argued that voluntary client–auditor realignment can generally be explained as an efficient response to competition among audit firms. This conclusion relies on the notion that economic considerations dictate the alignment of clients and audit firms. We have argued that public accounting firms specialize by adopting distinctive production technologies that reduce the costs of supplying audit services to particular market segments, that clients purchase audit services from the least cost supplier, and that clients change auditors when the incumbent can no longer provide the level and type of services required at the lowest cost. According to this perspective, voluntary auditor changes arise as a consequence of competitive forces: incumbent audit firms can lose their comparative cost advantage for a given client when changes in the client enterprise over time shift the client along the incumbent's cost curve.

Several predictions about client–auditor realignments were supported by our analysis of the relation between relative audit firm size and the characteristics of realignment clients. Admittedly, these tests rely on a rather crude proxy for differences in audit firm cost structures. Yet, selected client characteristics (e.g., enterprise growth and financing activities) were found to be associated with this proxy in a manner consistent with our predictions. Moreover, the explanatory power of our cross-sectional model was not enhanced by the incorporation of variables thought to proxy for accounting policy-induced auditor changes. In this regard, our results imply that audit qualifications and accounting disputes do not (on average) have a dominant impact on the direction of auditor realignment.

Our analysis of the contemporaneous share price reaction to realignment announcements indicate the general absence of systematic abnormal returns and increased return variance over the three days centered on the 8-K filing date. This result held for various portfolios of realignment clients, including partitions formed on characteristics of the audit firms involved as well as portfolios constructed using residuals from the cross-sectional realignment model. Therefore, our results imply that auditor changes provide little information that is relevant for the pricing of securities, even though realignments are related to change in corporate policies.

Several regularities were uncovered when common stock returns for longer trading periods were examined. For example, clients that changed to a comparatively large (small) audit firm exhibited significant positive (negative) abnormal returns over the sixty days preceding realignment. Finally, our results document a systematic decline in common stock values of all change clients over the 36 months before realignment, and these clients were significantly less profitable before changing auditors than were the matched comparison companies.

References

AICPA, 1986, Public oversight board: Annual report 1985–1986 (American Institute of Certified Public Accountants, New York, NY).

Balvers, R.J., B. McDonald, and R.E. Miller, 1988, Underpricing of new issues and the choice of auditor as a signal of investment banner reputation, The Accounting Review, 605–622.

Beatty, R.P., 1986, The initial public offerings market for audit services, Working paper (University of Pennsylvania, Philadelphia, PA).

Bedingfield, J. and S. Loea, 1974, Auditor changes: an examination, Journal of Accountancy, 66–69.

Benston, G.J., 1979-80, The market for public accounting services: Demand, supply and regulation, The Accounting Journal, 2–46.

Carpenter, C.G. and R.H. Strawser, 1971, Displacement of auditors when clients go public, Journal of Accountancy, 55–58.

Chow, C.W. and S.J. Rice, 1982, Qualified audit opinions and auditor switching, The Accounting Review, 326–335.

Danos, P. and J. Eichenseher, 1982, Audit industry dynamics: Factors affecting changes in client-industry market shares, Journal of Accounting Research, 604–616.

DeAngelo, L. E., 1981, Auditor size and audit quality, Journal of Accounting and Economics, 183–200.

Dopuch, N. and D. Simunic, 1980, The nature of competition in the auditing profession, in: J.W. Buckley and J.F. Easton, eds., Regulation and the accounting profession (Lifetime Learning, Belmont, CA) 77–94.

Eichenseher, J., 1984, The effects of foreign operations on domestic auditor selection, Journal of Accounting, Auditing and Finance, 195–209.

Eichenseher, J. and P. Danos, 1981, The analysis of industry-specific auditor concentration: Towards an explanatory model, The Accounting Review, 479–492.

Eichenseher, J.W. and D. Shields, 1983, The correlates of CPA-firm change for publicly-held corporations, Auditing: A Journal of Practice and Theory, 23–37.

Eichenseher, J.W. and D. Shields, 1986, Corporate capital structure and auditor 'fit', Working paper (University of Wisconsin, Madison, WI).

Fama, E., 1976, Foundations of finance (Basic Books, New York, NY).

Francis, J. and D. Simon, 1987, A test of audit pricing in the small-client segment of the U.S. audit market, The Accounting Review, 145–57.

Francis, J. and E.R. Wilson, 1988, Auditor changes: A joint test of theories relating to agency costs and auditor differentiation, The Accounting Review, 663–682.

Fried, D. and A. Schiff, 1981, CPA switches and associated market reaction, The Accounting Review, 326–341.

Halpren, P., 1983, Corporate acquisitions: A theory of special cases?, Journal of Finance, 297–317.

Healy, P., 1985, The effect of bonus schemes on accounting decisions, Journal of Accounting and Economics, 85–108.

Healy, P. and T. Lys, 1986, Auditor changes following big eight takeovers of non-Big Eight audit firms, Journal of Accounting and Public Policies, 251–265.

Jensen, M.C. and W.H. Meckling, 1976, Theory of the firm: Managerial behavior, agency costs and ownership structure, Journal of Financial Economics, 305–360.

Jensen, M. And R. Ruback, 1983, The market for corporate control: The scientific evidence, Journal of Financial Economics, 5–50.

Klein, B. and K.B. Leffler, 1981, The role of market forces in assuring contractual performance, Journal of Political Economy, 615–641.

Magee, R. and M. Tseng, 1987, Audit pricing and independence, Unpublished manuscript (Kellogg Graduate School of Management, Northwestern University, Evanston, IL).

Marais, M.L., 1984, An application of the bootstrap method to the analysis of squared standardized market model prediction errors, Journal of Accounting Research, Suppl., 34–58.

McConnell, J. and C. Muscarella, 1985, Corporate capital expenditure decisions and the market value of the firm, Journal of Financial Economics, 399–422.

McNichols, M. and J. Manegold, 1983, The effect of information environment on the relationship between financial disclosure and security price variability, Journal of Accounting and Economics, 49–74.

Miles, J. and J. Rosenfeld, 1983, An empirical analysis of the effects of spin-off announcements on shareholder wealth, Journal of Finance, 1597–1606.

Nichols, D.R. and D.B. Smith, 1983, Auditor credibility and auditor changes, Journal of Accounting Research, 534–544.

Palmrose, Z., 1984, The demand for quality-differentiated audit services in an agency-cost setting: An empirical investigation, Auditing Research Symposium (University of Illinois, Urbana, IL) 229–252.

Ruback, R.S., 1982, The effect of discretionary price control decisions on equity values, Journal of Financial Economics, 83–106.

Schipper, K. and A. Smith, 1983, Effects of recontracting on shareholder wealth: The case of voluntary spin-offs, Journal of Financial Economics, 437–467.

Schipper, K. and A. Smith, 1986, A comparison of equity carve-outs and seasoned equity offerings: Share price effects and corporate restructuring, Journal of Financial Economics, 153–186.

Scholes, M. and J. Williams, 1977, Estimating betas from nonsynchronous data, Journal of Financial Economics, 309–327.

Schwartz, K.B. and K. Menon, 1985, Auditor switches by failing firms, The Accounting Review, 248–261.

Simunic, D., 1980, The pricing of audit services: Theory and evidence, Journal of Accounting Research, 117–161.

Simunic, D. and M. Stein, 1986, Product differentiation in auditing: A study of auditor choice in the market for new issues, Unpublished Canadian Accounting Association monograph.

Smith, C., 1986, Investment banking and the capital acquisition process, Journal of Financial Economics, 3–29.

Smith, D.B. and D.R. Nichols, 1982, A market test of investor reaction to disagreements, Journal of Accounting and Economics, 109–120.

Titman, S. and B. Trueman, 1986, Information quality and the valuation of new issues, Journal of Accounting and Economics, 159–172.

Watts, R. and J. Zimmerman, 1986, Positive accounting theory (Prentice–Hall, Englewood Cliffs, NJ).

[15]

THE ACCOUNTING REVIEW
Vol. LXIV, No. 3
July 1989

The Relation of Audit Contract Type to Audit Fees and Hours

Zoe-Vonna Palmrose

ABSTRACT: Audit contract type—fixed fee or cost-reimbursement—may affect audit fees and audit hours because of differences in both risk-sharing and incentives for efficiencies between the two types of contracts. It was hypothesized that under fixed fee contracting (1) audit fees would be higher or unaffected, and (2) audit hours would be lower. Instead, results indicate fixed fee contracts are associated with significantly lower audit fees and audit hours are not affected by contract type. The study also found that type of auditor (Big Eight or non-Big Eight), company ownership (public or closely-held), and time frame of audit performance (auditors' busy or non-busy season) was not related to contract choice. Finally, fixed fee contracting tended to be used more in early years of auditor/client relations. However, any pricing unique to initial engagements (e.g., price cutting behavior) did not explain significantly lower audit fees with fixed fee contracting.

I N contracting for audit services, contract type is one choice variable. Contracts can be classified into two general types: fixed fee and cost-reimbursement. Under fixed fee contracts, auditor and client agree on a fee prior to the audit. The choice of contract type can alter assignment of risks between auditor and client and can influence auditors' incentives to conduct engagements in the most efficient (least cost) manner. Because of differences in risk-sharing and incentives for audit efficiencies, contract type can potentially affect both audit fees and audit hours. This study investigates the relation of contract type to audit fees and hours. It also provides insights into conditions surrounding the use of fixed fee and cost-reimbursement contracts in the audit services market.

The professional literature has long recognized contract type as an important choice variable in audit contracting (see Arens and Loebbecke [1984, p. 199] and Williams [1952]). In addition, regulators have revealed concern for this choice. For example, the SEC in ASR No. 250

The research assistance of H. Y. Chung, C. Ham, and Jianmin Liu; financial assistance of the University of California at Berkeley Professional Accounting Program; and helpful comments of Mike Duffy, Bill Felix, Clancy Houghton, Gene Imhoff, Jim Jiambalvo, Marcia Niles, and especially Bill Kinney and Jim Ohlson are all gratefully acknowledged.

Zoe-Vonna Palmrose is Associate Professor at the University of Southern California.

Manuscript received June 1987.
Revisions received May 1988 and February 1989.
Accepted February 1989.

(effective September 30, 1978 and rescinded January 28, 1982) required proxy statement disclosure of direct or indirect understandings limiting current or future years' audit fees, including fixed fees not subject to reconsideration when encountering unexpected accounting or auditing issues. However, empirical research on the pricing of audit services has not pursued issues related to contract type (e.g., Francis and Simon [1987], Palmrose [1986], Simon [1985], Simon and Francis [1988], and Simunic [1980]).

Section I develops a conceptual framework for hypotheses tested in the study. Section II discusses sample selection and characteristics. Section III presents results. Final remarks and conclusions appear in Section IV.

I. CONCEPTUAL FRAMEWORK

In conducting audits, auditors require sufficient evidence to support rendering assurances that financial statements contain no material omissions or misstatements. Irrespective of contract type, professional and regulatory standards (e.g., AICPA [1983]), along with a penalty structure for noncompliance with standards, impose general requirements for sufficient evidence to support the auditor's assurances. Although auditing standards and procedures serve as a framework for acquiring evidence, each engagement is unique as to both audit entity and time-period. During the period under audit, clients' information processing and control systems, events and transactions, and cooperation, all influence the auditor's evidence acquisition. Therefore, at the time of contracting for an audit, uncertainty exists as to the nature and magnitude of evidence to be acquired. The term task uncertainty [Williamson, 1975] is used to describe this evidence acquisition uncertainty.

At audit contract negotiation, clients and auditors do not have identical information regarding potential evidence acquisition. Auditors may have more information than clients on audit procedures to be used to acquire evidence. Clients have more information than auditors on organization-specific factors (systems, cooperation, transactions, and events) related to the audit period that influence actual auditor evidence acquisition.

Contract type, fixed fee or cost-reimbursement, shifts task uncertainty risk between auditor and client. In general, with cost-reimbursement contracts, clients bear task uncertainty risk. Under cost-reimbursement contracting, total audit fees are determined after both contracting and audit evidence acquisition based on hourly or daily charges for actual time devoted to an engagement. A common approach develops standard rates for each category of audit personnel and applies these standard rates to time charged by that category plus any direct expenses. In essence, with cost-reimbursement contracts, auditors determine the nature and magnitude of audit evidence and clients provide reimbursement for actual time spent in acquiring evidence and forming an opinion. Under fixed fee contracting, fees are set in advance of performance and task uncertainty risk shifts to auditors. Auditors bear the consequences of deviations between expected and actual evidence acquisition.

In addition to differences in risk-sharing between clients and auditors, incentives for efficiencies in performance of audits are not necessarily similar for fixed fee and cost-reimbursement contracts. Fixed fee contracts generally provide greater incentives for least-cost performance of engagements since auditors retain any differences between costs and fees, when prespecified fees exceed costs.[1]

These differences in risk-sharing and incentives between fixed fee and cost-reimbursement contracts have implications for audit fees. But, unfortunately, the net effect is not unambiguous. To compensate auditors for assuming greater risk of task uncertainty, expected audit fees would be higher with fixed fee contracts. However, increased incentives for efficiencies with fixed fee contracts translate into lower expected audit fees.

Given this ambiguity, examination of the implications of contract type requires a second variable, in addition to audit fees. The second variable is total audit hours. Because of the labor-intensive nature of auditing, any efficiencies in audit performance would decrease the amount of time incurred by audit team members. This means that expected audit hours would be less with fixed fee contracts. Note, it is the reduction in audit hours that decreases expected audit fees under fixed fee contracting.

To summarize, the study examines the effects of contract type on total audit fees and audit hours. Two null hypotheses are tested:

H_{0_1}: There is no difference in audit fees between fixed fee and cost-reimbursement contracts.

H_{0_2}: There is no difference in audit hours between fixed fee and cost-reimbursement contracts.

Under *ceteris paribus* conditions, rejection of H_{0_2} in the direction of lower audit hours with fixed fee contracts, accompanied by either a failure to reject H_{0_1} or rejection of H_{0_1} with higher fees for fixed fee contracts, would be consistent with both increased efficiencies and greater risk of task uncertainty borne by auditors with fixed fee contracts.

The *ceteris paribus* conditions under which the hypotheses are formulated require some discussion. In reality, contract type, expected audit fees, and expected audit hours are jointly determined. This determination may be influenced by factors, including: audit quality, time frame for audit performance, and length of auditor/client relation. These factors require recognition in testing.

The predictions assume constant quality (level of audit assurance that financial statements are free of material error) across audits. If audit quality differs systematically between fixed fee and cost-reimbursement contracts, any lower audit hours or lower audit fees would be indicative of lower levels of service. To assess whether contract choices appear associated with any differential supply or demand for audit quality, two variables are used—type of auditor (Big Eight or non-Big Eight) and company ownership (public or closely-held). These variables are based on extant evidence. For example, Francis and Simon [1987] and Palmrose [1986] present findings consistent with the Big Eight as higher quality suppliers. Research on differential demand for quality in an agency cost setting [Francis and Wilson, 1988; Palmrose, 1984] suggests that public companies are a class of auditees with a potential demand for higher quality audit services.

Time frame of audit performance, i.e., off-season or busy-season audits, represents another factor that may influence contract choice, audit fees, and audit hours. To provide work for staff during slack periods, auditors might be willing

---

[1] Under cost-reimbursement contracts, auditors can agree to charge clients less than 100 percent of standard. Such contracts may provide incentives for efficiencies if audit firms have alternate higher-valued uses for audit personnel.

to contract on a fixed fee basis at lower than normal fees, despite assuming greater risk of task uncertainty. Furthermore, fixed fee contracts during periods of slack demand would not necessarily create strong incentives for audit efficiencies. Client year-ends are used to proxy for the time frame of audit performance. Year-ends during November, December, and January are defined as busy season audits. Year-ends during all other months are defined as off-season audits.

Finally, the study considers length of auditor/client relation. Given risks associated with task uncertainty, fixed fee contracts should be less likely to occur in early years of auditor/client relations when information disparities between client and auditor are likely to be greatest regarding organization-specific information.[2] Yet, evidence suggests that fixed fee contracts may be part of a response to competition for clients in an environment where auditors can benefit from advantages to incumbency (see Bowman [1985] and DeAngelo [1981]).[3] Tests are conducted for any systematic differences in the choice of contract types over the term of auditor/client relations to assess the role of this factor in contracting.

Audit quality, time frame for audit performance, and length of auditor/client relations do not exhaust the potential conditions that may influence the joint determination of contract type, audit fees, and hours. For example, the use of total audit hours does not consider any differences in the mix of audit firm personnel (e.g., partners, managers, seniors, and staff accountants) across engagements. To ensure that any differences in audit fees or hours do not reflect utilization of less experienced personnel, it would be desirable to examine for systematic differences between fixed fee and cost-reimbursement contracts in

the use of categories of audit personnel. However, this analysis was precluded as audit hours by personnel categories were unavailable from data sources utilized for the study.[4]

To examine the relation of contract type to total audit fees and hours, relevant control and test variables are incorporated in a multiple regression model adapted from Palmrose [1986], as follows:

$$
\begin{aligned}
\ell n(\text{Audit Fees}) & \\
\text{or} \qquad & = b_0 + b_1 \ell n(\text{Assets}) \\
\ell n(\text{Audit Hours}) & + b_2 \ell n(\text{Reports}) \\
& + b_3 \ell n(\text{Locations}) \\
& + b_4 RAI \\
& + b_5 PNP + b_6 ST \\
& + b_7 B8NB8 \\
& + b_8 YE + b_{9\text{-}18} IIV \\
& + b_{19} FFNFF \\
& + u \qquad (1)
\end{aligned}
$$

where, the dependent variable is either:

$\ell n(\text{Audit Fees})$ = natural log of audit fees,
or
$\ell n(\text{Audit Hours})$ = natural log of total hours worked by audit team,

---

[2] This is consistent with historical professional literature. The *CPA Handbook* [1952] emphasizes that fixed fee contracting is not recommended on initial engagements, because auditors may not have the knowledge to make reasonable fee estimates [Williams, 1952, p. 10].

[3] Professional standards requiring communications between predecessor and successor auditors may help mitigate some risk of task uncertainty borne by auditors under fixed fee contracts with new clients.

[4] Because auditors considered client-specific information sought by the questionnaire as confidential, all data, including audit hours, were obtained from auditees. However, discussions with auditors supported the reasonableness of using auditees for data on audit hours. As a practical matter, on both fixed fee and cost-reimbursement engagements, auditors normally furnish clients with planned and actual hours. In addition, evidence suggests that clients do monitor audit team time incurred on engagements [Macchiaverna, 1981].

492   The Accounting Review, July 1989

the independent control variables are:

ln(Assets) = natural log of total assets of client,

ln(Reports) = natural log of number of separate audit reports,

ln(Locations) = natural log of number of locations requiring on-site visits by auditors,

RAI = percentage reduction in audit fee or hours from auditee inputs (i.e., internal audit, internal control, and utilization of client personnel) as assessed by participants,

PNP = ownership indicator variable,

    (1) public company, or
    (0) closely-held company,

ST = report modification indicator variable,

    (1) report modified (other than consistency exceptions from changes in GAAP), or
    (0) all others,

$B8NB8$ = type of audit firm,

    (1) Big Eight, or
    (0) non-Big Eight,

YE = client year-end indicator variable,

    (1) busy season audit, or
    (0) non-busy season audit,

and

IIV = (ten) industry indicator variables;

and the test variable is:

$FFNFF$ = indicator variable for type of contract,

    (1) fixed fee, or
    (0) cost-reimbursement;

and

u = error term.

Independent control variables are included to allow for possible effects of cross-sectional differences in client size (assets and reports), audit complexity (locations), client participation/substitution (RAI), audit risk (PNP, ST, IIV), type of audit firm ($B8NB8$), and client year-end (YE). Positive coefficients are expected for these variables except for RAI variable coefficient and coefficients for IIV variables in regulated industries (see Francis and Simon [1987], Palmrose [1986], Simon [1985], Simon and Francis [1988], and Simunic [1980]). A variable for length of auditor/client relation is added to the basic model using several different formulations for initial engagements as discussed in Section III.

To determine effects of contract type on both audit fees and hours, the model includes a test variable. The test variable ($FFNFF$) is an indicator variable, where (1) fixed fee engagement, and (0) cost-reimbursement engagement.

II. THE SAMPLE

Data from 361 companies issuing audited financial statements were obtained via questionnaires sent to an individual in the company considered most likely to be knowledgeable about contracting with public accounting firms (see Palmrose [1986]). The individual was usually a financial vice president, treasurer, or controller. The sample consists of both public and closely-held companies from a variety of industries, including: manufacturing, transportation, communications, electric and gas services, retail trade, financial services, and other services. Questionnaires were sent to companies from these industries using *Standard & Poor's*

TABLE 1

MEANS AND STANDARD DEVIATIONS OF THE INDEPENDENT AND DEPENDENT VARIABLES[1]

(1980–1981)

	Total Sample (n = 361)[2]	Fixed Fee Engagements (n = 183)	Cost-Reimbursement Engagements (n = 178)
Audit Fees	$179,669 (424,251)	$172,392 (419,546)	$187,150 (430,090)
Audit Hours	3,414 (7,925)	3,382 (8,481)	3,446 (7,364)
Assets	$ 1,260MM (6,832MM)	$ 1,382MM (9,316MM)	$ 1,135MM (2,380MM)
Number of Reports	3.5 (7.9)	3.4 (8.2)	3.7 (7.6)
Number of Locations	3.1 (7.6)	3.3 (7.8)	2.9 (7.5)
Percentage Reduction in Fees or Hours from Auditee Inputs	17% (13%)	17% (13%)	17% (13%)
Percentage of Public Companies	75%	76%	73%
Percentage of Report Modifications	8%	10%	6%
Percentage of Big Eight Auditors	83%	83%	82%
Percentage of Busy Season Audits	69%	68%	71%
Years Client Had Retained Auditor	21 (16)	17 (16)	24 (15)

[1] Variables not transformed.
[2] For audit hours the number of observations is 302, 150, and 152 (respectively).

Register of Corporations, Directors, and Executives [1981] and *Who Audits America* [Harris, 1980] with a response rate of approximately 30 percent. Data represent the 1980–1981 time-period.

The type of fee contracting was assessed from responses to the following question:

> Was the total cost of the audit for the last fiscal year agreed on in advance as a fixed amount?
>
> (Yes or No) _____

Overall, 51 percent of the participants indicated that total audit cost was agreed on in advance as a fixed amount. As discussed in Section IV, some participants commented that their fixed fee contracts were subject to adjustment for changed or unexpected circumstances.[5]

[5] Discussions with auditors reinforced that "yes" responses capture engagements where auditors provide clients with fixed estimates or quotations in advance of audit performance and both auditors and clients expect audit fees to equal prespecified amounts. Auditors were not surprised that 51 percent of the participants indicated fixed fee contracts, as fixed fee arrangements subject to adjustment for unexpected circumstances are considered common. However, arrangements not subject to renegotiation under any circumstances are considered rare. That is consistent with results of an Ernst & Whinney (EW) survey of 4,300 proxy statements filed from October 1, 1978 through June 30, 1979. The survey found only 12 had disclosures of fee limitations as required by the SEC [EW, 1980]. Perhaps more importantly, this illustrates that audit contracting involves a continuum of contract types not just the dichotomous classification used in this study. Section IV discusses this issue.

TABLE 2

REGRESSION RESULTS FOR AUDIT FEES AND AUDIT HOURS
(1980–1981)

ln(Audit Fees) or ln(Audit Hours) $= b_0 + b_1 ln$(Assets) $+ b_2 ln$(Reports) $+ b_3 ln$(Locations)
$+ b_4 RAI + b_5 PNP + b_6 ST + b_7 B8NB8 + b_8 YE$
$+ b_{9-18} IIV + b_{19} FFNFF + u$

| | Dependent Variable | | | |
| | ln(Audit Fee) ($n=361$) | | ln(Audit Hours) ($n=302$) | |
	Coefficient	t-statistic	Coefficient	t-statistic
Intercept	1.978	6.131*	−1.551	−3.336*
Assets (log)	.467	26.933*	.446	17.779*
Number of Reports (log)	.194	5.596*	.122	2.458**
Number of Locations (log)	.232	6.365*	.276	5.353*
Reduction From Auditee Inputs	−.498	−2.907*	−.701	−2.869*
Public Ownership or Closely-Held	.342	5.592*	.320	3.683*
Audit Report Modification	.348	4.242*	.395	3.170*
Audit Firm Type	.232	3.314*	.210	2.043**
Busy Season Audit	−.005	−.082	.109	1.364
Industry Indicator Variables[1]				
Contract Type	−.100	−2.174**	−.025	−.377
F-statistic	157.676*19,360		73.461*19,301	
Adjusted R^2	.89		.82	

* Significant at the .01 level.
** Significant at the .05 level.
[1] The following industry indicator variable coefficients are significant at the .05 level, for ln(Audit Fee) as the dependent variable: electric/combination utilities (negative), savings and loans (negative), office equipment (positive), and retail trade (positive); and for ln(Audit Hours) as the dependent variable: electric/combination utilities (negative) and savings and loans (negative).

III. RESULTS

Table 1 provides means and standard deviations for dependent and independent variables (not transformed) in the model. Data are presented for total sample and two subsets of participants— those with fixed fee and those with cost-reimbursement engagements. As noted in Table 1, a reduced number of participants (302 of 361) furnished data on total audit hours. Of the auditees not furnishing audit hour data, 33 had fixed fee and 26 had cost-reimbursement engagements. However, the frequency with which audit hours data were furnished did not differ significantly ($p = .10$) be-

tween fixed fee and cost-reimbursement engagements (computed chi-square (1) is .78).

Table 2 presents regression results with ln(Audit Fees) and ln(Audit Hours) each as dependent variables. In each regression, control variable coefficients have the expected signs. The reasonableness of combining both fixed fee and cost-reimbursement engagements in one regression was examined and a Chow test could not reject the null hypothesis of equal regression parameters across data subsets.

Table 2 shows that contract type ($FFNFF$) coefficient is negative and statistically significant at the .05 level with *ln*(Audit Fees) as dependent variable.[6] Thus, participants with fixed fee engagements do tend to have lower audit fees. Also, Table 2 shows the *FFNFF* coefficient is not statistically significant with *ln*(Audit Hours) as the dependent variable. Audit hours do not differ between fixed fee and cost-reimbursement engagements. These results suggest that the greater task uncertainty borne by auditors under fixed fee contracts is not reflected in a higher audit fee. The greater incentives for efficiencies under fixed fee contracts do not result in a reduction in audit hours.

The indicator variable for busy season audits is not significant at the .05 level in either regression. However, the busy season coefficient is significantly positive at the .10 level for audit hours. Since results appear consistent with contracting on a fixed fee basis to provide work for staff during slack periods, chi-square tests were conducted for differences between fixed fee and cost-reimbursement engagements regarding time-period of audit performance. Similar tests encompass the type of auditor and client company ownership. All tests are reported in Table 3.

The use of fixed fee contracts does not appear to be more characteristic of slack period audits (see panel A of Table 3). The computed chi-square is .469 and it cannot reject the null hypothesis of no association at even the .40 level.[7] Likewise, the use of fixed fee contracts does not appear to be more characteristic of Big Eight/non-Big Eight auditors or public/closely-held companies. Computed chi-squares cannot reject the null hypothesis of no association ($p = .40$) in either case (see panels B and C of Table 3). This analysis provides indirect evidence that choice of contract type does not reflect any systematic differences in supply or demand for audit quality.

Finally, the influence of length (term)

of auditor/client relations on contract choice was examined. Table 1 shows number of years retained averages 17 years for fixed fee and 24 years for cost-reimbursement engagements. Higher usage of fixed fee contracts in earlier years of auditor/client relations becomes more evident in Table 4. Nearly 30 percent of participants with fixed fees retained their audit firm for five years or less, and 50 percent (29 percent + 21 percent) for ten years or less. In addition, 75 percent of companies that retained their audit firm for five years or less used fixed fee contracts. The computed chi-square for a 2×6 contingency table is significant at the .01 level in the direction of a greater number of fixed fee engagements than expected in earlier years of auditor/client relations.

The predominance of fixed fee contracts in early years of auditor/client relations suggests that auditors may assume greater risk of task uncertainty as part of a competitive process for initially obtaining and maintaining clients. As a consequence, the contract type variable (*FFNFF*) could be proxying for pricing unique to initial engagements. For example, Simon and Francis [1988] provide evidence on price cutting behavior during the first three years of continuing audit engagements.

To help determine whether pricing unique to initial engagements, rather than contract type, drives pricing regression results (i.e., lower audit fees on

---

[6] Results for the *FFNFF* variable are not substantially altered if the regression with *ln*(Audit Fees) as the dependent variable is run using only the 302 observations with audit hours.

[7] The sample was also partitioned into two subsets—busy season audits ($n = 250$) and non-busy season audits ($n = 111$)—and the regressions estimated for each subset. With *ln*(Audit Fees) as the dependent variable the *FFNFF* coefficient was significant only in the busy season subset (coefficient $-.120$, t-statistic -2.178). With *ln*(Audit Hours) as the dependent variable the *FFNFF* variable coefficient was not significant in either subset.

496   The Accounting Review, July 1989

TABLE 3

CLASSIFICATION OF FIXED FEE/COST-REIMBURSEMENT ENGAGEMENTS

($n = 361$)

	Fixed Fee Engagements	Cost-Reimbursement Engagements	Total
Panel A. By Auditee Year-End (Auditor's Busy or Non-Busy Season):			
Year-End During Busy Season[1]	124	126	250
Year-End During Non-Busy Season	59	52	111
Total	183	178	361
Computed $\chi^2 = .469_{ns}$			
Panel B. By Type of Auditor:			
Big Eight Auditor	152	146	298
Non-Big Eight Auditor	31	32	63
Total	183	178	361
Computed $\chi^2 = .077_{ns}$[2]			
Panel C. By Type of Auditee:			
Public Company	139	130	269
Closely-Held Company	44	48	92
Total	183	178	361
Computed $\chi^2 = .526_{ns}$			

[1] Year-ends during November, December, and January are classified as busy season year-ends. All other year-ends are classified as non-busy season.

[2] χ^2 statistics are not significant at the .40 level.

fixed fee engagements), the *FFNFF* variable was deleted and an indicator variable—(1) initial engagement, and (0) otherwise—was substituted in the regression with ℓn(Audit Fees) as dependent variable. Several specifications of initial engagements (see SEC [1978, p. 36] and Simon and Francis [1988]) were used including the following:

- years retained—two years or less (6 percent of sample),
- years retained—three years or less (11 percent of sample), and
- years retained—five years or less (20 percent of sample).

None of the coefficients for the indicator variable was significant at any meaningful level under any specification of initial engagement (remaining regression results were not substantially altered from those reported in Table 2). Thus, it appears lower audit fees with fixed fee contracting cannot be attributed to pricing unique to initial engagements.[8]

[8] Regressions were also conducted with a variable for ℓn(Years Auditor Retained). The coefficient of this variable was not significant with ℓn(Audit Fees) as dependent variable, but it was significant with ℓn(Audit Hours) as dependent variable (coefficient −.085, t-statistic −2.170). This may indicate profit margins on engagements improve over time as audit fees do not

TABLE 4

CLASSIFICATION OF FIXED FEE/COST-REIMBURSEMENT ENGAGEMENTS
BY NUMBER OF YEARS CLIENT HAD RETAINED AUDITOR

	Total	Years					
		5 or Less	6-10	11-20	21-30	31-40	Over 40
Cost-Reimbursement	178	18 (10% 25% 5%)[1]	24 (13% 38% 6%)	49 (28% 57% 14%)	35 (20% 62% 10%)	24 (13% 63% 6%)	28 (16% 60% 8%)
Fixed Fee	183	53 (29% 75% 15%)	39 (21% 62% 11%)	37 (20% 43% 10%)	21 (12% 38% 6%)	14 (8% 37% 4%)	19 (10% 40% 5%)
Total	361	71	63	86	56	38	47

Computed $\chi^2_{(5)} = 29.95$
Table $\chi^2_{\alpha=.01} = 15.09$
[1] Row percentage/Column percentage/Overall percentage

IV. FINAL REMARKS AND CONCLUSIONS

Dichotomization of contract types into fixed fee and cost-reimbursement fails to consider that neither type of contract is of a single form. Recall, some participants commented that their fixed fee contracts were subject to adjustment for changed or unexpected circumstances. This provision is of interest because, in addition to avoiding the need for proxy statement disclosures under SEC ASR No. 250, such a provision may help mitigate some risk of task uncertainty otherwise assumed by auditors with fixed fee contracts. Furthermore, cost-reimbursement contracts can include an estimated fee (or fee range) with auditors agreeing to communicate to clients when it is known estimated amounts will be exceeded. This commitment may somewhat alter risk-sharing and incentives for efficiencies.

While the study provides insights into the nature and effect of differences in audit fee contracts, further research would be required to satisfactorily explain lower fees on fixed fee engagements (with audit hours remaining unaffected). However, assuming total hours worked by audit firm personnel in conducting engagements reflect audit evidence acquisition, these results should alleviate concerns that reducing audit fees necessarily compromises audit performance (see Work [1985, p. 58]). In part, such concerns were behind the SEC

ASR No. 250 disclosure requirements regarding fixed fee arrangements.

With fixed fee contracting, auditors bear greater risk of task uncertainty and auditors have greater incentives for efficiencies. As a consequence, it was hypothesized audit hours would be lower and audit fees would be unaffected or higher under fixed fee contracts. Instead, audit hours were not significantly affected by contract type and audit fees were significantly lower with fixed fee contracting.

In addition, the study found that type of auditor (Big Eight or non-Big Eight), company ownership (public or closely-held), and time frame of company year-end (auditors' busy or non-busy season) did not influence contract choice. However, it was found that fixed fee contracting tended to be used more in early years of auditor/client relations. Even so, price cutting behavior on initial engagements did not explain significantly lower audit fees with fixed fee contracting. Finally, the study recognized contract provisions that mitigate some differences between the two contract types in both risks of task uncertainty assumed by auditors and auditors' incentives for efficiencies.

---

adjust downward but audit hours decrease. This would be consistent with DeAngelo's [1981] arguments as to pricing advantages to incumbency.

REFERENCES

American Institute of Certified Public Accountants (AICPA), *Audit Risk and Materiality in Conducting an Audit*, Statement on Auditing Standards No. 47 (December 1983).

Arens, A. A., and J. K. Loebbecke, *Auditing: An Integrated Approach*, Third Edition (Prentice-Hall, Inc., 1984).

Bowman, A. W., "Statement of Editor, *Public Accounting Report*, before the Subcommittee on Oversight and Investigations, Committee on Energy and Commerce, U.S. House of Representatives" (March 6, 1985).

DeAngelo, L. E., "Auditor Independence, 'Low-Balling,' and Disclosure Regulation," *Journal of Accounting and Economics* (August 1981), pp. 113–127.

Ernst & Whinney, "Survey of ASR No. 250 Disclosures in Proxy Statements" (EW No. 40117, March 1980).

Francis, J. R., and D. T. Simon, "A Test of Audit Pricing in the Small-Client Segment of the U.S. Audit Market," THE ACCOUNTING REVIEW (January 1987), pp. 145–157.

———, and E. R. Wilson, "Auditor Changes: A Joint Test of Theories Relating to Agency Costs and Auditor Differentiation," THE ACCOUNTING REVIEW (October 1988), pp. 663–682.

Harris, S., Ed., *Who Audits America* (The Data Financial Press, 1980).

Macchiaverna, P. E., *Corporations and Their Outside Auditors: A Changing Relationship* (The Conference Board, 1981).

Palmrose, Z., "Audit Fees and Auditor Size: Further Evidence," *Journal of Accounting Research* (Spring 1986), pp. 97–110.

———, "The Demand for Quality-Differentiated Audit Services in an Agency-Cost Setting: An Empirical Investigation," *Auditing Research Symposium* (University of Illinois, 1984), pp. 229–252.

Securities and Exchange Commission, *Report to Congress on the Accounting Profession and the Commission's Oversight Role* (U.S. Government Printing Office, 1978).

Simon, D. T., "The Audit Services Market: Additional Empirical Evidence," *Auditing: A Journal of Practice and Theory* (Fall 1985), pp. 71–78.

———, and J. R. Francis, "The Effects of Auditor Change on Audit Fees: Tests of Price Cutting and Price Recovery," THE ACCOUNTING REVIEW (April 1988), pp. 255–269.

Simunic, D. A., "The Pricing of Audit Services: Theory and Evidence," *Journal of Accounting Research* (Spring 1980), pp. 161–190.

Standard & Poor's Corporation, *Standard & Poor's Register of Corporations, Directors, and Executives,* Volumes 1 and 3 (Standard & Poor's Corp., 1981).

Williams, T. D., "Fees for Services," in R. L. Kane, Jr., Ed., *CPA Handbook,* Volume I (AIA, 1952), pp. 1–12.

Williamson, O. E., *Markets and Hierarchies: Analysis and Antitrust Implications* (The Free Press, 1975).

Work, C. P., "Accounting's Bottom Line: Big Troubles," *U.S. News & World Report* (October 21, 1985), p. 58.

[16]

Journal of Accounting Research
Vol. 32 No. 2 Autumn 1994
Printed in U.S.A.

The Production of Audit Services: Evidence from a Major Public Accounting Firm

TERRENCE B. O'KEEFE,* DAN A. SIMUNIC,†
AND MICHAEL T. STEIN‡

1. Introduction

In this research, we examine the empirical relation between client characteristics and the nature and mix of labor resources used by an international *CPA* firm to obtain a desired level of assurance that clients' financial statements are free of material misstatement. The level of assurance is the output of an audit, while the input resources measure the effort required to produce that output, under varying client circumstances.

We use disaggregated labor hours by rank within the firm (partner, manager, senior, and staff) as the measure of inputs, in order to examine now client characteristics affect both the amount and mix of labor used. To the extent that client characteristics have differential effects on the various types of labor, only disaggregated data can reveal changes in labor mix and may also provide a more powerful test (relative to tests

* University of Oregon; †University of British Columbia; ‡ University of Calgary. The authors would like to thank faculty workshop participants at the University of British Columbia, the University of Indonesia, Lehigh University, New York University, Rutgers University, the University of Southern California, Washington University—St. Louis, and the joint UBC/University of Oregon/University of Washington accounting research symposium for their comments on earlier versions of this paper. The comments of Nick Dopuch, Ramy Elizur, Theresa John, Josh Livnat, Jim Rebele, and two anonymous referees were especially useful. Of course, our greatest debt is to the executives of the firm who provided the data and made this study possible.

based on aggregate hours as in Palmrose [1989]) of the influence of these characteristics on audit production.

In addition to providing evidence about which client characteristics have significant effects on auditor effort, hence audit costs, our research tests for knowledge spillovers between services and auditor learning over time. A test based on audit fees only can be contaminated by pricing policies. For example, the inferences from the behavior of audit fees concerning knowledge spillovers between services in Simunic [1984, p. 685] are predicated on the assumption that services are billed consistent with the "physical flow of knowledge." Or, a test for auditor learning using audit fees (e.g., Simon and Francis [1988]) can be contaminated by multiperiod pricing strategies and/or cross-subsidization of services. Thus direct examination of auditor effort can be expected to constitute a more powerful test of these issues. Recently, Davis, Ricchiute, and Trompeter [1993] failed to find evidence of knowledge spillovers for a small sample of clients of one *CPA* firm using aggregated audit hours. Our use of disaggregated labor hours can further increase the power of tests if knowledge spillovers and learning have differential impacts on different grades of labor.

Our research also complements previous studies which have tested hypotheses concerning unit prices using audit fees. Examples are tests of price competition, as in Simunic [1980], and tests for differentiated products, as in Palmrose [1986] and Francis and Simon [1987]. Inferences about prices in such studies can be erroneous if the cross-sectional variations in auditor effort caused by differences in client characteristics are not adequately controlled. Our direct tests on disaggregated audit inputs help validate the choice of control variables and functional forms used in such studies. Of course, our use of data from a single (albeit major) public accounting firm limits the generalizability of the results.

In this research then, we investigate the following specific issues:

1. The nature of the relationship between size, complexity, and risk characteristics of the client and the quantity and mix of labor inputs necessary to produce a fixed level of audit assurance.
2. The effect of auditor reliance on a client's internal control system on the nature and mix of audit inputs.
3. Whether there exists a learning curve in auditing a client over time.
4. Whether there exist knowledge spillovers from nonaudit to audit services. That is, does the production of tax and general management consulting services for a client affect the nature and mix of audit inputs?

Examining any one (or combination) of these issues requires a control for the others. For example, to infer the existence of a learning curve, it is necessary to hold client characteristics constant. In addition, we believe these issues encompass the major sources of variation in auditor effort which are plausible and/or have been identified in previous literature.

Our tests are conducted using data for 249 U.S. audits performed by an international public accounting firm in 1989. We find that the cross-sectional variation in the quantity of labor inputs can largely be explained by the same client size, complexity, and risk measures found to be important in previous research on auditors' fees. However, client size and risk measures are also associated with significant changes in the mix of labor inputs. That is, audit labor inputs are not used in fixed proportion, and certain risk measures have a statistically significant effect only on some classes of labor. Disaggregated labor hours can therefore provide a more powerful test for such effects than an aggregation of hours. We find no evidence of auditor learning over time for any class of labor. Finally, reliance on client controls and/or the joint production of nonaudit services seem to have no systematic effects on either the level or mix of audit labor inputs.

In section 2 we develop a framework for our tests by describing an auditor's decision problem as the production of a desired level of assurance at least cost. In section 3 we discuss the structure of the tests and the strengths and limitations of our data. Section 4 describes the data and principal variables. In section 5 we report, analyze, and evaluate results. A summary and conclusions are in the last section.

2. The Audit Production Problem

Because the level of assurance produced by a given audit is not directly observable, we assume that it is inferred from the audit firm's brand name (e.g., Dopuch and Simunic [1980] and Simunic and Stein [1987]). In addition, we assume that a particular audit firm delivers a fixed level of assurance (quality) at a moment in time. This assumption allows us to interpret cross-sectional differences in inputs used by a specific firm on different audit engagements.[1]

We take the client firm's structure (e.g., size, geographic dispersion of operations, product, and industry diversification), including an internal control system, as predetermined. In addition, owners and managers are assumed to select an audit firm which is expected to deliver a desired level of audit assurance. Finally, we assume the audit firm operates

---

[1] Simunic and Stein [1987] argue that multiple unobservable levels of audit quality cannot, in principle, be sold under a single brand name. In addition, if investments in reputation associated with the delivery of a specific level of assurance are not movable, the auditor is motivated to maintain intertemporal stability in the delivered quality level. Even absent brand incentives, O'Keefe and Westort [1992] show that in competitive markets, audit firms will tend to have limited range in the audit quality delivered to clients. This holds because an audit firm's investments, particularly in knowledge, make it the cost-efficient auditor only for clients who demand an audit quality consistent with those investments. Empirically, the audit manual of the public accounting firm from which our data is obtained explicitly states that, on every audit engagement, staff should design and execute an audit program which results in a specific numeric assurance level.

244   T. B. O'KEEFE, D. A. SIMUNIC, AND M. T. STEIN

in a competitive market and is therefore motivated to produce the desired level of assurance at least cost.[2]

Given these assumptions, the auditor's decision problem for a specific audit engagement can be written as:

$$\underset{\mathbf{h}}{\text{minimize}} \quad c(h,\gamma)$$

$$\text{such that} \quad \bar{q} = p(h,\gamma)$$

where:

$c(\cdot)$ = audit cost function,

$\mathbf{h}$ = $(h_1, \ldots h_J)$, a vector of audit service inputs, where h_j denotes the quantity of each type of input,

γ = $(\gamma_1, \ldots \gamma_I)$, a vector of exogenous (from the auditor's perspective) client firm characteristics,

$\bar{q}$ = the level of assurance associated with audit firm's brand name,

$p(\cdot)$ = audit production function.

This is the standard problem of minimizing costs for a given output; the solution requires that input quantities are determined simultaneously and that the ratio of the marginal factor cost to the marginal "assurance" product of each input be the same, where aggregate input utilization is such that the required level of assurance is, in fact, produced. This optimum combination of audit service inputs for a given client is denoted $\mathbf{h^*}$.

Consistent with the previous discussion, a potential audit supplier for a client is characterized by an assurance level, $\bar{q}$, and a minimum cost of producing that assurance, $c(\mathbf{h^*},\gamma)$. As is typical for services (Fuchs [1968]), client characteristics are parameters in the audit production function and cost function. The locus of assurance levels and minimum cost points constitutes a client-specific supply function of audit services.[3]

3. Structure of the Empirical Tests

Based on this conceptual framework, we investigate the cross-sectional relations between audit inputs and client characteristics. For-

[2] Formulating the auditor's decision as a constrained cost minimization is a simplification of the auditor's problem. Auditors frequently speak of "value billing" their services, which suggests profit maximization is the relevant objective. However, our data do not include information on factors which could be associated with variations in the price competitiveness, hence profitability, of individual engagements. Furthermore, there are likely to be other valued aspects of the audit service, beyond the production of a level of assurance. We ignore these secondary service attributes as we have no knowledge of client-specific factors which might be associated with variations in the demand for these ancillary aspects of auditing from a particular CPA firm.

[3] An auditor's client-specific cost minimization problem with a fixed (and constraining) assurance level can be thought of as his short-run problem. In the long run, the assurance level, q, is also a decision variable. However, we do not model this larger problem because it is not relevant to our empirical tests.

mally, we estimate the factor demand for audit service inputs, given relative prices and a particular level of audit quality. That is, we study the properties of the relations:

$$\mathbf{h^*}_j = p^{-1}(\bar{q}, \gamma) \qquad \forall\, j = 1, \ldots, J.$$

In principle, the components of the vector $\mathbf{h^*}$ are the units of labor, capital, and other resources utilized in audit service production. We measure $\mathbf{h^*}$ using the hours of the J grades of professional labor (e.g., partners, managers, etc.) charged to an engagement.[4] We do not consider capital inputs, such as the intensity of use of computer-assisted audit techniques, because we believe they are of second-order importance.

3.1 DISAGGREGATED LABOR HOURS

As noted in the introduction, disaggregated labor hours are appropriate measures of auditor effort if resources are used in different proportions as client characteristics vary. Given variable factor proportions, measurement of auditor effort using a simple sum of hours can lead to a loss of information and perhaps a loss of statistical efficiency in estimating the effects of changes in client characteristics. For example, if a change in a client characteristic decreases the quantity utilized of one input while increasing the quantity of another, using the sum of hours would represent an extreme case of information loss. But even when all input changes are nonnegative, simple summation assigns inappropriate equal weights to each change.

A loss of efficiency can occur when a change in a client characteristic has little or no effect on some class(es) of labor. The t-value for the estimated regression coefficient for that characteristic using aggregated hours as the dependent variable is likely to be smaller than in disaggregated hour regressions, because aggregation increases the standard error of the coefficient with little or no increase in the coefficient itself. The loss of efficiency is most severe when the standard errors of the estimate for the disaggregated regression equations are positively correlated. This issue is analyzed further in an Appendix, which is available from the authors.

While the optimum combination of resources used in audit service production depends on the marginal factor costs and the marginal assurance products of the resources, we have no data on marginal input costs, and assume that the ratios of marginal costs of the various grades of professional labor are constant across engagements. Our discussions with personnel of the firm providing the data indicate that although the absolute levels of audit labor costs vary geographically, the cost ratios among the labor categories are approximately the same in all locations.

---

[4] We recognize that the hours charged may not represent actual hours spent on a job. However, to the extent that any unreported hours simply reflect idiosyncratic inefficiencies, or even idiosyncratic learning, the hours charged are the appropriate empirical measure of $\mathbf{h^*}$.

246   T. B. O'KEEFE, D. A. SIMUNIC, AND M. T. STEIN

Thus cross-sectional variations in the mix of professional labor are assumed to reflect variations in marginal assurance products associated with different client characteristics, and not the results of price-induced substitution.

3.2 FUNCTIONAL FORM AND ACROSS-EQUATION TESTS

There is no theory of production from which the specific form of the $p^{-1}(\bar{q},\gamma)$ function can be deduced. We therefore investigated the properties of several variations of the empirical model used in the existing literature on audit fees. The basic statistical problems encountered by prior researchers are a need to linearize the relationship between total fees (here labor hours) and client size (typically the client firm's total assets) and to reduce heteroscedasticity. These problems are usually resolved by regressing the natural logarithm of fees on the log of total assets and other (usually not logged) explanatory variables.

We use the following empirical model in our tests:[5]

$$\ln h_j = \beta_{j0} + \beta_{j1} \ln A + \sum_{i=2}^{K} \beta_{ji} \gamma_i \ln A \qquad \forall j \qquad (1)$$

where A denotes client size and γ_i represents all other client (engagement) characteristics. This linear model is derived from an underlying relationship of the form:

$$h_j = e^{\beta_{j0}} A^{\beta_{j1} + \sum_{i=2}^{K} \beta_{ji} \gamma_i} \qquad \forall j. \qquad (2)$$

This underlying function recognizes the key role of client size as a determinant of audit hours.[6] All other characteristics are assumed to affect hours by changing the curvature of the hours–size relationship. However, none of our empirical results is sensitive to the choice of functional form, among those considered.

The elasticities of hours with respect to client characteristics in this empirical model are important for understanding the factors which

---

[5] We considered two other empirical models: $\ln h_j = \beta_{j0} + \beta_{j1} \ln A + \sum_{i=2}^{K} \beta_{ji} \ln \gamma_i$ (used by

Ashton, Elliott, and Willingham [1989]); and $\ln h_j = \beta_{j0} + \beta_{j1} \ln A + \sum_{i=2}^{K} \beta_{ji} \gamma_i$. These are de-

rived from the following underlying functional relationships, respectively: $h_j = e^{\beta_{j0}} A^{\beta_{j1}} \prod_{i=2}^{K} \gamma_i^{\beta_{ji}}$,

and $h_j = e^{\beta_{j0} + \sum_{i=2}^{K} \beta_{ji} \gamma_i} A^{\beta_{j1}}$. The first model is analogous to a Cobb-Douglas formulation. In the model, all client characteristics are deemed to be equally important. The second model has been most commonly used in the audit fee literature. Both models have the disadvantage that the elasticity of hours with respect to assets does not change with changes in other characteristics. If client size is the key independent variable in the production function, this is unreasonable.

[6] Previous studies have shown that client size alone explains more than 50% of the cross-sectional variation in audit fees, although many other client characteristics are correlated with size.

affect the mix of labor used in an engagement. Let η_{ji} denote the elasticity of the jth grade of professional labor with respect to the ith client characteristic. From equation (2), these elasticities are $\eta_{ji} = \beta_{ji} \gamma_i \ln A$, for all client characteristics except for client size, while the elasticities of hours with respect to client size are $\eta_{jA} = \beta_{j1} + \sum_{i=2}^{K} \beta_{ji} \gamma_i$.

For characteristics other than client size, the elasticities will vary if the relevant β_j vary, while elasticities with respect to client size depend on β_{j1} as well as all the β_{ji}. Finally, the intercept values, β_{j0}, in the empirical model are important in determining the initial factor shares. We perform tests of the equality of estimated β-coefficients across the labor hour (h_j) equations. These are effectively tests for factors which influence the mix of labor hours used in performing an audit, since by definition of an elasticity, a change in a particular client characteristic has no effect on the mix of hours if the η_j for that characteristic are equal across types of labor (h_j).

3.3 OTHER ISSUES

The data on audit hours and client characteristics were obtained from a single major public accounting firm. While a single firm data source limits generalizability, previous research (e.g., Kinney [1986]) has shown that the major (Big Six) public accounting firms can be characterized by at least two broadly different types of production technologies (structured vs. unstructured), and there are probably other technological differences as well. In addition, the major firms may deliver systematically different levels of audit quality. For example, litigation rates for the Big Six firms are not homogeneous (Palmrose [1988]). Thus pooling of observations across CPA firms can introduce potential biases. Also, because our data are for audits performed in a single year (cross-section), the firm's technology during the sample period can reasonably be assumed to be constant.

An uncontrolled potential source of variability in audit technology is our use of data from various U.S. offices of the firm. However, the firm's top management expends significant resources (through training, publication of audit manuals, etc.) to standardize audit quality (the assurance level) and audit methods nationwide. Probably the greatest weakness of our data is that, to preserve confidentiality, we were not informed of the identity of individual clients. Thus we could not supplement information obtained from the firm about the clients with publicly available information.

4. Data and Variables

The data were obtained via questionnaires sent to the partners in charge of a stratified random sample of 1,000 audits (100 from each of 10 broad industry categories). The objective was to develop a data base on 1989 audit engagements for internal purposes, independent of our research. The staff received 606 usable responses to this survey, plus a "large number" of responses which indicated that the service performed was a review or compilation.

We limit our analyses to a subsample of audits of companies whose primary operations are in three industries with similar asset structures: high technology, manufacturing, and merchandising. There were 125 responses for audits in these industries (300 requests) from the initial sample. We requested the research staff to expand the sample of clients in these industries by sending out 300 additional questionnaires. This supplementary sample was also stratified by client size to obtain a representative number of larger clients. Imposing the restriction that each observation had to be complete with respect to the variables used in this research yielded a supplementary sample of 124 audits and a final sample of 249 observations.

Descriptive statistics developed from responses received from the engagement partners are shown in table 1. The descriptive statistics indicate that the sample companies cover a broad size range, but that 80% are private companies. The CPA firm's total client base is 90% non-public companies.

While this research is concerned with the determinants of audit hours, we also use the audit fee as the dependent variable in some of our tests. *FEE*, the amount billed to the client, is an aggregation of the hours charged to the engagement priced at effective (not standard) billing rates. In our sample, the audit fee billed averages 71% of the standard fee (actual hours multiplied by standard billing rates) and ranges from 24% to 145% of that value. Our discussions with the firm's research staff indicate that the billing is normally determined after negotiation with the client. Thus, fee billed should closely approximate the actual fee collected, but there can be some (usually minor) losses in collection.

4.1 SIZE AND COMPLEXITY

Previous research assumes that *ASSETS, FRGN, CMPLX,* and *TRE-PORTS* effectively control for cross-sectional variations in the quantity or effort component of fees. Studies that have directly examined the determinants of audit effort (e.g., Palmrose [1989] and Davis, Ricchiute, and Trompeter [1993]) use aggregate audit hours. We examine the effect of these variables on both the level and mix of audit labor inputs. Except for complexity, these measures represent objective characteristics of the client firm. However, because we do not know the identity of individual clients, the values of the variables cannot be verified using alternative information sources.

The variable *CMPLX* is assessed by each questionnaire respondent, presumably the engagement partner. By its nature, the variable measures the basic construct of interest as perceived by the engagement partner. Again, because we do not know client identity, we cannot correlate this measure with client characteristics—such as number of subsidiaries and degree of diversification across industries—which have been used to measure client complexity in audit fee research. In regressions of input hours on the size and complexity variables, the estimated coefficients are expected to be positive.

4.2 RISK

The variables *LEVERAGE, PBLC,* and *INHRISK* measure various aspects of risk and are expected to increase input hours. *LEVERAGE* is intended to capture the client's business risk which in turn affects the auditor's business risk. Greater business risk may, in and of itself, motivate the auditor to produce a more "defensible" audit, involving production of better documentation and, perhaps, tests which are helpful in forming a legal defense.[7] *LEVERAGE* may also measure the prior (to the audit) probability of material misstatement in the financial statements. The greater the risk of bankruptcy, the greater the risk that management may attempt to misrepresent financial position and results of operations (Palmrose [1987]). A higher prior probability of material misstatement will require greater auditor effort to attain the target level of assurance.

The variable *PBLC* also measures both auditor business risk and the probability of misstatement in the financial statements. Previous research (e.g., St. Pierre [1983]) suggests an auditor is more likely to be sued if the client is publicly held. In addition, managers of public firms are generally viewed as having greater incentives to overstate financial position and results of operations to maximize their compensation and maintain their employment. Thus the effects of *PBLC* on auditor effort are expected to be essentially the same as the effects of greater *LEVERAGE.*

The variable *INHRISK,* by definition, measures the prior probability that the financial statements contain material misstatement. As with complexity, this assessment was also made by each engagement partner. Note that auditing standards (AICPA [1992, AU Section 316]) require an assessment of inherent risk at the overall financial statement level, as well as at the class of transactions and account balances level. *INHRISK* is a single measure, which presumably represents this overall assessment of risk as well as some average of the detail risks. The validity of this measure is enhanced by the fact that the firm provides extensive

---

[7] Formally, in our simplified characterization of audit service production as a constrained cost minimization, the level of assurance is fixed. However, auditing standards (AICPA [1992, AU Section 312]) recognize that an auditor may minimize expected costs by increased testing if the exposure to loss or injury from litigation and adverse publicity is deemed to be unusually high. In the language of the risk model, an auditor may decrease the desired audit risk (increase assurance), thereby reducing the required level of detection risk. This complication creates no special problems for our empirical tests but would tend to increase the size of the coefficients of the business risk measures, relative to the constant assurance situation.

250   T. B. O'KEEFE, D. A. SIMUNIC, AND M. T. STEIN

TABLE 1

Names, Definitions, and Descriptive Statistics for Variables for 249 U.S. Audit Engagements of Companies
Engaged in High Technology, Manufacturing, or Merchandising Performed by a Big Six Firm in 1989

Variable Name and Definition	Mean	Std. Deviation	Minimum	Maximum
FEE: Audit fee billed.	$107,169	$342,330	$5,385	$2,875,000
PRTHRS: Partner hours charged to audit.	88	314	3	3,550
MNGHRS: Manager hours charged to audit.	199	621	8	6,413
SENHRS: Senior hours charged to audit.	486	1,435	31	15,155
OTHRS: Other staff hours charged to audit.	863	3,199	28	36,329
ASSETS: Client's total assets at end of fiscal year (thousands).	$151,753	$635,879	$101	$5,408,000
FRGN: Client's percentage foreign to total assets.	2.78%	9.11%	0	65%
CMPLX: Client's assessed operational complexity.[a]	2.61	.99	1	5
TREPORTS: Number of separate audit reports issued.	2.63	5.81	1	73
LEVERAGE: Book value of client's liabilities + total assets.	.68	.53	0	6.57

Categorical: Variable Name and Definition	Proportion of Cases Where Value = 1
PBLC: (0,1) where 1 indicates company's shares or debt securities are publicly held.	.20
INHRISK: Assessed inherent risk (0,1), where 1 denotes a more risky than average firm client.	.65
EXRELY: (0,1) variable, where 1 denotes extensive auditor reliance on internal controls.	.01
MODRELY: (0,1) variable, where 1 denotes moderate reliance on internal controls.	.09
LTDRELY: (0,1) variable, where 1 denotes limited reliance on internal controls.	.19
YR1CLNT: (0,1) variable, where 1 denotes a first-year engagement.	.08
YR2CLNT: (0,1) variable, where 1 denotes a second-year engagement.	.12
YR3CLNT: (0,1) variable, where 1 denotes a third-year engagement.	.09
YR4CLNT: (0,1) variable, where 1 denotes a fourth-year engagement.	.06

Coded Variables[b]		Proportion of Cases
MC:	Percentage of management consulting fee to audit fee.	
	0—no management services provided.	.39
	1—consulting fee less than 10% of audit fee.	.04
	2—consulting fee 10% to 19% of audit fee.	.04
	3—consulting fee 20% to 29% of audit fee.	.02
	4—consulting fee 30% to 39% of audit fee.	.01
	5—consulting fee 40% to 49% of audit fee.	.01
	6—consulting fee 50% to 75% of audit fee.	.04
	7—consulting fee more than 75% of audit fee.	.45
		1.00

TAX: Percentage of tax services fee to audit fee.

0—no tax services provided.	.08
1—tax fee less than 10% of audit fee.	.07
2—tax fee 10% to 19% of audit fee.	.14
3—tax fee 20% to 29% of audit fee.	.20
4—tax fee 30% to 39% of audit fee.	.17
5—tax fee 40% to 49% of audit fee.	.14
6—tax fee 50% to 75% of audit fee.	.10
7—tax fee more than 75% of audit fee.	.10
	1.00

[a]Audit partners assessed a client's complexity on a 5-point ordinal scale where 1 denotes "very simple" and 5 denotes "very complex."

[b]Audit partners provided data on nonaudit services in coded form. The percentage of nonaudit service fee to audit fee was classified into discrete categories (0 to 7). The dollar amounts of management consulting and tax fees were not provided by respondents.

detailed guidance on the various aspects of inherent risk assessment to field auditors through its audit manual. However, we recognize that as a (0,1) variable, the measure contains limited information and, since it was developed after the fact, may be a biased measure of the auditor's ex ante assessment of risk.

4.3 INTERNAL CONTROLS

The dependence of the nature, extent, and timing of substantive audit procedures on the auditor's assessment of the client's internal control risk is a basic principle of auditing (see AICPA [1992, AU Section 319]). Thus research which seeks to explain auditor effort should, in principle, control for the cross-sectional variability of internal control systems. However, previous researchers (e.g., Simunic [1980]) have been limited to the use of plausible surrogates to control for such variations.

We use three variables (*EXRELY, MODRELY,* and *LTDRELY*) to measure the degree of auditor reliance on internal controls. The variables are derived from assessments made by the partner in charge of each engagement (questionnaire respondent). We obtained from the survey data the auditor's assessment of overall internal control quality for the entire client entity (including any subsidiaries) and a measure of the auditor's reliance on internal controls to reduce substantive procedures. As with the inherent risk assessment, the internal control quality and degree of reliance measures represent overall characterizations of the client and auditor's strategy as a whole. Our 1989 data precede *Statement on Auditing Standards No. 55* (current AU Section 319) which requires an auditor to obtain an understanding of a client's internal control structure in every engagement. Thus, in the absence of early adoption of this standard, the "no reliance" situation implies that the audit consisted solely of substantive tests. A cross-tabulation of these measures is shown in table 2.

Since the substitution between tests of controls and substantive tests is made purely on cost/benefit grounds (see AICPA [1993, AU Section

252   T. B. O'KEEFE, D. A. SIMUNIC, AND M. T. STEIN

TABLE 2

Cross-Tabulation of Auditors' Assessments of Internal Control Quality and Degree of Reliance upon Controls for 249 U.S. Audit Engagements of Companies Engaged in High Technology Manufacturing, or Merchandising Performed by a Big Six Firm in 1989

Control Assessment[a]	Control Reliance[b]				
	None	Limited	Moderate	Extensive	Total
None	3	2	0	0	5
Poor	11	2	0	0	13
Fair	96	19	3	0	118
Good	66	19	15	0	100
Excellent	2	5	4	2	13
Total	178	47	22	2	249

[a]Engagement partner's assessment of the quality of internal control for the client as a whole.
[b]Engagement partner's assessment of the degree of reliance on client internal controls in the audit as a whole.

319.44]), even when controls are excellent (13 firms in the sample) auditors need not rely on them (2 firms in the sample). The infrequency of even limited reliance on internal controls (40% of audits) can be partially explained by the fact that 80% of the sample companies are closely held.

Since auditors can (optimally) ignore the quality of controls, the appropriate measure of the potential effect of controls on auditor effort is the degree of control reliance. The coefficients of the three variables are all expected to be negative and ordered as follows: *EXRELY < MODRELY < LTDRELY*. The "no reliance" situation is included in the intercept. Note also that the impact of control reliance on auditor effort is best tested using disaggregated hours since it is reasonable to expect the effect of internal controls to be greatest on the hours of persons who performed the audit fieldwork (*SENHRS* and *OTHRS*).

4.4 LEARNING

The existence of a learning curve in auditing can lead to lowballing (pricing below cost) when auditors bid to perform a new engagement (DeAngelo [1981]). While previous research (e.g., Simon and Francis [1988]) has found that "price cutting" exists in early periods, fee discounting can also arise if a client incurs significant incremental costs when changing auditors. Thus previous research results are consistent with but do not imply the existence of a learning curve in auditing.

When audit technologies are constant, the best way to establish the existence and nature of learning curves in auditing would be through longitudinal analysis. However, because the firm was unable to provide longitudinal data, we estimate the learning curve by analyzing inputs for a cross-section of clients who have retained the audit firm for varying numbers of years, while controlling for the other factors which can affect the nature and quantities of inputs utilized. In addition, to the extent that audit technologies changed in recent years (e.g., greater use of analytical procedures, less reliance on statistical sampling), a cross-sectional test may be more powerful than a longitudinal test. The variables *YR1CLNT* through *YR4CLNT* identify audit engagements performed by the firm for relatively few years, when the greatest learning should occur. The coefficients of these variables are expected to be positive and ordered as follows: *YR1CLNT* > *YR2CLNT* > *YR3CLNT* > *YR4CLNT*. Clients serviced for five or more years are included in the intercept. If learning effects vary across the four classes of labor hours, then use of disaggregated input data can enhance the power of the test for learning.

4.5 KNOWLEDGE SPILLOVERS

While possible interactions between the production of auditing and other services are complex and varied (see Simunic [1984] and Beck, Frecka, and Solomon [1988]), in our simple model the output of the audit is assumed to be unidimensional (a single service characteristic—assurance) and fixed. If the production of nonaudit services reduces an audit setup cost or makes audit staff members more efficient in audit production, the effect will be the same—audit hours should decrease. Based on this argument, the coefficients of both *MC* and *TAX* are expected to be negative. Since the strength of spillover effects may vary across the types of labor hours, use of disaggregated input data is again appropriate.

5. Results

5.1 INDIVIDUAL SOURCES OF FACTOR DEMAND FOR LABOR

Because the logarithms of labor hours (the dependent variables) are highly correlated in our sample (pairwise correlations range from .85 to .89), it is reasonable to expect that the residuals from the four labor hour regressions will also be correlated. This implies that the set of four factor demand equations should be estimated as seemingly unrelated regressions. However, the *SURE* estimator reduces to ordinary least squares when, as in our case, the independent variables are identical for all the equations (Amemiya [1985, p. 187]).

Thus, the coefficients of five regression equations were estimated by ordinary least squares using each of the four types of labor input hours and the audit fee as the dependent variables. As noted earlier, the regression using *FEE* constitutes a reference for evaluating the reasonableness of results. Breusch-Pagan tests for heteroscedasticity indicate that residual variances are not constant for the *FEE* and *SENHRS* regressions. As a result, the *t*-statistics reported for these regressions are calculated using White's heteroscedastic-consistent covariance matrix estimation method.

Two aspects of the four labor hour regression equations are important for understanding the production of audit services. The coefficients (and statistical significance) of the independent variables in each equation identify the sources of "factor demand" for various classes of labor. The homogeneity (heterogeneity) of these coefficients across equations indicates whether the classes of labor are utilized in fixed or variable proportions as client characteristics vary. For each independent variable, significant differences in estimated regression coefficients across equations imply that the elasticities of hours with respect to that client (engagement) characteristic also vary. Different elasticities imply changes in factor mix.

The results for the complete (all independent variables) regression models are shown in table 3. The pairwise correlations for the independent variables are mostly quite small, both in absolute values and relative to the R^2 for the overall models. This suggests that collinearity among independent variables is unlikely to have a significant effect on the standard errors of estimated coefficients (see further test below).

Table 3 shows that the size (*ASSETS*), complexity (*FRGN*, *CMPLX*, and *TREPORTS*), and risk (*LEVERAGE*, *PBLC*, and *INHRISK*) measures are all significant determinants of at least some class of labor hours. In addition, consistent with previous research, all of these variables are significant determinants of the audit fee billed. The differences in coefficients across types of labor are examined later.

Table 3 also shows that the degree of reliance on internal control (*EXRELY*, *MODRELY*, and *LTDRELY*), the number of years the engagement has been performed by this public accounting firm (*YR1CLNT* to *YR4CLNT*), and the degree of auditor involvement in management consulting (*MC*) and tax services (*TAX*) have no systematic statistically significant effects on hours in any labor category or on the audit fee. To ensure that this lack of significant results was not caused by inflated standard errors of the coefficients of *EXRELY*, *MODRELY*, *LTDRELY*, *YRXCLNT*, *MC*, and *TAX* due to multicollinearity, we regressed each of these variables (in turn) on the other independent variables in each labor hour model and computed the variance inflation factors, $1/(1-R^2)$ (Kennedy [1985]). These range from 1.03 to 1.28, which confirms that multicollinearity is not a problem.

Our failure to find any effect of internal control reliance on audit hours is surprising. Not only are the coefficients of *EXRELY*, *MODRELY*, and *LTDRELY* small and statistically insignificant in all regression equations, but they are also insignificant in a partial *F*-test when the three levels of reliance are combined (the *F* statistics range from .10 to 1.43 with 3, 232 degrees of freedom). Since our data are limited to companies involved in manufacturing and wholesale/retail trade, there could be an industry effect. Alternatively, auditors in the field may not be very effective in mapping internal control quality and reliance into subsequent reductions in substantive testing. This conjecture is consistent with findings in the behavioral literature in auditing (e.g., Mock and Turner [1979] and Emby [1993]).

TABLE 3
Regression of Audit Fee and Disaggregated Labor Hours on Client Characteristics for 249 U.S. Audits of Companies Engaged in High Technology, Manufacturing, or Merchandising Performed by a Big Six Firm in 1989 (Complete Model)

Independent Variable Name	(Expected Sign)	Dependent Variables				
		Audit Fee[1]	Partner Hours	Manager Hours	Senior Hours[1]	Staff Hours
ASSETS	(+)	.340[3]	.301	.260	.241	.360
		14.00**	9.69**	8.83**	10.00**	12.00**
FRGN	(+)	.001	.001	.001	.001	.001
		4.88**	3.09**	3.94**	4.47**	2.55**
CMPLX	(+)	.007	.006	.007	.008	.011
		3.18**	2.21**	3.00**	3.83**	4.18**
TREPORTS	(+)	.001	.001	.001	.001	.001
		4.01**	3.25**	2.80**	4.15**	2.75**
LEVERAGE	(+)	.007	.010	.012	.002	.005
		1.92*	2.08**	2.72**	.43	1.02
PBLC	(+)	.022	.043	.033	.018	.017
		5.17**	7.69**	6.26**	4.10**	3.09**
INHRISK	(+)	.011	.005	.002	.008	.015
		3.03**	1.07	.51	2.29**	3.26**
EXRELY	(−)	.011	.003	.027	−.005	.008
		.63	.16	1.33	−.27	.35
MODRELY	(−)	−.001	−.006	.001	−.002	.006
		−.08	−.81	.10	−.36	.82
LTDRELY	(−)	.008	.009	.007	.001	.006
		1.88	1.67	1.44	.21	1.10
YR1CLNT	(+)	−.003	.002	.003	.009	−.006
		−.56	.29	.46	1.43	−.73
YR2CLNT	(+)	−.016	.002	−.009	−.004	−.016
		−2.90**	.35	−1.46	−.86	−2.45**
YR3CLNT	(+)	.006	.008	.016	.003	.007
		1.05	1.00	2.16**	.51	.92
YR4CLNT	(+)	.003	−.003	.005	.005	−.008
		.47	−.32	.57	.72	−.95
MC	(−)	.000	−.000	−.000	.000	−.000
		.23	−.53	−.83	.89	−.47
TAX	(−)	.000	−.000	.001	−.001	.000
		.02	−.47	1.25	−1.27	.01
CONSTANT		—[2]	−2.161	−.697	.878	−1.206
			−4.71**	−1.60	2.47**	−2.63**
R^2		.86	.78	.78	.80	.81
F		91.21**	51.48**	50.22**	58.43**	62.83**

[1]Reported *t*-statistics are calculated using White's heteroscedastic-consistent covariance matrix estimation method.
[2]Value of intercept deleted at the request of the firm that provided our data.
[3]Top number in each pair is the estimated β coefficient and the bottom number is the *t*-statistic.
*Significant at .05 level (one-tail test).
**Significant at .01 level (one-tail test).

With respect to the test for learning over time, the estimated coefficients of the *YRXCLNT* variables show no systematic pattern, and most (14/16) are statistically insignificant (one is significant in the direction opposite to our hypothesis). There is some (weak) evidence of fee cutting in the first two years, but no clear pattern of fee discounts across years, as in Simon and Francis [1988]. That study, as well as similar results reported by Ettredge and Greenberg [1990] and Turpen [1990], is based on both industrial and other client types. Thus there could again be industry effects. While our finding that audit hours do not decline with the tenure of the engagement is consistent with an absence of learning, it could also be that audit hours are systematically underreported in the early years of an audit, or the firm may fail to produce the target level of assurance in those years. The latter conjecture is consistent with evidence on auditor litigation (e.g., St. Pierre [1983]) which shows that a large proportion of lawsuits occur during the first few years of auditor association with a client.

Finally, there is no evidence of knowledge spillover from management consulting and/or tax work to audit services, consistent with results in Davis, Ricchiute, and Trompeter [1993] who failed to find knowledge spillovers in a test using aggregate audit hours for 98 U.S. clients of one public accounting firm. The fact that the firm from which our data were obtained is highly decentralized may influence the transmission of knowledge across its organization boundaries, or the direction of spillover could be from the audit to the cost of other services. However, a consistent failure to find evidence of knowledge spillovers between services using similar tests and data from other public accounting firms would cast serious doubt on the validity of the basic argument justifying the joint performance of nonaudit services for a public accounting firm's audit clients.

5.2 TESTS FOR CHANGES IN FACTOR MIX

We turn now to tests of the equality of regression coefficients across the four labor hour equations. Because of the insignificant results in the tests for the effects of internal control reliance, learning, and nonaudit services, these variables are dropped from subsequent analyses. The simplified empirical model containing only client size, complexity, and risk measures is termed the basic model. Regression results analogous to table 3 using the basic model are shown in table 4. To test the homogeneity of coefficients, we use the Q-statistic and evaluate its significance following de Jong and Thompson [1990]. The results of joint tests across all four equations are shown in table 4 and tests of pairwise equality are shown in table 5.

Note from table 4 that regression constants are different for each equation, and that the differences are highly significant (both for the joint test and for adjacent pairs—partner/manager, manager/senior, senior/staff—shown in table 5). These constants set the proportion of the various grades of professional labor for vanishingly small audits. Taking antilogs and calculating percentage shares yields the following labor mix for a hypothetical, very small audit with the other independent variables assumed to be zero: Partner–3%, Manager–14%, Seniors–76%, Staff–7%.

TABLE 4

Regression of Audit Fee and Disaggregated Labor Hours on Client Characteristics for 249 U.S. Audits of Companies Engaged in High Technology, Manufacturing, or Merchandising Performed by a Big Six Firm in 1989 (Basic Model)

Independent Variable Name	Dependent Variable					
	Fees[1] Billed	Partner Hours	Manager Hours	Senior[1] Hours	Staff Hours	Q-Statistic[2]
ASSETS	.352[4]	.310	.270	.236	.380	27.64**
	15.80**	10.81**	9.77**	10.33**	13.14**	
FRGN	.001	.001	.001	.001	.001	1.31
	2.97**	2.94**	3.44**	3.14**	2.57**	
CMPLX	.006	.005	.007	.007	.010	3.11
	2.76**	2.10*	3.05**	4.01**	3.96**	
TREPORTS	.001	.001	.001	.001	.001	.91
	2.97**	3.24**	3.10**	3.49**	2.80**	
LEVERAGE	.007	.011	.012	.002	.005	6.89*
	1.86*	2.32**	2.68**	.61	.94	
PBLC	.024	.042	.034	.017	.019	28.02**
	5.48**	7.76**	6.58**	4.18**	3.57**	
INHRISK	.010	.006	.002	.009	.014	7.72*
	3.06**	1.33	.50	2.73**	3.08**	
Constant	—[3]	-2.319	-.767	.929	-1.522	69.74**
		-5.55**	-1.90*	2.88**	-3.61**	
R^2	.85	.77	.75	.79	.79	
F	200.25**	118.23**	110.64**	134.41**	141.16**	

[1]Reported *t*-statistics were calculated using White's heteroscedastic-consistent covariance matrix estimation method.
[2]The *Q*-statistics test the null hypothesis that coefficients are equal across the four labor hour equations.
[3]Value of intercept deleted at the request of the firm that provided our data.
[4]Top number in each pair is the estimated β coefficient and the bottom number is the *t*-statistic. All coefficients of the independent variables are expected to be positive.
*Significant at .05 level (one-tail test).
**Significant at .01 level (one-tail test).

As clients increase in size, this mix changes, as shown by the heterogeneity of coefficients on *ASSETS*. Note from table 5 that the factor mix change arises mostly from the behavior of staff hours. The coefficient on *ASSETS* in that regression is significantly larger than all the other asset coefficients (particularly the coefficients in the manager and senior hours regressions), and no other adjacent coefficient pairs are significantly different. Thus, as clients increase in size, the proportion of staff hours continues to increase, while the proportion of manager and senior hours decreases.

When *ASSETS* total about $100 million, the labor proportions become relatively constant at the following mix.[8] Partners–5%, Managers–12%, Seniors–33%, Staff–50%.

---

[8] Given the nature of the power function, the share of staff hours continues to increase, albeit extremely slowly, for clients with *ASSETS* greater than $80,000,000.

258   T. B. O'KEEFE, D. A. SIMUNIC, AND M. T. STEIN

TABLE 5
*Q-Statistics for Pairwise Tests of Equality of Regression Coefficients
across Labor Hour Equations for Basic Model*

		Manager	Senior	Staff
Constant		β_{20}	β_{30}	β_{40}
	Partner[a]–β_{10}	16.13**[b]	61.57**	3.11
	Manager–β_{20}		20.45**	3.39
	Senior–β_{30}			33.86**
ASSETS		β_{21}	β_{31}	β_{41}
	Partner–β_{11}	2.24	6.77**	5.13*
	Manager–β_{21}		1.76	15.27**
	Senior–β_{31}			24.88**
FRGN		β_{22}	β_{32}	β_{42}
	Partner–β_{12}	0.16	0.52	0.10
	Manager–β_{22}		0.14	0.54
	Senior–β_{32}			1.12
CMPLX		β_{23}	β_{33}	β_{43}
	Partner–β_{13}	0.84	0.71	3.09
	Manager–β_{23}		0.25	1.15
	Senior–β_{33}			1.12
TREPORTS		β_{24}	β_{34}	β_{44}
	Partner–β_{14}	0.72	0.20	0.14
	Manager–β_{24}		0.59	0.28
	Senior–β_{34}			0.72
LEVERAGE		β_{25}	β_{35}	β_{45}
	Partner–β_{15}	0.08	3.49*	1.60
	Manager–β_{25}		5.50*	2.73
	Senior–β_{35}			0.22
PBLC		β_{26}	β_{36}	β_{46}
	Partner–β_{16}	2.33	21.52**	14.73**
	Manager–β_{26}		12.57**	7.77**
	Senior–β_{36}			0.19
INHRISK		β_{27}	β_{37}	β_{47}
	Partner–β_{17}	0.85	0.55	2.69
	Manager–β_{27}		3.15	7.16**
	Senior–β_{37}			1.05

[a]Partner, Manager, Senior, and Staff denote the labor hour regression from which the coefficient is taken.
[b]Q-statistics reported in the body of the table test the null hypothesis that pairs of coefficients are equal.
*Significant at .05 level (one-tail test).
**Significant at .01 level (one-tail test).

These results confirm the basic nonlinearity between client size and
auditor effort which has been inferred from studies of audit fees. They
also show that the nonlinearity between audit fees and client size is
caused by both an underlying production nonlinearity which exists for
all labor inputs and substitution of relatively cheaper labor (audit staff
vs. seniors and managers) as client size increases.

Turning to the complexity measures, table 4 shows that increases in *FRGN, CMPLX,* and/or *TREPORTS* increase the level of audit hours in all labor categories while leaving the mix of inputs unchanged. Finally, the risk measures have heterogeneous coefficients in table 4. For *LEVER-AGE,* the coefficients for partners and managers are both positive, similar in value, and statistically significant while the coefficients for seniors and staff are not significantly different from zero. Table 5 confirms that managers/seniors are different, and this is the only significantly different adjacent pair. Thus, increasing the risk of bankruptcy results in the use of relatively more "high level" labor in an engagement while having no significant effect on the level of senior and staff hours. This is reasonable. Greater bankruptcy risk may lead to consideration of the appropriateness of the going-concern assumption and to assessment of the possibility of deliberate manipulation of accounting numbers, which likely require high levels of audit expertise.

The coefficients of *PBLC* show a similar but stronger pattern. Again, the proportion of partner and manager hours increases while, in this case, the levels of all labor hours also increase significantly. Thus, the fact that a client is a publicly vs. closely held company seems to have a major effect on audit service production.[9]

The third risk variable, *INHRISK,* which measures the probability of financial statement error (not client business risk) shows a pattern opposite to *LEVERAGE.* Increasing inherent risk increases the amount of "low level" labor used in the audit while having no significant impact on partner and manager hours. Again, this is reasonable as greater inherent risk can be expected to result in more substantive testing with seniors and staff.

With regard to aggregation, the losses of information and efficiency discussed in section 3.1 occur in our data. When the log of the sum of labor hours is regressed on the independent variables in our basic morel, the *t*-values for the coefficients of *LEVERAGE* and *PBLC* are 1.78 and 5.81, respectively. Here the effect of *LEVERAGE* on total hours is only marginally significant. Recall, from table 4, that the effect is more strongly significant when partner and manager hours are disaggregated. The significance levels of the coefficients of *PBLC* display the same pattern. The effect can also be seen in table 4 by comparing the audit fee regression with the disaggregated labor hour regressions. This is not surprising since an audit fee is just a weighted aggregate of hours, where the weights are effective billing rates for each labor class, while equal weights are used in calculating the sum of hours.

---

[9] The empirical model whose coefficients are reported in tables 3 and 4 restricts the possible effect of a publicly vs. closely held firm to be a shift in the regression constant. However, we also investigated a more general formulation by introducing slope interaction variables (*ASSETS* × *PBLC* through *INHRISK* × *PBLC*). When this is done, the coefficients of *ASSETS* tend to be larger while the coefficients of *CMPLX* and *TREPORTS* decrease. This general pattern occurs for all labor categories and 8 of these 12 interactions are statistically significant at the 5% level. None of the other interaction variables is statistically significant.

6. Summary and Conclusions

In this paper we investigate the cross-sectional relation between a single *CPA* firm's use of different grades of professional labor and various client characteristics. Our data consist of a stratified random sample of 249 audit engagements performed by various U.S. offices of this international public accounting firm. The sample clients are primarily private firms involved in manufacturing, merchandising, or high technology.

We regress audit hours (by grade of labor) on measures of client size, complexity, business, and inherent risk, the degree of auditor reliance on internal controls, the number of years an engagement has been performed, and the extent of nonaudit services. The objective is to understand the factors which determine the level and mix of labor inputs (auditor effort) used in performing audit engagements. Because our "effort" data come from a single major public accounting firm, our study eliminates the potential confounding effects of audit firm pricing policies and possible economic rents in prices, as well as differences in audit product (level of assurance) and production technologies across firms. As a result, we believe our tests are relatively more powerful than any reported in the existing literature.

We find that size, complexity, and risk measures explain about 80% of the cross-sectional variation in audit hours. Tests of the equality of coefficients across equations indicate that several of these explanatory variables have different (but plausible) effects on the different grades of professional labor. We find clear evidence that, ceteris paribus, audit effort is a concave (from below) function of client size. In addition, the previously documented concave relationship between audit fees and size is found to be caused partially by the use of a relatively larger proportion of low-level (and therefore relatively inexpensive) professional labor as clients increase in size. However, we find no systematic effect of internal control reliance, or the number of years an audit has been performed, or the joint performance of nonaudit services on the levels of audit hours in any of the staff categories. These results imply that the effects of those three factors on audit production are subtle and may vary across client industries and, perhaps, *CPA* firms. Thus (at least for the types of clients in our sample) these complexities can probably be ignored in research designed to investigate other (more basic) issues. Finally, our results are not sensitive to the choice of specific functional form for the audit effort–client characteristics relationship, within the class of forms where effort—and fees—are a power function of client assets.

REFERENCES

AMEMIYA, T. *Advanced Econometrics.* Cambridge, Mass.: Harvard University Press, 1985.
AMERICAN INSTITUTE OF CERTIFIED PUBLIC ACCOUNTANTS. *Statements on Auditing Standards (AU).* New York: AICPA, 1992.

ASHTON, R.; R. ELLIOT; AND J. WILLINGHAM. "The Pricing of Audit Services: Evidence from a Big Eight Firm." Working paper, July 1989.

BECK, P.; T. FRECKA; AND I. SOLOMON. "A Model of the Market for MAS and Audit Services: Knowledge Spillovers and Auditor–Auditee Bonding." *Journal of Accounting Literature* (1988): 50–64.

DAVIS, L.; D. RICCHIUTE; AND G. TROMPETER. "Audit Effort, Audit Fees, and the Provision of Non-Audit Services to Audit Clients." *The Accounting Review* (January 1993): 135–50.

DEANGELO, L. "Auditor Independence, 'Lowballing,' and Disclosure Regulation." *Journal of Accounting and Economics* (1981): 113–27.

DE JONG, P., AND R. THOMPSON. "Testing Linear Hypotheses in the Sur Framework with Identical Explanatory Variables." *Research in Finance* 8 (1990): 59–76.

DOPUCH, N., AND D. SIMUNIC. "The Nature of Competition in the Auditing Profession: A Descriptive and Normative View." In *Regulation and the Accounting Profession*, edited by J. Buckley and F. Weston. Belmont, Calif.: Lifetime Learning Publications, 1980.

EMBY, C. "Framing Effects in Professional Judgement: The Link between Auditors' Judgements of Internal Control and Substantive Testing Decisions." Working paper, Simon Fraser University, May 1993.

ETTREDGE, M., AND R. GREENBERG. "Determinants of Fee Cutting on Initial Audit Engagements." *Journal of Accounting Research* (Spring 1990): 198–210.

FRANCIS, J., AND D. SIMON. "A Test of Audit Pricing in the Small-Client Segment of the U.S. Audit Market." *The Accounting Review* (January 1987): 145–57.

FUCHS, V. *The Service Economy.* Chicago: National Bureau of Economic Research, 1968.

KENNEDY, P. *A Guide to Econometrics.* Cambridge, Mass.: The M.I.T. Press, 1985.

KINNEY, W. R. "Audit Technology and Preferences for Auditing Standards." *Journal of Accounting and Economics* (March 1986): 73–89.

MOCK, T., AND J. TURNER. "A Field Test of the Effects of Changes in Internal Controls on Audit Programs." In *Behavioral Experiments in Accounting II,* edited by T. Burns, pp. 277–321. Columbus, Ohio: Ohio State University, 1979.

O'KEEFE, T., AND P. WESTORT. "Conformance to GAAS Reporting Standards in Municipal Audits and the Economics of Auditing: The Effect of Audit Firm Size, CPA Examination Performance, and Competition." *Research in Accounting Regulation* 6 (1992): 39–77.

PALMROSE, Z. "Audit Fees and Auditor Size: Further Evidence." *Journal of Accounting Research* (Spring 1986): 97–110.

_____. "Litigation and Independent Auditors: The Role of Business Failures and Management Fraud." *Auditing: A Journal of Practice and Theory* (Spring 1987): 90–103.

_____. "An Analysis of Auditor Litigation and Audit Service Quality." *The Accounting Review* (January 1988): 55–73.

_____. "The Relation of Audit Contract Type to Audit Fees and Hours." *The Accounting Review* (July 1989): 488–99.

ST. PIERRE, K. E. *Auditor Risk and Legal Liability.* Ann Arbor, Mich.: UMI Research Press, 1983.

SIMON, D., AND J. FRANCIS. "The Effects of Auditor Change on Audit Fees: Tests of Price Cutting and Price Recovery." *The Accounting Review* (April 1988): 255–69.

SIMUNIC, D. "The Pricing of Audit Services: Theory and Evidence." *Journal of Accounting Research* (Spring 1980): 161–90.

_____. "Auditing, Consulting, and Auditor Independence." *Journal of Accounting Research* (Autumn 1984): 679–702.

SIMUNIC, D., AND M. STEIN. *Product Differentiation in Auditing: Auditor Choice in the Market for Unseasoned New Issues.* Research Monograph no. 13. Vancouver: The Canadian Certified General Accountants' Research Foundation, 1987.

TURPEN, R. A. "Differential Pricing on Auditors' Initial Engagements: Further Evidence." *Auditing: A Journal of Practice and Theory* (Spring 1990): 69–76.

[17]

Auditing:
A Journal of Practice
& Theory
Vol. 11, No. 1
Spring 1992

1

Audit Quality Attributes: The Perceptions of Audit Partners, Preparers, and Financial Statement Users

Joseph V. Carcello, Roger H. Hermanson, and Neal T. McGrath

SUMMARY

Numerous studies have addressed audit quality. Archival studies have focused on differences among individual firms or classes of firms (*e.g.,* large versus small). Some behavioral studies have also related audit quality attributes in a similar fashion. Other behavioral studies have elicited the attributes of audit quality from auditors, and one from chairpersons of audit committees. However, in an increasingly competitive environment, it seems important to understand the perceptions of both users and preparers as they relate to audit quality. Any differences may allow for audit firms to deliver more satisfaction to both groups and simultaneously improve their own audit quality.

This study surveyed high-ranking auditors, preparers, and users as a basis for comparing their perceptions of the underlying components of audit quality. Usable responses from 245 audit partners, 264 *Fortune 1000* controllers, and 120 sophisticated users were distilled into 12 salient components using factor analysis. Using these 12 components, the perceptions of the three groups were then compared to isolate significant differences.

Characteristics related to members of the audit team were generally perceived to be more important to audit quality than characteristics related to

Joseph V. Carcello, Assistant Professor of Accounting, College of Business Administration, University of North Florida, Jacksonville, FL. Roger H. Hermanson, Regents Professor, Ernst & Young Professor, School of Accountancy, Georgia State University, Atlanta, GA 30303. Neal T. McGrath, Partner, Ernst & Young, Atlanta, GA.

The authors acknowledge the helpful comments of Merwyn Elliott, Zoe-Vonna Palmrose, Jerry Strawser, Robert Strawser, Georgia State University Accounting workshop participants, and an anonymous reviewer. The suggestions made by Willard Alexander, Vice Chairman of C&S Bank, Jay Halton, Chief Securities Officer at the Life Insurance Company of Georgia, David McClung, Partner at Ernst & Young, and Jack Stahl, Chief Financial Officer (formerly controller) at The Coca-Cola Co., during their review of the questionnaire were particularly helpful.

the audit firm itself, such as litigation record. The four factors reported to be most important in determining audit quality were audit team and firm experience with the client, industry expertise (especially within the audit team), responsiveness to client needs, and compliance with the general standards (competence, independence, and due care) of generally accepted auditing standards (GAAS). However, among the three groups, there were significant differences in the importance assigned to each factor. Both preparers and users placed significantly more importance on adherence to the general standards of GAAS than did audit partners. Auditor responsiveness to client needs was seen as more important by preparers than by partners. On the other hand, audit partners placed more emphasis on a skeptical attitude than did preparers. Finally, users also placed significantly less emphasis on involvement of high-ranking members of the audit team than did partners.

INTRODUCTION

THE external auditing profession has been buffeted by a number of events over the past 15 years that have heightened competition among different firms (Cowan 1990). During this time period, the AICPA has modified its prohibitions against advertising and against solicitation of clients (AICPA 1979). The large number of mergers among client companies during the 1980s served to diminish the pool of companies in need of audit services (Palmer 1989). The recession of 1981–82, increased global competition, and the current economic downturn are additional forces that make clients more sensitive to the relationship between audit services and audit fees (Cowan 1990).

As competition within the profession has grown, auditing firms have become more cognizant of the need to market their services (Bernstein 1978; Kotler and Bloom 1984; Congram and Dumesic 1986). In attempting to compete on other than a price basis, auditing firms seek to differentiate their services (Bernstein 1978). It is often difficult for firms to do so, for at least two reasons: (1) unlike goods, services cannot be experienced in advance, and (2) even after the service is provided, the purchaser often does not have the technical expertise to evaluate the quality of the service provided

(Bloom 1984). The purchaser may focus more on the process of rendering the service rather than on the output of the service itself (Parasuraman *et al*. 1985). One of the dimensions on which firms have attempted to differentiate themselves is the quality of services provided. Auditors often believe that they know the criteria used by clients (*i.e.*, both client management and the third-party users of their reports) in evaluating audit quality. However, Bishea (1982) found that auditors do not accurately perceive the expectations and needs expressed by clients.

This study attempts to define the attributes that are perceived by participants in the financial reporting process as being related to audit quality. It also investigates whether the three primary groups in the financial reporting process (preparers, auditors, and users) evaluate audit quality attributes differently.

BACKGROUND

Audit quality has been examined using various approaches. Researchers (Simunic 1980; Simon 1985; Palmrose 1986; Francis and Simon 1987; Simon and Francis 1988; Palmrose 1989; Turpen 1990) have examined a number of issues related to audit quality by reference to pricing differentials. Other studies (Palmrose 1982; Nichols and Smith 1983; Shockley and Holt 1983; Simunic and Stein 1987; Ettredge *et al*. 1988;

Imhoff 1988; Palmrose 1988; Beatty 1989; Eichenseher *et al.* 1989; Wilson and Grimlund 1990) have examined audit quality differences among types of firms and among individual firms using various surrogate measures of quality performance. For example, Palmrose (1988) used litigation against firms to measure the quality of audits provided by individual firms.

This study examines the issue of audit quality from a behavioral perspective and identifies attributes that are perceived by financial statement preparers, auditors, and users as being related to audit quality. Various researchers (see Mock and Samet 1982; Schroeder *et al.* 1986; Sutton and Lampe 1990) have used this approach.

The Mock and Samet (1982) and Sutton and Lampe (1990) studies were similar in that they both relied on input from practicing auditors in developing a model to evaluate audit quality. Mock and Samet employed a hierarchical multi-attribute evaluation model to develop a list of attributes that could be used in evaluating audit quality. Sutton and Lampe relied on structured group processes in developing their audit quality evaluation model. Neither study considered the perceptions of the two other primary participants in the financial reporting process, preparers and users.

Schroeder *et al.* (1986) surveyed audit committee chairpersons of the *Fortune 500* to determine how these individuals defined audit quality. The audit committee chairpersons were sent a questionnaire asking them to rank 15 factors as to their importance to audit quality. The factors contained in their questionnaire had been mentioned in the auditing literature as affecting audit quality. The main conclusion of the Schroeder *et al.* study was that audit-team factors (*e.g.,* partner/manager involvement, independence of audit team members, etc.) were viewed as more important in determining audit quality than were firm-wide factors (*e.g.,* quality control procedures and regulatory agency experience of the firm, etc.). This finding is particularly important since

much of the auditing profession's efforts to improve the quality of practice have been at the firm-wide level.

This study expands upon these prior studies in three important ways. First, potential audit quality attributes are evaluated by all three primary groups in the financial reporting process (preparers, auditors, and users). Second, the study is conducted using an expanded set of audit quality attributes. Third, differences between the groups are identified and discussed.

METHOD

The first phase of the present study involved developing a specific list of the attributes of audit quality. Attributes that may be associated with audit quality were identified by reviewing the literature and by referring to the personal experiences of the authors.[1] Financial statement preparers, auditors, and users were asked to evaluate the relative importance of each of the attributes to overall audit quality. No definition of a high quality audit was provided since respondents were to evaluate the attributes from their own frame of reference. One drawback to this approach is that it cannot be determined if differences in group perceptions are due to differing evaluations of the attributes or to different definitions of audit quality. However, from a practice development perspective, the cause of differences between groups is not as important as knowing that the participants in the financial reporting process focus on different attributes in evaluating audit services (whether it is because the attributes are weighted differently or because audit quality itself is viewed differently). Following the approach used by Schroeder *et al.* (1986), a

---

[1] All of the authors have experience in public accounting and one of the authors has extensive SEC experience as a Big Six partner. The attributes on the questionnaire were also reviewed by at least one individual from each of the three groups of interest in this study (preparers, auditors, and users) before the instrument was finalized.

questionnaire listing attributes that may influence audit quality was sent to a random sample of each of three groups—auditors, preparers, and users.

Survey Instrument

The questionnaire contained 41 attributes. Included among these attributes were the factors listed in the Schroeder *et al.* study. Additional attributes were included to provide a more extensive examination of audit quality. Using a five-point Likert scale, the survey participants were asked to evaluate the degree to which each attribute enhances audit quality. The audit quality attributes included in the questionnaire and the scale response format are presented in the appendix.

Participants

Controllers were used to represent the financial statement preparer group. Questionnaires were sent to the controllers of the companies included in the 1987 *Fortune 1000*. The names and addresses of the controllers were obtained from *Dun & Bradstreet's Million Dollar Directory*. A number of the *Fortune 1000* did not list their controller, and, since no known systematic bias would result from their exclusion, these companies were not included in the sample. The final sample size was 653.

Auditors were represented by Big Six audit partners, whose names were obtained from a directory of partners provided by each of the Big Six firms. Using a random number generating program, a random sample of 650 audit partners was selected.

The two primary financial statement user groups are investors (both institutional and individual) and creditors. Individual investors were not included in the study, on the premise that the typical individual investor may not have the expertise to identify the attributes of a high quality audit. Mutual fund investment managers, pension fund investment managers, and the chief securities officers of life insurance companies were used to represent institutional investors.

Questionnaires were sent to 108 fund managers of equity mutual funds with net assets in excess of $300 million.[2] The *Mutual Fund Sourcebook* (Morningstar 1988) was the data source used. Pension fund managers of the 100 largest domestic pension funds (based on assets) were selected from the *Money Market Directory of Pension Funds and their Investment Managers* (1988). Using *Best's Insurance Reports (Life-Health)* (1987), it was found that nearly half of the 200 largest domestic life insurance companies (based on assets) did not identify their chief securities officer. A decision was made to exclude these companies from the sample, resulting in a sample size of 103.[3]

Creditors, the other primary financial statement user group, were represented by the chief lending officers at the 250 largest domestic commercial banks (based on total assets). *Rand McNally's Bankers Directory*, the selection source, did not list the chief lending officer in some cases, resulting in a final sample of 203.

RESULTS

Response Rate

As shown in table 1, the response rates were 38 percent for audit partners, 40 percent for controllers, and 23 percent for users.[4] Given the nature of this research, and the

---

[2] A cut-off of $300 million in net assets was established for selecting equity mutual funds in an attempt to (approximately) equalize the sample selected from the three institutional investor groups (mutual fund investment managers, pension fund investment managers, and the chief securities officers of life insurance companies). The dollar amount of net assets that would produce a sample size of approximately 100 individuals was determined to be $300 million.

[3] There is no *a priori* reason for expecting chief securities officers from excluded companies to evaluate audit quality attributes differently from the chief securities officers who responded to the survey. There was no apparent systematic pattern as to which life insurance companies did not list the name of their chief securities officer in *Best's Insurance Reports*. Similar logic was used in selecting chief lending officers as discussed in the following paragraph.

[4] No differences between early and late respondents were noted by the authors. Non-response bias was not considered to be a problem.

TABLE 1
Sample Characteristics

Respondent Group	Sample Size	Usable Responses	Response Rate
Big Six Audit Partners	650	245	37.7%
Fortune 1000 Controllers	653	264	40.4%
Financial Statement Users (mutual fund managers, pension fund managers, chief securities officers of life insurance companies, chief lending officers of domestic commercial banks)	514	120	23.3%

nature of the groups contacted, the response rates were deemed satisfactory.

Analysis of Pooled Responses

Mean Values. To determine the overall importance of each audit quality attribute, the combined responses of all three groups were first analyzed. The initial analysis of the combined responses focused on determining mean values of each attribute as presented on the data instrument. Table 2 presents the ten attributes receiving the highest and lowest mean ratings. Each of the ten highest rated attributes had a mean score above 4.0, with a mean value of 4 or above indicating that most respondents either agreed or strongly agreed that the attribute enhanced audit quality. Each of the ten lowest rated attributes had a mean score of 3.1 or below, with a mean value of 3 or below indicating that most respondents were neutral about the attribute or disagreed with the statement that the attribute enhanced audit quality.

The six highest rated attributes all relate to characteristics of the audit team (rather than CPA firm characteristics). The two attributes that were viewed as least important were: (1) that cost is a major factor in determining whether an audit step is performed, and (2) that the firm did not provide consulting services to the audit client.

Clearly, using cost as a major factor in deciding whether an audit step is to be performed would detract from audit quality. The respondents recognized this, assigning the lowest mean score to this attribute. A decision not to provide consulting services to audit clients might enhance audit quality through greater actual, or apparent, independence. However, the respondents did not view an auditing firm's decision to refrain from providing consulting services as enhancing audit quality.

Although a number of attributes were included here that were not present in the Schroeder *et al.* study, the results of this study nevertheless are generally consistent with their findings. Both studies found that audit team factors were viewed as significantly more important than firm-wide factors in enhancing audit quality. For example, the active involvement of the engagement partner and the ethics of audit team members, both audit team factors, were found to be highly important in both studies.

Factor Analysis. Factor analysis is a statistical procedure used to reduce a large number of attributes to a smaller set of composite components. It summarizes the information in the original attributes and makes informed interpretation more manageable (Hair *et al.* 1987, 235). To achieve the desired reduction, only the 12 factors with

TABLE 2

Ten Highest Rated Attributes of Audit Quality—Groups Analyzed Together

Attribute	Description	Mean
A8	Very knowledgeable audit team—A&A*	4.655
A11	Active engagement partner	4.615
A34	High ethical standards—audit team	4.584
A19	Partner knowledgeable about client industry	4.537
A25	Frequent communication—auditors & mgmt.	4.524
A21	Senior mgr./mgr. knowledgeable—client industry	4.413
A13	Firm has strict guidelines against signing off on uncompleted audit steps	4.403
A1	Partner/senior mgr. make frequent visits to audit site	4.348
A41	Firm keeps client informed during year on financial reporting developments	4.336
A32	Thorough study of internal control	4.184

*A&A stands for accounting and auditing.

Ten Lowest Rated Attributes of Audit Quality

Attribute	Description	Mean
A16	Cost is a major factor in whether an audit step is performed	2.004
A28	Firm provides no consulting services to the client	2.201
A30	Firm has a policy on the maximum hours per day and per week that its staff can work	2.654
A10	Audit fee is immaterial to the engagement partner	2.684
A2	Audit fee is immaterial to firm	2.700
A29	Firm skillful in devising accounting treatments for transactions that generate results management wants	2.775
A14	Auditors are mindful of how busy the CFO and controller are and contact only as necessary	2.889
A31	Firm expects staff members to meet strict budgets	2.961
A7	Firm tends to have large (centralized) offices rather than small (decentralized) offices	3.026
A3	Personnel on the engagement below the senior level have passed the CPA exam	3.136

eigenvalues[5] greater than 1 were retained. Table 3 presents the 12 factors along with their "names," which were determined by

examining each original attribute that correlated with the factor at a .4 or higher level.[6]

The first four factors, and the attributes that loaded on these factors, merit further discussion. Collectively, these factors contain approximately 60 percent (.353/.59) of the total explanatory power of the model. Audit team and firm experience with the client (factor 1) proved to be the most im-

[5] An eigenvalue can be used in calculating the percentage of the total variance that is explained by any one factor. To calculate the percentage of the total variance explained by a factor, the factor's eigenvalue is divided by the trace of the model. The trace is equal to the number of original attributes, in this case, 41. Since the eigenvalue associated with the first factor is 5.29, and the trace is 41, the first factor accounts for approximately 12.9 percent of the total variance [(5.29/41) × 100]. An eigenvalue cutoff of one is reasonably standard, the rationale being that any factor retained for further analysis should at least explain the variance contained in any single variable.

[6] A number of texts in multivariate data analysis (Green 1978, 368; Hair et al. 1987, 247, 249) have suggested extracting factors with an eigenvalue greater than one and the consideration of variables with a loading of .4 or higher.

TABLE 3

Derived Factors

Note: The first number in parentheses after the factor label is the variance accounted for by the factor; the second number is the cumulative variance accounted for by that factor and the preceding factor(s), if any. The numbers in parentheses after the original attribute descriptions represent the factor loadings.

Attribute	Description

FACTOR 1—AUDIT TEAM & FIRM EXPERIENCE WITH CLIENT (.1292, .1292)

A23	Senior manager on audit at least past 2 years (.87)
A20	Manager on audit at least past 2 years (.85)
A22	Firm has been performing audit at least past 3 years (.80)
A4	Partner on audit at least past 3 years (.75)

FACTOR 2—INDUSTRY EXPERTISE (.0942, .2234)

A21	Senior mgr. and mgr. are very knowledgeable about the client's industry (.81)
A24	Senior is very knowledgeable about the client's industry (.77)
A19	Partner is very knowledgeable about the client's industry (.76)
A38	Firm has other clients in the same industry (.59)

FACTOR 3—CPA FIRM RESPONSIVENESS TO CLIENT NEEDS (.0712, .2946)

A37	Firm agreeable to completing audit by a date management has set (.70)
A31	Firm expects staff to meet stringent time budgets (.64)
A29	Firm skillful in devising acceptable accounting treatments for transactions that generate results that management wishes to obtain (.62)
A14	Audit team members contact CFO and controller only to the extent necessary (.55)
A17	Overall firm reputation is positive (.50)
A16	Cost is a major factor in whether an audit procedure is performed (.48)

FACTOR 4—CPA FIRM COMPLIANCE WITH GENERAL AUDIT STANDARDS (.0584, .3530)

A3	Audit team personnel below senior have passed the CPA exam (.68)
A28	Firm provides no consulting services to the audit client (.68)
A10	Audit fee is immaterial to the engagement partner (.65)
A5	Senior is a CPA (.64)
A18	Firm has rarely been found negligent in lawsuits (.45)

FACTOR 5—CPA FIRM COMMITMENT TO QUALITY (.0393, .3923)

A9	Firm is a member of SEC Practice Section or the Private Companies Practice Section (.75)
A26	Firm participates in the peer review process, and its most recent report was a clean one (.75)
A27	Firm encourages staff members to take courses in areas where they have major clients (.51)

FACTOR 6—CPA FIRM EXECUTIVE INVOLVEMENT (.0344, .4266)

A1	Partner/senior mgr. make frequent visits to audit site (.74)
A11	Active engagement partner (.62)
A25	Frequent communication between the audit team and management (.41)

FACTOR 7—CONDUCT OF AUDIT FIELD WORK (.0306, .4572)

A33	Firm makes extensive use of microcomputers in conducting the audit (.68)
A12	Firm makes extensive use of statistical techniques in conducting the audit (.64)
A32	A thorough study of internal control is performed (.61)

FACTOR 8—INVOLVEMENT OF AUDIT COMMITTEE (.0299, .4871)

| A35 | Frequent communication between audit team and audit committee (.75) |
| A40 | Client has a knowledgeable and active audit committee (.62) |

continued overleaf

TABLE 3 (continued)
Derived Factors

FACTOR 9—INDIVIDUAL TEAM MEMBER CHARACTERISTICS (.0271, .5142)
A34   Audit team members have high ethical standards (.74)
A8   Audit team members are very knowledgeable about accounting and auditing (.65)

FACTOR 10—CPA FIRM PERSONNEL MAINTAIN SKEPTICAL ATTITUDE (.0258, .5400)
A6   Firm performs a background search on senior management before accepting a new client (.60)
A2   Audit fee is immaterial to the firm (.50)
A36   Firm maintains an attitude of a skeptic, not a client advocate (.44)

FACTOR 11—
      CPA FIRM PERSONNEL MAINTAIN FRESHNESS OF PERSPECTIVE (.0255, .5655)
A30   Firm has a policy on the maximum number of hours per day and per week that its staff can work (.68)
A39   Audit team members are rotated off the audit periodically (.58)

FACTOR 12—DEGREE OF INDIVIDUAL RESPONSIBILITY (.0245, .5900)
A7   Large centralized offices vs. small decentralized offices (.76)
A13   Firm has strict guidelines against signing off on uncompleted audit steps (−.44)

portant attribute contributing to audit quality. Based on the loadings, the participants ranked continuity of individual audit team members more highly than continuity of the CPA firm. Expertise of audit team members and of the CPA firm with regard to the client's industry received the second highest rating. Once again, the expertise of individual audit team members was ranked more highly than was the expertise of the firm. This seems logical as the perceived quality of any particular audit is more dependent on individual, as opposed to firm, expertise.

CPA firm responsiveness to client needs (factor 3) included: (1) completing the audit by a date established by management, (2) being able to devise acceptable accounting treatments for transactions that generate results wanted by management, and (3) only contacting the CFO and controller during the audit to the extent necessary. It can be argued that responsiveness to clients does not measure audit quality but rather measures audit service quality. The attributes that loaded on this factor may contribute to a lower quality audit (while at the same time contributing to higher audit service quality). For example, completing the audit by a date management has set may lower audit qual-

ity when the audit deadline is unrealistically tight (often resulting in excessive procedures being performed at an interim date rather than at year-end).

CPA firm compliance with general standards (of generally accepted auditing standards) constituted the fourth factor. The general standards relate to competence, independence, and due professional care. Two of the attributes that loaded on this factor related to whether the engagement senior and sub-senior personnel were CPAs. These attributes pertain to the competence of the audit team. Two other attributes addressed the audit fee being immaterial to the engagement partner and the failure to provide consulting services to the client, attributes which relate to the actual and/or apparent independence of the audit firm/team. The last attribute that loaded on this factor pertained to the firm rarely being found negligent in lawsuits brought against it; this attribute provides a measure of due professional care. As discussed later, this factor proves to be the most significant in terms of differences between the three groups studied.

The remaining factors, and the attributes that loaded on these factors, are presented in table 3. In total, the 12 factors accounted for 60 percent of the variance in the original 41 variables. In the social sciences a factor analysis that explains 60 percent of the original variance is generally considered adequate (Hair *et al.* 1987, 247).

Comparison with the Mock/Samet and Sutton/Lampe Studies

As noted, both of these studies relied on auditors' perceptions of attributes to determine audit quality. The five characteristics identified by Mock and Samet (1982) were: (1) planning, (2) administration, (3) procedures, (4) evaluation, and (5) conduct. The administration factor in the Mock and Samet study was represented by many of the same attributes that loaded on the first two factors in this study (*i.e.*, audit team and firm experience with client, industry expertise). The other four factors identified by Mock and Samet, and the attributes pertaining to each, generally differed from the remaining factors identified by this study. Some of the underlying attributes used by Mock and Samet were of a procedural nature (*e.g.*, Were standardized forms appropriately employed?). The attributes used in this study tended not to be procedural, which may contribute to the different findings between the two studies.

Sutton and Lampe (1990) categorized audit quality factors as relating to one of three operations: (1) planning, (2) fieldwork, and (3) administration. They related 19 factors to one of the above three operations. Four of the factors that related to fieldwork in the Sutton and Lampe study were similar to factors identified in this study. These factors were: (1) audit team expertise, (2) rapport with the client, (3) availability of firm-wide resources, and (4) budgetary constraints. The factors related to planning and administration did not have similar counterparts in this study.

Analysis of Group Differences

As noted at the outset, a major aim of this study is to determine if the three groups

(auditors, preparers, and users) differ in their perceptions of audit quality. To achieve this end, a multivariate analysis of variance (MANOVA) was performed using factor scores as the dependent variables and group membership as the independent variable. This procedure indicated that auditors, preparers, and users had significantly different views on the 12 factors ($p < .0001$).[7] To determine in what ways the individual groups differed from each other, additional MANOVAs were run on a pairwise basis. This led to significant differences between audit partners and controllers ($p < .0001$), audit partners and users ($p = .0001$), and controllers and users ($p = .0001$). These results indicate that the three groups involved in the financial reporting process evaluate the attributes of audit quality differently.

The next phase of the analysis was directed at determining the factors on which the three groups differed.[8] Table 4 shows the comparison between audit partners and controllers, between partners and users, and between controllers and users.

Comparison of Audit Partners with Controllers

Audit partners exhibited a statistically significant difference from controllers on all factors except factors 5 (firm specific factors), 6 (CPA firm executive involvement), 9 (characteristics of individual team members), and 11 (maintaining freshness of per-

---

[7]This finding may be due to differences in how attributes are evaluated or to differences in how attributes are aggregated into factors. It cannot be stated that the groups evaluated the attributes differently. However, the groups did differ on the underlying audit quality dimensions (*i.e.*, factors) identified.

[8]Following an analysis of variance on each factor, multiple comparison procedures (*i.e.*, Tukey and Scheffé) were employed in evaluating the extent to which any two groups differed on the factor scores. These procedures allow multiple comparisons to be performed while maintaining a constant alpha rate (*i.e.*, they allow the user to maintain a constant probability of incorrectly concluding that there is a significant difference between groups across a number of different comparisons).

TABLE 4
Comparison of Mean Factor Scores Between Groups

Factor Label	Audit Partners and Controllers		Audit Partners and Users		Controllers and Users	
	F Statistic	P-Value	F Statistic	P-Value	F Statistic	P-Value
1. Audit team & firm experience with client	14.19	.0002	2.09	.1492	2.82	.0939
2. Industry expertise	16.71	.0001	.33	.5632	7.26	.0074
3. CPA firm responsiveness to client needs	121.39	.0001	.31	.5789	58.21	.0001
4. CPA firm compliance with general audit standards	157.45	.0001	358.68	.0001	106.42	.0001
5. CPA firm commitment to quality	.34	.5622	.01	.9201	.16	.6916
6. CPA firm executive involvement	1.38	.2415	68.47	.0001	38.46	.0001
7. Conduct of audit field work	16.48	.0001	10.03	.0017	.001	.9789
8. Involvement of audit committee	14.84	.0001	3.51	.0617	1.55	.2137
9. Individual team member characteristics	1.89	.1702	8.02	.0049	2.62	.1062
10. CPA firm maintains skeptical attitude	66.66	.0001	1.60	.2072	29.89	.0001
11. Maintain freshness of perspective	1.77	.1836	.02	.9012	.99	.3216
12. Degree of individual responsibility	18.23	.0001	.15	.6980	13.10	.0003

spective). There were particularly large differences between the two groups on factors 3 (CPA firm responsiveness to client needs), 4 (CPA firm compliance with general audit standards), and 10 (CPA firm maintains skeptical attitude). Partners viewed maintaining a skeptical attitude (10) as more important than did the controllers. Controllers considered CPA firm responsiveness to client needs (3) and CPA firm compliance with general audit standards (4) to be more important than did audit partners.

The greater importance placed on CPA firm compliance with general audit standards (4) by controllers may be reflective of the importance they assign to the attributes underlying this factor. The two groups may both view compliance with professional standards as important, while differing in their assessment of the role played by each attribute in achieving this compliance. For example, attributes dealing with not providing consulting services to an audit client and an audit fee immaterial to the engagement partner loaded highly on this factor. The mean value of both of these attributes was much lower for partners than for controllers. These findings indicate that partners consider these attributes as less important in complying with generally accepted auditing standards (GAAS) than do controllers.

Comparison of Audit Partners with Users

There were no statistical differences between the groups for eight of the 12 factors (although, when all 12 factors were considered, the groups differed). The factors on which the two groups differed were factors 4 (CPA firm compliance with general audit standards), 6 (CPA firm executive involvement), 7 (conduct of audit field work), and 9 (characteristics of individual team members). The differences were particularly pronounced for factors 4 and 6. Users evaluated compliance with general audit standards (4) as more important than did partners. Partners considered the active

involvement of CPA firm executives (partners/senior managers/managers), factor 6, as more important than did users. Users may not be aware of how important CPA executive involvement is in the audit process.

Comparison of Controllers with Users

There was a statistically significant difference between these groups on six of the factors. Controllers thought that the responsiveness of the CPA firm to client needs (3) was much more indicative of a high quality audit than did users. As discussed previously, this factor measures audit service quality, not audit quality. Audit service quality is likely to be of most importance to controllers and of least importance to users. (It is somewhat important to partners since they are charged with satisfying their clients' needs.) Users considered the CPA firm's compliance with general audit standards (4) as more important than did controllers. This result is not surprising since the value of an audit to users is dependent on the CPA firm's competence, independence, and due professional care. There were smaller differences between the two groups in their evaluations of factors 2 (industry expertise), 6 (CPA firm executive involvement), 10 (CPA firm maintains skeptical attitude), and 12 (degree of individual responsibility).

CONCLUSIONS

This study examined how the three primary groups (auditors, preparers, and users) involved in the financial reporting process perceived various audit quality attributes. The factors viewed as most important to audit quality were: (1) audit team and firm experience with the client, (2) industry expertise, (3) CPA firm responsiveness to client needs, and (4) CPA firm compliance with general audit standards. These factors were all more closely tied to the characteristics of audit team members than to firm-wide attributes.

The results of this study indicate that the

constituencies of CPA firms, preparers and users, evaluate audit quality differently than do partners. CPA firms may want to focus more effort on factors where there were particularly large differences between the perceptions of audit partners and those of preparers and users. Both preparers and users felt that compliance with general audit standards (factor 4) was more important than did partners. CPA firms may want to closely examine their policies and procedures dealing with: (1) the nature and extent of consulting services provided to audit clients, (2) professional certification for firm personnel, and (3) quality control standards as they relate to minimizing potential legal liability. Also, improved responsiveness to client needs (factor 3) may enhance retention rates,

a key service quality indicator, among existing clients.

Ideally, this study should serve as a springboard for future studies in this area. A number of important questions remain unanswered. First, are the findings in this study driven by differences in how auditors, preparers, and users evaluate the attributes of audit quality or by fundamentally different definitions of audit quality that each group uses? Second, are there appreciable differences in how CPA firms perform on these measures of audit quality? If so, do the firms that provide superior audit service quality have higher client retention rates and greater success in attracting new clients? Finally, what is the relationship between audit service quality and audit fees?

APPENDIX
AUDIT QUALITY ATTRIBUTES INSTRUMENT

Instructions

The following are factors that may influence the quality of audits performed by CPA firms. Using the below scale, please evaluate the impact of the following factors on audit quality. If any factor is unclear, or if you feel you do not have enough expertise to evaluate the factor, please leave that factor blank.

Scale Response Format

1-Strongly Disagree
2-Disagree
3-Neutral
4-Agree
5-Strongly Agree

Audit Quality Attributes

1. The engagement partner and senior manager make frequent visits to the audit site.
2. The percentage that the audit fee represents to total billings of the CPA firm is not material.
3. The personnel on the engagement below the senior level have passed the CPA exam.
4. The engagement partner has been on the audit for at least the past three years.
5. The senior on the engagement is a CPA.
6. Before accepting a new client the CPA firm conducts a background search on the senior management of the prospective client.
7. The CPA firm tends to have large (centralized) offices rather than small (decentralized) offices.
8. The auditors assigned to the engagement are very knowledgeable about accounting and auditing standards.
9. The CPA firm is a member of the SEC Practice Section for CPA firms or the Private Companies Practice Section for CPA firms.
10. The audit fee paid by the client does not represent more than 25 percent of the total audit fees controlled by the engagement partner.

11. The engagement partner is actively involved in the engagement beginning with initial planning and throughout the audit process, culminating with final sign off.
12. The CPA firm makes extensive use of statistical techniques in conducting the audit.
13. The CPA firm has strict guidelines against signing off on audit steps that are not completed.
14. The auditors are mindful of how busy the CFO and controller are and contact these individuals only to the extent necessary.
15. The CPA firm has regulatory agency (*i.e.*, SEC, etc.) expertise.
16. The cost of different audit procedures, in terms of time expended, is the major criterion as to whether the procedure is used.
17. The overall reputation of the CPA firm is positive.
18. The CPA firm has rarely been found negligent in lawsuits brought against it (alleging inadequate audit performance).
19. The partner assigned to the engagement is very knowledgeable about the industry.
20. The manager has been on the audit for at least the past two years.
21. The senior manager and manager assigned to the engagement are very knowledgeable about the industry.
22. The CPA firm has been performing the audit for at least three years.
23. The senior manager has been on the audit for at least the past two years.
24. The senior assigned to the engagement is very knowledgeable about the industry.
25. There is frequent communication between the audit team and management.
26. The CPA firm participates in the peer review process, and its most recent peer review report was a clean one.
27. The CPA firm actively encourages staff members to take courses and examinations in fields where they have major clients.
28. The CPA firm that is conducting the audit performs no consulting services for the client.
29. The CPA firm is skillful in devising acceptable accounting treatments for transactions that generate results that management wishes to obtain.
30. The CPA firm has a policy on the maximum number of hours per day and per week that its staff can work.
31. The CPA firm develops stringent time budgets for each audit area and expects their people to meet them.
32. The CPA firm conducts a thorough study of the client's system of internal control.
33. The CPA firm makes extensive use of micro-computers in conducting the audit.
34. The auditors assigned to the engagement have very high ethical standards.
35. There is frequent communication between the audit team and the audit committee.
36. The CPA firm's attitude is one of a skeptic, not one of a client advocate.
37. The CPA firm is agreeable to completing the audit by a date the client has set.
38. The CPA firm conducting the audit has other clients in the industry.
39. Audit team members are rotated off the audit periodically.
40. The company has a knowledgeable and active audit committee.
41. The CPA firm keeps company management informed during the year about accounting and financial reporting developments that may affect them.

REFERENCES

A. M. Best Co. 1987. *Best's Insurance Reports Life-Health*. Oldwick, NJ: A. M. Best Company.

American Institute of Certified Public Accountants. 1979. *Professional Standards: Ethics, Bylaws, Quality Control*. Volume 2, ET Section 502. New York: AICPA.

Beatty, R. 1989. Auditor reputation and the pricing of initial public offerings. *The Accounting Review* (October): 693–709.

Bernstein, P. 1978. Competition comes to accounting. *Fortune* (July 17): 88–96.

Bishea, M. & Associates, Inc. 1982. *Opinion Study for the Wisconsin Institute of Certified Public Accountants*. Milwaukee, WI: M. Bishea & Associates, Inc..

Bloom, P. 1984. Effective marketing for professional services. *Harvard Business Review* (September–October): 102–110.

Congram, C. and R. Dumesic. 1986. *The Accountant's Strategic Marketing Guide*. New York: Wiley.

Cowan, A. 1990. How desperate can auditors get? *The New York Times* (November 5): C1, C5.

Dun's Marketing Services. 1988. *Million Dollar Directory*. Parsippany, NJ: Dun's Marketing Services.

Eichenseher, J., M. Hagigi, and D. Shields. 1989. Market reaction to auditor changes by OTC companies. *Auditing: A Journal of Practice & Theory* (Fall): 29–40.

Ettredge, M., P. Shane, and D. Smith. 1988. Audit firm size and the association between reported earnings and security returns. *Auditing: A Journal of Practice & Theory* (Spring): 29–39.

Fortune. 1987. The largest 500 U.S. industrial corporations. (April 27): 364–383.

———. 1987. The service 500. (June 8): 196–215.

Francis, J. and D. Simon. 1987. A test of audit pricing in the small-client segment of the U.S. audit market. *The Accounting Review* (January): 145–157.

Green, P. 1978. *Analyzing Multivariate Data*. Hinsdale, IL: Dryden Press.

Hair, J., R. Anderson, and R. Tatham. 1987. *Multivariate Data Analysis*. Second Edition. New York: Macmillan.

Imhoff, E. 1988. A comparison of analysts' accounting quality judgments among CPA firms' clients. *Auditing: A Journal of Practice & Theory* (Spring): 182–191.

Kotler, P. and P. Bloom. 1984. *Marketing Professional Services*. Englewood Cliffs, NJ: Prentice-Hall.

Mock, T. and M. Samet. 1982. A multi-attribute model for audit evaluation. In *Proceedings of the VI University of Kansas Audit Symposium*.

Money Market Directories, Inc. 1988. *The Money Market Directory of Pension Funds and their Investment Managers*. Charlottesville, VA: Money Market Directories Inc.

Morningstar, Inc. 1988. *Mutual Fund Sourcebook*. Chicago, IL: Morningstar, Inc.

Nichols, D. and D. Smith. 1983. Auditor credibility and auditor changes. *Journal of Accounting Research* (Autumn): 534–544.

Palmer, R. 1989. Accounting as a 'mature industry.' *Journal of Accountancy* (May): 84–88.

Palmrose, Z. 1982. Quality-differentiation, surrogates, and the pricing of audit services: An empirical investigation. Ph.D. dissertation, University of Washington, Seattle, WA.

———. 1986. Audit fees and auditor size: Further evidence. *Journal of Accounting Research* (Spring): 97–110.

———. 1988. An analysis of auditor litigation and audit service quality. *The Accounting Review* (January): 55–73.

———. 1989. The relation of audit contract type to audit fees and hours. *The Accounting Review* (July): 488–499.

Parasuraman, A., V. Zeithaml, and L. Berry. 1985. A conceptual model of service quality and its implications for future research. *Journal of Marketing* (Fall): 41–50.

Rand McNally & Co. 1987. *The Rand McNally Bankers Directory*. Chicago, IL: Rand McNally & Co.

Schroeder, M., I. Solomon, and D. Vickrey. 1986. Audit quality: The perceptions of audit-committee chairpersons and audit partners. *Auditing: A Journal of Practice & Theory* (Spring): 86–94.

Shockley, R. and R. Holt. 1983. A behavioral investigation of supplier differentiation in the market for audit services. *Journal of Accounting Research* (Autumn): 545–564.

Simon, D. 1985. The audit services market: Additional empirical evidence. *Auditing: A Journal of Practice & Theory* (Fall): 71–78.

——— and J. Francis. 1988. The effects of auditor change on audit fees: Tests of price cutting and price recovery. *The Accounting Review* (April): 255–269.

Simunic, D. 1980. The pricing of audit services: Theory and evidence. *Journal of Accounting Research* (Spring): 161–190.

——— and M. Stein. 1987. *Product Differentiation in Auditing: Auditor Choice in the Market for Unseasoned New Issues, Research Monograph No. 13*. Vancouver,

British Columbia: The Canadian Certified General Accountants' Research Foundation.

Sutton, S. and J. Lampe. 1990. Formulating a process measurement system for audit quality. In *Proceedings of the 1990 University of Southern California Audit Judgment Symposium*.

Turpen, R. 1990. Differential pricing on auditors' initial engagements: Further evidence. *Auditing: A Journal of Practice & Theory* (Spring): 60–76.

Wilson, T., and R. Grimlund. 1990. An examination of the importance of an auditor's reputation. *Auditing: A Journal of Practice & Theory* (Spring): 43–59.

Part III
Governance and the Audit Committee

[18]

The Incentives for Voluntary Audit Committee Formation

Michael E. Bradbury

This study uses an agency theory framework to analyze the incentives for voluntary formation of audit committees. Empirical variables are chosen to proxy for costs of conflicts of interest between stockholders, bondholders, and managers. Also tested is the influence of size and the incentives of (Big Eight) auditors and directors to establish audit committees. Univariate and multivariate tests are undertaken on 135 firms listed on the New Zealand Stock Exchange. The results indicate that voluntary audit committees are not related to auditor incentive variables or to agency cost variables arising from the separation of (residual) ownership and (decision) control. A relation is found between voluntary audit committee formation and directors' incentives. Both the number of directors on the board and intercorporate ownership were found to be the more important determinants of voluntary audit committees.

1. Introduction

An important issue in the regulation of corporate behavior is the appropriate monitoring configuration for top management. This is reflected in the efforts of stock exchanges, the Securities and Exchange Commission (SEC), and the American Institute of Certified Public Accountants (AICPA) to promote the use of audit committees. As early as 1940, the SEC recommended the use of audit committees (Birkett 1986, p. 109). During 1967 the AICPA executive committee recommended that public companies have audit committees (Birkett, 1986, p. 116). On January 6, 1977, the New York Stock Exchange directed each domestic company, as part of its listing requirement, to have an audit committee (Birkett, 1986, pp. 115–116). More recently, the National Commission on Fraudulent Financial Reporting (NCFFR) recommended that the SEC require that every public company form an audit committee "of independent directors" (NCFFR, 1987, p. 40).[1]

Address reprint requests to: Michael E. Bradbury, Department of Accounting and Finance, Private Bag, University of Auckland, New Zealand.

[1] For a more comprehensive review of the recent history of audit committees and attempts to promote their use, see Birkett (1986).

Journal of Accounting and Public Policy, 9, 19–36 (1990)
© 1990 Elsevier Science Publishing Co., Inc.

0278-4254/90/$03.50

The justification for imposing mandatory audit committees is by no means obvious, inasmuch as firms have incentives to voluntarily establish monitoring mechanisms, including the formation of audit committees. If cross-sectional differences exist in the costs or benefits of monitoring packages, then the regulation of audit committees can potentially impose costs unevenly across firms.[2] Alternatively, if firms undertake the same amount of monitoring, then audit committee regulation will cause some firms to reduce expenditure on other monitoring activities. Furthermore, the regulation of audit committees also removes the ability of firms to signal information by the choice of monitoring technologies employed.[3] This study attempts to assist accounting policy makers evaluate the need for regulation by providing empirical evidence on the incentives for corporations to voluntarily engage in audit committee formation.

This study examines the characteristics of firms that voluntarily create an audit committee. New Zealand provides a suitable setting for investigating this question as there are no regulations or professional requirements that prescribe or recommend audit committees. Furthermore, with the exception of Bradbury (1979), there appears to be no discussion of audit committees in the New Zealand professional literature. This contrasts strongly with the experience in the United States, where audit committee formation has become a political issue (e.g., refer to the actions of Congress in Birkett, 1986, p. 118–120).

The remainder of this paper is organized as follows. The hypotheses to be tested are developed in Section 2. This research design and the sample selection are discussed in Section 3 and the empirical results are reported in Section 4. Section 5 provides a summary and discussion.

2. Development of Hypotheses

2.1 The Functions of Audit Committees

In developing hypotheses of the corporate incentives for forming audit committees, the firm is characterized by the separation of ownership and control (Jensen and Meckling, 1976, pp. 305–312). Large corporations, particularly those listed on stock exchanges, are further characterized by the separation and specialization of residual claimholders, decision control, and decision management (Fama and Jensen, 1983, p. 313). Fama and Jensen (1983, p. 313) state:

> Internal control in the open corporation is delegated by residual claimants to a board of directors. Residual claimants generally retain approval rights (by vote) on such matters as board membership, auditor choice, mergers, and new stock issues. Other management and control functions are delegated by the residual claimants

---

[2] For example, see Maher (1981) for a discussion of the penalties imposed by the regulation of internal control systems under the Foreign Corrupt Practices Act.

[3] Bar-Yosef and Livnat (1984) discuss the use of auditing as a signaling mechanism. Voluntary audit committee formation can be viewed as a signal that enhances audit quality.

to the board. The board then delegates most decision management functions and many decision control functions to internal agents, but it retains ultimate control over internal agents—including the rights to ratify and monitor major policy initiatives and to hire, fire and set the compensation of top level decision managers.

This characterization is important because it explicitly recognizes the role of the board of directors in the firm. Audit committees establish a formal communication between a subcommittee of the board of directors (comprising mainly outside directors), the internal monitoring system, and the auditor. Audit committees are established to (1) increase the credibility of annual audited financial statements, (2) assist directors in meeting their responsibilities, and (3) enhance audit independence.[4] These audit committee functions provide the underlying basis for developing hypotheses about the incentives for audit committee formation.

2.2 The Quality of Financial Reporting

Audit committees are commonly viewed as monitoring mechanisms that enhance the audit attestation function of external financial reporting. Auditing provides assurance about the quality of information reported between principal and agent.[5] Chow (1982) and Watts and Zimmerman (1983) provide evidence that firms voluntarily engage external auditing in situations of high agency costs. Hence, it is likely that audit committees will be voluntarily employed in situations of high agency cost to enhance the quality of information flows between principal and agent. However, Eichenseher and Shields (1985, pp. 21–27) compare 67 firms that change auditors with a random control sample of 61 firms over the period 1973–1978, but find no support for the relation between audit committee formation and corporation characteristics: size, agency relations, and industry.

Number of Outside Stockholders. Watts (1977, pp. 57–59) and Leftwich, Watts, and Zimmerman (1981, pp. 56–62) suggest that managers will reduce the stockholder–manager conflict by voluntarily providing financial statements. External financial reporting is most likely to be an effective monitoring mechanism when there exists a large *number* of outside stockholders. If audit committees enhance the external reporting function, we can make the following hypothesis.

H1: *Ceteris paribus, firms with a larger number of outside (nonexecutive) shareholders are more likely to employ audit committees.*

---

[4] Several studies report the functions and objectives of audit committees. For example, refer to Canadian Institute of Chartered Accountants (1981), Mautz and Neumann (1977), and Accounting International Study Group (1977).

[5] For example, Ng (1978, p. 917) suggests that auditing can limit the size of the reporting bias. See Wallace (1980) for a detailed discussion of the role of auditing in reducing agency costs.

Financial Leverage. The potential for wealth transfers from debtholders to stockholders increases as the proportion of debt in a firm's capital structure increases (Jensen and Meckling, 1976; Smith and Warner, 1979). Chow (1982, pp. 280–287) reports that leverage and the number of accounting-based debt covenants are related to voluntary audits. On the other hand, Watts and Zimmerman (1983, p. 627) find no direct relation between auditing and the level of debt. Furthermore, because debt contracts have provisions written in terms of audited financial statement numbers, there is indirect support that the level of voluntary auditing is positively related to leverage. If audit committees reduce agency costs of wealth transfers from debtholders to stockholders, then the probability that a firm will establish an audit committee is positively related to the level of debt in the firm's capital structure. Hence:

H2: *Ceteris paribus, the higher the leverage, the greater the likelihood that the firm has an audit committee.*

Assets-in-place. The value of the firm can be viewed as the sum of growth opportunities (or assets yet to be acquired) and assets-in-place (Myers, 1977). Wealth transfers between owners and creditors are more difficult, and hence agency costs are lower, for firms with a greater proportion of assets-in-place. Leftwich, Watts, and Zimmerman (1981, p. 61) and Chow and Wong-Boren (1987, p. 534) suggest that voluntary disclosure is inversely related to assets-in-place. Thus:

H3: *Ceteris paribus, the lower the value of assets-in-place, the greater the likelihood that the firm has an audit committee.*

2.3 Director Incentives

Outside directors are widely believed to play a larger role in monitoring management than inside board members. Fama (1980, p. 294) indicates that outside directors can be regarded "as professional referees whose task is to stimulate and oversee the competition among the firm's top management." Outside directors have an incentive to ensure the effective running of the company because being a director of a well-run company enhances their reputation and signals their competence to the market.

A particular benefit of the audit committee is that it strengthens the role of outside or nonexecutive directors by providing them with direct access to the external auditor and often the internal auditing system. Hence, audit committees provide a potentially efficient means of reducing information asymmetries between inside and outside directors. The increasing legal responsibilities of directors during the mid-1970s has increased the impetus for audit committees. (See, for example, Birkett 1986, pp. 120–122).

The increasing cost of personal liability provides outside directors with incentives to form audit committees in order to reduce information asymmetries within the board. Hence, it is hypothesized that firms with more nonexecutive directors are more likely to establish audit committees. The test of this hypothesis requires the determination of whether each director is an executive or outside director—information that is not directly available for New Zealand firms. Hence, suitable proxy measures must be found.

Intercorporate Ownership. A possible measure to proxy for the existence of outside directors relates to intercorporate ownership. In New Zealand many external directors are appointed by large intercorporate stockholders of the firm. Nominated directors are appointed to exercise decision control functions on behalf of the investing firm. This leads to the following hypothesis:

> H4: *Ceteris paribus, the existence of a large intercorporate stockholding will increase the probability that a firm will have outside directors, thereby increasing the probability that a firm maintains an audit committee.*

Directors' Ownership. The board of directors is itself a monitoring device. Agency costs will increase as the directors' ownership share of the firm decreases (Jensen and Meckling, 1976, pp. 312–330). In such cases the quality of monitoring can be enhanced if shareholders elect outside directors as their independent representatives. Thus:

> H5: *Ceteris paribus, the lower the directors' ownership of the firm, the greater the probability that a firm will have outside directors, thereby increasing the probability that a firm will maintain an audit committee.*

2.4 Auditor Incentives

It is generally recognized that audit committees can (at little or no cost to the auditor) enhance auditor independence. Hence, audit firms have an incentive to encourage the formation of audit committees.[6] However, Eichenseher and Shields (1985, pp. 25–27) provide evidence that newly hired small (other than Big Eight) auditors are reluctant to encourage formation of audit committees because audit committees have a preference for Big Eight auditors. Given this evidence, we state the following hypothesis:

> H6: *Ceteris paribus, the demand for audit committees increases when the incumbent auditor is a member of the Big Eight.*

2.5 Economies of Scale

It would appear, however, that audit committee formation requires nontrivial expertise (Eichenseher and Shields, 1985, p. 29). If the cost of maintaining an

---

[6] However, auditor incentives will not necessarily increase the supply of audit committees, which will depend primarily on directors' incentives.

audit committee is relatively fixed, then the net benefits of audit committees will increase with firm size. Mautz and Neary (1979, p. 83) report that a high percentage of large U.S. corporations have formed audit committees. Given this evidence, we hypothesize as follows:

H7: *Ceteris paribus, larger firms are more likely to employ an audit committee.*

However, firm size per se is unlikely to be a determinant of audit committee formation. For example, a large firm with a single director would not need an audit committee. The delegation of boardroom tasks to specialist subcommittees is feasible only in cases in which there are a large number of directors.[7] Note that the direction of causation is not clear, for it is possible that the decision to form an audit committee increases the size of the board. Hence, the last hypothesis:

H8: *Ceteris paribus, audit committees are more likely in corporate boards containing a large number of directors.*

2.6 Other Factors

At least one potential explanation for audit committee formation can be discounted in the New Zealand context. The image value of audit committee formation to reducing political costs is not a plausible hypothesis, as none of the sample firms having an audit committee indicated this fact in their annual report.[8] This raises doubts about the validity of hypotheses H1 through H3. If audit committees in fact reduced agency costs by improving the quality of financial statements, it would seem likely that at least one manager would advertise that such monitoring technology was being employed.

In this situation, a researcher must choose between including a potentially irrelevant variable in the regression (which leads to higher variances of the estimated coefficients) or leaving a potentially relevant variable out of the regression (which is likely to bias the remaining estimates). It was decided to leave the "financial statement improvement" variables relating to hypotheses H1 through H3 in the initial analysis because these variables are supported by theory and have been important determinants in other voluntary disclosure studies.[9] However, the sensitivity of the test results to their exclusion will also be examined.

3. Sample and Data Selection

The New Zealand companies that voluntarily formed audit committees were identified from the results of a questionnaire by Chandler (1982). Chandler examined the role of directors and surveyed all 208 companies listed on the New

---

[7] It is recognized that firm size is likely to be a major determinant of the size of the board.

[8] Eichenseher and Shields (1985, pp. 24–27) report an increasing awareness of the image value of audit committee formation in the United States.

[9] For example, Leftwich, Watts, and Zimmerman (1981), Chow (1982), and Chow and Wong-Boren (1987).

Zealand Stock Exchange as of March 31, 1981. The useable replies resulted in a sample of 135 firms (20 with voluntary audit committees) from the following industry groups: 71 (12) industrial companies, 10 (2) natural resource firms, 24 (4) service companies (including transportation), 11 (1) retailer wholesale firms, and 19 (1) financial services (including insurance and property investment). To check the representativeness of the sample I performed a binomial test for each industry to determine the probability of randomly obtaining in the given industry as many companies as, or more companies than, were actually observed. These results suggest that there is no strong industry effect in this sample of firms. Thus, the same 135 firms were used in the current study. For each of the 135 firms, I collected the following data from their 1981 financial statements:

1. Information on the number of outside stockholders is not readily available. However, an effective proxy is the total number of shares issued by the firm $(NUMSH)$.[10]
2. Leverage (LEV) is measured as the ratio of total liabilities to firm size.
3. The variable assets-in-place (AIP) is measured as the ratio of fixed assets to firm size.
4. The intercorporate control variable $(ICTRL)$ is set at 1 if another company owns 10 percent or more of the voting stock with a nominee seat on the board of directors; otherwise it is set at 0.
5. The directors' ownership $(DCTRL)$ is measured as the ratio of the total number of shares held by the board to the total number of shares issued.
6. A dummy variable is used to measure the impact of a Big Eight audit firm. *BIG8* is set to 1 if the auditor is a member of the Big Eight and 0 otherwise.
7. Firm size $(SIZE)$ is measured as the sum of the market value of ordinary share capital and the book values of preference capital and debt.
8. The number of directors $(NUMDIR)$ is a measure of size that is expected to be positively related to the decision to form an audit committee.

4. Empirical Results

A two-sample design is used to test the hypotheses developed in Section 2. The treatment group consists of firms that voluntarily formed audit committees, whereas the control group did not employ audit committees.

4.1 Descriptive Statistics and Univariate Results

Table 1 contains a summary of the descriptive statistics and the results of the univariate tests for each explanatory variable. The means and medians for all variables are in the predicted direction. A nonparametric Mann–Whitney U test

---

[10] Fogelberg (1980) examines the ownership and control of 43 New Zealand companies listed in 1974. From the details in Fogelberg's paper I calculated a Pearson correlation between outside stockholders and the number of shares issued that equaled 0.96 and was significant at the 0.01 level.

Michael E. Bradbury

Table 1. Summary Statistics and Univariate Tests of the Relation Between Independent Variables and Audit Committee Formation

Hypothesis	Direction	Variable[a]		Firms without audit committee (n = 115)	Firms with audit committee (n = 20)	Univariate tests[b]	
H1	<	NUMSH	Median	1.200	3.200	MWU	2.446
			Mean	3.509	6.492		(p = 0.007)
			Std. dev.	7.810	9.335		
H2	<	LEV	Median	0.598	0.601	MWU	0.027
			Mean	0.545	0.559		(p = 0.488)
			Std. dev.	0.215	0.183		
H3	>	AIP	Median	0.358	0.368	MWU	0.027
			Mean	0.444	0.386		(p = 0.488)
			Std. dev.	0.543	0.233		
H4	<	ICTRL	Median	1.000	1.000	χ^2	2.398
			Mean	0.513	0.700		(p = 0.060)
			Std. dev.	0.502	0.470		
H5	>	DCTRL	Median	0.022	0.003	MWU	2.010
			Mean	0.212	0.043		(p = 0.022)
			Std. dev.	0.589	0.112		

						Test statistic
H6	<	BIG8	Median	1.000	1.000	χ^2 0.367
			Mean	0.791	0.850	($p = 0.274$)
			Std. dev.	0.408	0.366	
H7	<	SIZE	Median	0.136	0.377	MWU 2.6107
			Mean	0.159	1.257	($p = 0.005$)
			Std. dev.	1.101	2.981	
H8	<	NUMDIR	Median	7.000	9.000	MWU 3.079
			Mean	6.913	8.950	($p = 0.001$)
			Std. dev.	1.976	3.219	

[a] Variables are defined as follows:

NUMSH = Number of shares issued by the firm $\times 10^{-6}$.
LEV = Total liabilities to firm size.
AIP = Ratio of fixed assets to firm size.
ICTRL = 1 if another company owns 10% of voting stock and a nominee on the board of directors; 0 otherwise.
DCTRL = Ratio of common stock held by the directors to total common stock issued.
BIG8 = 1 if auditor was a Big 8 firm; 0 otherwise.
SIZE = (Market value of common equity + book value of preferred stock and debt) $\times 10^{-6}$.
NUMDIR = Number of directors.

[b] The test statistics reported are as follows:

MWU = For continuous variables the nonparametric Mann–Whitney U test was employed. A parametric Student's t test (not reported) yielded similar results.
χ^2 = For dichotomous variables a χ^2 test statistic is reported. One-tailed probabilities are reported.

was used to assess the null hypotheses of no statistical differences in the hypothesized variables between the treatment and control groups.[11] For dichotomous variables *ICTRL* and *BIG8*, a χ^2 test was employed. *NUMSH*, *DCTRL*, *SIZE*, and *NUMDIR* are significant at the 0.05 level or lower, thereby providing support for hypotheses H1, H5, H7, and H8. *ICTRL* is significant at the 0.10 level. No statistical support is found for *LEV*, *AIP*, or *BIG8*.

In Section 2 it was suggested that it is the number of directors rather than firm size that acts as a constraint to audit committee formation. Size has been included in the analysis because evidence established by Mautz and Neumann (1977, p. 47) and Eichenseher and Shields (1985, p. 23) has suggested a relation between audit committees and size. In order to focus on marginal contribution of firm size, the following cross-sectional regression was estimated:[12]

$$\log(SIZE) = \hat{a} + \hat{b}\,NUMDIR \tag{1}$$

This regression yielded values of -7.777 and 0.508 for $\hat{a}$ and $\hat{b}$, respectively. The t statistics were -22.7 and 11.24, the adjusted R^2 was 0.483 and the F statistic of 126.4 was significant at the 0.01 level. The estimated parameters were applied to each observation to obtain a residual *SIZE*, designated *SIZERES*, which is calculated as follows:

$$SIZERES = \log(SIZE) + 7.777 - 0.508(NUMDIR) \tag{2}$$

The Mann–Whitney U test for differences in *SIZERES* between firms with audit committees and firms without, yields a Z statistic of 0.703 ($p = 0.241$). That *SIZERES* is orthogonal to *NUMDIR* indicates that firm size does not make a marginal contribution on the decision to maintain an audit committee once the number of directors has been considered.

As a complementary test this process was inverted and the marginal contribution of *NUMDIR*, once firm size has been considered, was examined. A residual *NUMDIR* was calculated from parameter estimates obtained from regressing *NUMDIR* on $\log(SIZE)$. A Mann–Whitney U test for differences in the residual *NUMDIR* between firms with and without audit committees was employed. This yields a Z statistic of 1.737 ($p = 0.041$), which suggests that the number of directors does make a marginal contribution to maintaining an audit committee after size has been considered.

Table 2 presents pairwise Spearman correlations among the independent variables. There exist significantly strong bivariate correlations between *NUMSH*, *NUMDIR* and *DCTRL*, and many other of the independent variables.[13] The degree of intercorrelation among the independent variables suggests that the col-

---

[11] Nonparametric tests are employed because there is no reason to expect the independent variables to be normally distributed.

[12] Logarithmic transformations were performed on *SIZE* to reduce skewness before regressions were run.

[13] Unexpectedly, no relation between *AIP* and *LEV* is evident. This is inconsistent with findings by Myers (1977) and empirical results reported by Leftwich, Watts, and Zimmerman (1981, p. 65).

Table 2. Spearman Correlations Among the Independent Variables

	NUMSH[a]	LEV	AIP	ICTRL	DCTRL	BIG8	SIZE
NUMSH	1.000						
LEV	0.130	1.000					
AIP	0.084	0.080	1.000				
ICTRL	−0.149	−0.077	0.024	1.000			
DCTRL	−0.796[b]	−0.133	−0.124	0.040	1.000		
BIG8	0.226[b]	−0.017	0.067	0.022	−0.281[b]	1.000	
SIZE	0.853[b]	0.266[b]	0.124	−0.075	−0.742[b]	0.182[c]	1.000
NUMDIR	0.697[b]	0.223[b]	0.112	−0.050	−0.527[b]	0.094	0.737[b]

[a] Variables are defined in Table 1.
[b] Significant at the 0.01 level (two-tailed).
[c] Significant at the 0.05 level (two-tailed).

lective results of the univariate tests may be overstated. A multivariate approach is an appropriate means to consider the simultaneous effect of the explanatory variables on voluntary audit committee formation.

4.2 Logit Analysis

Logistic regression is employed as a multivariate test of the explanatory variables. The dependent variable is set to one if the firm has voluntarily formed an audit committee and zero otherwise. The logit model can be written as follows:

$$\text{logit } (p) = B_1 + B_2 NUMSH + B_3 LEV + B_4 AIP + B_5 ICTRL$$
$$+ B_6 DCTRL + B_7 BIG8 + B_8 SIZE + B_9 NUMDIR, \quad (3)$$

where p is the probability that the dependent variable equals one and the independent variables are as previously defined. A log transformation was applied to $NUMSH$ and $SIZE$ because the raw variables were found to have limited dispersion.[14] Table 3 reports the logistic regression results for the full model (Model 1) and for three reduced models (Models 2, 3, and 4). The Model 1 χ^2 is 17.76 ($8df$), meaning the null hypothesis of no statistical relationship can be rejected at the .01 level of confidence. The likelihood ratio index, which provides an indication of the explanatory power of the model, is 0.163. The coefficients have the predicted signs except for $BIG8$. The coefficients for $NUMDIR$ and $ICTRL$ are significant (at the 0.05 level), supporting hypotheses H4 and H8. However, no support is provided for hypotheses H1, H2, H3, H5, H6, and H7 (variables $NUMSH$, LEV, AIP, $DCTRL$, $BIG8$, and $SIZE$, respectively).

---

[14] Logit analysis involves no distributional assumptions. Consequently transformations are not generally necessary. In this case, log transformations corrected the limited dispersion of $NUMSH$ and $SIZE$ for the logit regression.

Table 3. Logit Analysis of the Voluntary Formation of Audit Committees and the Explanatory Variables

Hypothesis	Variable[a]	Predicted sign	Coefficients (parameter χ^2)			
			Model 1	Model 2	Model 3	Model 4
H1	log (*NUMSH*)	+	0.186 (0.20)	0.186 (0.20)	0.139 (0.20)	
H2	*LEV*	+	0.046 (0.00)	0.046 (0.00)	-0.050 (0.00)	
H3	*AIP*	-	-0.724 (0.51)	-0.724 (0.51)	-0.702 (0.50)	
H4	*ICTRL*	+	1.238 (4.14)^f	1.238 (4.14)^f	1.219 (4.17)^f	1.176 (4.08)^f
H5	*DCTRL*	-	-1.048 (0.40)	-1.048 (0.40)	-1.029 (0.40)	-1.131 (0.47)
H6	*BIG8*	+	-0.075 (0.01)	-0.075 (0.01)	-0.080 (0.01)	-0.087 (0.01)

Voluntary Audit Committee Formation

		Expected sign				
H7	log (SIZE)	+	−0.055 (0.03)			0.055 (0.05)
H7	SIZERES	+		−0.055 (0.03)		
H9	NUMDIR	+	0.356 (4.67)^f	0.328 (2.99)^f	0.347 (5.08)^f	0.353 (4.80)^f
Constant			−5.233 (3.64)^f	−4.806 (9.91)^e	−4.859 (10.38)^e	−4.862 (5.24)^f
Likelihood ratio index^b			0.163	0.163	0.163	0.155
Model χ^2 statistic^c			17.76 (8 df)	18.46 (8 df)	18.44 (7 df)	17.57 (5 df)
Somers's D_{xy}^d			0.533	0.533	0.532	0.529

[a] See Table 1 for the definition of variables.
[b] The log-likelihood ratio idex is 1 − (log-likelihood at convergence/log-likelihood at zero). It is similar to an R^2 measure in a multiple regression and provides an indication of the logit model's explanatory power.
[c] The model χ^2 statistic is calculated to test the hypothesis that all the parameters in the model are simultaneously equal to zero.
[d] Somers' D_{xy} provides an assessment of the predictive ability of the model. It is a rank correlation between the predicted probabilities and the dependent variable.
[e] Significant at the 0.01 level (one-tailed).
[f] Significant at the 0.05 level (one-tailed).

SIZE is replaced with *SIZERES* in Model 2 and is omitted from Model 3. Model 2 has the same likelihood ratio index, Somers's D_{xy}, and is econometrically equivalent to Model 1 (see Christie et al., 1984). Model 2 is not estimated to reduce collinearity problems but to complement the univariate results and emphasize the marginal explanatory power of board size and firm size.

The coefficient for *LEV* becomes negative in Model 3, but remains insignificant at conventional levels. In Model 2 the parameter χ^2 for *NUMDIR* is reduced but still remains significant at the 0.05 level. *SIZERES* is not significant at the 0.10 level. Models 2 and 3 confirm the univariate analysis that firm size does not make a contribution to the audit committee formation decision, once the number of directors has been considered.

As an additional test, the marginal contribution of *NUMDIR*, once firm size has been considered, was examined. A logit model similar to Model 2 was estimated, by replacing *SIZERES* with $\log(SIZE)$ and *NUMDIR* with a residual *NUMDIR*). The parameter χ^2 for $\log(SIZE)$ was not significant at the 0.10 level, but χ^2 for the residual *NUMDIR* was significant at the 0.01 level. As a further test, *NUMDIR* was eliminated from Model 1. The results show a reduced model χ^2 of 12.88 (significant at only the 0.10 level), a likelihood ratio index of 0.114 and a Somers's D_{xy} of 0.468. *ICTRL* has the only significant parameter χ^2 (at 0.05) in the model. The parameter χ^2 for $\log(SIZE)$ is not significant at the 0.10 level. These results suggest that it is the number of directors rather than firm size that influences the voluntary formation of audit committees.

In Section 2.6, it was observed that none of the firms in the sample published the existence of their audit committee. This is quite surprising, as it would be costless to inform investors about audit committee formation in the annual report and costly for lower-quality firms to imitate by forming audit committees with outside directors. This suggests that audit committees are not used to reduce agency costs by increasing the quality of financial reporting. Furthermore, many of the contracts written to reduce agency costs could easily specify the formation of an audit committee. In Model 4, the variables *NUMSH*, *LEV*, and *AIP* were omitted from the regression.

Model 4 exhibits a lower likelihood ratio index, model χ^2, and Somers's D_{xy} than Model 1. Both *ICTRL* and *NUMDIR* parameter χ^2 values remain significant at the 0.05 level. A comparison between two logit models can be made by taking the differences between log-likelihoods of the models:

$$-2 \log L_{M_2 - M_1} = (-2 \log L_{M_2}) - (-2 \log L_{M_1}).$$

This statistic has an asymptotic χ^2 distribution with $M_2 - M_1$ degrees of freedom. In comparing Model 4 with Model 1, this statistic was 0.89 ($3df$), which is not significant at the 0.10 level. Hence, the variables proxying for agency cost incentives to improve the quality of financial reporting (hypotheses H1 through H3) are not important influences in the decision to form audit committees.

5. Summary and Discussion

This study investigates the association between corporate characteristics and voluntary formation of audit committees. The corporation characteristics employed reflect the benefits of audit committee formation as a monitoring mechanism to improve the quality of financial reporting. Also examined is the influence of directors and auditors on formation of audit committees.

The results do not support empirical variables generally found to be significant in studies of voluntary accounting policy choices. Variables such as the proportion and distribution of nonmanagerial ownership, financial leverage, assets-in-place, and size are not found significant in the multivariate logit analysis. This finding is consistent with the view that audit committees are not voluntarily employed to reduce the incentive problems arising from the separation of (residual) ownership and decision control. Also, the results do not support the use of audit committees to signal increased quality (independence) of audited information. Nor is Big Eight auditor support for audit committee formation found, which is inconsistent with the results of Eichenseher and Shields (1985, pp. 25–27).

Both multivariate and univariate results support a relation between voluntary audit committees and the number of directors and intercorporate ownership. Several reasons could exist for this association. First, audit committees might be an efficient mechanism for reviewing the audited financial statements and accounting controls as the size of the board of directors increases. Second, large boards are more likely to contain nonexecutive directors. Increasing directors' liability provides incentives for directors, and in particular nonexecutive directors, to form an audit committee in order to document "due care" and compliance with professional responsibilities. Third, the separation and specialization of decision management (executive directors) and decision control (outside directors) creates incentive problems within the boardroom. In particular, incentive problems will arise with large (but not necessarily controlling) intercorporate ownership.

Perhaps the most obvious result of this study is that in a purely voluntary environment, very few firms form audit committees. This contrasts strongly with the observed increase in voluntary audit committee formation in the United States (Mautz and Neary, 1979, p. 83; Pincus et al., 1989, pp. 239–265). Differences in institutional arrangements in New Zealand could influence the incentives for voluntary audit committee formation. For example, audit committees have not become a political issue in New Zealand. The high level of voluntary formation of audit committees in the United States can be interpreted as a means of forestalling regulation and quieting the press.[15] Another differ-

---

[15] Refer to Wallace (1980, p. 46) for a discussion of this point. The politization and "image value" of audit committees is reported by Birkett (1986), Eichenseher and Shields (1985, p. 14), and Pincus et al. (1989).

ence in the institutional arrangements is that New Zealand is a low-litigation environment because there are no contingency-based legal fees and no class action privileges (DeJong, 1985). Hence, the use of audit committees to insure against directors' liability is likely to be less strong in New Zealand. For the same reasons incentives to form audit committees arising from potential auditors' liability is not likely to be strong in New Zealand. Furthermore, there have been few or no instances of audits being put out for competitive bids (Firth, 1985, p. 25). Hence, there might be few incentives for New Zealand auditors to create product differentiation by offering expertise in audit committee formation.

This study provides preliminary evidence on the existence of private incentives to form audit committees. Any interpretation of this study for accounting policy regulators will depend on the explanatory variables surrogating for the costs and benefits of forming an audit committee. Furthermore, some caution is necessary in interpreting these results for other domains because different institutional arrangements (for example, directors' and auditors' liability, the competitiveness of the audit market) could provide different incentives for audit committee formation. The results suggest that making an audit committee obligatory for all firms would have a greater impact on firms with few directors, which are likely to be those without the necessary technical capability (Eichenseher and Shields, 1985, p. 27). The results also indicate that voluntary audit committee formation is not directed towards increasing the quality of annual financial statements, which is a major concern of the SEC and Congress. However, the issue of whether the social benefits of forming audit committees might outweigh the private costs has not been addressed by this paper. For example, the NCFFR (1987, p. 29) recognized that smaller firms might bear a disproportionately greater risk of fraudulent financial reporting.

This research was completed while the author was a visiting faculty member at the Sloan School of Management, Massachusetts Institute of Technology. I would like to thank Richard Chandler for making his survey results available. I am grateful to Ravi Bhushan, Paul Healy, Mark Rusbarsky, Lydia Schleifer, and Wanda Wallace, for comments on earlier drafts of this manuscript. Any errors and omissions are my responsibility.

References

Accounting International Study Group (AISG). 1977. *Audit Committees—Current Practices in Canada, the United Kingdom and the United States.* London: AISG.

Bar-Yosef, S. and Livnat, J. Autumn 1984. Auditor selection: An incentive-signalling approach. *Accounting and Business Research* 14(56):301–309.

Birkett, B. S. Fall 1986. The recent history of corporate audit committees. *The Accounting Historians Journal* 13(2):109–124.

Bradbury, M. E. 1979. Audit committees. *The Accountants' Journal* 58(12):430–431.

Canadian Institute of Chartered Accountants (CICA). 1981. *Audit Committees*. Toronto: CICA.

Chandler, R. F. 1982. *Corporate Directorship Practices in New Zealand Public Companies*. Unpublished Master of Commerce thesis, University of Auckland.

Chow, C. W. April 1982. The demand for external auditing: Size, debt and ownership influences. *The Accounting Review* 57(2):272–291.

Chow, C. W. and Wong-Boren, A. July 1987. Voluntary financial disclosure by Mexican corporations. *The Accounting Review* 62(3):533–541.

Christie, A. A., Kennelley, M. D., King, J. W., and Schaefer, T. F. December 1984. Testing for incremental information content in the presence of collinearity. *Journal of Accounting and Economics* 6(3):205–217.

DeJong, D. V. Fall 1985. Class-action privileges and contingent legal fees: Investor and lawyer incentives to litigate and the effect on audit quality. *Journal of Accounting and Public Policy* 4(3):175–200.

Eichenseher, J. W. and Shields, D. Spring 1985. Corporate director liability and monitoring preferences. *Journal of Accounting and Public Policy* 4(1):13–31.

Fama, E. F. April 1980. Agency problems and the theory of the firm. *Journal of Political Economy* 88(2):288–307.

Fama, E. F. and Jensen, M. C. June 1983. Separation of ownership and control. *Journal of Law and Economics* 26(2):301–325.

Firth, M. Spring 1985. An analysis of audit fees and their determination in New Zealand. *Auditing: A Journal of Practice and Theory* 4(2):23–37.

Fogelberg, G. 1980. Ownership and control in 43 of New Zealand's largest companies 1962 and 1974. *New Zealand Journal of Business* 2:54–78.

Jensen, M. C. and Meckling, W. H. October 1976. Theory of the firm: Managerial behavior, agency costs, and ownership structure. *Journal of Financial Economics* 3(4):305–360.

Leftwich, R. W., Watts, R. L., and Zimmerman, J. L. 1981. Voluntary corporate disclosure: The case of interim reporting. *Journal of Accounting Research* (Supplement) 19:50–77.

Maher, M. W. October 1981. The impact of regulation on controls: Firms' response to the Foreign Corrupt Practices Act. *The Accounting Review* 56(4):751–770.

Mautz, R. K. and Neary, R. D. October 1979. Corporate audit committee—quo vadis? *Journal of Accountancy* 148(4):83–88.

Mautz, R. K. and Neumann, F. 1977. *Corporate Audit Committees: Policies and Practices*. Cleveland: Ernst and Ernst.

Myers, S. C. November 1977. Determinants of corporate borrowing. *Journal of Financial Economics* 5(2):147–175.

National Commission on Fraudulent Financial Reporting (NCFFR). 1987. *Report of the National Commission on Fraudulent Financial Reporting*.

Ng, D. S. October 1978. An information economics analysis of financial reporting and external auditing. *The Accounting Review* 53(4):910–920.

Pincus, K., Rusbarsky, M., and Wong, J. Winter 1989. Voluntary formation of corporate audit committees among NASDAQ firms. *Journal of Accounting and Public Policy* 8(4):239–265.

Smith Jr., C. W., and Warner, J. B. June 1979. On financial contracting: An analysis of bond covenants. *Journal of Financial Economics* 7(2):117–161.

Wallace, W. A. 1980. *The Economic Role of Audit in Free and Regulated Markets.* Graduate School of Management, University of Rochester.

Watts, R. L. 1977. Corporate financial statements: A product of the market and political processes. *Australian Journal of Management* 2:53–75.

Watts, R. L., and Zimmerman, J. L. October 1983. Agency problems, auditing, and the theory of the firm: Some evidence. *Journal of Law and Economics* 26(3):613–633.

[19]

The Use of Audit Committees for Monitoring

Krishnagopal Menon and Joanne Deahl Williams

The Treadway Commission (National Commission on Fraudulent Financial Reporting 1987, p. 40) has recommended that companies be required to maintain audit committees (ACs). Some recent papers (Eichenseher and Shields 1985; Pincus et al. 1989; Bradbury 1990) in this journal have identified characteristics of firms which voluntarily formed ACs. The mere formation of an AC does not mean that the board of directors actually relies on the AC to enhance its monitoring ability. Companies may form ACs for their image value. In this study, we look for evidence that firms actually rely on ACs. We consider two indicators of a board's reliance on ACs as a mechanism to control management, the frequency of AC meetings and AC composition.

Our sample consisted of firms which faced no requirement to form ACs. Although the majority of firms formed ACs, many of these firms did not appear to rely on them. Some ACs did not meet at all or met only once during the year studied. In many instances ACs included at least one manager which is inconsistent with the role of ACs as a monitor of management. The results of the analysis suggest that reliance on audit committees is related to board of directors composition. As the proportion of outside directors on the board increases, firms seem more likely to exclude officers from ACs, and ACs are more active. Our study also found that frequency of meetings is associated with firm size.

1. Introduction

Audit committees (ACs) have been advocated by many as a deterrent to fraudulent financial reporting. The National Commission on Fraudulent Financial Reporting (Treadway Commission) recently recommended that the Securities and Exchange Commission (SEC) should require public companies to maintain ACs (National Commission on Fraudulent Financial Reporting 1987, p. 40). Although the SEC has yet to issue such a

Address correspondence to Professor Krishnagopal Menon, School of Management, Boston University, 704 Commonwealth Avenue, Boston, MA 02215.

Journal of Accounting and Public Policy, 13, 121–139 (1994)
© 1994 Elsevier Science Inc.

0278-4254/94/$7.00

mandate, it has in the past recommended that publicly-held companies should establish ACs (SEC 1972).

Some recent papers in this journal have identified characteristics of firms which voluntarily formed ACs (Eichenseher and Shields 1985; Pincus et al. 1989; Bradbury 1990). Pincus et al. (1989), for example, examined firms which were not subject to stock exchange regulations requiring them to form audit committees. Firms voluntarily forming ACs were found to be different from those without ACs along several dimensions, such as extent of management's ownership of stock, proportion of outsiders on the board of directors, and firm size (Pincus et al. 1989, p. 260).

In this paper we look beyond the formation of ACs for evidence that boards of directors actually use or rely on ACs. Mandating that companies should form ACs does not assure that boards will rely on ACs to assist in the monitoring function. A board of directors is more likely to rely on an AC if it is viewed as adding to the board's ability to monitor managers. Using simple indicators of firms' reliance on ACs, we identify characteristics of firms which appear to rely on ACs. In doing so, we add to the literature on the use of accounting mechanisms to monitor management.

The next section of our paper discusses the function of audit committees in carrying out the monitoring role of the board of directors. We review relevant prior literature on ACs, identify indicators of reliance on ACs, and develop hypotheses. Section 3 describes the research method employed and the result obtained. Section 4 presents some conclusions.

2. Audit Committees and Monitoring

Although ACs have a long history in the United States (Mautz and Neumann 1970, p. 8), their importance recently has been highlighted by the Treadway Commission. The Commission recommended that all public companies be required to have ACs, maintaining that ACs are instrumental in ensuring the integrity of financial reporting and the audit process (National Commission on Fraudulent Financial Reporting 1987, pp. 40–41).

Some companies face exchange requirements to form ACs. Companies listed on the New York Stock Exchange (NYSE), since 1978 (Bacon 1988, p. 9), and the National Association of Security Dealers' (NASD) National Market System, since 1989 (Bacon 1988, p. 8), are required by exchange rules to establish and maintain ACs. Although the American Stock Exchange does not require its members to have ACs, it does recommend their formation (Pincus et al. 1989, p. 240).

2.1 Benefits of ACs in Monitoring

The AC is a committee of the board of directors which assumes some of the board's responsibilities. The responsibilities of the AC typically include selecting the independent auditor, overseeing the audit process and ensuring the integrity of financial reporting. There are two potential monitoring advantages to be gained from assigning these board oversight responsibilities to a board committee: 1) independence, and 2) board efficiency.

First, the independence and integrity of monitoring may be enhanced by having internal and external auditors report to a subset of the board which consists of outside directors. The full board of directors includes the CEO and other officers of the company, whose performance may be questioned by the auditors.

Second, board committees could help improve the efficiency of board functioning. This is particularly important when the board size is large. Zahra and Pearce (1989, p. 309) contended that the structure of the board can be instrumental in the directors' involvement in control activities and in strengthening the position of directors relative to that of the CEO. They view a well-run audit committee as essential in allowing the board to monitor managerial performance (Zahra and Pearce 1989, p. 310). Jemison and Oakley (1983, p. 506) cited the establishment of ACs as one of the important methods by which a board actually exercises its oversight responsibilities. According to Merchant (1987, p. 33), adequate attention can be paid to the board functions of reviewing financial reporting policies and coordinating with auditors only if a subset of the board is charged with these responsibilities.

Despite the apparent monitoring advantages, the absence of an AC in a company need not indicate the absence of monitoring. Rather, it may reflect the belief that monitoring can be accomplished by the full board without any formal committees. If outside directors are vigilant monitors of management (which would be a prerequisite for effective ACs), they could still carry out their monitoring obligations without formal Acs.

Pincus et al. (1989) investigated factors associated with the voluntary formation of audit committees in a sample of 100 U.S. companies. Pincus et al. (p. 243) hypothesized that ACs would be formed voluntarily when high agency costs exist as the monitoring provided by ACs would help to limit agency costs. The results generally supported this position (Pincus et al. 1989, p. 260).

2.2. ACs and the Appearance of Monitoring

Benefits may accrue from having an AC because of the appearance of monitoring, even if the AC is not used by the board for this purpose. The board may not perceive a need to use an AC for monitoring purposes, yet may form an AC to satisfy external constituencies such as stockholders, regulators or even the company's independent auditor.

One potential benefit of ACs is to aid against litigation. Eichenseher and Shields (1985, p. 17) suggested that an AC can help limit the exposure

of boards to director liability by providing evidence that the board exercised due care in carrying out its obligations.

Bradbury (1990) referred to ACs as having high "image value" (1990, p.
24) in the United States, where they provide "a means of forestalling
regulation and quieting the press" (1990, p. 33). Bradbury examined
incentives for voluntary audit committee formation in a sample of 135 New
Zealand Stock Exchange companies (1990, p. 25). Only 20 of the firms
formed ACs which Bradbury attributes to the low image value of ACs in
New Zealand (1990, pp. 24–25). Variables used to represent agency costs
were not significant in differentiating between firms forming ACs and firms
without ACs (Bradbury 1990, p. 33). However, both univariate and multivariate results supported a relationship between voluntary AC formation
and two other variables, the number of directors and intercorporate
ownership (Bradbury 1990, p. 33).

2.3 Reliance on Audit Committees

The formation of an AC does not mean that the board actually relies on
the AC to enhance its monitoring ability. Two potential indicators of the
board's reliance on the AC as a monitoring mechanism are the frequency
of the AC's meetings and its composition. In this study we have extended
the research on AC formation by examining factors associated with frequency of AC meetings and the existence of insiders on the AC.

Zahra and Pearce (1989, pp. 309–310) suggested that board processes
(e.g., the intensity and quality of directors' interactions, and the compre-
hensiveness and formality of meetings) are important influences on the
functioning of the board. An AC which intends to play a major role in
oversight would need to maintain a high level of activity (National Commission on Fraudulent Financial Reporting 1987, p. 180). In order to carry
out its functions, it would need to hold a minimum of two meetings during
the year, a planning meeting with the independent auditor at the com-
mencement of the audit and a second meeting upon completion of the
audit to review the results (KPMG Peat Marwick 1988, p. 6). Merchant
(1987, p. 33) recommended a minimum of three meetings a year. The
Treadway Commission (National Commission on Fraudulent Financial
Reporting 1987, p. 180) suggested that the AC meet regularly with the
internal auditor, the external auditor and the company counsel. However,
boards are likely to be willing to incur the significant cost of an active
committee which meets frequently only if they feel it is necessary to
monitor managers.

The frequency of meetings is only a crude measure of AC activity. It
does not provide any indication of the work accomplished during these
meetings or of the committee's effectiveness in achieving financial reporting integrity. At the same time, there is some information conveyed by the

frequency of meetings. ACs which do not meet or meet only once are unlikely to be effective monitors. Several AC meetings would generally indicate a more serious effort to monitor management.

A critical aspect of AC structure is the composition of its membership. Although the background and experience of AC members influence its functioning, perhaps the most basic characteristic of the audit committee is whether it is staffed by insider (manager) directors or outside directors. An AC with inside directors cannot be viewed as an objective monitor of management. Such an AC is unlikely to provide the company's external auditor with a forum to express candid opinions on management. Jemison and Oakley (1983, p. 519) suggested that an active AC, staffed totally by outsiders, is a key element of corporate governance. Indeed, even such a strong advocate of the AC as the SEC notes that having insiders on an AC may be worse than having no committee at all, as such an AC would mislead stockholders into believing effective monitoring is taking place (SEC 1980, p. 491).

2.4 Development of Hypotheses

We considered six factors which might describe characteristics of firms which use ACs for monitoring. These factors are management stock ownership, leverage, firm size, auditor type, proportion of outsiders on the board, and board size. Each of these factors has been found to be associated with AC formation in at least one prior study. However, their explanatory power for AC reliance has not been investigated.

2.4.1 Management Stock Ownership. From an agency theoretic perspective, the need to monitor management stems from the divergence of interests between managers and stockholders (Jensen and Meckling 1976, pp. 312–313). The higher the managers' ownership stake in the company, the greater the alignment of managers' and stockholders' incentives (Jensen and Meckling 1976, p. 313). Thus a decrease in managers' holdings of ownership securities increases the stockholders' need to monitor. Although Pincus et al. (1989, p. 258) found a significant association between management stockholdings and AC formation, Eichenseher and Shields (1985, p. 27) did not.

According to the agency perspective, the higher level of monitoring required as managers' holdings decrease should be reflected in an increase in AC activity. The board's incentive to use an AC for monitoring purposes should result also in a higher likelihood that insiders will be excluded from AC membership.

H1A: AC activity tends to increase as management stockholdings decrease.

H1B: Firms tend more to exclude managers from ACs as management stockholdings decrease.

2.4.2 Leverage. Agency theory also posits that problems arising out of conflicting incentives of debtholders and managers can be mitigated by increased monitoring (Jensen and Meckling 1976, pp. 337–339). The use of monitoring mechanisms such as ACs should increase with leverage. Highly-leveraged firms should be more likely to maintain active, independent ACs.

The evidence on the association between leverage and AC formation does not provide strong support for the agency explanation. Pincus et al. (1989, p. 258) found mixed support for the leverage hypothesis, while Eichenseher and Shields (1985, p. 27) and Bradbury (1990, p. 33) found no support.

H2A: AC activity tends to increase with the degree of leverage.

H2B: Firms tend more to exclude managers from ACs as the degree of leverage increases.

2.4.3 Size. An AC, like any other control mechanism, is not costless. Small firms may see it as costly to maintain an active and independent AC (Bull and Sharp 1989, p. 48). Pincus et al. (1989, p. 246) contended that economies of scale result in net monitoring benefits increasing with size. They found some association between size and AC formation (1989, pp. 253–254), as did Jemison and Oakley (1983, p. 517) and Eichenseher and Shields (1985, p. 27). However, Bradbury (1990) did not find any incremental contribution from the firm size variable when a variable representing the number of directors on the board was included in the model (1990, p. 28). A plausible explanation is that because of the great attention paid to large firms in the United States these firms form ACs for their image value.

If net monitoring benefits increase with firm size, then AC activity should increase with size. Larger firms also should be more likely to exclude managers from ACs than smaller firms. This would be consistent with the image value argument as well, as the image of an AC is enhanced when it is staffed entirely with outside directors.

H3A: AC activity tends to increase with firm size.

H3B: Firms tend more to exclude managers from ACs as firm size increases.

2.4.4 Auditor. The public accounting profession sees the AC as a means to enhance the perception of auditor independence, and many external auditors aid their clients in forming ACs. The SEC has urged the American Institute of Certified Public Accountants (AICPA) to require ACs as a condition of an independent audit (AICPA 1978, p. 4). Big Eight accounting firms have been especially prominent in their advocacy of ACs.[1] Several of the Big Eight firms have published booklets and other materials for clients on how to form and use ACs (e.g., Coopers & Lybrand 1988; KPMG Peat Marwick 1988). Eichenseher and Shields (1985, p. 17) suggested that smaller CPA firms are less in favor of ACs for fear that ACs prefer larger auditing firms.

Pincus et al. (1989, p. 255) found that Big Eight auditors were more likely to be associated with U.S. firms voluntarily forming ACs. However, Kunitake (1981, p. 45) found no association between a company's inclination to form an AC and the type (i.e., Big Eight or non-Big Eight) of auditor engaged by the company, and Bradbury (1990, p. 29) also did not find such an association for his sample of New Zealand firms. Eichenseher and Shields (1985, p. 29) found that companies were more likely to form ACs following auditor changes if the new auditor was a Big Eight firm. They also found that companies switching to Big Eight auditors were more likely to have ACs than companies switching to non-Big Eight auditors (Eichenseher and Shields 1985, p. 23). They attributed this second finding to the directors' interest in limiting legal exposure by engaging a prestigious independent auditor (1985, p. 17).

If Big Eight CPAs persuade their clients to form ACs, as these results suggest, it is likely that the committee so formed will be the active and independent AC advocated by the Big Eight. Equally, if boards tend to appoint Big Eight CPAs in an attempt to reduce potential liability, then it is likely that there will be a similar incentive to form an outsider-based AC. However, an AC formed primarily to reduce liability by conveying the appearance of independence may not have the incentive to be active. The hypotheses are stated to be consistent with a Big Eight influence on AC reliance.

H4A: AC activity in Big Eight-audited firms tends to be greater than AC activity in non-Big Eight-audited firms.

H4B: Big Eight-audited firms tend more to exclude managers from ACs than non-Big Eight-audited firms.

2.4.5 Board Composition. Pincus et al. (1989, p. 254) found that the proportion of board seats held by outside (nonmanager) directors was significantly associated with AC formation. They (1989, p. 260) explained this relationship as stemming from the liability exposure of outside directors. An alternative explanation comes from the management literature,

---

[1] As the empirical analysis in this paper covers a period prior to the Ernst & Whinney/Arthur Young, and Deloitte Haskins & Sells/Touche Ross mergers, we use the term "Big Eight" rather than "Big Six."

where the proportion of insiders on the board has been used as a measure of management's influence in several studies (Kesner et al. 1986; Kosnik 1987; Singh and Harianto 1989). According to Mizruchi (1983, p. 429), a high proportion of insiders on the board is a strong signal that the company will be dominated by its officers. As incentives of managers can conflict with those of stockholders, the board's effectiveness in execution of its duties depends in large part on its independent outside directors (Jemison and Oakley 1983, p. 515).

If the proportion of outsiders on the board is an indication of the dominance of outside directors in board matters, an increase in this proportion should be associated with increasing use of mechanisms to monitor management. Reliance on ACs should then be seen to increase with the proportion of outsiders on the board. This should be reflected both in an increase in AC activity and in staffing the AC solely with outsiders.

If the proportion of outsiders serves as a surrogate for liability exposure, an increase in the proportion of outsiders on the board should provide a greater incentive to exclude insiders from the AC, as an AC with insiders conveys a weak appearance of monitoring. However, an AC formed to limit liability exposure may not have the incentive to be active in monitoring.[2]

H5A: AC activity tends to increase with the proportion of outsiders on the board.

H5B: Firms tend more to exclude managers from ACs as the proposition of outsiders on the board increases.

2.4.6 Board size. Bradbury's (1990, p. 29) analysis of New Zealand companies showed an association between AC formation and board size. The relationship between board size and ACs is likely to stem from the operational efficiencies to be gained from assigning responsibilities to designated board members once some threshold board size has been reached. Larger boards should obtain greater monitoring benefits than smaller boards, and should be more likely to rely on ACs. The ACs formed by these boards should then be more active and independent than ACs formed by smaller boards.

H6A: AC activity tends to increase with board size.

H6B: Firms tend more to exclude managers from ACs as the board size increases.

---

[2] The test of a relationship between the proportion of outsiders on the board and the exclusion of outsiders from the AC could be problematic because if an AC is randomly selected from all board members, a board with more insiders has a greater chance of including an insider on the AC. However, a randomly-selected audit committee implies that insiders have not been systematically excluded, contrary to the spirit of the Treadway Commission, the rules of the NYSE, and the preference of the SEC.

The next section presents the research method employed, the description of dependent and independent variables, the sample used and the results obtained.

3. Method and Results

3.1 Sample and Variables

The sample for our study consisted of 200 randomly selected over-the-counter (OTC) firms for which data on AC existence were available in 1986–1987. We chose this period because OTC firms were not required, at the time, to form audit committees.[3] The variables of interest were measured as described below.

Variables used to represent audit committee presence (AUDCOMM, set equal to 1 if the firm maintained an AC, and to 0 otherwise), the actual number of AC meetings (MEETINGS) and whether the AC included officers were obtained directly from annual proxy statements. Proxies from 1986 were used where available; in a few cases 1987 proxies were used. For the purposes of our study, only officers of the company were treated as insiders, although it could be contended that former officers, legal counsel, consultants and relatives of officers are insiders of the company.

Management ownership (MGRHOLD) was measured as the percentage of stock owned by the managers of the firm. Data for this variable were obtained from proxies.[4] The firm's leverage (LEVERAGE) was represented by its debt-assets ratio. Firm size (SIZE) was surrogated by total assets. The log of total assets was used in the multivariate analyses. Data for LEVERAGE and SIZE were obtained from 10-Ks or annual reports for 1986. The company's independent auditor was generally identified from proxies, though in a few cases annual reports were used. The auditor was classified as being a Big Eight or non-Big Eight auditor to construct the categorical variable CPATYPE (Big Eight = 1; non-Big Eight = 0). The proportion of outside directors on the board (BRDPROP) was measured by dividing the number of non-officer directors (identified from proxies) by the total number of directors. The total number of directors (BRDSIZE) was obtained from proxies.

Forty-four firms out of the sample of 200 firms did not maintain an AC. Of the sample, 174 firms had Big Eight CPAs. Other descriptive data on the sample are presented in Table 1, Panel A.

Panel B of Table 1 provides some descriptive information on the size of ACs, the number of ACs with insiders, and the frequency of meetings. The

---

[3] The sample was randomly drawn from the listing of OTC firms in the October 26, 1987 *The Wall Street Journal*. This listing of OTC firms included firms traded on the NASDAQ National Market System and other OTC firms.

[4] The annual proxy discloses the stock ownership of individuals holding more than five percent of the firm's stock.

Table 1. Descriptive Statistics[a]

Panel A: Sample Characteristics

	n	Mean	Median	Std. dev.
MGRHOLD (%)	199	18.4	11.3	21.4
LEVERAGE	200	0.55	0.55	0.30
SIZE ($ millions)	200	737.0	49.9	2144.7
BRDPROP	200	0.65	0.67	0.20
BRDSIZE	200	8.83	7.0	4.92

Panel B: Frequency Distribution of AC Size and AC Activity

AC Size		AC Activity	
Number of AC Member	n	Number of AC Meetings	n
1	1	0	9
2	24	1	48
3	81	2	41
4	25	3	18
5 or more	24	4	19
	155	5 or more	13
			148
(Firms with missing data: 1)		(Firms with missing data: 8)	

Panel C: Availability of Outside Directors for ACs

Number of Outside Directors on Board	Number of ACs with Insiders	Number of ACs without Insiders
1	2	0
2	2	5
3	5	16
4	3	24
5 or more	7	90
	19	135

(Firms with missing data: 2)

[a] Panel A presents descriptive statistics for sample firms. Variables are defined as follows: MGRHOLD = managers' stockholdings; LEVERAGE = the debt-to-assets ratio; SIZE = total assets; BRDPROP = the proportion of outside directors; BRDSIZE = the number of directors. Panels B and C provide descriptive data for the 156 firms with ACs.

Treadway Commission (National Commission on Fraudulent Financial Reporting 1987, p. 179) recommended that no fewer than three members should constitute the AC. Twenty-five firms in our sample had fewer than three members on the AC, though in some of these cases the board size was also small. Fifty-seven of the ACs had fewer than two meetings during the year.[5] In general, the number of ACs with insiders, the low activity

---

[5] Of the ACs which held fewer than two meetings, 14 had a committee size of not more than two members. One company reported having a one-member audit commitee which met once in the year examined.

level, and the small committee sizes support the contention that many of the ACs may have been established for cosmetic purposes.

One constraint on forming an independent AC composed of outside directors is the availability of outsiders on the board. If a board of directors is composed entirely of officers of the company, then the formation of an outsider AC becomes infeasible. At the same time, such boards of directors may choose to maintain ACs. Table 1, Panel C, shows the availability of outside directors for firms with ACs in our sample. In 15 of the 19 instances in which insiders were appointed to the AC there were at least three outside board directors. Each of these firms had a sufficient number of outsiders on the board of directors to form the three-member committee recommended by the Treadway Commission (1987, p. 179).

3.2 Characteristics of AC-Forming Firms

Prior studies have found that the six independent variables used in our study explain differences between AC-forming and AC-absent firms (Eichenseher and Shields 1985; Pincus et al. 1989; Bradbury 1990). We tested to see if these differences exist for our sample, which is larger than samples in previous studies (e.g., Bradbury 1990, p. 25; Pincus et al. 1989, p. 250). Univariate tests showed differences for every variable. The Wilcoxon rank sums test showed that firms with ACs were larger ($p <$ 0.001, two-tailed), had lower managerial stockholdings ($p < 0.001$), higher leverage ($p < 0.05$), larger boards ($p < 0.001$), and a higher proportion of outside directors ($p < 0.001$) than firms without ACs. Firms with Big Eight auditors also were more likely to form ACs (χ^2 test, $p < 0.001$).

We conducted a logistic regression analysis, using the following model:[6]

$$\text{AUDCOMM} = a + b_1 \text{ MGRHOLD} + b_2 \text{ LEVERAGE} + b_3 \text{ SIZE}$$
$$+ b_4 \text{ CPATYPE} + b_5 \text{ BRDPROP} + b_6 \text{ BRDSIZE} + e$$

The variables are defined in the previous section. Table 2 shows the results of the analysis. The model statistics, reported in the table, indicated good fit. Two of the independent variables were significant, CPATYPE and BRDPROP.[7]

---

[6] The form of the logistic model used is (Pindyck and Rubinfeld 1981, p. 310):

$$\text{Prob}(Y) = 1 / \{1 + exp[-\alpha - X\beta]\},$$

where Prob(Y) is the probability the dependent variable equals 1, X is the set of independent variables, and α, β are unknown parameters to be estimated from the data.
[7] The same independent variables proved significant when OLS regression was used rather than logistic regression. The adjusted R^2 was 0.13. We computed variance inflation factors and condition indexes to assess multicollinearity, but no problem was indicated. Also, we reran the logistic regression, omitting from the group of AC-forming firms those whose ACs included insiders or met fewer than twice during the year. The model had better fit (model χ^2 = 101.14; R = 0.74) but the only significant variables continued to be BRDPROP and CPATYPE.

Table 2. Formation of Audit Committees: Logistic Regression Results[a]

($n = 199$)	Coefficient (Std. Error)
Intercept	-4.890***
	(1.207)
MGRHOLD	-0.010
	(0.010)
LEVERAGE	0.936
	(0.801)
SIZE	0.157
	(0.149)
CPATYPE	1.344*
	(0.529)
BRDPROP	5.279***
	(1.405)
BRDSIZE	0.160
	(0.100)

Model $\chi^2 = 68.89$***
$R = 0.52$; Somer's $D_{yx} = 0.76$
* $p < 0.05$
*** $p < 0.001$

[a] The model is AUDCOMM $= a + b_1$ MGRHOLD $+ b_2$ LEVERAGE $+ b_3$ SIZE $+ b_4$ CPATYPE $+ b_5$ BRDPROP $+ b_6$ BRDSIZE $+ e$. AUDCOMM indicates whether the firm maintained ($=1$) or did not maintain ($=0$) an AC. Independent variables: MGRHOLD = managers' stockholdings; LEVERAGE = the debt-to-assets ratio; SIZE = the log of total assets; CPATYPE = Big Eight auditor ($=1$) or non-Big Eight ($=0$); BRDPROP = the proportion of outside directors; BRDSIZE = the number of directors. One firm out of the original sample was deleted from the analysis because of missing data. Significance levels for coefficients were determined using two-tailed χ^2 tests.

The significance and sign of CPATYPE agreed with the findings of Eichenseher and Shields (1985, p. 27) and Pincus et al. (1989, p. 255) that firms with ACs tend to have Big Eight independent auditors. BRDPROP was significant in our study, as in the Pincus et al. study (1989, p. 259). MGRHOLD, reported significant by Pincus et al. (1989, p. 258) but not by Eichenseher and Shields (1985, p. 27), did not prove significant in our analysis. BRDSIZE, a significant variable in Bradbury's multivariate analysis (1990, p. 28), and LEVERAGE and SIZE, which showed mixed results in the Pincus et al. (1989, p. 258) study, were not significant in our analysis.[8]

---

[8] Following Pincus et al. (1989, p. 253), we substituted the log of the debt-to-assets ratio for the variable LEVERAGE in the logistic regression. The substitution made little difference and essentially similar results were obtained.

3.3 Tests of Hypotheses

The hypotheses of interest in our study relate to reliance on ACs rather than formation. The two indicators of reliance used are frequency of meetings and composition of membership. The hypotheses were tested on firms which maintained ACs. To test hypotheses 1A-6A, related to AC activity, we ran an OLS regression, using the following model:

$$\text{MEETINGS} = a + b_1 \text{ MGRHOLD} + b_2 \text{ LEVERAGE} + b_3 \text{ SIZE}$$
$$+ b_4 \text{ CPATYPE} + b_5 \text{ BRDPROP} + b_6 \text{ BRDSIZE} + e$$

where MEETINGS, the dependent variable, represented the number of meetings held by the AC, and the independent variables were defined as before. Nine firms could not be included in the regression because of missing data (eight firms did not report the number of AC meetings, one did not report managerial holdings), leaving 147 observations in the analysis.

Pearson correlations were computed for the six independent variables used in the model, and are shown in Table 3. Each of these variables was significantly correlated with the dependent variable.[9] The significant correlations between some pairs of independent variables raised the issue of potential multicollinearity in the regression. We examined the variance inflation factors and condition indexes. The levels of these indicators were within acceptable ranges, and did not indicate a multicollinearity problem.

Table 4 shows the results of the regression. The adjusted R^2 was 0.37 and the F statistic was significant. Two of the independent variables, firm size and proportion of outsiders on the board, were significant and in the direction hypothesized, providing support for hypotheses 3A and 5A. Hypotheses 1A and 2A, related to the agency variables management ownership and leverage, and hypotheses 4A and 6A were not supported.[10, 11]

In selecting MEETINGS as a measure of AC activity, we had a variable which helped to distinguish between active and inactive ACs. We reran the

---

[9] Firms with Big Eight CPAs had more meetings than those with non-Big Eight auditors (Wilcoxon rank sums test, $p = 0.07$, two-tailed test).

[10] Despite the assurance of no harmful multicollinearity from the diagnostics that we used, the high pair-wise correlations are troublesome. We reran the regression without SIZE. As might be expected, three additional variables became significant: BRDSIZE ($p < 0.01$), MGRHOLD ($p < 0.05$), and LEVERAGE ($p < 0.05$). These variables did not make an incremental contribution at conventionally significant levels in the presence of SIZE. However, should the multicollinearity indicators be misleading, the coefficient tests reported in Table 4 would be biased.

[11] It could be argued that an AC which meets two or fewer times could accomplish just as much as one which meets more frequently. To consider this possibility, we redefined MEETINGS as a dichotomous variable (set to 0 if there were no or one AC meeting, and to 1 if there were two or more meetings). We ran a logistic regression, using this dichotomous variable as the dependent variable and the same set of independent variables as before. Only SIZE and BRDPROP were significant, as when a continuous dependent variable is used. However, these results are sensitive to the way in which the dichotomous dependent variable is constructed.

Table 3. Correlation Matrix[a]

	MGRHOLD	LEVERAGE	SIZE	CPATYPE	BRDPROP	BRDSIZE
MEETINGS	−0.32	0.35	0.56	0.14	0.42	0.45
	(0.00)	(0.00)	(0.00)	(0.09)	(0.00)	(0.00)
MGRHOLD		−0.10	−0.29	−0.05	−0.46	−0:14
		(0.24)	(0.00)	(0.51)	(0.00)	(0.10)
LEVERAGE			0.47	−0.02	0.12	0.42
			(0.00)	(0.83)	(0.14)	(0.00)
SIZE				0.15	0.39	0.59
				(0.07)	(0.00)	(0.00)
CPATYPE					0.06	0.07
					(0.46)	(0.43)
BRDPROP						0.41
						(0.00)

[a] This table shows Pearson correlation coefficients for the 147 firms in the sample for which data on meetings were available. Probabilities are given in parentheses. Variables: MEETINGS = the number of AC meetings; MGRHOLD = managers' stockholdings; LEVERAGE = the debt-to-assets ratio; SIZE = the log of total assets; CPATYPE = Big Eight auditor (= 1) or non-Big Eight (= 0); BRDPROP = the proportion of outside directors; BRDSIZE = the number of directors.

Table 4. Frequency of Audit Committee Meetings: OLS Regression Results[a]

(n = 147)	Hypothesis Reference	Expected Sign	Coefficient (Std. Error)
Intercept			−1.304
			(0.739)
MGRHOLD	1A	−	−0.009
			(0.006)
LEVERAGE	2A	+	0.636
			(0.458)
SIZE	3A	+	0.274***
			(0.076)
CPATYPE	4A	+	0.376
			(0.380)
BRDPROP	5A	+	1.938*
			(0.892)
BRDSIZE	6A	+	0.040
			(0.029)

Adjusted R^2 = 0.37; F value = 14.99***
* $p < 0.05$
*** $p < 0.001$

[a] This table shows OLS regression results for the model MEETINGS = $a + b_1$ MGRHOLD + b_2 LEVERAGE + b_3 SIZE + b_4 CPATYPE + b_5 BRDPROP + b_6 BRDSIZE + e. The sample was restricted to the 147 firms which had ACs. MEETINGS represents the number of AC meetings. Independent variables: MGRHOLD = managers' stockholdings; LEVERAGE = the debt-to-assets ratio; SIZE = the log of total assets; CPATYPE = Big Eight auditor (= 1) or non-Big Eight (= 0); BRDPROP = the proportion of outside directors; BRDSIZE = the number of directors. Significance levels for coefficients were determined using two-tailed t tests.

regression, omitting ACs which either included insiders or had fewer than two meetings a year. Omitted firms were more likely to have instituted ACs for cosmetic purposes. Their exclusion allowed the correlates of the frequency of AC meetings to be more clearly ascertained. The sample for this analysis contained 81 firms. SIZE was the only significant independent variable.[12] As SIZE is a surrogate for net monitoring benefits, this result is consistent with the explanation that in companies which form ACs for noncosmetic purposes, AC activity is driven by monitoring needs. As the size of the company increases, the complexity of the monitoring function increases as well, resulting in more work for the AC and necessitating more meetings.

To test hypotheses related to the composition of ACs (1B–6B), we compared firms whose ACs were staffed solely by outside directors with firms whose ACs included at least one officer. The following logistic regression model was employed.

$$\text{INSIDERS} = a + b_1\, \text{MGRHOLD} + b_2\, \text{LEVERAGE} + b_3\, \text{SIZE}$$

$$+ b_4\, \text{CPATYPE} + b_5\, \text{BRDPROP} + b_6\, \text{BRDSIZE} + e$$

where INSIDERS was set equal to 1 if there was an insider on the AC, and equal to 0 otherwise, and the independent variables were defined as before. Of the 156 firms which maintained ACs, 19 had at least one officer-director on the AC, while 135 had committees staffed completely by outsiders. AC composition data were unavailable for two firms.

Table 5 reports the results of the analysis. BRDPROP was the only significant variable ($p < 0.01$). The model was significant ($p < 0.001$). We reran the regression omitting the two firms with fewer than two outside board members. BRDPROP continued to be significant, though at a lower level than previously ($p < 0.05$). These results provide support only for H-5B.

The inferences from the logistic regression were limited by the small number of observations (19) in one of the response categories. According to Stone and Rasp (1991, p. 179) the effect of reducing sample size in logit analysis is to introduce an anticonservative bias into model statistics and a conservative bias into tests of individual variables.[13]

In view of the concern about sample size, we also used univariate tests to test hypotheses 1B–6B. The Wilcoxon rank sums test showed significant

---

[12] These results appear to be driven by the exclusion of inactive ACs in the sample. Ten of the ACs with insiders met at least twice. Adding these firms back into the regression did not significantly change the result. On the other hand, excluding only firms with insiders on their ACs and retaining inactive ACs in the sample obtained results similar to those reported in Table 4.

[13] Again, OLS regression results were similar, with the same independent variables proving significant. The adjusted R^2 in the OLS regression was 0.28. Diagnostic tests did not indicate a multicollinearity problem.

Table 5. Insiders on ACs: Logistic Regression Results[a]

(n = 153)	Hypothesis Reference	Expected Sign	Coefficient (Std. Error)
Intercept			−0.090 (1.782)
MGRHOLD	1B	−	−0.010 (0.013)
LEVERAGE	2B	+	−0.747 (1.154)
SIZE	3B	+	−0.138 (0.186)
CPATYPE	4B	+	−1.357 (1.260)
BRDPROP	5B	+	6.665** (2.092)
BRDSIZE	6B	+	0.036 (0.090)

Model χ^2 = 23.08***
R = 0.31; Somer's D_{yx} = 0.61
** p < 0.01
*** p < 0.001

[a] The model is INSIDERS = a + b_1 MGRHOLD + b_2 LEVERAGE + b_3 SIZE + b_4 CPATYPE + b_5 BRDPROP + b_6 BRDSIZE + e. INSIDERS indicates whether the AC included (=0) or did not include (=1) an officer. Independent variables: MGRHOLD = managers' stockholdings; LEVERAGE = the debt-to-assets ratio; SIZE = the log of total assets; CPATYPE = Big Eight auditor (=1) or non-Big Eight (=0); BRDPROP = the proportion of outside directors; BRDSIZE = the number of directors. One firm in the category INSIDERS = 1 was deleted because of missing data. Significance levels for coefficients were determined using two-tailed χ^2 tests.

differences between the two groups only in the case of one variable, BRDPROP (p < 0.001, two-tailed test). When the two firms which had fewer than two outside directors on the board were omitted from the analysis, BRDPROP continued to be significant (p < 0.01). Differences between ACs with insiders and ACs without insiders were not significant for MGRHOLD, LEVERAGE, SIZE or BRDSIZE, though the signs were all in the expected direction. A χ^2 test of independence bewteen INSIDERS and CPATYPE showed no significant association. A small expected frequency in one of the cells violated the assumptions of the χ^2 test. However, Fisher's exact test yielded similar results.

Both AC activity and AC composition are important in reliance. A frequently-meeting AC which includes an insider, for example, may be ineffective for monitoring. In an additional analysis we constructed a new dichotomous dependent variable. For this variable, we combined firms which did not form ACs and firms which formed cosmetic ACs into one group, where cosmetic ACs were defined as those with at least one insider or which held fewer than two meetings. The other group consisted of outside director-composed ACs which held two or more meetings. A logistic regression was employed, using the same independent variables as in the other regressions. BRDPROP was highly significant ($p < 0.001$), and SIZE, CPATYPE and BRDSIZE were all significant ($p < 0.05$) in the expected direction. The results appear to reflect the association of each of the significant independent variables with one of the three constructs (formation, activity, composition) which were combined to form the dependent variable.

4. Conclusions

Our study examined the use of audit committees, one mechanism available to boards of directors to limit conflicts of interests between managers and stockholders. Although the majority of firms voluntarily formed ACs, many of these firms did not appear to rely on them. Fifty-seven ACs did not meet at all or met only once during the year studied, and 19 were staffed by insiders.

This reluctance to rely on standing ACs provides support to Bradbury's (1990, p. 33) claim that ACs are often created for the purposes of appearances rather than to enhance stockholders' control of management. The multivariate analysis showed AC formation to be related to the type of auditor employed by the firm and the proportion of outsiders on the board of directors. However, auditor type is not associated with measures of reliance on ACs, suggesting that the big accounting firms may encourage the formation of ACs, but go no further in persuading boards to rely on them.

Board composition appears to influence reliance on audit committees. The higher the proportion of outside directors, the more likely it is that the AC will exclude officers of the company. Also, as the proportion of outside directors on the board increases, ACs are found to meet more frequently. This association between board composition and frequency of meetings appears to reflect the board's inclination to use ACs for monitoring. The results of our study may indicate that boards with high outsider participation assert themselves as representatives of owners, and are more likely to employ mechanisms to monitor managers. However, an alternative explanation is possible. The proportion of outside directors may surrogate in our analysis for director liability, and the formation of an AC composed of outside directors which exhibits a minimum level of activity may be viewed as a mechanism to reduce this potential liability.

An important finding of our study is the association of the frequency of AC meetings with firm size, both in the sample of all firms with ACs and in the subsample of firms with noncosmetic ACs. Larger firms appear to have more active ACs than smaller firms. Firm size was used here as a surrogate for the net monitoring benefits from employing an AC, following the argument that an AC is a costly control mechanism, and that large firms are more likely to accrue sufficient benefits to justify an active AC. It appears that the monitoring complexities which are associated with greater size provide incentives for ACs to be active. However, as size may also surrogate for other attributes, this implication should be viewed with caution. Although the empirical analyses provided little support for the agency variables, management stock ownership and leverage, the significance of size suggests that monitoring needs may drive AC activity.

The results have important implications for regulators and public policy makers who face the question of the extent to which audit committee formation and operation should be mandated as part of a move towards the reform of boards of directors. The tendency for many companies in our sample to maintain ACs which were structurally weak or inactive indicates that merely requiring ACs may not achieve the intended purpose. Although the structure of ACs can be mandated, their vigilance cannot. At the same time, it appears that as firms grow larger, their boards have a greater incentive to employ active ACs, which may mitigate the need for regulatory requirements.

The authors would like to thank Dorothy Feldmann and Atiq Shaikh for their able research assistance on this project. Helpful comments were provided by an editor and three reviewers. This project was supported by the Institute for Accounting Research and Education at Boston University.

References

American Institute of Certified Public Accountants (AICPA). March 1978. *An AICPA Requirement for Audit Committees: An Analysis of the Issues*. AICPA.

Bacon, J. 1988. *The Audit Committee: A Broader Mandate*. New York: The Conference Board.

Bradbury, M. E. Spring 1990. The incentives for voluntary audit committee formation. *Journal of Accounting and Public Policy* 9(1):19–36.

Bull, I. and Sharp, F. Feb. 1989. Advising clients on Treadway audit committee recommendations. *Journal of Accountancy* 167(2):46–52.

Coopers & Lybrand. 1988. *Audit Committee Guide*. Coopers & Lybrand.

Eichenseher, J. and Shields, D. Spring 1985. Corporate director liability and monitoring preferences. *Journal of Accounting and Public Policy* 4(1):13–31.

Jemison, D. and Oakley, P. Dec. 1983. Corporate governance in mutual insurance companies. *Journal of Business Research* 11(4):501–522.

Jensen, M. C. and Meckling, W. H. Oct. 1976. Theory of the firm: Managerial behavior, agency costs and ownership structure. *Journal of Financial Economics* 3(4):305–360.

Kesner, I. F., Victor, B. and Lamont, B. T. Dec. 1986. Board composition and the commission of illegal acts: An investigation of Fortune 500 companies. *Academy of Management Journal* 29(4):789–799.

Kosnik, R. D. June 1987. Greenmail: A study of board performance in corporate governance. *Administrative Science Quarterly* 32(2):163–185.

KPMG Peat Marwick. 1988. *The Audit Committee*. KPMG Peat Marwick.

Kunitake, W. Aug. 1981. Do audit committees favor the large CPA firms? *Journal of Accountancy* 152(2):43–45.

Mautz, R. and Neumann, F. 1970. *Corporate Audit Committees*. Urbana, IL: Bureau of Economics and Business Research, University of Illinois.

Merchant, K. 1987. *Fraudulent and Questionable Financial Reporting: A Corporate Perspective*. Morristown, NJ: Financial Executives Research Foundation.

Mizruchi, M. S. July 1983. Who controls whom? An examination of the relation between management and boards of directors of large American corporations. *Academy of Management Review* 8(3):426–435.

National Commission on Fraudulent Financial Reporting. 1987. *Report of the National Commission on Fraudulent Financial Reporting*.

Pincus, K., Rusbarsky, M. and Wong, J. Winter 1989. Voluntary formation of corporate audit committees among NASDAQ firms. *Journal of Accounting and Public Policy* 8(4):239–265.

Pindyck, R. and Rubinfeld, D. 1981. *Econometric Models and Economic Forecasts*, 2nd ed. New York: McGraw-Hill.

Securities and Exchange Commission (SEC). 1972. *Accounting Series Release No. 123* (The Federal Register, vol. 37, p. 6850). Washington, D.C.: U.S. Government Printing Office.

Securities and Exchange Commission. 1980. *Staff Report on Corporate Accountability*. Washington, D.C.: U.S. Government Printing Office.

Singh, H. and Harianto, F. March 1989. Management-board relationships, takeover risk, and the adoption of golden parachutes. *Academy of Management Journal* 32(1):7–24.

Stone, M. and Rasp, J. Jan. 1991. Trade-offs in the choice between Logit and OLS for accounting choice studies. *The Accounting Review* 66(1):170–187.

Zahra, S. A. and Pearce, J. A., II. June 1989. Boards of directors and corporate performance: A review and integrative model. *Journal of Management* 15(2):291–334.

[20]

JOURNAL OF MANAGERIAL ISSUES
Vol. X Number 2   Summer 1998: 129-150

Organizational and Economic Explanations
of Audit Committee Oversight*

Lawrence P. Kalbers
KPMG Peat Marwick LLP
Accounting Professor in International Business
John Carroll University

Timothy J. Fogarty
KPMG Peat Marwick Faculty Fellow
Case Western Reserve University

Corporate governance plays an important role in the production of corporate results. The setting of corporate objectives, and the concomitant measuring and reporting of results, depend in fundamental ways upon the caliber of corporate oversight. Although considerable attention has been focused on the forms that are necessary for such direction, less is known about their effectiveness.

The establishment of audit committees in the United States was recommended by the Securities and Exchange Commission (SEC) as early as 1940. However, the place of audit committees in the corporate governance structure has increased dramatically only over the past twenty-five years (Birkett, 1986; Braiotta, 1994). Studies show that the percentage of firms with audit committees has gone from nearly ten percent in 1958 to nearly forty percent in 1972, to over ninety percent in 1982 (as summarized in Harrison, 1987, Figure 1, p. 110). Similar findings were shown in two early studies of audit committees by Mautz and Neumann (1970, 1977). In their first study (1970), they found one-third of their sample to have adopted audit committees. In their second study (1977), eighty-seven percent of responding chief executive officers indicated their corporations had audit committees. Thus, an increasingly rapid adoption of audit committees took place from the late 1950s through the early 1980s.

The genesis of audit committees suggests that their inclusion in the

* The authors gratefully acknowledge the financial support for this project from the Peat Marwick Foundation and a Wasmer Summer Research Grant from John Carroll University. The generous contribution of efforts and time by the anonymous reviewers are also appreciated.

130   KALBERS AND FOGARTY

structure of corporate governance should be understood as part of the reaction to corporate abuses occurring over the last three decades. Instances of fraudulent financial reporting, defalcations, accounting method choice abuses, and opinion shopping served as evidence that management was not effectively accountable to the full board of directors. The audit committee was an attempt to specifically designate responsibility for accounting-related matters, to provide a reporting structure for insiders that would circumvent managerial retribution, and to supervise relations with the external auditor. In fact, the SEC has forced a number of corporations to adopt audit committees as a remedial measure (see Birkett, 1986). Although many large companies had voluntarily formed audit committees by the mid-1970s, pivotal points occurred when audit committees were mandated for New York Stock Exchange firms in 1978, and for those listed on the National Market System by the National Association of Security Dealers in 1989.

This article contrasts two competing theoretical orientations. Agency theory, now considered mainstream thought on control, proposes a primarily economic explanation of the existence and form of control mechanisms. Institutional theory offers a sociological approach that questions the sufficiency of technical rationality for understanding corporate governance. A review of previous empirical studies in the audit committee literature suggests that traditional agency cost measures do not provide an adequate basis to explain the formation of audit committees. Further, the studies on audit committee formation require a presumption that audit

committees actually will reduce information asymmetry between principals and agents (i.e., audit committees are effective in carrying out their responsibilities). Other empirical studies link audit committee effectiveness to factors internal to the corporate governance and organization structure, but do not determine the extent to which these internal factors are influenced by external monitoring demands. In the next two sections, agency theory and institutional theory approaches are extended to analyze the contribution of each theory to understanding audit committee activities and effectiveness. Then, the hypotheses, design and results of a study are described. The empirical evidence suggests that neither theory alone is as useful as their synthesis. The last section discusses the results and their implications for the management of corporations.

Theoretical Perspectives

This section outlines two theoretical approaches for the appreciation of audit committees. Since agency theory is well represented in the accounting and finance literature, more attention will be devoted to the description of institutional theory.

Agency Theory

The separation of management from ownership in the modern corporation provides an ideal context for the operation of agency theory. Shareholders (and debtholders) act as the principal with interests in deriving maximum utility from the actions of management, serving as the agent. Problems arise because of the separation of ownership and management and the resulting inability of the owners to observe the actions of management (Jensen and Meckling, 1976; Berle and Means, 1932). Owners and agents have incentives to invest in various information systems and control devices to reduce agency costs associated with information asymmetry (Jensen and Meckling, 1976; Fama, 1980; Fama and Jensen, 1983). These control devices might offer Pareto optimality (i.e., maximum gains for all parties) since the agent would otherwise bear agency costs that occur when principals discount the value of the firm, based on the likelihood of adverse selection, shirking, and moral hazard (Alchian and Demsetz, 1972; Jensen and Meckling, 1976).

Management may use various means to indicate to others the quality of the information they are providing. Demands for monitoring may result in external audits (see Wallace, 1980; Chow, 1982; Anderson *et al.*, 1993), the use of outside directors (Fama, 1980; Watts and Zimmerman, 1986; Anderson *et al.*, 1993) and audit committees (Eichenseher and Shields, 1985; Pincus *et al.*, 1989; Bradbury, 1990; Menon and Williams, 1994). The use of audit committees can be considered an important part of the decision control system for internal monitoring by boards of directors (see Fama, 1980; Fama and Jensen, 1983). Agency theory suggests some firms will have incentives to incur costs to differentiate themselves from others. For example, in order to assert their higher quality, companies would submit to audits (Bar-Yosef and Livnat, 1984). Additional private information can be signaled through the selection of higher quality audits (see DeAngelo, 1981; Francis and Wilson, 1988; Bachar, 1989; Dye, 1991; Menon and Williams, 1991). However, when information is difficult to verify, an agent may attempt to mimic quality messages, which may lead to adverse selection (Akerlof, 1970). In a realistic multi-period world, agents have to be concerned about their human capital in the labor market. False communications may therefore have negative consequences for the agent as well as the principal (see Fama, 1980).

In sum, agency theory places economic self-interest at the center of theoretical expectations. Certain contractual relationships, combined with information asymmetry, indicate a corresponding demand for investment in control and monitoring mechanisms. Therefore, the effectiveness of audit committees should be influenced by the factors believed to alter agency costs.

Institutional Theory

Institutional theory, initiated in one form by Meyer and Rowan (1977), suggests that organizational structures in such an environment become symbolic displays of conformity and social accountability. Simultaneously, the real work of the organization is accomplished by internal operating processes loosely coupled from the observable structures. Organizations with the appropriate structures in place avoid in-depth investigations of their operating core by external parties (see Meyer and Rowan, 1977; Zucker, 1988; Orton and Weick, 1990). This theoretical perspective has been applied to a wide set of social phenomena, including choice of accounting methods (Mezias, 1990), the use of accounting by public sector organizations (Covaleski and Dirsmith, 1991), and the adoption of innovative technologies (King *et al.*, 1994).

The external expectations that have crystallized about corporate governance indicate the existence of an institutionalized environment which serves as the threshold for the application of institutional theory (Zucker, 1988). The recent concern over corporate control has reached the highest levels of government in the U.S. Demands for greater accountability have lead to threats of more regulation and to a new wave of interest in oversight and self-regulation (e.g., National Commission on Fraudulent Financial Reporting, 1987; Committee of Sponsoring Organizations of the Treadway Commission, 1992).

Various forces can be identified that suggest that organizations will conform to the central elements of an institutional environment. Following the categorization developed by DiMaggio and Powell (1983), coercive, mimetic, and normative mechanisms predict that control structures will gravitate toward common social forms. For these purposes, regulatory bodies (New York Stock Exchange, NASDAQ, Securities and Exchange Commission) have used coercive influence that has led to the formation of audit committees. Corporate mimicry occurs through formal and informal channels, such as industry guidelines, common practices, and interaction through interlocking boards of directors. Normative influence emanates primarily from the professionalism of involved individuals. Accountants and auditors, through their professional bodies such as the American Institute of Certified Public Accountants and the Institute of Internal Auditors, have pushed for the creation of audit committees and guidelines for their activities.

Institutional theory posits that the employment of structures fails to be directly related to the production of expected outcomes. Due to the importance of creating ceremonial structures for the benefit of constituencies, control structures may not exist primarily to accomplish control objectives. The theory suggests that outcomes, such as effectiveness, are more attributable to an internal "core" logic not derivable from external structures (see Thompson, 1967). This core escapes the attention of external parties and is therefore unconstrained by their influence. Little evidence exists as to whether audit committees are successful in achieving their intended levels of corporate control. If effectiveness proves more directly the result of internal factors than the result of those characteristics observable to external parties, institutional theory is supported.

Agency and Institutional Theories in Audit Committee Research

Positive agency theory has been used to study various aspects of management and organizational action. Empirical regularities have been found between certain firm variables and firms' accounting choice (see Watts and Zimmerman, 1990). Agency theory has also been applied to audit committees. Four recent studies used agency theory as a theoretical basis for developing expected relationships between agency costs and the formation of audit committees and other audit committee activities. Pincus *et al.* (1989) found a number of significant relationships between variables that proxied for agency costs (i.e., leverage, size, ownership, structure) and the formation

ORGANIZATIONAL AND ECONOMIC EXPLANATIONS   133

of audit committees for a sample of U.S. companies prior to the requirement for formation of audit committees. Bradbury (1990), in his study on New Zealand companies, found no significant relationships with variables proxying for auditor incentives or agency costs. He did, however, find audit committee formation to be related to board size and intercorporate ownership. Menon and Williams (1994) found selected agency variables (i.e., outside directors, auditor type) to be associated with the existence of audit committees, the percentage of outside directors on audit committees, and the frequency of audit committee meetings. Eichenseher and Shields (1985), whose study also had agency theory implications, also had mixed results. To date, the audit committee formation studies using agency theory perspectives have not provided overwhelming, or consistent, findings.

A major implication of the demand for monitoring by audit committees is that audit committees will actually contribute to corporate control. The development of the hypotheses in studies such as Pincus *et al.* (1989) implies actual reductions of agency costs and information asymmetry resulting from the formation of audit committees. The effectiveness of corporate control mechanisms is a judgment that has not often been empirically examined. Little is known about the effectiveness of audit committees as a monitoring control. Unlike audit quality, there have been few attempts to systematically evaluate the activities or effectiveness of audit committees. Available evidence reveals that companies with audit committees are not immune to fraudulent reporting (see, for example, National Commission on Fraudulent Financial Report-

ing, 1987; Wechsler, 1989; Verschoor, 1989b, 1990; Beasley, 1996).

In the audit committee literature, Menon and Williams (1994) have come closest to examining the links among agency theory variables, the formation of audit committees, and audit committee effectiveness. Menon and Williams used the absence of insiders on the audit committee and the frequency of audit committee meetings to proxy for the audit committee's monitoring effectiveness. They found two agency variables to be significantly associated with the two proxies. First, organizations with higher percentages of outside directors on the board had fewer insiders on audit committees and audit committees that met more often. They also found that organization size was highly associated with the number of audit committee meetings. However, these two agency theory variables were not the same ones they found to be highly associated with audit committee existence. This suggests that there is not a direct link between the formation or existence of audit committees and the activities or effectiveness of audit committees.

A recent study of the relationship between the composition of boards of directors and financial statement fraud also provides empirical evidence about the corporate governance structure, including audit committees, with regard to fraudulent financial statements. Beasley's (1996) primary finding was that firms with financial statement fraud had a significantly lower percentage of outside directors compared to a matched sample of no-fraud firms. He also found that certain variables (i.e., increased stock ownership of outside directors, increased outside director tenure, decreased number of direc-

torships of outside directors, and decreased board size) were associated
with a decreased likelihood of fraud.
Even more relevant to this study,
Beasley found no significant differences between the fraud and no-
fraud firms for the presence, composition, or number of meetings of
audit committees.

The pattern and rate of adoption
of audit committees cited earlier is
similar to other social diffusions observed in institutional theory studies.
Tolbert and Zucker's (1983) work on
civil service and the Dobbin *et al.*
(1988) analysis of affirmative action
demonstrate the temporal sequence
of adoption that can be used to observe isomorphic forces. Early adopters of a new structure should be responding to technical dictates and
constraints, whereas late adopters
should be more influenced by isomorphic forces in the decision to
adopt. The increasing velocity of audit committee adoption during the
1970s suggests an explanation other
than a cost beneficial reaction to demands for monitoring. Audit committees could be adopted as a symbolic gesture that legitimates a
corporation's governance structure
to other parties.

Baysinger and Butler's (1985) study
of boards of directors and organizational performance used agency theory for its underpinnings, but it also
had institutional theory implications.
Against the background of the overall
increase in the number of independent board members from 1970 to
1980, they found that early increases in
independent directors led to better financial performance later. Conversely, good financial performance
in early years did not explain subsequent board composition. Early
adoption of independent board

members was evidently based on the
need or desire for oversight and input, whereas late adoption of independent board members was not for
substantive reasons.

Several studies provide evidence
for symbolic displays of conformity.
Maher (1981) found that firms were
more likely to invest in resources to
prove compliance with the Foreign
Corrupt Practices Act of 1977 than to
actually make expenditures to improve existing controls. Eichenseher
and Shields (1985) suggested that audit committee formation in the late
1970s was primarily a response to the
Foreign Corrupt Practices Act and to
the increased legal exposure of directors. The relatively consistent finding
that companies with Big-Eight auditors were more likely to form an audit
committee (Eichenseher and Shields,
1985; Pincus *et al.*, 1989) indicates an
implicit normative persuasion is
transmitted through accounting professionals such that a higher level of
similarity of practice is attained.

Consistent with the nature of corporate mimicry, institutional theory
studies have found certain accounting and control practices concentrated by industry. For example, Neu
(1992) found that social variables
were better for explaining voluntary
disclosures of financial forecasts in
particular industries than were economic variables. Different influences
present within distinct institutional
environments tend to determine appropriate forms of corporate governance and their rate of diffusion.
Mautz and Neumann (1977) found
that eighty-nine percent of the Fortune 500 Industrial companies and
eighty-six percent of the Fortune 50
corporations in other industries indicated that they had an audit committee. However, banking and retail-

ing companies reported the highest rate of audit committees (approximately ninety-five percent). The financial industry also had the highest percentage of audit committees in Mautz and Neumann's earlier study (1970). These concentrations support the prospect that institutional influence may be variable.

Institutional theory has not previously been specifically applied to the study of the work of audit committees. However, two previous studies on audit committee effectiveness are consistent with the premise that actual operations of audit committees are linked to more proximate and less publicly observable factors than to agency costs and the traditional agency theory variables. Spangler and Braiotta (1990) found audit committee effectiveness to be associated with the personal leadership of audit committee members. Kalbers and Fogarty (1993) found that audit committee effectiveness was associated with organizational and personal bases of audit committee power. Because these studies did not use agency theory or agency theory variables, any further link to the more observable agency conditions is unknown.

Development of Hypotheses

For purposes of these research expectations, we initially adopt a commonplace understanding of effectiveness as an ability to accomplish meaningful objectives. Although judgments of effectiveness vary, we presume that effectiveness connotes efficaciousness, willfulness, and timeliness. As applied to audit committees, effectiveness entails increasing the level of control and accountability experienced by the corporation.

If the research concerned with the formation of audit committees has importance, it must presume a consistent demand for *effective* corporate monitoring. Therefore, agency variables should be highly correlated with the effectiveness of audit committees. Accordingly, the variables to proxy for agency costs used by Pincus *et al.* (1989) are used in this study. These are managerial ownership, leverage, size, and proportion of outside directors.

The level of managerial ownership is thought to proxy for the separation between owners and managers (Niehaus, 1989). High levels of management ownership suggest a better alignment with the interests of owners. Low levels of ownership by management can trigger significant information asymmetries that are lessened with particular forms of corporate governance. Dhaliwal *et al.* (1982) suggested that accounting method choice is a function of firm position on an owner control-manager control continuum. Several agency studies have employed variables that measured this differentiation (see Morck *et al.*, 1988; Francis and Wilson, 1988; Niehaus, 1989). Agency costs should be lower as managers' ownership increases. Conversely, as the ownership of outside directors increases, it would be expected that the outside directors would have increased incentive to demand effective monitoring since their own wealth would be at risk (Patton and Baker, 1987; Jensen, 1993).

H₁: Corporations with higher percentages of ownership by management are less likely to invest in effective audit committees.

H₂: Corporations with higher percentages of ownership by outside directors are more likely to invest in effective audit committees.

Leverage has been used extensively in agency theory (see Watts and Zimmerman, 1990). High levels of debt financing create new agency dimensions through the introduction of debtholders with differing interests. This should lead to an increased demand for monitoring (see, for example, Smith and Warner, 1979; Chow, 1982).

H₃: **Corporations with higher leverage are more likely to invest in effective audit committees.**

Larger firms should be more visible and, therefore, be more likely to form audit committees to forestall regulation (see Watts and Zimmerman, 1986, 1990; Wallace, 1980). Also, larger firms can benefit from economies of scale in monitoring activities. Therefore, the cost of forming and maintaining an audit committee would be more cost effective for larger firms (Pincus *et al.,* 1989; Anderson *et al.,* 1993).

H₄: **Larger corporations are more likely to invest in effective audit committees.**

The final agency hypothesis examines the composition of the board of directors. Corporate governance at this level varies with the relative presence of insiders and outsiders on the board (see Pfeffer, 1972). Since greater information asymmetry normally exists for outside directors than inside directors (Baysinger and Hoskisson, 1990), a greater percentage of outside directors on the board will involve higher agency costs for managers. Effective audit committees would provide an efficient way for outside directors to reduce information asymmetry (Pincus *et al.,* 1989; Bradbury, 1990, especially as related to intercorporate holdings) and legal exposure (Eichenseher and Shields, 1985).

H₅: **Corporations with higher percentages of outside directors on their boards are more likely to invest in effective audit committees.**

Institutional theory requires hypotheses that question the primacy of the technical rationality of corporate control mechanisms. The very existence of an audit committee suggests the authority to conduct the business of control. However, institutional theory would suggest that formal symbols of power exist for public consumption and are only marginally related to outcomes such as control. Instead, more proximate and less publicly observable forms of power affect results in a more direct fashion (Spangler and Braiotta, 1990; Kalbers and Fogarty, 1993). Institutional theory, at least as presently developed, does not provide a direct test for the factors that will be associated with the inner workings of corporate governance and audit committees. In the context of this study, the lack of significant results for the association between agency theory variables and audit committee effectiveness in previous studies is consistent with the premise of institutional theory. To the extent that the first four hypotheses (H₁-H₄) can be rejected, the following hypothesis will be accepted.

H₆: **The level of agency costs are not directly related to audit committee effectiveness.**

In order to provide an alternative test of the distinctiveness of external imagery and organizational results, constructs not conceptually tied to agency theory can be used. Menon and Williams (1994) used two publicly available proxies for audit committee "effectiveness" or board "reliance" on audit committees. Institutional theory would suggest that publicly available measures exist primarily for the consumption of external constituents and would not be directly associated with core organization results. A second institutional hypothesis formalizes this premise with regard to audit committees.

H₇: Publicly available measures of audit committee attributes are not directly associated with audit committee effectiveness.

The final institutional theory hypothesis pertains to the nature of the coupling of formal structure and the operational core. Although this key aspect of institutional theory has been interpreted in several ways (see Orton and Weick, 1990), it conventionally posits that a weak empirical relationship exists between the observable external structure of the organization and internally generated organizational results (see Weick, 1976). Organizational structures, such as boards of directors, should therefore have some influence on the operational core that creates levels of organizational control. However, this is expected to be modest in degree so as to result in what has been called "loose coupling" (Weick, 1976). Since coupling is usually not measured, but instead documented with qualitative methods (see Ritti and Silver, 1986; Covaleski and Dirsmith, 1988), the exact nature of the empirical expectation can only be generally expressed. Therefore, it may be hypothesized that public displays of appropriate forms of corporate governance are linked to audit committee effectiveness through more consequential and precise organizational commitments to audit committees. For example, written mandates and practical authority provided to the audit committee may be more likely to exist in certain control environments than in others. If these condi-

tions contribute to greater organizational effectiveness, they are coupled with external factors.

Although a variety of approaches might be specified for the purpose of understanding core operating processes, the concept of power provides an excellent choice. Although power has been underutilized in institutional theory (Perrow, 1985), it produces a means to specify the micro-level of institutionalism at which organizational change is thought to occur (see Powell, 1991; Friedland and Alford, 1991). Power is closely related to institutional projects (DiMaggio, 1991) in which the actions of insiders are critical to the organization's position in its environment. How resources are mobilized through the "rules of the game" also often underlies the emergence of revised structures and organizational results (see Singh et al., 1991; Galashiewiez, 1991). Power can be seen as a critical medium for expression of institutional constraints upon organizational results (see DiMaggio and Powell, 1991). Also, power has contributed to the progressive elaboration of institutional theory in ways that make it less monolithic and more sensitive to changes in the interorganizational field (Jepperson, 1991).

Institutional theory has focused considerable attention upon the professions as potential change agents (see Galashiewiez, 1991; DiMaggio, 1991). Building upon previous work recognizing the power exerted by professions (see Abbott, 1988; Esland, 1980), the accounting literature has begun to incorporate the recognition of power in organizational settings. Kalbers and Fogarty (1993) show how power relates to effectiveness and therefore is suggestive of an efficacious internal operation apart

138 KALBERS AND FOGARTY

Table 1
Agency Cost Variables Used in the Study

LOGSIZE   Log of sum of market value of common stock and book values of liabilities and preferred stock

LOGLEV   Log of long-term debt to total assets

LOGLEV2   Log of total debt to total assets

INOWN   Proportion of ownership by inside directors

OUTOWN   Proportion of ownership by outside directors

OUTDIR   Proportion of outside directors on the board of directors

OUTAC   Proportion of outside directors on the audit committee

from external visibility. In turn, other studies have shown how power within the organization is conditioned and altered by the existence of institutionalized expectations not confined to the organization (Covaleski and Dirsmith, 1988; Covaleski et al., 1993). Thus, some links between external demands for monitoring and sources of audit committee power within the organization can be expected.

H₆: **Demands for monitoring (as captured by agency cost variables) are weakly related to organizational bases of power for audit committees.**

Method and Results

The sample for this study is based on that used by Kalbers and Fogarty (1993). It consists of data related to 79 companies selected from the Value Line Investment Survey (1988) and from 164 individuals (chief financial officers, external audit partners, and directors of internal audit) who responded to a survey instrument. All organizations in the sample had audit committees and internal auditing functions. Based on their original sample frame, this represents an 87.8% company response rate and a 60.7% response rate for individuals.

Variables used to proxy for agency costs were operationalized in conformity with established traditions of the literature. The data for these variables were obtained from publicly available financial statements and proxy statements. Table 1 provides details about the measures used to calculate the agency variables used in Hypotheses 1-4. The classification of outside directors was based on the more rigorous criterion used by Molz (1988) and Weisbach (1988). Based on proxy statements, any director that was a former employee of, or had any business relationship with, the organization was not considered to be an outside director. The importance of this distinction has also been noted in other studies of boards of directors (see Baysinger and Butler, 1985) and audit committees (Verschoor, 1989a, 1989b, 1990).

The data related to audit committee effectiveness and the organizational bases of audit committee power are taken from the data set developed by Kalbers and Fogarty (1993). They used six constructs for

ORGANIZATIONAL AND ECONOMIC EXPLANATIONS   139

Table 2
Effectiveness Measures

EFFECTIVENESS-FINANCIAL REPORTING (4 items, 7-point scale: Ineffective/Very Effective):

1. Review and analysis of the application of alternative generally accepted accounting principles (GAAP).
2. Review and analysis of significant changes in accounting policies and year-end adjustments.
3. Review and analysis of accounting estimates and judgments.
4. Review of the annual financial statements and interim reports, in general.

EFFECTIVENESS-ANNUAL AUDIT AND THE EXTERNAL AUDITORS (6 items, 7-point scale: Ineffective/Very Effective):

5. Selection of the independent auditors.
6. Evaluation of independent auditors' performance, including determination of independence.
7. Review and analysis of the scope and activities of the annual audit by the independent auditors.
8. Review and analysis of the results of the annual audit by the independent auditors.
9. Monitoring of corrections by management of reported deficiencies in the independent auditor's management letter.
10. The audit committee enhances the effectiveness of the independent auditors (Strongly Disagree/Strongly Agree).

EFFECTIVENESS-INTERNAL CONTROLS AND THE INTERNAL AUDITORS (6 items, 7-point scale: Ineffective/Very Effective):

11. Review and analysis of the adequacy and effectiveness of the internal accounting and financial controls of the company.
12. Review and analysis of the internal audit reports, budgets, and findings.
13. Evaluation of internal auditors' performance.
14. Review and analysis of the scope and activities of the internal auditors.
15. Monitoring of corrections by management of reported deficiencies reported by the internal auditors.
16. The audit committee enhances the independence of the internal auditors (Strongly Disagree/Strongly Agree).

EFFECTIVENESS-OVERALL (5 items, 7-point scale: Strongly Disagree/ Strongly Agree):

17. The audit committee accomplishes very little.

    Overall effectiveness measures used by Grinaker *et al.* (1978):

18. Beyond meeting legal or other regulatory requirements, the audit committee serves an important need in this company.
19. The audit committee in this company is very effective.
20. The performance of this audit committee is probably better than most other audit committees.
21. Other audit committees would do well to use this audit committee as a model.

audit committee power—three types of organizationally based power and three types of individually based power. The three institutionally based forms of power, considered exogenous in their model, are legitimate power, sanctionary power, and institutional support. They represent forms of audit committee power mandated or empowered through internal organizational policies or actions. For purposes of this study, they represent a potential link for the loose coupling that may exist between agency costs and audit committee effectiveness. Kalbers and Fogarty (1993) measured audit committee effectiveness both in the specific areas

140   KALBERS AND FOGARTY

Table 3
Power Variables Used in the Study

Type of Power	Description and Measurement in the Study
Sanctionary	1. The perceived level of the audit committee's responsibility to determine the budgets and compensation of internal auditors. 2. The perceived level of the audit committee's responsibility to determine the scope and compensation of external auditors.
Legitimate	1. Existence and perceived adequacy of written authority of the audit committee. 2. The perceived general authority and importance of the audit committee.
Institutional Support	1. The perceived timeliness, usefulness, and reliability of information provided to the audit committee by the chief executive officer, chief financial officer, chief internal auditor, and external auditors. 2. The perceived tone of top management in providing a supportive atmosphere for the audit committee. 3. The perceived working relationship with the audit committee and the chief executive officer, chief financial officer, chief internal auditor, and external auditors.

of financial reporting, the annual audit and external auditors, internal controls and the internal auditors, and with an overall effectiveness construct. A more detailed description of the measurements are provided in Tables 2 and 3.

The data in this study are based on both individual responses and company attributes. Two data sets were produced and each was used to test the hypotheses. One data set used the companies as the sample. For companies with more than one individual responding, the mean of the responses was computed. The second data set kept all of the individual responses and matched the company data to the respondents.

Before testing the hypotheses, the Pearson correlations for the seven agency variables used for testing were computed, and are shown in Table 4. As would be expected, the two measures of leverage are highly correlated. However, the two measures of leverage have different patterns of significance related to other agency

variables. The more typically used measure of total debt to total assets (LOGLEV2) is negatively associated with the level of inside director ownership (INOWN), but positively associated with the percentage of outside directors on the board. Using the leverage measure of long-term debt to total assets (LOGLEV), a negative association with the percentage of outside director ownership was found. This suggests that neither inside or outside directors are favorably disposed toward debt. Further, as total debt increases, the proportion of outside directors increases.

The agency hypotheses were tested by first computing the Pearson correlations of the agency variables with the audit committee effectiveness variables. The results are displayed in Table 5. Only one association of the 28 pairs was significant at $p < .05$. This result strongly suggests that to a great extent, agency variables are not directly related to audit committee effectiveness. Only mild support for H_4, which related firm size to audit com-

Table 4
Correlation Matrix: Agency Variables; n=79

	LOGLEV	LOGLEV2	INOWN	OUTOWN	OUTDIR	OUTAC
LOGSIZE	-.144	.178	-.274	-.006	.091	.117
	(.205)	(.117)	(.015)	(.960)	(.424)	(.305)
LOGLEV		.401	.055	-.311	-.011	-.099
		(.000)	(.630)	(.005)	(.926)	(.383)
LOGLEV2			-.248	-.138	.298	.046
			(.028)	(.225)	(.008)	(.690)
INOWN				-.027	-.336	-.181
				(.813)	(.002)	(.111)
OUTOWN					.164	.074
					(.150)	(.519)
OUTDIR						.524
						(.000)

Note: Probabilities are shown in parentheses. Correlations significant at p<.05 are in **boldface**.

mittee effectiveness, existed. Company size (LOGSIZE) was positively correlated with a measure of overall effectiveness (EFFECTO), but not to any of the specific measures of effectiveness.

Because each of the first five hypotheses must be rejected (usually without exception), the institutional theory hypothesis, H_6, which specified that the composite results of the first five hypotheses would be in the direction of nonsignificant relationships with effectiveness, can be accepted. Since agency costs are not directly associated with audit committee effectiveness, evidence against a strictly economic-based result is produced.

The second institutional theory hypothesis, H_7, posited that publicly available measures of audit committee activity would not be associated with effectiveness. This was tested with the Pearson correlations between the two measures used by Menon and Wil-

liams (1994) as proxies for the board of directors' reliance on audit committees and the effectiveness measures. Their two measures were the number of audit committee meetings and the absence of insiders on the audit committee. Instead of a dichotomous variable for the absence of insiders, the proportion of outsiders on the audit committee (OUTAC) was used for this test.

The results of the relationship between outside directors (OUTAC) and the effectiveness measures can be found within Table 5. The proportion of outside directors on the audit committee has no direct relationship to audit committee effectiveness. However, it should be noted that the definition of outsiders used in this study is more stringent than those in other audit committee studies. Also, significant discretion is provided to management and boards of directors in determining whether a board member is to be considered inde-

Table 5
Correlations: Agency Variables with Effectiveness Measures; n=164

	LOGSIZE	LOGLEV	LOGLEV2	INOWN	OUTOWN	OUTDIR	OUTAC
EFFECTFR	-.048	.009	-.049	.001	.069	.039	-.005
	(.543)	(.909)	(.541)	(.991)	(.388)	(.625)	(.952)
EFFECTEA	-.025	-.104	-.042	.028	.079	.002	.016
	(.750)	(.190)	(.592)	(.722)	(.320)	(.978)	(.836)
EFFECTIA	.136	-.137	-.002	.003	.077	-.038	.007
	(.088)	(.085)	(.981)	(.969)	(.335)	(.638)	(.928)
EFFECTO	.185	-.093	-.003	-.085	.040	.050	-.025
	(.019)	(.240)	(.974)	(.283)	(.616)	(.531)	(.756)

Note: Detailed results are shown for the sample of individuals. Although total sample size is 164, missing data reduced n for certain variables. Probabilities are shown in parentheses. The correlation significant at p<.05 is in **boldface**. For the company data set of 79 companies, no results were significant.

pendent (see Verschoor, 1989a). This finding challenges the conventional wisdom and regulatory edicts about the need for independent directors on audit committees and related concerns about "grey" directors (e.g., Treadway Commission 1987; Vicknair *et al.*, 1993). These results are also consistent with those of Beasley (1996), who found that the composition of audit committees had no significant effect on the likelihood of financial statement fraud.

Menon and Williams' (1994) other measure, the number of audit committee meetings, was obtained from company proxy statements. The results of the Pearson correlations between the effectiveness measures and the number of meetings (MEETGS) are presented in Table 6. Two measures of effectiveness (EFFECTIA and EFFECTO) are highly associated with the number of meetings. On the surface, it appears that the number of meetings provides a reasonable proxy for certain dimensions of committee effectiveness. However, the EFFECTO measure of effectiveness had

the least specificity about committee tasks. It may be that respondents were influenced by the number of meetings in their general impressions about audit committee activities. The traditional focus of audit committee meetings has been on the external audit and meeting with external auditors. Additional meetings may reflect more reporting by, or interaction with, internal auditors. H_7, therefore, is differentially supported by the results. Although there is no association with effectiveness with regard to financial reporting and the external auditor, the results do suggest that frequency of meetings may provide some evidence about the attention paid to internal controls and internal auditing by audit committees.

The last institutional theory hypothesis, H_8, expected a weak association between demands for monitoring (in agency theory terms) and power held by the audit committee. This hypothesis was tested by computing the Pearson correlations between the agency variables and the

Table 6
Correlations: Number of Meetings with Effectiveness Measures; N=164

	EFFECTFR	EFFECTEA	EFFECTIA	EFFECTO
MEETGS	.120	.085	.251	.303
	(.130)	(.282)	(.001)	(.004) **

Note: Detailed results are shown for the sample of individuals. Although total sample size is 164, missing data reduced n for certain variables. Probabilities are shown in parentheses. Correlations significant at p<.05 are in **boldface**. For the company data set of 79 companies **p<.01.

organizational power bases. Table 7 reveals that several significant associations exist. The strongest results relate to one measurement of leverage (LOGLEV). Unexpectedly, the relationship is negative. That is, the more long-term debt that exists, the less that sanctionary responsibility and institutional support exists for the audit committee. Three other significant associations are in what can be considered the expected direction. The level of inside director ownership (INOWN) is negatively associated with the legitimacy of the audit committee (LEGITIM), the level of outside director ownership (OUTOWN) is positively associated with institutional support, and the proportion of outside directors on the board (OUT-

DIR) is positively associated with audit committee legitimacy. The modest results provide general support for H_8. As would be expected by institutional theory, some association exists between agency variables and certain mandates and conditions under which audit committees operate. The coupling between external economic conditions and the power environment is aptly described as "loose." Both the limited number of these associations and some unexpected directions suggest the precise method of coupling is not simple or predictable. This amplifies the need for further theoretical elaboration of this tenet of institutional theory (see Orton and Weick, 1990; Oliver, 1990; Scott, 1987).

Table 7
Correlations: Agency Variables with Exogenous Power Variables; n=164

	LOGSIZE	LOGLEV	LOGLEV2	INOWN	OUTOWN	OUTDIR	OUTAC
LEGITM	.029	-.132	.053	-.191	.088	.161	.111
	(.710)	(.093)*	(.504)	(.014)	(.264)	(.040)	(.158)
SANCTION	-.051	-.178	-.072	-.040	.061	.014	.076
	(.527)	(.025)	(.367)	(.618)	(.448)	(.864)	(.342)
INSTITUT	.171	-.176	-.109	-.010	.179	.064	.180
	(.054)	(.048)	(.219)	(.907)	(.043)	(.469)	(.193)

Note: Detailed results are shown for the sample of individuals. Although total sample size is 164, missing data reduced n for certain variables. Probabilities are shown in parentheses. Correlations significant at p<.05 are in **boldface**. For the company data set of 79 companies *p<.05.

The specific role of leverage in the results across hypotheses provides some support for both agency and institutional predictions. The proportion of outside directors does increase with increases in the percentage of total debt, consistent with agency theory. However, it appears that the composition of the board may be largely symbolic. The negative or non-significant findings for the two measures of leverage and both the measures of audit committee effectiveness and internal institutional support suggest that outside directors do not translate into an effective monitoring mechanism for debtholders.

Discussion and Implications

This study compared and contrasted agency theory and institutional theory in an attempt to better understand the effectiveness of audit committees. The study focused on effectiveness because of the possibility that the formation of an audit committee itself does not achieve expected control for a corporation.

The results of the present research reveal that economic variables, such as those embraced by agency theory, fail to provide an explanation for the implied consequence of audit committee formation. It is not safe to assume that all committees naturally possess a certain degree of effectiveness. The present research posits that agency variables, at least as currently conceived in the literature, cannot differentiate qualitative *degrees* of corporate control.

This study extends previous studies on audit committees by broadening the theoretical and empirical approaches to understanding actual effectiveness of monitoring. In addition

to challenging the suggestion that economic rationality dictates levels of corporate control, the institutional variables pertaining to the power environment constitute a fertile area to find the medium through which core operating processes lead to this organizational result. The findings of this study, and those of both Spangler and Braiotta (1990) and Kalbers and Fogarty (1993), support the conclusion that audit committee effectiveness emanates from sources close to the actual functioning of the committee. The formal empowerment of the audit committee appears to be designed for the consumption of external parties with some interest in the adherence to adequate forms of corporate control.

The empirical findings of some significant correlations between agency variables and internal institutional forms of power also yield the potential for combining agency and institutional premises to better explain activities within organizations. The true relevance of corporate structures that establish and maintain audit committees is the linkages that they forge with the power exerted by the individuals that serve monitoring functions within organizations. However, precise enumeration of the effect of outside factors on internal activities is still lacking in both theoretical approaches.

The results of this study indicate that the presumption that corporate control can be bureaucratically accomplished through the adoption of the correct forms is not viable. More broadly, this study calls into question the various analyses of controls that assume economic rationality. The results suggest that firms that have higher agency costs, and therefore greater incentive to communicate high levels of corporate control, do not necessarily have better audit committees, as judged by knowledgeable parties. Economic rationality may provide a more satisfactory explanation of the process of adoption and diffusion of certain mechanisms of corporate governance and control. This study signifies the need to elaborate the conditions under which such processes do or do not take place.

This study suggests that changes in the structure of corporate governance may be primarily symbolic. Policy makers should be aware that the mandatory creation of entities such as audit committees is only a first step toward the enhancement of the control environment. Laws or guidelines for future changes should consider substantive results of such changes in a more qualitative fashion. Rather than use specific laws and guidelines for implementation, policy makers should address more directly the desired outcomes of corporate control. The academic community could contribute by conducting research on the psychometric qualities of the measurements that this would entail.

This study also indicates the need for further research of audit committees and other control and monitoring devices in corporations using both agency theory and institutional theory. Although agency cost variables may suggest conditions for increased demand for monitoring, the results of this study demonstrate that demand does not directly translate into effective corporate monitoring. It may be that alternative control and monitoring mechanisms exist in corporate structures and demands for monitoring may vary among constituents. Additional specification and tests are necessary in agency theory to identify such relationships. More re-

finement or expansion of both agency cost variables and organizational variables could provide a better single explanation of the conditions under which particular controls would be instituted effectively. In this regard, it appears that publicly available information may be of limited use in understanding actions that exist at the core of corporate governance. Research that is limited to these sources may provide unsatisfactory closure on the key issues.

The managerial implications of this work present a broad challenge to those interested in corporate governance. The results strongly suggest the corporations will not naturally invest in a level of board oversight that provides the appropriate degree of protection to constituents. For these purposes, factors such as the distribution of ownership, the preponderance of debt and company size do not serve as useful predictors for the substantive level of monitoring attained. In sum, corporate governance cannot be left to rational economic incentives. Furthermore, effective oversight cannot be predicated on the background characteristics of those entrusted with it. Only in a limited sense can the activity level of audit committees be taken as a reliable indicator of effectiveness.

The inability for us to accept such appearances at their face value testifies to the deep incentives that exist in creating the facade of effectiveness in corporate governance. We need to go beyond these first appearances. We recommend examining power as a means to do this. The results suggest that economic variables create a climate for power distributions which, in turn, translate into effectiveness. Since this is likely to be more highly idiosyncratic, those interested in effective governance must realize that it cannot be done by mandate or fiat. Instead, the structures that will deliver a check upon management must be consistently embedded within the culture of the organization. To be otherwise, will force a departure of form and substance.

References

Abbott, A. 1988. *The System of Professions.* Chicago, IL: University of Chicago Press.

Akerlof, G.A. 1970. "The Market for "Lemons": Quality Uncertainty and the Market Mechanism." *Quarterly Journal of Economics* (August): 488-500.

Alchian, A. A. and H. Demsetz. 1972. "Production, Information Costs, and Economic Organization." *American Economic Review* 62(5): 777-795.

Anderson, D., J.R. Francis, and D.J. Stokes. 1993. "Auditing, Directorships and the Demand for Monitoring." *Journal of Accounting and Public Policy* 12: 353-375.

Bachar, J. 1989. "Auditing Quality, Signaling, and Underwriting Contracts." *Contemporary Accounting Research* Fall: 216-241.

Bar-Yosef, S. and J. Livnat. 1984. "Auditor Selection: An Incentive Signalling Approach." *Accounting and Business Research* Autumn: 301-309.

Baysinger, B.D. and H.N. Butler. 1985. "Corporate Governance and the Board of Directors: Performance Effects of Changes in Board Composition." *Journal of Law, Economics and Organization* 1(1): -124.

Baysinger, B. and R. E. Hoskisson. 1990. "The Composition of Boards of Directors and Strategic Control: Effects on Corporate Strategy." *Academy of Management Journal* 15(1): 72-87.

Beasley, M.S. 1996. "An Empirical Analysis of the Relation Between the Board of Director Composition and Financial Statement Fraud." *The Accounting Review* 71(4): 443-465.

Berle, A. A., and G. C. Means. 1932. *The Modern Corporation and Private Property.* New York, NY: Macmillan Publishing Co.

Birkett, B. S. 1986. "The Recent History of Corporate Audit Committees." *The Accounting Historians Journal* 13(Fall): 109-124.

Bradbury, M. E. 1990. "The Incentives for Voluntary Audit Committee Formation." *Journal of Accounting and Public Policy* 9: 19-36.

Braiotta, L. 1994. *The Audit Committee Handbook.* New York, NY: John Wiley & Sons, Inc.

Chow, C. W. 1982. "The Demand for External Auditing: Size, Debt and Ownership Influences." *The Accounting Review* 57(2): 72-291.

Committee of Sponsoring Organizations of the Treadway Commission. September 1992. *Internal Control—Integrated Framework.* New York, NY: Committee of Sponsoring Organizations of the Treadway Commission.

Covaleski, M. and M. Dirsmith. 1988. "An Institutional Perspective on the Rise, Social Transformation, and Fall of a University Budget Category." *Administrative Science Quarterly* 33(4): 562-587.

_____ and _____. 1991. "The Management of Legitimacy and Power in Public Sector Administration." *Journal of Accounting and Public Policy* 10(2): 135-156.

_____, _____, and J. Michelman. 1993. "An Institutional Theory Perspective on the DRG Framework, Case-Mix Accounting Systems and Health-Care Organizations." *Accounting, Organizations and Society* 18(1): 65-80.

DeAngelo, L. 1981. "Auditor Size and Audit Quality." *Journal of Accounting and Economics* 3(3): 183-189.

Dhaliwal, D., G. Salamon, and E. Smith. 1982. "The Effect of Owner Versus Management Control on the Choice of Accounting Methods." *Journal of Accounting and Economics* 4(2): 41-53.

DiMaggio, P. 1991. "Constructing an Organizational Field as a Professional Project: U.S. Art Museums 1920-1940." In *The New Institutionalism in Organizational Action*. Eds. W. Powell and P. DiMaggio. Chicago, IL: University of Chicago Press.

_____ and W. Powell. 1983. "The Iron Cage Revisited: Institutional Isomorphism and Collective Rationality in Organizational Fields." *American Sociological Review* 48(April): 147-160.

_____ and _____. 1991. Introduction. In *The New Institutionalism in Organizational Action*. Eds. W. Powell and P. DiMaggio. Chicago, IL: University of Chicago Press.

Dobbin, F., L. Edelman, J. Meyer, J. Scott, and A. Swidler. 1988. "The Expansion of Due Process in Organizations." In *Institutional Patterns and Organizations: Culture and Environment*. Ed. L.G. Zucker. Cambridge, MA: Ballinger.

Dye, R. A. 1991. "Informationally Motivated Auditor Replacement." *Journal of Accounting and Economics* 14(2): 347-374. Eichenseher, J. W. and D. Shields. 1985. "Corporate Director Liability and Monitoring Preferences." *Journal of Accounting and Public Policy* 4(1): 13-31.

Esland, G. 1980. "Professions and Professionalism." In *The Politics of Work and Occupations*. Eds. G. Esland and G. Salaman. Keyes, U.K: Open University Press.

Fama, E. F. 1980. "Agency Problems and the Theory of the Firm." *Journal of Political Economy* 88(2): 288-307.

_____ and M. C. Jensen. 1983. "Separation of Ownership and Control." *Journal of Law and Economics* 26(June): 301-325.

Francis, J. and E. Wilson 1988. "Auditor Changes: A Joint Test of Theories Relating to Agency Costs and Auditor Differentiation." *The Accounting Review* 63(4): 663-682.

Friedland, R. and R. Alford. 1991. "Bringing Society Back In: Symbols, Practices, and Institutional Contradictions." In *The New Institutionalism in Organizational Action*. Eds. W. Powell and P. DiMaggio. Chicago, IL: University of Chicago Press.

Galashiewiez, J. 1991. "Making Corporate Actors Accountable Institution-Building in Minneapolis-St. Paul." In *The New Institutionalism in Organizational Action*. Eds. W. Powell and P. DiMaggio. Chicago, IL: University of Chicago Press.

Harrison, J. R. 1987. "The Strategic Use of Corporate Board Committees." *California Management Review* 30(1): 109-125.

Jensen, M. C. and W. H. Meckling. 1976. "Theory of the Firm: Managerial Behavior, Agency Costs and Ownership Structure." *Journal of Financial Economics* 3(4): 305-360.

Jensen, M.C. 1993. "The Modern Industrial Revolution, Exit, and the Failure of Internal Control Systems." *The Journal of Finance* 48(July): 831-880.

Jepperson, R. 1991. "Institutions, Institutional Effects and Institutionalism." In *The New Institutionalism in Organizational Action*. Eds. W. Powell and P. DiMaggio. Chicago, IL: University of Chicago Press.

Kalbers, L.P. and T.J. Fogarty. 1993. "Audit Committee Effectiveness: An Empirical Investigation of the Contribution of Power." *Auditing: A Journal of Practice & Theory*, 12(1): 24-48.

King, J., V. Gurbaxani, K. Kraemer, F. McFarlan, K. Raman, and C. Yap. 1994. "Institutional Factors in Information Technology Innovation." *Information Systems Research* 5(2): 139-169.

Maher, M. W. 1981. "The Impact of Regulation on Controls: Firms' Response to the Foreign Corrupt Practices Act." *The Accounting Review* 56(4): 751-770.

Mautz, R. K. and F. L. Neumann. 1970. *Corporate Audit Committees*. Urbana, IL: University of Illinois.

Mautz, R. K. and F. L. Neumann. 1977. *Corporate Audit Committees, Policies and Practices*. Cleveland, OH: Ernst & Ernst.

Menon, K. and D. D. Williams. 1991. "Auditor Credibility and Initial Public Offerings." *The Accounting Review* 66(2): 313-332.

_____ and _____, 1994. "The Use of Audit Committees for Monitoring." *Journal of Accounting and Public Policy* 13(1): 121-139.

Meyer, J.W. and B. Rowan. 1977. "Institutional Organizations: Formal Structure as Myth and Ceremony." *American Journal of Sociology* 82 (September): 340-363.

Mezias, S. J. 1990. "An Institutional Model of Organizational Practice: Financial Reporting at the Fortune 200." *Administrative Science Quarterly* 35(4): 431-457.

Molz, R. 1988. "Managerial Domination of Boards of Directors and Financial Performance." *Journal of Business Research* 16(2): 235-249.

Morck, R., A. Shleifer, and R. Vishny. 1988. "Management Ownership and Market Valuation: An Empirical Analysis." *Journal of Financial Economics* (January/March): 293-315.

National Commission on Fraudulent Financial Reporting. October 1987. *Report of the National Commission on Fraudulent Financial Reporting*. New York, NY: American Institute of Certified Public Accountants.

Neu, D. 1992. "The Social Construction of Positive Choices." *Accounting, Organizations and Society* 17(3/4): 223-237.

Niehaus, G. R. 1989. "Ownership Structure and Inventory Method Choice." *The Accounting Review* 64(2): 269-284.

Oliver, C. 1990. "Determinants of Interorganizational Relationships: Integration and Future Developments." *Academy of Management Review* 15(2): 241-265.

Orton, J. D. and K. E. Weick. 1990. "Loosely Coupled Systems: A Reconceptualization." *The Academy of Management Review* 15(1): 203-223.

Patton, A. and J. Baker. 1987. "Why Do Not Directors Rock the Boat?" *Harvard Business Review* 65 (November): 10-12.

Perrow, C. 1985. "Overboard with Myth and Symbols." *American Journal of Sociology,* 90(1): 151-153.

Pfeffer, J. 1972. "Size and Composition of Corporate Boards of Directors: The Organization and Its Environment." *Administrative Science Quarterly* 17(2): 218-228.

Pincus, K., M. Rusbarsky, and J. Wong. 1989. "Voluntary Formation of Corporate Audit Committees Among NASDAQ Firms." *Journal of Accounting and Public Policy* 8(2): 239-265.

Powell, W. 1991. "Expanding the Scope of Institutional Analysis." In *The New Institutionalism in Organizational Action.* Eds. W. Powell and P. DiMaggio. Chicago, IL: University of Chicago Press.

Ritti, R. R. and J. H. Silver. 1986. "Early Processes of Institutionalizations: The Dramaturgy of Exchange in Interorganizational Relations." *Administrative Science Quarterly* 31 (March): 25-42.

Scott, W. R .1987. "The Adolescence of Institutional Theory." *Administrative Science Quarterly* 32 (December): 493-511.

Singh, J., D. Tucker, and A. Meinhard. 1991. In *The New Institutionalism in Organizational Action.* Eds. W. Powell and P. DiMaggio. Chicago, IL: University of Chicago Press.

Smith, C. W. and J. B. Warner. 1979. "On Financial Contracting: An Analysis of Bond Covenants." *Journal of Financial Economics* (June): 117-161.

Spangler, W. D. and L. Braiotta, Jr.1990. "Leadership and Corporate Audit Committee Effectiveness." *Group and Organizational Studies* (June): 134-157.

Thompson, J. D. 1967. *Organizations in Action.* New York, NY: McGraw-Hill.

Tolbert, P. and L. Zucker. 1983. "Institutional Sources of Change in the Formal Structure of Organizations: the Diffusion of Civil Service Reform." *Administrative Science Quarterly.* 28(March): 22-39.

Treadway Commission (see National Commission on Fraudulent Financial Reporting).

Value Line Investment Survey. 1988. *Value Line Investment Survey.* New York, NY: Value Line, Inc.

Verschoor, C.C. 1989a. "Measuring Audit Committee Effectiveness in the Defense Industry." *Internal Auditing* 4(3): 13-25.

_____. 1989b. "A Case Study of Audit Committee Effectiveness at Sunstrand." *Internal Auditing* 4(4): 11-19.

_____. 1990. "MiniScribe: A New Example of Audit Committee Ineffectiveness." *Internal Auditing* 5(4): 13-19.

Vicknair, D., K. Hickman, and K.C. Carnes. 1993. "A Note on Audit Committee Independence: Evidence from the NYSE on "Grey" Directors." *Accounting Horizons* 7(1): 53-57.

Wallace, W. 1980. *The Economic Role of the Audit in Free and Regulated Markets.* Sarasota, FL: American Accounting Association.

Watts, R. and J. Zimmerman. 1986. *Positive Accounting Theory.* Englewood Cliffs, NJ: Prentice-Hall.

_____ and _____. 1990. "Positive Accounting Theory: A Ten Year Perspective." *The Accounting Review* 65(1): 131-156.

Wechsler, D. 1989. "Giving the Watchdog Fangs to Deal With Management and Outside Auditors." *Forbes* 144 (November): 130.

150   Kalbers and Fogarty

Weick, K. 1976. "Educational Organizations as Loosely Couple Systems." *Administrative Science Quarterly* 21(1): 1-19.

Weisbach, M. S. 1988. "Outside Directors and CEO Turnover." *Journal of Financial Economics* 20: 431-460.

Zucker, L. G. 1988. "Where Do Institutional Patterns Come From? Organizations as Actors in Social Systems." In *Institutional Patterns and Organizations: Culture and Environment.* Ed. L. G. Zucker. Cambridge, MA: Ballinger.

Corresponding author: Timithy J. Fogarty (216-368-3938)

[21]

THE ACCOUNTING REVIEW
Vol. 77, No. 2
April 2002
pp. 435–452

Economic Determinants of Audit Committee Independence

April Klein
New York University

ABSTRACT: This paper provides empirical evidence that audit committee independence is associated with economic factors. I find that audit committee independence increases with board size and board independence and decreases with the firm's growth opportunities and for firms that report consecutive losses. In contrast, no relation is found between audit committee independence and creditors' demand for accounting information. Although the analyses are based on data from 1991 to 1993, these results have implications for NYSE and NASDAQ listing requirements for audit committees adopted in December 1999. Specifically, the new requirements give firms the option of including non-outside directors on their audit committees if it is in the best interests of the firm to do so.

Keywords: audit committee; outside directors; corporate governance; board of directors.

Data Availability: Data used for this study are derived from a proprietary database.

Just as "one size doesn't fit all" when it comes to board governance, "one size can't fit all" audit committees. Within broad parameters, each audit committee should evolve and develop its own guidelines suited to itself and its corporation.
—New York Stock Exchange and National Association of Securities Dealers (1999)

I. INTRODUCTION

In December 1999, in response to the SEC's call for improving the effectiveness of corporate audit committees in overseeing the financial-reporting process (Levitt 1998), the NYSE and NASDAQ modified their listing requirements for large U.S. companies. Under the new standards, firms must maintain audit committees with at least three directors, "all of whom have no relationship to the company that may interfere with the exercise of their independence from management and the company" (*NYSE Listed Company Manual*

Financial support is provided by a summer grant from the Stern School of Business. I thank Ashiq Ali, Eli Bartov, Stephen Bryan, Eric Koh, Baruch Lev, James Ohlson, Jeffrey Simonoff, the editor (Michael Bamber), two anonymous referees, and the NYU Accounting and Statistics Departments for their constructive comments.

Submitted April 2000
Accepted November 2001

§303.01[B][2][a]). Although this statement implies that firms must maintain audit committees with outside members only, listing requirements provide for the appointment of certain affiliated directors if the board determines it is in the best interests of the corporation for these individuals to serve on its audit committee (see NYSE Rule §303.01[B][3][b] and NASDAQ Rule 4310[c][26][B][ii]). Thus, firms have some flexibility in determining audit committee composition.

Because enforcement standards are constantly evolving, one question of interest is to what degree the SEC and the exchanges should allow firms to exercise this option. I provide insights into this question by examining economic determinants behind differences in audit committee independence for a sample of more than 400 large U.S. firms that were publicly traded during most of 1991–1993. During this time, exchange rules allowed more flexibility with respect to audit committee independence and many firms opted for audit committees with less than 100 percent outside directors (Vicknair et al. 1993; Verschoor 1993; Klein 1998, 2001; Parker 2000).

I develop predictions and test determinants of audit committee independence. I expect and find that the percentage of outside directors on the audit committee is limited by board size and overall board independence. Firms incur costs in expanding the board to include more outside directors (e.g., Yermack 1996) and in enlisting outside directors instead of inside directors who have firm-specific knowledge (e.g., Fama and Jensen 1983; Klein 1998). Thus, audit committee independence is costly to the firm.

I expect the demands for audit committee independence to emanate from management, shareholders, and creditors. Consistent with my expectation that managers' demand for directors with inside expertise increases in proportion to the complexities and uncertainties associated with growth opportunities (Williamson 1975), I find that audit committee independence decreases with the firm's growth opportunities. Consistent with the hypothesis that shareholders' demand for accurate, unbiased financial accounting data depends on the published financial accounting data's potential informativeness for equity valuation, I find that firms that have experienced two or more consecutive losses (which typically are less value-relevant than positive profits) have less independent audit committees. However, I find no evidence that audit committee independence is associated with the degree of debt in the firm's capital structure. This result is inconsistent with the expectation that creditors' demand for unbiased accounting data for use in debt covenants increases with debt.[1]

One implication of these findings is that firms tailor audit committee composition to suit their specific economic environments. This suggests that the SEC and the stock exchanges may wish to continue to allow firms some flexibility to include non-outside directors on their audit committees.

II. THE AUDIT COMMITTEE
The Audit Committee's Role as Monitor of the Firm's Financial-Reporting Process

By state law, boards of directors may conduct their work through the full board or delegate their authority to standing committees responsible to the board—for example, Delaware General Corporate Law §141(c) allows boards to set up committees. One such committee is the audit committee.

The audit committee provides, on behalf of the board of directors, oversight responsibility for the firm's financial-reporting process. According to the *Blue Ribbon Committee*

---

[1] Creditors also use accounting numbers to assess firm value in liquidation (as in the abandonment option). See, for example, Barth et al. (1998).

Report, the audit committee is the "the ultimate monitor" of the financial accounting reporting system (NYSE and NASD 1999, 7). The audit committee selects the outside auditor and meets separately with senior financial management and with the external auditor. The committee also questions management, internal auditors, and external auditors to determine whether they are acting in the firm's best interests.[2]

Consistent with the *Blue Ribbon Committee Report* and with prior studies (e.g., Carcello and Neal 2000), I assume that audit committee members who are independent of management are better monitors of the firm's financial accounting process.[3] Benefits of effective monitoring include transparent financial statements, active trading markets, and the ability to use unbiased financial accounting numbers as inputs into contracts among shareholders, senior claimants, and management.

NYSE and NASDAQ Audit Committee Requirements

Before December 1999, stock exchanges' and NASDAQ's rules for audit committee composition were vague at best. They required or encouraged large, U.S.-listed companies to maintain audit committees with all or a majority of their members independent of management. However, the listing requirements did not define "independence."[4]

In December 1999, the NYSE and NASDAQ modified their audit committee requirements, based on their *Report and Recommendations of the Blue Ribbon Committee on Improving the Effectiveness of Corporate Audit Committees,* which they had issued in the previous February. Simultaneously, the SEC adopted new rules to improve disclosures related to audit committees (see SEC Release No. 34-42266, *Adopting Rules Regarding Disclosure by Audit Committees, Including Discussions with Auditors Regarding Financial Statements*). All large, U.S.-listed companies must now maintain audit committees with at least three independent directors.[5] Both exchanges disallow directors from serving on the audit committee if they are current employees, have been employees within the last three years, have cross-compensation committee links, or are immediate family members of an executive officer. In addition, the NASDAQ bars from the audit committee directors who accept more than $60,000 in non-director compensation from the firm, or whose employers received at least $200,000 from the firm in any of the three past years.

However, both the NYSE and NASDAQ allow the firm to appoint to the audit committee directors who have business relationships with the firm if the board determines that the individual's membership on the committee is in the corporation's best interests. NASDAQ Rule 4310(c)(26)(B)(ii) allows the board under "limited circumstances" to appoint one former employee or family member to the audit committee if the board determines this is in the best interest of the corporation and its shareholders. NYSE §303.01(B)(3)(b) gives the board greater discretion. If the board determines that the business relationship does not

---

[2] For example, see *Audit Committee Effectiveness—What Works Best,* a guide for audit committees written by PricewaterhouseCoopers (2000), under the aegis of the Institute of Internal Auditors Research Foundation.

[3] Fama and Jensen (1983) and Fama (1980) also argue that outside directors have incentives to effectively monitor top management.

[4] Advocacy of independent audit committees has a long tradition. In 1940, the SEC first recommended that firms establish audit committees with only nonofficer board members (Accounting Series Release No. 19). In October 1987, the Treadway Commission advocated that audit committees include only independent directors (National Commission on Fraudulent Financial Reporting 1987).

[5] See *NYSE Listed Company Manual,* New York Stock Exchange, §303.01(B)(2)(a), and *The NASDAQ Stock Market Listing Requirements,* National Association of Securities Dealers, §4310(c)(26)(B). See also SEC Release Nos. 34-42231, 34-42232, and 34-42233, *Adopting Changes to Listing Requirements for the NASD, AMEX, and NYSE Regarding Audit Committees.*

438 The Accounting Review, April 2002

compromise the individual's independence, then that director may serve on the board's audit committee. Thus, despite recent changes in exchange requirements, audit committee independence is still an open issue.

III. DETERMINANTS OF AUDIT COMMITTEE INDEPENDENCE
Board Size and Board Independence

I develop hypotheses relating audit committee independence to the supply of available outside directors. Because the audit committee is a subset of the full board, its composition depends on the board's overall structure.

Lipton and Lorsch (1992), Jensen (1993), and Yermack (1996) argue that the board's decision-making quality decreases with board size because the more people in the group, the lower the group's coordination and processing skills (see Steiner 1972; Hackman 1990). Yermack (1996) finds evidence consistent with this argument. Specifically, Tobin's Qs, several accounting profitability ratios, and CEO turnover rates are negatively related to board size.

If the firm limits board size, then the number of directors available to serve on the audit committee also will be limited. The typical board has between three and six board committees to staff, with each committee having at least two members (Klein 1998). Two committees, the executive compensation committee and the nominating committee, require independent directors to ensure monitoring. Thus, a smaller board may have to choose one or more nonindependent directors to serve on the audit committee to meet overall committee staffing needs.

Stated in the alternative form:

H1: Audit committee independence is positively related to the number of directors sitting on the entire board.

The larger the pool of outside directors on the board, the easier it is for the board to have an independent audit committee. However, boards require both outside and non-outside directors to fulfill their duties. Outside directors serve as monitors and help alleviate agency conflicts between shareholders and upper management. Inside and affiliated directors have the specialized expertise about the firm's activities to evaluate and ratify its future strategic plans (Williamson 1975; Fama and Jensen 1983). Consistent with this argument, Klein (1998) finds that the percentage of inside directors on board investment or finance committees is positively associated with firm value. Thus, board independence reflects the trade-off between director independence and director expertise, which, in turn, reflects the balancing of the firm's monitoring needs and its requirements for specialized information.

If board independence varies across firms, then, in the alternative form:

H2: Audit committee independence is positively related to board independence.

The Demands for Audit Committee Independence
Growth Opportunities

Williamson (1975) and Fama and Jensen (1983) argue that a firm structures its board in response to its needs to obtain unbiased, expert information. Both papers assert that a board's demand for knowledgeable directors increases with the firms' complexity and uncertainties. Inside directors have direct knowledge about their firm's operations and investment horizons. Affiliated directors or their companies have ties with the firm and often provide expertise to the firm about suppliers, customers, financial opportunities, or legal issues. Because of the complexities and uncertainties associated with growth opportunities, I expect high-growth opportunity firms' managers and shareholders to demand less independent boards, resulting in less independent audit committees.

In the alternative form:

H3: Audit committee independence is negatively related to the firm's expected growth in earnings or cash flows.

Consecutive Losses

Hayn (1995), Lipe et al. (1998), Amir et al. (1999), and Collins et al. (1999) show that the cross-sectional returns (or price) earnings relation is much weaker for firms reporting losses than for firms reporting profits. In addition, Hayn (1995) reports negative coefficients on the regression of returns on earnings, with R^2 values near 0.0 percent, for her sample of firms posting losses over two or more consecutive years. These studies suggest that financial statements on the whole are less value-relevant for firms suffering repeated losses than for profitable firms. Thus, I expect shareholders of firms with past consecutive losses to demand less scrutiny of the financial-reporting system and, consequently, to have a lower demand for audit committee independence.

In the alternative form:

H4: Audit committee independence is lower for firms reporting a series of consecutive, past losses.

Creditors

Creditors write debt contracts that contain accounting-based covenants to monitor management and shareholders (Jensen and Meckling 1976; Smith and Warner 1979; Leftwich 1983; Watts and Zimmerman 1990). However, managers sometimes manipulate earnings to delay or avoid debt covenant violations. For example, DeFond and Jiambalvo (1994) conclude that managers overstate earnings in the year before debt covenant violations. Thus, creditors' demand for audit committee independence should increase with the firm's debt-to-assets ratio due to their increased demands for monitoring the integrity of the firms' financial accounting reports.

In the alternative form:

H5: Audit committee independence is positively related to the firm's debt-to-assets ratio.

CEO on Compensation Committee

Although exchange and NASDAQ regulations restrict the CEO from serving on the board's audit committee, no regulations prohibit the CEO from sitting on the board's executive compensation committee. I make no prediction, *ex ante*, about the sign of the relation between the CEO serving on the compensation committee and audit committee independence. On the one hand, a board that allows its CEO to sit on its executive compensation committee may be CEO-friendly, thus providing less monitoring of the firm's financial accounting reporting process. For example, Klein (2001) finds that earnings management is higher in firms where the CEO serves on the board's compensation committee. On the other hand, shareholders may want to curb the CEO's ability to distort financial statements by demanding greater audit committee independence. Thus, Hypothesis 6 is nondirectional:

H6: Audit committee independence is different if the CEO sits on the board's executive compensation committee than if the CEO does not.

Substitute Monitoring Mechanisms

Nonmanagement blockholders (or their representatives) sometime serve on the audit committee, giving them the opportunity to monitor the firm's financial-reporting process. Klein (1998, 2001) finds that firms with large, non-inside stockholders on audit committees are more productive and exhibit less earnings management. If large, nonmanagement block-holders on the audit committee actively monitor the financial-reporting process, then there is less need for outside directors on the audit committee.

In the alternative form:

H7: Audit committee independence is lower if a large, non-inside shareholder sits on the board's audit committee.

Jensen and Meckling (1976) argue that directors' shareholdings act as a monitoring device. If outside director shareholdings substitute for outsiders on the audit committee, then in the alternative form:

H8: Audit committee independence is negatively related to the percentage of shares held by outside directors.

Firm Size

I also control for firm size. Larger firms have stronger internal controls systems than smaller firms (O'Reilly et al. 1998). If the firms' internal controls act as in-house monitoring mechanisms, then larger firms require less alternative monitoring of their reporting systems and therefore need lower levels of audit committee independence. Alternatively, if shareholders are more apt to sue larger firms for misstated or fraudulent financial statements, then larger firms may try to inoculate themselves against lawsuits by adopting stronger monitoring mechanisms, such as greater audit committee independence. Thus, the association between firm size and audit committee independence is indeterminate.

IV. RESEARCH DESIGN

Sample Selection

I hand-collected data about boards and board audit committees from SEC-filed proxy statements. Initially, I include all U.S. firms listed on the S&P 500 as of March 31, 1992 and 1993, with annual shareholder meetings between July 1, 1991, and June 30, 1993. I exclude 65 bank and financial institution firm-years and 38 insurance company firm-years. I also delete three firm-years with missing audit committee composition data, and 58 firm-years with missing Compustat or CRSP data. The final sample has 803 firm-year observations.

Schedule 14A (the proxy statement) requires firms to disclose each director's name, current directorships; family relationships between each and any director, nominee or executive officer; significant current or proposed transactions with management; significant business relationships with the firm, current firm shareholdings, and business experience during the last five years.[6] Schedule 14A (Item 7[e][1]) requires firms to state whether they

---

[6] Items 404(a) and 404(b) of Regulation S-K of the 1934 Securities and Exchange Act define significant business transactions. Item 404(a) specifies a threshold of $60,000 for a transaction to be considered significant. Item 404(b) defines "certain business relationships" to include significant payments to the firm in return for services or property, significant indebtedness by the firm, outside legal counseling, investment banking, consulting fees, and other joint ventures.

have standing audit, compensation, or nominating board committees. If such committees exist, then firms must disclose their functions and responsibilities, their members, and the number of times each committee met during the last fiscal year.

I define *outside directors* as having no affiliation with the firm other than serving as directors. Consistent with NYSE and NASD (1999) and with exchange definitions, *affiliated directors* include former employees, relatives of the CEO, those with significant transactions or business relationships with the firm as defined by Items 404(a) and (b) of Regulation S-K, and those on interlocking boards. *Inside directors* are current employees.

Regression Model

I measure the associations between audit committee independence and the explanatory variables by estimating the following regression:

$$\%\text{Audout} = \alpha + \beta_1\text{Board Size} + \beta_2\%\text{Outsiders} + \beta_3\text{Growth Opportunities}$$
$$+ \beta_4\text{Losses} + \beta_5\text{Debt-to-Assets} + \beta_6\text{CEO on Compensation Committee}$$
$$+ \beta_7 5\%\text{Blockholder on Audit Committee} + \beta_8\%\text{Outside Director Holdings}$$
$$+ \beta_9\text{Firm Size} + \mu.$$

%Audout is the logistical transformation of the percentage of outsiders on the audit committee.[7] Board Size is the natural log of the number of board members (Yermack 1996) and %Outsiders is the logistical transformation of the percent of outside directors on the board.[8] I obtain data for these three variables from the shareholders' meeting proxy statement. Following Smith and Watts (1992), I define Growth Opportunities as the three-year market value of equity plus the book value of liabilities divided by the three-year book value of assets, all ending on the fiscal year prior to the shareholders' meeting.[9] This metric captures the proportion of firm value represented by growth opportunities relative to assets in place. Losses equals 1 if the firm reported losses for each of the two years prior to the firm's shareholders' meeting (Compustat item 18 is negative for fiscal years t and t−1), and 0 otherwise. Losses captures the diminished value-relevance of financial reporting for firms experiencing extended periods of losses. Debt-to-Assets is the three-year long-term debt-to-assets ratio at the end of the fiscal year prior to the shareholders' meeting (three-year Compustat item 9 divided by three-year item 6). CEO on Compensation Committee is a dichotomous variable set to 1 if the CEO sits on the board's compensation committee, and 0 otherwise. 5%Blockholder on Audit Committee is a dichotomous variable set to 1 if a nonmanagement director holding at least 5 percent of the firm's shares sits on the board's audit committee, and 0 otherwise.[10] %Outside Director Holdings is the percentage of shares held by outside directors. The latter two items are in the firm's proxy statement. Firm Size is the natural log of the firm's assets (Compustat item 6) at the end of the fiscal year prior to the shareholders' meeting.

---

[7] The logistical transformation is ln(%Audout/(1−%Audout)+1). I use this transformation because the values of %Audout are confined to the interval from 0 to 1, whereas the logistically transformed values extend from −∞ to +∞. Thus, an intrinsically non-normal distribution is transformed into a more normal distribution.

[8] I use the latter transformation to be internally consistent with the transformed %Audout variable. Results based on untransformed values as well as the natural log of %Outsiders are qualitatively the same as those reported in the text and are not shown separately.

[9] The numerator is Compustat items (6 − 60 + (24 × 25)) summed over fiscal years t, t − 1, and t − 2. The denominator is Compustat item 6 summed over fiscal years t, t − 1, and t − 2.

[10] I would like to thank Lee-Seok Hwang for these data.

V. EMPIRICAL RESULTS

Descriptive Statistics

Table 1 reports data on board and audit committee composition. Consistent with other board composition studies or surveys, 58.4 percent of the board is outsiders, less than one quarter (22.5 percent) is insiders, and the rest (19.1 percent) are affiliated directors.[11] In contrast, the audit committee includes a preponderance of outsiders (79.6 percent) and few insiders (1.4 percent), but about the same percentage of affiliated directors (19.0 percent). Because of these affiliated directors, 43.4 percent of firms have audit committees with outside directors only, and 86.7 percent have a majority of independent directors.

Table 2 presents the mean, median, and 1st and 3rd quartiles of the untransformed variables used in the regression analysis. The interquartile range for board size is 10–14 members. The interquartile range for %Outsiders is 50.0 percent to 70.6 percent, consistent with Fama and Jensen's (1983) argument that boards should include some insiders and affiliated directors for their expertise.

Growth Opportunities and the Debt-to-Assets ratio have means of 1.40 and 0.27, respectively. 4.6 percent of firms report losses in two or more consecutive years; 9.1 percent of firms allow the CEO to sit on the executive compensation committee; and 5.7 percent

---

[11] Yermack (1996) reports 54 percent outsiders for his sample of 452 firms listed on the *Forbes* 500 between 1984 and 1991. Bhagat and Black (1999) report similar percentages of insiders for 957 large U.S. firms in 1991.

TABLE 1
Composition of Overall Boards of Directors and Audit Committees[a]

	(1) *Overall* *Boards of* *Directors*	*(2)* *Audit* *Committee*
Percentage of Directors Who Are:		
Insiders	22.5	1.4
Outsiders	58.4	79.6
Affiliates	19.1	19.0
Percentage of Firms that Have at Least One *Member Who Is:*		
Inside Director	99.7	4.8
CEO	99.0	1.9
Outside Director	99.0	97.9
Affiliated Director	85.5	54.3
Relative of CEO	11.3	4.3
Former Employee of Firm	51.5	12.3
Percentage of Firms that Have at Least *51% Outside Directors*	73.8	86.7
Percentage of Firms that Have 100% *Outside Directors*	0	43.4

[a] Sample is for 803 U.S. firm-years with audit committees listed on the S&P 500 as of March 31, 1992 and 1993 with annual shareholder meetings between July 1, 1991 and June 30, 1993. Banks, financial institutions, insurance companies, and firms with missing Compustat or CRSP data are excluded.

TABLE 2
Descriptive Statistics for Untransformed Variables Used in the Analysis of Audit Committee Independence for a Pooled Sample of 803 Firm-Years 1991–1993

Variable[a]	Hypothesis Number[b]	Mean	Median	1st Quartile	3rd[d] Quartile
%Audout		79.7%	80.0%	66.7%	99.0%
Board Size	1	12.0	12.0	10.0	14.0
%Outsiders	2	58.4%	60.0%	50.0%	70.6%
Growth Opportunities	3	1.40	1.29	1.11	1.61
%Losses	4	4.6%	0	0	0
Debt-to-Assets	5	0.27	0.27	0.16	0.36
CEO on Compensation Committee	6	9.1%	0	0	0
5% Blockholder on Audit Committee	7	5.7%	0	0	0
%Outside Director Holdings	8	1.58%	0.47%	0.15%	1.82%
Assets ($ million)	Control Variable	8,526	3,190	1,330	8,554

[a] Variable definitions:

　　　　　　　　　　%Audout = the percent of outside directors on the audit committee;
　　　　　　　　　Board Size = the number of board members;
　　　　　　　　　%Outsiders = the percent of outside directors on the board;
　　Growth Opportunities = the three-year market value of the total firm (Compustat items $(6 - 60 + (24 \times 25))$ divided by three-year assets-in-place (Compustat item 6) ending on the fiscal year prior to the shareholders' meeting;
　　　　　　　　　　%Losses = the percent of firms that reported losses (Compustat item 18) in each of the two years prior to the shareholders' meeting;
　　　　　　Debt-to-Assets = the three-year ratio of the book value of debt (Compustat item 9) divided by the book value of assets (Compustat item 6) ending on the fiscal year prior to the shareholders' meeting;
　CEO on Compensation Committee = 1 if the CEO sits on the board's compensation committee, and 0 otherwise;
5% Blockholder on Audit Committee = 1 if a non-inside director with at least 5 percent of the firm's shares sits on the audit committee, and 0 otherwise;
　　%Outside Director Holdings = the percentage of shares owned by all outside directors; and
　　　　　　　　　　　Assets = the firm's book value of assets (Compustat item 6).
[b] Hypothesis number refers to the hypotheses in Section III.

include a non-inside director/blockholder on the audit committee. Outside director shareholdings have an interquartile range of 0.15 percent to 1.82 percent, with a mean of 1.58 percent.

Correlations
　　Table 3 presents Pearson correlations between the transformed dependent and independent variables. Spearman correlations yield similar results. The following correlations support several hypotheses: %Audout is significantly positively correlated with Board Size

TABLE 3
Pearson Correlations (and p-values) among the Dependent and Explanatory Variables[a]

	%Audout	Board Size	%Outsiders	Growth Opportunities	Losses	Debt-to-Assets	CEO on Compensation Committee	5% Blockholder on Audit Committee	%Outside Director Holdings
Board Size	0.06 (0.10)								
%Outsiders	0.50 (0.01)	0.09 (0.01)							
Growth Opportunities	-0.12 (0.01)	-0.16 (0.01)	-0.21 (0.01)						
Losses	-0.03 (0.44)	-0.01 (0.81)	0.02 (0.51)	-0.11 (0.01)					
Debt-to-Assets	0.04 (0.24)	0.19 (0.01)	0.13 (0.01)	-0.30 (0.01)	0.08 (0.03)				
CEO on Compensation Committee	-0.17 (0.01)	-0.15 (0.01)	-0.25 (0.01)	0.20 (0.01)	-0.03 (0.42)	-0.15 (0.01)			
5% Blockholder on Audit Committee	-0.16 (0.01)	-0.01 (0.84)	-0.06 (0.08)	0.07 (0.06)	-0.03 (0.42)	-0.09 (0.02)	0.03 (0.34)		
%Outside Director Holdings	0.05 (0.20)	-0.01 (0.69)	0.09 (0.01)	0.06 (0.08)	0.03 (0.33)	0.02 (0.56)	-0.02 (0.55)	0.36 (0.01)	
Firm Size	0.03 (0.47)	0.54 (0.01)	0.12 (0.01)	-0.25 (0.01)	-0.05 (0.14)	0.31 (0.01)	-0.17 (0.01)	-0.08 (0.03)	-0.09 (0.02)

[a] Variable definitions:
%Audout = ln(%Audout/(1 − %Audout) + 1);
Board Size = the natural log of the number of board members; and
%Outsiders = ln(%Outsiders/(1 − %Outsiders) + 1).
See Table 2 for other variable definitions.

(H1) and %Outsiders (H2). %Audout is significantly negatively correlated with Growth Opportunities (H3), CEO on Compensation Committee (H6), and 5%Blockholder on Audit Committee (H7). In contrast, the correlations between audit committee independence and Losses (H4), Debt-to-Assets (H5), %Outside Director Holdings (H8), and Firm Size are insignificantly different from zero.

Table 3 also reveals that many explanatory variables are significantly correlated with each other. The formal hypothesis tests are based on multiple regression analysis.

Multiple Regression Results

The data encompass two consecutive years, with many firms represented in both years. OLS error terms will suffer from serial correlation, resulting in unbiased coefficients but understated standard errors. I use Froot's (1989) procedure to adjust the variance-covariance matrix for dependence among observations from the same firm.

Table 4 presents the empirical results. %Audout is significantly positively associated with Board Size ($p < 0.01$) and with %Outsiders ($p < 0.01$). These findings are consistent with H1 and H2, supporting the view that audit committee independence increases with the supply of available, outside directors.

%Audout is significantly negatively associated with Growth Opportunities ($p < 0.10$), Losses ($p < 0.05$), 5%Blockholder on Audit Committee ($p < 0.01$), and Firm Size ($p < 0.05$). These findings are consistent with H3, H4, and H7, with Firm Size serving as a control variable. The negative coefficient on Growth Opportunities supports the view that managers of growth firms require more board members with specific expertise about their firms. The negative coefficient on Losses is consistent with shareholders demanding lower audit committee independence when financial statements are less value relevant. The negative coefficients on 5%Blockholder on Audit Committee and on Firm Size suggest that large nonmanagement blockholders and strong internal controls substitute for audit committee independence. The coefficients on the debt-to-assets ratio (H5), CEO on Compensation Committee (H6), and Outside Director Holdings (H8) are insignificantly different from zero.

In summary, audit committee independence increases with the supply of available, independent directors and with the demand for monitoring, and decreases with the availability of substitute monitoring mechanisms. %Outsiders plays the biggest role in explaining audit committee independence. A simple regression of %Audout on %Outsiders yields an R^2 of 0.22, compared with the R^2 of 0.25 from the full multiple regression. Nonetheless, the other factors collectively play a significant incremental role in explaining the percentage of outsiders on the audit committee variation in audit committee independence; testing for the differential in R^2s yields an F-statistic of 5.07, significant at the 0.01 level.

Additional Tests
Are Growth Opportunities Primarily Capturing Hi-Tech Firms?

The variable, Growth Opportunities, may capture disproportionate numbers of firms in high-tech industries or with high research and development expenditures.[12] Reingold (1999) reports that according to Korn/Ferry and Spencer Stuart, high-tech companies such as Internet firms have fewer outsiders on their boards and smaller board sizes than do other types of companies.

---

[12] Contrary to this conjecture, Smith and Watts (1992) test and find that R&D expenditures cannot substitute for this measure of growth opportunities in their analyses. Lev and Zarowin (1999) also find no relation between R&D expenditures and future growth.

TABLE 4
**Explanators of Audit Committee Independence Based on Time-Series Adjusted Regressions[a]
for a Pooled Sample of 803 Firm-Years 1991–1993**

$$\%Audout = \alpha + \beta_1 Board\ Size + \beta_2 \%Outsiders + \beta_3 Growth\ Opportunities$$
$$+ \beta_4 Losses + \beta_5 Debt\text{-}to\text{-}Assets + \beta_6 CEO\ on\ Compensation\ Committee$$
$$+ \beta_7 5\% Blockholder\ on\ Audit\ Committee + \beta_8 \%Outside\ Director\ Holdings$$
$$+ \beta_9 \%Firm\ Size^b$$

Independent Variables	Predicted Sign	Hypothesis Number	Coefficients and (t-statistics)
Intercept			0.39 (0.56)
Board Size	+	1	0.78 (2.62)***
%Outsiders	+	2	1.89 (13.50)***
Growth Opportunities	−	3	−0.06 (−1.86)*
Losses	−	4	−0.55 (−2.32)**
Debt-to-Assets	+	5	−0.26 (−0.59)
CEO on Compensation Committee	+/−	6	−0.25 (−1.39)
5% Blockholder on Audit Committee	−	7	−0.97 (−3.80)***
%Outside Director Holdings	−	8	0.62 (1.06)
Firm Size	+/−	Control Variable	−0.15 (−2.22)**
Adjusted R^2			0.24

***, **, * Significant at the 0.01, 0.05, and 0.10 levels, respectively.
[a] t-statistics are after using the Froot (1989) procedure to adjust the variance-covariance matrix for dependence among observations from the same firm.
[b] Variable definitions:
  %Audout = ln(%Audout/(1 − %Audout) + 1);
  Board Size = the natural log of the number of board members; and
  %Outsiders = ln(%Outsiders/(1 − %Outsiders) + 1).
See Table 2 for other variable definitions.

I therefore re-estimate the regression in Table 4, substituting R&D Expenditures and a proxy, Hi-tech, for my growth opportunity measure. I define R&D Expenditures as research and development expenditures divided by total assets. Hi-tech is a dummy variable equal to 1 if the firm is in a high-tech industry, and 0 otherwise.[13] Growth Opportunities is insignificantly positively correlated with R&D Expenditures ($\rho = 0.18$) and Hi-tech ($\rho = 0.13$).

---

[13] Following Field and Hanka (2000), Hi-tech encompasses all firms with primary three-digit SIC codes in computer and office equipment (357), electronic components and accessories (367), miscellaneous electrical machinery, equipment, and supplies (369), laboratory apparatus and analytical, optical, measuring, and controlling instruments (382), surgical, medical, and dental instruments and supplies (384), and computer programming, data processing, and other computer-related services (737).

The coefficients on R&D Expenditures and Hi-tech are not significant in the multiple regression, suggesting that neither R&D Expenditures nor Hi-tech substitute for Growth Opportunities. I also re-estimate the regression in Table 4 after including Growth Opportunities along with R&D Expenditures and Hi-tech, respectively. The coefficients on Growth Opportunities exhibit virtually no change, and the coefficients on R&D Expenditures and Hi-tech remain insignificantly different from zero.

Accounting Losses and Legal Liability for Poor Performance

%Audout is lower for firms reporting losses in the previous two years. These results are consistent with the argument that investors in loss firms require less independent audit committees because financial information is less value-relevant for loss firms. A competing explanation for the negative association between losses and audit committee independence is that firms experiencing sustained losses have difficulty attracting outside directors to serve on their audit committees due to liability concerns. However, most large companies have director and officer insurance indemnifying non-inside directors from legal damages, and many states (especially Delaware and New York) severely limit lawsuits against non-inside directors.

Using the probability of bankruptcy as a proxy for legal liability, I substitute Altman's Z-statistic for Losses and also use Altman's Z-statistic as an additional regressor in the original multiple regression. In each regression, the coefficient on Altman's Z-statistic is insignificant at the 0.10 level, suggesting no systematic association with audit committee independence.

Alternative Definition of Audit Committee Independence

Current SEC and exchange rules suggest all members must be outside directors for the audit committee to be considered independent. As Table 1 shows, only 43.4 percent of sample firms had 100 percent independent audit committees in 1991–1993. To assess whether full independence is associated with the same economic factors as %Audout, I estimate a probit model using full independence (rather than %Audout) as the dependent variable. The inferences from the probit model are identical to those in Table 4, except the coefficient on CEO on Compensation Committee is significantly negative at the 0.05 level for the probit model.

Simultaneity

Some variables that explain %Audout also likely explain Board Size and %Outsiders. To account for simultaneities, I use a two-stage least squares (2SLS) method, in which %Audout is regressed on the factors used in Table 4, and either %Outsiders or Board Size is regressed on a set of endogenous and exogenous factors. The 2SLS estimator of %Outsiders or Board Size can be described as an instrumental variables estimator because this method substitutes instruments for %Outsiders or Board Size based on predicted values obtained from regressions of each variable on its set of factors.

Table 5 presents the 2SLS coefficients for each set of equations. The first two columns present the results with %Outsiders as the instrumental variable. To determine the simultaneous factors, I estimate stepwise regressions explaining %Outsiders and explaining Board Size, respectively. The set of possible explanatory variables include those used for the regression explaining %Audout and other potential determinants of board independence and board size described in the literature. I keep all explanatory variables from the stepwise regressions with p-values less than 0.15.

TABLE 5

Two-Stage Least Squares (2SLS) Regression of %Audout on %Outsiders, Board Size, and Other Endogenous and Exogenous Variables[a]
(coefficients and t-statistics)

	2SLS on %Audout and %Outsiders		2SLS on %Audout and Board Size	
	%Audout	%Outsiders	%Audout	Board Size
Intercept	1.09 (1.50)	1.41 (7.52)***	0.55 (0.92)	1.64 (28.52)***
%Outsiders	1.38 (3.70)***		1.84 (14.85)***	
Board Size	0.62 (2.35)**	−0.10 (−1.58)	0.67 (2.61)***	
Growth Opportunities	−0.08 (−2.31)**	−0.05 (−3.07)***	−0.05 (−1.88)*	
Losses	−0.54 (−1.91)*		−0.53 (−1.90)*	0.06 (1.94)*
Debt-to-Assets	−0.46 (−1.24)		−0.51 (−1.39)	
CEO on Compensation Committee	−0.62 (−2.95)***		−0.52 (−2.68)***	−0.06 (−2.28)**
5% Blockholder on Audit Committee	−1.24 (−4.82)***		−1.15 (−4.67)***	
%Outside Director Holdings	1.13 (1.63)	0.20 (0.92)	0.83 (1.27)	
Firm Size	−0.10 (−1.93)*		−0.12 (−2.17)**	
%Inside Director Holdings		−1.58 (−6.22)***		
CEO on Nominating Committee		−0.13 (−4.05)***		
CEO Tenure		−0.04 (−1.97)**		0.02 (2.14)**
R&D Expenditures		−0.88 (−2.03)**		−0.57 (−2.41)**
Beta		−0.13 (−3.18)***		−0.05 (−2.72)***
Institutional Ownership		0.41 (3.74)***		

(Continued on next page)

TABLE 5 (Continued)

	2SLS on %Audout and %Outsiders		2SLS on %Audout and Board Size	
	%Audout	%Outsiders	%Audout	Board Size
5% Outside Blockholder		0.21 (2.00)*		0.05 (1.16)
Lagged Stock Returns				0.08 (2.88)***
Hi-tech				−0.13 (−4.11)***
Adjusted R²	0.10	0.16	0.28	0.37

***, **, * Significant at the 0.01, 0.05, and 0.10 levels, respectively.

ª Variable definitions:

%Inside Director Holdings = the percentage of shares owned by all inside directors;

CEO on Nominating Committee = 1 if CEO sits on the board's nomination committee, and 0 otherwise;

CEO Tenure = the natural log of the number of years the CEO has been on the board;

R&D Expenditures = research and development expenses divided by total assets;

Beta = the 120-day beta of the stock prior to the end of the last fiscal year;

Institutional Ownership = the percentage of stock owned by institutions;

5% Outside Blockholder = 1 if an outside director owns 5% or more shares, and 0 otherwise;

Lagged Stock Returns = the one-year stock return prior to the shareholders' meeting; and

Hi-tech = 1 if firm is in a high-technology industry, and 0 otherwise.

See Tables 2 and 4 for other variable definitions.

The endogenous variables for %Audout and %Outsiders are Board Size, Growth Opportunities, and %Outside Director Holdings. The exogenous variables for %Outsiders are %Inside Director Holdings (Hermalin and Weisbach 1988), CEO on Nominating Committee (Klein 1998), CEO Tenure (Hermalin and Weisbach 1988), R&D Expenditures (Reingold 1999), Beta, Institutional Ownership, and 5% Outside Blockholder. The last two columns present the results using Board Size as the instrumental variable. The endogenous variables are Losses and CEO on Compensation Committee. The exogenous variables for Board Size are CEO Tenure (Yermack 1996), R&D Expenditures (Reingold 1999), Beta, 5% Outside Blockholder, Lagged Stock Returns, and Hi-tech (Reingold 1999).

The inferences from the 2SLS analyses are similar to those derived from the multiple regression reported in Table 4. The one exception is that the coefficients on CEO on Compensation Committee are significantly negative at the 0.01 level for the 2SLS analyses, but insignificantly negative for the multiple regression. Thus, simultaneity does not affect the primary inferences drawn from Table 4, suggesting that the empirical results are robust to both procedures.

VI. CONCLUSIONS

Beginning in December 1999, the SEC and stock exchanges require listed firms to maintain audit committees with at least three directors, "all of whom have no relationship to the company that may interfere with the exercise of their independence from management and the company" (*NYSE Listed Company Manual* §303.01[B][2][a]). Although this statement suggests that firms must maintain audit committees composed solely of outside directors, exchange regulations allow for non-outside directors if the board determines it is in the firm's best interests for these individuals to serve on its audit committee.

I examine if variations in audit committee independence are associated with economic factors for a sample of S&P 500 firms over 1991–1993, a time period when firms had greater latitude in placing affiliated directors on their audit committee. I find that audit committee independence increases with board size and the percentage of outsiders on the board, consistent with the hypothesis that audit committee independence depends on the supply of available outside directors on the board. In contrast, audit committee independence decreases with the firm's growth opportunities and when the firm reported net losses in each of the two preceding years, supporting the hypothesis that audit committee independence is related to management's and shareholders' demand for scrutiny of the firm's financial accounting process. I also find a negative association between audit committee independence and the presence of alternative monitoring mechanisms, that is, for larger firms or when a nonmanagement director owning at least 5 percent of the firms' shares sits on the audit committee. Overall, my findings are consistent with the Blue Ribbon Commission's observation that "one size doesn't fit all" when it comes to audit committees. Thus, the stock exchanges may wish to allow boards of directors flexibility in determining their audit committee composition.

Several possible avenues for future research arise from this study. First, does the lower level of audit committee independence for higher growth firms and for firms with sustained losses result in higher incidences of financial fraud? Second, the Blue Ribbon Commission suggests that all audit committee members should have expertise in financial accounting. To what extent do audit committees comply with this suggestion, and what factors, if any, are related to fulfilling this mandate? Third, examining the interdependence between audit committee independence and competing corporate governance structures could further our understanding as to how corporations make trade-offs among these alternative mechanisms.

REFERENCES

Amir, E., B. Lev, and T. Sougiannis. 1999. What value analysts? Working paper, Tel Aviv University, New York University, and University of Illinois at Urbana–Champaign.

Barth, M. E., W. H. Beaver, and W. R. Landsman. 1998. Relative valuation roles of equity book value and net income as a function of financial health. *Journal of Accounting & Economics* 25: 1–34.

Bhagat, S., and B. Black. 1999. The uncertain relationship between board composition and firm performance. *Business Lawyer* 54: 921–963.

Carcello, J. V., and T. L. Neal. 2000. Audit committee composition and auditor reporting. *The Accounting Review* 75: 453–467.

Collins, D. W., M. Pincus, and H. Xie. 1999. Equity valuation and negative earnings: The role of book value of equity. *The Accounting Review* 74: 29–61.

DeFond, M. L., and J. Jiambalvo. 1994. Debt covenant violation and manipulation of accruals. *Journal of Accounting and Economics* 17: 145–176.

Fama, E. F. 1980. Agency problems and the theory of the firm. *Journal of Political Economy* 88: 288–307.

———. and M. C. Jensen. 1983. Separation of ownership and control. *Journal of Law & Economics* 26: 301–325.

Field, L. C., and G. Hanka. 2000. The expiration of IPO share lockups. *Journal of Finance* 56: 471–500.

Froot, K. A. 1989. Consistent covariance matrix estimation with cross-sectional dependence and heteroskedasticity in financial data. *Journal of Financial and Quantitative Analysis* 24: 333–355.

Hackman, J. R., ed. 1990. *Groups That Work and Those That Don't: Conditions for Effective Teamwork.* San Francisco, CA: Jossey-Bass.

Hayn, C. 1995. The information content of losses. *Journal of Accounting & Economics* 20: 125–153.

Hermalin, B. E., and M. S. Weisbach. 1988. The determinants of board composition. *RAND Journal of Economics* 19: 589–606.

Jensen, M. C., and W. H. Meckling. 1976. Theory of the firm: Managerial behavior, agency costs and ownership structure. *Journal of Financial Economics* 3: 305–360.

———. 1993. The modern industrial revolution, exit and the failure of internal control systems. *Journal of Finance* 48: 831–880.

Klein, A. 1998. Firm performance and board committee structure. *Journal of Law and Economics* 41: 275–303.

———. 2001. Audit committees, board of director characteristics and earnings management. Working paper, New York University.

Leftwich, R. 1983. Accounting information in private markets: Evidence from private lending agreements. *The Accounting Review*: 23–42.

Lev, B., and P. Zarowin. 1999. The boundaries of financial reporting and how to extend them. *Journal of Accounting Research* 37: 353–385.

Levitt, A. 1998. The numbers game. Remarks delivered at the NYU Center for Law and Business, New York, NY, September 28.

Lipe, R. C., L. Bryant, and S. K. Widener. 1998. Do nonlinearity, firm-specific coefficients, and losses represent distinct factors in the relation between stock returns and accounting earnings? *Journal of Accounting & Economics* 25: 195–214.

Lipton, M., and J. W. Lorsch. 1992. A modest proposal for improved corporate governance. *Business Lawyer* 48: 59–77.

O'Reilly, V. M., P. J. McDonnell, B. N. Winograd, J. S. Gerson, and H. R. Jaenicke, eds. 1998. *Montgomery's Auditing.* 12th edition. New York, NY: John Wiley & Sons.

The NASDAQ Stock Market Listing Requirements. Undated. New York, NY: National Association of Securities Dealers.

National Commission on Fraudulent Financial Reporting (the Treadway Commission). 1987. *Report of the National Commission on Fraudulent Financial Reporting.* Washington, D.C.: Government Printing Office.

NYSE Listed Company Manual. Undated. New York, NY: New York Stock Exchange.

New York Stock Exchange and National Association of Securities Dealers. 1999. *Report and Recommendation of the Blue Ribbon Committee on Improving the Effectiveness of Corporate Audit Committees.* New York, NY: NYSE and NASD.

Parker, S. 2000. The association between audit committee characteristics and the conservatism of financial reporting. Working paper, Santa Clara University.

PricewaterhouseCoopers LLP. 2000. *Audit Committee Effectiveness—What Works Best.* 3rd edition. Altamonte Springs, FL: The Institute of Internal Auditors Research Foundation.

Reingold, J. 1999. Dot.com boards are flouting the rules. *Business Week* (December 20): 130–134.

Smith, C. W., and J. B. Warner. 1979. On financial contracting: An analysis of bond covenants. *Journal of Financial Economics* 7: 117–161.

———, and R. L. Watts. 1992. The investment opportunity set and corporate financing, dividend and compensation policies. *Journal of Financial Economics* 32: 263–292.

Steiner, I. D. 1972. *Group Process and Productivity.* New York, NY: Academic Press.

Verschoor, C. C. 1993. Benchmarking the audit committee. *Journal of Accountancy* (September): 59–64.

Vicknair, D., K. Hickman, and K. C. Carnes. 1993. A note on audit committee independence: Evidence from the NYSE on "grey" area directors. *Accounting Horizons* 7 (March): 53–57.

Watts, R. L., and J. L. Zimmerman. 1990. Towards a positive theory of positive accounting: A ten year perspective. *The Accounting Review* 65: 131–156.

Williamson, O. E. 1975. *Markets and Hierarchies: Analysis and Antitrust Implications: A Study in the Economics of Internal Organization.* New York, NY: The Free Press.

Yermack, D. 1996. Higher market valuation of companies with a small board of directors. *Journal of Financial Economics* 40: 185–212.

[22]

THE ACCOUNTING REVIEW
Vol. 78, No. 1
January 2003
pp. 95–117

Audit Committee Characteristics and Auditor Dismissals following "New" Going-Concern Reports

Joseph V. Carcello
University of Tennessee

Terry L. Neal
University of Kentucky

ABSTRACT: One important role of audit committees is to protect external auditors from dismissal following the issuance of an unfavorable report. We examine auditor dismissals following *new* going-concern reports that Big 6 firms issued between 1988 and 1999. Our findings suggest that audit committees with greater independence, greater governance expertise, and lower stockholdings are more effective in shielding auditors from dismissal after the issuance of new going-concern reports. In addition, we find that the relation between audit committee independence and auditor protection from dismissal has grown stronger over time. Finally, independent audit committee members experience a significant increase in turnover rate after auditor dismissals. These findings, coupled with those from Carcello and Neal (2000), suggest that when affiliated directors dominate the audit committee, management often can (1) pressure its auditor to issue an unmodified report despite going-concern issues, and (2) dismiss its auditor if the auditor refuses to issue an unmodified report.

Keywords: *audit committee characteristics; auditor dismissals; going-concern reports.*

Data Availability: *The data are available from public sources. A list of sample firms is available from the second author.*

We thank Mark Beasley, Dana Hermanson, Linda McDaniel, Mark Nelson (the associate editor), Bob Ramsay, two anonymous reviewers, and workshop participants at the University of Georgia, University of Oklahoma, and Louisiana State University for their helpful comments. We also thank Mike Barnhisel, Mike Borth, Becky Cassill, Marie Dothard, and especially Sandra Holt for research assistance.

Submitted April 2002
Accepted August 2002

I. INTRODUCTION

The sudden collapse of Enron amid questionable accounting practices has led Congress and regulators to call for more effective audit committee performance as one means of enhancing external auditor independence (Pitt 2001; Ruder 2002). This study contributes to the growing literature on corporate governance by investigating the relation between audit committee characteristics (independence, governance expertise, financial expertise, and stock ownership[1]) and auditor dismissals following the issuance of *new* going-concern reports. We define a going-concern report as new if the client received an unmodified (clean) report in the previous year.[2]

One of the primary functions of an audit committee is to safeguard the independence of the external auditor. Auditor independence is essential to audit quality because it minimizes "the possibility that any external factors will influence an auditor's judgments" (SEC 2000, 5). The independence of the auditor is particularly critical in financial accounting and reporting situations that are ambiguous, such as when a client is experiencing financial distress and the "temptation to 'see it the way your client does' is subtle, yet real" (Levitt 2000, 5). In their examination of an ambiguous reporting situation, Carcello and Neal (2000) find that audit firms are less likely to issue going-concern reports to financially distressed clients whose audit committees lack independence. Auditors may hesitate to issue a going-concern report if management implicitly or explicitly suggests that the client will dismiss the auditor if the auditor issues a going-concern report.

Prior research finds that clients receiving a going-concern report are more likely to switch auditors (e.g., Chow and Rice 1982; Mutchler 1984; Geiger et al. 1998). We test the hypothesis that management is less likely to terminate the auditor following the issuance of a going-concern report if the audit committee—which reviews all auditor-management disputes—embodies certain characteristics (PricewaterhouseCoopers 2000).

As shareholder representatives, the audit committee plays an important role in the auditor dismissal process. The NYSE-NASDAQ-sponsored Blue Ribbon Committee (BRC) (1999, 14) recognized the audit committee's "ultimate authority and responsibility to select, evaluate, and where appropriate, dismiss the outside auditor." Moreover, Securities and Exchange Commission Chairman Harvey Pitt has recently proposed additional safeguards to prevent management from firing the auditor without audit committee approval (Pitt 2002b).

Audit committee performance should be of high quality when members are independent (Public Oversight Board [POB] 1994; BRC 1999; PricewaterhouseCoopers 2000), when they have more governance expertise (Fama 1980; Fama and Jensen 1983), and more financial expertise (BRC 1999). Since critics have alleged that higher levels of stock ownership motivate corporate directors (and management) to artificially boost reported performance (Millstein 2002; Pitt 2002a), we expect that owning large stockholdings in the company will impair audit committee members' performance. In sum, we expect that audit committees whose members are more independent, have more governance expertise, more financial expertise, and own less of the company's stock, will be more likely to resist managerial attempts to dismiss an auditor following the issuance of a going-concern report.

Our results generally support our expectations. Auditors who issue a going-concern report are more likely to be dismissed if audit committees have a larger percentage of affiliated directors on the audit committee, or if audit committee members: (1) have less

---

[1] Throughout this paper, when we refer to the percentage of stock owned by audit committee members, we include their stock options.

[2] Subsequent references to going-concern reports denote new going-concern reports.

governance expertise, or (2) own a larger percentage of the company's stock. We do not find a significant relation between the percentage of audit committee members with financial expertise and auditor dismissals following going-concern reports.

These results, coupled with the evidence reported by Carcello and Neal (2000), indicate potential problems in the interactions among auditors, audit committees, and management of financially distressed companies. Carcello and Neal (2000) suggest that auditors often believe that they are more likely to be dismissed following a going-concern report if there is a greater percentage of affiliated directors on the audit committee. The current study provides explicit evidence that this concern is valid. Therefore, we conclude that when affiliated directors dominate the audit committee, management often can (1) pressure its auditor to issue an unmodified report despite going-concern issues, and (2) dismiss its auditor if the auditor refuses to issue an unmodified report.

We organize the remainder of this paper as follows. Section II provides further background on the link between audit committee characteristics and auditor dismissals and develops our empirical predictions. We present the research design and sample selection procedure in Section III, and our results in Section IV. Section V contains supplemental analyses, and the last section discusses the study's implications and limitations.

II. BACKGROUND AND EMPIRICAL PREDICTIONS

Previous research suggests that opinion shopping is generally unsuccessful (e.g., Chow and Rice 1982; Smith 1986; Krishnan and Stephens 1995; Geiger et al. 1998). Nonetheless, clients receiving a going-concern report are more likely to switch auditors (e.g., Chow and Rice 1982; Mutchler 1984; Geiger et al. 1998) perhaps because management *believes* that once an incumbent auditor is dismissed, the company will find a more pliable auditor (Craswell 1988, 26). Alternatively, management might dismiss an auditor solely as punishment for issuing a going-concern report, or due to irreparable damage to its relationship with the auditor as a result of the conflict.

We posit that an audit committee whose members have more independence, governance expertise, financial expertise, and who own less of the company's stock will be more likely to block a managerial attempt to dismiss an auditor who issued a going-concern report. We now consider in more detail why we expect each of these four audit committee characteristics to affect auditor dismissals.

In our view, the independence of the audit committee is the primary mechanism for reducing the likelihood that the company will dismiss its auditor in retaliation for issuing a going-concern report. We classify audit committee members as either independent or affiliated directors. *Affiliated directors* (who have strong economic or personal ties to the company or its management) include current or former officers or employees of the company or of a related entity, relatives of management, professional advisors to the company (e.g., consultants, bank officers, legal counsel), officers of significant suppliers or customers of the company, and interlocking directors (Vicknair et al. 1993; Beasley 1996; Carcello and Neal 2000).

Given the strong economic or personal ties between affiliated directors and the company or its management, affiliated audit committee members have more incentive to side with management in disputes with the auditor (Baysinger and Butler 1985). Affiliated committee members also typically own more stock in the company than independent members, and stock ownership may increase the likelihood that a director sides with management. Indeed, we expect independent directors to be more objective and to possess greater expertise than affiliated directors, and the legal system appears to hold independent directors to a higher standard (Braiotta 1999, 104).

An audit committee with greater *governance expertise* should also reduce the likelihood that the company will dismiss its auditor in retaliation for issuing a going-concern report. Fama (1980) and Fama and Jensen (1983) suggest that directors make costly investments to develop reputations as effective monitors of corporate performance. Moreover, prior research concludes that directors of companies experiencing adverse events such as poor performance or financial distress subsequently serve less often as directors for other companies (Gilson 1990; Kaplan and Reishus 1990). We expect a director's reputation to suffer when the company fires its auditor after issuing a going-concern report. Directors who sit on more boards will have more to lose and therefore we expect them to be more likely to oppose the auditor's dismissal.

An audit committee with greater *financial expertise* should reduce the likelihood that the company will dismiss its auditor for issuing a going-concern report. The BRC (1999, 25) recommends that every audit committee have at least one member who possesses financial expertise, defined as "past employment experience in finance or accounting, requisite professional certification in accounting, or any other comparable experience or background which results in the individual's financial sophistication, including being or having been a CEO or other senior officer with financial oversight responsibilities." We expect that a financial expert will understand and support an auditor's decision to issue a going-concern report, and that an audit committee whose members have greater financial expertise will be more effective in preventing management from dismissing its auditor in this event.

An audit committee with a lower level of *stock ownership* should reduce the likelihood that the company dismisses its auditor after receiving a going-concern report. Audit committee members who own more company stock are likely to suffer losses if the going-concern report triggers a negative stock price response (Jones 1996; Melumad and Ziv 1997), so we expect them to be more willing to accede to auditor dismissals.[3]

III. RESEARCH DESIGN AND SAMPLE

Model

We use the following logistic regression model to test the relation between the likelihood that the client dismisses its auditor and audit committee characteristics:

$$
\begin{aligned}
\text{DISMISSED} = {}& b_0 + b_1\text{AFFILIATED} + b_2\text{AFFILIATED} \times \text{GC\_OPINION} \\
& + b_3\text{GOVEXPERT} + b_4\text{GOVEXPERT} \times \text{GC\_OPINION} \\
& + b_5\text{FINEXPERT} + b_6\text{FINEXPERT} \times \text{GC\_OPINION} \\
& + b_7\text{STOCKOWN} + b_8\text{STOCKOWN} \times \text{GC\_OPINION} + b_9\text{SIZE} \\
& + b_{10}\text{INDSHARE} + b_{11}\text{TENURE} + b_{12}\text{ZFC} + b_{13}\text{MGMTCHG} + \varepsilon.
\end{aligned}
$$

We define the dependent, test, and control variables as follows:

---

[3] Agency theory (e.g., Jensen and Meckling 1976) would suggest an opposite relation because a higher level of stock ownership should align the interests of management (audit committee members) with the interests of stockholders. Stock ownership is most likely to align the interests of audit committee members and stockholders if audit committee members are *long-term investors*. However, many audit committee members (and management) have a short-term perspective with respect to their ownership stake (Leonhardt 2002), and financial distress is likely to increase this myopia because the company's long-term existence is in doubt.

DISMISSED = identifies whether a client dismissed its auditor before the client's next annual report (1 = client dismissed auditor, 0 = client did not dismiss auditor);

AFFILIATED = the percentage of audit committee members classified as affiliated directors: current or former officers or employees of the company or of a related entity, relatives of management, professional advisors to the company, officers of significant suppliers or customers of the company, and interlocking directors;

GOVEXPERT = a proxy for audit committee members' governance expertise, the average number of directorship positions they hold in other public companies;

FINEXPERT = the percentage of audit committee members possessing financial expertise, per the BRC (1999) recommendations;[4]

STOCKOWN = the percentage of the client's common stock (and stock options) held by its audit committee members; and

GC_OPINION = a going-concern opinion indicator variable (1 = GC, 0 = clean).

Although we do not hypothesize significant relations between audit committee characteristics and auditor dismissals following a clean opinion, our analysis includes dismissals after both types of opinions. As explained later, we use a matched-pairs design where companies dismissing their auditor are matched on opinion, year, size, and industry, with companies not dismissing their auditor. This design allows us to determine the incremental relation between audit committee characteristics and dismissals following a going-concern (GC) opinion (relative to a clean opinion), which, in turn, enables us to address one potential alternate explanation for our results—audit committees with certain characteristics could be associated with auditor dismissals in all contexts, not just when management wants to dismiss the auditor because of a GC report.

The coefficients associated with the main effects of each of the four audit committee characteristics (b_1, b_3, b_5, b_7) measure the relation between the characteristic and auditor dismissals following clean opinions. However, we are primarily interested in the relation between audit committee characteristics and auditor dismissals following GC opinions. For each audit committee characteristic, we sum the coefficient on the main effect of that characteristic plus the coefficient on the term that interacts that characteristic with the going-concern opinion indicator variable.[5]

We expect that the higher the percentage of affiliated directors on the audit committee, the more likely the client is to dismiss its auditor following the receipt of a GC report ($b_1 + b_2 > 0$). We expect that the more directorship positions audit committee members hold, the less likely the client is to dismiss its auditor ($b_3 + b_4 < 0$). We also expect that the higher the percentage of audit committee members with financial expertise, the less likely the client is to dismiss its auditor ($b_5 + b_6 < 0$). Finally, we expect that the more of

---

[4] The BRC (1999) recommends that an audit committee contain at least one financial expert. As 95.2 percent of the audit committees in our study had at least one member with financial expertise, we measured financial expertise as the percentage of audit committee members possessing financial expertise as defined by the BRC (1999), rather than using a dichotomous measure.

[5] Because we use a matched-pairs design, including the base level of GC_OPINION as a main effect in the model would provide no incremental explanatory power (the dismissal rate is 50 percent for both the GC and clean samples).

the client's common stock and options audit committee members hold, the more likely the client is to dismiss its auditor ($b_7 + b_8 > 0$).

In addition to the audit committee characteristics of interest, we control for the effects of other factors that likely affect a client's decision to dismiss its auditor: client size, auditor industry share, auditor tenure, financial distress, and managerial change.

SIZE. Large clients are less likely to dismiss their auditors (Francis and Wilson 1988; Haskins and Williams 1990; Krishnan 1994). Large clients wield more bargaining power as a result of the higher audit fees that they pay (McKeown et al. 1991, 11), and thus we expect fewer disagreements leading to auditor dismissals. Larger companies also have more incentive than smaller companies to retain their auditors, since financial analysts and the financial press scrutinize their auditor dismissals more closely. We measure size as the natural log of total assets (expressed in thousands of dollars). We expect that larger clients are less likely to dismiss their auditor.

INDSHARE. Prior studies provide evidence that a client is less likely to dismiss an auditor who specializes in the client's industry (Haskins and Williams 1990; Williams 1988). Williams suggests that clients commonly perceive that auditors with a greater market share in the industry are likely to be more effective, so clients would not want to change to a less effective auditor (i.e., an auditor with a lower market share). We measure an auditor's industry share as the percentage of the square root of total assets that the auditor audits for all companies in the client's industry (Hogan and Jeter 1999).[6] We expect that the larger the auditor's market share in the client's industry, the less likely the client is to dismiss its auditor.

TENURE. Levinthal and Fichman (1988) and Williams (1988) provide evidence that longer auditor tenure reduces the likelihood of auditor dismissal. As the tenure of the auditor-client relationship lengthens, the auditor develops client-specific knowledge that would be lost if the client changed auditors. We measure auditor tenure as the number of consecutive years that the client has retained the auditor.[7] We expect that the longer the auditor's tenure, the less likely the client is to dismiss its auditor.

ZFC. The financial condition of a company affects the likelihood that it will change auditors (Krishnan and Stephens 1995; Schwartz and Menon 1985). We compute the Zmijewski financial condition (ZFC) score using the PROBIT coefficients from Zmijewski's (1984, 69) 40 bankrupt/800 nonbankrupt estimation sample.[8] Higher ZFC scores indicate greater financial distress, so we expect that the higher the ZFC score, the more likely the client is to dismiss its auditor.

MGMTCHG. A change in top management is often associated with a change in auditors (Chow and Rice 1982; Williams 1988). A new CEO could change auditors to obtain a fresh perspective on the company's financial results, or because he or she had positive experiences with another audit firm. A new chief financial officer (CFO) could seek an auditor change for similar reasons, and CFOs with prior experience in public accounting often prefer to work with their former employers (Iyer 1998). We use a dummy variable (1 = CEO or CFO change, 0 = no change) to measure whether top management changed

---

[6] We based industry share measures on three-digit SIC codes for all industries with at least ten companies. For the 21 industries with fewer than ten companies, we determined the industry share measures at the two-digit level.

[7] We truncate auditor tenure at ten years to reduce the effect of extreme values for clients that have retained their auditors for many years.

[8] A number of prior studies have used Zmijewski's (1984) ZFC score to control for financial distress level (e.g., Bamber et al. 1993; Carcello et al. 1995).

in the year the opinion was issued or in the following year, provided the change in top management preceded the date of the auditor dismissal.[9] We expect a change in the company's CEO or CFO to increase the likelihood that the client dismisses its auditor.

Sample

We identified all publicly traded companies (except financial institutions and service companies [i.e., SIC codes 6000–9999]) included on the Compact D/SEC database that (1) received a new GC report from a Big 6 firm during the period 1988 to 1999, and (2) dismissed their auditor prior to the issuance of the client's next annual report. We limit our sample to companies with SIC codes below 6000 because Zmijewski (1984) excluded financial and service companies when he developed his financial condition index (ZFC), which is our control variable for client financial condition. Although auditor changes include dismissals and resignations, we limit our study to auditor dismissals because we are interested in whether audit committee characteristics enhance auditor independence by making it less likely that the client dismisses its auditor, not whether audit committee characteristics make it less likely that the auditor dismisses its client.

One hundred seventy-four companies met our sample selection criteria. We then exclude companies that filed for bankruptcy during the fiscal year under audit or the next year (n = 30), because the bankruptcy itself sometimes precipitates the auditor dismissal (Williams 1988; DeFond 1992; Krishnan 1994). Since we focus on the relation between audit committee characteristics and auditor dismissals, we exclude companies that did not maintain an audit committee (n = 45). We also exclude companies for which we were unable to obtain the relevant proxy statement or Form 10-K (n = 33), from which we gathered data on audit committee characteristics.

We then matched each GC client that dismissed its auditor with a GC client that did not dismiss its auditor.[10] We matched on year, industry, and to the extent possible, size.[11] We were unable to locate a suitable matching client for four GC dismissal companies because the number of GC companies that dismissed their auditors in that industry and year exceeded the number of potentially matching GC companies that did not dismiss their auditors. Table 1 shows that this resulted in a final sample of 62 clients receiving GC reports that dismissed their auditors, matched with 62 clients receiving GC reports that retained their auditors.

To provide a benchmark for assessing the relation between audit committee characteristics and auditor dismissals, we gathered a sample of companies that received clean opinions between 1988 and 1999 and dismissed their auditors during the following year. Approximately 1,000 public companies (with SIC codes below 6000) received clean reports from Big 6 firms between 1988 and 1999 and then changed their auditors during the following year. Due to the large sample size, we selected a random sample of 200 companies. From this sample, 24 companies did not maintain audit committees and 13 other companies did not have financial statement or other required data.

---

[9] For companies that did not change auditors, we determined whether top management changed during the year corresponding with the financial statements, or in the first nine months of the next year.

[10] The nondismissal category includes two clients that changed auditors in the second year after the GC opinion. Excluding these clients from our analyses does not affect our inferences.

[11] We matched 13 clients at the four-digit SIC code level, 16 at the three-digit level, 16 at the two-digit level, and 17 at the one-digit level. We then selected the GC client retaining its auditor that was closest in total assets to the GC client that dismissed its auditor. Given the limited number of GC observations, we chose not to use a stricter match on size (e.g., match on assets within ±20 percent).

TABLE 1
Sample Selection Criteria

	Going-Concern Opinion Sample[a]	Clean Opinion Sample[b]	Combined Sample
Initial sample	174	200	374
Companies that filed for bankruptcy	(30)		(30)
Companies with no audit committee	(45)	(24)	(69)
Proxy statement and/or Form 10-K not available	(33)	(13)	(46)
Disagreement over accounting or auditing issues		(7)	(7)
Auditor resigned		(14)	(14)
No companies meeting matching criteria existed	(4)	(17)	(21)
Dismissal sample	62	125	187
Nondismissal sample[c]	62	125	187
Total sample	124	250	374

[a] The going-concern opinion sample frame is publicly held companies that dismissed their auditors after receiving *new* going-concern reports from Big 6 audit firms during the period 1988–1999 (financial institutions and service companies excluded).

[b] The clean opinion sample frame is publicly held companies that dismissed their auditors after receiving clean reports from Big 6 audit firms during the period 1988–1999 (financial institutions and service companies excluded). Due to the large sample size, we selected an initial random sample of 200 companies.

[c] We matched every company in the sample that dismissed its auditor with a company that received the same type of opinion but did not dismiss its auditor. We matched companies on year, industry, and to the extent possible, size.

We are particularly interested in controlling for the relation between audit committee characteristics and auditor dismissals that do not result from a conflict between the auditor and management (i.e., benign auditor changes). We are interested in benign changes because we would expect the same relation between audit committee characteristics and auditor dismissals following an auditor-client disagreement over accounting and auditing issues as between audit committee characteristics and dismissals following a GC opinion. Including non-GC contentious auditor dismissals in the clean opinion sample would blur the distinction between the GC and clean opinion samples. (Unfortunately, given the limited number of auditor dismissals following an accounting/auditing disagreement [n = 7], we cannot test the relation between audit committee characteristics and non-GC contentious auditor dismissals.)

We examined the 8-Ks filed after each auditor change to determine the reasons the client gave for changing auditors. We excluded observations where the client and auditor disagreed over accounting or auditing issues (n = 7) and where the auditor resigned (n = 14). We then matched each company that received a clean opinion and dismissed its auditor with a company that received a clean opinion and did not change its auditor. We matched on year, industry, and size. We could not match on size for 17 of the dismissal companies in the clean opinion sample.[12] As shown in Table 1, our final sample includes

---

[12] Of our 125 matched pairs, we matched 61 at the four-digit SIC code level, 20 at the three-digit level, and 44 at the two-digit level. We matched on size using total assets, if possible, within ±20 percent. For ten matched-pairs, the size match was ±30 percent.

125 clients that received a clean opinion and dismissed their auditor, matched with 125 companies that received a clean opinion and did not change their auditor.

Therefore, our final sample includes 250 companies receiving clean opinions and 124 companies receiving GC opinions. By sample construction, 50 percent of the companies receiving each type of opinion dismissed their auditor.

IV. RESULTS

Univariate Analysis

Table 2 presents descriptive statistics for the audit committee characteristics and control variables. Since we are primarily interested in the relation between audit committee characteristics and dismissals following a GC report, we present separate descriptive statistics for the audit committee characteristics for clients receiving GC and clean reports. As we expect, three of the four characteristics differ significantly between clients dismissing their auditor following a GC opinion and those clients retaining their auditor after receiving a GC opinion. For GC clients who dismissed their auditors, 49 percent of the audit committee are affiliated directors, whereas for GC clients that did not dismiss their auditor, only 24 percent of the audit committee are affiliated directors ($p < 0.01$). GC clients that dismissed their auditors had audit committee members who held an average of only 0.84 directorships in other companies, while GC clients who retained their auditors had audit committee members holding an average of 1.83 directorships ($p < 0.01$). Audit committee members' average percentage stock ownership for GC clients dismissing their auditors is 9 percent compared to 3 percent for GC clients retaining their auditors ($p < 0.01$). There is no significant difference in the percentage of audit committee members with financial expertise between those clients dismissing their auditors vs. those clients retaining their auditors. In addition, there are no significant differences for any of the audit committee characteristics for clients dismissing their auditors following a clean opinion vs. clients retaining their auditors after receiving a clean opinion.

With respect to the control variables, clients are more likely to dismiss auditors when there has been a recent change in the client's top management ($p < 0.05$). There is no significant relation between auditor dismissals and auditor industry-market share, auditor tenure, and client financial distress level. In addition, there is no significant relation between client size[13] and auditor dismissals in our sample, although this result is not surprising given that we matched on client size.

Table 3 presents the correlations among the independent variables. The correlations are all below 0.35.[14] A higher percentage of affiliated directors on the audit committee is associated with more stock ownership (rho = 0.29, $p < 0.01$). In results not separately reported, we find that affiliated audit committee members on average own 3.3 percent of their companies' shares, whereas independent audit committee members own only 1.0 percent. As discussed previously, affiliated directors' higher stock ownership can increase their incentive to support managerial efforts to replace an auditor issuing a GC report.

In addition, audit committees with a higher percentage of affiliated directors are on average smaller (rho = −0.19, $p < 0.01$), have members with less governance expertise (rho = −0.21, $p < 0.01$), and experience more financial distress (rho = 0.12, $p < 0.05$).

---

[13] Although we control for client size in our logistic regression model using the natural log of total assets, we present descriptive statistics on client size for total assets (untransformed).

[14] The generally modest correlations suggest that multicollinearity is unlikely to be a problem, but we nonetheless computed variance inflation factors. Only two of the variance inflation factors are above 3.0 and the largest is 3.7; Gujarati (1995, 339) suggests that multicollinearity is unlikely to be problematic if the variance inflation factors are below 10.0.

TABLE 2
Descriptive Statistics for Audit Committee Characteristics and Control Variables
Mean (Median) [Standard Deviation]

Variable[a]	Combined Sample			Going-Concern Sample			Clean Sample		
	Dismissal (n = 187)[b]	No Dismissal (n = 187)[c]	(Dismissal – No Dismissal)[d]	Dismissal (n = 62)[b]	No Dismissal (n = 62)[c]	(Dismissal – No Dismissal)[d]	Dismissal (n = 125)[b]	No Dismissal (n = 125)[c]	(Dismissal – No Dismissal)[d]
Audit Committee Characteristics									
AFFILIATED	0.31 (0.33) [0.32]	0.24 (0.00) [0.30]	0.07* (0.33)**	0.49 (0.50) [0.36]	0.24 (0.07) [0.28]	0.25*** (0.43)***	0.22 (0.00) [0.26]	0.25 (0.00) [0.31]	−0.03 (0.00)
GOVEXPERT	1.02 (0.67) [1.11]	1.49 (1.00) [1.41]	−0.47*** (−0.33)***	0.84 (0.50) [1.01]	1.83 (1.37) [1.63]	−0.99*** (−0.87)***	1.11 (0.75) [1.15]	1.32 (1.00) [1.26]	−0.21 (−0.25)
FINEXPERT	0.79 (1.00) [0.27]	0.75 (0.75) [0.28]	0.04 (0.25)	0.80 (1.00) [0.30]	0.79 (1.00) [0.28]	0.01 (0.00)	0.78 (1.00) [0.25]	0.73 (0.75) [0.28]	0.05 (0.25)
STOCKOWN	0.05 (0.00) [0.11]	0.03 (0.00) [0.07]	0.02 (0.00)	0.09 (0.01) [0.15]	0.03 (0.00) [0.07]	0.06*** (0.01)	0.03 (0.00) [0.07]	0.03 (0.00) [0.08]	0.00 (0.00)
Control Variables									
SIZE	352.74 (51.68) [1,065.39]	334.26 (55.22) [995.75]	18.48 (−3.54)						
INDSHARE	0.18 (0.15) [0.11]	0.19 (0.17) [0.11]	−0.01 (−0.02)						
TENURE	6.54 (6.00) [3.07]	6.97 (7.00) [3.04]	−0.43 (−1.00)						

(continued on next page)

TABLE 2 (continued)

Variable[a]	Combined Sample			Going-Concern Sample			Clean Sample		
	Dismissal (n = 187)[b]	No Dismissal (n = 187)[c]	(Dismissal – No Dismissal)[d]	Dismissal (n = 62)[b]	No Dismissal (n = 62)[c]	(Dismissal – No Dismissal)[d]	Dismissal (n = 125)[b]	No Dismissal (n = 125)[c]	(Dismissal – No Dismissal)[d]
ZFC	−1.97 (−2.55) [2.61]	−1.59 (−2.47) [3.72]	−0.38 (−0.08)						
MGMTCHG	0.35 (0.00) [0.48]	0.24 (0.00) [0.43]	0.11** (0.00)***e						

*, **, and *** indicate significance at p < 0.10, p < 0.05, and p < 0.01, respectively, based on two-tailed tests, except for the going-concern sample, which is based on one-tailed tests.

a Variable definitions:
  AFFILIATED = percentage of "affiliated" directors on the audit committee;
  GOVEXPERT = average number of directorships in other public companies held by directors on the audit committee;
  FINEXPERT = percentage of directors on the audit committee with financial expertise;
  STOCKOWN = percentage of the company's stock (including stock options) owned by directors on the audit committee;
  SIZE = total assets (in millions of dollars);
  INDSHARE = auditor's market share in the client's industry, based on the percentage of the square root of total assets of all the companies in the client's industry, audited by the auditor;
  TENURE = number of consecutive years the client has engaged the auditor (truncated at ten years);
  ZFC = Zmijewski's (1984) financial condition index, where higher values indicate weaker financial condition; and
  MGMTCHG = 1 if client changed CEO or CFO during the year the opinion was issued or during the following year, provided the management change preceded the auditor dismissal, else 0.

b Companies that dismissed their auditor before the company's next annual report.
c Companies that did not dismiss their auditor before the company's next annual report.
d Tests for differences in the means are based on t-statistics (Z-statistics) for continuous variables (proportions). Nonparametric tests for differences in location are based on the Wilcoxon rank sum test.
e The Wilcoxon rank sum test does not test whether the medians for the two groups are different. Instead, the test identifies a difference in location; specifically, whether the observations in the two groups are from populations with different medians. Thus, the test indicates a significant difference even though the medians for the two groups are the same.

TABLE 3

Correlations among Audit Committee Characteristics and Control Variables[a]

	GOVEXPERT	FINEXPERT	STOCKOWN	SIZE	INDSHARE	TENURE	ZFC	MGMTCHG
AFFILIATED	-0.21***	0.08	0.29***	-0.19***	-0.07	-0.08	0.12**	0.04
GOVEXPERT		0.06	-0.11**	0.16***	0.05	0.05	0.10	0.08
FINEXPERT			0.03	-0.07	0.00	-0.11**	0.06	0.15***
STOCKOWN				-0.24***	-0.04	-0.06	0.08	0.03
SIZE					0.19***	0.34***	-0.28***	-0.09
INDSHARE						0.10	-0.02	-0.03
TENURE							-0.21***	-0.14***
ZFC								0.09

** and *** indicate significance at $p < 0.05$ and $p < 0.01$, respectively.

[a] We report Spearman rank correlation coefficients for MGMTCHG, and Pearson correlations otherwise. Variables are defined in Table 2.

Audit committee members with more governance expertise are more likely to serve on the boards of larger companies (rho = 0.16, p < 0.01) and to own less stock in the company (rho = −0.11, p < 0.05). Surprisingly, audit committees with greater financial expertise are associated with shorter auditor tenures (rho = −0.11, p < 0.05) and with more changes in top management (rho = 0.15, p < 0.01). Audit committee members also own more of the stock of smaller companies (rho = −0.24, p < 0.01).

Finally, in terms of the control variables, larger companies are more likely to use an industry specialist auditor (rho = 0.19, p < 0.01), to have retained their auditor for more years (rho = 0.34, p < 0.01), and are less likely to be financially distressed (rho = −0.28, p < 0.01). Auditors have shorter tenure in financially distressed companies (rho = −0.21, p < 0.01) and those with changes in top management (rho = −0.14, p < 0.01).

Logit Analysis
Audit Committee Characteristics and Auditor Dismissals
Model 1 in Table 4 shows that the overall logit model is significant (p < 0.01), and the pseudo-R^2 is 10 percent.[15] As expected, the likelihood that the client dismisses its auditor after receiving a GC report is: (1) increasing in the proportion of the audit committee composed of affiliated directors ($b_1 + b_2 > 0$; p < 0.01) and audit committee members' stock ownership level ($b_7 + b_8 > 0$; p < 0.05), and is (2) decreasing in audit committee members' governance expertise ($b_3 + b_4 < 0$; p < 0.01). We find no significant relation between the likelihood of auditor dismissal and audit committee members' financial expertise ($b_5 + b_6$ is not significantly different from 0, p = 0.99).[16]

In contrast to the positive relation between affiliated directors and auditor dismissals following GC opinions, there is no significant relation between the percentage of affiliated directors on the audit committee and auditor dismissals following a clean opinion (b_1 is not significantly different from 0, p = 0.20). There is a marginally significant negative relation, albeit weaker than in the GC sample, between audit committee members' governance expertise and auditor dismissals following clean opinions ($b_3 < 0$; p < 0.10). Unlike the GC sample, there is a marginally significant *positive* relation between audit committee members' financial expertise and auditor dismissals following clean opinions ($b_5 > 0$; p < 0.10), and no relation between audit committee members' stock ownership level and auditor dismissals (b_8 is not significantly different from 0, p = 0.96).

---

[15] The model's explanatory power is modest because the logit model does not include some likely causes of auditor dismissals (e.g., a desire to obtain lower fees, dissatisfaction with the audit firm or team, etc.). Clients rarely disclosed these reasons for changing auditors in their 8-Ks. However, our matched-pairs design helps control for these other causes of auditor dismissals, and enables us to ascertain the incremental effects of audit committee characteristics on auditor dismissals.

[16] Thirty-two of the 62 clients that dismissed their auditor after receiving a GC report switched from a Big 6 auditor to a non-Big 6 auditor, and 20 of the 125 clients that dismissed their auditor after receiving a clean report switched from a Big 6 auditor to a non-Big 6 auditor. We reran our analysis excluding these clients and their matched pairs. Since agency costs may affect both auditor changes and audit committee characteristics, we investigate whether our results hold when the subsequent auditor is of the same type as the predecessor auditor (i.e., an intra-Big 6 change). We continue to find that the likelihood of auditor dismissals following a GC report increases with the percentage of the audit committee composed of affiliated directors (p < 0.01) and decreases with audit committee members' governance expertise (p < 0.05). The coefficient on audit committee members' stock ownership is comparable to the coefficient reported in Table 4 (3.980 as compared to 3.985 in Table 4), but is not significant at conventional levels because the GC sample size in this sensitivity test is only half that in the primary analysis reported in Table 4. The relation between audit committee characteristics and auditor dismissals following clean opinions is qualitatively unchanged from that reported in Table 4.

TABLE 4
Logistic Regression of Auditor Dismissals on Audit Committee
Characteristics and Control Variables

$DISMISSED = b_0 + b_1 AFFILIATED + b_2 AFFILIATED \times GC\_OPINION + b_3 GOVEXPERT$
$+ b_4 GOVEXPERT \times GC\_OPINION + b_5 FINEXPERT$
$+ b_6 FINEXPERT \times GC\_OPINION + b_7 STOCKOWN$
$+ b_8 STOCKOWN \times GC\_OPINION + b_9 SIZE + b_{10} INDSHARE + b_{11} TENURE$
$+ b_{12} ZFC + b_{13} MGMTCHG + \varepsilon$

		Model 1		Model 2	
Variable[a]	Predicted Relation	Estimated Coefficients	Wald Chi-Square	Estimated Coefficients	Wald Chi-Square
INTERCEPT	none	−0.461	0.277	−0.712	0.448
Board Members on the Audit Committee					
AFFILIATED	none	−0.628	1.675	−0.784	2.417
AFFILIATED × GC_OPINION	+	2.738	11.258***	3.306	13.674***
Joint Test ($b_1 + b_2$)	+	2.110	9.954***	2.522	11.624***
GOVEXPERT	none	−0.200	3.004*	−0.174	2.018
GOVEXPERT × GC_OPINION	−	−0.341	2.801**	−0.360	2.687**
Joint Test ($b_3 + b_4$)	−	−0.541	9.872***	−0.534	8.471***
FINEXPERT	none	0.842	3.574*	0.805	2.768*
FINEXPERT × GC_OPINION	−	−0.838	2.489*	−0.513	0.341
Joint Test ($b_5 + b_6$)	−	0.004	0.000	0.292	0.140
STOCKOWN	none	0.091	0.002	0.325	0.028
STOCKOWN × GC_OPINION	+	3.894	1.635*	3.442	1.292
Joint Test ($b_7 + b_8$)	+	3.985	2.728**	3.767	2.500*
Board Members Not on the Audit Committee					
AFFILIATED	none			0.312	0.372
AFFILIATED × GC_OPINION	+			−1.560	2.948
Joint Test	+			−1.248	2.427
GOVEXPERT	none			−0.349	1.476
GOVEXPERT × GC_OPINION	−			−0.093	0.028
Joint Test	−			−0.442	0.801
FINEXPERT	none			−0.161	0.071
FINEXPERT × GC_OPINION	−			0.401	0.161
Joint Test	−			0.240	0.069
STOCKOWN	none			−0.487	0.671
STOCKOWN × GC_OPINION	+			1.754	2.036*
Joint Test	+			1.267	1.370

(continued on next page)

Carcello and Neal—Audit Committee Characteristics and Auditor Dismissals   109

TABLE 4 (continued)

		Model 1		Model 2	
Variable[a]	Predicted Relation	Estimated Coefficients	Wald Chi-Square	Estimated Coefficients	Wald Chi-Square
Control Variables					
SIZE	−	0.032	0.190	0.080	1.000
INDSHARE	−	−1.494	2.144*	−1.467	2.025*
TENURE	−	−0.022	0.314	−0.026	0.395
ZFC	+	−0.041	0.790	−0.023	0.239
MGMTCHG	+	0.737	7.881***	0.780	8.482***
Number of Observations		374		374	
Chi-Square for Model (degrees of freedom)		51.700 13		58.507 21	
p-value		0.0001		0.0001	
Pseudo R^2		0.10		0.11	
Concordant Pairs		70.1%		71.1%	

*, **, and *** indicate significance at $p < 0.10$, $p < 0.05$, and $p < 0.01$, respectively, based on one-tailed tests for variables that we predict an expected difference and two-tailed tests for variables that we do not predict an expected difference.

[a] Variable definitions:

DISMISSED = 1 if client dismissed its auditor before the company's next annual report, else 0;
AFFILIATED = percentage of "affiliated" directors;
GOVEXPERT = average number of directorships in other public companies held by directors;
FINEXPERT = percentage of directors with financial expertise;
STOCKOWN = percentage of the company's stock (including stock options) owned by directors;
SIZE = natural log of total assets (in thousands);
INDSHARE = auditor's market share in the client's industry, based on the percentage of the square root of total assets of all the companies in the client's industry, audited by the auditor;
TENURE = number of consecutive years the client has engaged the auditor (truncated at ten years);
ZFC = Zmijewski's (1984) financial condition index, where higher values indicate weaker financial condition; and
MGMTCHG = 1 if client changed CEO or CFO during the year the opinion was issued or during the following year, provided the management change preceded the auditor dismissal, else 0.

Finally, each of the four interactions between an audit committee characteristic and the GC indicator variable is statistically significant in the predicted direction, indicating that the relations between audit committee characteristics and auditor dismissals are significantly different for clients receiving GC reports than for clients receiving clean reports. Our collective results suggest that the significant relations between (1) auditor dismissals and (2) audit committee member independence, governance expertise, and stock ownership level, are unique to the GC-reporting context and do not generalize to the more common situation where the auditor issues a clean opinion.

With respect to the control variables, we find that a client is less likely to dismiss an industry-specialist auditor ($p < 0.10$) and more likely to dismiss its auditor after a recent change in top management ($p < 0.01$). There is no significant relation between the client's decision to dismiss its auditor and any of the other control variables.

Board of Director Characteristics and Auditor Dismissals

The BRC (1999, 14) views both the audit committee and the board of directors as clients of the auditor. Because the audit committee is composed of members of the board of directors, audit committee independence is positively associated with board of director independence (Klein 2002b). Since audit committee characteristics could simply mirror the characteristics of the full board of directors, we investigate the possibility that the characteristics of the audit committee that are associated with auditor dismissals are merely instruments for characteristics of board composition.

We test the relation between board of director characteristics and auditor dismissals by expanding the model to include both the audit committee characteristics and the characteristics of non-audit-committee board members. Model 2 in Table 4 presents these results.

The overall model is significant ($p < 0.01$), and the model's pseudo-R^2 is 11 percent. As was the case in Model 1 of Table 4, the likelihood that the client dismisses its auditor after receiving a GC report is: (1) increasing in the proportion of the audit committee composed of affiliated directors ($b_1 + b_2 > 0$; $p < 0.01$) and audit committee members' stock ownership level ($b_7 + b_8 > 0$; $p < 0.10$), (2) decreasing in audit committee members' governance expertise ($b_3 + b_4 < 0$; $p < 0.01$), and (3) unrelated to audit committee members' financial expertise ($b_5 + b_6$ is not significantly different from 0, $p = 0.71$). Moreover, there are no significant relations between auditor dismissals after a GC opinion and the characteristics of non-audit-committee board members (although the interaction between non-audit-committee board members' stock ownership and GC opinion is significant; $p < 0.10$).

Although the BRC (1999, 14) argues that the external auditor is ultimately accountable to the board of directors and the audit committee, our results suggest that it is the members of the audit committee, and not the other members of the board, who play a significant role in the auditor dismissal process. This result likely reflects the fact that most boards of directors delegate oversight of the external auditing function, including the hiring and firing of auditors, to the audit committee.

V. SUPPLEMENTAL ANALYSES
Subsequent Changes in Audit Committee Membership

We expect the turnover rate of independent audit committee members to be greater for clients that dismiss their auditors following GC reports than for clients that retain their auditors, because: (1) clients that dismissed their auditors might also dismiss independent audit committee members who voted to retain those auditors, possibly against the wishes of management and the affiliated directors, and (2) independent committee members who failed to prevent the dismissal of auditors might resign. To provide preliminary evidence on subsequent governance changes, we examine the proxy statements in the year following the GC report to determine the percentage of audit committee members who left their committees following GC reports.

Panel A of Table 5 shows that independent directors have a 56 percent turnover rate following an auditor dismissal pursuant to a GC report, compared to only a 27 percent turnover rate when the client retains the auditor after receiving a GC report. This significant ($p < 0.001$) difference supports our conjecture that independent directors who likely opposed management are more likely to be removed or to resign from the audit committee. Unfortunately, the proxy statements do not provide enough information to allow us to

---

TABLE 5
Percentage of Audit Committee Members Who Did Not Serve on the Audit Committee in the Following Year

Panel A: Going-Concern Opinion Sample (n = 124)[a]

	Client Dismissed Auditor	Client Did Not Dismiss Auditor	Difference	p-value[c]
Affiliated members (n = 79)[d]	52%	47%	5%	0.620
Independent members (n = 108)[e]	56%	27%	29%	0.001

Panel B: Clean Opinion Sample (n = 250)[b]

	Client Dismissed Auditor	Client Did Not Dismiss Auditor	Difference	p-value[c]
Affiliated members (n = 119)[d]	30%	20%	10%	0.205
Independent members (n = 236)[e]	24%	24%	0%	0.960

[a] Companies that received *new* going-concern reports from Big 6 audit firms during the period 1988–1999 (financial institutions and service companies excluded).
[b] Companies that received clean reports from Big 6 audit firms during the period 1988–1999 (financial institutions and service companies excluded).
[c] Based on Z-statistics for differences in proportions across dismissal vs. nondismissal clients.
[d] We performed this analysis only on clients with at least one "affiliated" director (e.g., current or former officers or employees, relatives of management, professional advisors to the company, officers of significant suppliers or customers, and interlocking directors) on the audit committee.
[e] We performed this analysis only on clients with at least one "independent" director on the audit committee. We classified directors as "independent" if the proxy statement discloses no ties to the company other than their service as a member of the board of directors.

---

disentangle whether that turnover is due to managerial action (termination, failure to re-nominate) or due to the director's initiative (resignation, choosing not to stand for re-election). We therefore leave further examination of this issue to future research.

Since we expect affiliated committee members to be more likely to support managerial attempts to dismiss the auditor, we do not expect turnover among the affiliated members to be related to dismissal of the auditor. Consistent with our expectation, Panel A of Table 5 shows that there is no relation between affiliated directors' turnover rate and auditor dismissals (p = 0.62). The high turnover rate among affiliated committee members after a GC report (approximately 50 percent whether or not the auditor is dismissed) likely reflects the high turnover rates of management and its advisors (both of whom would be considered affiliated directors) in companies experiencing financial difficulties.

To rule out the possibility that independent directors are more likely to leave the audit committee after any type of auditor dismissal, Panel B of Table 5 reports turnover rates of audit committee members following clean opinions. As expected, there is a lower level of turnover on the audit committee following clean reports (20–30 percent) than following GC reports (30–60 percent). More importantly, however, when the client receives a clean opinion, turnover rates for both affiliated and independent committee members are unrelated to auditor dismissal (p > 0.20).

Managerial Characteristics and Auditor Dismissals

Top management, particularly the CEO or the company's founder, sometimes has sufficient power to cause the auditor's dismissal, and to staff the audit committee with directors who are less effective monitors (e.g., affiliated directors, directors with little expertise, etc.). To ensure that the relations we observe between audit committee characteristics and auditor dismissals following GC opinions do not merely reflect the dominance of top management, we repeat our analysis after controlling for characteristics of top management dominance: (1) whether the same individual is both CEO and chairman of the board (Beasley 1996; Dechow et al. 1996); (2) the percentage of the entity's outstanding common stock the CEO owns (Klein 2002a); (3) the number of other corporate directorships the CEO holds; (4) whether the client's founder serves on the board of directors (Dechow et al. 1996); and (5) the percentage of the entity's outstanding common stock owned by all officers and directors (Beasley 1996; Dechow et al. 1996).

None of these proxies for top management dominance is significantly associated with auditor dismissals following a GC opinion, and our other results are consistent with those reported in Table 4. We therefore conclude that the relation between audit committee characteristics and auditor dismissals following GC reports is not driven by top management characteristics.

Over-Time Change in the Relation between Affiliated Audit Committee Members and Auditor Dismissals

Regulators' increasing scrutiny of audit committee performance (BRC 1999; Levitt 1998a, 1998b) is more likely to concern independent directors than affiliated directors who are more concerned with their direct economic incentives. Moreover, given the recent calls for audit committee independence, the continuing presence of affiliated directors on audit committees is more likely to be attributable to opportunistic motivations than has been the case in the past. We therefore expect the positive relation between the percentage of affiliated directors on the audit committee and auditor dismissals following GC reports to become stronger over time.

To test this conjecture we split our GC sample at its midpoint in time and compare the relation between affiliated directors and auditor dismissals in each period. Specifically, we add a dummy variable, TIME, (1 = post-1993, 0 = 1993 and earlier) to our primary logit model and an interaction between AFFILIATED and TIME to measure the differential relation between affiliated directors and dismissals after GC reports in the latter half of the sample period. We find that the likelihood that the client dismisses its auditor after receiving a GC report is increasing in the proportion of the audit committee composed of affiliated directors, in both the earlier and latter periods ($p < 0.05$ and $p < 0.001$, respectively), and that this positive relation is significantly stronger in the latter period ($p < 0.10$).[17]

Although the frequency with which affiliated directors sit on audit committees is likely to diminish in response to the recently enacted stock-exchange listing requirements, the adverse effects of allowing affiliated directors to sit on audit committees appear to have grown stronger over time (at least in the context of auditor dismissals). This result is of particular concern because the new stock-exchange listing requirements still provide some opportunities for affiliated directors to serve on audit committees.

---

[17] There is no significant interaction between time period and any of the other audit committee characteristics (GOVEXPERT, FINEXPERT, STOCKOWN). However, with the exception of financial expertise, which was not significant across the entire time period, the independence of the audit committee is the only audit committee characteristic receiving significant regulatory focus in recent years.

Opinion Shopping
We examine the relation between audit committee independence and potential opinion shopping for those clients receiving a GC opinion and then dismissing their auditor. We expect that a client with a greater percentage of affiliated directors on the audit committee is more likely to dismiss its auditor as part of an effort to shop for a more favorable audit opinion. We find that for those clients where the percentage of affiliated directors serving on the audit committee is above the median, 37.1 percent of the clients dismissing their auditors receive clean opinions in the following year; but where the percentage of affiliated directors serving on the audit committee is below the median, only 18.5 percent of the clients dismissing their auditors receive clean opinions in the following year ($p < 0.05$).[18] Although prior research finds that opinion shopping is generally unsuccessful (Chow and Rice 1982; Smith 1986; Krishnan and Stephens 1995; Geiger et al. 1998), our results suggest that opinion shopping following a GC report is more likely to be successful for companies that have a higher percentage of affiliated directors on the audit committee.

VI. SUMMARY, IMPLICATIONS, AND LIMITATIONS
This paper presents evidence on the relations between audit committee characteristics and the committee's ability to effectively discharge one of its primary responsibilities—protecting the auditor from the potential consequences of decisions that are unpopular with client management. More specifically, we find that the higher the percentage of affiliated directors on the audit committee, the more likely a client will dismiss its auditor following the receipt of a going-concern report, and there is some evidence that this relation has grown stronger in recent years. We also find that the probability the client dismisses the auditor following a going-concern report increases as audit committee ownership of client stock increases. On the other hand, clients whose audit committees have more governance expertise are less likely to dismiss their auditor. We find no significant relation between audit committee members' financial expertise and auditor dismissals following going-concern opinions. Finally, for clients receiving a going-concern report, the subsequent turnover rate among independent audit committee members is significantly greater when the client dismisses the auditor than when the client retains the auditor.

The documented relations between audit committee characteristics and auditor dismissals appear to arise from the contentious environment surrounding the issuance of a going-concern report. There is no significant relation between either the percentage of affiliated directors on the audit committee or audit committee members' stock ownership level and auditor dismissals following clean opinions. There is a marginally significant negative relation between audit committee members' governance expertise and auditor dismissals following clean opinions, and a counter-intuitive *positive* relation between audit committee members' financial expertise and dismissals following clean opinions. Moreover, our results are not driven by the characteristics shared by non-audit-committee members of the board of directors or by characteristics of top management.

Our results suggest that an audit committee that is more independent, with members who sit on more boards (governance expertise) and who own less company stock, is more

---

[18] We find no relation between the proportion of audit committee members who are affiliated and the nature of the audit report the client receives in the following year for clients that receive a GC report and retain their existing auditor.

effective in protecting the auditor from dismissal following the issuance of a going-concern report.[19] These results provide empirical support for recent calls to further strengthen audit committee independence (Levitt 2002; Millstein 2002; Teslik 2002; Turner 2002). In addition, the evidence that an audit committee holding more of the client's stock is more likely to dismiss the auditor after an unfavorable audit report supports calls to reduce the use of stock, particularly stock options, to compensate audit committee members (Millstein 2002). Finally, the higher turnover rate among independent audit committee members following auditor dismissals than following nondismissals—potentially driven by the desire of management and affiliated directors to replace these individuals—supports recent calls for (1) corporations to establish nominating committees composed entirely of independent directors (Millstein 2002), and (2) clients to disclose turnover of audit committee members in a Form 8-K filing (Turner 2002).

This study is subject to a number of limitations. Although we believe that the characteristics of the audit committee affect the committee's ability to effectively protect the independence of the external auditor, this study documents only association, not causation. Our model may have inadvertently omitted variables that are correlated with both the characteristics of the audit committee and the likelihood that the client will dismiss its auditor following the receipt of a going-concern report. We have attempted to minimize this risk by controlling for other factors that could be correlated with both the characteristics of the audit committee and auditor dismissal (i.e., company size, auditor industry market share, auditor tenure, client financial condition, and whether the client's top management recently changed), and by exploring potential alternative explanations for our results.

The new listing requirements related to audit committee members' independence and financial expertise became effective in June 2001 for companies traded via Amex or NAS-DAQ.[20] Our results suggest that the incidence of auditor dismissals following going-concern reports will decline as these new audit committee guidelines take effect. A decline in the incidence of auditor dismissals following going-concern reports should strengthen the auditor's position in disputes with management over the audit report, and presumably improve the quality of auditor communications with investors and creditors for companies experiencing financial distress.

---

[19] However, Klein (2002b) finds that companies with higher growth prospects have a higher percentage of affiliated directors on the audit committee than companies with lower growth prospects. The possible trade-off between company financial performance and threats to auditor independence as it relates to audit committee composition remains unresolved, although regulators appear more concerned with minimizing threats to auditor independence.

[20] The new listing requirements are effective for NYSE companies when new directors join the audit committee, or upon the reappointment of existing audit committee members.

REFERENCES

Bamber, E. M., L. S. Bamber, and M. P. Schoderbek. 1993. Audit structure and other determinants of audit report lag: An empirical analysis. *Auditing: A Journal of Practice & Theory* 12 (Spring): 1–23.

Baysinger, B. D., and H. N. Butler. 1985. Corporate governance and the board of directors: Performance effects of changes in board composition. *Journal of Law, Economics and Organization* 1 (Fall): 101–124.

Beasley, M. S. 1996. An empirical analysis of the relation between the board of director composition and financial statement fraud. *The Accounting Review* 71 (October): 443–465.

Blue Ribbon Committee (BRC). 1999. *Report and Recommendations of the Blue Ribbon Committee on Improving the Effectiveness of Corporate Audit Committees.* New York, NY: New York Stock Exchange and National Association of Securities Dealers.

Braiotta, L., Jr. 1999. *The Audit Committee Handbook.* 3rd edition. New York, NY: Wiley.

Carcello, J. V., D. R. Hermanson, and H. F. Huss. 1995. Temporal changes in bankruptcy-related reporting. *Auditing: A Journal of Practice & Theory* 14 (Fall): 133–143.

———, and T. L. Neal. 2000. Audit committee composition and auditor reporting. *The Accounting Review* 75 (October): 453–467.

Chow, C. W., and S. J. Rice. 1982. Qualified audit opinions and auditor switching. *The Accounting Review* 57 (April): 326–335.

Craswell, A. T. 1988. The association between qualified opinions and auditor switches. *Accounting and Business Research* 19 (Winter): 23–31.

Dechow, P. M., R. G. Sloan, and A. P. Sweeney. 1996. Causes and consequences of earnings manipulation: An analysis of firms subject to enforcement actions by the SEC. *Contemporary Accounting Research* 13 (Spring): 1–36.

DeFond, M. L. 1992. The association between changes in client firm agency costs and auditor switching. *Auditing: A Journal of Practice & Theory* 11 (Spring): 16–31.

Fama, E. F. 1980. Agency problems and the theory of the firm. *Journal of Political Economy* 88 (April): 288–307.

———, and M. C. Jensen. 1983. Separation of ownership and control. *Journal of Law & Economics* 26 (June): 301–325.

Francis, J. R., and E. R. Wilson. 1988. Auditor changes: A joint test of theories relating to agency costs and auditor differentiation. *The Accounting Review* 63 (October): 663–682.

Geiger, M., K. Raghunandan, and D. V. Rama. 1998. Costs associated with going-concern modified audit opinions: An analysis of auditor changes, subsequent opinions, and client failures. *Advances in Accounting* 16: 117–139.

Gilson, S. C. 1990. Bankruptcy, boards, banks, and blockholders. *Journal of Financial Economics* 27 (October): 355–387.

Gujarati, D. N. 1995. *Basic Econometrics*. 3rd edition. New York, NY: McGraw-Hill.

Haskins, M. E., and D. D. Williams. 1990. A contingent model of intra-Big Eight auditor changes. *Auditing: A Journal of Practice & Theory* 9 (Fall): 55–74.

Hogan, C. E., and D. C. Jeter. 1999. Industry specialization by auditors. *Auditing: A Journal of Practice & Theory* 18 (Spring): 1–17.

Iyer, V. M. 1998. Characteristics of accounting firm alumni who benefit their former firm. *Accounting Horizons* 12 (March): 18–30.

Jensen, M. C., and W. H. Meckling. 1976. Theory of the firm: Managerial behavior, agency costs and ownership structure. *Journal of Financial Economics* 3 (October): 305–360.

Jones, F. L. 1996. The information content of the auditor's going concern evaluation. *Journal of Accounting and Public Policy* 15 (Spring): 1–27.

Kaplan, S. N., and D. Reishus. 1990. Outside directorships and corporate performance. *Journal of Financial Economics* 27 (October): 389–410.

Klein, A. 2002a. Audit committee, board of director characteristics and earnings management. *Journal of Accounting and Economics* 33 (September): 1–26.

———. 2002b. Economic determinants of audit committee independence. *The Accounting Review* 77 (April): 435–452.

Krishnan, J. 1994. Auditor switching and conservatism. *The Accounting Review* 69 (January): 200–215.

———, and R. G. Stephens. 1995. Evidence on opinion shopping from audit opinion conservatism. *Journal of Accounting and Public Policy* 14 (Fall): 179–201.

Leonhardt, D. 2002. Anger at executives' profits fuels support for stock curb. *The New York Times on the Web* (July 9). Available at: http://www.nytimes.com/2002/07/09/business/09PAY.html.

Levinthal, D. A., and M. Fichman. 1988. Dynamics of interorganizational attachments: Auditor-client relations. *Administrative Science Quarterly* 33 (September): 345–369.

Levitt, A. 1998a. Corporate governance: Integrity in the information age. Remarks delivered at Tulane University's Corporate Law Institute, New Orleans, LA, March 12. Available at: http://www.sec.gov/news/speech/speecharchive/1998/spch206.txt.

———. 1998b. "The numbers game." Remarks delivered at the NYU Center for Law and Business, New York, September 28. Available at: http://www.sec.gov/news/speech/speecharchive/1998/spch220.txt.

———. 2000. Renewing the covenant with investors. Remarks delivered at the NYU Center for Law and Business, New York, May 10. Available at: http://www.sec.gov/news/speech/spch370.htm.

———. 2002. *Oversight Hearing on "Accounting and Investor Protection Issues Raised by Enron and Other Public Companies."* Senate Committee on Banking, Housing, and Urban Affairs. 107th Cong., 2nd sess. 12 February. Available at: http://www.senate.gov/~banking/02_02hrg/021202/levitt.htm.

McKeown, J. C., J. F. Mutchler, and W. Hopwood. 1991. Towards an explanation of auditor failure to modify the audit opinions of bankrupt companies. *Auditing: A Journal of Practice & Theory* 10 (Supplement): 1–13.

Melumad, N. D., and A. Ziv. 1997. A theoretical examination of the market reaction to auditors' qualifications. *Journal of Accounting Research* 35 (Autumn): 239–256.

Millstein, I. M. 2002. *Oversight Hearing on "Accounting and Investor Protection Issues Raised by Enron and Other Public Companies."* Senate Committee on Banking, Housing, and Urban Affairs. 107th Cong., 2nd sess. 27 February. Available at: http://www.senate.gov/~banking/02_02hrg/022702/millstn.htm.

Mutchler, J. F. 1984. Auditors' perceptions of the going-concern opinion decision. *Auditing: A Journal of Practice & Theory* 3 (Spring): 17–30.

Pitt, H. L. 2001. How to prevent future Enrons (Commentary). *The Wall Street Journal* (December 11): A18 or available at: http://interactive.wsj.com/archive/retrieve. cgi?id=SB1008029427565622280.djm.

———. 2002a. Remarks by Chairman Harvey Pitt, U.S. Securities and Exchange Commission, at the inaugural lecture of the JD/MBA lecture series, Kellogg Graduate School of Management and Northwestern University Law School, Evanston, IL, April 4. Available at: http://www.sec.gov/news/speech/spch547.htm.

———. 2002b. *Testimony Concerning The Corporate and Auditing Accountability, Responsibility, and Transparency Act.* House of Representatives Committee on Financial Services. 107th Cong., 2nd sess. 20 March. Available at: http://financialservices.house.gov/media/pdf/032002hp.pdf.

PricewaterhouseCoopers. 2000. *Audit Committee Effectiveness: What Works Best.* 2nd edition. Altamonte Springs, FL: The Institute of Internal Auditors Research Foundation.

Public Oversight Board (POB). 1994. *Strengthening the Professionalism of the Independent Auditor.* Stamford, CT: POB.

Ruder, D. S. 2002. *Oversight Hearing on "Accounting and Investor Protection Issues Raised by Enron and Other Public Companies."* Senate Committee on Banking, Housing, and Urban Affairs. 107th Cong., 2nd sess. 12 February. Available at: http://www.senate.gov/~banking/02_02hrg/021202/ruder.htm.

Schwartz, K. B., and K. Menon. 1985. Auditor switches by failing firms. *The Accounting Review* 60 (April): 248–261.

Securities and Exchange Commission (SEC). 2000. *Final Rule: Revision of the Commission's Auditor Independence Requirements.* Release No. 33-7919. Washington, DC: SEC. Available at: http://www.sec.gov/rules/final/33-7919.htm.

Smith, D. B. 1986. Auditor "subject to" opinions, disclaimers, and auditor changes. *Auditing: A Journal of Practice & Theory* 6 (Fall): 95–108.

Teslik, S. 2002. *Oversight Hearing on "Accounting and Investor Protection Issues Raised by Enron and Other Public Companies."* Senate Committee on Banking, Housing, and Urban Affairs. 107th Cong., 2nd sess. 20 March. Available at: http://www.senate.gov/~banking/02_03hrg/032002/teslik.htm.

Turner, L. 2002. *Testimony Concerning The Corporate and Auditing Accountability, Responsibility, and Transparency Act.* House of Representatives Committee on Financial Services. 107th Cong., 2nd sess. 13 March. Available at: http://financialservices.house.gov/media/pdf/031302lt.pdf.

Vicknair, D., K. Hickman, and K. C. Carnes. 1993. A note on audit committee independence: Evidence from the NYSE on "grey" area directors. *Accounting Horizons* 7 (March): 53–57.

Williams, D. D. 1988. The potential determinants of auditor change. *Journal of Business Finance & Accounting* 15 (Summer): 243–261.

Zmijewski, M. E. 1984. Methodological issues related to the estimation of financial distress prediction models. *Journal of Accounting Research* 22 (Supplement): 59–82.

Part IV
The Relationship between Internal and External Auditors

[23]

Accounting and Business Research, Vol. 24. No. 96. pp. 335–348. 1994

Evaluating the Work of Internal Audit: A Comparison of Standards and Empirical Evidence

James C. Lampe and Steve G. Sutton*

Abstract—Numerous changes have recently been proposed or made to audit standards providing guidance for external auditors' evaluations of internal audit work. This paper reports the results of a study to compare the UK's Accounting Practices Board Statement of Auditing Standard 500, first, with similar standards promulgated by international, Canadian and US societies, and second, with audit quality factors derived from practising internal auditors. The data for the latter comparison was obtained from a two-phase study that first generated a set of potential quality factors through intensive structured interviews with audit groups from six different and diverse organisations, and then obtained evaluations of these factors from a large sample of internal auditors worldwide. Results first indicate that there are strong similarities between the guidance provided by SAS 500 and that proposed or promulgated by the UK, international, Canadian and US audit groups. Furthermore, the guidance provided by these SASs for items to consider in evaluating the quality of internal audit work are largely in agreement with the factors determined by practising internal auditors. There are, however, several items listed in SAS 500 that are not considered useful by internal auditors and there are other factors considered crucial by internal auditors but not mentioned in the SASs.

Introduction

Changes in the global business environment over the past two decades have brought about reconsideration and re-engineering of the manner in which business organisations are managed and audited. Many organisations are downsizing in numbers with flatter management structures to curb costs. Consumers are demanding higher quality products for less money and with fewer delays. Internal audit departments within these organisations are expected to parallel the general economic movement by providing greater value services with fewer personnel and less expenditure of corporate resources.

Strong competitive bidding among external audit firms for audit clients has also forced the profession to identify ways to audit clients more efficiently while maintaining or improving the degree of confidence when issuing opinions. These cost pressures have been exacerbated by increasing legal sanctions for erroneous decisions, decreasing audit fees, and normal inflationary increases in the cost of performing audit services. A necessary by-product of these influences has been increased motivation for external auditors to reduce cost by relying more heavily on the work performed by

clients' internal auditors when the quality and type of their work justify it.

Numerous changes have recently been made (or proposed) to auditing standards and guidelines for assisting auditors in meeting the challenges generated by the rapidly changing global business community. For example, from an independent external audit perspective, the Auditing Practices Board (APB), the International Auditing Practices Committee (IAPC), the American Institute of Certified Public Accountants (AICPA) and the Canadian Institute of Chartered Accountants (CICA) have all promulgated standards and guidelines intended to help improve the effectiveness and efficiency of audits performed in the remainder of the decade and into the 21st century. One of the changes common to the APB's SAS 500 Exposure Draft, *Considering the Work of Internal Auditors*, and the other standards (APB, IAPC, CICA and AICPA) has been guidance for increased reliance on internal auditors' work. Beyond the new or proposed standards for external auditors' evaluation of internal audit work, the Institute of Internal Auditors (IIA) has adopted and updated a worldwide set of standards for internal auditors. Although only a minority of UK internal auditors belong to the IIA, the IIA-UK has incorporated the worldwide standards, interpretive Statements on Internal Audit Standards (SIASs), and IIA code of ethics into the 1992 reprint of the *Standards and Guidelines*. Most internal audit groups indicate that they are largely in compliance

*James C. Lampe is at Texas Tech University and Steve G. Sutton at Arizona State University-West. Correspondence should be addressed to Professor Lampe, Area of Accounting, College of Business Administration, Texas Tech University, PO Box 4320, Lubbock, Texas 79409-2101, USA.

with these standards (Burnaby et al., 1994). Other countries (France, Italy, New Zealand, Australia, Canada) have chapter affiliates that have similarly adopted the worldwide IIA standards that serve to promote higher quality work by participating internal auditors.

The purposes of this study are, first, to identify and compare the standards and guidelines promulgated by the respective professional societies; and second, to determine the extent to which guidance in these standards agrees with responses from large samples of internal auditors concerning the factors that most influence the quality and productivity (effectiveness and efficiency) of internal audit work. The second stated purpose, and the research approach, used here, are based on the premise that the collective group of internal auditors performing the day-to-day internal audit programmes can aid external auditors in identifying the facts that best determine when internal audit work is of sufficiently high quality to be reliable and usable. The remainder of this study and discussion of external auditor evaluations of internal audit work is split as follows:

- A recognition of the changes in both the internal and external audit professions leading to both the need and ability to further rely on internal audit work.
- A comparison of specific guidance provided in the SAS 500 Exposure Draft with similar standards promulgated by international, US and Canadian societies.
- A description of the study performed to identify and rank the factors considered by internal auditors performing day-to-day internal audit process tasks as most critically affecting the quality and reliability of their work.
- The implications of the areas in which internal auditors are in agreement and disagreement with the considerations recommended by SAS 500.

Changing environments

Over the past two decades, auditors have witnessed massive conceptual, procedural and reporting changes. These changes have been partially driven by efforts to improve service, and partially by survival instincts to remain viable in a rapidly changing business environment. Most successful business organisations have become more global, more competitive, more cost efficient, more timely in producing goods or services, more productive per capita (downsized personnel), and more focused on customer wants and needs. Many of these organisations have adopted a total quality management (TQM) philosophy to achieve the difficult goal of continual quality and productivity improvements.

One clear indication of the TQM impact on the current business environment is the establishment of production and service quality standards by the International Organisation for Standardisation (ISO). In the UK, the British Standards Institution had previously adopted a series of standards (BS 5750) with the objective of establishing, documenting and maintaining effective quality assurance systems. The combined series of BS 5750/ISO 9000 quality standards provides a consistent set of quality assurance guidelines for application by organisations to provide evidence of commitment and ability to provide quality goods and services to their customers.

The ISO standards have subsequently been adopted by over 50 countries and are considered essential to doing business in the post-1992 European Economic Community. The standards also include guidelines for the training and certification of 'quality systems auditors' and the methodology for auditing their company's quality system internally. Many internal audit departments are involved in establishing and monitoring BS 5750/ISO 9000 quality assurance systems operations. There is little doubt that overlap exists between the audit activities promulgated for external, internal and quality systems auditors via APB, IIA-UK and BSI/ISO organisations.[1] If traditionally educated and trained auditors are to remain viable in the global environment reflected by the quality award criteria and standards mentioned above, the changes in all areas of audit standards, guidelines and practices will need to parallel the changes in the global marketplace.

The Changing Internal Audit Environment
Traditionally, internal audit departments:

1. review accounting and other control systems and compliance with laws, regulations and other requirements to provide company management with an appraisal of service to the organisation;
2. examine financial and operational reports to determine accuracy and usefulness to organisation management;
3. co-ordinate work with independent external auditors to better accomplish total audit objectives and reduce total audit fees incurred by the organisation; and
4. review auditable subunits of the organisation with respect to their adequacy, efficiency and effectiveness in conducting primary operations (operational auditing).

---

[1] For greater detail on the overlap of IIA-UK/BSI/ISO standards, see Professional Briefing Note One, *Total Quality Management: Implications for Internal Audit Departments*, IIA-UK, London, 1992.

When external auditors evaluate internal audit work, attention is focused on the first three traditional functions with little emphasis on operational auditing. While providing these traditional services to the traditional customers (executive management, operating management and external auditors), leading internal audit organisations have recognised the need to continually improve their service performance and also to expand non-traditional services adding value to their respective organisations.

Perhaps greater in importance than the expanded scope of these traditional services are the extended set of internal audit stakeholders now considered to be 'customers' and the non-traditional approaches used to achieve the expanded services. One view of internal auditing is that it serves at the discretion of, and reports to, the audit committee. With adoption of the TQM philosophy, most IA departments also now consider the operating level auditee as a direct customer with wants to be satisfied. Additionally, the wants and needs of executive management, operating management and external auditors, as well as other stakeholders such as consumer groups, regulators, legislators and news media, must be considered when these persons or groups are likely to have direct impact on the auditable unit under examination.

Not only are the concepts of internal audit 'customers' being extended to persons and groups not previously considered, but the methods of obtaining and evaluating evidence are also changing rapidly. Use of advanced computer queries, data retrieval and communication networking are essential tools for increased audit efficiency. When internal auditors seek to improve service as consultants to operating management, a much broader scope of technical and interpersonal skills are required. Another change adopted by many leading internal audit groups is that auditee personnel are increasingly taught and relied upon to provide self-assessments of risk. The self-assessments help internal auditors to efficiently identify the trouble spots on which they concentrate with less attention paid to other less risky areas of operation. All of the above mentioned changes in the ways that internal audit services are performed, who is considered the customer, and who performs the activities, will affect the external auditor's planning of the nature, timing and extent of external audit activities.

The Changing External Audit Environment

The recent changes in the public accounting profession are numerous and complex. Given the global information age in which accounting and auditing professionals now practice, services must be responsive to the international capital markets in which information professionals operate. Although proposals of the International Accounting Standards Committee (IASC) are influential over only those professional societies that voluntarily choose to associate and adopt the proposals and standards issued, it is clear that most accounting professionals are aware of the need for common accounting and auditing standards to properly serve existing international capital markets and their investors.

Deregulation of the London stock market, emergence of the 'stock around the clock' euphemism, rapid increases and dominance of Japanese market investments, and availability of electronic trading media are all products of the past decade. In order to better service these markets, the accounting and auditing profession has sought to improve reporting for both the financial statements and internal control structure as evidenced by the Rutteman Exposure Draft on *Internal Control and Financial Reporting*. On the one hand, these developments have brought about increased awareness of the need for international accounting and auditing standards, but on the other, they have also brought about increased competition with non-accounting advisory and consulting firms as well as with other accounting firms about who is to provide such a service.

Whether the global information markets and increased price competition (bidding between firms) have been beneficial or detrimental to the accounting profession and the overall quality of audit service is beyond the scope of this study. These market changes are, however, forcing other movements in the profession that directly affect the auditor's consideration of, and reporting on, financial statements, supplementary data and internal controls. Increased competition has required audits to become more effective in terms of assurance and goal accomplishment as well as more efficient in terms of utilising fewer resources. Greater utilisation of inherent risk analyses and improved assessments of internal control risks are two procedural changes intended to achieve the joint effectiveness and efficiency desired. Use of internal auditor's work is another means of achieving these objectives.

The Use of Internal Audit Work

It is apparent that there is an overlap between the work of internal and external auditors. Furthermore, results from this and prior studies (Burnaby, 1994) indicate that most internal audit directors wish to co-ordinate activities with those of the external auditors in order to reduce the total audit fees charged. It does not follow, however, that the external auditors can automatically use the work of internal auditors. Nor does it follow that internal auditors best utilise their time and resources by perfunctorily performing procedures assigned by the external auditor. The goals of each unit can be accomplished at marginally lower total cost when internal auditors recognise the objectives of the external audit, modify their programmes to help achieve those objectives, and the external auditors recognise that internal auditors have performed needed procedures with acceptable levels of quality.

As an example, the general area of risk analysis is one in which clear overlap between internal and external auditors exists. Furthermore, both groups of auditors are using similar and expanded definitions and assessments of internal control such as in the Rutteman Exposure Draft on *Internal Control and Financial Reporting*, or the US equivalent COSO document entitled, *Internal Control-integrated Framework*. The external auditor performing an audit in accordance with promulgated standards will identify and assess inherent risks, general control risks, and specific cycle or application control risks. This is necessary to plan the audit, determine the tests to be performed and evaluate the evidence collected in order to form an opinion on the fair and accurate presentation of the financial statements. Internal auditors also assess these same risks but with the primary objectives of appraising their effectiveness and efficiency in order to assist the members of the total organisation to achieve continual improvement goals.

The selection of auditable units for scheduled internal audit assignments is commonly driven by risk assessment procedures. Following selection for audit, but prior to fieldwork, most internal auditors perform additional and more specific risk analyses of the units selected for audit. There is little marginal cost involved in co-ordinating the overall risk analyses and the more specific audited unit risk assessments to accomplish external auditor objectives and documenting the work for review by the external auditors.

Based on both the general inherent and specific item risk analyses performed, internal auditors direct the testing performed within the fieldwork phase. Fur the auditable units selected, reviewing and monitoring control structure policies and procedures are often primary objectives of internal audit assignments. The internal audit reports for these engagements include an evaluation and conclusion on the controls tested. When the quality of the internal auditors' work in these areas is judged to have been performed adequately, external auditors may use this work to reduce other audit evidence gathering procedures and concurrently achieve greater efficiency whilst gaining higher degrees of confidence about the true and accurate presentation of the financial statements.

Prior research on internal audit work has followed two major avenues: the nature and quality of internal audit work; and, the external auditors'

judgment processes when evaluating internal auditors' work. In both professional promulgations and academic research, the clear majority of prior studies have been oriented toward the external auditor's judgment process. Several studies concluded that subjective evaluations of competence and work performance were considered most important by external auditors (Clark, Gibbs and Schroeder, 1980; Brown, 1983; Schneider, 1984; Margheim, 1986; Messier and Schneider, 1988). A subsequent study alternatively concluded that the level of materiality of the area under audit was the most important determinant of the extent to which internal audit work was relied upon (Moiser, Turley and Walker, 1986). Other recent studies indicate that external auditors also use assessments of inherent and control risks in the evaluation of internal audit work (Maletta, 1993; Maletta and Kida, 1993).

The published research on the nature of internal auditors' work has been largely survey based and oriented toward the extent to which external auditors rely on the internal audit function (Ward, 1979; Ward and Robertson, 1980). Results of these studies indicate that respondents believe there is increasing reliance on internal auditors and that this reliance is primarily focused on the evaluation of the internal control structure. However, none of these publications has directly addressed the specific determinants of what constitutes high quality internal audit work performance.

A comparison of standards and guidelines

Following significant pronouncements in the Cadbury Report, *The Financial Aspects of Corporate Governance*, the APB has adopted a massive project to review and update all existing auditing standards and guidelines. Exposure drafts of the proposed overall structure of Statements of Auditing Standards (SASs), and in particular SAS 500, *Considering the Work of Internal Auditors*, have been issued for public comment. When issued as final, SAS 500 will replace the current Auditing Guideline 3.408, *Reliance on Internal Audit*. An equivalent International Standard on Auditing (ISA), *Considering the Work of Internal Auditors*, was published by the IAPC in late 1992. There are four broad requirements in both the SAS 500 Exposure Draft and the ISA:

SAS 500.1. The external auditors should consider the activities of internal audit and their effect, if any, on external audit procedures.
SAS 500.2. The external auditors should obtain a sufficient understanding of internal audit activities to assist in planning the audit and developing an effective audit approach.
SAS 500.3. During the course of their planning the external auditors should perform a

preliminary assessment of the internal audit function when it appears that certain internal audit work is relevant to the external audit of the financial statements.

SAS 500.4. When the external auditors use specific internal audit work to reduce the extent of their audit procedures, they should evaluate that work to confirm its adequacy for their purposes.

North American professional accounting and auditing societies (CICA and AICPA) have also recently promulgated audit standards that expand and replace prior guidance on evaluating the work of internal auditors. A joint study group report, *Independent Auditors' Consideration of the Work on Internal Auditors* (CICA, 1989; AICPA, 1989), provides the basis for these standards including three general areas of consideration that overlap the four requirements proposed by the APB and IAPC: understanding the internal audit function; assessing the competence and objectivity of internal auditors; and determining the extent and effect of internal auditors' work. Because AICPA SAS 65 contains very similar general recommendations to SAS 500 but more specificity in items to be considered, the SAS 65 content will first be summarised, with noticeable differences to SAS 500 discussed subsequently.

Understanding the Internal Audit Function
SAS 65 specifies that the auditor should inquire of management and internal audit personnel the internal auditors': organisational status; application of professional standards; audit plan(s); access to records and possible limitations on scope; and mission statement. Specific procedures recommended to assess the relevancy of internal audit activities include:

- reviewing internal audit resource allocation in accordance with risk assessments;
- considering prior audit knowledge; and
- reading internal audit reports to obtain information about the scope of internal audit activities.

Assessing Competence and Objectivity
Auditors are encouraged to obtain or update prior information about the internal auditors': education and experience level; professional certification and continuing education; audit policies, programmes and procedures; auditor assignment practices; supervision and review activities; quality of documentation and reporting; and performance evaluations. In order to assess internal auditor objectivity, information should be initially obtained or prior information updated concerning:

- the organisational status of the director of internal audit;

- the level of management to whom reports are directed;
- the access of internal auditors to the audit committee or equivalent;
- policies with respect to auditing relatives or relatives' work; and
- auditing policies with respect to the internal auditors' recent or future assignments.

Extent and Effect of Internal Audit Work
Determining the extent of the effect of internal auditors' work on the nature, timing and extent of external audit procedures follows two primary streams. In the first stream, external auditors consider the materiality, risk and degree of subjectivity involved in the investigation. These considerations are necessary to determine the extent to which internal audit work is used, but are not directly related to an evaluation of the work's quality. The second stream involves direct assessment of internal audit quality as a determinant of the degree to which the work is usable in restricting the nature, timing or extent of other audit procedures.

Suggestions to help co-ordinate the work of external and internal auditors include: holding periodic meetings; joint scheduling of work; access to internal audit working papers; and, reviewing internal audit reports issued. Additional procedures recommended in the evaluation of internal audit work quality are the consideration of:

- the adequacy of scope on assignments;
- the adequacy of programmes;
- the adequacy of work paper documentation; and
- the consistency of reports with audit results obtained.

It is further recommended that the external auditor re-perform some tests and compare independent results with those obtained by the internal auditors when the financial statements assertions are deemed to be significant to the total audit.

APB, IAPC and AICPA Differences
The first, and most important, comparison between the APB's proposed SAS 500, the proposed ISA, AICPA's SAS 65 and the CICA standard is that all four standards guide auditors to similar overall considerations of internal auditor work quality. At different ends of the spectrum, however, the AICPA SAS 65 provides the greatest specificity in items listed for auditor consideration while the SAS 500 guidance lists fewer specific items and allows auditors greater freedom of ultimate judgment in the degree of internal auditor impact on the nature, timing and extent of external audit procedures. The proposed ISA, however, requires the most specific action when the external auditor intends to use specific internal auditor

work. The ISA states that auditors 'should evaluate and test the work to confirm its adequacy'. SAS 500 requires only that auditors 'evaluate that work to confirm its adequacy'. The noticeable difference is that no requirement is stated for testing the work. SAS 65 recommends, but does not require, specific re-performance of some internal auditor tests as a method of evaluation.

Another commonality of virtually all SASs is that they require auditors to exercise professional judgment in the application of standards to specific audit engagements. Because all the SASs (especially SAS 500) permit substantial latitude in the evaluation of internal audit work, additional comparison of the internal audit quality assessment considerations with the factors identified by practising internal auditors may lead to even greater effectiveness and efficiency.

Study methodology and results

In the previous sections, it has been recognised that both external and internal auditors have significant and direct interest in evaluating the quality of internal audit work performance. Beyond these auditor groups, the management of the entity under audit, the audit committee, and industry regulators also share a common desire to make objective evaluations of internal audit quality. An immediately recognised barrier to all these groups sharing a common assessment of quality is that they have dissimilar perceptions and often have conflicting motivations for evaluating internal audit quality. Service quality research and applications outside auditing provide some direction for generating objective measures of service process quality that can be used by internal audit groups to motivate continual process improvements and by external auditors in their evaluation of internal audit work.

A Process View of Internal Audit Quality
Most of the published research on process quality has been performed in the area of manufacturing production with some direct extensions into service industries. In order to circumvent the problems generated by differing perceptions and motivations, production quality literature typically concentrates on more objective quantitative measures of the production process used as an intermediate indicator of quality rather than more subjective customer utilisation (output) measures (Adam et al., 1986; Van de Ven and Ferry, 1981; and Tuttle, 1982). More specific definitions of these two alternative approaches applied to the evaluation of internal audit work can be dichotomised as:

● *Process measures* that concentrate on the work performed in the audit process and how well it

compares with established service criteria in the form of professional and self-developed standards.
● *Outcome measures* that concentrate on the amount of increased value perceived by the auditee, the auditee's superiors, the audit committee and/or other company management as a result of the auditor's report.

In the context of process versus output measures of internal audit quality, it is evident that many of the suggestions provided in SAS 500 for external auditor consideration are oriented towards the final output of internal auditors' work. The alternative presented in this study is for external auditors to also consider process measures of the work quality performed by internal auditors. The following sections of this paper compare: (1) benchmark factors identified by practising internal auditors to be indicative of quality across most engagements they perform with (2) the considerations of internal audit work quality suggested via the SASs. The results of these comparisons indicate the degree to which empirically determined factors agree with those promulgated for external auditor consideration.

Data Collection Process
The research process used to collect and analyse quality factors considered important by internal auditors comprises two distinct phases. In the first phase, six different groups of internal auditors from a diverse set of industries participated in six independent and intensive structured group interviews—three full days with each different group of five to eight internal auditors. Results obtained from these structured interviews included: definitions of the boundaries around and major phases (segments) in the internal audit process applied by nearly all internal audit departments; identification of the key factors that may vary between audit and are associated with internal auditors' achievement of desired quality levels; and, generation of potential measures for each identified quality factor for the purpose of indicating the degree of quality achieved. The structured group interview processes used in this study led to consensus within each of the six separate participating audit groups when generating these boundaries, factors and measures. The reliability of these study results was confirmed via comparisons that yielded highly similar results obtained from all six different and independent groups.

In the second phase of the study, responses to a combined listing of the Phase I factors and measures were obtained from a large sample[2] of practising internal auditors. These responses were analysed to better define the relative importance of the 15 key quality factors identified in Phase I[3] and to rate the perceived usefulness of

---

Table 1
Profiles of the Participating Internal Audit Groups
Industry: National bank
Size of internal audit group: 60
Organisational profile: This firm hired primarily new graduates directly out of university. A more traditional pyramid structure (similar to external auditing firms) with staff, senior, manager and senior manager levels was used. A percentage of the employees made internal auditing a career position while most eventually left the internal audit group.

Industry: Oil and gas firm
Size of internal audit group: 120–140
Organisational profile: This firm hired primarily experienced internal and external auditors. A very flat structure was used where all audit staff were considered to be at essentially the same level. Median time on staff was approximately three years with auditors primarily moving to other positions within the company.

Industry: Chemical manufacturer
Size of internal audit group: 110
Organisational profile: This firm hired primarily new graduates directly out of university. A more traditional pyramid structure was used. While most staff eventually left internal audit, there were career path opportunities within the internal audit group.

Industry: Retail sales
Size of internal audit group: 85
Organisational profile: This firm hired a cross-section of new graduates and experienced auditors. The upper echelon of the audit staff had a pyramid structure, while the staff auditor level consisted primarily of personnel from other areas of the corporation that joined the audit staff on a three-year rotation.

Industry: Natural gas firm
Size of internal audit group: 15
Organisational profile: This firm hired primarily experienced internal and external auditors. A very flat structure was used where all audit staff were considered to be at essentially the same level. Roughly half of the positions were simply interim (approximately three-year) positions before entering other parts of the company, while the other half were career internal auditors.

Industry: Multi-product manufacturing
Size of internal audit group: 60–80
Organisational profile: This firm hired a cross-section of new graduates and experienced auditors. A more traditional pyramid structure with staff, senior and manager levels was used. A percentage of the employees made internal auditing a career position while most eventually left the internal audit group.

---

the associated potential measures. Results of the analyses provide objective rankings of the factors that many practising internal auditors believe to most affect the quality of their work and two or more objective measures of each identified factor.

The six organisations selected for participation in Phase I of the study represent a broad range of industries and organisational structures in which internal audit groups operate. The range in terms of size, industry and organisational structure provides strong validity for the commonly identified audit quality factors. With respect to organisational structure, the entities participating in this study include internal audit groups that rotate staff on a three-year basis, groups that hire experienced auditors from external audit firms or other internal

audit groups, and groups that provide career track audit positions. The participating internal audit group staff sizes ranged from small (15 auditors) to large (150–200 auditors). Table 1 provides a more in-depth profile of the internal audit groups from participating companies.

Although there are obvious industry and entity differences, the data collected from the diverse groups of auditors indicate strong commonalities in both the approach to the internal audit process and key factors individually identified as affecting audit quality. These results have important implications for the external auditors' evaluation of internal audit work quality.

Defining the Internal Audit Process
All six groups defined the starting boundary of the internal audit, for process quality evaluation purposes, as beginning subsequent to an auditee being selected for inclusion in the current year's set of audits but prior to contact of the auditee and initial planning of the audit. The end point for the process was identified either at the issuance of the

---

[2] Over 700 responses were obtained from a randomly selected sample of 3,000 from approximately 30,000 worldwide IIA members.
[3] For a more detailed discussion of the Phase I and Phase II methodology, refer to Sutton and Lampe (1991).

audit report (including closing conference with auditee) or right after receiving a response to the audit report from the auditee.

Based on these boundaries, participants then broke the entire audit process into smaller, but major, sequential stages. Again, the results indicate virtual consensus among the six diverse audit groups concerning the segmentation of the audit process (see Table 2). In all cases, a planning stage that includes a preliminary survey of the auditee is followed by a fieldwork segment conducted at the auditee site and a final phase that includes the reporting and closing conference with the auditee.

Because of the strong agreement between groups about the day-to-day tasks within the planning and fieldwork phases, discussion in this paper focuses on the apparent differences in the reporting phase of the audit. In addition to format differences between the six audit groups, it was also observed that the demeanour and content of reports varied within each individual group based on the various purposes of different audit engagements. From a format perspective, some groups present their reports at a closing conference with the auditee, while others require a formal response to the audit results. In these organisations, the auditees' formal responses are then included in the final audit report issued at a later date. Beyond such timing differences, variations in reporting demeanour are also observable. In some companies the internal audit group is perceived as, and works more like, a consultant using a reporting process oriented to value-added recommendations for improvement. In other organisations, the report is independently generated by the internal auditors with a specific rated evaluation of auditee controls. These differences in reporting tasks are also observable in the quality factors identified by the different audit groups as key to the completion of a quality audit. Furthermore, all the participating auditors considered the variations that occur during the reporting phase to have the most critical impact on audit quality.

Identified Key Audit Quality Factors

Following each group's consensus definition of the audit process, the objective of the structured

group interviews was shifted to identification of key factors perceived to affect completion of an internal audit engagement at a desired quality level. Each group independently generated a large number of potential factors that was subsequently reduced to a smaller and more manageable number of factors considered to most critically affect audit quality. Table 3 presents both the larger number of factors initially identified via the structured brainstorming technique and the reduced number of audit quality factors identified by each individual group as having a critical affect on internal audit quality.

Two important observations can be made of the data in Table 3. Although each of the six different internal audit groups identified a large number of varied quality factors, those considered to be critical by each group are similar. Many of the quality factors considered as key (critical) by any one individual group were also considered as critical by the auditors from the other organisations. Out of the total of 85 key quality factors, 51 are repeats resulting in only 34 unique factors that were subsequently reduced to the set of 15 considered to be most critical.

Additional analysis of the consistency between the six groups' selections and ratings of audit quality factors is provided via Kendall's Coefficient of Concordance. Because Kendall's test uses rank data to measure the level of concordance, the test was run separately for each of the three phases of the audit (i.e., planning, fieldwork and reporting).

The results show high correlation between the six groups for the planning and fieldwork phases of the audit, but little agreement on the critical factors during the reporting phase (see Table 4). These results are highly consistent with those found during the sessions used to identify the major audit phases and process tasks. While the processes defined for planning and fieldwork were common across all six organisations, the tasks defined within the reporting phase fluctuated from one organisation to the next. This deviation in the definability of the reporting phase is followed by predictably low levels of concordance between the participating groups.

Table 2
Composite of Audit Phases Identified by the Six Internal Audit Groups

Banking	Oil and gas	Chemical manufacturer	Retail sales	Natural gas	Multi-product manufacturer
Planning	Planning/risk analysis	Planning	Preliminary survey	Preliminary survey	Preliminary survey
Fieldwork	Transaction flow review				
	Audit testing	Fieldwork	Fieldwork	Fieldwork	Fieldwork
Wrap-up	Final evaluation and reporting	Reporting	Reporting	Reporting	Reporting

Table 3
Audit Quality Factor Identification

Participating audit groups	Banking	Oil and gas	Chemical manufacturer	Retail sales	Natural gas	Multi-product manufacturer
Total quality factors generated	55	83	91	65	75	81
Quality factors considered key	18	22	17	13	15	16

Key factors by phase and group

Planning

	Banking	Oil and gas	Chemical manufacturer	Retail sales	Natural gas	Multi-product manufacturer
Audit team experience and training	X	X	X	X	X	X
Audit manager (supervisor) involvement and support	X	X		X	X	
Auditee co-operation and availability	X		X	X	X	X
Time available for planning	X	X	X		X	X
Understanding of risks (objectives)	X	X		X		X

Fieldwork

	Banking	Oil and gas	Chemical manufacturer	Retail sales	Natural gas	Multi-product manufacturer
Audit team experience and training	X	X	X		X	X
Time pressures (constraints)	X		X	X	X	X
Auditee availability and co-operation	X	X	X	X	X	X
Level of auditee documentation (automation)		X			X	
Complexity (technical) of issues		X	X		X	X

Reporting and review

	Banking	Oil and gas	Chemical manufacturer	Retail sales	Natural gas	Multi-product manufacturer
Audit manager (supervisor) involvement and support		X		X	X	X
Audit team experience and training (emphasis on primary report writer)	X	X	X		X	X
Complexity (sensitivity) of report findings	X	X	X	X	X	
Auditee co-operation and availability	X	X	X		X	X
Timing of the report	X	X		X		X

Relative Importance of Audit Quality Factors

In order to further evaluate the data aggregated from Phase I, the factors most highly and commonly rated by the six participating internal audit groups were combined into a questionnaire for distribution to a larger sample of practising internal auditors. A common benchmark factor was selected as a basis for adjusting the individual data sets to a common standard for evaluation by the Phase II survey respondents. The single most commonly identified factor, 'Audit team experience and training', was assigned the value of 100. The survey respondents were instructed to assign value weightings for each of the remaining 14 quality factors relative to the benchmark factor valued at 100. The composite set of audit quality factors and the associated factor weightings are presented in Table 5. Results indicate that

'Understanding risks' is the single most important factor, but that the reporting phase has the greatest overall affect on audit work quality.

Best Measures for the Key Quality Factors

Separate sets of sessions with each of the six audit groups in Phase I were used to generate an initial set of potential measures for each identified audit quality factor. An iterative approach (similar to that used to identify factors) resulted in numerous potential measures being generated for each factor. Subsequent rankings of measure usefulness reduced the large number of potential measures to a more manageable set of 'best measures'. A total of 45 measures (about three each for the 15 factors) were synthesised from the rankings provided by the six audit groups and included in the questionnaire distributed to the large sample of

Table 4
Test of Consensus Among Auditors on Selected Quality Measures (Kendall's Coefficient of Concordance)

Audit quality factor	Degrees of freedom	X^2	p-value
All audit factors	44	4394.14	<0.0001
Planning			
Audit team experience and training (emphasis on primary planner)	3	117.04	<0.0001
Audit manager (supervisor) involvement and support	2	142.66	<0.0001
Auditee co-operation and availability	3	479.08	<0.0001
Time available for planning	1	36.51	<0.0001
Understanding of risks (objectives)	1	185.01	<0.0001
Fieldwork			
Audit team experience and training	2	105.69	<0.0001
Time pressures (constraints)	3	167.12	<0.0001
Auditee availability and co-operation	2	220.53	<0.0001
Level of auditee documentation (automation)	2	224.34	<0.0001
Complexity (technical) of issues	2	182.15	<0.0001
Reporting and review			
Audit manager (supervisor) involvement and support	1	15.81	.0001
Audit team experience and training (emphasis on primary report writer)	2	201.40	<0.0001
Complexity (sensitivity of report findings)	3	139.68	<0.0001
Auditee co-operation and availability	2	12.16	0.0023
Timing of the report	1	6.32	0.0119

practising auditors in Phase II of the study. Two dimensions of usefulness were provided to facilitate participants' evaluations. The first dimension presented for evaluation was the 'strength' element that represents the relevancy and meaningfulness of the measure to the given audit quality factor being measured. 'Confidence' was defined as the second element and represents the precision, objectivity and feasibility of the given measure. Both of these dimensions were evaluated separately using a 0–5 scale. The values obtained for each of the two dimensions were multiplied to form a composite rating of measure usefulness[4] that could range from 0 (both dimensions rated 0) to 25 (both dimensions rated 5).

Results of the individual composite usefulness ratings for each measure in the planning, fieldwork and reporting phases of the internal audit process are shown in Tables 6, 7 and 8 respectively. Readers are reminded that all these measures were individually considered as the best for the given audit quality factor by one or more of the six audit teams participating in the Phase I group processes. All these measures, therefore, are considered to have potential for being a useful indicator of internal audit quality. The benefit of additional

rankings by larger numbers of internal auditors is that external auditors can compare specific evaluations of internal audit work using measures that many internal auditors performing similar tasks consider to be most meaningful. The greater the average composite usefulness value for a given measure, the greater the overall belief among survey respondents that the measure provides a reliable indication of audit quality in most audit engagements. These results indicate primary agreement with SAS 500. There are, however, several noticeable discrepancies from the guidance provided in the SASs. More specific implications of these inconsistencies between the two sources are examined in the next section.

Discussion and implications

The first sections of this paper presented and compared recently adopted or proposed standards to guide external auditors in evaluating the quality of internal audit work. Many of the items recommended in SAS 500 and the other SASs for external auditor consideration are representative of internal audit quality output measures. The research results reported in the latter sections of this paper propose additional consideration of process oriented measures to aid external auditors in evaluating internal audit work. Comparisons of the empirical research results based on practising internal auditor responses with the four major

---

[4]The multiplication of the two items is recommended by Adam, Hershauer and Ruch (1986) and is based on the Expectancy Theory foundations for the development of the methodology.

Table 5

Magnitude Measures for Audit Quality Factors

Audit quality factor	Magnitude measure
Planning	
Audit team experience and training (emphasis on primary planner)	117
Audit manager (supervisor) involvement and support	101
Auditee co-operation and availability	80
Time available for planning	85
Understanding of risks (objectives)	153
Fieldwork	
Audit team experience and training	100
Time pressures (constraints)	81
Auditee availability and co-operation	105
Level of auditee documentation (automation)	86
Complexity (technical) of issues	115
Reporting and review	
Audit manager (supervisor) involvement and support	121
Audit team experience and training (emphasis on primary report writer)	121
Complexity (sensitivity) of report findings	124
Auditee co-operation and availability	89
Timing of the report	94

recommendations of SAS 500 Exposure Draft reveal many similarities and overlap, but also indicate differences of which external auditors should be aware.

Consider Internal Audit Activities (SAS 500.1)

The scope and objectives of internal audit functions are briefly defined in SAS 500.1. Results of this study provide greater specificity in the definition of internal auditing and provide external auditors with the knowledge that most internal audit engagements comprise three major phases with fairly consistent activities in the planning and fieldwork phases, but that objectives and activities in the reporting phase vary significantly between companies and engagements.

These results may not provide new knowledge to many external auditors, but are beneficial in confirming and/or adding to knowledge already used in evaluating internal audit work. There is, however, one additional organisational aspect of internal audit departments (groups), not discussed in the SASs but identified in the current study, that deserves additional consideration by external auditors. The political nature of the corporate environ-

ment was identified as affecting all audit assignments. SAS 500 recognises the importance of the internal audit group position within the organisational structure and clearly states that it must be 'free of any other operating responsibility'. The additional factor discovered in this research is that many companies follow the practice of rotating staff auditors to other organisational operating areas after three or four years' service in internal audit. In this environment, many staff level internal auditors feel much greater pressure not to issue negative reports for an auditee in an operating area where they may be transferred in future years.

Understanding and Assessing the Internal Audit Function (SAS 500.2,3)

General considerations recommended in SAS 500 include: organisational status; scope of function; technical competence; and due professional care. The additional listings of considerations in AICPA SAS 65 include: audit team experience; assignment of individual auditors; adequacy of audit programmes and procedures; supervision and review; workpaper documentation; and report consistency. Most of these factors were also recognised by the internal auditors in this study. It is interesting to note, however, that several of the SAS 65 recommendations were specifically considered by all six groups of internal auditors and subsequently excluded from the list of factors considered to have a critical impact on audit quality. The auditors' education level, professional certification and whether or not auditor relatives are at the audit site, were all considered sufficiently unimportant by all six groups of internal auditors to be excluded from a quality monitoring system. The question arises, therefore, of whether external auditor investigation of such matters is cost beneficial in evaluating internal audit work.

Perhaps of greater significance are the factors the group of internal auditors considered critical but which are not discussed in the SASs. For example, although external auditors recognise the importance of time constraints on external audits, neither the SAS 500 Exposure Draft nor the other standards compared with it mention this as a consideration of internal audit quality. Internal auditors agree that the amount of time budgeted and spent on different assignments has a critical influence on audit quality. Other factors not recognised by any of the SASs, but which internal auditors considered critical, include corporate political pressures, sensitivity of audit findings and the level of internal audit manager involvement with the on-site internal audit team. External auditors should also consider these factors when evaluating the extent of potential reliance on internal audit work.

Table 6
Mean Ratings for Audit Quality Measures (Planning Phase)

Audit quality measure	Mean rating*
Audit team training and experience	
(Emphasis on primary planner on the team)	
● No. of new staff on audit ÷ total no. of people on audit team	7.71
● No. years of planner's experience ÷ minimum years to planning position	9.35
● No. years of audit experience (total and in company)	12.34
● No. prior audits in area of current audit	12.39
Audit manager involvement and support	
● Did manager complete review of scope prior to fieldwork? (Y/N)	12.95
● Did manager attend opening conference with auditee? (Y/N)	8.44
● Did manager meet with audit team prior to fieldwork? (Y/N)	11.48
Auditee co-operation and availability	
● % of days auditee executive(s) on-site during first week	6.23
● Was access to desired auditee information available? (Y/N)	15.60
● Is auditee an ex-auditor? (Y/N)	4.72
● Do audit findings affect auditee's formal evaluation? (Y/N)	6.82
Time available for planning	
● Total hours used in planning ÷ scheduled hours for planning	7.87
● Total hours planning ÷ total audit hours	9.78
Understanding audit risks (objectives)	
● % risk analysis completed before fieldwork	12.20
● % audit programme completed before fieldwork	6.22

*A higher rating is better. Ratings above nine are considered to represent robust measures for audit quality factors.

Table 7
Mean Ratings for Audit Quality Measures (Fieldwork Phase)

Audit quality measure	Mean rating*
Audit team training and experience	
● No. of new employees on audit ÷ total no. of people on audit team	9.48
● % of audit team with prior audit experience in area of current audit	13.12
● Average number years audit experience of audit team	10.95
Time constraints	
● (Actual hours − scheduled hours) ÷ scheduled hours	7.95
● Overtime hours for fieldwork ÷ total hours for fieldwork	5.43
● Days from planned to actual completion of fieldwork	7.43
● No. of overtime hours in last two weeks of audit ÷ total hours worked in last two weeks	4.69
Auditee co-operation and availability	
● % of days auditee executive(s) and key personnel are at site during fieldwork	8.70
● Was formal (written) auditee feedback obtained? (Y/N)	13.84
● Type of previous audit opinion	7.07
Level of auditee documentation (automation)	
● Was access to desired auditee documentation available? (Y/N)	15.39
● Has auditee assigned a primary contact person? (Y/N)	10.60
● Are auditee data in electronic format? (Y/N)	8.04
Complexity (sensitivity) of audit	
● Dollar amount of questioned costs (recommended savings)	9.02
● No. of reported findings ÷ average no. reported findings	4.88
● No. of reported findings ÷ no. potential items in workpapers	5.31

*A higher rating is better. Ratings above nine are considered to represent robust measures for audit quality factors.

Table 8
Mean Ratings for Audit Quality Measures (Reporting Phase)

Audit quality measure	Mean rating*
Audit manager involvement and support	
• Days from receipt of draft to return of completed review	9.77
• Did manager attend final review meeting? (Y/N)	11.58
Audit team training and experience	
(Emphasis on primary report writer)	
• Years of audit experience (total and in company)	11.36
• No. prior audit reports written	11.68
• Years of audit experience ÷ minimum years to report writing	
position	7.25
Complexity (sensitivity) of findings	
• Is report issued to higher than normal level? (Y/N)	11.70
• No. of conference attendees above auditee level	7.21
• Is an ethics violations involved? (Y/N)	11.02
• Dollars of questioned costs (recommended savings)	10.22
Auditee co-operation and availability	
• Are audit results part of formal auditee evaluations? (Y/N)	7.47
• Type of previous audit opinion	6.70
• No. of rebuttals at final opinion	8.02
Timing of report issuance	
• Days from informal exit conference with auditee to issuance	10.96
• Days from end of fieldwork to issuance	11.35

*A higher rating is better. Ratings above nine are considered to represent robust measures for audit quality factors.

Evaluating Specific Internal Audit Work (SAS 500.4)

General considerations listed in SAS 500.4 include the supervision of assistants, conclusions reached, reports prepared and resolution of internal auditors' findings. Factors that are both identified in this study and mentioned for consideration by the SASs include the scope of audit programme and procedures, workpaper documentation, and consistency of report conclusions with audit findings. A caveat is necessary, however, when external auditors review internal audit reports. The current study has concluded that while many similarities exist between internal audit groups in the planning and fieldwork phases on internal audit assignments, there is a wide variety of reporting formats and purposes in different entities and in different types of internal audit engagements. External auditor consideration and review of internal audit reports should recognise such differences, especially because the reporting phase is considered to have the greatest overall impact on audit quality.

Another aspect of audit quality internal auditors surveyed in this study considered critical—auditee attributes—is approached from a different perspective in the SASs. The risk, materiality and subjectivity associated with a given work area are discussed in general in the SASs and overlap many of the internal auditor concerns identified in this study. Above and beyond the areas of general concern, internal auditors recognise that the timing, co-operation and availability of key auditee personnel further affect the ultimate quality achieved by the internal audit process.

The final, and most important, difference between SAS 500 Exposure Draft guidance and that recommended in the current study deals with specific measures of internal audit quality. SAS 500 does not list or recommend any quantitative measures of internal audit quality or any re-performance of internal audit testing. There is an implication that external auditors are better served by broad and general considerations that lead to a qualitative judgment of internal audit quality. The current study identifies and evaluates 45 specific measures for use in comparing quality between engagements. It is not recommended that internal or external auditors should invest the time or resources to track all 45 of these measures across internal audit engagements. External auditors may, however, wish to select only a few of these 'best' measures to be tracked across the internal audit engagements for which they have evaluation responsibilities. It is critical that the reduced set of measures are comprehensive of the total audit engagement. If the measures are believed to be robust, even one or two measures from each of the audit phases (planning, fieldwork and reporting) could provide reliable and comprehensive quantitative assessments of engagement quality. We firmly believe that relatively few but comprehensive quantitative measures used for common comparisons between engagements will result in improved evaluations and greater adequacy of corresponding documentation.

Conclusion

This study's overall conclusion is that empirical data collected from six internal audit groups representing a wide variety of industries and subsequently evaluated by a large sample of internal auditors identify a comprehensive set of audit quality considerations separate from those listed in the SASs. Comparisons of the two sets of factors (considerations) indicate that:

- many of the considerations listed in SAS 500 are confirmed by the empirical data collected from practising internal auditors;
- some of the items suggested in SAS 500 and the other SASs are not considered critical by internal auditors—efficiencies may be gained if these factors are not evaluated by external auditors; and
- several factors that internal auditors believe to strongly influence the quality of their work are not suggested by SAS 500—audit effectiveness may be improved if these factors are evaluated.

Other important questions are not directly addressed or answered by this research. It has been pointed out that IAPC standards require re-performance of internal auditors' work before placing reliance on it, but SAS 500 does not even recommend re-performance. If specific work is not re-performed, what constitutes an adequate basis for reliance on internal auditors' work? Alternatives include: review of IA working papers; review and discussion of findings written for the auditee; or a special report by internal auditors for the external auditors similar to that from other professional experts such as petroleum engineers or surveyors.

Another recent development has been in contracting out (outsourcing) some or all of the internal audit functions. When such activities are contracted out, especially to the external audit firm, does the quality evaluation need to take a different form? Should ethical issues of independence between internal and external auditors override quality issues when the external auditor is determining the extent of reliance on internal auditors' work? Consideration of additional factors identified and rated in this study should provide an improved and expanded basis for the evaluation of the work of internal auditors, by external auditors, regardless of the situation in which it is taking place. The list of factors to be considered is organised in a logical order in the internal audit process sequence. These factors provide a more comprehensive and detailed view of the internal audit process while adding the ability to compare empirically determined measures of internal audit quality across the engagements in which evaluation responsibility is present. As always, the ultimate decision must rely on the judgment of the professional auditor.

References

Adam, E. E. Jr., Herschauer, J. and Ruch, W. (1986), *Productivity and Quality Measurement as a Basis for Improvement* (University of Missouri College of Business Research Center).

Brown, Paul R. (1983), 'Independent Auditor Judgment in the Evaluation of Internal Audit Functions', *Journal of Accounting Research*, Autumn, pp. 444–455.

Burnaby, Priscilla A., Powell, N. C. and Strickland, S. (1994), 'Internal Auditing Internationally: Another Step Toward Global Harmonization', *Internal Auditing*, Winter, pp. 38–53.

Clark, M., Gibbs, T. E. and Schroeder, R. B. (1980), 'Evaluating Internal Audit Departments Under SAS No. 9', *The Woman CPA*, July, pp. 8–11 and 22.

Maletta, M. J. (1993), 'Auditors' Decisions to Use Internal Auditors as Assistants: The Effect of Inherent Risk', *Contemporary Accounting Research*, Spring.

Maletta, M. J. and Kida, T. (1993), 'The Effect of Risk Factors on Auditors' Configural Information Processing', *Accounting Review*, July, pp. 681–691.

Margheim, Loren L. (1986), 'Further Evidence of External Auditors' Reliance on Internal Auditors', *Journal of Accounting Research*, Spring, pp. 194–205.

Messier, W. F. and Schneider, A. (1988), 'A Hierarchical Approach to the External Auditor's Evaluation of the Internal Auditing Function', *Contemporary Accounting Research*, Spring, pp. 337–353.

Moizer, P., Turley, S. and Walker, D. (1986), 'Reliance on Other Auditors: A UK Study', *Accounting and Business Research*, Autumn, pp. 343–352.

Schneider, Arnold (1984), 'Modeling External Auditors' Evaluations of Internal Auditing', *Journal of Accounting Research*, Autumn, pp. 657–678.

Sutton, S. G. and Lampe, J. C. (1991), 'A Framework for Evaluating Process Quality and Audit Engagements', *Accounting and Business Research*, Summer, pp. 275–288.

Tuttle, T. C. (1982), 'Measuring Productivity and Quality of Working Life', *National Forum*, Spring.

Van De Ven, A. and Ferry, D. (1981), *Measuring and Assessing Organizations* (New York: John Wiley & Sons).

Ward, D. D. (1979), 'A Delphi Survey of Reliance Upon Internal Auditors and Their Work by External Auditors During Financial Audits', unpublished doctoral dissertation, University of Texas at Austin.

Ward, D. D. and Robertson, J. C. (1980), 'Reliance on Internal Auditors', *Journal of Accountancy*, October, pp. 62–73.

[24]

Journal of Accounting Research
Vol. 39 No. 3 December 2001
Printed in U.S.A.

The Contribution of Internal Audit as a Determinant of External Audit Fees and Factors Influencing This Contribution

WILLIAM L. FELIX, JR.,* AUDREY A. GRAMLING,†
AND MARIO J. MALETTA‡

Received 4 January 1999; accepted 26 March 2001

ABSTRACT

Despite extensive research on the determinants of external audit fees, there is little empirical evidence on the effect of internal audit contribution on the external audit fee. Using a cross-sectional regression model based on prior audit fee research, this study provides evidence that internal audit contribution is a significant determinant of the external audit fee. Further, a second model that provides evidence on the determinants of internal audit contribution is developed and tested. This second model indicates that internal audit contribution is influenced by internal audit quality and, conditional on the level of inherent risk, the availability of internal audit and the extent of coordination between internal and external auditors. These results are based on a unique data-set comprised of publicly available data matched with survey responses from internal and external auditors affiliated with 70 non-financial services Fortune 1000 firms. The sample includes all of the former "Big 6" international accounting firms and clients from twenty-nine different industries.

*University of Arizona; †Georgia State University; ‡Northeastern University. We gratefully acknowledge the financial support of The Institute of Internal Auditors Research Foundation and the accounting department at the University of Arizona. We are also very appreciative of the internal and external audit professionals who took their time to talk with us and to provide data used in this study. This project would not have been possible without their valuable input. We appreciate comments received from Abbie Smith (editor),

513

514   W. L. FELIX JR., A. A. GRAMLING, AND M. J. MALETTA

1. Introduction

Professional auditing standards recognize that internal auditors may contribute to the financial statement audit by either working as assistants under the direct supervision of the external auditors or independently performing relevant work throughout the audit year on which the external auditors can rely (see SAS No. 65, AICPA [1997]). This study investigates the relation between the contribution that internal audit makes to the financial statement audit via these two approaches and the magnitude of the external audit fee.[1]

Our analysis is based on a unique data-set comprising publicly available archival data and matched survey responses from internal and external auditors affiliated with 70 non-financial services Fortune 1000 firms. Our sample includes all of the Big 6 firms, while the client firms represent twenty-nine industries. Using a cross-sectional regression model based on prior audit fee research, we use a continuous measure of internal audit contribution and analyze the extent to which this contribution measure affects the external audit fee. We also develop and test a model that provides evidence on the determinants of internal audit contribution.

Our findings indicate that the extent to which internal audit contributes to the financial statement audit is a significant determinant of external audit fees. We find that the greater the contribution made by internal audit, the lower the external audit fee. For example, if an audit client were to increase the contribution made by internal audit to the financial statement audit from no contribution to the mean level found in our sample (i.e., internal audit completes 26.57% of the financial statement audit), the audit fee would decrease by approximately 18 percent, or $215,961. Further analysis suggests that clients can affect the extent of internal audit contribution by investing in internal audit quality and, depending on the level of inherent risk, by either managing internal audit availability or facilitating greater coordination between internal and external auditors.

Allen Craswell, Jere Francis, Willie Gist, Tom Linsmeier, Arnie Schneider, Dan Simunic, Mike Stein, Mark Taylor, Greg Trompeter, Richard Turpen, Wanda Wallace, Dave Ziebart, and workshop participants at the 1998 ISAR, 1999 AAA Audit Midyear Meeting, 1999 AAA Annual Meeting, 2000 AAA-BAA Second Globalization Conference, the University of Arizona, the University of Florida, Georgia State University, and Wake Forest University. Finally, we thank Cassandra J. Walsh for her very useful research assistance.

[1] Professional auditing standards (see SAS No. 78 (AICPA [1997]) also recognize that a client's internal audit department may affect the financial statement audit given that it is a component of a client's internal controls. Accordingly, internal audit could affect the external auditor's assessment of control risk, and hence the audit procedures performed (see SAS No. 78). Our investigation does not consider this type of contribution but focuses solely on the contribution that internal audit can make through completion of audit procedures that can be used by the external auditors (see SAS No. 65).

2. Background and Expectations

2.1 INTERNAL AUDIT AND THE EXTERNAL AUDIT FEE

Extensive empirical research documents the determinants of external audit fees in the market for audit services.[2] This research has important economic implications for both audit firms and audit clients. While clients generally are concerned with controlling external audit costs (Elgin [1992], Elliott [1994]), they also have an interest in obtaining the greatest benefit possible from their internal audit investments (Aldhizer and Cashell [1996]). Given the potential for internal and external auditors to serve as alternative monitoring mechanisms (Simunic [1980], Anderson et al. [1993], and Craswell et al. [1995]), both external auditors and their clients have an interest in the mix of internal and external audit costs expended on the external audit. While the potential for a reduction in external audit fees due to internal audit contribution has been discussed in the internal auditing literature for at least five decades (Thurston [1949], Wallace [1984a,b,c], and Whittington and Winters [1990]), only Elliott and Korpi [1978] and Stein et al. [1994] have directly investigated the relation between internal audit contribution and the external audit fee.

In the more recent study, Stein et al. [1994] model the determinants of audit fees for financial services clients and industrial clients of one external audit firm. Their model includes a variable of internal audit contribution that represents the level of internal audit assistance provided on the external audit. This variable is dichotomous, with the level of assistance represented as either extensive/moderate or limited/none, and likely only captures the type of contribution in which internal auditors act as assistants to the external auditor. Contrary to expectations, this variable is not a significant determinant of external audit fees for either financial services or industrial firms. Possibly this lack of significance is due to the use of a restricted dichotomous measure or to the fact that the measure does not fully capture both forms of internal audit contribution.

By comparison, Elliott and Korpi [1978] use a continuous measure of internal audit contribution and report that the percentage reduction of audit scope due to internal audit contribution is significant in predicting audit fees. While these results provide support for an inverse relation between internal audit contribution and the external audit fee, Elliott and Korpi's [1978] sample consists of only manufacturing companies and financial institutions from a single external audit firm, suggesting that the results might be industry and/or audit firm specific. Also, with respect to the current relevance of the findings, a number of significant changes have occurred in the

---

[2] For example, see Craswell et al. [1995]; Davis et al. [1993]; Francis and Simon [1987]; Gist [1992, 1994]; Maher et al. [1992]; O'Keefe et al. [1994]; Palmrose [1986a,b, 1989]; Pearson and Trompeter [1994]; Simon [1985]; Simunic [1980]; Stein et al. [1994]; Turpen [1990]; and Ward et al. [1994]. Also, see Turpen [1995] for a summary of the major findings of research examining the determinants of audit fees.

audit environment in the 20 years since their study was published. For example, the importance of internal audit contributing to the financial statement audit has received increased emphasis (Treadway Commission [1987], IIA [1995], and AICPA [1997]). Further, competition in the market for audit services suggests that external auditors might more aggressively choose to use internal audit as a means of reducing external audit fees. While these factors suggest that the contribution of internal audit to the completion of the financial statement audit may be increasing, there is no current evidence regarding the effect of such contribution on the external audit fee.

If, as permitted by SAS No. 65, external auditors use work completed by internal audit to reduce the evidence/effort required to complete the financial statement audit, a corresponding reduction in the external audit fee should occur. Consistent with this notion, Felix et al.'s [1998] recent survey suggests that the primary reason external auditors use internal audit work in the performance of the financial statement audit is to lower external audit costs.[3] Based on professional guidance provided in SAS No. 65, survey work by Felix et al. [1998] and the findings of Elliott and Korpi [1978], we expect external audit fees to be inversely related to the contribution made by internal audit to the financial statement audit.

2.2 FACTORS AFFECTING INTERNAL AUDIT CONTRIBUTION

Given the potential for internal audit contribution to reduce audit fees, it is important to understand the factors that affect external auditors' decisions to use work completed by the internal auditors. Based on prior research and professional auditing standards, we investigate whether the contribution that internal audit makes to the financial statement audit is a function of the availability of the internal auditors at the end of the audit year, internal audit quality, and the extent of coordination throughout the year between the internal and external auditors. We also examine whether the effects of these factors are contingent on the level of risk present in the audit environment. Specifically, based on research in cognitive psychology and auditing, we examine whether the level of inherent risk exacerbates or mitigates the effects of these factors on internal audit contribution.

2.2.1. Internal Audit Availability. The simplest factor for the external auditors to consider in determining the participation of internal audit in the financial statement audit is availability. That is, the more time internal auditors have available during the time period of the financial statement audit, the greater their potential contribution. At some clients, internal audit may be organized so as to have time available to provide direct assistance to the external auditors, while at other clients internal audit may have very limited availability near the time period of the financial statement audit (AICPA

---

[3] Survey results also suggest that these cost savings are passed on to the audit client in the form of a lower audit fee and do not result in an increase in the realization rate for the external auditor (Felix et al. [1998]).

[1997] and Felix et al. [1998]). We expect that the greater the availability of the internal auditors to assist the external auditor, the greater the contribution internal audit will make to the financial statement audit.

2.2.2. Internal Audit Quality. SAS No. 65 indicates that the internal audit function must be of a sufficient level of quality before external auditors can consider internal audit's work to be competent evidential matter for purposes of completing the financial statement audit (AICPA [1997]). Prior experimental research supports a positive relation between internal audit quality and the contribution made by internal audit to the financial statement audit (Abdel-khalik et al. [1983], Brown [1983], Clark et al. [1983], Schneider [1984, 1985], Maletta and Kida [1993], and Maletta [1993]). Thus, professional auditing standards and extant research suggest that the contribution made by internal audit to the financial statement audit is positively related to the level of quality of internal audit.

2.2.3. Extent of Coordination Between Internal and External Audit. Internal and external auditors concerned with audit costs and quality may attempt to coordinate their activities throughout the year. In fact, both internal and external auditing standards encourage the two audit groups to coordinate their efforts related to completing the financial statement audit (IIA [1995] and AICPA [1997]). Coordination efforts can involve assigning specific audit work throughout the audit year to internal audit and managing internal audit availability at year-end. Coordination has the potential to maximize the effectiveness of the internal auditors' contribution to the financial statement audit and increase overall audit efficiency through the minimization of duplicate audit efforts (Felix et al. [1998]). Inadequate levels of coordination between the two audit groups can lead to a failure to fully utilize the potential of internal audit to contribute to the financial statement audit. Thus, we expect a positive relation between the level of coordination between internal and external auditors and the extent of internal audit contribution to the financial statement audit.

2.2.4. Risk in the Audit Environment. SAS No. 65 indicates that audit risk factors should be considered by external auditors in determining the contribution of internal audit to the financial statement audit. Maletta and Kida [1993] and Maletta [1993] find that inherent risk affects internal audit reliance decisions by interacting with factors related to internal audit. Consistent with the effects of inherent risk found by Libby, Artman, and Willingham [1985], these two studies indicate that as inherent risk increases, certain internal audit factors will increase in importance. These findings are consistent with the premise that the nature of an individual's decision process changes with the criticality of the decision. Specifically, research in psychology has shown that as decisions become more critical, the decision processes become more analytical and complex (see, e.g., Petty and Cacioppo [1984]; Hagafors and Brehemer [1983]; Chaiken [1980];

518   W. L. FELIX JR., A. A. GRAMLING, AND M. J. MALETTA

Gabrenya and Arkin [1979]; Beach and Mitchell [1978]; Bybee [1978]; Murnighan and Leung [1976]; and Heslin et al. [1972]).

In the context of this study, these findings suggest that increases in inherent risk should not simply cause a change in the use of internal audit but instead should cause the process by which internal audit reliance decisions are made to become more complex and analytical. In effect, auditors should move away from simple decision rules that utilize only simple factors and toward more analytical decision functions that emphasize more complex and substantive factors. Thus, in lower risk conditions, simple factors such as the general availability of the internal auditors may be significant in determining internal audit contribution. However, in higher risk conditions, more complex factors such as internal audit quality and the extent of internal/external audit coordination may emerge as the primary factors that influence internal audit contribution.[4] Stated more specifically, the literature suggests, and we expect, general availability to be less important in determining the level of internal audit contribution when inherent risk is higher than when it is lower. However, more complex factors, such as overall internal audit quality and the level of coordination between the two audit groups, should have a significantly greater effect on external auditors' reliance decisions in higher versus lower risk environments.

3. Data and Model Specification

3.1 SAMPLE AND DATA

We obtained our data from surveys and publicly available information. The survey data consists of responses to questions that were designed for directors of internal audit departments of Fortune 1000 firms[5] and public accounting partners responsible for conducting the financial statement audits at these organizations. The Institute of Internal Auditors (IIA) provided the names of IIA members (e.g., internal audit director) at 603 Fortune 1000 firms. We sent two questionnaires to each of these firms. We instructed the internal audit directors to complete the questionnaire designed for internal auditors, and to forward the other to the external audit partner responsible for completion of the firm's annual financial statement audit.

---

[4] Our discussion is not meant to suggest that external auditors in settings with low inherent risk consider internal audit quality irrelevant. In fact, SAS No. 65 requires that internal auditors have some minimum level of quality if external auditors are going to permit them to contribute to the completion of the financial statement auditor. Rather, our discussion posits that internal audit quality will be more important in the presence of higher inherent risk than in the presence of lower inherent risk.

[5] Prior research suggests that the fee model for financial services firms differs from the fee model for non-financial services firms (Elliott and Korpi [1978], Stein et al. [1994]). We focus only on non-financial services firms. Thus, throughout the paper, the term Fortune 1000 firms refers only to the 827 non-financial services firms in the Fortune 1000 (Fortune [1997]).

TABLE 1

Comparison of Fortune 1000 Firms, Survey Recipients, and Survey Respondents[a]

mean

(standard deviation)

n = number of firms for which this information is provided on the Fortune 1000 database

Variable[b] (1)	Fortune 1000 firms (2)	Survey Recipients (3)	t^1 (4)	Survey Respondents (5)	t^2 (6)
Revenue (millions)	5,780.11	6,819.10	−1.51 ns	9,238.66	1.25 ns
	(12,168.67)	(13,730.09)		(17,244.57)	
	n = 827	n = 603		n = 67	
Assets (millions)	6,201.06	7,352.82	−1.17 ns	9,409.09	0.90 ns
	(17,224.51)	(17,781.89)		(14,929.05)	
	n = 824	n = 601		n = 67	
Profits (millions)	308.64	390.28	−1.82***	661.54	1.81***
	(778.39)	(867.99)		(1,351.68)	
	n = 815	n = 594		n = 67	
Equity (millions)	1,888.77	2,219.65	−1.67***	3,279.67	1.56 ns
	(3,462.88)	(3,831.67)		(6,086.54)	
	n = 822	n = 599		n = 66	
Market Value (millions, as of March 14, 1997)	8,684.14	10,675.01	−0.60 ns	14,460.91	0.49 ns
	(56,946.65)	(66,224.07)		(28,233.78)	
	n = 793	n = 583		n = 65	
EPS	1.64	1.91	−1.70***	1.99	0.20 ns
	(2.98)	(2.76)		(3.49)	
	n = 786	n = 575		n = 66	
Return to Investors (includes price appreciation and dividend yield)	18.71	18.36	0.18 ns	14.06	−1.05 ns
	(37.21)	(34.71)		(28.31)	
	n = 759	n = 569		n = 64	
Number of Employees	26,553.63	31,527.65	−1.66***	36,129.15	0.68 ns
	(51,613.02)	(58,972.49)		(67,002.57)	
	n = 825	n = 602		n = 67	

[1] T-statistic (adjusted for unequal variances, as appropriate) for test of equality of means between the 827 non-financial services Fortune 1000 firms and the 603 survey recipients. *p < .01 **p < .05 ***p < .10 ns: p ≥ .10 (all are two-tailed)

[2] T-statistic (adjusted for unequal variances, as appropriate) for test of equality of means between the 70 survey respondents (column 5) and the remaining 533 survey recipients from whom we did not obtain completed surveys. *p < .01 **p < .05 ***p < .10 ns: p ≥ .10 (all are two-tailed)

[a] Data relates only to non-financial services firms. See text for additional discussion.

[b] Descriptive data are from the Fortune 1000 database (Fortune [1997]), which is based on 1996 publicly available data.

Columns (2), (3), and (4) of table 1 provide comparative descriptive statistics of the Fortune 1000 firms and the 603 firms to whom we sent questionnaires. The 603 survey recipient firms do not differ significantly from the Fortune 1000 firms on a number of characteristics including firm revenue, assets, and market value.

We received completed questionnaires from both the internal and external auditor respondents for 76 (12.6%) firms. Our tests are based on 70 firms for which we have complete data available.[6] Columns (5) and (6) of

---

[6] Testing of Model 2 (i.e., table 6) is based on 66 observations because of missing data constraints.

TABLE 2
Respondents' Firms

Panel A: External Audit Firms Included in Sample

	Sample Frequency	Sample Percent
Arthur Anderson	14	20.0
Coopers & Lybrand	8	11.5
Deloitte & Touche	14	20.0
Ernst & Young	10	14.3
KPMG Peat Marwick	11	15.7
Price Watehouse	12	17.1
OTHER	1	1.4
	70	100.0

Panel B: Industries of Client Firms Included in Sample

Industry Classifications*	Sample Frequency	Sample Percent
Mining	1	1.4
Construction	4	5.7
Manufacturing	37	52.8
Transportation, Communications, Electric, Gas and Sanitary Services	18	25.7
Wholesale Trade	2	2.9
Retail Trade	2	2.9
Services	6	8.6
	70	100.0

* The 70 firms represent 29 industries at the 2-digit SIC level.

table 1, respectively, provide comparative descriptives for the 70 respondent firms that we do include and the 533 survey recipients from whom we did not obtain completed surveys. Overall, the respondent firms are not significantly different from the survey recipients from whom we did not obtain completed surveys. The respondent firms are large economically significant entities. On average, these firms have revenue of $9,239 million, assets of $9,409 million, a market value of $14,461 million, and employ 36,129 individuals.

Panels A and B of table 2 provide additional detail on the firms with which the external and internal auditor respondents were associated. As detailed in panel A, all of the Big 6 audit firms are represented in our sample.[7] Panel B indicates that the client firms represent twenty-nine industries. This information suggests that we have a broad sample of client industries and external audit firms.

---

[7] Only one audit firm is not a Big 6 audit firm. The inclusion of essentially only Big 6 firms in our sample serves as a mechanism to increase the homogeneity of the quality of the audit (Dopuch and Simunic [1982], Francis and Wilson [1988], Beatty [1989], DeAngelo [1981], Knapp [1991], Teoh and Wong [1993], and Craswell et al. [1995]). Our results are not sensitive to the inclusion of the one observation for which the audit firm is a non-Big 6 audit firm.

3.2 RESEARCH DESIGN AND MODEL SPECIFICATION

A cross sectional regression model based on prior audit fee research is used to examine the effect of internal audit contribution on external audit fees. The model we specify is represented as equation (1).

$$FEE = \beta_0 + \beta_1 \text{ IACONTRB} + \beta_2 \text{ NUMLOC} + \beta_3 \text{ NUMRPTS} + \beta_4 \text{ ASSETS}$$
$$+ \beta_5 \text{ LEVERAGE} + \beta_6 \text{ LENGTH} + \beta_7 \text{ RELCON} + \beta_8 \text{ NONAUDIT} + \varepsilon$$

$$(1)$$

where:

FEE = Audit fee paid by the client, as reported by internal auditor respondent (natural log used in regression model).

IACONTRB = External auditor assessment of percentage of internal audit contribution to financial statement audit work. (0% = internal audit did not perform any of the work required to complete the audit to 100% = internal audit performed all of the work required to complete the audit).

NUMLOC = Number of client locations (natural log used in regression model).

NUMRPTS = Number of reports issued for client (natural log used in regression model).

ASSETS = Total assets for client at the end of the fiscal year (natural log used in regression model).

LEVERAGE = Total liabilities divided by total assets for client at the end of the fiscal year.

LENGTH = Length of the auditor relationship with the client, in years (natural log used in regression model).

RELCON = Extent of reliance placed on the overall system of internal controls, as reported by external auditor respondent. (0 = moderate; 1 = extensive).[8]

NONAUDIT = A dichotomous variable indicating whether the client's external audit firm also provides significant non-audit services (tax, consulting) to the client. (0 = no; 1 = yes).

3.2.1. Control Variables.[9] Audit fee models employed in prior research have used a variety of variables to control for cross-sectional differences associated

---

[8] A three-point scale was used in the survey instrument to obtain measures of reliance on internal controls (limited, moderate, extensive). None of the external auditors in our sample indicated that they relied on the client's internal controls at a limited level. Accordingly, we use this variable as a dichotomous measure.

[9] Additional control variables included in preliminary analyses, but not discussed in this section, include the level of inherent risk perceived by the external auditor, net income,

522   W. L. FELIX JR., A. A. GRAMLING, AND M. J. MALETTA

with auditee size, complexity and risk, and quality of internal controls. These empirical models have demonstrated good explanatory power and have been robust across different samples and different time periods. Inclusion of these control variables in our fee model is necessary for a careful analysis of the effect of internal audit contribution to the financial statement audit on external audit fees.

Our control variables include total assets (cf. Palmrose [1986a,b], Turpen [1990], Stein et al. [1994], and Craswell et al. [1995]), total number of audit locations (cf. Palmrose [1986a,b], Turpen [1990], Gist [1992], and Stein et al. [1994]), total number of audit reports issued annually (cf. Palmrose [1986], Gist [1992], and Stein et al. [1994]) and the length of the external auditor's relationship with the client (see e.g., O'Keefe et al. [1994], and Stein et al. [1994]). The natural log of these variables is used, as it has been consistently documented in prior audit fee research that the relation between audit fees and these size/complexity measures is nonlinear (see e.g., Gist [1992]). The coefficients for these four variables are expected to be positive.

We include three additional control variables. Cross-sectional differences in client risk are captured with a measure of financial leverage, calculated as the proportion of total liabilities to total assets at fiscal year-end (cf. Gist [1992], Stein et al. [1994]). The coefficient for this variable is expected to be positive. To control for differences in the client's internal control environment, a variable indicating the extent of reliance placed on the client's system of internal control is included in the model (cf. Stein et al. [1994]). This variable is dichotomous with "0" indicating that a moderate level of reliance was placed on controls and "1" representing an extensive level of reliance on controls. Finally, we include a dichotomous variable indicating whether the external audit firm also provided significant non-audit services to its audit client.[10]

3.2.2. Experimental Variable: Internal Audit Contribution. The contribution of the internal audit department to the financial statement audit is measured as the percentage of the financial statement audit performed by the internal auditors, where 0% indicates that the internal auditors did not perform any work that was used by the external auditors during the audit, and

---

alternative measures of financial leverage, a variable indicating whether the client had suffered a loss within three years of the financial statement date, a variable indicating whether the client industry is regulated, and a variable indicating whether the client perceives that the audit firm is an industry specialist. None of these variables were significant and their inclusion did not produce results different from those reported in this research. Other studies have included a control variable to indicate whether an unqualified opinion was issued. In our sample, almost all of the clients received an unqualified opinion and thus it was not statistically possible to include this variable in an analysis. An examination of the data including only those firms with unqualified opinions did not produce results different from those reported in this research.

[10] While several studies have provided empirical evidence on the relation between external audit fees and the provision of non-audit services, the nature of that relation is an unresolved issue (Solomon [1990]).

100% indicates that the internal auditors performed the entire audit. This variable, which was obtained from the external auditor respondent, includes both the contribution made by internal auditors acting as assistants under direct supervision of the external auditors and by completing relevant work throughout the year.[11] Consistent with prior research (Elliott and Korpi [1978]) and profession auditing guidance (AICPA [1997]), the coefficient for this variable is expected to be negative in a model predicting external audit fees, as the greater the internal audit contribution to the financial statement audit, the lower the external audit fee.

3.3 DETERMINANTS OF INTERNAL AUDIT CONTRIBUTION

The second portion of this study examines the factors that influence the extent to which internal audit contributes to the financial statement audit. The model we specify is represented as equation (2).

$$IACONTRB = \beta_0 + \beta_1 \, AVAIL + \beta_2 \, IAQUAL + \beta_3 \, COORD + \beta_5 \, IRxAVAIL$$
$$+ \beta_6 \, IRxIAQUAL + \beta_7 \, IRxCOORD + \varepsilon \quad (2)$$

where:

IACONTRB	=	External auditor assessment of percentage of internal audit contribution to financial statement audit work (0% = internal audit did not perform any of the work required to complete the audit to 100% = internal audit completed all of the work required to complete the audit).
AVAIL	=	Extent to which external auditors agree that the internal audit department has time available to assist in the performance of the financial statement audit (-2 = strongly disagree to $+2$ = strongly agree).
IAQUAL	=	External auditor assessment of overall internal audit quality (0 = very low to 100 = very high).
COORD	=	External auditor assessment of relationship with internal auditors (1 = coexistence, 2 = coordination, 3 = integration, 4 = partnering).
IR	=	Risk of material misstatement occurring in the client's financial statements, in the absence of controls (inherent risk), as reported by external auditor respondent (0 = low, 1 = moderate/high).[12]

---

[11] The reader should note that the experimental variable of interest, internal audit contribution, was obtained from the external auditor respondent. The dependent variable, audit fee, was obtained from the internal auditor respondent. When completing their survey questions the auditors were not aware of our interest in the relation between internal audit contribution and the external audit fee.

[12] A three-point scale was used to obtain measures of inherent risk (high, moderate, low). However, only three of the clients in our sample were deemed by their auditors to have a high level of inherent risk. To eliminate the computational problems associated with this situation, the variable was made dichotomous by combining the moderate and high categories.

3.3.1. Independent Variables. The first independent variable, AVAIL, represents the extent to which the external auditor agreed that the internal auditors had time available to assist in performing the financial statement audit. This variable is measured on a five-point scale (-2 = strongly disagree, to $+2$ = strongly agree) and is expected to have a positive coefficient. The greater the external auditor perception that the internal auditors had available time, the greater the expected contribution of the internal auditors to the financial statement audit.

The second experimental variable, IAQUAL, is overall internal audit quality. External auditors assessed internal audit quality on an eleven-point scale ranging, in increments of 10, from "0," very low overall quality, to "100," very high overall quality. The coefficient for this variable is expected to be positive, with higher levels of internal audit quality being associated with higher levels of internal audit contribution.

The third variable (COORD) captures the external auditor's perception of the relationship between the internal and external auditors in coordinating and planning the financial statement audit and is expected to have a positive coefficient, as the more integrated the relationship the greater the expected contribution of the internal auditors. Coordination was measured using a four-point scale ranging from a relationship characterized as coexistence ("1") to a relationship labeled as "partnering" ("4"), with midpoints labeled as coordination ("2") and integration ("3"). Thus, the more integrated the relationship, the greater the numerical score.

The inherent risk variable, IR, captures the external auditor's assessment of the client's level of inherent risk (i.e., the risk of a material misstatement occurring in the client's financial statements, in the absence of controls). The variable is dichotomous, with "0" representing a low level and "1" representing a moderate/high level of inherent risk. The coefficient for the IRxAVAIL interaction term is expected to be negative, as the availability of the internal auditors should be less critical in higher versus lower risk conditions. The interaction terms IRxIAQUAL and IRxCOORD are expected to have positive coefficients, as internal audit quality and coordination are expected to have a greater effect on internal audit contribution in higher versus lower inherent risk conditions.

3.4 DESCRIPTIVE STATISTICS

Tables 3 and 4 provide descriptive statistics regarding the variables used in the specified audit fee model (equation 1) and the internal audit contribution model (equation 2), respectively. As highlighted in table 3, Panel A, the mean audit fee paid by clients in our sample is $1,169,369 and on average, the internal auditors completed 26.57% of the work necessary to complete the financial statement audit. The correlations between the variables included in the fee model are included in table 3, panel B.

TABLE 3

Variables Used in Audit Fee Regression

Panel A: Descriptive Statistics

Variable	Mean	Std. Dev.	Min	Max
FEE	$1,169,369	1,403,548	171,000	9,600,000
IACONTRB	26.57%	16.36	0.00	70.00
NUMLOC	19.64	41.21	1	300
NUMRPTS	24.13	39.59	1	200
ASSETS (000)	$9,096,432	14,680,123	346,590	95,527,000
LEVERAGE	.66	.17	.23	1.3
LENGTH	33.17	22.99	2	107
RELCON	.63	.49	0	1
NONAUDIT	.60	.49	0	1

Panel B: Correlation Matrix

	(1)	(2)	(3)	(4)	(5)	(6)	(7)	(8)	(9)
FEE (1)	1.00	−.15	.65*	.67*	.79*	.12	.36*	.15	−.01
IACONTRB (2)		1.00	−.08	−.10	.12	−.15	.06	.25*	−.20*
NUMLOC (3)			1.00	.63*	.34*	−.10	.25*	.10	.18
NUMRPTS (4)				1.00	.59*	.04	.21*	.20	.19
ASSETS (5)					1.00	−.01	.19	.24*	−.03
LEVERAGE (6)						1.00	−.12	−.35*	.19
LENGTH (7)							1.00	.09	.02
RELCON (8)								1.00	.04
NONAUDIT (9)									1.00

* Correlation is significant at p ≤ .05 level.

NOTE:

FEE = Audit fee paid by the client, as reported by internal auditor respondent (natural log used in regression model).

IACONTRB = External auditor assessment of percentage of IA contribution to financial statement audit work (0% = internal audit did not perform any of the work required to complete the audit to 100% = internal audit performed all of the work required to complete the audit).

NUMLOC = Number of client locations (natural log used in regression model).

NUMRPTS = Number of reports issued for client, as reported by external auditor respondent (natural log used in regression model).

ASSETS = Total assets for client at the end of the fiscal year (natural log used in regression model).

LEVERAGE = Total liabilities divided by total assets for client at the end of the fiscal year.

LENGTH = Length of the auditor relationship with the client, in years (natural log used in regression model).

RELCON = Extent of reliance placed on the overall system of internal controls, as reported by external auditor respondent (0 = moderate; 1 = extensive).

NONAUDIT = A dichotomous variable indicating whether the client's external audit firm also provides significant non-audit services (tax, consulting) to the client. (0 = no; 1 = yes).

Table 4, panel A indicates that the internal auditors included in our sample are perceived to be high quality. The mean quality assessment provided by the external auditors is 71.98 (on a scale ranging from 0 to 100). The mean level of coordination is 2.30 (on a scale ranging from 1 to 4), while the mean of the AVAIL variable is .68 (on a scale ranging from −2 to +2). The correlation matrix for the variables included in the contribution model is included in table 4, panel B.

526   W. L. FELIX JR., A. A. GRAMLING, AND M. J. MALETTA

TABLE 4
Variables Used in Internal Audit Contribution Regression

Panel A: Descriptive Statistics

Variable	Mean	Std. Dev.	Min	Max
AVAIL	.68	1.36	−2	+2
IAQUAL	71.98	16.67	30	100
COORD	2.30	.72	1	4
IR	.50	.50	0	1

Panel B: Correlation Matrix

	(1)	(2)	(3)	(4)	(5)	(6)	(7)
IACONTRB (1)	1.00	.33*	.27*	.48*	−.02	.09	.17
AVAIL (2)		1.00	−.01	.15	.59*	.13	.10
IAQUAL (3)			1.00	46*	−.02	.16	.02
COORD (4)				1.00	−.08	.02	.17
IRxAVAIL (5)					1.00	.45*	.40*
IRxIAQUAL (6)						1.00	.92*
IRxCOORD (7)							1.00

* Correlation is significant at p ≤ .05 level.

NOTE:
AVAIL   = Extent to which external auditors agree that the internal audit
           department has time available to assist in the performance of the
           financial statement audit (+2 = strongly agree to −2 = strongly disagree).
IAQUAL = External auditor assessment of overall internal audit quality (0 = very
           low to 100 = very high).
COORD = External auditor assessment of relationship with internal auditors
           (1= coexistence, 2 = coordination, 3 = integration, 4 = partnering).
IR   = Risk of material misstatement occurring in the client's financial
           statements, in the absence of controls (inherent risk), as reported by
           external auditor respondent (0 = low; 1 = moderate).

4. Test Results

4.1 AUDIT FEE MODEL: TEST OF INTERNAL AUDIT CONTRIBUTION

Table 5 presents the regression results of our audit fee model. The overall model is significant (p < .0001), with an adjusted R^2 of .80.[13] Consistent with prior research, several of the control variables are significant and have coefficients in the expected direction. For example, the variables representing the number of client locations (NUMLOC) and total assets (ASSETS) are both significant (p ≤ .001 level) and have positive coefficients. The variable

---

[13] Standard regression diagnostics were performed. The VIF scores reported in the regression results are well below the level that would suggest problems with multicollinearity (Neter et al. [1990]). The distribution of the residuals from Model 1 was examined using the Kolmogorov-Smirnov test and the assumption of normality was not rejected at conventional levels. Tests for serial correlation (Durbin Watson test) and heteroscedasticity (Breusch and Pagan [1979]) revealed no evidence of problems in either of these areas. Finally, checks for outliers revealed that one observation was among the top ten percent in terms of total assets but reported an audit fee that was three and one-half times smaller than the next lowest audit fee in the sample (e.g., it has been verified that the company has assets totaling over $1.5 billion, while the audit fee indicated on the questionnaire was only $50,000). Our analyses identified this observation as being an outlier by more than four standard deviations. We believe that the audit fee provided is in error and we deleted this observation. No additional outliers were identified.

THE CONTRIBUTION OF INTERNAL AUDIT 527

TABLE 5

Regression Results: Audit Fee Model

FEE $= \beta_0 + \beta_1$ IACONTRB $+ \beta_2$ NUMLOC $+ \beta_3$ NUMRPTS $+ \beta_4$ ASSETS $+ \beta_5$ LEVERAGE
$+ \beta_6$ LENGTH $+ \beta_7$ RELCON $+ \beta_8$ NONAUDIT $+ \varepsilon$

Variables	β	VIF	t-value	p-value*
Intercept	9.056		20.717	.001
Experimental Variable				
IACONTRB	−.007	1.142	−2.395	.009
Control Variables				
NUMLOC	.273	1.781	5.739	.001
NUMRPTS	.012	2.416	.238	.405
ASSETS	.378	1.665	8.351	.001
LEVERAGE	.672	1.265	2.162	.017
LENGTH	.173	1.101	2.790	.007
RELCON	.165	1.337	1.519	.134
NONAUDIT	−.215	1.177	−2.134	.037

* p-values represent 1-tailed tests when direction of coefficient is consistent with expectations.
Model:
R Square $= .83$
Adjusted R Square $= .80$
F-Ratio $= 36.26$
Signif. F $< .0001$
n $= 70$
NOTE:

FEE	= Audit fee paid by the client, as reported by internal auditor respondent (natural log used in regression model).
IACONTRB	= External auditor assessment of percentage of IA contribution to financial statement audit work. (0% = internal audit did not perform any of the work required to complete the audit to 100% = internal audit performed all of the work required to complete the audit).
NUMLOC	= Number of client locations (natural log used in regression model).
NUMRPTS	= Number of reports issued for client, as reported by external auditor respondent (natural log used in regression model).
ASSETS	= Total assets for client at the end of the fiscal year (natural log used in regression model).
LEVERAGE	= Total liabilities divided by total assets for client at the end of the fiscal year.
LENGTH	= Length of the auditor relationship with the client, in years (natural log used in regression model).
RELCON	= Extent of reliance placed on the overall system of internal controls, as reported by external auditor respondent (0 = moderate; 1 = extensive).
NONAUDIT	= A dichotomous variable indicating whether the client's external audit firm also provides significant non-audit services (tax, consulting) to the client (0 = no; 1 = yes).

capturing the duration of the auditor/auditee relationship (LENGTH) is significant (p = .007) with a positive coefficient, indicating that as the length of the relationship increases, the audit fee increases.

The variable capturing whether the external auditing firm also provided non-audit services to its client (NONAUDIT) is significant (p = .037), indicating a negative relation between audit fees and the provision of non-audit services. This result contrasts with prior studies that have used data from the 1970s and 1980s. These studies find either a positive relation between non-audit services and audit fees (i.e., Simunic [1984]; Simon [1985]; Palmrose [1986b]; Turpen [1990]; Davis et al. [1993]) or provide no evidence of a relation between non-audit services and audit fees (i.e., Abdel-khalik [1990]; O'Keefe et al. [1994]). Our finding may be indicative of a change in the audit environment over the last two decades. That is, the increased competitiveness in the audit marketplace may now be motivating auditors to discount the

528   W. L. FELIX JR., A. A. GRAMLING, AND M. J. MALETTA

financial statement audit in an effort to procure more lucrative consulting service fees rather than vice versa. However, additional research is needed before definitive conclusions can be drawn regarding the relation between non-audit services and audit fees.[14] Finally, LEVERAGE is significant ($p = .017$), while RELCON[15] and NUMRPTS are not significant ($p = .134$ and $.405$, respectively).

Most important to this study is internal audit contribution, IACONTRB, which is significant ($p = .009$) and, consistent with expectations, has a negative coefficient ($-.007$). This result indicates that as the extent of internal audit contribution increases, there is a significant decrease in external audit fees. In fact, the results indicate that for every one percent increase in the extent to which internal auditors complete work that would otherwise be completed by external auditors, the audit fee decreases by approximately $8,000. Accordingly, if an audit client were able to increase the contribution made by internal audit to the financial statement audit from no contribution to the mean level of contribution in our sample (i.e., internal audit completes 26.57% of the work necessary to complete the financial statement audit), the audit fee would decrease by approximately 18 percent.[16] Thus, the contribution of internal audit to the financial statement audit plays an important role in the determination of external audit fees. Given the significance of this relation, we now explore the factors that influence the extent of internal audit contribution.

4.2 FACTORS AFFECTING INTERNAL AUDIT CONTRIBUTION

Table 6 presents the regression results of the internal audit contribution model. The overall model is significant ($p = .001$), with an adjusted

---

[14] We use a dichotomous measure for capturing whether non-audit services are provided to the audit client. While Abdel-khalik [1990] argues that the use of a dichotomous measure is appropriate when examining this relation, future research examining this relation may want to further explore the appropriateness of using a dichotomous or continuous measure.

[15] The insignificance of RELCON in our fee model is consistent with prior archival work. Specifically, we are aware of only one prior audit fee study that archivally examines the relation between reliance on internal controls and the external audit fee (see O'Keefe et al. [1994]). They report that the degree of reliance on internal control has no systematically significant effect on the audit fee. This insignificant relation might suggest the presence of contracting inefficiencies, since greater reliance on controls does not yield a corresponding fee reduction. Alternatively, increased (decreased) reliance on controls, which typically results in increased (decreased) control testing and decreased (increased) substantive testing, may not impact the audit production in a manner that would yield a fee reduction. Future research could profitably explore the relation between reliance on controls and audit fees. Since RELCON is not significant at conventional levels in our model, the model was also run without the RELCON variable. Our results and interpretations remain substantially unchanged when this variable is not included in the model.

[16] The log of our mean audit fee is 13.972. Subtracting the model coefficient for the variable of interest (.007) from that mean yields 13.965. The anti-log of 13.965 is $1,161,241. Thus, a one unit (percent) increase in IACONTRB leads to a fee decrease of $8,128 ($1,169,369–$1,161,241). If an audit client were to move from no IACONTRB (0%) to the mean level of contribution in our sample (26.57%), the fee reduction would be $215,961 (8,128 × 26.57), an 18.47% decrease (215,961/1,169,369).

TABLE 6

Regression Results: Internal Audit Contribution Model

$$IACONTRB = \beta_0 + \beta_1 \ AVAIL + \beta_2 \ IAQUAL + \beta_3 \ COORD + \beta_5 \ IRxAVAIL$$
$$+ \beta_6 \ IRxIAQUAL + \beta_7 \ IRxCOORD + \varepsilon$$

Variables	β	VIF	t-value	p-value*
INTERCEPT	−4.355		−.542	.590
AVAIL	6.509	1.793	3.925	.001
IAQUAL	.246	2.356	1.584	.056
COORD	3.980	2.495	1.081	.142
IRxAVAIL	−6.662	2.095	−2.538	.007
IRxIAQUAL	−.211	14.818	−1.211	.231
IRxCOORD	9.133	14.780	1.723	.045

* p-values represent 1-tailed tests when direction of coefficient is consistent with expectations.

Model:
R Square = .40
Adjusted R Square = .34
F-Ratio = 6.540
Signif. F <.001
n = 66

NOTE:

IACONTRB = External auditor assessment of percentage of IA contribution to financial statement audit work (0% = internal audit did not perform any of the work required to complete the audit to 100% = internal audit completed all of the work required to complete the audit)

AVAIL = Extent to which external auditors agree that the internal audit department has time available to assist in the performance of the financial statement audit (+2 = strongly agree to −2 = strongly disagree).

IAQUAL = External auditor assessment of overall internal audit quality (0 = very low to 100 = very high).

COORD = External auditor assessment of relationship with internal auditors (1 = coexistence, 2 = coordination, 3 = integration, 4 = partnering).

IR = Risk of material misstatement occurring in the client's financial statements, in the absence of controls (inherent risk), as reported by external auditor respondent (0 = low; 1 = moderate).

R^2 of .34.[17] As for individual coefficients, AVAIL is significant (p = .001) and, as expected, its sign is positive (6.509). This result indicates that the greater the availability of the internal auditors, the greater the contribution that internal audit makes to the financial statement audit. We also find, consistent with expectations, that the coefficient for the inherent risk by availability variable (IRxAVAIL) is significant (p = .007) and negative, indicating a diminishing importance of availability as inherent risk increases. That is, availability is a more important determinant of internal audit contribution in low inherent risk situations than in high.

---

[17] It is important to recognize the potential for endogeneity issues in Model 2. Specifically, if there is a demand for internal auditors to contribute to the financial statement audit, it may be that they will make their services available and work toward greater coordination. Hence, a higher demand for internal audit contribution may cause high values of availability and coordination, as well as high values of observed internal audit contribution. Standard regression diagnostics were performed. The VIF scores reported in the regression results are well below the level that would suggest problems with multicollinearity (Neter et al. [1990]). The distribution of the residuals from the internal audit contribution regression was examined using the Kolmogorov-Smirnov test and the assumption of normality was not rejected at conventional levels. Finally, tests for serial correlation (Durbin Watson test) and heteroscedasticity (Breusch and Pagan 1979) revealed no evidence of problems in either of these areas.

530   W. L. FELIX JR., A. A. GRAMLING, AND M. J. MALETTA

Consistent with expectations, IAQUAL is significant (p = .056), with a positive coefficient (.246), indicating that as the overall quality of the internal auditors increases, the extent of their contribution to the financial statement audit also increases. However, the inherent risk by internal audit quality variable (IRxIAQUAL) is not significant (p = .231). Thus, it appears that internal audit quality is an equally important determinant of internal audit contribution across differing levels of inherent risk.

The level of coordination between the internal and external auditors (COORD) is not significant at conventional levels (p = .142), however, the IRxCOORD interaction is significant at the p = .045 level. Thus, the extent of coordination between internal and external auditors does affect internal audit contribution; however, this effect is contingent on the level of inherent risk. Consistent with expectations, the positive coefficient on the interaction term indicates that the importance of coordination in determining internal audit contribution increases as inherent risk increases. Stated differently, the extent to which the coordination between internal and external audit positively affects the contribution of internal audit to the financial statement audit is greater when inherent risk is high than when it is low.[18]

5. Summary, Limitations, and Future Research

Our results indicate that internal audit contribution is a significant determinant of the external audit fee. Specifically, the greater the contribution of the internal auditors to the financial statement audit, the lower the audit fee. Our examination of the factors influencing internal audit contribution suggests that internal audit contribution is influenced by internal audit quality. We also find that as inherent risk increases, the effect of internal audit availability on contribution diminishes, while the effect of coordination on contribution increases. Overall, our findings suggest that internal audit contribution can result in reduced external audit fees, and that client firms can potentially affect internal audit contribution by investing in internal audit quality, managing availability, and facilitating coordination between the internal and external auditors.

---

[18] A high degree of correlation was noted between IAQUAL and COORD. Consistent with the possibility that the extent of coordination between internal and external auditors is a function of the level of internal audit quality (e.g., if the internal auditors are of unacceptable quality there may be no need for coordination (IIA [1995] and AICPA [1997])) we performed two supplemental analyses. First, we re-ran the regression in table 6 without IAQUAL and the IR*IAQUAL interaction term. This analysis indicates that the coefficient for COORD is positive and significant (p = .011) and the interaction between IR and COORD is significant (p = .042). Next, we re-ran the regression in table 6 without COORD and the IR*COORD interaction. This analysis indicates that the coefficient for IAQUAL is positive and significant (p = .019) and, the interaction between IR and IAQUAL is significant at p = .095 level. While not highly significant, the nature of this interaction suggests that, consistent with prior research (Maletta and Kida [1993]), external auditors appear to consider internal audit quality to a greater extent in higher versus lower inherent risk environments.

THE CONTRIBUTION OF INTERNAL AUDIT 531

While this study relies on a unique database comprising survey and publicly available data, such an approach has limitations. First, response bias may exist. While table 1 notes that the survey recipients and respondents are not significantly different, these two groups may differ in terms of internal audit quality and internal audit contribution. The extent to which our results are robust to the inclusion of clients with other levels of internal audit quality or contribution remains an opportunity for future research. Second, given that our analysis required proprietary data, we were limited to including firms that responded to our survey. The sensitive nature of the data we requested (e.g., audit fees), and the necessity of receiving responses from both internal and external auditor respondents, placed downward pressures on sample size. Accordingly, possible response bias and small sample size potentially limit the generality of our results.

A final limitation results from possible endogeneity concerns. Specifically, a question arises as to whether model 2 should be estimated separately from model 1. Because of the possibility of endogeneity of the internal auditor contribution variable, it is reasonable to consider models 1 and 2 as a system of simultaneous equations. Accordingly, the audit fee variable was included in the internal audit contribution model and a simultaneous estimation of the two models was performed. The results are fully consistent with those presented in tables 5 and 6. That is, no measurable differences in the coefficients or their significance result from simultaneously estimating these equations.

Our results suggest additional opportunities for future research. For example, research that can provide insights into why the relation between audit fees and external auditor reliance on the client's internal controls appears to be insignificant (see also Stein et al. [1994]) would enhance understanding of the audit production process. Relatedly, our research establishes an inverse relation between internal audit contribution and the external audit fee, but we cannot indicate whether the fee is decreased because auditors have reduced the price or the quantity of their services. Research addressing how internal audit contribution affects audit production technology would be valuable. Finally, our data do not allow for assessment of the relative significance of each form of internal audit contribution (i.e., internal auditors working as assistants to the external auditors; internal auditors completing relevant work throughout the year) on the audit fee. Research that obtains measures of both types of contribution could provide interesting insights related to audit fees, and would also allow for assessment of the relative importance of the independent variables in model 2 (i.e., AVAIL, IAQUAL, COORD) across these two forms of contribution.

REFERENCES

ABDEL-KHALIK, A. R. "The Jointness of Audit Fees and Demand for MAS: A Self-selection Analysis." *Contemporary Accounting Research* (Fall 1990): 295–322.

532   W. L. FELIX JR., A. A. GRAMLING, AND M. J. MALETTA

ABDEL-KHALIK, A. R.; D. SNOWBALL; AND J. H. WRAGGE. "The Effects of Certain Internal Audit
   Variables on the Planning of the External Audit." *The Accounting Review* (April 1983): 215–27.
ALDHIZER, G. R., III, AND J. D. CASHELL. "A Tale of Two Companies: The Decision to Outsource
   Internal Auditing." *Internal Auditing* (Winter 1996): 10–15.
AMERICAN INSITITUE OF CERTIFIED PUBLIC ACCOUNTS (AICPA). *Statements on Auditing Standards.*
   New York: AICPA, 1997.
ANDERSON, D.; J. R. FRANCIS; AND D. J. STOKES. "Auditing, Directorships and the Demand for
   Monitoring." *Journal of Accounting and Public Policy* (1993): 353–75.
BEACH, L. R., AND T. R. MITCHELL. "A Contingency Model for the Selection of Decision Strate-
   gies." *Academy of Management Review* (1990): 439–49.
BEATTY, R. "Auditor Reputation and the Pricing of Initial Public Offerings." *The Accounting
   Review* (October 1989): 693–709.
BREUSCH, T. S., AND A. R. PAGAN. "A Simple Test of Heterscedasticity and Random Coefficient
   Variation." *Econometrica* (1979): 1287–94.
BROWN, P. R. "Independent Auditor Judgment in the Evaluation of Internal Audit Functions."
   Journal of Accounting Research (Autumn 1983): 444–55.
CHAIKEN, S. "Heuristic versus Systematic Processing and the Use of Source versus Message Cues
   in Persuasion." *Journal of Personality and Social Psychology* (November 1980): 752–6.
CLARK, M.; T. E. GIBBS; AND R. B. SCHROEDER. "Evaluating Internal Audit Departments Under
   SAS No. 9." *The Woman CPA* (July 1980): 8–11 and 22.
CRASWELL, A.; J. FRANCIS; AND S. TAYLOR. "Auditor Brand Name Reputation and Industry Spe-
   cialization." *Journal of Accounting and Economics* (December 1995): 297–322.
DAVIS, L. R.; D. N. RICCHIUTE; AND G. TROMPETER. "Audit Effort, Audit Fees, and the Provision
   of Nonaudit Services to Audit Clients." *The Accounting Review* (January 1993): 135–50.
DEANGELO, L. "Auditor Independence, "Low Balling," and Disclosure Regulation." *Journal of
   Accounting and Economics* (August 1981): 113–27.
DOPUCH, N., AND D. SIMUNIC. "Competition in Auditing: An Assessment." *Illinois Audit Sympo-
   sium,* 1982.
ELGIN, P. "Huge Liability Judgments Pressure CPAs to Raise Prices." *Corporate Cashflow* (July
   1992): 12–13.
ELLIOTT, R. K. "Confronting the Future: Choices for the Attest Function." *Accounting Horizons*
   8, No. 3 (September 1994): 106–24.
ELLIOTT, R. K.; AND A. R. KORPI. "Factors Affecting Audit Fees, Appendix Commission on
   Auditors' Responsibilities." *Cost-Benefit Analysis of Auditing,* Research Study No. 3 by Melvin
   F. Shakun (AICPA): (1978).
FELIX, W. L., JR.; A. A. GRAMLING; AND M. J. MALETTA. *Coordinating Total Audit Coverage: The
   Relationship Between Internal and External Auditors.* Altamonte Springs, FL: The Institute of
   Internal Auditors, 1998.
Fortune. "America's Largest Corporations: Fortune 500." (April 28, 1997).
FRANCIS, J. R., AND D. T. SIMON. "A Test of Audit Pricing in the Small-Client Segment of the
   U. S. Audit Market." *The Accounting Review* (January 1987): 145–57.
FRANCIS, J. R., AND E. R. WILSON. "Auditor Changes: A Joint Test of Theories Relating to
   Agency Coasts and Auditor Differentiation." *The Accounting Review* (October 1988): 663–82.
GABRENYA, W., AND R. M. ARKIN. "The Effect of Commitment on Expectancy Value and Ex-
   pectancy Weight in Social Decision Making." *Personality and Social Psychology Bulletin* (1979):
   86–90.
GIST, W. E. "Explaining Variability in External Audit Fees." *Accounting and Business Research*
   (Winter 1992): 79–84.
GIST, W. E. "Empirical Evidence on the Effect of Audit Structure on Audit Pricing." *Auditing:
   A Journal of Practice and Theory* (Fall 1994): 25–40.
HAGAFORS, R., AND B. BREHMER. "Does Having to Justify One's Judgments Change the Nature
   of the Judgment Process?" *Organizational Behavior and Human Decision Processes* (April 1983):
   223–32.
HESLIN, R.; B. BLAKE; AND J. ROTTON. "Information Search as a Function of Stimulus Uncer-
   tainty and the Importance of the Response." *Journal of Personality and Social Psychology* (1972):
   333–9.

THE CONTRIBUTION OF INTERNAL AUDIT   533

INSITITUE OF INTERNAL AUDITORS (IIA). *Standards for the Professional Practice of Internal Auditing.* Altamonte Springs, FL. IIA, 1995.

KNAPP, M. C. "Factors That Audit Committee Members Use as Surrogates for Audit Quality." *Auditing: A Journal of Practice and Theory* (Spring 1991): 35–52.

LIBBY, R.; J. T. ARTMAN; AND J. J. WILLINGHAM. "Process Susceptibility, Control Risk, and Audit Planning." *The Accounting Review* (April 1985): 212–30.

MAHER, M. W.; P. TIESSEN; R. COLSON; AND A. J. BROMAN. "Competition and Audit Fees." *The Accounting Review* (January 1992): 199–211.

MALETTA, M. J. "An Examination of Auditors' Decisions to Use Internal Auditors as Assistants: The Effect of Inherent Risk." *Contemporary Accounting Research* (Spring 1993): 508–25.

MALETTA, M. J., AND T. KIDA. "The Effect of Risk Factors on Auditors' Configural Information Processing." *The Accounting Review* (July 1993): 681–91.

MURNIGHAN, J. K., AND T. K. LEUNG. "The Effects of Leadership Involvement and the Importance of the Task on Subordinates' Performance." *Organizational Behavior and Human Decision Processes* (1976): 299–310.

NETER, J.; W. WASSERMAN; AND M. H. KUTNER. *Applied Linear Statistical Models. Third Edition.* Homewood, IL: Irwin, 1990.

O'KEEFE, T. B.; D. A. SIMUNIC; AND M. T. STEIN. "The Production of Audit Services: Evidence from a Major Accounting Firm." *Journal of Accounting Research* (Autumn 1994): 241–61.

PALMROSE, Z. V. "Audit Fees and Auditor Size: Further Evidence." *Journal of Accounting Research* (Spring 1986a): 97–110.

PALMROSE, Z. V. "The Effect of Nonaudit Services on the Pricing of Audit Services: Further Evidence." *Journal of Accounting Research* (Autumn 1986b): 405–11.

PALMROSE, Z. "The Relation of Audit Contract Type to Audit Fees and Hours." *The Accounting Review* (July 1989): 488–99.

PEARSON, T., AND G. TROMPETER. "Competition in the Market for Audit Services: The Effect of Supplier Concentration on Audit Fees." *Contemporary Accounting Research* (Summer 1994): 115–35.

PETTY, R. E., AND J. T. CACIOPPO. "The Effects of Involvement on Responses to Argument Quantity and Quality: Central and Peripheral Routes to Persuasion." *Journal of Personality and Social Psychology* (1984): 69–81.

Report of the National Commission of Fraudulent Financial Reporting (Treadway Commission). October 1987.

SCHNEIDER, A. "Modeling External Auditors' Evaluations of Internal Auditing." *Journal of Accounting Research* (Autumn 1984): 657–78.

SCHNEIDER, A. "The Reliance of External Auditors on the Internal Audit Function." *Journal of Accounting Research* (Autumn 1985): 911–19.

SIMON, D. T. "The Audit Services Markets: Additional Empirical Evidence." *Auditing: A Journal of Practice and Theory* (Fall 1985): 71–8.

SIMUNIC, D. A. "The Pricing of Audit Services: Theory and Evidence." *Journal of Accounting Research* (Spring 1980): 161–90.

SIMUNIC, D. A. "Auditing, Consulting, and Auditor Independence." *Journal of Accounting Research* (Autumn 1984): 679–702.

SOLOMON, I. "Discussion of the Jointness of Audit Fees and Demand for MAS: A Self-Selection Analysis." *Contemporary Accounting Review* (Spring 1990): 323–38.

STEIN, M. T.; D. A. SIMUNIC; AND T. B. O'KEEFE. "Industry Differences in the Production of Audit Services." *Auditing: A Journal of Practice and Theory* (Supplement 1994): 128–42.

TEOH, S. H., AND T. J. WONG. "Perceived Auditor Quality and the Earnings Response Coefficient." *The Accounting Review* (April 1993): 346–66.

THURSTON, J. B. *Basic Internal Auditing Principles and Techniques.* Scranton, Pennsylvania: International Textbook Company, 1949.

TURPEN, R. A. "Differential Pricing on auditors' Initial Engagements: Further Evidence." *Auditing: A Journal of Practice and Theory* (Spring 1990): 60–76.

TURPEN, R. A. "Audit Fees—What Research Tells Us." *CPA Journal* (January 1995): 54–6.

WALLACE, W. A. *A Time Series Analysis of the Effect of Internal Audit Activities on External Audit Fees.* The Institute of Internal Auditors, Inc.: Altamonte Springs, FL, 1984a.

534   W. L. FELIX JR., A. A. GRAMLING, AND M. J. MALETTA

WALLACE, W. A. "Internal Auditors Can Cut Outside CPA Costs." *Harvard Business Review* (March-April 1984b): 16, 20.

WALLACE, W. A. "Enhancing Your Relations with Internal Auditors." *The CPA Journal* (December 1984c): 46–53.

Ward, D. D.; R. J. ELDER; AND S. C. KATTELUS. "Further Evidence on the Determinants of Municipal Audit Fees." *The Accounting Review* (April 1994): 399–411.

WHITTINGTON, O. R., AND A. J. WINTERS. "Considering the Work of an Internal Auditor." *The CPA Journal* (April 1990): 28–34.

[25]

PERGAMON

Accounting, Organizations and Society 26 (2001) 617–641

Accounting,
Organizations
and Society

www.elsevier.com/locate/aos

Internalization versus externalization of the internal audit function: an examination of professional and organizational imperatives

Larry Rittenberg, Mark A. Covaleski*

School of Business, University of Wisconsin — Madison, 975 University Avenue, Madison, WI 53706, USA

Abstract

This paper examines the recent trend towards the outsourcing of internal audit services to the public accounting profession. Here we draw from two dominant literature perspectives (the sociology of professions literature and the outsourcing literature) to examine this clash between the public accounting profession and the internal auditing profession over the provision of internal audit services. Two major research propositions are postulated from which to consider these issues. These propositions concern themselves with the efforts of both the public accounting profession and the internal audit profession in this outsourcing debate. We examine these professions both in terms of volitional professional behavior (as espoused in the sociology of professions literature) and organizational arguments (inherent advantages and disadvantages of the externalization of work as typically espoused by the outsourcing literature). © 2001 Elsevier Science Ltd. All rights reserved.

1. Introduction

A marketing brochure of Arthur Andersen (1995) stated that the outsourcing of internal audit services is a "strategic concept — a way to add value to a business — that converts an in-house cost center into a customer-focused service operation with you as the customer." The firm appealed to corporations to focus on the critical "core" areas of the business that create and sustain competitive advantage and outsource non-core competencies such as internal auditing. The alternative view to these alleged advantages of the outsourcing of internal audit services comes from, as might be expected, in-house internal audit departments

such as the one at J. C. Penney. The internal audit department at this company espoused its commitment to "value-added services" and argued that their internal audit department achieves a competitive advantage through knowing the business and performing comparative analysis and benchmarking within units. In fact, J. C. Penney has an *Internal Auditor's Bill of Rights* which states that its internal auditors have "the right to feel important — indispensable, in fact — to corporate management."

To some extent, these opposing views as to the appropriate manner in which to have internal audit services provided — to have such services outsourced to a public accounting firm (as argued by a public accounting firm providing these services) or to have such services maintained in-house (as argued by an in-house internal audit department) — are no surprise. Such self-serving expressions of

* Corresponding author. Tel.: +1-608-262-4239; fax: +1-608-263-0477.

E-mail address: mcovaleski@bus.wisc.edu (M.A. Covaleski).

618   *L. Rittenberg, M.A. Covaleski/Accounting, Organizations and Society 26 (2001) 617–641*

optimal internal audit practices are a reflection of Hopwood's recent (1998, p. 515) observation as to the changing nature of the audit industry:

> ...changes afoot are taking place in the audit industry, including the audit itself. Ernst & Young, for example, now claim that it "has challenged all aspects of the traditional audit". Professionalism has been replaced by business acumen. Notions of independence seem curiously antiquated in a world where audit is conducted in the very same business unit as the promotion of consultancy products and services. Even ideas of "paper walls" between the professional and the commercial are now remnants of the past in audit organizations that pro-actively structure their operations to facilitate the commercial potential of the joint operation of the two.

At a very general level, these contrasting views as to the provision of internal audit services provide a meaningful arena for more research which addresses some of the more macro behavioral issues which are shaping the internal auditing profession (Kalbers & Fogarty, 1995). At the heart of the development of the internal auditing profession are such issues as the battle for professional turf (Abbott, 1988; Freidson, 1986; Reed, 1996) in terms of efforts towards self-motivated market control, as well as changing organizational structures and processes such as outsourcing (Bettis & Hitt, 1995; Davis-Blake & Uzzi, 1993; Halal, 1994; Matusik & Hill, 1998; Wallace, 1995) within which internal auditing is embedded.

The purpose of our paper is to draw from two dominant literature perspectives to examine the changing nature of the internal auditing profession. The next section of this paper presents these theoretical arguments supporting the paper and the resultant research propositions to be examined: the sociology of professions literature which provides a theoretical basis from which the volitional behavior of both the public accounting firms and the corporate internal audit departments can be recognized and the outsourcing literature which frames the organizational arguments (changing organizational structures and processes) which are challenging all internal support services — not just internal auditing — in terms of their inherent "value-added" relative to the outsourcing of such services.

The third section of the paper provides a discussion of the research methods used in this study.

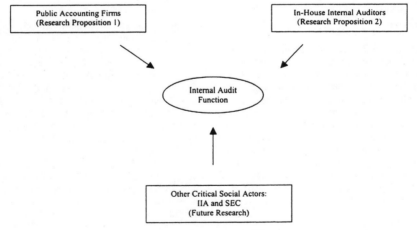

Fig. 1. An overview of the research study.

L. Rittenberg, M.A. Covaleski / Accounting, Organizations and Society 26 (2001) 617–641 619

The fourth section will be guided by the first research proposition which presents observations related to the efforts of the public accounting profession to stake to claim internal auditing work (see Fig. 1). Here we will consider both the volitional professional behavior of the public accounting profession (as espoused in the sociology of professions literature) and organizational arguments (inherent advantages of the externalization of organizational processes as espoused by the outsourcing literature). This public accounting profession perspective will be grounded by observations from recent positions taken by the AICPA and the active role of three public accounting firms (Arthur Andersen, Ernst & Young, and KPMG) which have taken aggressive positions in the effort to market their delivery of internal audit services. The second research proposition which pertains to the internal audit profession perspective (see Fig. 1) will then be presented in section five both in terms of the volitional professional behavior of the internal audit profession as well as the organizational arguments as to the inherent advantages of the internalization of organizational processes. This internal audit profession perspective will be grounded by observations from: early IIA positions on this issue as well as the advocacy from internal audit departments (S.C. Johnson Wax and J. C. Penney) which have thus far successfully defended their delivery of internal audit services. The sixth section of the paper offers additional observations and suggestions for future research revolving around some of the dynamics identified in this research pertaining to other critical social actors (the IIA and the SEC — see Fig. 1) who, although not the major focus of the study, seemed to be making a significant impact on the changing public accounting and internal audit professions. The final section of the paper provides a closing discussion.

2. Two major forces: inter-professional competition and organizational imperatives

The tension that was apparent in the differing views of Arthur Andersen versus J. C. Penney as to the nature of the internal audit function can be addressed from the sociology of professions literature which recognizes that both sides (the internal and external auditors) are capable of engaging in volitional professional behavior in the protection and/or advancement of their respective professional turf. These differing views can also be addressed through the outsourcing literature which recognizes that both sides can stake claim to traditional organizational arguments regarding the inherent advantages and disadvantages of externalized work. This section of the paper will provide a theoretical backdrop from the sociology of professions literature and the outsourcing literature from which to consider these dramatic changes in the internal audit profession.

2.1. Sociology of professions

Abbott's (1988) work on the manner in which occupations define their jurisdiction in terms of the right to control the provision of particular services and activities becomes helpful to address the increasing trend in outsourcing of professional work. Abbott (1988) was concerned with the manner in which the work content of a profession may become routine and cast off, while other parts of work content may become elaborated and defined as the core of the profession (Tolbert, 1990). Thus, as Abbott (1988) suggested, an occupation's ability to assume exclusive control of work activities depends largely on inter-professional competition. This point is important because it basically states that one professional occupation such as internal auditing cannot be studied in isolation from other occupations such as the external audit profession. Similarly, Hopwood (1998, p. 516) stated, "Rather than taking professional claims for granted, the ways in which they are sustained must be investigated, as should their consequences."

On this point, the sociology of professions literature has increasingly probed the dynamic processes by which professions establish and defend their jurisdictional domains. It focuses in particular on inter and intraprofessional competition in socially constituting both jurisdiction and the right to control the provision of services in that domain,

620   *L. Rittenberg, M.A. Covaleski / Accounting, Organizations and Society 26 (2001) 617–641*

as well as the abstract system of knowledge that undergirds these services. Abbott (1988, pp. 8–9) reasoned that it is essential for an occupational group to control its abstract system of knowledge in order to claim professional stature it is through this control that a profession can define and redefine the societal problems it addresses, develop the services and practical techniques to be performed to address these problems (that Abbott defines as the profession's jurisdiction), and defend this resultant jurisdiction against competing professions or factions within the profession. With time and legal sanction, this jurisdiction may eventually comprise a monopoly over performing specified activities. This jurisdiction includes formal control over both key definitions of professional service and the language used in describing the techniques performed, the practitioners that perform them and the actual conduct of the work (Abbott, 1988, p. 62).

On this theme, Crozier (1964, p. 165) observed that the expert's success is constantly self defeating. The rationalization process provides a basis for power, but the end results of rationalization curtail this power. As soon as a field is well covered, as soon as the first institutions and innovations can be translated into rules and programs, the expert's power disappears. This simultaneously enabling and disabling (Zuboff, 1988), Janus-faced (Reed, 1996) effect of codified knowledge contributes to a profession's downward spiral unless it regenerates its abstract system of knowledge and thereby extends its jurisdictional domain to possibly encroach upon that of adjacent professions.

Subsequent work in the sociology of professions area has sought to extend Abbott's general thesis of jurisdictional disputes. Key, once more, is a profession's command over an abstract body of knowledge that is storable, controllable, indeterminable, and deployable to convince constituents that the profession has expertise that is of utility to them (Derber, Schwartz, and Magrass, 1990; Drazin, 1990; Larson, 1990). Such a body of knowledge must be:

> effectively protected from incursion by predatory competitors if it is to remain the specialized preserve of a particular expert group.

The political strategies and tactics through which such expert jurisdictional domains are constructed and policed need to be supported by ideological resources and moral prohibitions that legitimate monopoly control for 'us''by delegitimating predatory incursions by 'them' (Reed, 1996, p. 575)

Similar to Abbott's (1988) concern for mapping disturbances, such jurisdictional disputes give rise to the "politics of expertise" that tend to be more intense and unstable during periods of professional transformation. According to Reed (1996), the politics of expertise, in turn, revolve around the knowledge base with which professional stature is claimed, the technical work and benefits for clients derived from this knowledge, the political strategies used to defend a jurisdiction, and the organizational forms used to mobilize expertise.

The basic power strategy and corresponding legitimating discourse for the entrepreneurial professions or knowledge workers, Reed (1996) theorized, also begins with displaying appropriate, though more general, credentials than organizational professionals [in our case, the Certified Public Accountant (CPA) is an older and more widely recognized credential]. In contrast with the specific and localized knowledge of organizational professions, knowledge workers, rely on developing, deploying and displaying a highly esoteric, intangible system of knowledge. This knowledge entails a "sophisticated combination of theoretical knowledge, analytical power and tacit or judgmental skills" (Reed, p. 588) that are refined, even partially codifiable, but transferable to other settings thus granting the knowledge worker a competitive advantage. As Reed (p. 576) reasoned, "...it is the putative universality, codificability, neutrality and mobility of modern, [entrepreneurial] expertise that sets it apart from the localism, particularlism and stability characteristic of traditional [organizational] expertise." It is by virtue of this very universality or generality of expertise, which can be communicated relatively easily to external constituents, that enables the client organization to be more mobile as it extends it global reach in that these constituents are comforted that appropriate expertise is being applied. Such globalization "offers to the entrepreneurial professions/knowledge workers the opportunity to exploit the potential for cognitive expansion, material advancement and socio-political enhancement that these developments present (Reed, 1996, p. 588).

The dark side of this universality and serving the client organization is that the entrepreneurial profession could be seen as too closely aligned to the vested interests of the client thereby undermining the professional claim of neutrality and independence in that the exercise of expertise is not objectified by a wholly codified knowledge base (see also Freidson, 1986). As Reed (p. 588) observed, "Once they become 'tainted" through a much closer incorporation into business practice, the disinterested claim to moral and cultural authority is increasingly difficult to sustain." Shaping the jurisdictional disputes of, for example, organizational and entrepreneurial professionals is an institutional environment that Reed (1996, p. 586) characterizes as being comprised of the "state, political ideologies and policies highly suspicious of, if not downright hostile to, professional power." Such an environment of regulation and suspicion tends to lead to both a strong fragmentation among the forms of expertise being mobilized, and more dramatic disputes over jurisdictions (Freidson, 1994).

This recognition of the importance of understanding professional claims is at the crux of Kalbers and Fogarty's (1995) point that there are more macro-behavioral forces which need to be considered as impacting the internal auditing profession. In short, the differentiation between the external and internal audit profession may be the possession of a body of abstract knowledge on which the occupation bases its claims for the exclusive right to control specific work activities. Such claims to work, from Abbott's (1988) perspective, is the critical, distinguishing characteristic of professional occupation. Abbott's (1988) approach emphasized that the analysis of the tasks or work activities of occupations is the key to understanding changes in professionalization. In this vein, we are interested in the manner in which the work of internal auditing is defined — from both sides of the competing professions. Similarly, Larson (1977) argued that professionalization is a collective assertion of special social status and upward social mobility where producers of special services seek to constitute and control a market for their expertise. Thus battles over marketable expertise is a crucial element in the structure of professionalism.

2.2. Outsourcing literature

Outsourcing is proving to be a growth industry, with employment growing by 250 percent between 1982 and 1992 (compared with overall employment growth of 20 percent; Morrow, 1993), with contingent workers comprising approximately 10 percent the US workforce (Cohany, 1996). Growth in and reliance on technical experts has been especially dramatic, with 43 percent of large US companies outsourcing professional and technical functions, thus potentially having a significant impact on the stock of knowledge available to them (Matusik & Hill, 1998; Wysock, 1996). The rationale for outsourcing organizational functions is predominantly stated in economic terms: within a "new competitive landscape" demanding a reduction in costs, organizations can manage their capacity more efficiently and enhance their flexibility by focusing on their "core activities" and outsourcing their "non-core activities" to an external, contingent workforce of independent contractors. The company thus averts the high costs of recruiting, training and paying an internal workforce, though it incurs both a higher marginal cost of paying contingent workers and a potential cost of giving up the advantage of utilitizing unique "local knowledge" in advancing the firm. Moreover, organizations may gain access to a wider range of publicly available information, though it may also "leak" proprietary information to contingent workers thus impacting the organization's competitive advantage (Bettis & Hitt, 1995; Davis-Blake & Uzzi, 1993; Matusik & Hill, 1998; Roodhooft & Warlop, 1999; Tsui, Pearce, Porter, & Hite, 1995).

The importance of understanding the manner in which workers adapt within organizational work settings was also recognized by Davis-Blake and Uzzi (1993) who stated that most research on internalization of work (traditional internal work force) provides considerable agreement that internal workers increase workforce stability and give the employing firm control over employees. These traditional internal labor markets provide these benefits by selecting workers capable of following the rules, and by embedding jobs in hierarchical structures that socialize workers, monitor behavior, provide opportunities, etc. However, because internal labor markets are designed to provide stability and control, this traditional internal approach may make it difficult and expensive for employers to adjust to changing internal and external conditions. Thus, firms may derive the benefits of a traditional internal labor force at a cost of reduced organizational flexibility.

In contrast to internalization, externalization (outsourcing) may increase a firm's flexibility in dealing with changing market conditions and organizational requirements (Davis-Blake & Uzzi, 1993). Externalization reduces many types of employment and administrative costs (benefits and administration of such benefits). Externalized workers are hired without the expectation of long term employment and therefore can be let go without tarnishing the firms image. Externalization may offer a firm a way to access highly specialized skills that are needed for only a short period of time, such as engineering skills. Essentially, Davis-Blake and Uzzi argued that internalization and externalization serve different but complementary purposes. Internalization enhances organizational control and stability, while externalization increases organizational flexibility. When used together, these two arrangements give a firm a mechanism for developing stable yet adaptable work arrangements.

Halal (1994) characterized this rapid expansion of the externalization of the work force as part of a trend toward structuring modern organizations as internal markets. Referring to several successful firms such as Hewlett Packard, Johnson & Johnson, and Clark as companies who have been novel in their creation of internal markets, Halal argued that just as the post-Communist bloc is adopting markets, so too are corporations moving to market systems. Halal drew from Tom Peters' battle cry to "Force the market into every nook and cranny of the firms" to emphasize the importance

of today's growing use of "intrapreneurs" "internal customers" and other equivalents of markets. This "market test" on internal markets is consistent with Davis-Blake and Uzzi's (1993) broad concept of the benefits of internalization of work being stability and the benefits of externalization being flexibility, and that the tradeoffs need to be considered within a corporation's assessment of costs pertaining to the respective alternatives this is the internal market test.

Matusik and Hill (1998) also made similar arguments regarding the tradeoffs in the internalization versus externalization debate when they stated that contingent work is an increasingly integral part of the world of work and that its use affects firms' abilities to accumulate knowledge, create value, and establish competitive advantage. The authors broadly define contingent workforce as consisting of several types of work groups, including those workers on site whose services are provided by contract firms such as outsourced internal audit services. Consistent with Davis-Blake and Uzzi (1993), Matusik and Hill acknowledge the typical arguments that depict contingent work use as an attempt by firms to drive down their cost structure (benefit, training, recruitment, capacity) and increase their ability to reduce or expand their workforce in order to match rapidly changing market conditions and the staffing demands of internal projects. However, Matusik and Hill (p. 681) go beyond these issues to further by stating that:

...the most significant impact of contingent work may be on the knowledge stock of the firm and, through that, on the firm's long term competitive position. Contingent work can be an important vehicle for importing valuable performance enhancing knowledge into the firm. At the same time, the unchecked use of contingent work can result in the leakage of valuable private knowledge into the public domain.

With this serious tradeoff in mind, Matusik and Hill (1998, p. 694) go on to "call into the question the one-size-fits-all adage to protect core functions and outsource liberally in non-core areas." As the

L. Rittenberg, M.A. Covaleski / Accounting, Organizations and Society 26 (2001) 617–641 623

authors argued, the internalization versus externalization decision is more complex. They observed that sources of technical knowledge are not necessarily contained within organizational boundaries. And similar to Davis-Blake and Uzzi (1993), Matusik and Hill stated that the effects of changing boundary conditions such as through outsourcing of organizational processes and outcomes have yet to receive much attention.

On this point, Davis-Blake and Uzzi (1993), in their analysis of trends in the outsourcing of corporate work, argued that future research needs to recognize that the majority of externalized workers no longer perform unskilled clerical tasks many are professionals such as nurses or accountants (see Ang & Cummings, 1997) The authors stated that as the externalized workforce becomes more numerous and diverse, it is important to explore why firms internalize and/or externalize these types of workers. This call for future work to recognize outsourcing in terms of professional work is particularly relevant to our work where the outsourcing decision pertaining to the internal audit involves professional work, i.e. internal auditors if the work is internalized, or external auditors if the work is externalized.

Matusik and Hill (1998) reasoned that command of knowledge is key in outsourcing work to external professionals and experts, and identified two important dimensions of knowledge: (1) private versus public knowledge, and (2) architectural versus component knowledge. Private or localized knowledge is the proprietary knowledge which an organization develops internally that involves idiosyncratic procedures, processes, routines, documentation and trade secrets that grant an organization its competitive advantage thus, there is great concern as to its leakage. Public knowledge resides in the external environment and includes tools, techniques processes, even accounting and auditing practices, etc. found in a society, economic sector, industry or professional group, that are applicable across a number of social settings and are often discussed using their acronyms — JIT, MBO, TQM, etc. As a public good, such knowledge cannot confer competitive advantage. The key issue concerns the possession of sufficient expertise to recognize its existence, understand it, tailor it to fit the unique features of an organization, and apply it. From a sociology of professions perspective, Reed (1996, p. 577), reasoned that it was precisely in the area of public knowledge that jurisdictional disputes would > be sharpest, and theorized that the entrepreneurial professions would eventually come to dominate because of their "putative universality, codifiability, neutrality and mobility" that set them apart from the "localism, politicularism and stability" of organizational professionals whose province is private knowledge.

Architectural knowledge, Matusik and Hill (1998) stated, relates to organization-wide philosophies, schemas and routines that are gleaned from deep, long term emersion in an organization's culture sufficient to develop a collective, tacit understanding of the overall system. Architectural knowledge is predominantly "private" in nature and is essential to the organization's competitive advantage. In contrast, component knowledge relates to the concrete operation of organizational subsystems that consume specific inputs and produce specific outputs. Such components may be either "core" or "non-core" to the organization, and either private or public in nature. Component knowledge is, in turn, embedded within architectural knowledge which is used to orchestrate subsystems.

Matusik and Hill (1998) hypothesized that because of the very nature of the forms of knowledge involved, organizations would most likely outsource professional and expert work to external contractors that predominantly concerned public versus private knowledge, and non-core component versus architectural knowledge. They reasoned that this work would be outsourced because it would allow the least leakage of proprietary knowledge of strategic importance, while simultaneously engendering the most importation of public knowledge due to external contractors being exposed to the discipline of market forces which would force them to be more abreast of public knowledge concerning such components as accounting, inventory, and personnel management techniques (e.g. ABC, JIT, and TQM) that are deemed generally necessary to compete in the marketplace.

In summary, the flow of logic begins the recognition by Davis-Blake and Uzzi (1993) that the

624   *L. Rittenberg, M.A. Covaleski | Accounting, Organizations and Society 26 (2001) 617–641*

outsourcing of work increasingly pertains to professional workers, including the internal audit function as the nature of control is changing dramatically in contemporary organizations (Simons, 1995). Furthermore, Matusik and Hill's (1998) provided a taxonomy to suggest the impact of outsourcing on the importing or exporting of valuable knowledge into and out of the firm. It appears that: the outsourcing of work such as internal auditing can be characterized as merely entailing public, non-core knowledge thus receptive to market testing or entailing valuable private, architectural knowledge too valuable to the competitive advantage of companies to risk leakage. Such characterizations and opposing views are rife with conflict and thus have the potential for enriching our understanding of the outsourcing of the internal audit function. Therefore, the following propositions will be examined:

P1: The sociology of professions literature suggests that public accounting firms will attempt to re-define the boundaries of the external and internal audits in an effort to justify their entrance into the provision of internal audit services. Furthermore, as suggested by the outsourcing literature, these public accounting firms will attempt to define their provision of internal audit in line with broader organizational imperatives — i.e. the internal audit function containing public, non-core component knowledge that should be exposed to the discipline of market forces.

P2: The sociology of professions literature suggests that corporate internal audit departments will attempt to re-affirm the boundaries of the external and internal audits in an effort to retain their provision of internal audit services. Furthermore, as suggested by the outsourcing literature, these corporate internal audit departments will attempt to define their provision of the internal audit function in line with broader organizational imperatives — i.e. internal auditing function containing private, architectural knowledge that is too valuable to the competitive position of the company to outsource.

3. Research methods

Consistent with our theoretical perspective that professional jurisdiction is socially constituted through the interactions of various constituent groups, evidence was gathered through qualitative analysis of archival material from both side of the professional dispute. This evidence was supplemented with extensive interviews with key organizational actors from the two professional sides to elicit their views and their guidance on accessing relevant material. Archival material took the form of both public and private records (Denzin, 1978) as well as business press coverage of the events examined (Allison, 1971; Herman & Chomsky, 1988; Zelizer, 1992). Public material included: IIA exposure drafts of proposed standards and definitions of internal auditing AICPA audit guides, speeches by Big Five firms members, and IIA officers and SEC officials. Private material included interview comments from key social actors pertaining to both the Big Five firms and the corporate internal audit departments (see Lincoln & Guba, 1985). These interviews were supplemented with internal memos, brochures, and documents from these studied organizations. Finally, IIA memoranda and correspondence files of key social actors were important sources of data. Press coverage includes minutes of CNBC broadcasts, and articles, editorials, and advertisements appearing in the *Wall Street Journal, Public Accounting Report, Internal Auditor,* and *Accounting Today.*

Latent or qualitative content analysis, in which the researcher serves as a research instrument in interpreting archival material (Van Maanen, 1979, 1988), was deemed especially relevant in order to place emphasis on the character of the archival material rather than on quantitative procedures of analysis. According to Berg (1989, p. 107), latent content analysis represents an "interpretive reading of the symbolism underlying the physically presented data" and thus provides a very useful approach in examining archival material complicit in the exercise of power and exertion of influence (Merton, 1968, pp. 366–370). Such exercise of power and influence underlie the two major research propositions of this study.

L. Rittenberg, M.A. Covaleski / Accounting, Organizations and Society 26 (2001) 617–641 625

The primary groups of social actors examined include the AICPA, the Big Five public accounting firms (increasingly relabeled as "profession service firms"), with a particular focus on Arthur Andersen, Ernst & Young, and KPMG Peat Marwick; two corporate internal audit departments (S. C. Johnson Wax and J. C. Penney) two professional associations — the AICPA and the IIA and the interests of the federal government in the form of the SEC. The Big Five firms are among the largest professional bureaucracies in the world (Mintzberg, 1979; Whittington, McNulty, & Whipp, 1994), are also *the* predominant form of under-researched, organization-based profession that has emerged as a direct consequence of commercial enterprise within which expertise may first be expected to become commodified to justify the expansion of CPA's jurisdictional domain (Abbott, 1988; Freidson, 1986).

4. Analysis: efforts by the public accounting profession to re-define the boundaries between the external and internal audit function

The AICPA Professional Ethics Division released an exposure draft in February 1996, proposing several interpretations and guidelines for the performance of extended audit services (such as internal auditing) for external audit clients. The 1996 AICPA Professional Ethics Committee's Exposure Draft effectively codified "best practices," affirming that extended audit services such as the provision of internal audit services would not impair independence with respect to attest clients. As the AICPA (1996) Exposure Draft concluded:

A member's performance of extended audit services would not be considered to impair independence with respect to a client for which the member also performs a service requiring independence, provided that the member of his or her firm does not act or does not appear to act in a capacity equivalent to a member of client management or as an employee.

In May of 1996, the Ethics Committee upgraded the Exposure Draft to an official interpretation, Extended Audit Services, and specifically concluded that outsourcing does not impair the external auditor's independence as long as someone from management remains in charge of the internal audit function, and the internal audit function does not perform "on-going" monitoring activities. The consequence of this "green light" into extended audit services by the AICPA was a dramatic growth in the performance of internal audits services by the Big Five. According to a *Public Accounting Report* (1997, p. 2) article, for example, these firms' "plotted annual growth rates of 80 to 100% through the year 2000 for this fledgling practice area."

As a specific example of the actual performance of such services, a *Wall Street Journal (WSJ)* (1996a) article described a situation where Arthur Andersen reached an agreement with the Camp Fire Boys and Girls to give up their external financial audit role due to the client's insistence (and a related $50,000 per year audit fee) in order to make possible an outsourcing agreement to provide full-time, on-site accounting and systems services at approximately $400,000 per year. Arthur Andersen defended this new arrangement by arguing that they could better serve their client through this outsourcing arrangement than through the attest arrangement. As the *WSJ* (1996a) summarized, this recent expansion of services by public accounting firms has also been characterized as "an outrageous conflict of interest" and as a trend which "could add to the accounting profession's credibility problems" (p. B8). It (*WSJ*, 1996a, p. B8) warned that the internal auditing profession as represented by the 60,000 member IIA, "wants double duty auditing stopped entirely."

According to two other 1996 *Wall Street Journal* articles, this expansion of services is attributable to a problematic external audit market. The first (*WSJ*, 1996b, p. B1), whose title succinctly captures the issues at hand (i.e. entitled "Who is Going to Audit the Auditor") stated that Big Five accounting firms, worried about slowing revenues, have tripled the amount of "double duty work" they perform in the past five years. The second (*WSJ*, 1996c. p. B1), further argued that accounting

626   L. Rittenberg, M.A. Covaleski / Accounting, Organizations and Society 26 (2001) 617–641

firms are trying to broaden the scope of the audit business. It noted that while the major public accounting firms have almost doubled their consulting business since 1990 (collectively they perform 23 percent of such services worldwide *Public Accounting Report,* 1998, 1999a, 1999b), their audit business has edged up only 16 percent. It characterized the external financial audit ("the plain vanilla audit") as having become "a stagnant commodity," where clients resist fee increases because "they increasingly feel that traditional audits don't help their business and that one is as good as another" (*WSJ,* 1996c, p. B1 see also SEC Commissioner Norman Johnson, 1999, p. 3). Also, the more lucrative outsourcing work does not simply consist of small engagements with camp fire boys and girls anymore: PWC just reported a $850 million outsourcing contract with a governmental agency in New Zealand (*WSJ,* 2000).

The"green light" provided into extended audit services by the AICPA and the corresponding movement by the major public accounting firms can be illustrated by the posturing of three of the Big Five firms in their efforts to re-define the internal/external audit relationship. The combined efforts of the AICPA and the firms themselves illuminate the issues raised in the *first research proposition* of this study which argued that *public accounting firms will attempt to re-define the boundaries of the external and internal audits in an effort to justify their entrance into the provision of internal audit services. Furthermore, these public accounting firms will attempt to define their provision of internal audit in line with broader organizational imperatives.* A common theme in these firm-specific efforts is the attempt to unfreeze the body of abstract knowledge on which the internal audit profession bases its claims for the exclusive right to control specific work activities — i.e. the internal audit function (Abbott, 1988; Reed, 1996). Furthermore, the three firms all seem to characterize the internal audit function in terms of public, non-core work (Matusik & Hill, 1998) that can best served by subjecting it to the discipline of market forces which, of course, would be the services offered by these firms (see also Cooper, Scarborough & Chilton, 1995; Preston, et al., 1995; Sikka & Willmott, 1995).

4.1. Arthur Andersen

The marketing brochure of Arthur Andersen (1995), the most active firm in internal audit outsourcing (*Public Accounting Report,* 1997), stated that outsourcing is a "strategic concept" — a way to add value to a business — that "converts an in-house cost center into a customer-focused service operation with you as the customer." The firm appealed to corporations to focus on the critical "core" areas of the business that create and sustain competitive advantage and outsource such non-core competencies (Matusik & Hill, 1998) such as internal auditing. Arthur Andersen (AA) defined its outsourcing services wrapped around internal auditing as including: assisting management in the planning and execution of the internal audit process identifying customer needs assessing risks supervising audits and communicating results and performing partial outsourcing services for peak period needs, international locations, regulatory compliance, and EDP audits on both recurring and non-recurring bases. Arthur Andersen's pamphlet listed the benefits of outsourcing in terms highly consistent with the traditional outsourcing literature: outsourcing eliminates the tasks of recruiting, training and maintaining employees helps manage costs engenders objectivity, expertise and consistent quality leverages existing internal audit resources focus on more key organizational needs offers technologies or geographical flexibility reduces fixed salary costs shifts liability for attestation assignments frees management to focus on core competencies *opens internal audit services to the discipline of market forces* and engenders a dynamic for continual improvement — all in a competitively priced package.

The position of AA as articulated by their Director of Contract Audit Services is that the audit business is evolving to meet the clients" needs in terms of broad business assurance as to their procedures, processes, systems, and risk areas. This view sees, and advocates, the traditional audit as migrating from auditing financial statements to auditing the business (Abbott, 1988; Reed, 1996). The historical focus of attestation remains important, according to this perspective, but is of less value today than the need to assure

L. Rittenberg, M.A. Covaleski / Accounting, Organizations and Society 26 (2001) 617–641   627

that business processes are in place to compete in a rapidly changing world. While the financial statement remains important in the integration of financial markets, this view argues that it is not as relevant in the management decision making process. Here, it is argued that the move to providing contract audit services is a natural move to providing greater relevance to clients in an area in which the public accounting firms have a competitive advantage. Essentially, AA is stating that business organizations want more than financial statement audits they want broader attestation service — business risk/internal audit/consulting services. Here, AA is interested in providing these broader assurances in terms of how the host organization benchmarks relative to best practice processes/operational efficiencies. At this point, the internal audit becomes the mechanism where AA attempts to blend the knowledge base of the client with the broad knowledge of the business and best practices.

Furthermore, the firm's views, as expressed by their Head of Contract Services believes that the line between internal and external auditing is not relevant (Abbott, 1988; Reed, 1996). Here the firms argues that independence is not a major issue when AA performs outsourcing as long as the client accepts the responsibility for the function as outlined in the AICPA position. Critical in this redefinition of the nature of the audit is the distinction between auditing and attestation. This views suggests that while attestation services requires an assertion (e.g. management's assertion that the financial statements are fairly presented) to a third party recipient, auditing and assurance services do not necessarily require these components. For example, an auditor can provide assurances to management on the efficiency of its practices or the likely effectiveness of its control practices without performing the attestation function. The resultant model for AA is a depiction of broad range of services provided by external auditors along the following continuum:

ATTEST—AUDIT—ASSURANCE—CONSULTING

Here, AA sees the challenge for the auditor is to provide relevance to management, including control

effectiveness and strategic decision making along this continuum. In other words, their changing external audit philosophy is to adapt to business needs or face the risk of becoming irrelevant. The resultant audit service that AA offers as the outsourcer of internal audit services emphasizes working as partners with the organization to control business risk. AA emphasizes three things to its potential client: (1) a standardized approach to address risk in the framework of strategic management and operational control (2) its access to "best practices" and (3) a one-step solution to risk management. This standardized, "one-stop" solution (Matusik & Hill, 1998) advocated in the AA (Arthur Andersen, 1995) brochure is revealed in the following:

> We work with many of the world's leading companies to provide rigorous internal audit and risk management services. We have the skills and tools to help you access risk, evaluate the effectiveness of your business and financial controls, and use best practices to continually improve them. We can help you anticipate, not simply react to risk, and put you in control.

Once the boundaries between external and internal auditing are re-defined in AA's terms, this allows AA to advocate the advantages that they perceive that their firm has in being the provider of internal audit services. The Head of Contract Services believes that the competitive marketplace drives the demands for services. AA is essentially justifying their position in terms of companies wanting broader attestation — i.e. business risk, internal audit, consulting services. This, in their view, is part of the natural migration a migration that "converts an in-house cost center into a customer focused service operations" and allows companies to sustain competitive advantage through outsourcing such non-core competencies as internal auditing (Arthur Andersen, 1995).

4.2. Ernst & Young

Ernst & Young's (E&Y) depiction of the changing nature of the internal audit function also advocates a continuing change in the boundaries between the external and internal audit processes

(Abbott, 1988; Reed, 1996). Essentially this perspective sees the job of internal auditing as moving closer to a consulting role. In this view, the "biggest issue the internal auditor faces today is not the perceived threat of outsourcing but the challenge from management to add value to the company" (*Internal Audit Alert*, 1996, p. 4). As to the future, their view is:

> Ten years from now, the internal auditor will be a high level management person who knows about a business, its products, and risk management. The internal auditor department will be smaller, more high-powered, and more flexible. It will be part of a broader risk management area, probably part of the CFO's world. There will also be more interaction and collaboration between internal and external auditors (*Internal Audit Alert*, 1996, p. 5).

E&Y's Director of Outsourcing Services argues that the idea of financial statement audits, internal audits, and consulting being able to operate as independent functions is a thing of the past (Abbott, 1988; Reed, 1996). E&Y feels that these functions need to become more focused on the business processes — thus, a potential blurring of the services. In serving the organization, internal auditing will be called upon to serve on task forces, while managers take on more of the control function by doing more self-assessment. In this view, the blending of these services allows the organization to focus on profitability, thus appealing to a market-solution to the delineation of the responsibilities of the internal audit function (Matusik & Hill, 1998). This view sees the audit market as existing on one common continuum (not as two distinct markets) where the continuum runs from exclusive internal auditing (and no external auditing) to exclusive external auditing (and no internal auditing), with any combination of the provision of internal auditing and external auditing services in between. Here, the Director of Outsourcing Services at E&Y argues that the extent of outsourcing of the internal audit function can be anywhere on the continuum. In their experience, they have started with a client

on exclusive external auditing side of the continuum and have helped the client move towards engaging E&Y in more-and-more internal audit services. The E&Y position concedes that both the internal and external audit groups need independence to determine the scope of activities. However, this independence often results in audit duplication. Therefore, it is argued that value can be added (Matusik & Hill) by "objectively" reconsidering the costs related to monitoring the boundaries between the external and internal audit groups (Abbott, 1988; Reed). E&Y is convinced that quality could be improved by removing the boundaries between the external and internal audits, while retaining the critical benefits of objectivity and independence. The perspective is this:

> A look at the businesses we audit suggests an answer. Time after time, in area after area, business mangers have been able to find ways to re-engineer redundant or layered work processes while both improving product or service quality and reducing all-in costs. Why should auditors, either internal or external, be held to a lesser performance standard? Why should the business practices and processes followed by auditors be any less innovative or flexible than those of their most successful clients? (Anderson, 1994, p. 13)

A more specific example of the changing nature of the business of internal auditing comes from E&Y's development of the outsourcing function in Great Britain. One of their selling points as to the non-core, public nature of the internal audit function (Matusik & Hill, 1998) is that internal auditing tends to be fixed in nature, but the risks of the company, or management's needs to have the audit function focus on particular risks, may vary over time (see Fig. 2). The E&Y partner in London then asks the question whether there should be a role that the outsourcer should play in assisting the internal audit function. The obvious answer, in his view, is that an outsourcer provides flexible staffing and expertise that will allow the internal audit department to best address unaddressed risks when they arise. His view then is a traditional economic argument (Davis-Blake & Uzzi, 1993) in

L. Rittenberg, M.A. Covaleski / Accounting, Organizations and Society 26 (2001) 617–641 629

terms of the benefits of outsourcing; i.e. flexible staffing can provide better coverage of risks throughout the year at no additional cost. E&Y then presents additional economic arguments for utilizing outsourcing much in the same manner as AA: organizations tend to underestimate the cost of the internal audit function employment, and other costs, e.g. benefits, are usually double salary costs specialists, in such areas as treasury, will reach issues (define, analyze, and suggest solutions) more quickly than non-specialists and implementation of modern audit methodologies and technology leads to savings in audit time of about 20 to 50%.

In summary, E&Y's approach to auditing has evolved to emphasize auditing and risk analysis as a core competency an approach which, in their view, "transcends" traditional external/internal audit boundaries (Abbott, 1988; Reed, 1996). E&Y particularly bases its new audit philosophy around the issue of information technology as the firm accelerates its development of a worldwide knowledge base to share information as key to the organization's future success with this audit philosophy. They believe that as organizations become more dependent on information systems, firms will be able to invest in the technology that visualizes the organizational processes, develop tools that will help management monitor controls, and develop audit techniques concurrent with the technology which can add value to the organization. Again, their view is that the value-added from

such inter-related use of the new technology would be strongly retarded by audit boundaries which only results in a duplication of services (Matusik & Hill, 1998).

4.3. KPMG

KPMG's new "Business Measurement Process"provides an excellent overview of their new audit approach which, as with the previous two firms, is justified as being a much broader and more meaningful than traditional financial statement audits (Abbott, 1988; Reed, 1996). This Business Measurement Process is an endorsement of the integrated audit approach because, in their view, part of this integration may be due to the fairly dramatic change taking place in their external audit philosophy. They describe their approach as follows:

> Our internal audit methodology is based on a *combined assurance approach*. It provides a model for your internal audit function to work closely with management and your external auditors, so as to maximize the internal control assurance provided to your Audit Committee and provide efficiency by avoiding duplication.

Furthermore, KPMG has restructured its audit approach along five industry lines that represent distinct service areas such as manufacturing,

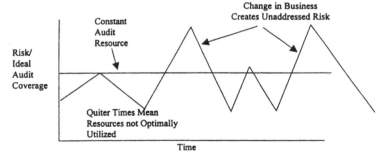

Fig. 2. Challenges for internal auditing.

finance, retail, entertainment, health care, and high technology to enhance their newly defined audit approach as one that focuses on operational and business risks.

KPMG described their audit approach as one that focuses on operational and business risks. This approach contains two other dimensions that blur the distinction between internal and external audit services (Abbott, 1988; Reed, 1996). First, it emphasizes a willingness to assist an organization in starting an internal audit function. The intent may to eventually bring the function in-house or retain it as an outsourcing function. Second, they have developed a "Quality Assurance Review and Re-engineering" service specifically for existing internal audit departments. They describe this latter approach as "an effective means of assessing the performance of the internal audit function against management expectations and best practices." The services emphasize the standardized, public nature of the internal audit function by including benchmarking against other organizations that are similar in industry and basic attributes (Matusik & Hill, 1998).

The contrasts that KPMG makes between the old traditional audit (where KPMG does the external audit and the company's internal audit department does the internal audit) versus their world-class audit (where KPMG does both the external and internal audit function) reveals their efforts to re-characterize the nature of internal audit work (Abbott, 1988; Reed, 1996). The traditional audit (and traditional boundaries) simply involves detection whereas the new world-class audit (which blurs and blends the boundaries) means that the company hires a risk partner. The traditional audit simply provides an audit focus the world-class audit provides business focus. Other contrasts are just as apparent in their efforts to re-define the audit process: cost focus versus customer focus functional focus versus process focus hierarchical versus horizontal green pen versus harnessing technology and fragmented approach versus integrated approach.

In summary, the actions of KPMG, as with AA and E&Y, are fully consistent with the recent AICPA (1996) document on Extended Audit Services. These combined efforts to redefine the nature

of internal audit work are indicative of the macro forces which are shaping the nature of the internal audit profession (Kalbers & Fogarty, 1995). At stake are traditional lines drawn between the work of the public accounting firms — the external financial audit — and the work of the internal audit profession — the internal audit (Abbott, 1988; Freidson, 1994; Reed, 1996). This line between respective jurisdictional claims and the efforts to blur these lines are at the core of Hopwood's (1998) concern as to the commercialism of the audit industry and, more specifically, support Abbott's (1983) contention as to the significance of claims for the exclusive right to control specific work activities as being the critical, distinguishing characteristic of professional occupation. In this vein, we are interested in the manner in which the work of internal auditing is defined — here from the side of three of the firms in the public accounting profession. According to Reed, the politics of expertise, in turn, revolve around the knowledge base with which professional stature is claimed, the technical work and benefits for clients derived from this knowledge, the political strategies used to defend a jurisdiction, and the organizational forms used to mobilize expertise. Also, more specifically, the positions taken by these three firms support Matusik and Hill's (1998) hypothesis that these firms would characterize internal audit work as being predominantly public, non-core knowledge that should be exposed to the discipline of market forces (Halal, 1994).

5. Analysis: efforts by the internal audit profession to re-affirm the boundaries between the external and internal audit function

The Institute of Internal Auditors (IIA) (1978) developed a codified set of *Standards for the Professional Practice of Internal Auditors* that includes the association's definition of internal auditing. Here, the IIA presented the case for internal audit services remaining a strictly in-house function and established the point that keeping the internal auditing function as an integral part of the organization offers clear advantages. Extending this view, the IIA's (1994, p. 2) own white paper

L. Rittenberg, M.A. Covaleski / Accounting, Organizations and Society 26 (2001) 617–641 631

emphatically stated that a "competent internal audit department that is properly organized with trained staff can perform the internal audit function more efficiently and effectively than [an externally] contracted service." Consistent with the political advantage of organizational professionals being localized knowledge (Reed, 1996), the primary rationale for this position was that internal auditors are "intimately acquainted with their organizations' policies, procedures, operating practices, and personnel" (IIA, 1994, p. 3). The IIA argued that through day-to-day experience in the business, internal auditors acquire — and operate from — an intimate knowledge of an organization's culture, processes, risks, and controls, and thereby obtain the "proprietary knowledge" that figures prominently in giving competitive management advantage to their client (Matusik & Hill, 1998). The insight and expertise of internal auditors, it was argued, enables them to provide management with tailored services, especially in the regulated areas of internal control risk analysis. In short, the IIA's position was that internal auditing professionals know and understand the organizations to a degree that such outsiders as public accountants cannot, and their loyalty and confidentiality are ensured by the internal nature of their function (Pelfrey & Peacock, 1995).

Moreover, consistent with the assertions of the outsourcing literature (Bettis & Hitt, 1995; Davis-Blake & Uzzi, 1993; Tsui et al., 1995), the IIA's position elaborated on the disadvantages of outsourcing which they defined as: the lack of independence on part of external auditor violates AICPA ethics it attempts to take away management's responsibility for internal control and thereby contributes to an irrevocable diminishment of the value of the external audit services in financial markets high learning curve costs high cost potential loss of direct management control over and orchestration of internal audit function possible loss of informal and potent communications disruption caused by a change in the locus of who performs the services potential loss of competitive advantage concerning proprietary information and a loss of checks and balances.

The most forceful expression of the IIA's position against the outsourcing of internal audit services to the external auditor came on 19 January 1996 when the IIA boldly presented its views at the open session of the Professional Ethics Executive Committee of the AICPA. This open session was part of the protocol whereby the Committee solicited input for its eventual 28 February exposure draft (described earlier) and, in turn, resultant May 1996 official interpretation, Extended Audit Services. At this 19th January meeting, the IIA (1996a, p. 1) made its position clear:

> The IIA is opposed to total outsourcing of the internal audit function to a company's external auditor because it impairs the [CPA] firm's independence. Internal auditing is a key management function that conflicts with the public accountants" responsibilities to be independent of management. (1996a, p. 1)

In this open hearing, the IIA also made strong reference to the frustration that the SEC was having over the lack of guidance from the AICPA regarding the implications of outsourcing on audit independence. The IIA stressed that its representative to the SEC was going to take the official position on behalf of the IIA that "monitoring and control activities" could not be assumed by external auditors without impairment of independence.

The assertive position by the IIA to defend the internal audit function against efforts to outsource these services can be exemplified by the strength of the internal audit departments of two major corporations in their efforts to re-affirm their primary role in the provision of internal audit services. The combined efforts of the IIA, and the two companies as illustrations of these efforts, illuminate the issues raised in the *second research proposition* of this study which argued that *corporate internal audit departments will attempt to re-affirm the boundaries of the external and internal audits in an effort to retain their provision of internal audit services. Furthermore, these corporate internal audit departments will attempt to define their provision of the internal audit function in line with broader organizational imperatives.* A common theme in these in-house efforts to retain their provision of internal audit services is the attempt to reaffirm the boundaries of the external and internal audits,

632　　　　*L. Rittenberg, M.A. Covaleski / Accounting, Organizations and Society 26 (2001) 617–641*

thus claiming the exclusive right to control specific work activities (Abbott, 1988; Reed, 1996). Furthermore, both companies all seem to characterize the internal audit function in terms of private, architectural knowledge that is much too valuable to the competitive position of the company to outsource (Matusik & Hill, 1998).

5.1. S. C. Johnson Wax

The Director of Corporate Audit suggested that the internal audit function at S. C. Johnson Wax is embedded within a commitment from the highest levels of management to a strong business process control environment within the company. This commitment is expressed in a document that is provided to all key managers. Here the CEO of the company stated:

> Wildly fluctuating economies and competitive situations, shifting customer demands and priorities... the business environment continues to change at a breakneck pace. To manage effectively, business must have solid management and internal controls in place.

Furthermore, the CEO wrote:

> I encourage you to read this brochure and partner with Corporate Audit in achieving our corporate objectives.

Essentially, the CEO's message emphasized the importance and value of controls in achieving business objectives. The CEO referred to Corporate Audit in terms of helping the company remain innovative by sharing ideas. Consistent with the importance of nature of private, architectural knowledge, the CEO perceived and advocated a very broad and significant mission for the internal audit function.

Likewise, the internal audit department, through its *Corporate Audit Vision and Mission Statement* promoted this significant role for itself (see Fig. 3). Note the key issues in their statement: This internal audit department provides "internal consulting and audit services that align with the company's business directions and priorities."

Consistent with Reed's (1996) notion of politics of expertise, the knowledge base as espoused by this internal audit department is indeed aligned with critical benefits for its clients. Furthermore, this department provides "value added" services that redesign business processes, increase operational efficiencies, assess risk to assets and operations, and provide solutions for improving controls, and perhaps most importantly, and consistent with Matusik and Hill (1998), this critical architectural knowledge is provided by an internal audit department that enjoys a "uniquely broad exposure to all business activities at different company locations" with such exposure providing unique "insight into S. C. Johnson Wax's methods, procedures and multinational operations."

The internal audit department has solidified its integration with the strong business process control environment within S. C. Johnson Wax. Here Corporate Audit's emphasis is essentially to identify the key core processes and the key control processes. Rather than perform risk analysis by Corporate Audit, they have moved to a model in which the risk issues are filled out by business managers (Simons, 1995). The internal audit group helped write a corporate policy on controls and have taken an active lead in facilitating control self assessment. The Director of Corporate Audit, consistent with the CEO's emphasis on business controls, has stressed that control is an integral part of the business and its importance ought to be ingrained in the basic business functions. From the risk issues, Corporate Audit describes the risk into definable audits and objectively determines priorities for the year. In their reports, they provide feedback to management and the auditee as to the progress made in dealing with the risks during the year and whether or not significant risks may have overlooked. From the risk analysis, Corporate Audit developed an audit plan for the coming year and presents the plan to the Audit Committee.

The Director of Corporate Audit is very cognizant of the trend towards the outsourcing of internal audit departments. As evidenced by the *Corporate Audit Vision and Mission Statement*, he has taken a strong position that the internal audit departments that are likely to get outsourced are

L. Rittenberg, M.A. Covaleski / Accounting, Organizations and Society 26 (2001) 617–641 633

those who do not add value to the organization (Matusik & Hill, 1998). Here it is believed that operational auditing is the key to the future of internal audit departments. In this regard, S. C. Johnson Wax benchmarks its audit function with a group of 30 internal auditing departments in the consumer product category which includes such companies as RJR, ConAgra, Kraft, Procter & Gamble, etc., to monitor the productivity of their own internal audit department. Furthermore,

S. C. Johnson Wax
Vision and Mission
Corporate Audit Services

Vision and Mission (excerpts)

The Corporate Audit mission is to provide our clients with proactive internal consulting and audit services that align with the company's business directions and priorities, contribute value to operations and promote a positive control environment.

To achieve this, the department will focus on:

- Working with clients to establish appropriate business controls through a positive and productive partnership
- Delivering value-added results and recommendations
- Service
- Continuous improvement in delivery of services
- Development of people

Responsibilities, Services, and Clients: (excerpts)

On behalf of the Audit Committee and management, Corporate Audit promotes a strong and positive control environment throughout the company. Their services can be structured to meet specific client requirements or objectives. These may include:

- Consulting engagements for redesigning business processes
- Determining opportunities for increasing operational efficiencies
- Monitoring management controls (financial/administrative/operational)
- Assessing risk to assets and operations
- Recommending constructive and actionable solutions for improving controls and meeting business objectives.

Looking Ahead:

As the Corporate Audit Department looks forward, it is striving to:

- Promote a positive control environment within the company
- Provide services that contribute value by offering solutions, not simply "audits"
- Provide accurate and actionable information to executive management, the Board of Directors, and other stakeholders on the state of the company's business controls
- Assist employees at all levels to design and maintain better, more efficient control systems to support business objectives
- Focus on issues important to our clients.

Staff Training, Development, and Growth: (excerpts)

Members of the Corporate Audit Department have a diverse background. Likewise, they enjoy a uniquely broad exposure to all business activities at different company locations. They gain insight into SC Johnson Wax's methods, procedures and multinational operations, and receive training in analytical and problem solving techniques. *Consequently, the group provides a bank of talent available for movement into other career positions within the company.* (emphasis added)

Fig. 3. S. C. Johnson Wax, Vision and Mission, Corporate Audit Services.

Corporate Audit at S. C. Johnson's Wax has re-defined its relationship with their external auditors. Corporate Audit is now looking to re-claim into operational audits all of what they had provided as support services to the external audit, and, in return, give all the financial audit work back to their external auditor. Such re-shuffling of the various audit responsibilities serves to delineate and re affirm traditional professional jurisdictions (Abbott, 1983; Reed, 1996).

5.2. J. C. Penney

The second company examined was J. C. Penney where corporate culture and strong management support is an integral part of the internal audit structure. The seriousness of this management support is evident in the auditor's *Bill of Rights* published by management. This *Bill of Rights* clearly defines important aspects of the corporate culture and internal audit's role in that culture. The *Bill of Rights* is published by management telling its internal auditors their rights, including: right to full understanding of the corporate policies they are expected to enforce right to be problem solvers as well as problem identifiers and, consistent with the notion of private, architectural knowledge (Matusik & Hill, 1998), a right to brought into the mainstream of the company. Furthermore, the *Bill of Rights* stresses that the internal auditors have a right to complete understanding of the company's goals and aspirations right to the total support of the company's top management and, most significantly, *the right to feel important — indispensable, in fact — to corporate management* (Abbott, 1983; Freidson, 1986; Reed, 1996).

The Director of internal auditing at J. C. Penney believes that the building and maintenance of this architectural knowledge ("the internal audit department achieves a competitive advantage") is done through (1) knowing the business and (2) performing comparative analysis and benchmarking within units. As an example of comparative analysis, the audit team will compare catalog desk operations with others in the company on approximately 50 dimensions to identify opportunities for improvement. Such benchmarking has

resulted in the company feeling that internal auditing has developed a unique skill in performing exception analysis and turning exceptions into constructive recommendations for improvement. Essentially, the internal audit department at J. C. Penney espouses that it is committed to "value-added services." Internal auditing is being asked to service on a number of study groups including JIT, merchandising, and streamlining. The Director points out that these are important, corporate-wide study groups that enhance the contribution of the internal audit department.

The Director viewed the future maintenance of the architectural foundation of internal auditing at J. C. Penney as one which the internal audit is to be intertwined with management. Here the emphasis is that the primary reporting is to management with a secondary reporting to the audit committee. The Director feels that by making the audit committee the primary user of internal audit only sets up internal audit for outsourcing because it can contribute to the audit committee wanting something even more removed from management such as outsourced internal audit services. The Director wants to be involved with more cross functionality diagnostic reviews and exception analysis — all contributing to the internal audit department retaining its competitive edge. The Director of internal auditing feels that if the organization believes in the integrity of its management and the commitment to the control environment, and a long run perspective, then it makes the most sense to report to management and to become involved in identifying business opportunities as does the internal audit department. Finally, the Director sees the future of his internal auditing group as being strongly tied to the use of the external auditors. Here the intent is return the work performed by internal auditing pertaining to the financial audit, such that the external auditors can do the entire financial audit. In turn, the internal audit department can concentrate on identifying business opportunities, thus clearly delineating and re-affirming traditional professional jurisdictions (Abbott, 1983; Reed, 1996).

In summary, the actions of J. C. Penney, like S. C. Johnson Wax, are fully consistent with the traditional IIA (1978, 1994, 1996a, 1996b) position to

L. Rittenberg, M.A. Covaleski / Accounting, Organizations and Society 26 (2001) 617–641 635

defend the internal audit function against efforts to outsource these services. These combined efforts to reaffirm the nature of internal audit work are indicative of the macro forces which are shaping the nature of the internal audit profession (Kalbers & Fogarty, 1995). At stake are traditional lines drawn between the work of the public accounting firms — the external financial audit — and the work of the internal audit profession — the internal audit (Abbott, 1988; Freidson, 1994; Reed, 1996). This line between respective jurisdictional claims and the efforts to reaffirm these lines are at the core of Abbott's (1983) contention as to the significance of claims for the exclusive right to control specific work activities as being the critical, distinguishing characteristic of professional occupation. In this vein, we are interested in the manner in which the work of internal auditing is defined — here from the side of two internal audit departments. According to Reed, the politics of expertise, in turn, revolve around the knowledge base with which professional stature is claimed, the technical work and benefits for clients derived from this knowledge, the political strategies used to defend a jurisdiction, and the organizational forms used to mobilize expertise. And, more specifically, the positions taken by these two in-house internal audit departments firms support Matusik and Hill's (1998) hypothesis that these departments would characterize internal audit work as being predominantly private, architectural knowledge that is too valuable to the competitive position of the company to outsource.

6. Beyond the public accounting firms and in-house internal auditors: implications for future research

As suggested in Fig. 1, although the major focus of this research has been to draw from the sociology of professions and the outsourcing literature to theoretically motivate the study of the tensions between the public accounting and internal audit professions over the internal audit function (research propositions 1 and 2), additional social actors were implicated in our analysis and need to be subject to more systematic analysis in future research for deeper understanding of their roles in

these battles between the professions. To some extent, this comment is a re statement of Kalbers and Fogarty's (1995) critical observation that the construct of professionalism in accounting and internal auditing is much more complex, needing recognition of the more macro-behavioral forces which need to be considered as impacting the professions. For example, the battle between the public accounting firms and the in-house internal auditors seemed to be also being played out at the professional association level — between the AICPA and the IIA. And, besides the AICPA and the IIA, the SEC (who, while not directly concerned with outsourcing, per se, becomes concerned in terms of the implications for external auditor independence) seemed to have more than an insignificant role in our study a role that might offer fruitful insight from future research.

6.1. The changing position of the IIA

The strong position that IIA took against the outsourcing of internal audit services to the external auditor at the open session of the Professional Ethics Executive Committee of the AICPA on 19 January, 1996 took a dramatic, immediate, and almost inexplicable change. The IIA's March/April newsletter reflected a more conciliatory position with the public accounting profession when they stated that as a result of a "meeting with representatives of major accounting firms that provide internal auditing services," the IIA's leadership concluded that there is a need to chart a new "enlightened" path for the future, which they articulated as follows:

The IIA and its membership must refocus energy spent in challenging the outsourcing issue to improving the quality of internal audit functions. The answer to "who does it best" should be determined in the competitive market place .... The door must be opened to include internal audit professionals regardless of employer. The trend toward outsourcing will continue, and third-party providers are an increasing segment of the IIA membership [roughly 500 members].... The path to this position has been a very difficult one. Even

636 *L. Rittenberg, M.A. Covaleski / Accounting, Organizations and Society 26 (2001) 617–641*

though we still have independence concerns and preferences for internal operations, the trend toward greater efficiencies and involvement by third-party providers is very evident. In order to maintain a position of leadership and authority, the IIA must begin to adapt our thinking and processes so that we can help all practitioners and ensure that the profession of internal auditing is well understood by its clients. Thus, the IIA intends to recognize internal auditors as potential members based on what they do rather than who employs them (IIA, 1996a, p. 4).

In a fairly candid confession of its acquiescence to the Big Five firms, the IIA newsletter acknowledged that:

Outsourcing is increasingly used as part of re-engineering and downsizing, and this trend is much larger than the function of internal auditing. All major public accounting firms now seem to be pursuing these services with some degree of enthusiasm. Given the growth and possible success of these efforts, the question for the IIA is whether it is postured to achieve its goals and objectives if it cannot help increase the internal audit efficiency and effectiveness of the contract (outsourced) providers (IIA, 1996a, p. 3).

The IIA newsletter also conceded that:

It is important for the IIA to reassess our bedrock mission and chart a course that identifies common ground on which future activity can take place. As more and more contract providers enter the public and private sectors, the IIA must address their professional needs. Otherwise we may end up trying to achieve objectives of leadership and authority, only to ignore a large segment of internal audit practitioners. At a minimum this calls for another look at who we consider to be internal auditors and how the IIA relates to major providers, e.g., public accounting firms that provide internal audit services (IIA, 1996a, p. 3).

The closing comments in the IIA newsletter provide a realistic perspective of: the needs of the IIA taking precedence over those of internal auditors the economic imperative of "clients" and trends of public accounting firms, now reclassified from being "affiliates" to "fellow" — not competing — practitioners, being in the relatively lucrative domain of internal auditing:

The IIA is postured to work with public accounting firms in all aspects of the profession and will not oppose the development of this market. The door is open to cooperation across the full range of IIA activities.... The greatest risk to both external and internal auditors is to be considered irrelevant to the successful attainment of corporate objectives (IIA, 1996a, p. 6).

The significant shift in the IIA position that took place in the Spring of 1996 came to be more formally embodied in the Fall of 1996 with the IIA's (1996b) official position being expressed in a *Exposure Draft of a Professional Issues Pamphlet on Internal Auditing and Outsourcing*. Thus, in terms of Abbott's (1988) notion of jurisdictional claims and control of work activities being at the core of the concept of profession, the dramatic change in position by the IIA seems to be recognizing the tensions inherent in the efforts to expand jurisdictional claims. As Hopwood (1998, p. 516) stated, "Faced with the stark commercialism of the new world of audit and consultancy, there is an increasing case for their analysis and appraisal." Indeed, the actions of the IIA do represent dramatic disputes over jurisdictions which are still in process of playing out as evidenced by the major shift in position by the IIA (Freidson, 1986, 1994; Reed, 1996). The turmoil in these professional disputes is somewhat encapsulated in the following petition:

At a growing number of companies, internal auditors are no longer performing internal auditing. Rather, such auditing is being performed by public accounting firms — in many instances by the same firm that does the

L. Rittenberg, M.A. Covaleski / Accounting, Organizations and Society 26 (2001) 617-641 637

annual financial statements. The IIA has taken no effective action to stop the public accountants efforts to displace internal auditors. To the contrary, the IIA has effectively supported the public accounting firms in this effort by changing the definition of internal auditing to encompass work done by external auditors.... and generally embracing as fellow internal auditors those public accountants who are working diligently to displace internal auditing departments.

We the undersigned are aware that internal auditing departments are being displaced by public accounting firms and that the IIA, rather than defending the profession, has chosen to welcome the public accounting firms as fellow internal audit practitioners and has taken various steps to accommodate the public accountants, with the most well-known being the revision of the definition of internal auditing.... We are not pleased with the IIA's actions to date nor with the IIA's current course in response to the challenge of our profession presented by the Big 5 public accounting firms.... [W]e do not wish to see any of the current [IIA Board] members re-elected (Petition amongst IIA members, January 4) (IIA, 2000).

Thus, the combination of the battles that the internal audit profession has with the public accounting profession, along with their own battles internally as suggested by these serious charges against the IIA leadership by a "few" disgruntled members of the professional, provides a greater appreciation for the comments made by Kalbers and Fogarty (1995) who stressed that the construct of professionalism in internal auditing is much more complex than typically presented in accounting research.

6.2. Auditor independence, outsourcing, and the SEC.

The developments in terms of this debate as to the boundaries of the internal and external audits, as reflected in the AICPA's Ethics Rulings as well

as the movements by the individual firms, have not gone un-noticed by the SEC. This is critical because while the AICPA and the three firms examined have argued that blurring of boundaries in the re-definition of the external and internal audits are a non-issue, important constituencies such as the government may feel otherwise. At issue is the public accounting profession's claim of neutrality and independence in the exercise of their new expertise (Freidson, 1986; Reed, 1996). As Reed (p. 588) observed, "Once they become 'tainted' through a much closer incorporation into business practice, the disinterested claim to moral and cultural authority is increasingly difficult to sustain." Shaping the jurisdictional disputes of these professional groups instigates the concerns of an institutional environment that Reed (p. 586) characterizes as being comprised of the "state, political ideologies and policies highly suspicious of, if not downright hostile to, professional power." Such an environment of regulation and suspicion tends to further accentuate the dramatic disputes over jurisdictions (Freidson, 1994). Signs of such concern and suspicions are evident in comments of Arthur Levitt, Chairman of the SEC at the time, who raised questions about the expansion of audit services in a speech given in the Summer of 1996:

> If I may digress for a moment: I'm deeply concerned that "independence" and "objectivity" are increasingly regarded by some as quaint notions.... There are those who say that increasing competition puts pressure on accountants to branch out and try new ways to generating profits. I caution the industry, if I may borrow a Biblical phrase, not to "gain the whole world, and lose [its] own soul (Levitt, 1996a).

Chairman Levitt (1996a, p. 5) noted the emerging services offered by public accounting firms and worries that the "traditional understanding of the need for auditors to be absolutely and unquestionably independent" may be slipping away. Chairman Levitt (1996a, p. 6), implying that the monopoly power granted external auditors could to revoked, discussed the benefits and

638   *L. Rittenberg, M.A. Covaleski / Accounting, Organizations and Society 26 (2001) 617–641*

costs to the profession for the special obligations that where in a professional monopoly:

> The price the profession pays for this special role is to accept important limitations on its activities.... To maintain both the fact and appearance of independence — and thus the confidence of investors — auditors must avoid all suggestions of mutuality of interests with management of registrants for which an auditor provides services.... [auditors] can't participate in management activities of audit clients. Moreover, auditors can't sell services that leave them auditing their own work. (See also Levitt, 1996b, 1998)

Extending this view, the SEC Chief Accountant at the time, Michael Sutton (1996), took direct aim at the AICPA's (1996) official position approving of a CPA's performance of internal audits for external audit clients fortified by their own self-policing of the independence issue:

> The continuing concern about auditor independence is an issue that has serious implications for the image and stature of the profession — one that the leadership of the profession, including its self-regulatory processes, needs to address.... We have to avoid seeking solutions that sound good, but that are 'fuzzy" and avoid taking meaningful action and, thus, raise independence to a higher level of concern.

Thus, in terms of Abbott's (1988) notion of jurisdictional claims and control of work activities being at the core of the concept of profession, the SEC seems to be recognizing the tensions inherent in the efforts to expand jurisdictional claims as they warn that such effort to "gain the whole world" not be done at a price of "losing its soul". Recasting this point more bluntly and without the use of Biblical metaphors, Hopwood (1998, p. 516) stated, "Faced with the stark commercialism of the new world of audit and consultancy, there is an increasing case for their analysis and appraisal." Indeed, the actions of the AICPA and public accounting firms do represent dramatic disputes over jurisdictions

where the eventual impact of the government (Freidson, 1986, 1994; Larson, 1977; Reed, 1996) seems to be just starting to play itself out.

7. Closing discussion

Our paper has attempted to advance several critical issues pertaining to the current turmoil surrounding the trend toward the provision of internal audit services on an outsourced basis to the external financial auditors. At the most general level, this study attempted to provide some initial effort towards Hopwood's (1998) charge that if auditing research "...is to be meaningful in the modern era the world view of the research community must change." Our study took serious the various *WSJ* articles with their tongue-in-cheek headlines ("Who is Going to Audit the Auditor" and "In with Outsourcing, Out with the Audit") that signaled that much is at stake here: for the public accounting firms seeking revenue growth for the internal auditors who are protecting their work for the host organizations attempting to assess the optimal manner in which to have these services provided for the respective professional associations and, obviously, for the SEC in the form of their biblical metaphors which have expressed broader social and economic concerns.

The differentiation between the external and internal audit profession may be the possession of a body of abstract knowledge on which the occupation bases its claims for the exclusive right to control specific work activities. Such claims to work, from Abbott's (1988) perspective, is the critical, distinguishing characteristic of professional occupation. Abbott's (1988, 1983) approach emphasized that the analysis of the tasks or work activities of occupations is the key to understanding changes in professionalization. In this vein, we are interested in the manner in which the work of internal auditing is defined–from both sides of the competing professions. Our results corroborate the theorizing found in the sociology of professions area (Abbott, 1988; Freidson, 1994; Reed, 1996), that the transformation of a jurisdiction should be accompanied by not only conflict, but by modification of codes of ethics, and the

L. Rittenberg, M.A. Covaleski / Accounting, Organizations and Society 26 (2001) 617–641 639

respective professions' abstract system of knowledge. Indeed, we found that the profession of knowledge work was highly abstract and reliant on a series of societally prized, though vaporous, even mythical (Alvesson, 1993) terms that have become institutionalized in their own right as demonstrating organizational/professional progressivism. The views from both sides of the professional arguments implied that surely a professional must be engaged (from an external source per the public accounting profession, from an internal source per the internal auditing profession) to assist the client survive in this new era of global relations and rapidly changing conditions (Abbott, 1988).

Here, the rhetoric used in establishing the jurisdictional claim of Big Five firms as to internal auditing appeared to almost draw on as script both the sociology of professions (e.g. Abbott, 1988; Reed, 1996) and outsourcing (e.g. Davis-Blake & Uzzi, 1993; Matusik & Hill, 1998) literatures in voicing, for example, their attributes of being global knowledge professionals having unparalleled access to public, albeit arcane information. Likewise, the IIA (at least initially) and the corporate internal audit departments drew upon as script this same literature in voicing its unique local knowledge and command of private information. Combined, both professional groups appeared to relegate the work of the external financial audit to service public, non-core component information leaving the disputable portion in terms of the degree of "architectural-level" character and strategic sensitivity of internal audit work (Matusik & Hill, 1998).

We anticipate that these public/private information and non-core/architectural distinctions raised by the outsourcing and sociology of profession's literatures will degenerate with the performance of internal audits by external auditors. As the Big Five firms perform these services, they will perform not only non-core component, but also architectural level work (and hence must gain access to private information), and this degeneration of jurisdictional claims to work and related implications of such degeneration is only beginning to reveal itself as the full force of all the critical social actors: actors beyond the public

accounting firms themselves and the corporate internal auditors.

Acknowledgements

The authors wish to thank two anonymous reviewers, Anthony Hopwood, and participants at the doctoral seminar at the University of Wisconsin-Madison for their many thoughtful comments on earlier versions of this paper.

References

Abbott, A. (1988). The system of professions: An essay on the division of expert labor. Chicago: University of Chicago Press.

Abbott, A. (1983). Professional ethics. American Journal of Sociology, 88(5), 855–885.

AICPA. (1996). Exposure draft: Extended audit services. New York: AICPA.

Allison, G. T. (1971). Essence of decision: Explaining the Cuban missile crisis. Boston: Little Brown.

Alvesson, M. (1993). Organizations or rhetoric: knowledge intensive firms and the struggle with ambiguity. Journal of Management Studies, 30, 997–1015.

Anderson, R. (1994). The truly integrated audit. Internal Auditing, December, 11–14.

Ang, S., & Cummings, L. (1997). Strategic response to institutional influences on information outsourcing. Organization Science, 8(3), 235–256.

Arthur, Andersen (1995). Are you in control? London: Business Risk Management.

Berg, B. L. (1989). Qualitative research methods for the social services. Boston: Allyn and Bacon.

Bettis, R. A., & Hitt, M. A. (1995). The new competitive landscape. Strategic Management Journal, 16, 7–20.

Cohany, S. (1996). Workers in alternative employment arrangements. Monthly Labor Review, 119(10), 31–45.

Crozier, M. (1964). The bureaucratic phenomenon. Chicago: University of Chicago Press.

Davis-Blake, A., & Uzzi, B. (1993). Determinants of employment externalization: a study of temporary workers and independent contractors. Administrative Science Quarterly, 38, 195–223.

Denzin, N. (1978). The research act. New York: McGraw Hill.

Derber, C., Schwartz, W. A., & Magrass, Y. (1990). Power in the highest degree: Professionals and the rise of a new mandarin order. New York: Oxford University Press.

Drazin, R. (1990). Professionals and innovation: structural–

640   *L. Rittenberg, M.A. Covaleski / Accounting, Organizations and Society 26 (2001) 617–641*

functional versus radical structural perspectives. *Journal of Management Studies, 27*(3), 245–264.

Freidson, E. (1986). *Professional powers.* Chicago: University of Chicago Press.

Freidson, E. (1994). *Professionalism reborn: Theory prophecy and policy.* Cambridge: Polity.

Halal, W. (1994). From hierarchy to enterprise: internal markets are the new foundation of management. *Academy of Management Executive, 8,* 69–83.

Herman, E. S., & Chomsky, N. (1988). *Manufacturing consent: The political economy of mass media.* New York: Pantheon Books.

Hopwood, A. (1998). Exploring the modern audit firm: an introduction. *Accounting, Organizations and Society, 23,* 515–516.

IIA (Institute of Internal Auditors) (1978). Standards for the professional practice of internal auditing. *The Internal Auditor,* October, 13–33.

IIA (Institute of Internal Auditors) (1994). Perspective on outsourcing internal auditing: a professional briefing for chief audit executives, Altamonte Springs, FL: The IIA.

IIA (Institute of Internal Auditors) (1996a). *March/April newsletter.*

IIA (Institute of Internal Auditors) (1996b). *Exposure draft.*

IIA (Institute of Internal Auditors) (2000). *Letter to IIA members.*

Internal Audit Alert. (1996, January 4). Interview sheds light on outsourcing.

Johnson, N. (1999, January 20). *Current regulatory and enforcement developments affecting the accounting profession.* Presented at the 26th Annual Securities Regulation Institute Conference (http://www.SEC.Gov/news/speeches/spch248.htm).

Kalbers, L., & Fogarty, T. (1995). Professionalism and its consequences: a study of internal auditors. *Auditing: A Journal of Practice & Theory, 14,* 64–86.

Larson, M. (1977). *The rise of professionalism: A sociological analysis.* Berkeley: University of California Press.

Larson, M. S. (1990). The matter of experts and professionals. In M. Burrage, & R. Torstendall (Eds.), *The formation of the profession* (pp. 24–50). London: Sage.

Levitt, A. (1996a, June 6). Remarks at the SEC and Financial Reporting Institute, University of Southern California. Washington, DC: US Securities and Exchange Commission.

Levitt, A. (1996b, December 10). Remarks at the AICPA's 24th Annual Conference on SEC Developments. Washington, DC: US Securities and Exchange Commission.

Levitt, A. (1998, December 8). *A partnership for the public trust.* Presented before the AICPA (http://www.SEC.Gov/news/speeches/spch230.txt.

Lincoln, Y. S., & Guba, E. (1985). *Naturalistic inquiry.* Beverley Hills, CA: Sage.

Matusik, S., & Hill, C. (1998). The utilization of contingent work, knowledge creation, and competitive advantage. *Academy of Management Review, 23,* 680–687.

Merton, R. K. (1968). *Social theory and social structure.* New York: Free Press.

Mintzberg, H. (1979). *The structuring of organizations.* Englewood Cliffs: Prentice Hall, NJ.

Morrow, L. (1993). The temping of America. *Time,* March 29, 40–41.

Pelfrey, S., & Peacock, E. (1995). A current status report on outsourcing. *Internal Auditing,* Fall, 26–32.

Public Accounting Report. (1999a, February 28). *Annual survey of national public accounting firms* (pp. 51–56.

Public Accounting Report. (1999b, September 30). *Profession watches for outsourcing boom* (pp. 1–6).

Public Accounting Report. (1998, January 31). *Big 6 firms account for 23% of global MCS services* (p. 1).

Public Accounting Report. (1997, September 15). *Internal audit outsourcing revives A&A practices* (pp. 2–4).

Preston, A. M., Cooper, D. J., Scarbrough, D. P., & Chilton, R. C. (1995). Changes in the code of ethics of the U.S. accounting profession, 1917 and 1988: the continual quest for legitimation. *Accounting, Organizations and Society, 20*(6), 507–546.

Reed, M. I. (1996). Expert power and control in late modernity: an empirical review and theoretical synthesis. *Organization Studies, 17*(4), 573–597.

Roodhooft, F., & Warlop, L. (1999). On the role of sunk costs and asset specificity in outsourcing decisions: a research note. *Accounting, Organizations and Society, 24,* 363–369.

Sikka, P., & Willmott, H. (1995). The power of 'independence': defending and extending the jurisdiction of accounting in the United Kingdom. *Accounting, Organizations and Society, 20*(6), 547–581.

Simons, R. (1995). Control in an age of empowerment. *Harvard Business Review,* March–April, 80–88.

Sutton, M. (1996, August 14). *Auditor independence: The challenge of fact and appearance.* Remarks by the Chief Accountant of the Securities and Exchange Commission, at the *American Accounting Association's 1996 Annual Meeting,* Chicago.

Tolbert, P. (1990). A review of "The system of professions: an essay on the division of expert labor," by A. Abbott. *Administrative Science Quarterly, 35,* 410–413.

Tsui, A. S., Pearce, J. L., Porter, L. W., & Hite, J. P. (1995). Choice of employee — organization relationship: influence of external and internal organizational factors. *Research in Personnel and Human Resource Management, 13,* 117–151.

Van Maanen, J. (1979). Reclaiming qualitative methods for organizational research: a preface. *Administrative Science Quarterly, 24,* 520–526.

Van Maanen, J. (1988). *Tales of the field.* Chicago: University of Chicago Press.

Wallace, J. (1995). Organizational and professional commitment in professional and nonprofessional organizations. *Administrative Science Quarterly, 40,* 228–255.

WSJ (Wall Street Journal). (1996a, April 22). In with outsourcing, out with audit (p. B1).

WSJ (Wall Street Journal). (1996b, March 5). Who is going to audit the auditors (p. B1).

WSJ (Wall Street Journal). (1996c, June 17). Accountants expand scope of audit work (p. B1).

WSJ (Wall Street Journal). (2000, January 7). Report by SEC says Price & Coopers violated rules of conflict of interest (p. A3).

Whittington, R., McNulty, T., & Whipp, R. (1994). Market-driven change in professional services: problems and processes. *Journal of Management Studies, 31*(6), 829–846.

Wysock, B. (1996). High tech nomads write new program for future work.

Zelizer, B. (1992). *Covering the body: The Kennedy assassination, the media and the shaping of collective memory*. Chicago: University of Chicago Press.

Zuboff, S. (1988). *In the age of the smart machine: The future of work and power*. London: Heinemann.

Name Index